BROADCAST/CABLE PROGRAMMING

FROM THE WADSWORTH SERIES IN MASS COMMUNICATION

General

The New Communications, 2nd, by Frederick Williams
Media/Impact: An Introduction to Mass Media by Shirley Biagi
Media/Reader by Shirley Biagi
Mediamerica: Form, Content, and Consequence of Mass Communication, 4th,
      by Edward Jay Whetmore
The Interplay of Influence: Mass Media & Their Publics in News, Advertising, Politics,
      2nd, by Kathleen Hall Jamieson and Karlyn Kohrs Campbell
Technology and Communication Behavior by Frederick Williams
Mass Media Research: An Introduction, 2nd, by Roger D. Wimmer
      and Joseph R. Dominick
Communication Research: Strategies and Sources by Rebecca B. Rubin, Alan M. Rubin,
      and Linda J. Piele
Creative Strategy in Advertising, 3rd, by A. Jerome Jewler
Fundamentals of Advertising Research, 3rd, by Alan Fletcher and Thomas A. Bowers

Broadcast/Cable/Film

Stay Tuned: A Concise History of American Broadcasting by Christopher H. Sterling
      and John M. Kittross
World Broadcasting Systems: A Comparative Analysis by Sydney W. Head
Broadcast/Cable Programming: Strategies and Practices, 3rd, by Susan Tyler Eastman,
      Sydney W. Head and Lewis Klein
Radio Station Operations: Management and Employee Perspectives
      by Lewis B. O'Donnell, Carl Hausman and Philip Benoit
Broadcast and Cable Selling by Charles Warner
Advertising in the Broadcast and Cable Media, 2nd, by Elizabeth J. Heighton
      and Don R. Cunningham
Copywriting for the Electronic Media: A Practical Guide by Milan D. Meeske
      and R. C. Norris
Writing for Television and Radio, 4th, by Robert L. Hilliard
Writing the Screenplay: TV and Film by Alan A. Armer
Newswriting for the Electronic Media: Principles, Examples, Applications
      by Daniel E. Garvey and William L. Rivers
Newstalk II: State-of-the-Art Conversations with Today's Broadcast Journalists
      by Shirley Biagi
Communicating Effectively on Television by Evan Blythin and Larry A. Samovar
Announcing: Broadcast Communicating Today by Lewis B. O'Donnell, Carl Hausman
      and Philip Benoit
Modern Radio Production by Lewis B. O'Donnell, Philip Benoit and Carl Hausman
Audio in Media, 2nd, by Stanley R. Alten
Television Production Handbook, 4th, by Herbert Zettl
Directing Television and Film by Alan A. Armer
Sight-Sound-Motion: Applied Media Aesthetics by Herbert Zettl
Electronic Cinematography: Achieving Photographic Control over the Video Image
      by Harry Mathias and Richard Patterson
Immediate Seating: A Look at Movie Audiences by Bruce Austin

BROADCAST/CABLE PROGRAMMING

FROM THE WADSWORTH SERIES IN MASS COMMUNICATION

General

The New Communications, 2nd, by Frederick Williams
Media/Impact: An Introduction to Mass Media by Shirley Biagi
Media/Reader by Shirley Biagi
Mediamerica: Form, Content, and Consequence of Mass Communication, 4th,
        by Edward Jay Whetmore
The Interplay of Influence: Mass Media & Their Publics in News, Advertising, Politics,
        2nd, by Kathleen Hall Jamieson and Karlyn Kohrs Campbell
Technology and Communication Behavior by Frederick Williams
Mass Media Research: An Introduction, 2nd, by Roger D. Wimmer
        and Joseph R. Dominick
Communication Research: Strategies and Sources by Rebecca B. Rubin, Alan M. Rubin,
        and Linda J. Piele
Creative Strategy in Advertising, 3rd, by A. Jerome Jewler
Fundamentals of Advertising Research, 3rd, by Alan Fletcher and Thomas A. Bowers

Broadcast/Cable/Film

Stay Tuned: A Concise History of American Broadcasting by Christopher H. Sterling
        and John M. Kittross
World Broadcasting Systems: A Comparative Analysis by Sydney W. Head
Broadcast/Cable Programming: Strategies and Practices, 3rd, by Susan Tyler Eastman,
        Sydney W. Head and Lewis Klein
Radio Station Operations: Management and Employee Perspectives
        by Lewis B. O'Donnell, Carl Hausman and Philip Benoit
Broadcast and Cable Selling by Charles Warner
Advertising in the Broadcast and Cable Media, 2nd, by Elizabeth J. Heighton
        and Don R. Cunningham
Copywriting for the Electronic Media: A Practical Guide by Milan D. Meeske
        and R. C. Norris
Writing for Television and Radio, 4th, by Robert L. Hilliard
Writing the Screenplay: TV and Film by Alan A. Armer
Newswriting for the Electronic Media: Principles, Examples, Applications
        by Daniel E. Garvey and William L. Rivers
Newstalk II: State-of-the-Art Conversations with Today's Broadcast Journalists
        by Shirley Biagi
Communicating Effectively on Television by Evan Blythin and Larry A. Samovar
Announcing: Broadcast Communicating Today by Lewis B. O'Donnell, Carl Hausman
        and Philip Benoit
Modern Radio Production by Lewis B. O'Donnell, Philip Benoit and Carl Hausman
Audio in Media, 2nd, by Stanley R. Alten
Television Production Handbook, 4th, by Herbert Zettl
Directing Television and Film by Alan A. Armer
Sight-Sound-Motion: Applied Media Aesthetics by Herbert Zettl
Electronic Cinematography: Achieving Photographic Control over the Video Image
        by Harry Mathias and Richard Patterson
Immediate Seating: A Look at Movie Audiences by Bruce Austin

SUSAN TYLER EASTMAN / *Indiana University*
SYDNEY W. HEAD / *University of Miami*
LEWIS KLEIN / *Temple University*
Gateway Communications, Inc.

Third Edition / **BROADCAST/CABLE PROGRAMMING**

STRATEGIES AND PRACTICES

Wadsworth Publishing Company

Belmont, California

A Division of Wadsworth, Inc.

Senior Editor: Rebecca Hayden
Editorial Assistant: Melissa Harris
Production Editor: Hal Humphrey
Text and Cover Designer: Andrew Ogus
Print Buyer: Karen Hunt
Copy Editor: Jean Mann
Compositor: G&S Typesetters, Inc.

Printed in the United States of America   50

   2 3 4 5 6 7 8 9 10——93 92 91 90 89

Library of Congress Cataloging in Publication Data

Eastman, Susan Tyler.
   Broadcast/cable programming : strategies and practices / Susan
Tyler Eastman, Sydney W. Head, Lewis Klein.—3rd ed.
        p.   cm.   —(Wadsworth series in mass communication)
   Bibliography: p.
   Includes indexes.
   ISBN 0-534-09354-X
   1. Television programs—Planning.   2. Radio programs—Planning.
3. Cable television—Planning.   I. Head, Sydney W.   II. Klein,
Lewis, 1927– .   III. Title.   IV. Series.
PN1992.55.E18   1989
791.44′0236′0973—dc 19   88-11791
                                                                CIP

PREFACE

In the decade since the original edition of this book, the subject matter has evolved dramatically. Broadcast networks have changed owners; cable television has developed a new form; a new measurement technique has been adopted for television ratings; satellites have stimulated radio syndication; public broadcasting has reorganized; and the process of broadcast deregulation has advanced. In response to changes in the industry and our publisher's survey of college teachers who use this book, we made the following changes in this third edition:

- We *shortened the book's length* from 21 to 19 chapters, making it more useful in the classroom. The material on superstations was distributed to the independent television station and basic cable network chapters, and portions of the afterword were incorporated in several chapters.

- We added information on *peoplemeters* throughout the book, especially expanding that portion of the ratings chapter. Chapter 2 also contains recent ratings book examples and updated descriptions of measurement practices.

- We added a *fresh chapter on the role of station representatives in programming,* providing details on the processes of negotiating and bidding for syndicated programs.

- We took account of the *major changes in ownership of the television and radio networks,* assessing their impact on programming. Chapter 4 also utilizes updated material on station groups and multiple system owners.

- We *recast the chapters on prime-time and nonprime-time network television,* updating industry strategies, providing new program examples and adding new programming topics such as the evening news and late-night news. Charts and graphs in both chapters were completed with the most recent data.

- We added entirely new material on the economics and technology of *pay-per-view* in the chapter on pay-television programming, also updating our descriptions of all the basic and pay-cable services.
- We *revised the radio chapters* to better illustrate satellite distribution's role in programming and added information on Westwood One's expanded position in the radio industry.
- Fresh alterations in *national public television*, especially the end of the core concept in prime-time programming, led to further reworking of these chapters.
- Deregulation rendered moot most of the material on regulation in the previous edition, leading us to once again *recast the entire introductory chapter* in this edition.
- Finally, we created a separate *instructor's guide*, providing chapter summaries, lists of videotapes, details of student projects and essay and multiple-choice test questions to aid new and ongoing users of this book.

Despite these changes, we believe our fundamental approach to the subject of programming proved viable and so have retained much of the first and second editions. As we said in the preface to the first edition, only on the most generalized level can one make statements about programmers and their functions that apply equally to all sorts of programming situations. We start with such generalizations because all types of broadcasting and cable ultimately share certain common attributes, no matter how diverse the surrounding circumstances. But the heart of our book is the testimony of actual practitioners in varied programming situations.

One caveat should be made at the outset: We do not attempt to evaluate programming except in the pragmatic way that programmers themselves judge programs—by their ability to attract targeted audiences. This approach does not mean that we discount the importance of program quality or absolve broadcasters from responsibility for taking quality into consideration. We feel, however, that there is sufficient critical literature available. Our task was to examine objectively how programming decisions are actually made, whatever the wider artistic or social implications of those decisions might be.

ORGANIZING PRINCIPLES

One of the more perplexing problems we faced at the start was the decision as to what we meant by programming and hence what types of program decision makers we should include. It was tempting, for example, to think in terms of program genres and therefore to seek out experts in such specializations as sports, news and feature film programming. We were also tempted to call upon specialists in the making of programs, such as the package producers responsible for fashioning most of the network television entertainment programming.

We needed some defining principle that would impose limits and logical coherence on the selection of authors and the subjects of the chapters. In the end, we decided that we should confine the book to situations in which program executives are responsible not only for choosing and shaping individual programs or program segments but also for organizing such separate program items into coherent program services. It is universally recognized that an important—in some situations even the most important—part of the broadcast programmer's job is **scheduling**. Significant though producing organizations are in the creative aspects of program making, such organizations have no responsibility for designing entire program services. Instead, they focus their energies on turning out specific program series, leaving it to broadcast and cable programmers to decide if, when and how to use these programs in designing the continuous sequences that constitute broadcast or cable services. We therefore selected authors who had responsibility for the design of entire network, station or cable services.

We divided the job of the programmer into three activities—*evaluation, selection* and *scheduling.* Part One opens with a chapter defining these activities, along with other basic programming concepts. The second chapter in this part reviews the central tools of evaluation—ratings—and the third and fourth chapters examine the roles of representatives and owners—all essential for background because they inevitably enter into nearly all programming decisions. The three activities of evaluation, selection and scheduling guide the organization of the remaining chapters, each of which deals with a particular programming situation from the perspective of a practitioner specializing in that type of programming.

STRUCTURE OF THE BOOK

The book divides into five major sections: Part One introduces the concepts and vocabulary for understanding the remaining chapters; Parts Two, Three, Four and Five look at programming strategy respectively for television, cable, radio and public broadcasting from the perspective of industry programming experts.

- Each *part* begins with a brief *overview,* relating the set of chapters to each other and the rest of the book.
- Each *chapter* starts with an *outline* of its headings and subheadings, providing a handy guide to its contents.
- A *summary* concludes each chapter, followed by *notes* and *selected reference sources.* The readings cite books, reports and trade publications that expand, support, complement or contrast with the point of view expressed in each chapter.
- A list of *abbreviations and acronyms* appears near the end of the book.
- A *glossary* summarizes the concepts and vocabulary pertaining to programming. Glossary entries appear **bold** in the text.
- An *annotated bibliography* of books, articles, reports, guides, theses and dissertations on programming follows the glossary. References

appearing in the notes are not repeated in the bibliography if they are highly topical or do not relate mainly to programming. For items on specific topics, readers should consult the selected sources, chapter notes and the bibliography.

• A complete *index to the movies and television and radio program titles* mentioned in the text precedes the *general index*.

ACKNOWLEDGMENTS

We want to thank warmly the individuals and organizations that assisted us: Bruce Austin, Rochester Institute of Technology; Joel Chaseman of Post-Newsweek Stations; Robert Klein of Klein &; James Miller of Showtime Entertainment; Martha Popowski of Cox Enterprises; David E. Wilson of KRON-TV, San Francisco; and Andy Yocom of WTTW in Chicago. All made useful suggestions that aided in the formation or refinement of specific chapters.

Rebecca Hayden of Wadsworth warmly supported and counseled us through all editions. Christopher Sterling of George Washington University made substantial contributions to the first edition's bibliography. Charles R. Bantz of the University of Minnesota, David Eshelman of Central Missouri State University, Donald G. Godfrey, then of the University of Washington, Daniel E. Gold of Comcast, Ralph L. Smith of Illinois State University, Jacob J. Wakshlag, then of Indiana University and Robert D. West of Kent State University commented beneficially on the first edition manuscript in draft, as did Norman Marcus of Boston University, Timothy Meyer of the University of Wisconsin–Green Bay and Mitchell Shapiro of the University of Miami on the second edition manuscript.

Most especially we thank Charles Clift III of Ohio University and George Mastroianni of California State University, Fullerton, who reviewed the third edition manuscript in painstaking detail and made many invaluable suggestions.

We are grateful to all these people for their help, to the National Association of Television Program Executives for sustaining a survey of its members and to the Department of Telecommunications at Indiana University for its support.

Susan Tyler Eastman
Sydney W. Head
Lewis Klein

CONTENTS

PART ONE / PROGRAMMING RESOURCES AND CONSTRAINTS

Part One has a dual purpose. Chapters 1 and 2 provide concepts and vocabulary used in the rest of the book. Chapters 3 and 4 introduce broad perspectives that span the contents of two or more subsequent parts.

Chapter 1 introduces the major concepts and vocabulary of **programming strategy,** providing a framework for the individual chapters that follow. It lays the groundwork for conceptualizing the essential nature of the programming function. Despite the tremendous variety of programming situations that occurs in broadcasting and cable, all programmers face similar problems and approach them with similar strategies. Common assumptions, then, underlie programming behaviors that can be understood by examining the programmer's options. Some of the constraints operating on programming situations are beyond the programmer's immediate control; others leave latitude for the exercise of the programmer's skills. This chapter spells out the wide range of skills and types of knowledge a programmer needs.

Chapter 2 introduces the major concepts of program and audience **ratings** crucial to understanding many of the strategies in the remainder of the book. Subsequent authors in this book draw on these concepts, assuming that the reader is familiar with them. This chapter describes the qualitative and quantitative research tools of broadcasting and cable, explains how they can be put to use and assesses their programming value. The authors focus on national and local market ratings because they are the industry's primary method of program evaluation, providing the major measures of success and failure and the means for setting advertising rates. Authors in the rest of the book, especially in Chapters 3, 5, 9 and 14, supplement the measurement tools introduced in this chapter by discussing more specialized data collection methods and by reviewing highly specialized research and ratings reports. Chapter 2, then, supplies the reader with a basic understanding of how the industry evaluates programs and audiences.

Chapter 3 introduces the role of the **station representative.** The station representative firms help their client stations purchase and schedule programming because stations in a dominant position are easy to sell to advertisers, the primary job of the rep firm. About a dozen major rep firms employ rep programmers who bring a nationwide perspective to program-decision making. Reps advise station and cable system programmers rather than program a station or service themselves. In Chapter 3, the author also discusses many of the research reports that reps interpret and relay to their clients. Rep programmers concentrate on television station programming; they are less involved in radio programming, a more local activity. In the cable industry, group owners generally advise their owned systems on programming from a national perspective.

Chapter 4 covers **group ownership** of broadcasting stations and cable systems and its impact on programming. Group ownership refers to common ownership of two or more television and/or radio stations or cable systems. There are over 150 group owners of television stations, averaging three stations each and including half of all television stations. Most of the 10,000 commercial radio stations in the United States are owned by individuals or companies that own more than one radio station, often also owning television stations and/or cable systems. And over 300 group owners of cable systems control from a few to hundreds of individual cable franchises, often with simultaneous financial interests in broadcasting. The author of Chapter 4 discusses the influence group ownership has on station and system programming.

The four chapters making up Part One, then, discuss programming strategies from broad perspectives. The authors of these chapters supply an overview of programming strategies and the tools to interpret the more specialized chapters in the rest of the book.

CHAPTER 1 \ A FRAMEWORK FOR PROGRAMMING STRATEGIES

Sydney W. Head

A Guide to Chapter 1

Sydney W. Head brings to this book a lifetime of experience with broadcasting, both as a practitioner and as an academic. After working as technical director of the university theater at the University of Colorado, he founded and administered as full professor and chairman the Department of Radio-Television-Film at the University of Miami (Florida). Later, he headed teams advising the governments of the Sudan and Ethiopia on radio broadcasting development. Between 1970 and 1980, he served as a senior faculty member at Temple University in Philadelphia. In 1980 he retired from Temple University only to be recalled to revise the curriculum of the department he had started at the University of Miami. During his teaching career, he wrote and produced many radio and television programs and, in addition to numerous journal articles, is senior author of *Broadcasting in America: A Survey of Television and Radio* (Houghton-Mifflin, 1987, fifth edition), editor of *Broadcasting in Africa: A Continental Survey* (Temple University Press, 1974), and author of *World Broadcasting Systems: A Comparative Analysis* (Wadsworth, 1985).

WHAT IS PROGRAMMING?

The program you see or hear on your receiving set arrived there at that moment and at that place on the dial or channel selector as the end result of two types of creative activity: *programming* and *production*. The two activities differ fundamentally. This book is about programming, not production, and because discussions of programming often get sidetracked into discussions about production, we want to draw the line between the two very explicitly at the outset.

Strategy vs. Tactics

We find it helpful to make the programming–production distinction in terms of *strategy* versus *tactics*. Strategy refers to the planning and directing of large-scale operations—in this case, entire schedules of broadcast stations and cable systems, and of broadcasting and cable networks. Tactics refers to the methods and techniques used to reach the goals that strategy has defined. Strategic considerations say that Hill No. 25 must be stormed and occupied; tactical operations carry out the assignment. It is no accident that terms associated with warfare fittingly describe the programmer's mission. Programmers work in a highly combative environment, besieged on all sides by rival programmers and competing media. The successful practitioner surveys the terrain, deploys the troops and goes on the attack. John Haldi concludes his chapter in this book on network affiliate strategies with the words, "Programming is war. You are a general. The object is to win!"

Programming generalship starts with searching out and selecting programming materials appropriate to a particular market and a predefined target audience. After negotiating to get the selected materials on the best possible terms, the programmer organizes the items into a coherent program service designed to appeal to the target audience. Finally, the programmer assesses results in terms of ratings reports, learns from mistakes, and returns to the fray with new insights. Boiling it down to a brief job description one can say:

> The programmer uses appropriate strategies in searching out and acquiring program materials designed to attract a defined audience in a

specific market, and in scheduling program items so as to create a coherent program service.

The last point should not be overlooked: A program service adds up to more than the sum of its parts. Decisions about how to combine programs (or program elements) into an effective whole are just as important as decisions about which program items to accept or reject. Programming is not merely collecting so many bricks and throwing them into a pile; the bricks must be put in place, one by one, according to a rational plan. In the end, they form a structure, not just a meaningless jumble. The art of the schedule-builder, like that of the architect, lends meaning to an otherwise meaningless assembly of parts.

In practice, programmers rarely have the luxury of starting up a brand-new program service. Usually they have to deal with an already existing set of programs, goals, assumptions and viewpoints. Therefore, the programmer's most likely first task will be to evaluate the strengths and weaknesses of an existing program schedule. Changes may have to be delayed while the new programmer straightens out the mess a predecessor left behind—at least that is the way it often seems to the newcomer.

Diversity of Programming Environments

Programming takes place under circumstances so varied that many people question whether they share any common principles. Picture a small-town **radio** station in a one-station market. A husband-and-wife team own the station and do most of the work. They have only a limited range of programming decisions to make because the entire day unrolls according to a music formula. Under the formula, the DJs have a good deal of personal input. Therefore, hiring a new DJ to cover an important daypart becomes not just a personnel decision but a major programming decision as well.

The husband and wife can barely see one another across desks piled high with stacks of unanswered mail, promotional pieces, equipment catalogs, giveaway discs, tapes, cartridges, old commercial copy and trade journals. They sip coffee from battered mugs as they go over the pros and cons of hiring a new DJ. At last they decide to hire the best of a dozen applicants they have already interviewed to take over the 10 A.M. to 3 P.M. daypart.

The cable television equivalent of this minimal programming situation might be a small-town **cable system** with 1,500 subscribers. Five of its 12 channels deliver television station signals. The remaining 7 supply a pay channel, a local origination channel and the five most popular basic cable networks—ESPN, Superstation WTBS, CNN, CBN and USA Network. Programming decisions for this system might consist of ordering a new alphanumeric service for the local origination channel, promoting a sports special on the superstation or (a more weighty decision!) changing to a different pay program supplier.

At the other extreme is the situation of a **network television prime-time** programmer. We can imagine him (we'll say it's a man because relatively few women as yet operate at this level in network hierarchies) in a luxuriously decorated executive office high above Manhattan's midtown traffic. Expensively tailored, he lounges at a marble-topped table that takes the place of a desk. He confers with several equally well-turned-out colleagues. Many weeks of close study and earnest debate have preceded this showdown meeting. Like the husband-and-wife team at the radio station, they are about to arrive at a momentous decision. One of their sitcoms, now scheduled at 8:30 Thursday nights, will be shifted to 8:00 Saturday nights!

This one decision will affect the viewing habits of millions of viewers. Millions of dollars in gross revenue are at stake. Some 210 television stations will feel the repercussions. Thousands of stockholders of affiliated stations as well as the network's own stockholders may eventually sense the shock waves. Prime-time network programmers make the most highly specialized, exacting and consequential decisions in the programming field. Their work has no parallel in other broadcasting or cable settings. Even the programming options and decisions of the country's largest cable system, Cox Cable in San Diego, or those of Tele-Communications Inc., the largest multiple system operator, or of the nation's largest pay-television supplier, HBO, are not on the scale of network television programmers' decisions.

Between these extremes exist many other programming situations, each presenting its own special problems and opportunities—programming by **group-owned** television stations, for example, by community groups on **access** channels, by the **public broadcasting** network, by **independent** (nonnetwork) television stations and so on. Because of this diversity, we thought it best to go to real-world specialized programmers for information about the strategies they use in various programming settings.

COMMON RADIO-TELEVISION ATTRIBUTES

All these programming environments, so different in size, scope and importance, share a number of attributes that have significant implications for both production tactics and programming strategies. For present purposes, four of these shared qualities seem especially relevant: (1) the *ease* with which radio and television *deliver* materials to consumers, (2) the continuous, day-and-night *availability* of program services, (3) the ease of consumer *access* and (4) the capacity for *realism*. Note that this book uses the terms **radio** and **television** programs to mean those delivered either directly from broadcasting stations or through the intermediary of cable systems. Many of the latter carry radio as well as television stations. When used alone, the words **broadcasting** and **cable** distinguish explicitly between the two methods of delivery.

Ease of Delivery

The attribute of *wirelessness* sets broadcasting apart from other communications media. Because of it, broadcasting can reach larger numbers of people simultaneously than any other medium. Moreover, unlike other media within a given area, it costs a television or radio station no more to reach a million people than to reach only one person.

To take advantage of this potential, programmers must motivate people to buy, to maintain and to use receiving sets. Audience members will make this investment of time and money only if they find programs worth-while by their own standards—not by the standards of other people or those of some ideal goal. Cable television relies on the same free-will investment in receivers as does broadcasting; indeed, in most cases, broadcasting alone moti-vated the initial receiver purchase. By definition, however, cable is not wire-less; therefore, it becomes cost ineffective if its customers are too widely dis-persed. Nevertheless, like broadcasting, it delivers programs directly to the home receiver; and, once the cable installation has been made, the consumer accepts both broadcast and cable signals on equal terms.

The fact that both broadcasting and cable deliver their services di-rectly to the home with minimum effort on the part of its occupants has im-portant consequences for programmers. Television remains essentially a *home-centered* activity. Studies of how people use their leisure time put television (whether broadcast or cable) at the top of the list as the primary leisure-time activity in the home, ahead of reading, music and yes—even ahead of sex. This attribute, home-centeredness, limits what programmers can safely schedule without raising a storm of protest about "undermining the family," but it also permits programmers to schedule programs to fit into the typical pattern of home activities. Cable programming, though also generally received in a home environment, is less constrained by that fact than broadcasting, so that cable programmers have more latitude in choice of program materials.

In view of the changing nature of the family, you might well ask whether the traditional view of broadcasting as home-and-family centered re-mains valid. Certainly programmers must take into account current trends to-ward single-person households and single-parent families. In the latter, the child has even greater control over television viewing and the choice of chan-nels than when two adults are present; in the after-school hours, in the absence of a lock on the tuner, **latchkey children** use all the home-delivered media without supervision, a situation with obvious implications for programming. Working adults comprising single-person homes find their time at a premium and spend it with television only when they feel they are getting adequate value. Adults not bound by child-centered activities want scheduling patterns that suit their convenience. Accordingly, videocassette recorders (**VCRs**) have made television a more convenient medium, to be recorded, edited and re-played (or not) at the user's whim. Using the past as a guide to programming strategies becomes increasingly problematic as **lifestyles** change.

Continuous Availability

Both cable and broadcasting are continuously available, making com-patibility strategies possible. Whereas books, newspapers, magazines or movies deliver discrete items of content, radio and television have a continuously un-folding nature. They are always *there*, but also always *imminent*. The most rou-tine program might be interrupted for an unscheduled and possibly vitally important message. This quality of incipience creates suspense and gives tele-vision and radio a special usefulness unique to them alone.

Their continuous availability also means radio and television con-sume program material relentlessly, compelling conservation of resources—

typically by using the same program over and over again in many different markets and countries. Chief among conservation mechanisms are **networking** and **syndication,** the primary means of reducing programming costs to manageable proportions by sharing them among many users, on an international as well as national scale.

Ease of Access

Broadcast and cable audiences need no preparation to become audience members. People need not learn to read, buy a ticket, get dressed or assemble at a special place outside the home. Thus these media reach a wider, more varied group of consumers than any other medium. Broadcasting, more than cable, can surmount geographic and economic barriers to reach rich and poor, old and young, rural and urban dwellers, the educated and the dropouts, the shut-ins and travelers, blue-collar workers and professionals, minorities and majorities. For economic reasons, cable will probably never be as accessible as broadcasting. Fees for cable services keep some people out of its audience, and the need for installing expensive connecting links to each individual home makes it uneconomical to install cable wires in rural areas. A new market niche emerged with the growth of **TVROs** (backyard satellite dishes), creating a need for someone to negotiate a supply of programs (actually, those of the satellite-to-cable networks) and to handle billing of the TVRO subscribers. Cable operators themselves usually take on these added functions within their franchise areas and in adjacent unfranchised rural areas, bringing "cable programming" to even more people.

The heterogeneity of people within reach of broadcasting and cable has important implications for programmers. It means the creation of larger audiences than ever before possible, generating the need for new types of program material. Prime-time broadcasting presents a unique challenge to programmers—how to interest and entertain audiences of unprecedented size and dissimilarity on a daily basis, year in and year out. Of course, most programmers aim at much smaller, more localized audiences than do those responsible for prime-time network television. But always they face the challenge of **maximizing and maintaining audience size,** even for the most narrowly defined subcategory of the population.

Capacity for Realism

Among the most memorable and highest rated of radio and television achievements have been their coverage of actual news and sports events— the burning of the zeppelin Hindenburg, the Kennedy funeral, the Apollo moon landings, the Super Bowl and World Cup games—real-life events picked up as they actually transpired. That the media deliver the sights and sounds of real events even as they take place compels our attention.

Cable has exploited this potential to good effect. The all-news cable services, lacking the time constraints of broadcast television newscasts, present extended live coverage of news events. Cable News Network (CNN) sometimes stays with a continuing story, such as a notable trial or congressional hearing, for hours on end. The Financial News Network (FNN) supplied 24-

hour coverage of the 1987 stock market crash. The Cable Satellite Public Affairs Networks (C-SPAN I & II), sponsored on a noncommercial basis primarily by the cable industry itself, bring the reality of government to the television screen in a way never done before. They provide live gavel-to-gavel coverage of both the Senate and the House of Representatives, as well as of many congressional hearings and other Washington events, such as conferences and public addresses. They convey an otherwise hidden reality with behind-the-scenes coverage of government and of news media operations.

In practice, the four previously mentioned attributes work together, giving radio and television unique power among the media to affect audiences, to reflect and shape social change. This impact comes from the combined weight of their ability to enter directly into the home, from their continuous and almost universal availability, from their easy accessibility, and from their realism. Government regulation, industry self-regulation and audience response constantly remind programmers that they must keep in mind the social consequences of their decisions.

COMMON STRATEGIC THEMES

Given that radio and television have the attributes just described, what can programmers learn from these attributes? What kinds of strategies for effective programming do they imply? Five themes emerge from a study of the chapters by programming specialists in this book. Briefly, they can be summarized as strategies capitalizing on (1) compatibility, (2) habit formation, (3) control of audience flow, (4) conservation of program resources and (5) breadth of appeal.

Compatibility

Scheduling strategies take advantage of the fact that programs can be timed to coincide with what people do throughout the daily cycle of their lives. The continuous unfolding nature of radio and television allows programmers to schedule different kinds of program material, or similar program materials in different ways, in the various dayparts. They strive to make their programming *compatible* with the day's round of what most people do—getting up in the morning and preparing for the day, driving to work, doing the morning household chores, breaking for lunch, enjoying an afternoon lull; the homecoming of the children after school, the accelerating tempo of home activities as the day draws to a close; relaxing during early prime time, indulging in the more exclusively adult interests of later prime time, the late fringe hours and the small hours of the morning. And, of course, compatibility calls for adaptation to the changed activity schedules of Saturdays and Sundays.

Compatibility strategies affect not only scheduling, but also the choice of program types and subject matters. The programmer must consider both who the audience is in each daypart and what the available audience members are most likely to be doing at the time. To apply the compatibility principle, the programmer studies the *lifestyles* of listeners and viewers. For this reason and for many others, programmers must know the community for which they design their program schedules. For example, in Chapter 14 on radio music programming, Edd Routt and Nick Alexander advise programmers to "observe lifestyles by visiting restaurants, shopping centers, gas stations, discotheques, bars, taverns and other places where people let their hair down."

Subsequent chapters will describe compatibility strategies in specific programming environments. Programmers speak of these strategies in terms of **dayparting,** the scheduling of different types of programs to match parts of the day known by such terms as **drivetime, early fringe** and **prime time.** Even in the rigid format of all-news radio, as Brewer and Eastman point out, the format must be carefully adjusted to suit the needs of different dayparts.

Cable television's approach to compatibility differs from broadcasting's approach. Because each broadcast station or network has only a single channel at its disposal, broadcast programmers must plan compatibility strategies for what they judge to be the "typical" lifestyles of their audiences. Cable systems, however, can devote entire channels to atypical audiences, ignoring dayparts. They can cater to the night-shift worker with sports at 6 A.M., to the single-person household with movies at 6 P.M., to the teenager with round-the-clock videos, using a different channel to serve each interest.

Time-zone differences work both for and against compatibility goals. A children's program on superstation WTBS in Atlanta at 7 A.M. would turn up on cable systems in California at 4 A.M.—hardly a compatible hour. On the other hand, an 8 P.M. sports event in Atlanta kicking off at 5 P.M. on cable in the West might be welcomed by sports enthusiasts having no interest in watching the late-afternoon/early-evening sitcoms and news that most stations carry then. Chapter 10 on programming for cable systems lists dozens of specialized services, about half of which are unique to cable, such as the all-weather and all-sports channels. Such **dedicated channels** (in the sense that they devote themselves to single subjects) will always be compatible with some of the people some of the time. Cable operators need not worry about the majority of subscribers not interested in weather at any particular moment because they can still serve those subscribers with other channels, and The Weather Channel's programmer knows that most people get interested in weather some of the time.

Habit Formation

Compatibility strategies acquire even more power because audience members form listening and watching *habits*. Scheduling programs for strict predictability (along with promotional efforts to make people aware of both the service as a whole and of individual programs) establishes **tuning habits** that eventually become automatic. Indeed, some people will go to extraordinary lengths to avoid missing the next episode in a favorite series. Programmers discovered this principle in the early days of radio when the *Amos 'n' Andy* habit became so strong that movie theaters in the 1930s shut down their pictures temporarily and hooked radios into their sound systems at 7:15 P.M. when *Amos 'n' Andy* came on. About that time the fanatic loyalty of soap-opera fans to their favorite series also became apparent, a loyalty still cultivated by today's televised serial dramas.

Ideally, habit formation calls for **stripping** programs—scheduling them Monday through Friday at the same time each day. To strip original prime-time programs, however, would require building up a backlog of these expensive shows, which would tie up far too much capital. Moreover, networks want maximum latitude for strategic maneuvers in the all-important prime-time schedule. If a broadcast network stripped its three prime-time hours with the same six half-hour shows each night, it would be left with only 6 pawns to move around in the scheduling chess game, instead of the 22 or so pawns that weekly scheduling of programs of varying length makes possible.

However, when weekly prime-time network shows go into **syndication,** stations and cable systems schedule them daily, a strategy requiring a large number of episodes. According to Ed Aiken in Chapter 8 on independent television station programming strategies, a prime-time series must have been on a network at least five years to accumulate enough episodes for a year's stripping in syndication (including a substantial number of reruns). Since few weekly shows survive five years of prime-time competition, the industry faces a nagging shortage of quality, off-network programs suitable for syndication.

Like all programming rules, those concerning habit formation are subject to selective violation. The most brilliant of the early television program strategists, Sylvester "Pat" Weaver, president of NBC, recognized that too much predictability can beget boredom. In the 1950s he invented the **spectacular** (nowadays called the **special**). Although at the time it seemed like a potentially destructive maneuver, Weaver boldly broke the established pattern of routine series scheduling in prime time with one-time, blockbuster programs, usually much longer than the normal series episodes they displaced. The interruption itself attracted attention, furnishing a peg on which to hang special promotional campaigns.

In the 1970s the number of specials increased greatly, spurred on by the discovery that audience members with the most purchasing power, the ones advertisers especially covet, tolerated schedule irregularities and found the specials attractive. The more habit-bound viewers, in both younger and older age ranges, interested advertisers less than the ones who favored change.

More recently, research data on people's feelings about television (as compared with simple tuning data) suggest that the increased variety of programs and schedule options made possible by cable television and home video recording may be weakening viewing habits. Only about half of viewers choose *in advance* the programs they watch. Furthermore, channel switching occurs more often in cable homes than in broadcast-only homes. But even so, one can hypothesize that some people may prefer to have only a limited number of choices. They may find it confusing and wearying to sift through scores of options before settling on a program. Broadcast scheduling, as a result of compatibility strategies, preselects a varied sequence of listening and viewing experiences, skillfully adapted to the desires and needs of a target audience. People can then choose an entire service—an overall pattern (or "sound" in the case of radio)—rather than individual programs.

No definitive research has settled the question of whether audiences find themselves more comfortable with the structured, compatible, predictable scheduling of traditional broadcasting than with a multitude of programming choices. However, researchers have often observed that when dozens or scores of options are available to listeners and viewers, most tune in to only a very few of the possible sources. For example, A. C. Nielsen surveys of homes with access to 20 or more television channels found that viewers watched only 8 to 10 of them for more than an hour per week. Among the most successful of the cable network programming services are superstations, which supply broadcast-like program schedules. As Susan Eastman points out in discussing cable programming strategies, some of the leading cable satellite channels have turned to **dayparting** for compatibility in the manner of broadcasting networks. She refers to such operations as "full-service" cable networks, citing CBN and USA Network as examples.

Control of Audience Flow

The assumption that audiences welcome, or at least tolerate, preselection of their programs most of the time accounts for strategies arising from the notion of **audience flow.** At scheduling breaks, when one program comes to an end and another begins, programmers visualize audience members as flowing from one program to the next, in any of three possible directions. They try to maximize the number that flow *through* to the next program on their own channel and the number that flow *in* from rival channels, at the same time minimizing the number that flow *away* to competing channels. Many strategies at all programming levels, described by authors in subsequent chapters, hinge on this concept. Audience flow considerations dominate the strategies of the commercial networks and affiliates, as well as of their rivals, the cable networks and independent television stations. Aiken, for example, stresses the role of **counterprogramming** (simultaneously scheduling programs with differing appeals) in the strategies of independent television stations seeking to direct the flow away from competing network affiliates.

Controlling audience flow becomes problematical, however, because listeners and viewers have a *freedom of choice.* Unlike the consumer faced with the limited decision of whether or not to buy a book, subscribe to a newspaper or attend a movie, broadcasting and cable consumers can choose instantaneously and repeatedly by switching back and forth among programs at will. Hence, the programmer cannot count on even the slight self-constraint that keeps a book buyer reading a book or a ticket buyer watching a movie so as not to waste the immediate investment. And, obviously, the polite social restraint that keeps a bored lecture audience seated does not inhibit radio and television audiences. Programmers have the job of holding the attention of a very tenuously committed audience. Its members take flight at the smallest provocation. Boredom or unintelligibility acts like a sudden shot into a flock of birds.

Fortunately for programmers, many audience members are afflicted by **tuning inertia.** People tend to leave the dial or key-pad alone unless stimulated into action by some forceful reason for change. For example, programmers believe that children can be used as a kind of stalking horse: Adults will tend to leave the set tuned to whatever channel the children chose for an earlier program.

Increased program options provided by cable and the convenience of **remote controls** have lessened the effect of tuning inertia; and, of course, video-cassette recording can remove programs from the exigencies of tuning entirely. Researchers recognize several ways the audience uses the remote control key-pad to manipulate programming: **flipping,** changing the channel before completion of a program; **zapping,** changing the channel to avoid a commercial interruption; and **zipping,** fast-forwarding a recording to avoid commercials or to reach a more interesting point. More than half of homes had VCRs by 1988, and nearly that number had remote controls (and these figures are expected to reach two-thirds by the early 1990s).[1] Tuning inertia continues therefore as a modest factor to consider in broadcast programming strategies.

However, formats such as all-news radio and cable channels invite audience flow in and out. They aim not at keeping audiences continuously tuned in but constantly coming back. As a widely used all-news radio slogan goes, "Give us 22 minutes, and we'll give you the world." One cable news service says "Around the world in thirty minutes."

In any case, the overall strategic lesson taught by the freedom-of-choice factor is that programs must always please, entertain and be easily understood. Much elitist criticism of program quality arises simply because of the democratic nature of the medium. Critics point out that programs must descend to the *lowest common denominator* of the audience they strive to attract. This fact need not mean dismissal of program quality. After all, some programs aim at elite audiences among whom the lowest common denominator can be very high indeed.

Conservation of Program Resources

Radio and television notoriously burn up program materials faster than other media—an inevitable consequence of the continuousness attribute. That fact makes *program conservation* an essential strategy. Satellite networks actively compete for channels on cable systems, suggesting an excess of programs. In fact, the reverse holds true. A high percentage of the programming on cable networks consists of repeats of the same items. The broadcast networks, too, also repeat many programs, in the form of summer **reruns,** for example. Cable has stimulated production of new programs and program types, but on the whole, cable heightens program scarcity rather than alleviating it. Cable makes parsimonious use of program resources all the more essential.

A popular fallacy holds that innumerable workable new program ideas and countless usable new scripts by embryonic writers await discovery and that only the perversity or shortsightedness of program executives keeps this treasure trove of new material off the air. But one can hardly blame programmers and their employers for being unwilling to risk huge production costs on untried talents and untested ideas. Even if they were willing, the results would not differ much as long as mass entertainment remains the goal. A national talent pool, even in a country the size of the United States (and even for superficial, imitative programming), is not infinitely large. It takes a certain unusual gift to create programs capable of holding the attention of millions of people hour by hour, day by day, week after week.

Anyone doubting the difficulty of appealing to mass audiences need only consider the experience of the older media. In a recent year, of 27,000 new books printed, only 33 sold 100,000 or more copies; of 13,000 records copyrighted, only 185 singles went gold; of 205 feature film releases, only 11 grossed the $20 million reckoned as the minimum to break even. And yet audiences for these media are small compared to the nightly prime-time television audience.[2]

Sometimes audience demands and conservation happily coincide, as when the appetite for a new hit song demands endless replays and innumerable arrangements. Eventually, however, obsolescence sets in, and the song becomes old hat. Radio and television are perhaps the most obvious indices of our throwaway society. Even the most massively popular and brilliantly successful program series eventually lose their freshness. Then they go into the limbo of the umpteenth rerun circuit.

Frugality must be practiced at every level and in every aspect of programming. Consider how often you see or hear "the best of so-and-so," a compilation of bits and pieces from previous programs; news actualities broken into many segments and parceled out over a period of several hours or days; the annual return of past year's special-occasion programs; the sports shows patched together out of stock footage; the weather report broken down into separate little packets labeled "marine forecasts," "shuttle-city weather," "long-term forecast," "weather update," "aviation weather" and so on.

The enormous increase in demand for program materials created by the growth of cable television would be impossible to satisfy were it not that the multichannel medium lends itself to repeating programs much more liberally than does broadcasting. A pay-cable channel operates full time by scheduling fewer than 50 or so new programs a month, mostly movies. As Jeffrey Reiss points out in Chapter 11 on premium cable networks, each one runs four to six times. Furthermore, films first scheduled one month turn up again in the following months in still more reruns, which pay-cable programmers euphemistically call **encores**.

A major aspect of the programmer's job consists, then, in devising ingenious ways to get the maximum mileage out of each program item, to develop formats that require as little new material as possible for the next episode or program in the series, to invent clever excuses for repeating old programs over and over. The first programming coup of Fred Silverman, a legendary programming executive who served each of the three national television networks in turn, consisted simply of inventing a new framework for presenting overused theatrical films. Soon after getting his master's degree from Ohio State University, Silverman found a job in the program department of WGN-TV, Chicago. He devised a simple but effective stratagem for reviving the old films in WGN's library by incorporating them into a series under a high-sounding but meaningless name, *Film Classics*. He built an impressive library setting in which an attractive presenter gave gracious live introductions. This window dressing gave the old turkeys a new lease on life. Today, some national cable services—such as American Movie Classics—use just this strategy.

The first question a programmer asks about any proposed series concerns its staying power. William Paley, as president and later chairman of CBS

Inc. from 1928 to 1983 (with a reprise as acting chairman starting in 1986), has had more top-level network programming experience than any other broadcaster. He made the point in his autobiography: "'What are you going to do for the next ten shows?' we might ask a writer. . . . What we really want to find out is how well the writer can handle his material over the long run."[3] Any tyro can design a winning schedule for a single week; a professional has to plan for the attrition that inevitably sets in as weeks stretch into the indefinite future.

Breadth of Appeal

Stations and cable systems recoup their high capital investment and operating costs only by appealing to a wide range of audience interests. This statement might seem self-evident, yet initially some public broadcasters made a virtue out of ignoring "the numbers game," leaving the race for ratings to commercial broadcasters. But as John Fuller explains in Chapter 17 on national public television programming, this fundamentally unrealistic viewpoint has given way to the strategy of aiming for a high *cumulative* number of viewers rather than for high ratings for each individual program. This strategy coincides with that of cable television, whose many channels enable it to program to small audiences on some channels, counting on the cumulative reach of all its channels to bring in sufficient subscriptions to make a profit.

The difference between the two goals has been expressed in terms of **broadcasting** versus **narrowcasting.** Gene Jankowski, president of the CBS/ Broadcast Group, uses the term *aggregation* and *disaggregation*, pointing out that the former deals with shared feelings and interests while the latter with highly personalized tastes and needs. Jankowski's terms take into account our complementary needs for belonging to the group while at the same time retaining our personal individualities.[4]

To *broadcast* originally meant to sow seed by hand, throwing it at random upon cultivated fields. Broadcasters began by throwing signals across the land, signals that blossomed by chance wherever receivers happened to be located. But as the medium developed, stations began to define audiences in demographic terms, adjusting the nature of their programs accordingly. Now, cable goes beyond the broad versus narrow dichotomy. Nevertheless, a broad-appeal service can have a narrowly defined clientele, as in the case of Univision, a hybrid broadcast-cable network having broad appeal but only for Spanish-speaking audiences. On the other hand, a narrow- (or vertical-) appeal service can nevertheless have a broadly defined clientele, as in the case of Lifetime, a cable channel that touches on a wide range of women's interests and lifestyles.

Only the national television broadcasting networks continue to "cast" their programs across the land from coast to coast with the aim of filling the entire landscape. Of course, no network expects to capture *all* the available viewers. A top-rated prime-time program draws only 20 to 25 percent of the potential audience, though extraordinary programs get up to three times that many viewers.

Nevertheless, by any standard, audiences for prime-time broadcast television networks are enormous. A single such program can draw an audience so large that it could fill a Broadway theater every night for a century. Such size can only be achieved by cutting across demographic lines and appealing to many different social groups. Network broadcasting can surmount differences of age, sex, education and lifestyle that would ordinarily segregate people into many separate sub-audiences.

A series such as *The Cosby Show,* the top-rated regularly scheduled network television program of 1986 and 1987, exhibits remarkably broad appeal. For example, it led in popularity with all age groups except the 12–17 teens (who rated it second after *Family Ties*).[5] The show was timely, tapping into a revived interest in promoting family values, yet with enough wry humor to save it from smugness. Its depiction of middle-class family life among blacks had positive appeal for both black and white viewers. Blacks welcomed the upbeat role models of the Huxtable family (notwithstanding a few intransigents who regarded the family as pandering unrealistically to white values). Even whites with a residue of racial bias found it easy to accept the attractive, all-black cast. (Note that the only recurrent white character, the chubby prepubescent friend of cute little Rudy Huxtable, minimized the possibility of raising racist hackles.)

AUDIENCE APPEALS

Programmers do well to ask themselves how well new program concepts, scripts, pilots and proffered ready-made programs exploit basic audience appeals. Specific major and secondary **appeals** can be identified and used in advance to appraise the probable success of mass media products. Sophisticated media critics might find it simplistic to use arbitrarily defined audience appeals as criteria of success, but television programmers do in fact work at this level. A committee of network vice-presidents appraising the merits of a pilot program for a new prime-time series will analyze it for its major and secondary mass-audience appeals; the programmers may then go on to select specific appeals for enhancement in future episodes and later identify others to downplay if the series fails to attract the desired audiences. Program researchers use focus groups and other methods (see Chapter 2) to predict whether the right number and combination of appeals have been incorporated in an as-yet-untried program.

Primary Appeals

Five major kinds of appeal have preeminent importance in any television program capable of attracting the kind of mass audience the national broadcast networks seek. As a rule of thumb, one might say that to succeed, any mass communication product must incorporate all five of these appeals, at least in some degree, and must maximize several of them. Try applying this appeals test to any well-known, successful product in any mass medium, whether a best-selling book, a blockbuster movie, a hit Broadway play or a wide-circulation newspaper or magazine:

1. Conflict.   Nearly all radio and television programs contain elements of conflict, rivalry or contention. Conflict is especially prominent in all types of drama, in sports and in most forms of comedy. In explaining why television drama tends toward violence, a professional scriptwriter pointed out that dramatic plots evolve out of conflicts between man and nature, man and God, man against himself, and man against man. Writers generally find it too difficult to use the first three types within the confines of television formats; therefore, most scriptwriters resort to man-against-man conflicts, which tend to result in violent confrontations before the plot finally works itself out.[6] Conflict appeal also figures prominently in many nondramatic formats such as song lyrics and news stories.

Conflict can also be analyzed in terms of *suspense*. We eagerly look forward to finding out who or what is going to win in a conflict. Well-constructed programs wring the maximum suspense out of conflict situations. Note how skillfully television game shows and soap operas exploit suspense. Sports announcers and commentators build verbally upon the visual suspense in athletic conflicts. Talk-show hosts create suspense by deliberate role-playing.

2. Comedy.   People love to be amused, though just what makes them laugh is not easy to pin down. Elements commonly found in comedy include incongruity, exaggeration, surprise, embarrassment and ridicule. Comedy comes in many different genres, such as satire, farce, fantasy, one-liners and parody. It may vary widely as to style, characterized by such terms as slapstick, romantic, social, bawdy, tragicomic and musical. Comedy sometimes plays a special role in providing comic relief—a momentary lightening of tension in tragedies and other serious presentations.

3. Sex.   Of course sexual appeals attract people universally, whether found in characters/performers, plots or dialogue. Television commercials, no less than prime-time dramas, utilize direct sexual appeals. Implicit sexual appeals are embodied not only in the physical appearance and deportment of those who appear but also in the personality traits identified by such terms as vitality, animation, warmth, vulnerability and charisma. The hosts and hostesses of quiz shows offer an interesting study in implied sexuality.

4. Information.   The universal interest in news illustrates the wide appeal of information. Journalism manuals emphasize that the appeal of news can be enhanced by proximity (nearness to the audience's own environment, social class, interests and so on), importance of the subject in the scheme of things, the notability or notoriety of news subjects, and elements of novelty ("man bites dog"). However, information lacking these qualities can also have appeal, that of quiz-show trivia, for example. Information also feeds the interest in self-improvement and in learning how to conduct oneself in specific social and economic situations (advice columns, "lifestyle" programs).

5. Human Interest.   As human beings, we have insatiable curiosity about the lives of other human beings. This curiosity is formally satisfied by information (news, biography, history) and informally by details of ordinary and extraordinary lives revealed in "human interest stories." Material exploiting this appeal varies widely, from scholarly anthropological documentaries to features on "the lifestyles of the rich and famous." Note how often news programs relieve the gloom of hard news with a concluding human interest story, not infrequently exploiting comedy appeal at the same time.

Overlapping as they do, these five appeals exist in only loosely defined compartments. If you try them out on familiar material, you will find, for example, that comedy often relies heavily on conflict—consider the slapstick episodes in Laurel and Hardy films. Comedy appeals can also have a sexual component, as almost any **situation comedy** series demonstrates. Could Lucy have gained such fame as a comedienne if she had looked dowdy and middle-aged? Sex can enhance the appeal of information, too. How often do you see ugly, sexually neutral news anchors? If you do, what compensating appeals do they have? An item having human interest appeal gains from the presence of conflict, sex, information and comedy appeals. Despite such overlaps, defining appeals under separate headings in this way has proved useful in analyzing the potential of mass media products.

Secondary Appeals

Nor do the five primary appeals stand alone. One can identify many well-defined secondary appeals, supporting the five major appeals. Some of the following appeals, as well as a long list of others, will be found in every successful mass audience production:

• *Identification.*   Any program that entices the audience into identifying emotionally with characters/participants has strong appeal. Such feelings enhance the interest in conflicts of all kinds, including sports in which fans become passionate partisans.

• *Sympathy.*   A special kind of identification comes with feelings of sympathy for the underdog, the victim or the loser. Babies and animals also tend to have intrinsic sympathetic appeal, which is why experienced actors tend to avoid sharing the spotlight with these unwitting scene-stealers. For the same reason, when the ratings of a prime-time dramatic series start to slip, the producers sometimes try to revive its appeal by adding dogs or children to the cast.

• *Nostalgia.*   Anything that reminds us pleasurably of past events, such as old songs, photographs or anniversary programs, has nostalgia appeal.

• *Acquisitiveness.*   Programs that offer opportunities for winning prizes, saving money, getting bargains or keeping up with the Joneses have strong appeal for some audience members. Cable shopping channels rely primarily on this appeal, enhanced by the sex appeal of the presenters. Because programs with few appeals draw only limited audiences, the shopping channels soon began adding other appeals such as conflict (contests) to supplement the acquisitiveness appeal.

• *Credibility.*   All appeals rely on an element of credibility. The plot must be plausible, the personality ring true, the offer sound genuine, the information appear authentic, the comedy seem spontaneous.

• *Importance.*   Association with someone or something important lends heightened significance to a communication. Advertisers constantly use this appeal by employing celebrity performers and endorsers. A star name automatically enhances the appeal of a program irrespective of other factors; but, illustrative of the need for multiple appeals, a star cannot single-handedly rescue a weak program.

• *Beauty.*   Sex appeal and beauty are closely linked, of course, but beauty in the broader sense of aesthetic quality enhances programs, for example, in terms of beautiful scenery, fine design and artistic use of light and color.

• *Novelty.*   Anything that breaks the monotony of humdrum repetition by introducing new ideas, personalities, styles, products, services and ways of doing things has novelty appeal. The prevalence of imitation in the mass media and the tendency to repeat successful performances place a special premium on superficially novel approaches.

Role of Social Trends

Novelty appeal relates to a more generalized appeal for which no single name exists. It includes elements of trendiness, modernity, stylishness, timeliness and being "with it." At the crudest level, programmers exploit this appeal by capitalizing on the notoriety of figures in the news who have captured that brief 15 minutes of fame that Andy Warhol promised everyone. Vanna White won such fame as the beautiful letter-turner in the game show, *Wheel of Fortune.* Every talk show wanted her as a guest; model photographers dug through their archives for long-forgotten poses; publishers urged a biography—all for a supernumerary performer who rarely spoke a word on her own show yet mysteriously acquired the status of a cult figure.

Programmers must be on the lookout to capitalize on such fleeting fame. More importantly, at a deeper level, programmers need to be sensitive to significant social trends and their implications for programming.

Market researcher Daniel Yankelovich once made the point that a good marketer—and a program executive is after all a marketer of programs—combines research findings on social trends with a "reading of the tea leaves."[7] Most of the social trends he listed more than a decade ago continue in evidence, though somewhat modified in the intervening years. He mentioned, for example, emphasis on creativity, meaningful work, mysticism, return to nature, ethnicity, liberalized sex attitudes, tolerance for disorder, challenge to authority, female careerism and reaction against the complexity of modern life.

Programmers today need the kind of background that the Yankelovich article calls for, with due awareness of how the pendulum has begun its swing in the opposite direction. New trends are emerging—the Protestant work ethic on the rise, a renewed emphasis on basic education, reaction against the drug culture, fear of AIDS, the return of dress codes, more disciplined treatment of children, harsher penalties for criminals, revived concern for the family. Are these genuine long-term trends, or merely aspects of a temporary political-social agenda? Programmers must assess such questions in terms of the audiences they want to reach and place their bets on what the future will bring. Programmers should in fact consider themselves futurists. By combining wide reading and observation, research and the messages of the tea leaves, good programmers foresee changes in public tastes, the rise and fall of fashions, the emergence of trends and the decline of current fads.

BASIC PROGRAMMER SKILLS

The preceding section on audience appeals concerns the programmer's arts of **evaluation.** Programmers also need specific practical skills relating to program **selection:** audience targeting, program acquisition and negotiation. But above all, programmers must understand **scheduling** and give time to keeping up-to-date on program availabilities.

Audience Targeting

Programmers spend a great deal of time and effort studying their market, their coverage, their competition and their prospective advertisers. They seek in these studies to define specific salable targets within the total population, reachable by their programs and of interest to advertisers. Merely striving to reach the largest possible audience can be self-defeating, for programs inevitably have a push-pull effect: What attracts one audience member repels another. Programmers must therefore decide which audience members to aim for, which to sacrifice. This process reaches its highest degree of precision in radio music programming, which in a large market involves highly refined audience **targeting.** In Chapter 14 on radio music programming, Edd Routt and Nick Alexander show how a programmer goes about finding an audience subgroup not already adequately served by competing music radio stations and devising a musical format to target that audience. **Cable systems** also pose interesting and intricate targeting questions because their multiplicity of channels enables appealing to many specific audiences simultaneously.

Essentially, targeting involves applying knowledge of **demographics**—audience composition, especially in terms of age and sex, but also often in such terms as income, ethnic identity and rural versus urban residence. Programmers acquire this knowledge from the study and practice of audience research. Well-rounded programming executives must master the basics of that somewhat arcane field. They must be able to read and interpret standard audience reports and understand their limitations; they must be able to analyze those reports to extract information with specific relevance for their own stations. They should be capable of conducting or commissioning special local research studies. Because of its fundamental importance, *audience research* occupies its own chapter in this book (Chapter 2), preceding the chapters on specific programming situations.

Broadcast audience research evolved during the last half-century, well supported financially because of the healthy condition of the broadcast advertising industry. **Cable television** challenged traditional broadcast research with a new set of problems, both in terms of cable programs as competitors for audiences and of cable advertising as a competitor for commercial revenue. Cable advertising initially earned insufficient revenue to justify developing a separate, new research service. Cable's needs, combined with broadcasting's need to deal with cable competition, led to experiments with a new version of traditional audience measurement devices, the **peoplemeter,** introduced as the basis for a regular audience measurement service in the United States only in 1987. As discussed in Chapter 2, by improving on previous methods of analyzing audience composition, the peoplemeter gives better reports on the all-important demographic aspects of measurement.

Program Acquisition

Would-be program suppliers are abundant, but they never have enough programs of just the right type to fit the target audience, to fit into the schedule, and to fit the user's pocketbook. Programmers must therefore know the program market. Speaking of a particular class of users, Ed Aiken says in Chapter 8 on independent stations, "Effective communication with program suppliers is the lifeblood of the independent programmer."

Three basic program sources exist: broadcast **network** programs, **syndicated** programs (including feature films) and **local** programs produced "in-house." These compartments, however, are by no means watertight. Locally produced shows sometimes develop into hybrid blends of local production and syndication. Network entertainment programs "go into syndication" to stations after their initial plays on the national network. Networks produce **made-for-TV movies.** Pay-television suppliers produce **made-for-pay movies** and entertainment specials—on-location taping of live performances at concerts, at nightclubs and in theaters. Live sports events crop up on both cable and broadcasting network services and also as syndicated local/regional productions.

1. *Network Programs.*   The national, full-service, interconnected network is broadcasting's distinctive contribution toward conservation of program resources. Newspapers had shared news and features by means of news agencies and syndicates long before broadcasting began, but broadcasting introduced the elements of instantaneous national distribution and simultaneity of programs. The three national television networks supply the bulk of all broadcast television programs, filling about 70 percent of their affiliates' schedules (about two-thirds of all commercial television stations have network affiliations). About 70 cable program networks similarly deliver the bulk of cable systems' content by means of satellite.

Aside from news and news-related public affairs materials, the broadcast networks buy their programs from independent production firms. In their discussion of prime-time broadcast programming in Chapter 5 Lewine, Eastman and Adams describe the tortuous route from program idea to finished, on-the-air network series. Each year, network programmers sift through five or six *thousand* initial proposals, shepherding them through successive levels of screening, ending up in the fall with twenty-odd new programs for their actual schedules. Outside authors write the scripts, and production houses do the rest of the creative work.

The veteran movie and television producers, the traditional **Big Seven studios** of the Hollywood entertainment motion-picture industry, are Columbia, Walt Disney Studios, MGM-UA, Paramount, 20th Century–Fox, Universal and Warner Brothers. Cannon, New World Pictures, Lorimar, Orion, Tri-Star and others fight to join this elite production group. However, the independent production houses also make Hollywood their base of operations. Among **independent producers,** Lorimar–Telepictures, MTM, Steven J. Cannell and Aaron Spelling and Steven Bochco are regular and prolific producers for the networks and syndication. As an example, the early lineup for the fall 1987 prime-time network television season consisted of 75 program series, 22 of them new that season. Of the 75, the networks themselves produced only ABC's *Moonlighting, Monday Night Football* and *20/20*, and CBS's *60 Minutes* and *West 57th.* A total of 25 Hollywood producers accounted for all the other program series, except for the feature film series. About five producers turned out nearly half the series. The most-used producer, Lorimar–Telepictures, had responsibility, along with various collaborators, for 11 series in the 1987–88 prime-time schedule. Such concentration of prime-time entertainment production in so few hands led to the **prime-time access rule** (**PTAR**), designed to break the stranglehold of the few elite producers, opening the top time period to a greater variety of independent producers.

The networks' surrender of the entertainment-program-production function has a legal basis in the resolution of an antitrust suit brought against them by the Justice Department in the early 1970s. At that time the department deemed network control of prime-time entertainment a near monopoly. Each network separately entered into a consent decree with the Justice Department. These decrees meant that, while admitting no wrongdoing, the networks consented to observe certain constraints, namely, (1) to refrain from syndicating any programs in the United States and any programs other than their own abroad (the **network syndication rule**) and (2) to limit their financial interests in entertainment program productions by others (the **financial interest rule**). They could still produce 17 percent of their own entertainment programs (amounting to $3\frac{1}{2}$ hours of the 22 hours of prime time). Ironically, though the networks chafe at these restrictions, they fail to take full advantage of the 17 percent allowance, as the above data on the 1987 season indicate. The only network-produced entertainment prime-time program in 1987 was ABC's *Moonlighting* (PTAR rules classify programs such as *60 Minutes* as public affairs, not entertainment).

A peculiar fiscal fact of life about prime-time entertainment is that the original license fees paid by the networks for the use of these programs by no means cover the costs of production. This loss-leader type of pricing is known as **deficit financing.** The producers count on recouping their losses by selling **off-network syndication** rights, and indeed they profit handsomely from these rights. Exposure of a successful series on a network creates tremendous demand for it in the syndication market. For example, as a result of its top-rated run on NBC, *The Cosby Show* grossed for Viacom International, holder of the syndication rights, something on the order of half a billion dollars in its first off-network season. Suffering as they are from cable and independent station competition, the networks look with envy on such windfalls. After all, they, the networks, created the appetite for the Cosby series, yet the network syndication and financial interest rules prevent their profiting further from such shows, once they have scheduled their two **plays** (original showing plus one repeat). The networks will experiment with new ways of handling prime-time productions after the consent decrees expire in 1990.

Cable networks differ in major respects from broadcast television networks. In technical delivery, they are similar: In both cases a central headquarters assembles programs and distributes them nationwide, using common-carrier relay facilities to reach individual broadcast stations or cable systems. But the financial and working relationships between broadcasting affiliates and their networks and between cable affiliates and their networks differ fundamentally. Cable systems depend almost totally on satellite-distributed programming to fill their channels, and because they have many channels, they deal with many networks. The symbiotic relationship between each broadcast network and its affiliates does not exist in the cable field. Chapter 9 on cable system programming points out that only a tiny percentage of cable programming originates locally, whereas television stations average 5 to 10 percent of local material (and many broadcast a great deal more local production than that). Retransmitted broadcast programs constitute one-quarter of cable scheduling, with over 70 national cable networks (some in decidedly shaky financial condition) supplying the remaining programming. Cable network programmers have far less input into the creative aspect of programming than their broadcasting counterparts.

The great bulk of cable network programming comes from the same sources as broadcast programming—from distributors of feature films and syndicated programs. Thus programmers find their negotiations complicated by increases in demand from a variety of users. However, specialized cable networks, such as Cable News Network, Lifetime, Nickelodeon and The Weather Channel have developed their own genres of program material. And pay-cable channels increasingly venture on their own production enterprises. Showtime picked up *Brothers,* an offbeat sitcom series, after it had been rejected by the broadcast networks. On the other hand, HBO prefers to create programming tailored especially for its needs rather than to compete with broadcasters for programming:

> Cable network executives say that introducing original product attracts fresh attention to the cable service from the press, enables a network to develop programming that suits its target audience and helps project an image of uniqueness.[8]

HBO has had considerable success with the production of original comedy specials that would not always have passed muster with broadcast network

censors but that have proved popular in cable's more permissive environment. Despite such supplementation, however, cable has so far contributed
relatively little to the total store of program materials.

Radio's networks no longer qualify as full-service networks. They
now resemble syndicators, supplying features and program inserts such as
newscasts. On the other hand, some radio program syndicators supply stations via satellite with complete schedules of ready-to-air music in various
established formats, much like networks. In Chapter 13 Cameron, Johnson
and McLaughlin illustrate radio's blending of networking and syndication.

Public broadcasting network programmers face still a different situation, as John Fuller explains in Chapter 17 on PBS. Designed as an alternative
to the commercial system, PBS programming comes ready-made from the
larger member stations specializing in production for the network, from small
independent producers and from foreign sources, notably the British Broadcasting Corporation. Foreign sources supply more elaborate productions than
PBS can generally afford to commission, costing PBS about one-tenth of what
a similar program would if produced in the United States. **Coproduction,** the
sharing of production costs by broadcasting organizations in different countries, accounts for an increasingly large proportion of Public Broadcasting Service programming.

A certain amount of crossover usage occurs in the varying programming situations. *The Paper Chase* exemplified such commercial-noncommercial
exchange. It began as a feature theatrical film in 1973. In 1978–79, CBS spun it
off into a critically acclaimed but unsuccessful prime-time commercial network series. After CBS dropped the series, PBS picked up the rights in 1981.
Still later, the pay-cable network Showtime obtained rights to the 22 original
episodes, producing further episodes on its own. Still later, the series appeared on CBN. Another example of crossover usage is the PBS movie review
program originated by the public broadcasting station in Chicago, *Sneak Previews*, then featuring Chicago-newspaper critics Roger Ebert and Gene Siskel.
When the stars failed to agree with the noncommercial station on contract
renewal, they accepted an offer from a commercial syndicator and retained
the same format under a new title, *At the Movies*, later shifting to Disney
Productions.

2. *Syndicated Programs and Feature Films.* Local broadcast programmers
come into their own when they select syndicated programs for their individual stations. They draw upon (a) *off-network series,* programs that have reverted to their copyright owners after the network that first ran them has
used up its contractual number of plays; (b) *first-run syndicated series and specials,* programs packaged independently by producers and marketed directly
to individual stations rather than being first seen as network shows; typical of
such series are *Wheel of Fortune, People's Court, Entertainment Tonight, Oprah
Winfrey* and holiday specials; and (c) *feature films,* movies made originally for
theatrical exhibition. Syndicators put these three classes of programs on display nationally and internationally at a number of annual meetings and trade
shows. For showcases, they rely especially on the annual conventions of the

Table 1-1 Some Major Distributors of Syndicated Off-Network Programs

DISTRIBUTOR	SAMPLE OFFERINGS (No. of Episodes)
Columbia/Embassy Television	*Diff'rent Strokes* (109)
DFS Dorland Program Exchange	*The Flintstones* (166)
Freemantle	*New Candid Camera* (130)
Globo TV Network (Brazil)	*Cambalache* (174)
King Features Entertainment	*Ask Dr. Ruth* (130)
Lionheart Television (BBC)	*Civilisation* (14)
Lorimar-Telepictures	*Dallas* (191)
MCA TV	*Miami Vice* (90)
Orion Television	*Hollywood Squares* (260)
Paramount Television	*Cheers* (121), *Happy Days* (255)
Republic Pictures	John Wayne Classic Westerns (29)
D. L. Taffner Ltd.	*Benny Hill* (95)
Turner Program Services	MGM Pre-1948 movies
20th Century–Fox	*M*A*S*H* (255)
Viacom International	*Cosby* (182), *I Love Lucy* (179)
Warner Brothers Television	*Tarzan* features (32), *Superman* (104)

Source: *Broadcasting*, 19 January 1987, p. 136.

National Association of Television Program Executives (**NATPE**) and the National Cable Television Association (**NCTA**) held each spring.

At the 1987 NATPE convention, hundreds of syndicators fought for the attention of television programming executives, offering a huge array of feature films (singly and in packages), made-for-television movies, off-network series, first-run series, specials, miniseries, documentaries, docudramas, news services, game shows, cartoons, variety shows, soap operas, sports shows, concerts, talk shows and so on. Trade publications carry lists of exhibitors and their offerings at the time of the conventions. Table 1-1 gives a selection of syndicators attending that conference, along with examples of their offerings.

Europe has a corresponding annual program trade fair, MIP-TV. Formerly at that fair, the flow of commercial syndicated programming between the United States and other countries ran almost exclusively *from* the United States. Public broadcasting first whetted American viewers' appetites for foreign programs. And with such specialized cable services as The Discovery Channel featuring foreign documentaries and Arts & Entertainment featuring foreign dramatic offerings, the international flow has become somewhat more reciprocal, though the United States still remains much more of an exporter than an importer.

Barter syndication deals often complicate the purchasing of syndicated programs. These deals generally come as offers from advertisers who, having acquired licenses to broadcast certain syndicated programs, offer these programs without charge to stations. The bartering advertisers retain some of the commercial spots for their own ads, offering the rest of the commercial minutes for the station to sell on its own behalf. The amount of commercial time retained by the advertiser varies, and some **barter** deals require the station to give *cash* as well as *advertising spot time*. As Aiken and Haldi explain, barter deals thus involve complex financial trade-off decisions: Does the value of the programs, including the potential earnings from the open spots within them, offset the lost revenue for the commercial spots the syndicator retains? Is the proffered program series so desirable that it warrants supplementing the time barter with cash payment?

Of all the program types, the feature film is the most in demand because of its popularity on so many different delivery systems. The term **windows,** borrowed from the world of space flight in which rockets can be launched only through certain time-space openings when conditions are just right, has been applied to the release-sequence by which feature films reach their various markets. First, of course, comes the traditional window of *theatrical release,* either simultaneously in several thousand theaters throughout the country or in stages of "limited release." Next, in the usual order of priority, as Reiss explains in Chapter 11, come releases through the windows of *home video* and *pay-per-view* cable, regular *pay cable,* broadcast *networks* and finally general broadcast and cable *syndication.* Prices for rentals decrease in each stage of release as products age and lose their timeliness.

The trade press prints directories of program suppliers for both broadcasting and cable. For example, the 1988 editions of *Broadcasting-Cablecasting Yearbook, Channels Field Guide* and *View* list the following:

- Over a thousand producers, distributors, and production service companies
- 55 basic cable services such as ESPN, MTV, Nickelodeon, USA Network, the superstations and shopping services
- 8 pay-cable services, such as HBO and Showtime
- 5 pay-per-view services, such as Viewer's Choice and Request Television

3. *Local Production.* As the chapters on television station programming will show, local news programs play an important role in broadcast station program strategies (even these programs, though locally produced, often contain a great deal of syndicated material as inserts). But aside from news, locally produced material plays only a minor role as a program source. True, all-news and all-talk radio stations depend almost entirely on local production, but those formats cost so much to run and have such a specialized appeal that they remain few in number. Stations simply find syndicated material cheaper to obtain and easier to sell to advertisers.

Some cable systems do make a stab at local news production but do not invest the kind of money in facilities and staff required for a competitive news department. As Agostino and Eastman point out in Chapter 12, even though metropolitan cable franchises usually mandate one or more **access** channels for use by the general public, municipal agencies and education, these sources account for only a tiny fraction of cable system programming. **Local origination** channels, used by cable systems for their own programming and syndicated material such as **electronic text,** likewise contribute only minimally in most cases to the total program service supplied by cable systems.

Negotiation

The preceding section makes it clear that programmers need to be skilled negotiators. They deal constantly with outside suppliers—networks, syndicated program distributors, barter advertisers, production houses. Business relations between stations or cable systems and their suppliers have few hard-and-fast rules. Bargaining and bartering characterize practically every transaction. For example, *group owners* and cable *multiple system operators*, because they purchase programs and services for several markets in a single transaction, enjoy a bargaining advantage. As big spenders, they can demand *discounts* that small individual stations or cable systems cannot command. Similarly, syndicators give special *incentives* to network owned-and-operated broadcast stations because they reach such a large and desirable percentage of the total national market. Syndicators especially want exposure on prestigious stations within the bellwether markets (top three), according to Klein's Chapter 4 on **group-owned stations.** Syndicators may also pressure stations to take lesser programs or movies along with good ones they distribute. This practice is called **block booking,** and it was once prohibited in the theatrical film industry but has become common practice today in both television and movie program licensing.

Program Selection

Having pegged out a suitable target audience, defined in terms of market, facilities and competition, and having identified program sources, the programmer next faces the task of program selection. One might expect an approach to the problem in the spirit of the critic, asking "Which of the affordable programs has the highest quality?" As a matter of fact, this sort of question is rarely asked. Instead, programmers and other executives ask about demographics, past performance, lead-in and lead-out, counterprogramming strategies and the like.

Certain basic questions need to be asked in evaluating additions to or replacements in a broadcast schedule. Surrounding circumstances may differ greatly: Network executives contemplating a prime-time series pilot program clearly operate in a different context than station executives appraising a syndicated offering for a prime-time access slot. Nevertheless, each needs to ask whether the contemplated change meets certain criteria. Does it:

1. Target a demographically desirable audience?
2. Entail reasonable costs for its type and time slot?

3. Compete well with the simultaneous offerings of competitors?

4. Articulate well with its neighboring programs?

5. Employ talent with high current audience recognition?

6. Come from a previously successful producer-writer team?

7. Deal with currently topical subject matter?

8. Resemble comparable high-rated series?

9. Rate high in terms of the five primary appeals and many secondary appeals discussed in the preceding section?

A programmer can devise numerical scales for evaluating a program series in terms of the above questions, reducing the answers finally to a composite score. Indeed, teams of researchers, time-buyers and analysts at major advertising agencies do just that in anticipation of the upcoming prime-time television season, predicting the shares each series is likely to earn. This is an essential exercise, for the initial prices charged for commercials will depend on the predicted audience shares and demographics earned by the shows.

Scheduling

Of all the programmer's basic skills, perhaps **scheduling** comes closest to qualifying as uniquely a radio and television specialty. One critic has referred to broadcast television scheduling as an "arcane, crafty, and indeed, crucial" operation; another has said that "half a (network) program director's job is coming up with new shows; the other half, some would say the other 90 percent, is in knowing how to design a weekly schedule, in knowing where to put shows to attract maximum attention."[9]

Scheduling a station, cable system or network is a singularly difficult process. It demands using the principles of compatability, habit formation, flow control and resource conservation. It requires understanding one's own and one's competitors' coverage patterns, market and audience demographics. Access commitments and owner policies complicate the scheduling of cable channels. Cable programmers also have to weigh the claims of competing services for specific channel locations. VHF television stations, for example, much prefer a cable channel that matches their over-the-air channel number, and UHFs would like a channel between 2 and 13 (there being no necessary relation between the cable channel number a station occupies and its own assigned broadcast channel number). Stations particularly object to **repositioning,** putting **VHF** stations (channels 2 through 13) on higher number cable channels. Cable operators, on the other hand, prefer to give the choicest positions to the most *popular* (or most lucrative) services, whether they are broadcast or cable-only.

Each of the specialist chapters later in the book deals with the strategies of scheduling within a particular programming environment. Each has its own strategies, yet all of them rest on fundamental programming principles. To give an idea of the range of scheduling considerations, here is a sampling from ensuing chapters:

1. Prime-time broadcast network television programmers are experts in fine-tuning their schedules. They have even invented names for special strategies, such as *stunting, hammocking* and *tent-poling*.

2. Non-prime-time network television programmers must be particularly conscious of *daypart demographics* because their programs must appeal to a disparate audience ranging from children on Saturday morning to adults in the after-midnight hours.

3. Broadcast network affiliate programmers have the luxury of being able to concentrate most of their energies on filling the 30 percent of their hours when the network is not feeding them programs. Attention here focuses particularly on the *prime access* period strategies, *early fringe* and *local evening news*.

4. Independents can take advantage of their greater scheduling flexibility in competing with affiliates in their markets by using *counterprogramming* strategies.

5. Radio station formula programming requires precision scheduling, sometimes calling for split-second timing. The all-news and music radio chapters illustrate the use of scheduling *clocks* that break an hour's programming into precisely defined short segments.

6. Cable television and cable radio use all the previously developed broadcast scheduling strategies and introduce many of their own. In choosing programming for cable at the system level, entire programming services (channels) rather than individual programs must be considered, and as a result, extraneous technical considerations intrude in the decision-making process. For example, Chapter 9 on cable systems mentions the need for matching program choices to the engineering parameters of the system. A cable programmer could be prevented from scheduling a desirable new satellite network if it came via a satellite other than the one relaying the rest of the system's programs since picking up the new program might require the installation of a new receiving dish—an expense many systems cannot afford.

7. Though some of its leaders at first thought that public broadcasting should and could ignore commercial strategies, programmers have increasingly adopted the familiar ploys of commercial stations, such as *counterprogramming* and *bridging*. Network programmers in public broadcasting have relatively little choice in program selection, as Fuller explains in Chapter 17 on national public television programming. Their strategies necessarily center on scheduling.

Modern programmers do well to understand the use of computers, which increasingly come to the programmer's aid in performing some evaluation, selection and scheduling tasks. They have long been used for program **logs** and keeping track of production personnel assignments and equipment allocations. The better news operations in both radio and television are highly *computerized* today, and new software packages computerize many of the day-to-day functions of a television station's program department. They can keep track of contract deadlines, the number of unused **plays** of a syndicated program and the details about possible program purchases (see Chapter 2 for more on this).

Keeping Up-to-Date

Executives concerned with programming, as indeed with every other aspect of broadcasting and cable television, need constantly to update their knowledge of their rapidly evolving fields. The trade press provides one source of updates, but even more important are the many trade and professional associations that provide for personal meetings, demonstrations, exhibits, seminars and publications. Dozens of such associations bring practitioners together at conferences on every conceivable aspect of the media, all of which touch upon programming in one way or another—conferences on advertising, copyright, education, engineering, finance, law, management, marketing, music, news, production, programs, promotion, research and satellites, to name a few.

Among the major associations that deal primarily with commercial programming from the practitioner's point of view, the oldest and largest broadcast trade association is the National Association of Broadcasters (**NAB**). It dates back to the early days of radio. The association emerged in 1923 specifically to present a united front on a vital issue in the economics of programming—the exorbitance, as the broadcasters saw it, of the license fees they had to pay for the use of music. The NAB fought the American Society of Composers, Authors and Publishers (**ASCAP**), then the sole American organization licensing the commercial use of copyrighted music. Since music was a principal source of radio programming, the fees charged by ASCAP on behalf of copyright holders had a vital bearing on the economic well-being of the industry. The NAB became a powerful Washington lobby for broadcasting and serves the medium in many other ways. At its annual convention in the spring, the association offers expert sessions on every aspect of programming. It also conducts a fall radio programming conference and prints reports on various aspects of the subject.

The NAB serves both radio and television. It has separate boards for the two media. Radio committees include those on Daytime Broadcasters, Group Radio, Local Radio Audience Measurement, Medium Market Radio and Small Market Radio. Nevertheless, radio interests sometimes complain that the economically more powerful television segment of the industry overwhelms their concerns in the NAB. Some have therefore formed a separate association, the National Radio Broadcasters Association (**NRBA**). The NAB and NRBA conduct a joint annual radio meeting; they also cooperate on an annual fall Radio Programming Conference (**RPC**). Radio programmers generally attend the RPC while station and sales managers attend the main NRBA meetings.

NATPE, the National Association of Television Program Executives, has already been mentioned. In addition to offering opportunities for program selling, buying and information exchange at its annual late-winter convention, it conducts several program management seminars each year and supports a college faculty internship program. Smaller and less structured than the NAB or NATPE, the Television Programmers' Conference (**TVPC**) serves the needs of small-market broadcasters with emphasis on the problems of local programmers.

In the late 1970s the independent (nonnetwork-affiliated) television stations, previously very weak in audience appeal, began to have a growing impact. Their emergence as viable competitors to network affiliates owed something to their trade organization, the Association of Independent Television Stations (**INTV**). Independent stations get valuable lobbying assistance from the INTV as well as sales advice and program information. Syndicators showcase programs of particular interest to independent operators at the annual INTV meetings. This meeting also brings programmers together to discuss problems peculiar to independent station operation.

The Radio-Television News Directors Association (**RTNDA**) is an example of a professional, as opposed to a trade, association. It enrolls individuals rather than stations and focuses more on the professional skills of broadcast journalists, the ethics of their profession and First Amendment issues, rather than on the business affairs of stations and networks. It has about 3,000 members, of which about a third actually function as radio or television news directors. Other relevant professionally oriented organizations include the Society of Motion Picture and Television Engineers (**SMPTE**) and the International Radio-Television Society (**IRTS**). Most of these organizations do not have direct programming functions, but their activities frequently have impact on programming decisions.

The cable equivalent of the NAB, the National Cable Television Association (**NCTA**), meets annually in late spring. Much younger and less highly developed than the NAB, the NCTA lacks the elaborate committee structure of the NAB and devotes a major part of its efforts to lobbying. However, it does play an important program role, with its meetings offering the second most important sales opportunity (after the NATPE meetings) for syndicated program distributors.

The cable industry supports two additional organizations involved in programming, the Cable Television Administration and Marketing Society (**CTAM**) and the National Federation of Local Cable Programmers (**NFLCP**). CTAM's annual August conference interweaves programming concerns with its marketing sessions. Attendees are mostly broadcast group and cable **MSO** executives. The NFLCP is devoted to local cable origination and local access cable programming. Sessions at its annual conference touch on production problems and the buying of syndicated feature films and shorts to be used as **interstitial programming,** items inserted to even up the time of odd-length programs. This conference attracts mostly system programmers responsible for local origination programming.

Some industry organizations concerned with programming more peripherally include the Television Bureau of Advertising (**TvB**), the Radio Advertising Bureau (**RAB**) and the Cable-Television Advertising Bureau (**CAB**). Based in New York, they mainly supply sales and promotional materials touting the advertising value of their media over others. They also conduct surveys, hold regional sales seminars and generate product information to aid station sales efforts. The Station Representatives Association (**SRA**) and the Association of Advertising Agencies (**AAA**) conduct occasional seminars on program issues as well as lobbying to influence legislation that affects programs.

REGULATORY CONSTRAINTS

Radio and television, more than most businesses (including other media), must live within constraints imposed by national, state and local statutes and administrative boards. Moreover, public opinion imposes its own limitations, even in the absence of government regulation. But even so, the hybrid nature of most of the newer communication technologies has created novel regulatory problems. The **Communications Act of 1934** covers *common carriers* in its Title II and *broadcasting* in Title III. An amendment incorporates the Cable **Communications Policy Act of 1984** as Title VI of the Communications Act. While Title III (broadcasting) speaks repeatedly of licensing for operation "in the public interest," Title VI (*cable*) imposes no such constraint. True, the deregulatory zeal of recent Federal Communications Commissions has resulted in abandoning many of the rules imposed by previous commissioners that sought to enforce operation in the public interest on broadcasters. In 1987 the courts voided the **must-carry** rules, and the FCC abolished one of its most controversial program-related rules, the **Fairness Doctrine.** The **equal-time** rule for political candidates also faces possible repeal, though that will take action by Congress, not just an FCC action, because the Communications Act spells out this rule. Nevertheless, from long custom as well as sensitivity to public opinion that demands more of broadcasting than of cable, broadcasters generally have a more highly developed sense of public interest concerns than do cable operators.

Regulation for both broadcasters and cable operators remains in a transitional state as the pendulum shows signs of swinging back from the extreme deregulatory ideology of the early 1980s. Fortunately for programmers, responsibility for compliance with the law devolves upon top management, guided by legal counsel. Programmers should keep informed about changes in the laws that affect their work. "Ignorance of the law is no excuse," so programmers need to be aware of possible violations within their jurisdiction. Following is a checklist of the chief regulatory constraints with which programmers should be familiar.[10]

Fairness and Equal Opportunity

Both broadcast and local cable-originated programming must observe the many rules governing appearances by candidates for political office (**equal-time**), station editorials and personal attacks. Although the FCC has formally abandoned its specific Fairness Doctrine concerning discussion of controversial issues of local importance, Congress could reintroduce the rule by amending the Communications Act. In any event, many managers are likely to continue adhering to the basic fairness concepts as a matter of station policy. Day-to-day enforcement of such rules and policies devolves largely upon the production staff in the course of operations, but programmers often articulate station policies regarding balance and stipulate compliance routines. Fairness looms large in talk radio, as indicated in Bruce Marr's Chapter 16, because the talk so often deals with controversial topics.

Equal Employment Opportunities (**EEO**) compliance might also be considered an aspect of fairness. EEO requirements affect all but the smallest stations and cable operations. Special consideration in hiring practices must be given to women and to minority groups with significant presence in the local work force. Hiring practices must be reported annually to the FCC, and employers must have an active affirmative action program. In general, employers must aim at ensuring that 50 percent of all full-time employees and 25 percent of top supervisory employees reflect the minority composition of the local labor force.

Monopoly

Various rules limit concentrations of media ownership, all of them aimed at ensuring diversity of information sources, in keeping with implicit First Amendment goals. Group owners of broadcast stations are particularly sensitive to regulatory compliance in this area. They have a high financial stake in compliance and of course are conspicuous targets, susceptible to monopoly charges. This sensitivity affects programming policies. Whether or not cable franchising agencies may grant monopolies within certain geographic areas remains a subject of legal dispute. In a way, cable franchises may be regarded as "natural monopolies," for it would normally seem uneconomic to duplicate cable installations (**overbuilds**). But if monopoly is construed as denial of freedom of speech, then even the "natural monopolies" created by franchising one operator may violate the First Amendment.

The broadcast networks have long been subject to antimonopoly regulation. The *financial interest* and *network syndication rules,* aimed at weakening network control over prime-time entertainment, were discussed in describing the networks as program sources. In addition, the *prime-time access rule* (**PTAR**) prevents network entertainment from monopolizing more than three of the four prime-time hours in the top 50 markets. This leaves one hour accessible in those valuable markets to nonnetwork-originated programs. PTAR has an important significance for station programmers, giving them an opportunity to make major programming decisions in filling the **access hour** (by common consent 7 to 8 P.M. eastern time, though the FCC left it to the industry to decide which of the prime-time hours to devote to access programming). Inasmuch as PTAR makes exemptions for public affairs programming, CBS was able to schedule *60 Minutes* from 7 to 8 P.M. Sundays, a prime slot that had much to do with the phenomenal success of this nonentertainment series.

Localism

The FCC nudges broadcasters toward a modicum of **localism** in their program mix. It expects licensees to find out about local problems in a station's service area and to offer programs dealing with such problems (the informal **ascertainment** requirement)—an annual list of local issues and programming dealing with these issues that stations must place in their public files). In licensing and license renewals, the FCC gives preferential points for local ownership, owner participation in management and program plans tailored to local needs. Management's catering to the FCC (or, to put it more generously, its desire to fulfill its public service obligations as defined by the FCC) generally constrains programmers to pay some attention to local programming, especially that of a public service nature. Deregulation has lightened these constraints, but so far the Communication Act's explicit requirement that licenses must be issued only insofar as they serve the public interest remains the law.

Cable operators are not licensed by the FCC and so have no such federal public-interest mandate. As a result, cable programmers differ fundamentally in their programming outlook from broadcast programmers. True, the 1984 Cable Act provides for **PEG** (public, education and governmental) access channels, but only at the discretion of the municipalities that franchise cable systems. PEG access requirements therefore vary widely with location; cable programmers must consult the terms of their systems' franchises to ascertain whether some channels must be left free to fulfill mandatory PEG allocations.

Copyright

Except for news and most public affairs programs and most local productions, all programs entail the payment of royalties to copyright owners. Programmers should understand how the **copyright royalty** system works, how users of copyrighted material negotiate licenses from distributors to use them, and the limitations on program use that the copyright law entails.

Broadcast stations and networks usually obtain **blanket licenses** for music from copyright licensing organizations, which give licensees the right to unlimited plays of all the music in their catalogs. For the rights to individual programs and films, users usually obtain licenses authorizing a limited number of performances ("plays") over a stipulated time period. One of the programmer's arts is to schedule the repeat plays at strategic intervals to get the best mileage possible out of the product.

Cable television systems introduced a new and exceedingly controversial element into copyright licensing. Stations and networks obtain licenses for the materials they broadcast, with fees calculated on the basis of a station's usual over-the-air coverage areas. The problem lurked in the background while early cable systems merely improved weak broadcast coverage but came to the forefront when cable companies began picking up distant television stations relayed to them by satellite and delivering them on the cable. Importation of distant signals stretched the original single-market program license to include hundreds of unrelated markets all across the country, to the obvious detriment of copyright owners (the producers).

The Copyright Law of 1976 (effective in 1978) tried to solve this problem. It introduced **compulsory licensing** of cable companies that retransmit television station signals. It provided retransmission compensation to the copyright owners in the form of a percentage of cable companies' revenues. The law also created a Copyright Royalty Tribunal (**CRT**) that sets the percentage cable companies must pay for retransmission rights, collects the money and distributes it to the copyright owners on a group basis. As of the mid-1980s (the CRT moves slowly), about three-fourths of the compulsory fee went to program suppliers (including movie makers); about 16 percent went to joint sports claimants; about 5 percent to commercial broadcasters through the NAB; about 5 percent to public broadcasters; and about 1 percent to music rights organizations (the **American Society of Composers, Authors and Publishers (ASCAP)**, **Broadcast Music Incorporated (BMI)** and other music rights societies which redistribute royalties to individual composers and lyricists).

In 1986 a federal court gave cable operators a measure of relief from compulsory licensing payments by ruling that cable operators, for purposes of calculating copyright payments, may exclude from their gross income money earned from the *nonbroadcast* services they carry. This ruling cut back substantially on the amount of compulsory license payments by cable companies.

A related copyright matter, the **syndicated exclusivity rule** (often called **syndex**), at one time gave television stations local protection (**blackout**) from the competition of signals from distant stations (notably superstations) imported by cable systems. The rule was based on the long-held principle that a station licensed to broadcast a given syndicated program normally paid for *exclusive* rights to broadcast that program within its established market area. Cable's ability to import programs licensed for broadcast in distant markets (especially the superstations) undermined this market-specific definition of licensing. The FCC dropped the syndicated exclusivity rule in 1980 but in 1987 invited comments on the desirability of reinstating it. If restored, the rule would require cable systems to black out imported programs that duplicate the same programs broadcast locally. Broadcasters divide on the issue. Some say that duplication helps the sale of first-run syndicated programs and that it fails to siphon off audiences for the same programs carried by local stations. Others argue that imported programs divide audiences, harming stations whose programs are duplicated in their local market areas.[11]

Cable Carriage Rules

One of the most controversial of the FCC regulations affecting cable, the **must-carry** rules, obligated cable systems to allot channels for broadcast television stations with substantial numbers of viewers within a cable system's coverage areas. These rules aimed at preventing cable companies from discriminating against stations by excluding them from their channels and then undercutting them by importing stations with the same network affiliations from other markets. However, the obligation to carry an arbitrary number of local stations constrained the cable programmer's freedom of action, especially in those cable systems located between two large television markets.

Must-carry rules created one of the most contentious clashes between cable and broadcasting interests. They originated as a means of ensuring that broadcast stations within a cable system's franchise area would not be frozen out by the cable operator. In 1985 and again in 1987, federal courts declared existing must-carry rules an unconstitutional infringement on cable operators' freedom of speech. Now cable operators may choose which broadcast services to carry and may drop unpopular or duplicative stations. In practice, however, most cable systems have retained the established local commercial stations, dropping only redundant broadcast network-affiliates and some public stations, and adding new independents only when there is excess channel capacity.[12]

Lotteries, Fraud, Obscenity, Indecency

Federal laws forbid **lotteries, fraud** and **obscenity,** and laws regarding them apply to locally originated cable as well as to broadcast programs. Programmers also need to be aware of special Communications Act provisions regarding **fraudulent contests, plugola** and **payola. Indecency,** a specialized interpretation of obscenity laws, appears to apply only to broadcasting.

The 1984 Cable Act sets specific penalties for transmitting "any matter which is obscene or otherwise not protected by the Constitution" (Sec. 639). A subsequent Supreme Court decision affirmed that cable operators qualify for First Amendment protection of their speech freedom. This puts the heavy burden on those alleging obscenity of proving the unconstitutionality of material to which they object; in fact, several court decisions have overthrown too-inclusive obscenity provisions in municipal franchises. In practice, cable operators have greater freedom to offend the sensibilities of their more straitlaced viewers than do broadcasters, whose wider reach and dependence on the "public airwaves" (electromagnetic spectrum) make them more vulnerable to public pressure.

A 1987 FCC ruling broadened its previous definition of prohibited words in broadcasting to cover **indecency.** That definition had been based on a 1973 case involving the notorious "seven dirty words" used by comedian George Carlin in a recorded comedy routine broadcast by WBAI-FM in New York. In 1987, responding to complaints about raunchy talk-radio hosts (**shock jocks**), the FCC advised broadcasters that censorable *indecent* language could include *anything* that "depicts or describes, in terms patently offensive as measured by contemporary community standards for the broadcast medium, sexual and excretory activities or organs." It is noteworthy that the commission used the words *for the broadcast medium,* implying that broadcasting should be treated differently from other media, a concept out of keeping with much FCC-sponsored deregulation. Also striking is the fact that the increased surveillance implied by the new indecency standard likewise contradicted the current FCC's usual zeal for decreasing government regulation.

Libel

News, public affairs programs, and radio talk shows in particular run the risk of inviting libel suits. Because of their watchdog role and the protection afforded them by the First Amendment, the media enjoy immunity from punishment for libel resulting from honest errors in reporting and commentary on public figures. However, due care must be taken to avoid giving rise to charges of malice or "reckless disregard for the truth." Even though the media win most libel cases brought against them, it costs a lot to defend cases in court. Managers responsible for news departments and radio talk shows need to be aware of libel pitfalls and to institute defensive routines. These defenses include issuing clear-cut guidelines, ensuring suitable review of editing and taking care that promotional and other incidental material does not introduce libelous matter. As an example of the National Association of Broadcasters' (NAB) assistance to programmers, it has issued a videocassette illustrating some of the common ways that news programs inadvertently open themselves to libel suit.

PROGRAMMING AS TEAMWORK

You may have noticed that this book avoids the term *program director*, using instead *programmer*. This less precise title reflects the fact that in most cases management *teams*, not just a program director, make programming decisions of any consequence. Indeed, most local cable operations do not even employ an executive with a programming title.

Programmers work in a highly charged atmosphere, full of pressures and counterpressures. In a speech before the International Radio and Television Society, Frederick S. Pierce, then president of ABC Television, summarized some of these pressures as they appear to a broadcasting network executive:

> Programming decisions are made only after the "votes" are in. And the "votes" take many forms and come from many directions. Input comes from ratings and research, from thousands of letters from viewers and from countless phone calls. It comes from advertisers, who aren't shy, believe me, about communication of their views; and it comes from the creative community.

> We also measure reactions from our affiliates, who are important in measuring response in over 200 separate communities. And we pay attention to polls, surveys, and to special interest groups, who are very vocal and visible.[13]

Programmers do not enjoy the luxury of autonomous decision making. In arriving at decisions, often sales or corporate image-making motives outweigh programming considerations. Programming may be an art, but it is not a fine art. Creativity in radio and television organizations is buried under layers of bureaucracy—more so than in other media. Radio and television are set apart by unique technology, their special legal status and the fact that so much of the creative work of program making takes place outside the walls of stations, cable systems and networks. This separation of functions explains why leading writers and producers like Norman Lear (what Pierce refers to as "the creative community" in the statement above) complain so bitterly about the frustrations of creating television entertainment. When Lear first offered *All in the Family*, network executives looked upon its innovative realism and satirical bite as far too risky for television. It survived only because Lear had far more clout with executives than do most producers. As Les Brown put it, television is an "executive's medium."[14]

When television programmers formed their own professional organization in 1962, they called themselves the National Association of Television Program *Executives*—tacitly acknowledging that membership would be dominated by general managers and other executives who play more important programming roles than those specifically designated as programmers. The programming team is usually made up of the general manager, sales manager and program manager. In cable organizations, the executive in charge of marketing plays a key management role and may be the one with the most influence on programming decisions.

Few U.S. cable systems have executives with the word *program* in their title. This fact does not mean, of course, that programming functions are not performed, but that they take less time than in broadcasting organizations and so can be treated as a part-time responsibility of the system manager or other primary executive. Only about one-third of cable operators employ full-time program managers, and most deal with many systems for an MSO.

If *salary* is any measure of perceived job importance (and it usually is), television station program executives rank in the middle range. According to recent surveys, program directors average lower salaries than top management (general managers, station managers), sales managers, news directors and chief engineers, and also often get less than top account executives (salespersons) and news, sports, weather and entertainment personalities. On the other hand, they usually make more than some other department heads, and the range of salaries differs widely depending on market size. Radio station programmers also find that top management, sales managers, local account executives and some sports and entertainment personalities make more money than they do.[15]

In general, cable system management-level employees earn less than those in comparable positions in broadcasting. According to recent *Cable Marketing* surveys, cable programmers receive lower average pay than general management, sales/marketing, operations, engineering and finance specialists in cable and somewhat less than their broadcast opposite-numbers at both the network and local levels.[16]

Program executives play an information-processing role. Paul Virts, in the course of his doctoral research, interviewed a group of television station executives in the Midwest. He concluded that *briefing* the other members of the programming team constituted one of the programmer's basic roles. The program managers he interviewed said they assembled the pertinent data on audience, scheduling, program availabilities and costs, then presented their findings to the sales manager and general manager.[17] The programmer defines the constraints within which the decision must be made from the programming point of view, the sales manager defines them from the advertiser's point of view, and the general manager defines them from the policy point of view. How much attention the others pay to the programmer's recommendations varies with the makeup of the team. If the sales manager happens to be aggressive and the general manager sales-minded, the programmer's viewpoint tends to get submerged. To cite a practical example at the most basic level, Bill Drake of Drake-Chenault Enterprises—one of the most influential figures in modern radio programming—recalled in an interview his start as a small-town Georgia disc jockey:

> Stations would sell everything they could, because most General Managers were sales oriented. . . . A lot of commercials would be recorded by the owners and the Sales Manager, who were tight with the account (i.e., advertiser) and the account wanted them to do the commercials. As it turned out, you'd have what were supposed to be one minute commercials and by the time they got through ad-libbing and recording the damned things, they were two minutes and fifteen seconds, which I guess was why the accounts loved them.[18]

Drake attributes much of his later success to his insistence on separating radio programming from sales. As he puts it, Cadillac dealers sell the product; they do not spend their time calling Detroit to tell General Motors how to design Caddies. The programmer's role is to persuade sales-minded executives to concentrate on selling, leaving program design to programmers. The best general managers referee the warfare between sales and programming fairly, encouraging the best efforts of both without giving too much firepower to either.

The previous sections mentioned the ability to **negotiate** effectively with *program suppliers* as one of the programmer's basic skills. Equally important, programmers must negotiate effectively within the *management team*. When a researcher asked professional broadcast programmers what qualities lead to success in the field, most mentioned the ability to work well with all kinds of people. Summarizing the personal characteristics of program executives, the investigator found they tended to be

> male, relatively young, likely to be college educated—especially those in the top markets and at the largest stations; have considerable experience in broadcasting—both in terms of longevity and in terms of variety of jobs held; believe that a person should start his or her career in a station where he or she can perform many different tasks, but also believe that it is not so much the possession of particular skills that will lead to success as it is the possession of an appropriate attitude. The program managers in this sample watch a lot of television as part of their job and at home, and they perceive themselves as having something less than complete freedom in decision-making, subject always to the scrutiny of the station manager.[19]

Most cable programmers have college degrees, and one-fourth have done graduate work. Their prior experience includes work in radio and television broadcast programming, film production, program syndication and distribution and satellite networks. A *Cable Marketing* survey concludes, "As much as cable systems need top notch specialists, they must employ them very often as generalists—with the ability to understand activities outside their prime area of responsibility and to make meaningful contributions wherever they must focus their attention."[20]

SUMMARY

Programming can be defined as the strategic use of programs arranged in schedules or tiers to attract target audiences. Programmers need the knowledge and skills to define such audiences and to select, acquire and place programs that will attract them. In carrying out their tasks, programmers use strategies based on the inherent characteristics of radio and television, whether delivered by broadcast signals, cable signals or other means. These strategies cluster around the concepts of compatibility, habit formation, audience flow, program conservation and wide audience reach. From these broad concepts come the specific strategies such as dayparting, stripping, counterprogramming and rerunning. Programmers evaluate the probable success of untried programs in terms of the types of appeals they have for audiences, expecting successful mass audience programs to exhibit conflict, comedy, sex, information and human interest, plus a number of secondary qualities. The extent to which programs reflect current social trends can also be important to their success. To reach a wide audience, programs need to incorporate several primary and secondary appeals simultaneously. Programmers need to know about audience targeting, program acquisition, negotiation, scheduling and personnel management. Computer programs aid in some of these operations. Programmers should have some knowledge of laws and regulations affecting programming decisions, such as fairness and equal employment opportunity, monopoly, localism, copyright, carriage rules, lotteries, fraud, obscenity and indecency. Programming is usually the product of teamwork among a number of executives in addition to the programmer and in terms of pay, programmers occupy a middle rank in the hierarchy of top radio and television executive salaries.

Notes

1. Mark Schone, "Agency View: Rating the Zippers and Zappers," *View*, 7 December 1987, p. 39.

2. Gene E. Jankowski, President of CBS/Broadcast Group, in "Choices and Needs: The Meaning of the New Technologies," address to Connecticut Broadcasters Association, 20 October 1982.

3. William S. Paley, *As It Happened: A Memoir* (New York: Doubleday, 1979), p. 260.

4. Jankowski.

5. Nielsen Media Research, *1987 Nielsen Report on Television* (Northbrook, Ill.: A.C. Nielsen Co., 1987).

6. This analysis came from an anonymous scriptwriter who was responding to queries by researchers analyzing violence in television, cited by Thomas F. Baldwin and Colby Lewis, "Violence in Television: The Industry Looks at Itself," in George Comstock and E. Rubenstein, *Television and Social Behavior: Media Content and Control*, vol. 1 (Washington, D.C.: U.S. Government Printing Office, 1972), pp. 290–365.

7. Daniel Yankelovich, "What New Life Styles Mean to Market Planners," *Marketing/Communications*, June 1971, pp. 38–45.

8. "Cable Goes Original," *Broadcasting*, 22 September 1986, p. 62.

9. William H. Read, *America's Mass Media Merchants* (Baltimore, Md.: Johns Hopkins University Press, 1976); Thomas Thompson, "The Crapshoot for Half a Billion: Fred Silverman Rolls the Dice," *Life*, 10 December 1971, pp. 46–48.

10. A convenient source for details on these regulations is the annual *Broadcasting-Telecasting Yearbook*, supplemented for more recent developments by "Where Things Stand," a weekly update in the trade journal *Broadcasting*. See also the *NAB Legal Guide to Broadcast Law and Regulation*, Washington, D.C.: National Association of Broadcasters, 1988.

11. Compare Shaun M. Sheehan, "The Perils of Resurrecting the FCC's Syndex Rules," *Broadcasting*, 1 June 1987, p. 26, with Charles Edwards, "Rebutting Arguments Against Reinstating Syndex," *Broadcasting*, 22 June 1987, p. 22. See also "In Anticipation of Syndex," *Broadcasting*, 14 March 1988, pp. 33–34.

12. The original cable rules in the 1984 Cable Act specified different requirements for different capacity cable systems. They required cable systems with 20 or fewer channels, for example, to carry only a single public broadcast station, if one were available, whereas systems with 21 to 26 channels had to carry seven broadcast stations, and those with 27 to 53 channels had to devote 25 percent of them to broadcast stations, while those systems with 54 or more channels had to include at least two noncommercial stations within the 25 percent. Then in 1987, a "must-carry compromise" was reached among broadcasters, cable and the FCC, simplifying these rules. The revised rules stated that a cable system was required to carry all full-power television stations that were licensed to communities within 50 miles of the system's principal head-end that could demonstrate an average total viewing share of 2 percent and a net weekly circulation of 5 percent in noncable homes in the cable system's county; noncommercial stations would be eligible for carriage without having to meet the viewing standards, as would new commercial stations for their first year of operation, and multiple affiliates of the same broadcast network would not have to be carried. In addition, cable operators were required to supply A/B switches (at the homeowner's expense), enabling home owners to switch from cable to over-the-air reception. This requirement reflected the fact that the cable connection normally disables the customer's outdoor antenna (or rabbit ears) lead-in, often making it impossible to receive local broadcast stations not carried by the cable system. However, the courts voided all of these rules in 1987 in favor of First Amendment rights for cable operators.

13. Frederick S. Pierce, remarks before the International Radio and Television Society, New York City, 6 November 1978.

14. Les Brown, "Is Silverman Worth it?" *New York Times*, 1 January 1978, p. 26. See also "Hollywood Fights Back," *TV Guide*, 27 August 1977, pp. 4–18; reprinted in part in Barry Cole, ed., *Television Today* (New York: Oxford University Press, 1981), pp. 331–336.

15. Broadcast Financial Management Association, *1985 Edition, Broadcast Industry Compensation Fringe Benefits Survey* (Des Plaines, Ill.: Broadcast Financial Management Association, 1985).

16. "*Cable Marketing's* Executive Compensation Survey," *Cable Marketing*, May 1987, p. 28.

17. Paul H. Virts, "Television Entertainment Gatekeeping: A Study of Local Television Directors' Decision Making" (Ph.D. dissertation, University of Iowa, 1979), p. 104.

18. Quoted in "The Top-40 Story: Bill Drake," *Radio & Records*, September 1977, p. 30.

19. Michael G. Fisher, "A Survey of Selected Television Station Program Managers: Their Backgrounds and Perceptions of Role" (M.A. thesis, Temple University, 1978).

20. "*Cable Marketing* Survey," May 1987, p. 17.

Selected Sources

Bortz, Paul I. *Great Expectations: A Television Manager's Guide to the Future.* Washington, D.C.: National Association of Broadcasters, 1986.

Channels of Communication, a monthly consumer and trade magazine covering issues affecting broadcasting, cable and new technologies, published in New York.

Head, Sydney W., and Sterling, Christopher H. *Broadcasting in America: A Survey of Television, Radio, and New Technologies.* 5th ed. Boston, Massachusetts: Houghton Mifflin, 1987.

Howard, Herbert H., and Kievman, Michael S. *Radio and TV Programming.* Columbus, Ohio: Grid Publishing, 1983.

NAB Legal Guide to Broadcast Law and Regulation. Washington, D.C.: National Association of Broadcasters, 1988.

Radioutlook: Forces Shaping the Radio Industry. Washington, D.C.: National Association of Broadcasters, 1988.

CHAPTER 2 \ PROGRAM AND AUDIENCE RESEARCH

Roger D. Wimmer

Susan Tyler Eastman

Timothy P. Meyer

A Guide to Chapter 2

Roger D. Wimmer is president of Surrey Research, Inc., a full-service media research company in Denver, Colorado. Before joining Surrey in 1985, Dr. Wimmer was the manager of research for Cox Enterprises, Inc. in Atlanta, Georgia, with responsibilities in radio, television, corporate and new technology research. Prior to joining Cox, he was an associate professor of broadcasting at the University of Georgia and, prior to that, an assistant professor at the University of Mississippi. He received his Ph.D. in Radio-Television-Film from Bowling Green State University and is senior author of *Mass Media Research: An Introduction* (Wadsworth, 1983, 1987) and author of other books and scholarly articles.

Susan Tyler Eastman, associate professor of telecommunications at Indiana University, contributed the sections on ratings services, market reports and computerized services. Her credentials appear at the start of Chapter 9.

Timothy P. Meyer, professor of communications at the University of Wisconsin—Green Bay, holds the Rosenberg chair in communications at that university and consults in marketing and advertising as a partner in Lucas Associates. He is co-author of *Advertising Research Methods* (Prentice-Hall, forthcoming), *Mediated Communication Effects* (Sage, 1988) and "Sports Programming: Economics and Scheduling," in *Media, Sport & Society*, Lawrence Wenner, editor (Sage, forthcoming). In addition, Dr. Meyer has published numerous reports and articles on programming and marketing in both the trade and scholarly press. He received his bachelor's degree from the University of Wisconsin and his master's and doctorate from Ohio University in Athens. Before joining the University of Wisconsin, he taught at the University of Texas at Austin and the University of Massachusetts, Amherst. Dr. Meyer contributed the sections on effects and qualitative research and peoplemeters, accompanied by an update on ratings interpretation and limitations for this edition.

DECISION-MAKING INFORMATION FOR PROGRAMMERS

"How could those idiots cancel that show? It was my favorite. Why do they always get rid of the good stuff and keep all the junk?" Sound familiar? It should. Most people have, at one time or another, heard the news that a favorite television show has been cancelled. The reason? Usually the one given is "low ratings," a way of saying not enough people watched the program. Why are the ratings so important? Why do so many shows fail? Can't a network executive tell whether a show will succeed in the ratings? This chapter looks at ratings and other forms of audience research and explains what they are, how they are used and misused and why.

Broadcast and cable programmers are interested in one goal: *reaching the largest possible salable audience.* Programmers define audiences differently depending on particular circumstances, but regardless of definition, determining audience size is the paramount concern. The separations between program creation and presentation and reception by the audience mean that programmers must always guess who will be there and how many there will be, estimating how predictable and accurate those guesses are. Because networks and stations sell commercial time at dollar rates based on predicted audiences, it is no surprise that program and audience research are critical for the financial health of the broadcast and cable industries. Program and audience research, usually involving ratings, guides the process of selecting and scheduling programs to attract the desired audience and provide feedback on programming decisions.

The broadcast and cable industries use many research approaches to evaluate programs and audiences, most of which fall into one of three groupings: (1) qualitative and quantitative measures of the *programs* themselves, (2) qualitative and quantitative measures of *audience preferences and reactions* and (3) quantitative measures of *audience size*. Qualitative research tries to explain *why* people make specific program choices and *what they think* about those programs. Quantitative data, in the form of ratings and surveys, report *what programs* (and commercials, presumably) people are listening to or watching. Programmers use qualitative information on programs to select and improve programs and to understand audiences' reactions to program content; qualitative audience data help explain people's reactions to programs. Quantitative audience data, on the other hand, generally provide measures of the size and demographic composition of sets of viewers, listeners or subscribers. Of all these findings, however, **ratings** are the major form of program evaluation, and they most influence the other concerns of this book, program selection and scheduling. This chapter examines the industry's current program research practices and qualitative audience measurement techniques and then, because of their special position in industry economics, explains and interprets audience ratings.

In the late 1980s, a sweeping change occurred in the national television ratings—the shift by ratings companies from measuring people's viewing by diaries and simple meters to peoplemeters, a much more elaborate measurement process. **Peoplemeters** are electronic, hand-held devices that individuals use to indicate when they are viewing. A "black box" computer sits on top of the television set, recording each viewer's selections, and stored in it is background demographic information (age and sex) on every viewer in the household. Other new forms of audience measurement are also being tested by competitors to the established ratings companies. It will take several years to judge the effectiveness and acceptance of new ratings services, but this chapter supplies a description of the major services and the measurement problems their practices create. But no way of measuring audience will ever be error-free or problem-free. We can only assess the competing methods with an eye to their advantages and drawbacks.

Effects vs. Industry Research

Research on how programs affect viewers' beliefs, attitudes and behaviors is rarely used in selecting and scheduling programs on television, cable or radio. While the broadcast and cable industries are concerned with the impact of their programs, their concern centers on the potential of a program to produce a predictably large audience of a given type. *Why* audiences are there and *how they are affected* as consequences of viewing are irrelevant issues to the industries unless these intangibles impair a program's ability to produce predictable audiences of a desired size and type.

The sole exception to this pattern is the topic of *violence*, especially its impact on *children*. The major commercial television networks have funded both outside and in-house investigations of the effects of violence within some kinds of television content. This research, however, was prompted by social and political pressures and generally has had minimal effect on programming practices or program content.

The broadcast and cable industries have little use for social science research into media effects for two reasons:

1. Research about media effects has not produced clear-cut findings because of inherent methodological limits and the enormous complexity of the problem. Despite many years and thousands of studies, the nature of the relationship between violent television content and its effects on viewers remains problematic. For some viewers, under some conditions, some kinds of television violence can produce negative effects or positive effects. Effects do not occur either uniformly or consistently; different people interpret the same program in different ways and thus will be affected differently.

2. The social effects of programs on audiences are largely irrelevant to the commercial industry. The ability of the advertiser-supported services to function hinges only on their continued capacity to attract known (by size and composition) audiences. If audiences became unpredictable, the economic foundation of broadcasting and cable would collapse. But as long as audience members remain predictable as a mass, the system operates smoothly and profitably. Little else beyond this concerns programmers and advertisers.

Some scholarly research in the social sciences, such as marketing research, has developed methods for approaching problems that transfer readily to industry research practices, and this kind of scholarly research is used by broadcasting and cable. But in general, the two arenas of science and industry are guided by different goals, needs and values.

PROGRAM TESTING

The enormous expense of producing television programs necessitates testing them before and during the actual production of a show. In addition, promotional announcements advertising programs (**promos**) are usually tested to gauge their effectiveness and ability to communicate a program's most attractive features.

Concept, Pilot and Episode Testing

Concept testing is asking audiences whether they like the ideas for proposed programs. Producers generally conduct it before a program has been offered to a broadcast or cable network. *Pilot testing* occurs when a network is considering purchase of a new series, and audiences are asked to react to the pilot episode. This process is described in detail in Chapter 5 on network prime-time programming. *Episode testing* happens when a series is under way. Plot lines, the relative visibility of minor and major characters, the appeal of the settings and so on can be tested to gauge audience preferences.

ASI Market Research, based in Los Angeles, is one of the best known of the companies conducting program tests (and tests of commercials). Typically, ASI researchers invite people into a *testing theater* to watch a television program, a film or a commercial, asking them to rate it by pushing "positive" and "negative" buttons attached to their seats. Generally the participants are paid, often in products rather than cash, for taking part in the test. Computers monitor individual responses, producing a graph of the viewer's "votes" over time. These data are correlated with demographic and other information (**psychographics**) obtained via questionnaires from each participant. ASI research has been criticized for its unrepresentative audience samples, yet it remains a major contributor to network and movie studio program testing in America. ASI provides valuable data because its audiences are consistent from one time to the next. It has established norms from all its previous testing of programs, films and commercials against which new findings are weighed. Given the many programs evaluated over past decades and that few programs are really "new" in any significant way, how well a new show tests compared to others like it in past tests is useful information. The results are especially noteworthy when a program produces a negative or low evaluation since the average ASI audience evaluates programs positively. Not all programs that test positively are successful when put on a network schedule (factors independent of the show's content have more influence on ratings), but very few of those that test negatively at ASI later succeed.

Frequently prime-time series that have slipped in the ratings are tested with live audiences to determine which aspects of the program, if any, can be manipulated to improve the popularity of the series. The testing instruments range from simple levers and buttons, such as used in ASI theaters, to more controversial methods, such as galvanic skin response meters measuring respiration and perspiration. Programmers seek aids in understanding the weaknesses and strengths of a series performing below expectations. Sometimes the research suggests a change of characters or setting that revitalizes a program. (If research results are no help, the cynical programmer usually suggests adding a dog or a child.)

Concept and pilot testing stress general plot lines and main characters, seeking to find out if they are understood and appeal to a variety of people. Ongoing program testing seeks subtler evaluations of the voices, manners, style and interactions of all characters. In fact, different actors and plot lines are sometimes used for separate screenings to find out which cast and plot audiences prefer. Postproduction research can discover a poor program opening or difficulty in understanding the main theme of an episode. Unfortunately, the theater environment cannot reflect at-home viewing conditions and is thus a less than ideal research method. It does, however, supply detailed data that can be matched to screen actions, adding fodder for programming decisions.

Promotion Testing

Competition for audiences requires that most programmers continually produce effective promotional materials. Promotional spots advertise particular episodes of a series, special shows, movies, newscasts or unique aspects of a station's or service's programming. These promos can be tested before they are aired to find out whether they communicated what was intended. Testing firms generally conduct tests in shopping centers, intercepting people at random to invite them to view promos in return for cash or merchandise. Demographic data are gathered and other questions are asked and associated with participants' opinions. Promo-copy testing has become a standard practice in the industry.

QUALITATIVE AUDIENCE RESEARCH

In addition to program testing, which applies mostly to television programs and movies, stations use qualitative research to get audience reactions to program materials, personalities and station or system image. Using focus groups is one such research method. Radio stations also use call-out research to test their programming, and network television and major-market stations make use of TvQs. All of this research is grouped under the heading "Qualitative Audience Research," its most common title in the industry.

Focus Groups

One method used to gather information from a group of people is to conduct focus groups.[1] A **focus group** is a set of ten or twelve people involved in a controlled discussion. A moderator leads a conversation on a predetermined topic, such as a music format or television newscast, and structures the discussion with a set of questions. Predetermined criteria guide group recruitment: Station management may want people who listen to country music or women aged 25 to 34, for example. Finding people who fit the predetermined criteria (**screening**) can be costly: More qualifications result in a greater turndown rate, increasing the price for screening. Assembling a typical focus group generally costs between $2,500 and $3,000, including the fee paid to each participant ($30 is the standard fee, although it is sometimes as high as $150 for individuals difficult to recruit, such as physicians and other professionals).

Focus group research provides preliminary information about a topic or provides questions that may be used later in field surveys of a large sample of people. It generates informal information about whether a station has enough news, how people react to the newscasters, whether music is too soft or loud, whether personalities are perceived as interesting or friendly and so on. One advantage of focus groups is that visual materials (videotapes, newspaper ads) and recordings can be evaluated in the session, providing immediate stimuli and avoiding confused recall.

Due to the small size of focus groups, research results cannot be generalized. However, focused discussions can elicit unusual perceptions that would be overlooked by techniques such as survey questionnaires used with larger groups of people. Focus groups are especially suited to answering some of programmers' *why* questions in depth.

Music Research

Radio programmers want to know their audiences' opinions of different songs and different types of music. They need to know which songs are well liked and which ones no longer have audience approval (which songs are "burned out"). **Call-out research** is one popular, although controversial, method for discovering what listeners think about music selection.[2]

Programmers conduct call-out research by selecting 5- to 15-second "hooks" from well-established songs and play them for respondents over the telephone. A **hook** is a brief segment or musical phrase that captures the song's essence, frequently its theme or title. Programmers ask randomly selected respondents to rate 15 or 20 song hooks on a predetermined scale. Often a scale of 1 to 10 is used, where 1 represents "don't like" and 10 represents "like a lot." If stations perform call-out research frequently (and some use it every day), a track record for each song develops, and based on it, the music programmer can decide whether to leave the song in the station's rotation or drop it. Chapter 14 describes a particular form of this research in detail and shows how it can be applied to radio programming decisions.

Call-out research indicates listeners' musical tastes at a given moment. When tied to the same songs for some time, it indicates their popularity but does not tell the programmer how often a particular song should be played. That remains the programmer's decision.

Another popular method of testing music is **auditorium research.** Programmers invite 75 to 150 people to a location where they jointly listen to and rate a variety of songs. Instead of rating just 15 or 20 hooks as in telephone research, auditorium tests involve from 200 to 400 hooks. Like call-out research, the method tells which songs are liked and disliked at the moment but not how often they should be aired.

Music testing is expensive. Call-out research requires an investment in employees to make the calls as well as computer time to analyze the results. Auditorium tests involve recruiting costs and "co-op" money for participants (usually $20–$35). Those stations lacking facilities and personnel for music testing can hire commercial firms specializing in such work.

TvQs

TvQ (Television Quotient) data are used by many programmers to supplement Nielsen and Arbitron ratings.[3] The latter two services provide information on *how many* people watched a program; TvQs measure the *popularity and familiarity* of a program and the performers in it (or in commercials). Programmers use TvQs as indicators of a star's potential by assessing both recognition and likeability. Some research companies own computer programs that use TvQs to project the eventual success of a network program in syndication. The models consider how the people who watched felt about a show, but not how many watched.

RATINGS SERVICES

The rest of this chapter focuses on how programmers use and interpret ratings data. Ratings exert a powerful influence on the industry. This phenomenon is powerfully illustrated in Chapter 3, on the role of station representatives in programming, and in chapters 5 and 6 on network television programming. Radio programmers also use ratings information to evaluate their market positions and convince advertisers to buy time, as discussed in chapters 14 and 15 in relation to other evaluation techniques. Ratings are also used in cable and public broadcasting in specialized ways as analyzed in chapters 9 and 17. In fact, all programmers use ratings as part of their program decision making.

Using audience ratings is not restricted to programming applications, however. In fact, ratings were originally intended to provide information for advertisers curious about audience size. But once ratings data were on "solid" statistical ground, programmers used them to gauge the success of their decisions. As competition among networks and stations increased, ratings became the most important decision-making data in commercial broadcasting. Broadcast revenues, programs, stations and individual careers depend on audience ratings. For insofar as it is a business, broadcasting is usually a very simple business: High ratings result in profits (and continuing careers). Of course broadcasting also has public service obligations and other aspirations and commitments. On the purely economic side, however, a network or station will eliminate a program that receives low "numbers" if other options are available.

Cable and broadcast ratings cannot be compared directly because cable's potential audience is only half (just over 50 percent) that of the commercial networks (as of the late 1980s), and cable's programs are scheduled in rotating rather than one-time-only patterns. Therefore, cable programmers analyze ratings to determine *audience reach*—how many people over a period of time viewed a program or channel, much as public television programmers use ratings. But the absence of cable ratings directly comparable to those of broadcast television results in conservative advertising purchases and has contributed to the unprofitability and subsequent demise of several advertiser-supported cable networks.[4]

Articulating the power of audience ratings may sound crass to those who consider broadcasting an art form, but the reality is that ratings are the most important measure of commercial success. The efforts of most people involved in commercial broadcasting focus on achieving the highest possible numbers.[5] Targeting more precisely defined audiences such as women 25–54 is a fall-back position for stations that cannot immediately achieve a number one position in the adults 18 + category.

Ratings affect television and radio programming and sales at stations and at networks; they affect independent producers, Hollywood studios, distributing companies and advertisers and their agencies. Understanding the basics of the all-powerful numbers is essential in all of these businesses. And because nearly all basic cable networks are advertiser-supported, they also need ratings information to convince advertising agencies to purchase time. The premium cable services, such as HBO, use their national ratings to convince local cable systems that their programs are watched and important to promoting the local system. High ratings, demonstrating television's widespread household penetration, also carry clout with Congress. Legislators generally use television to get elected and reelected and tend to pay attention to their local broadcasters and the three national networks because they reach such enormous numbers of people.

Television Services

The most important distinction in television ratings is between *national* and *local* (called *market*) ratings. Two companies in the United States produce nationally-syndicated **network audience** measurements, A.C. Nielsen and AGB Peoplemeter. Nielsen and the Arbitron Ratings Company produce most of **local station** ratings for television. Other companies, such as Percy and regional research firms, collect and analyze television audience measurements of specialized types or for only a portion of the country. Nielsen and AGB cover the entire country continuously for network ratings, each using a separate sample of households. The three broadcast networks contract with Nielsen and/or AGB for this ratings service.

Nielsen and Arbitron conduct the four nationwide **sweeps** in November, February, May and July that produce the most important *local television reports*. These market–by–market reports allow stations to compare themselves with the other stations in their market. A separate **ratings book** is published (by each company) for each of the 210+ markets in the country for each ratings period. This data is based on a mix of *diaries* and local tuning-sensors (*meters*) in the larger markets, diaries only in the smaller markets.

In addition to the four major nationwide sweeps, large-market stations purchase ratings for as many as four more ratings periods (most commonly two more books in October and January, and sometimes books for March and September). A **ratings period** consists of four sequential weeks of data, reported week by week and averaged for the month. Midsized and smaller television markets purchase only one or more ratings books beyond the four sweeps (and the very smallest markets even skip the July sweep book). The stations in a market must contract with Nielsen or Arbitron (or both) for a ratings book, paying the cost of data collection, analysis and reporting. Other companies such as advertising agencies, station representatives and syndicators can then purchase the network and local ratings books.

Normally, station programmers purchase only the books for their own market, but programmers dealing with groups of stations may purchase all 210+ local market reports for the entire country or a subset of books for markets where they have stations. These books can be used to cross-compare the performance of programs in different markets, at different times of day, with different lead-in shows and so on. Subsequent chapters in this book discuss how these ratings are used in specific sets of circumstances.

1. *A.C. Nielsen Company.* Headquartered in Northbrook, Illinois, Nielsen gathers and interprets data on a wide range of consumer products and services as well as television (no radio). Nielsen's *network* audience estimates are reported in a form called the *National Television Index* (**NTIs**) twice a year, and in the abbreviated weekly booklets called *The Pocketpiece Report* (see Chapter 5 for a sample pocketpiece page). Besides the network-by-network ratings based on the audience for their affiliates, **pocketpieces** now include the collective ratings for independent television stations, superstations, national public broadcasting (PBS), basic cable networks and premium cable networks, giving network programmers a handy tool for comparing the performance of the networks and their competitors. (Eventually, VCR viewing may be incorporated in these reports.) National viewing data are also reported in other forms described in Chapter 3, often combined with product purchase and usage data.

Nielsen also collects nightly ratings called **overnights** in 11 large, metered markets, publishing this information every morning for the benefit of network executives and purchasing stations. Overnights, because of the smaller samples used and the big-city nature of the viewers, are only indicators of what the network ratings probably will be when the six-monthly NTIs are issued. Network viewing estimates now come from a nationwide sample of 4,000 households, with and without cable television (for many years, Nielsen's national sample was 1,700 households). To be included in Nielsen reports, however, at least 3 percent of viewer meters (or diaries in local reports) must record viewing of a cable service. This means only the top dozen or so cable networks figure in most ratings calculations. Multiple-set households are only counted once in total households (**TVHH**), though the sum of the audiences to several programs telecast simultaneously may be bigger than the number of households said to be viewing at one time (**HUT**) because one household may tune more than one program. Network data come from a mix of older Nielsen tuner-sensing devices and peoplemeters, gradually shifting entirely to peoplemeters as all 4,000 units are installed by the early 1990s.

Nielsen also measures *local market* television viewing (like Arbitron). These reports are known as the *Nielsen Station Index* (**NSIs**) and published in a form called *Viewers in Profile* for each market. These ratings books are purchased by most television stations and advertising agencies. Nielsen household samples are drawn from the most recent national census, and its ratings are not **weighted** (adjusted to fit national or local population percentages).

2. *AGB Peoplemeter.* AGB is a British-owned television-advertising measurement service. In 1986 it began challenging Nielsen by field-testing the first operational **peoplemeters** in the United States. AGB's national sample of 5,000 metered homes first showed that as much as 5 percent fewer viewers watch the three national broadcast networks than previous projections. Moreover, AGB's daytime ratings for women and prime-time ratings for cable networks average substantially higher than Nielsen's older audimeter and diary reports. AGB annually supplements its peoplemeter data with 20,000 household interviews, asking about viewing habits and cable, VCR and backyard satellite dish use. The company provides *local* television data in a few markets (such as Boston) but primarily supplies a *nationwide* television rating service.

AGB ratings differ significantly from Nielsen ratings (with AGB's typically lower), and the advertising industry commonly uses both in weighing a program's performance. Sampling error (and other characteristics possibly) contribute to varying numbers for the same program. Crafty programmers always cite the service reporting the higher numbers for their programs.

3. *Arbitron Ratings Company.* A subsidiary of Control Data Corporation and based in Laurel, Maryland, Arbitron rates *radio* (like Birch) as well as *local television* audience size (like Nielsen). It uses diaries alone for radio, a combination of its own meters and diaries for the large television markets and diaries only for the midsized and small television markets. Its diaries are offered in Spanish-language versions for those who request them, and Arbitron samples unlisted as well as listed telephone subscribers (using the **Expanded Sample Frame** technique—**ESF**) and encourages responses from black and Hispanic households by increasing the premium ($) enclosed with the diary and the number of follow-up reminder calls (called **Differential Survey Treatment**—**DSF**). Arbitron data is *weighted* to match the proportions of demographic subgroups in the local market. Arbitron's version of the peoplemeter (called **ScanAmerica**) is scheduled for a full roll-out sometime after 1988. It will combine product-purchase data (from the electronically scanned bars on most retail products) with television viewership research.

Arbitron provides only local ratings, not national ratings. Its metered homes generate local *overnight* ratings for several major cities, in competition with Nielsen's overnights, allowing station programmers to track the daily performance of their programs in those urban markets. Its peoplemeters are being progressively installed in markets where most stations subscribe to Arbitron's *Local TV Market Reports.* The company produces the same number of reports as Nielsen—excepting those for national network television.

4. *R.D. Percy Company.* Percy has its own 1,200 peoplemeters installed in New York City and anticipates samples in other major cities. The Percy **VOX-BOX** system enables in-home program testing and allows product-sales information to be combined with television viewing within each household. Percy will probably remain a supplementary major-market service, not a nationwide service.

Radio Services

1. *Birch Radio.* Founded in 1978 as the *Birch Report* and based in Florida, Birch is Arbitron's chief competitor in radio audience measurements. In 1982, the company absorbed both Mediastat and Mediatrend, expanding into branch offices in several cities. It has subscribers in over 230 (out of about 275 total) radio markets. Because the service combines radio ratings with **product-purchase** information (unlike Arbitron), it has become a standard tool for advertising agencies in the top 100 radio markets.

Birch uses **aided-recall telephone surveys** (giving lists of station call letters) rather than diaries to gather its listening data. It surveys only one person in a household in daily telephone interviews. In contrast, Arbitron uses seven-day written diaries and asks respondents to report on the listening habits of an entire household. Birch Radio issues 12 monthly *Standard Reports* covering one month's survey and comparing it to the previous month's report (using rolling averages). Quarterly by season, it summarizes ratings, ranks stations by AQH and cume audiences for target demographic groups, and presents qualitative information on product usage. Stations and advertising agencies can purchase the Birch Radio service for around a thousand dollars per month (in the top ten markets), the price decreasing as a station's market size decreases. These rates are about one-tenth the cost of Arbitron reports for comparable markets.

2. *Arbitron Radio Ratings.* Arbitron's *Radio Market Reports* track both *in-home* and *out-of-home* listening (in cars and other places) for local radio stations. The data come from weekly *diaries* mailed to a sample of households in each market. The size of the sample depends on the past history of response in the market and how much data collection the stations are willing to pay for (larger samples cost more money). Arbitron collects ratings for 48 weeks each year (called **continuous radio measurement**) in the larger markets and as few as 16 weeks in the smaller markets.

3. *RADAR Reports.* RADAR (Radio's All Dimension Audience Research), produced by Statistical Research, Inc. (SRI) in Westfield, New Jersey, reports on the performance of the national radio services. RADAR reports cover the size and demographics composition of 20 major radio services, including ABC's six radio networks, CBS's two radio services, Westwood's services (NBC Radio, Westwood One and Mutual), US I and II, Sheridan, Satellite Program Network's multiple services and others. Called the **network radio ratings,** RADAR reports are published twice annually, fall and spring, based on analyses of 32 weeks of continuous measurement beginning at the end of August and running through the end of April. Statistical Research, Inc., collects the data by *telephone.* These are the *only* nationwide radio network ratings.

In general, rating procedures are very similar from company to company, although each competes to sell more information to its clients. The quantity of demographic detail in local television and radio market reports steadily increased in the late 1970s and early 1980s because of increased competition between Nielsen and Arbitron (and Birch in radio) and pressure from programmers and advertisers for more information about an increasingly fragmented audience. The advent of cable and the larger audience share captured by independent television stations created demand for an even more precise understanding of audience viewing habits. Thus, in local market reports, the rating companies broke demographic information into smaller units (such as ten-year jumps for radio) and into more useful categories for different groups of advertisers (both women 18–34 and women 25–49 are now included, for example, as well as similar subgroups of men, children and teens).

In addition to local and national ratings reports, the largest companies offer a variety of *customized* reports covering narrower views of the audience (women 18–49 only or blacks or Hispanics or children, for example) and

Figure 2-1 Map of a Television Market Survey Area

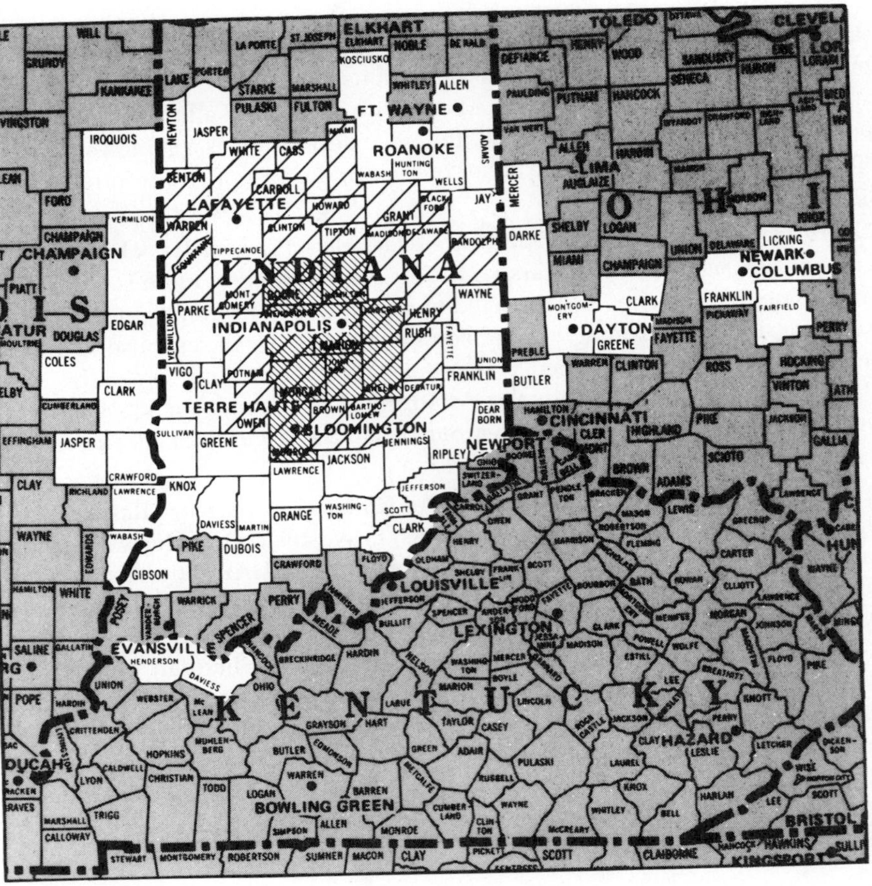

The "Total Survey Area" of this market is shown in white on the accompanying map. Where appropriate, the "Area of Dominant Influence" is indicated by coarse cross-hatching and the Arbitron "Metro (or Home County) Rating Area" by fine cross-hatching.

Source: Reproduced with the permission of the American Map Corporation. Further reproduction prohibited.

specialized programming, such as the Nielsen and Arbitron's analyses of *syndicated program ratings,* which are particularly useful to stations making program purchases. Chapters 3 and 8 make a special point of the importance of syndicated program reports, which are illustrated later in this chapter.

RATINGS TERMINOLOGY AND MEASUREMENT COMPUTATIONS

Arbitron and Nielsen collect audience estimates by randomly selecting listeners and viewers from the approximately **210 U.S. broadcast markets.**

The number of markets varies slightly from year to year and from company to company, but it has remained between 205 and 213 for several years. In technical terms, Arbitron calls the markets **Areas of Dominant Influence (ADIs)**, and Nielsen uses the term **Designated Market Areas (DMAs)**.

Survey Areas

However, Arbitron and Nielsen collect ratings data from more than ADIs/DMAs, as shown in Figure 2-1. In the illustration, the smallest measurement unit is the *Metro Area* (also called Metro Rating Area, Metro Survey Area, and Metro Sampling Area by Arbitron); next largest is the *ADI/DMA*; the largest unit is the *Total Survey Area* (TSA), called NSI Area by Nielsen.

1. *TSA/NSI Area.* The TSA or NSI Area includes all counties measured in an Arbitron or Nielsen survey, including counties outside the ADI/DMA when substantial viewing of stations inside the ADI/DMA occurs in them—viewership usually attributable to the presence of cable systems. Rarely used by commercial television programmers, TSA/NSI Area figures show a station's total estimated reach or circulation. As indicated earlier, **reach** tells how many people have viewed or listened to a station in the past, and it therefore suggests how many could view or listen in the future. In cable, **reach** tells how many households subscribe to basic cable service. Reach is an important measure for radio, public television and cable. Another name for reach is *cumulative* audience, or **cume.**

2. *ADI/DMA.* Each *county* in the United States is assigned to only one ADI or DMA. Occasionally, Arbitron's ADIs and Nielsen's DMAs differ in size because each company independently decides which counties belong to the particular market. Generally, an ADI/DMA centers on a single city, such as Indianapolis or Denver or New York, but in some cases two or even three cities are linked, as in the Dallas–Ft. Worth and Springfield–Decatur–Champaign markets. All stations in these multiple markets reach most viewers, making the cities one television viewing market. Arbitron and Nielsen rank each ADI/DMA according to the estimated number of television households within its counties.

As of 1988, the top five ADIs/DMAs were:

ADI		DMA	
Rank	Market	Rank	Market
1	New York*	1	New York
2	Los Angeles	2	Los Angeles
3	Chicago	3	Chicago
4	Philadelphia	4	Philadelphia
5	San Francisco	5	San Francisco–Oakland

*Nearly seven million television households.

The bottom five ADIs/DMAs in 1988 were:

ADI		DMA	
Rank	Market	Rank	Market
208	Mankato, Minn.	205	Twin Falls, Idaho
209	Helena, Mont.	206	Helena, Mont.
210	North Platte, Neb.	207	Alpena, Mich.
211	Alpena, Mich.	208	North Platte, Neb.
212	Glendive, Mont.	209	Glendive, Mont.*

*About 5,000 television households.

These lists indicate overall agreement between Arbitron's and Nielsen's major market surveys but show differences at the small-market end. Nielsen rates slightly fewer total markets (209 versus 212 in 1988) because it collapses more cities into double markets.

3. *Metro Areas.* The third geographical area, the Metro Survey Area (MSA) in radio and Metro Rating Area (MRA) or simply "Metro," is the smallest of the three survey areas and is the one most frequently used for radio programming. The Metro includes only a small number of counties closest to the home city of the ADI/DMA and consists of only a single, large county in some parts of the United States—especially in the West. Since competing big-city radio signals generally blanket the Metro, urban radio programmers use it to determine the success or failure of programming decisions. (Coverage patterns in outlying areas may vary too widely to compare.) The Metro represents the majority of the urban listeners, the bulk of office and store listening, and a large part of in-car listening. Altogether, **259** Metro areas were measured by Arbitron for radio listening in 1988 (as in television, the number of radio markets varies slightly from year to year). Radio stations on the fringe of the Metro area are more likely to refer to TSA/NSI Area measures. Television programmers, on the other hand, rarely use Metro ratings because no demographic breakouts are available.

But to use any of these ratings services for programming decisions, programmers must understand how the estimates are produced. Using ratings without this knowledge is like trying to play chess without ever learning the rules; pieces can be moved, but winning the game is unlikely. The following subsections, therefore, provide an overview of the basics of audience computations.

Ratings/Shares/HUTs

A **rating** is an estimate of the *percentage of the total* number of people or households in a population *tuned* to a specific station or network during a specific time period (**daypart**) such as morning drive or access. A **share** is an estimate of the percentage of people or households actually *using* radio or television and who *are tuned* to a specific station or network during a specific daypart. Ratings depend on a count of **all receivers;** shares on a count of **all users.** Shares are always bigger percentages than ratings for the same program or station because some people who *could* watch television (or listen to radio) are always *not* watching (they are sleeping or playing or working).

Ratings are always an estimate (percentage) of an entire population, whether the population refers to all households in the country or all people age 25–54 or all adults 12 + or all women 18–49 and so on. A share is always a percentage of those households or people in that population *using* the particular medium at a specific time. To repeat, *shares always appear larger than ratings* because they are based on a smaller sample of people; fewer people use television (or radio or cable) than *could* use it if all were at home, awake and choosing television above other activities. Both estimates are always percentages of an entire group—although the percent designation (%) is often omitted.

Sales staffs use **ratings** to set ad rates; **shares** *are used most typically in decisions about programming because they show how well a program does against its competition.* Broadcast networks and stations and cable services typically refer to their shares of an actual audience, not their percentage of all households having receivers (or cable service).

The combined ratings of all stations or networks during a particular daypart provide an estimate of the number of **households using television (HUTs)** or the persons using television (PUTs) or using radio (PURs). HUTs, PUTs, and PURs are used to compute the shares for each station or network.

To illustrate these concepts, assume only three television options in the United States. Also assume that Nielsen's 4,000 metered households indicate the following data:

Network	Household Viewing
ABC	691
CBS	827
NBC	774
Not watching	1708
	4000

The HUT level is .573 or 57.3% (2292/4000), calculated by adding households watching television and dividing by the total number of households with television (691 + 827 + 774 divided by 4000 equals .573). The answer is changed from a decimal to a percent by multiplying by 100. A HUT of 57.3 means an estimated 57 percent of all households had a television set on at the time of the measurement.

The individual ratings and shares for the three networks can now be calculated.

$$\text{Rating} = \frac{\text{Households Watching a Network}}{\text{Households with Receivers}}$$

Network	Ratings		Share
ABC	$\dfrac{691}{4000} = .172$ or 17.2%		$\dfrac{691}{2292} = .301$ or 30.1%
CBS	$\dfrac{827}{4000} = .207$ or 20.7%		$\dfrac{827}{2292} = .360$ or 36.0%
NBC	$\dfrac{774}{4000} = .194$ or 19.4%		$\dfrac{774}{2292} = .337$ or 33.7%

To calculate a *rating*, the number of households watching a network was divided by the total number of households having receivers (for example, for ABC, 691 divided by 4000 equals 17.2%). To calculate *shares*, the number of households watching ABC, for example, was divided by the total number of households watching television (691 divided by 2292 equals 30.1%).

Network programmers primarily use rating and share estimates to compare program audiences, but often they also will be interested in the specific number of **persons** in the audience. Ratings can be used to project to any particular population. For example, the data for the three networks above produce these estimates for the entire United States (having a total population of about 88 million households).

Network	Rating	×	Population	=	Population HH Estimate
ABC	.172	×	88 million	=	15,136,000
CBS	.207	×	88 million	=	18,216,000
NBC	.194	×	88 million	=	17,072,000
	.573				50,424,000

The number 15,136,000 represents the 15+ million homes estimated to be watching ABC (at this specific time). These calculations can be verified by multiplying the HUT, 57.3, by the total number of households: .573 × 88 million = 50,424,000, the total for the three networks.

Using part of a page from an Atlanta Nielsen book (Table 2-1), we can see how ratings and shares were computed for the local television stations WTBS, WAGA and WANX.

To calculate the rating and share for WTBS, in this early morning example, Nielsen first analyzed diaries from a sample of households (**HH**) in the Atlanta DMA. It then projected the sample returns to the DMA household population. Approximately 2 percent of the total diaries were tuned to WTBS from 7 A.M. to 9 A.M. If one assumes that 2 percent of the diaries reflects 2 percent of the total households, the number of homes watching WTBS can then be calculated. An estimated 1,117,400 households in the Atlanta DMA (this information is supplied on another page) produces a 2 rating for WTBS (22,000/1,117,400 = .02 or 2 percent). The share for WTBS was computed by using the HUT (see the HUT/PUT/TOTALS), which was 17 or 17 percent. Seventeen percent of 1,117,400 yields 189,958 HH, and when that figure is divided into WTBS's 22,000 HH, a share of 11 results.

Table 2-1 Portion of Arbitron Local Market Report, Atlanta Market

ATLANTA, GA

D A Y P A R T	METRO HH	DAYPART TIME (ETZ) STATION	DMA HH		DMA RATINGS		
	R T G / S H R		R T G / S H R	SHARE TREND	PER	WOMEN	FEM PER MEN
	1 / 2		7 / 8	JUL '82 / MAY '82 / FEB '82 / NOV '81 (9 10 11 12)	18-49 / 16	18+ / 18-34 / 18-49 / 25-43 / 25-54 / WKG (18 19 20 21 22 23)	12-24 / 12-24 / 18+ / 18-34 / 18-49 / 25-49 / 25-54 (24 25 26 27 28 29 30)

S U M M A R Y

MON.-FRI.
7.00AM-9.00AM

2 10	WAGA 5 C	2 10	11 8 10 7	1 1 1 1 1 1 1		1 1 1 1
2 12	WANX 46 I	2 12	10 10 14 8	1 1 1 1 1 1	1 1	
<<	WATL 36 I	<<	NR NR NR NR			
<<	WGTV 8 P	<<	NR			
7 40	WSB 2 A	7 42	33 39 37 37	3 5 3 4 5 5 3	2 1	3 1 2 2 3
2 11	WTBS 17 I	2 11	13 11 12 15	1 1 2 2 2 1 1	2 1	1 1 1 1 1
4 23	WXIA 11 N	3 19	25 23 21 29	1 2 1 2 2 2 2	1 1	2 1 1 1 2
18	HUT/PUT/TOTALS *	17	15 17 18 16	7 12 9 10 11 11 8	5 5	8 5 5 6 7

9.00AM-NOON

6 32	WAGA 5 C	6 30	32 31 34 33	3 5 4 4 4 4 2	2 2	2 1 1 1 1
1 6	WANX 46 I	1 5	4 4	1 1 1 1 1		
<<	WATL 36 I	<<	NR NR NR NR			
<<	WGTV 8 P	<<	NR			
4 23	WSB 2 A	4 22	29 30 27 31	2 4 4 3 3 3 1	3 2	1 1 1 1 1
2 10	WTBS 17 I	2 9	7 7 8 8	1 1 1 1 1 1	1	1 1 1 1 1
5 25	WXIA 11 N	4 22	20 21 15 16	2 4 3 3 3 3 1	2 1	1 1 1 1 1
19	HUT/PUT/TOTALS *	19	22 16 21 16	9 16 15 13 13 13 7	9 7	6 5 5 5 5 2

NOON-4.30PM

6 23	WAGA 5 C	7 26	31 24 27 24	3 6 4 4 4 4 3	3 2	2 2 1 1 1
2 9	WANX 46 I	2 8	9 6 6 5	1 1 1 1 1 1	1 1	1
<<	WATL 36 I	<<	NR NR NR NR			
<<	WGTV 8 P	<<	NR			
8 32	WSB 2 A	9 29	28 36 30 36	4 7 8 7 6 6 3	6 4	2 1 1 1 1
2 6	WTBS 17 I		5 7 7 6	1 1 1		1 1 1 1
	11		2 21	5 4		1 1

Source: Arbitron Ratings Company (1982), used with permission.

Arbitron and Nielsen always round rating and share figures to the nearest whole number, making numbers easier to read but creating some interpretive problems. If you refer again to the 7 A.M.–9 A.M. time period on the Nielsen report, you will see that WAGA, WANX and WTBS all have "2" ratings, but each station's share is different. We can compute more accurate ratings by manipulating the basic formula, usually written as:

$$\frac{\text{Rating}}{\text{HUT}} \times 100 = \text{Share}$$

The calculated value is multiplied by 100 to create whole numbers instead of decimals for shares and ratings. If we transpose to:

$$\text{Rating} = \frac{\text{Share} \times \text{HUT}}{100}$$

we can rate more accurately.

$$\text{WAGA Rating} = \frac{10 \times 17}{100} = 1.7$$

$$\text{WANX Rating} = \frac{12 \times 17}{100} = 2.04$$

$$\text{WTBS Rating} = \frac{11 \times 17}{100} = 1.87$$

Keep in mind that all ratings and shares are percentages and must include decimal points for all calculations although to make their reports easy to read ratings companies do not print the decimals.

One final point concerning the 7 A.M.–9 A.M. example is that the HUT/PUT/TOTAL line is 17, but if we add all of the stations, the total rating is actually 16. The uncounted rating point means that 1 percent of the households in the ADI/DMA were using their television sets for other things—viewing cable stations from other markets, playing video games or displaying for a computer.

PUTs/PURs

Also remember that ratings and shares for television generally represent households, but occasionally refer to specific demographic groups such as women 18–49. Radio ratings always represent individuals or persons, and therefore, the term *persons using radio* (PUR) is used. *Persons using television* (PUT) is appropriate when calculations of individual viewers are made. Sales staffs and time buyers tend to be more interested in these calculations than programmers, and one of the big advantages of peoplemeters is that they supply individual person as well as household data for the advertising industry.

AQH/Cume

Programmers use two very important computations in calculating ratings: average quarter-hour audiences (**AQH**) and cumulative audience estimates (**cume**). Program audiences are typically measured in 15-minute intervals, hence "quarter-hour audience." Meters can, in fact, measure one-minute audiences, but a person or household is counted in a quarter-hour if the television was turned on for a minimum of five minutes during the measurement period.

Although radio and television diaries also measure audience size in 15-minute intervals, programmers utilize these data in much larger units—by whole program or daypart. Quarter-hours are the particular concern of those who try to count fickle radio listeners. (Both time units may be too gross for measuring remote control flippers and radio button pushers.)

Cumulative audience measures, on the other hand, are appropriate for *small audiences* that would not show up in rating/share measures. Cume measurements indicate the number of different people tuned in during a 15-minute (or longer) time period. *Cume figures are always larger than AQH figures.*

The basic difference between AQH and cume is that in the average quarter-hour calculation persons can be counted more than once in a total daypart. For instance, a person could tune to a station for five minutes, switch stations or tune out, and then tune back into the original station during a later quarter-hour. This viewer would be counted twice in an AQH calculation, but not in a cume calculation since it counts only the number of different persons listening. *Cume* is considered the *reach* of a station because it tells you *how many different persons* were in the audience during a time period or daypart. It also reflects the growth or decay of an audience over time.

Public television and basic cable audiences are often too small for accurate measurement within one quarter-hour, but cumulative ratings over a longer period of time may reflect more substantial audiences. Cumes can also be calculated for a single program over several airings, a common pattern in public television and cable measurements, permitting programmers to estimate the total number of people who watched a program. Commercial broadcasting with its special interest in the number of people watching one commercial spot generally uses AQH ratings.

Reach and Frequency Analysis

Sales people most often use the concepts of *reach* and *frequency*. As we said earlier, **reach** refers to circulation, or the net size of the audience; **frequency** indicates the number of times a person was exposed to a particular advertising message (or program). A high frequency means exposure to a message several times and indicates the "holding power" of a station, network or program. Programmers usually schedule several interesting programs in succession, trying to create audience flow and achieve a high frequency for advertisers among successive programs appealing to the same viewers.

TELEVISION MARKET REPORTS

Market reports (or "books") are divided into sections to allow programmers, sales people and advertisers to examine an audience from many perspectives. In television, the major sections are: Daypart Audiences, Network Dayparts, Time Period Averages, and Program Audience. (The section names vary slightly between Nielsen and Arbitron—and their order differs.)

Daypart Audience

The Daypart Audience section divides viewing into roughly 21 **dayparts,** a highly useful format for analyzing a station's overall performance in specific time blocks. For instance, Monday through Friday early fringe (4:00 P.M.–6:00 P.M. EST) provides a quick summary of the ratings and shares for all stations during this daypart. Table 2-2, a page from an Arbitron book, shows the weekday 4–6 P.M. period in the Los Angeles market.

Arbitron uses 21 demographic categories. Nielsen divides the viewers into 22 age and sex classifications for both the DMA and the TSA. For just one station, then, 462 ratings cells are required to fill out all 22 Nielsen people categories and 21 daypart categories for TSA ratings alone. A single ratings book page contains an immense amount of data.

A look at Table 2-2 shows that KABC-TV was the strongest station in the market in the early fringe daypart, with a 9 rating/21 share in the ADI and

Table 2-2 Arbitron Local Market Report, Daypart Audience Section

Daypart Audience Estimates Summary

DAYPART AND STATION	ADI TV HH		ADI TV HH SHARE/HUT TRENDS				METRO TV HH		TV HH	TOTAL SURVEY AREA, IN THOUSANDS (000's)																			
										PERSONS						WOMEN							MEN					TEENS TOTAL
	R T G	S H R	JUL '87	MAY '87	FEB '87	NOV '86	R T G	S H R	TV HH	TOT 2+	18+	18-49	12-24	12-34	18-34	TOT 18+	18-49	12-24	18-34	25-49	25-54	WKG WMN 18+	TOT 18+	18-49	18-34	25-49	25-54	12-17
	5	6	58	59	60	61	8	9	11	12	13	14	15	16	17	18	19	20	21	22	23	24	25	26	27	28	29	30
MON–FRI																												
4:00P–6:00P																												
KCBS	4	9	8	7	8	9	4	10	194	297	282	117	26	55	45	169	64	11	25	55	61	30	112	53	19	46	52	10
KNBC	6	14	13	13	13	13	6	13	305	458	442	135	19	65	56	266	76	9	32	70	84	35	175	59	24	54	66	8
KTLA	4	9	11	9	9	10	4	9	199	313	248	144	63	109	71	150	87	31	37	77	89	37	98	58	34	42	49	37
KABC	9	21	20	19	20	19	9	22	436	641	612	257	50	149	137	360	130	23	74	111	144	50	253	128	63	108	121	12
KHJ	4	10	12	12	13	14	4	10	219	345	281	183	102	143	98	170	104	55	48	81	87	29	111	79	50	46	51	45
KTTV	6	13	9	11	13	11	6	13	292	530	179	156	121	177	114	101	88	60	66	54	57	25	78	68	49	43	45	63
KCOP •	5	13	11	12	10	12	5	13	266	536	181	155	186	223	95	106	90	106	62	52	53	18	74	65	33	45	47	128
KWHY			**	**					8	1	1												1					
KMEX	2	4	6	4	4	4	2	5	89	170	109	72	43	78	49	76	49	31	33	42	53	6	33	23	16	16	17	29
KVEA	1	1	3	4	3	3	1	2	30	20	19	18	5	8	7	12	12	2	5	10	10	2	7	6	2	4	5	
KDOC					2	1			16	38	24	21	22	26	18	7	7	9	5	4	4	2	16	14	13	3	4	8
KCET	1	1	2	2	2				27	41	26	11	2	7	6	17	8	2	5	7	7	2	8	4	1	4	4	2
KOCE									2																			
HUT/TOT	43		39	39	44	43	41		2083	3390	2404	1269	639	1040	696	1434	715	339	392	563	649	236	966	557	304	411	461	342
4:00P–7:30P																												
KCBS	4	9	9	8	8	8	4	9	212	338	321	132	23	51	ᴸ	185	71	11	2ᴸ	63	70	40	136	61ᴵ	18	55	64	9
KNBC	6	12	12	⁻	ˢ	12	6	12	299	46ᶜ	⁴	168	32	86	⁻3	90	16				94	48	181			68	82	11
KTLA	5	11	⁻		⁻1		5	11	274	⁻		221	97	1ᴵ		128	4ᶜ				ᵉ9	56	14ᶜ			⁵7	76	5
KABC	9	1ᶜ					9	20	44ᶜ		⁻4	66				⁻4						68	⁻		1	165	20	
ᵛHJ	F						5	10	⁻																			41

Source: Arbitron Ratings Co. (1987), used with permission.

9/22 in the Metro. It was very strong with both women 18–49 and men 18–49. No doubt this station's programmer was delighted since these demographics are very easy to sell to advertisers.

Programmers normally compare the most current numbers to previous performances. **Tracking** a daypart shows how the station or program is doing *over time*. It is also important in selecting syndicated programs, as explained in chapters 3 and 8. Rarely will program decisions be based on only one book unless the numbers are very low and very credible, and no hope for improvement is in sight.

Network Daypart/Time Period Averages

The Network Daypart section provides broad time-segment information for network programming (ABC, CBS, NBC). Arbitron and Nielsen divide data on dayparts and demographic groups for the networks just as they do for stations in each market's report. An example is not included here since the layout of the Network Daypart section is similar to that of Table 2-2. This ratings book section shows how network programming performed on the local station—which on occasion is very different from national averages. The section lets programmers compare the three networks in market-by-market performance.

Television programmers are interested not only in broad dayparts but in quarter-hour or half-hour segments within them. This information, found in the Time Period Averages section of ratings books, is useful in determining a program's strength against the competition for a specific quarter-hour or half-hour. Managers of affiliates look here, for example, to see how their local newscast stacks up against its competitors. It also has an overview of access time and early fringe competition and shows lead-in and lead-out effects. Programmers use it to analyze performance in *time* segments. (Sales people use it to determine spot ratings.)

Daypart Audience Estimates Summary

DAYPART AND STATION	TSA (000's) CHILDREN 2-11	6-11	TSA TV HH	CUMES (000's)	ADI TV HH	PERSONS TOT 2+	18+	18-49	12-24	12-34	18-34	WOMEN TOT 18+	18-49	12-24	18-34	25-49	25-54	WKG WMN 18+	MEN TOT 18+	18-34	25-49	25-54	TNS TOT 12-17	CHILD 12-	2-	6-	METRO	PERCENT DISTRIBUTION HOME ADI	#1	#2	#3	TV HH RTGS IN ADJACENT ADI'S #1	#2	#3
	31	32	111		105	35	36	37	38	39	40	41	42	43	44	45	46	47	48	49	50	51	52	53	54	55	62	65	66	67	68	70	71	72
MON-FRI 4:00P-6:00P																																		
KCBS	5	3	1249		1205	2	3	2	1	1	1	3	2	1	1	2	2		2	2	2	1	2	2	1		77	95	1		1	1	2	1
KNBC	8	5	1565		1471	3	4	2	1	1	1	5	2	1	2	3	3	2	4	2	2	2	1				68	93	1		3	2	1	4
KTLA	28	18	1195		1107	2	2	2	2	2	2	2	2	2	3	3	2	2	2	1	2	2	1				74	91	2	2	2		2	
KABC	17	7	1986		1926	5	6	4	2	3	3	7	4	2	4	5	3	5	4	3	4	4	1	1	1		79	97		1	1	1		3
KHJ	19	11	1117		1075	3	3	3	4	3	2	3	3	4	2	4	3	3	4	3	4	4		1	1		79	97		1	1	1		
KTTV	288	146	1585		1447	4	2	2	4	3	2	2	4	3	2	2	1	2	2	2	2	4	1	1	72	94	1	1	1	2		1	
KCOP	227	162	1500		1428	4	2	2	7	4	2	2	3	8	3	2	2	1	2	2	2	2	6	14	12	71	91	2	3	1	3	1	2
* KWHY			41		40																		12	12	15	74	96			2	1	1	1
KMEX	32	22	298		295	1	1	1	2	2	1	1	2	2	2		1	1	1	1	3	2	2	99	99							
KVEA			179		179																			82	99	1					
KDOC	6	5	165		165		1	1				1						1						82	99						
KCET	13	3	340		321																1		1	62	89	2	1	7			1
KOCE			16		16																			99	99						
TOT/PVT	643	382				28	26	20	24	22	19	30	23	27	21	23	24	15	22	18	17	18	18	31	32	32	75	94	1	2	1			
4:00P-7:30P																																		
KCBS	7	4	1854		1767	3	3	2	1	1	1	4	2	1	1	2	2	2	3	2	1	2	2	1		79	95		1	1	1		2
KNBC	15	10	2206		2055	3	4	2	2	2	1	5	3	1	2	3	3	2	2	2		1	1	71	93	1	1	2	3	2	1	4
KTLA	61	42	2143		1946	3	3	2		3	3	4	3		3	3	2	2	3	3	2	3		1	74	91		3	2	1	4
	20	9	2810		2700	5	3		4	4	4	3	4		3	2	3	4	6	5	4	1	80	97			3	1	2
	27	15	19		1854					3	4	4	3		2		75						3
	39	132			224																										

Averages for the whole week, Monday–Friday, are also included in the Time Period Averages section, as well as most prime-time network programming since it varies from night to night. These figures show performance during a daypart or time period when all days are averaged together, crucial data when a programmer is looking at stripped programming in early fringe and prime-time access.

Program Audience

The last major section of a television ratings book, one television programmers most often use, is the Program Audience section. Rather than lumping a program into a daypart, this section breaks each daypart and program into 30-minute segments (and some 15-minute ones)—to isolate individual programs on different days of the sweep weeks. The Program Audience section is considered the "pure programming" section since each program is analyzed individually. It shows the titles of the shows and any scheduling variations from night to night. This allows programmers to examine ratings for their local news, say, night by night, and to eliminate the odd night when a sporting event, for example, cut into the news time.

Look at the Program Audience data for Los Angeles at 6 P.M. in Table 2-3. The highlighted numbers are the ADI rating/share and Metro rating/share for all weekdays (WKD). Notice that in ADI measurements, KABC and KTTV are neck and neck (carrying local news and *Three's Company* reruns) and that KTLA is only a hair behind (carrying *Magnum P.I.* reruns). KCBS and KNBC, two other network-owned stations (in addition to KABC), have local newscasts that average two or three rating points less than those of KABC and the two independents carrying reruns. KCBS's news at 6 P.M. was not even doing as well as reruns of *Gimme a Break* (in this particular ratings book covering only the November 1987 sweep). Also, notice that when KHJ preempted *T.J. Hooker* for Lakers basketball games on Tuesdays, the station's ratings went up a point (to 7) over the *Hooker* average (6), whereas the *Lakers Pregame Show* hurt the station's

Table 2-3 Arbitron Local Market Report, Program Audience Section

Weekly Program Estimates / **Program Audience Estimates** — TOTAL SURVEY AREA, IN THOUSANDS (000's)

DAY	TIME AND STATION / PROGRAM	TELECASTS # OF TEL	TELECASTS # OF QTR-HRS	WEEK-BY-WEEK ADI TV HH RATINGS WK 1 10/28	WK 2 11/4	WK 3 11/11	WK 4 11/18	ADI TV HH RTG	ADI TV HH SHR	ADI TV HH HUT	METRO TV HH RTG	METRO TV HH SHR	METRO TV HH HUT	TV HH	PERSONS TOT 2+	PERSONS 18+	PERSONS 18-49	PERSONS 12-24	PERSONS 12-34	PERSONS 18-34	WOMEN TOT 18+	WOMEN 18-49	WOMEN 12-24	WOMEN 18-34	WOMEN 25-49	WOMEN 25-54	WKG WMN 18+
				1	2	3	4	5	6	7	8	9	10	11	12	13	14	15	16	17	18	19	20	21	22	23	24
	▲ RELATIVE STD-ERR THRESHOLDS (1 σ) 25%			3	3	3	3	2			2			78	85	54	50	63	58	57	41	41	57	47	37	37	42
	50%			-	-	-	-	-			-			19	21	13	12	16	14	14	10	10	14	11	9	9	10
	6:00P																										
	KCBS																										
MON	6OCLCK NEWS	4	8	4	5	5	6	5	9	59	5	9	58	256	425	414	165	12	47	41	231	78	7	19	74	88	39
TUE	6OCLCK NEWS	4	8	6	5	5	6	6	10	56	6	11	55	274	463	454	152	16	40	34	255	87	3	15	86	89	41
WED	6OCLCK NEWS	4	8	6	4	4	5	5	9	55	5	8	55	230	388	380	128	10	31	29	215	71	7	18	66	74	36
THU	6OCLCK NEWS	4	8	4	6	6	4	5	9	55	5	10	54	246	383	368	138	15	34	29	216	79	8	14	75	82	45
FRI	6OCLCK NEWS	4	8	5	4	5	3	4	8	50	5	9	50	207	364	348	128	16	34	23	196	66	3	13	65	67	47
WKD	6OCLCK NEWS	20	40	5	5	5	5	5	9	55	5	9	54	243	405	393	142	14	37	31	223	76	5	16	73	80	41
SAT	CBS NEWS-SAT	3	6	5	5	7		6	11	51	6	11	51	282	477	468	180	9	57	57	243	73	6	23	68	102	28
	JOHN ROBNSON	1	2				2	2	4	50	2	3	49	91	150	150	86	28	67	67	66	46	28	28	18	22	8
SUN	CH2 NW WKD 6	4	16	11	9	9	8	9	17	57	10	17	58	466	767	751	257	38	86	76	427	131	16	35	116	151	87
ALL	JOHN ROBNSON	4	8	2	2	4	2	3	5	49	3	5	48	127	210	168	119	71	89	48	51	32	25	8	25	26	13
	KNBC																										
MON	CH 4 NEWS 6	4	8	7	6	6	6	6	11	59	7	11	58	310	481	433	186	44	104	84	259	95	23	32	84	104	54
TUE	CH 4 NEWS 6	4	8	6	6	6	8	6	12	56	6	10	55	317	468	452	197	29	110	100	247	100	19	57	82	98	58
WED	CH 4 NEWS 6	4	8	6	6	6	5	6	10	55	5	9	55	284	432	410	197	35	90	80	215	87	18	35	74	94	47
THU	CH 4 NEWS 6	4	8	6	7	6	6	6	12	55	6	11	54	318	509	470	210	31	104	97	252	110	15	54	96	113	71
FRI	CH 4 NEWS 6	4	8	6	5	4	6	5	11	50	5	10	50	271	438	415	177	25	71	65	207	78	12	27	66	84	60
WKD	CH 4 NEWS 6	20	40	6	6	6	7	6	11	55	6	10	54	300	466	436	193	33	96	85	236	94	17	41	80	99	58
SAT	FIGHT BACK	4	8	8	10	8	9	9	17	51	9	17	51	429	742	672	255	54	132	92	391	133	28	42	131	145	65
SUN	ENTRTN TS WK	4	16	7	7	6	8	7	13	57	7	13	58	348	522	465	254	85	151	112	297	141	50	62	111	136	102
	KTLA																										
MON	MAGNUM PI-S	4	16	8	7	7	5	6	11	61	6	11	60	329	564	436	294	133	245	196	277	185	73	129	129	137	62
TUE	MAGNUM PI-S	4	16	9	8	8	9	9	15	57	9	16	57	449	717	590	373	158	254	188	357	231	75	118	183	190	114
WED	MAGNUM PI-S	4	16	7	8	8	8	8	14	56	8	14	56	416	670	573	381	127	293	246	307	198	52	114	163	185	107
THU	MAGNUM PI-S	4	16	6	8	8	7	7	13	56	8	14	56	381	683	550	369	126	280	226	291	189	41	108	159	172	90
FRI	MAGNUM PI-S	4	16	7	9	8	6	8	15	51	8	15	51	387	624	547	362	114	248	210	305	190	42	101	161	180	83
WKD	MAGNUM PI-S	20	80	7	8	8	7	8	14	56	8	14	56	393	652	539	356	131	264	213	308	199	56	114	159	173	91
SAT	MV SAT EVE	3	24		9	8	8	8	15	54	8	15	53	422	966	645	556	195	476	385	330	276	122	194	210	222	115
	RTRN TITAN-R	1	8	6				6	12	52	6	12	52	307	528	452	272	86	193	154	211	127	52	70	94	110	57
SUN	MV SUN EVE	4	32	7	10	5	7	7	12	61	7	12	61	360	793	519	427	206	412	297	291	240	110	167	194	202	96
	KABC																										
MON	NFL MON FTBL	4	57	19	16	22	22	20	30	66	20	30	66	947	1504	1362	876	233	559	470	450	284	67	157	244	281	156
TUE	CH7 EYEWT NW	4	8	8	10	8	10	9	16	56	9	17	55	433	655	622	315	77	213	196	325	142	40	96	112	132	101
WED	CH7 EYEWT NW	4	8	9	11	7	8	9	16	55	10	17	55	425	681	642	336	52	187	169	337	169	16	85	158	185	93
THU	CH7 EYEWT NW	4	8	11	8	8	8	9	16	55	9	16	54	408	624	594	322	63	176	163	306	158	33	85	132	157	101
FRI	CH7 EYEWT NW	4	8	7	5	7	7	6	13	50	6	12	50	311	460	443	213	37	92	85	246	111	17	48	95	125	63
WKD	CH7 EYEWT NW	16	32	9	8	7	8	8	15	54	8	16	54	394	605	575	296	57	167	153	304	145	26	79	124	150	90
SAT	CH7 EYW NEWS	4	8	7	7	6	8	7	14	51	8	15	51	338	528	508	247	40	134	124	271	126	14	59	121	146	76
SUN	CH7 EYEW NWS	4	8	7	5	5	6	6	11	55	6	11	55	279	466	422	221	35	134	110	224	101	26	58	95	114	64
	KHJ																										
MON	TJ HOOKER	4	16	5	5	6	6	5	9	61	6	10	60	261	387	330	167	34	110	90	219	114	26	47	100	105	70
TUE	LAKER PREGME	1	2		4			4	8	56	4	8	56	214	285	240	142	28	123	95	155	59	15	40	59	59	31
	LAKERS BKBL	1	9	6				6	11	58	6	10	57	296	408	351	227	74	183	136	147	95	19	61	81	110	21
	TJ HOOKER	2	8			5	5	5	9	59	5	9	59	256	458	369	210	46	124	102	201	112	34	47	97	99	69
WED	TJ HOOKER	4	16	6	7	7	4	6	11	56	6	12	56	289	450	361	229	92	170	123	196	112	52	53	87	99	71
THU	TJ HOOKER	4	16	6	6	5	7	6	11	56	6	11	56	292	492	376	221	90	166	130	244	145	55	68	117	128	60
FRI	TJ HOOKER	4	16	5	5	4	5	5	9	51	5	10	51	240	385	303	152	64	106	60	203	106	41	32	89	91	48
WKD	TJ HOOKER	18	72	5	6	5	6	6	10	56	6	10	56	269	432	345	194	68	137	101	214	118	43	50	98	105	63
SAT	HRDCSTL-MC-S	4	16	6	5	6	7	6	11	51	5	10	51	274	367	317	145	35	80	52	209	93	8	21	91	104	60
SUN	MILN $ MOV 3	4	32	6	3	4	3	4	6	61	4	6	61	186	253	210	146	61	143	106	103	71	23	52	57	61	46
ALL	LAKER PREGME	4	8	3	4	2	4	3	6	57	3	6	55	157	271	238	152	44	85	65	122	75	19	34	65	78	47
ALL	LAKERS BKBL	4	37	6	9	7	7	7	12	61	7	12	60	345	555	500	327	87	216	184	179	105	23	63	96	119	56
	KTTV																										
MON	THREES CMPNY	4	8	8	7	9	7	8	13	59	8	14	58	394	875	560	405	222	408	307	316	231	106	175	175	180	87
TUE	THREES CMPNY	4	8	9	11	9	7	9	16	56	9	16	55	444	820	550	396	265	387	248	284	211	147	126	146	152	99
WED	THREES CMPNY	4	8	8	11	8	10	9	17	55	10	18	55	476	828	573	421	178	370	292	310	239	75	166	193	202	85
THU	THREES CMPNY	4	8	7	8	8	9	8	15	55	8	15	54	401	699	445	316	213	332	230	247	175	116	119	126	138	50
FRI	THREES CMPNY	4	8	9	7	7	10	8	17	50	9	18	50	408	806	561	424	208	389	297	316	245	105	173	192	194	68
WKD	THREES CMPNY	20	40	8	9	8	9	8	15	55	9	16	54	425	806	538	392	217	377	275	295	220	110	152	166	173	78
SAT	SMALL WONDER	4	8	6	6	4	6	6	11	51	5	10	51	286	514	303	230	115	183	123	169	134	67	67	104	111	25
SUN	WORLD-DISNEY	3	12	7	8		6	7	13	56	7	13	57	362	888	472	384	172	312	199	224	183	66	95	161	162	85
	KCOP																										
MON	GIMME BRK-S	4	8	5	5	5	6	6	9	59	5	9	58	268	545	298	225	181	239	134	219	159	132	103	89	106	37
TUE	GIMME BRK-S	4	8	5	6	6	6	6	11	56	6	10	55	289	578	329	257	184	289	192	214	159	109	121	107	110	45
WED	GIMME BRK-S	4	8	5	7	6	6	6	11	55	7	12	55	301	631	330	259	191	278	155	235	174	136	110	124	135	45
THU	GIMME BRK-S	4	8	6	7	4	5	6	11	55	6	10	54	280	516	275	215	165	229	135	178	129	80	79	101	110	42
FRI	GIMME BRK-S	4	8	6	6	7	4	6	11	50	6	11	50	275	517	323	241	163	220	123	228	170	118	97	121	129	54
WKD	GIMME BRK-S	20	40	6	6	6	6	6	11	55	6	11	54	283	558	311	239	177	251	148	215	158	115	102	109	118	44
SAT	STR TK NX-R	4	16	5	5	6	6	6	11	51	6	11	51	291	517	401	333	94	239	206	192	150	28	95	126	134	100
SUN	SU FILM FEST	4	32	8	8	9	7	8	13	61	8	13	61	407	872	539	420	160	353	266	259	207	90	139	171	177	101
	KMEX																										
MON	NOTICIERO	4	8	4	2	3	2	3	5	59	3	5	58	128	323	243	154	91	144	97	126	74	62	46	56	66	9
TUE	NOTICIERO	4	8	3	3	3	3	3	5	56	3	6	55	140	372	301	217	81	161	145	151	102	28	66	87	104	17
WED	NOTICIERO	4	8	3	3	4	3	3	6	55	4	7	55	156	372	285	199	92	161	118	145	93	30	51	86	99	33
THU	NOTICIERO	4	8	2	3	3	2	2	4	55	3	5	54	113	284	203	131	82	135	87	111	67	54	43	57	67	14
FRI	NOTICIERO	4	8	2	4	3	3	3	6	50	4	7	50	152	362	273	192	124	184	120	138	97	71	52	84	94	20
WKD	NOTICIERO	20	40	3	3	3	3	3	5	55	3	6	54	138	342	261	178	94	157	113	134	87	49	52	74	86	19
	KVEA																										
MON	VEA NOTICIAS	4	8	2	-	2	1	1	2	59	1	2	58	57	144	112	103	44	62	55	51	47	28	27	26	26	1
TUE	VEA NOTICIAS	4	8	1	1	2	2	2	3	56	2	3	55	73	282	173	164	87	98	68	95	87	50	44	52	52	10
WED	VEA NOTICIAS	4	8	1	1	1	2	1	2	55	1	3	55	58	128	97	89	25	47	34	29	20	18	7	15	17	5
THU	VEA NOTICIAS	4	8	2	1	1	2	1	2	55	2	3	54	61	163	130	119	15	41	41	50	38	8	16	30	30	11
FRI	VEA NOTICIAS	4	8	1	-	1	1	1	2	50	1	2	50	43	128	111	105	27	47	47	52	48	16	25	33	33	9
WKD	VEA NOTICIAS	20	40	1	1	1	1	1	2	55	1	3	54	58	169	125	116	40	59	49	55	48	24	24	31	32	7
SAT	BUTACA 52	4	32	2	1	2	1	1	3	53	2	3	53	63	142	93	78	33	73	48	41	32	20	20	29	37	3
SUN	CUSTU ODISEA	4	16	2	1	1	1	1	2	57	1	2	58	49	121	108	104	40	71	58	46	46	24	30	34	34	17
	KDOC																										
MON	COMBAT	4	16	1	1	-	1			61			60	23	18	6	4	3	7	4							
TUE	COMBAT	4	16	-	-	-	-			57			57	10	24	12	7	4	10	6							
WED	COMBAT	4	16	1	1	-	-	1	1	56	1	1	56	28	49	33	21	15	26	19	5					3	
THU	COMBAT	4	16	1	-	1	1	1	1	56	1	2	56	33	27	24	21	3	11	8	6	6			6	6	
FRI	COMBAT	4	16	1	-	1	1	1	1	51	1	1	51	26	26	19	17	8	12	8	1	1			1	1	1
WKD	COMBAT	20	80	1	-	-	1	1	1	56	1	1	56	24	29	19	14	7	13	9	2	1			1	2	
SAT	JAPANESE	4	32	-	1	-	1	1	1	53			53	25	20	18	11	2	5	3	10	6		1	6	7	3
ALL	JAPANESE	8	72	-	-	-	1			57			56	21	15	14	6	1	2	1	8	4			4	5	3

LOS ANGELES 183 NOVEMBER 1987 PROGRAM AUDIENCES

~ INCLUDED IN TYPICAL AVERAGE
* SAMPLE BELOW MINIMUM FOR WEEKLY REPORTING
\- DID NOT ACHIEVE A REPORTABLE WEEKLY RATING
‡ TECHNICAL DIFFICULTY
\+ COMBINED PARENT/SATELLITE
▲ SEE TABLE ON PAGE v

Source: Arbitron Ratings Co. (1987), used with permission.

ratings (only a 3). This section permits analysis of individual programs without interference from ratings for other programs.

In summary, then, the sections of a television book provide programmers with at least four different ways to evaluate station performance. Daypart Audience examines broad time periods without regard to specific programs; Network Daypart includes only network programming; Time Period Averages provide programming data by quarter-hours and half-hours on a daily basis and are useful in analyzing competitive performance. Finally, Program Audience information isolates the "pure program" data. Each section answers different questions, and television programmers use every section as their questions shift.

OTHER PROGRAMMING AIDS

Ratings companies issue reports on specific demographic groups or types of programs or station market sizes in easy-to-use formats, and stations, reps and ad agencies rely heavily on them. They also depend on other companies to reanalyze Arbitron's and Nielsen's ratings data and to supplement them with other research. Of all these additional services, programmers find analyses of syndicated television programs the most valuable.

Syndicated Program Reports

Affiliates and independents rely on *off-network* and *first-run* syndicated programming to fill parts of their broadcast days. But because syndicated programs are expensive, station decision makers want to know about a program's past performance. Will a program perform well in their market? Will its ratings justify its cost? Reps and program consultants especially want this information since they advise station programmers. Projecting or estimating ratings success for a first-run product is an involved process that, finally, comes down to an educated guess. The potentials of off-network programs are somewhat easier to evaluate, but even here no hard-and-fast rules exist. Lead-in programs, local competition and audience fads always influence ratings. Even the most successful network program may fail in syndication or perform below its network numbers at a given time or in a given market.

In making decisions about syndicated programs, Arbitron's *Syndicated Program Analysis* (Nielsen's publication is called the *Report on Syndicated Programs*) is helpful. The major television rep firms also provide similar analyses in less bulky and unwieldy formats. A page from the Arbitron analysis for *Barney Miller* is shown in Table 2-4. At the top of the page, the program, program type and overall ADI rating and share for all markets where the program is currently broadcast are specified. The number of markets carrying the program and the number of previous syndicated program analyses (SPAs) reporting on that program also appear.

The second section provides overall ratings and share data by daypart and by market size. For example, in prime access, *Barney Miller* had a 10 rating and 17 share in 14 markets with 4 or more stations. This section indicates the dayparts and market sizes where the program has played most effectively,

Table 2-4 Syndicated Program Analysis

BARNEY MILLER

129 MARKETS TELECASTING	PROGRAM TYPE: SITUATION COMEDY
129 STATIONS TELECASTING	PROGRAM DURATION: 30 MINUTES
7 PREVIOUS SPA'S	TVHH IN ADI MKTS: 69,757,800
NOV 80 FIRST SPA	ADI MKTS % U.S. 83.58

DISTRIBUTOR: COLUMBIA PICTURES TV — BARNEY MILLER
ADI TVHH RATING: 8.8
ADI TVHH SHARE: 18.8

AVG ADI ESTIMATES BY STATIONS PER MARKET

DAYPARTS IN WHICH TELECASTS BEGAN	4+ STA NO MKTS	R	SH	3 STA NO MKTS	R	SH	2 STA NO MKTS	R	SH	1 STA NO MKTS	R	SH	ALL STA NO MKTS	R	SH	NO. OF STNS BY DAY-PART
M-F MORNING	1	3	16										1	3	16	1
M-F AFTERNOON	1	7	17										1	7	17	1
M-F TOTAL DAYTIME	2	6	17										2	6	17	2
M-F EARLY FRINGE	33	8	17	19	10	23	5	8	16				57	8	17	57
MN-SA PRIME ACCESS	14	10	17	10			5	11	20	3	12	24	32	12	19	32
SU-SA PRIME	3	13	24	2	13	25				1	8	37	6	13	25	6
M-F LATE NIGHT	12	7	22	9	7	24	1	12	36				23	7	23	23
SAT MORNING																
SU-SA SGN/ON-SGN/OFF	70	8	18	42	11	25	13	11	24	4	10	27	129	9	19	TOTAL PRGM 129

AGGREGATE TSA PROGRAM TOTALS FOR HOME STATIONS — IN THOUSANDS (000)

DAYPART	TOTAL TVHH	WOMEN 18+	WOMEN 18-49	MEN 18+	MEN 18-49	TEENS 12-17	CHILD 2-11
M-F MORNING	28	19	11	12	6	1	4
M-F AFTERNOON	295	217	111	171	84	35	20
M-F TOTAL DAYTIME	323	236	122	183	90	36	24
M-F EARLY FRINGE	3698	2635	1469	2370	1464	548	710
MN-SA PRIME ACCESS	1837	1426	807	1336	825	242	303
SU-SA PRIME	240	183	90	163	92	31	40
M-F LATE NIGHT	757	583	359	490	334	53	32
TOTAL	7188	5307	2977	4771	2938	944	1146

MARKET DATA

ALBANY, GA — M-F 7:30P 20T/C — Competing programs: THE JEFERSNS / VARIOUS

TSA

CALL	HH RTG	RT IDX	HH SH	SH IDX	W18+ R/SH	W18-49 R/SH	M18+ R/SH	M18-49 R/SH	TEENS 12-17 RTG	CHILD 2-11 RTG	LEAD-IN HALF HOUR PROGRAM
WALB (55S/S)	32	367	51	271	23/48	17/39	26/53	19/44	17	12	NBC NGHT NWS
WTSG*	10	68	16		9/20	12/26	7/14	8/18	15	13	SANFORD-SON
WVGA*	1		1		1/2	1/2	1/2	1/1	1	1	VARIOUS

ADI

CALL	TVHH R/SH	W18+ R/SH	W18-49 R/SH	M18+ R/SH	M18-49 R/SH	TEENS RTG	CHILD RTG	LEADOUT TVHH R/SH
WALB	39/58	28/58	20/48	32/62	22/51	12	7	35/51
WALB TSA (000)	71	59	48	55	26			71
WTSG*	9/13	7/15	9/21	6/11	7/17	15	12	4/5
WVGA*	1/1	1/1	1/2	1/1	1/2	1	1	3/4

ALBNY-SCHDY-TROY — M-F 5:00P 19T/C — Competing programs: MASH-S HR / HPY DAYS AGN

TSA

CALL	HH RTG	RT IDX	HH SH	SH IDX	W18+ R/SH	W18-49 R/SH	M18+ R/SH	M18-49 R/SH	TEENS 12-17 RTG	CHILD 2-11 RTG	LEAD-IN HALF HOUR PROGRAM
WNYT (20S/S)	8	86	18	96	6/22	4/17	5/20	3/14	2	3	THE JEFERSNS
WTEN+	13		32		9/34	9/36	10/39	9/40	13	6	CHIPS-S
WRGB	8		18		5/18	5/20	4/15	4/17	11	9	LITTLE HOUSE

ADI

CALL	TVHH R/SH	W18+ R/SH	W18-49 R/SH	M18+ R/SH	M18-49 R/SH	TEENS RTG	CHILD RTG	LEADOUT TVHH R/SH
WNYT	6/18	4/20	4/20	3/20	2/16	7	11	8/17
WNYT TSA (000)	38	21	13	21	6			
WTEN+	8/23	4/21	4/23	4/29	3/25	9	6	15/34
WRGB	8/25	6/33	6/32	3/18	3/19	10	6	9/21

ALBNY-SCHDY-TROY — AVG 5:00P> 23T/C — Competing programs: VARIOUS

TSA

CALL	HH RTG	RT IDX	HH SH	SH IDX	W18+ R/SH	W18-49 R/SH	M18+ R/SH	M18-49 R/SH	TEENS 12-17 RTG	CHILD 2-11 RTG	LEAD-IN HALF HOUR PROGRAM
WNYT (20S/S)	8	91	19	101	6/23	4/17	5/19	3/14	3	3	THE JEFERSN
WTEN+	12		30		9/33	9/34	9/36	9/37	11	6	CHIPS-S

ADI

CALL	TVHH R/SH	W18+ R/SH	W18-49 R/SH	M18+ R/SH	M18-49 R/SH	TEENS RTG	CHILD RTG	LEADOUT TVHH R/SH
WNYT	7/20	5/23	4/20	4/20	3/17	3	6	8/18
WNYT TSA (000)	41	26	13	23	8			
WTEN+	8/22	4/21	4/21	5/26	4/24	8	8	14/30

Source: Arbitron Ratings Co. (1982), used with permission.

quite useful information for programmers. Demographic data by daypart fill out the rest of this section.

The third section of the page shows a market breakout of specific stations carrying the syndicated *Barney Miller*. For example, in Albany, Georgia, *Barney Miller* ran on WALB-TV during prime access in November 1982. The program had a 32 ADI rating and a 51 ADI share. This strong showing overpowered the competition—*The Jeffersons* on WTSG-TV and various programs on WVGA-TV. Other programmers, then, use this information either to purchase the show or to schedule it during a daypart where it seems to be most successful.

This third section also provides ADI demographic ratings and shares for a program in key demographic groups. In Albany, for example, *Barney Miller's* strength was with men and women 18+. Further analysis shows that since it did less well with women and men 18–49 (only 17 and 19 ratings), it appeals strongly to the older audience (50+) in this market. The data in the market section show how a syndicated program has performed against specific competition.

Before purchasing a syndicated program, station programmers typically choose markets that are similar to their own in size and regional characteristics and chart the performance of that program to determine its best daypart, its strength and weaknesses against specific competing programs and its demographic appeal. The *Syndicated Program Analysis* enables programmers to estimate the likely performance of a syndicated program and then to schedule it effectively in their lineup. If a program proves unsuitable (demographically or in terms of ratings projections), the analysis is helpful in targeting another program to meet a station's programming needs.

The *Syndicated Program Analysis* is limited since it contains program data only about syndicated programs already on the air, and quite often stations must decide whether or not to purchase a program *before* it is released in syndication (or even produced). This is particularly the case with **first-run** syndicated programs (never on a network) and popular off-network programs (often purchased before any station has tried them out). (The subject of purchasing **futures** on programs is covered in chapters 7 and 8.) In the case of off-network programming, national and local data from the program network performance can be projected to the local market—though many markets differ substantially from the national market. However, airing programs in first-run syndication is riskier since they lack both network and station track records.

A ratings book represents only a fraction of the data available from Arbitron and Nielsen. The books exclude each diarist's age, county of residence, zip code and specific viewing and listening patterns. A diary also tells what the diarist was watching at 5:45 P.M. before he/she began watching the 6:00 P.M. news. Arbitron and Nielsen store this raw diary information on computer tapes that stations can examine for a substantial fee, by means of a computer terminal. Arbitron's terminal system is called *AID* (Arbitron Information on Demand); Nielsen calls theirs *Data Command*. The information on these computer tapes allows programmers to analyze nonstandard dayparts, specific groups of zip codes, nonstandard demographics, county-by-county viewing and audience flow patterns. In addition, sales staffs use the terminals to compute audience reach and frequency.

Computerized Services

Several other companies provide ratings analysis services to stations and advertising agencies. Two of them, Marketron in radio and Telmar in television, have copyrighted software that analyzes Arbitron data. They use the local Arbitron market reports on computer tape. Because they have access only to published ratings reports and not raw diary data, these companies cannot provide customized demographic analysis or daypart analysis. However, Marketron and Telmar's analyses have many features that Arbitron and Nielsen reports lack. For example, they rank stations in a market and give audience distribution information.

The management of any station, network or cable service that subscribes to Arbitron (or Nielsen) can personally review listener or viewer diaries. The main reason for inspecting diaries is to search for unexpected entries—such as how listeners or viewers recorded the station's or service's name or call letters (or slogan or air personalities). Sometimes diarists name things differently than stations expect them to. A station can remedy incorrect attributions in subsequent ratings periods by submitting a limited number of different "nicknames" to Arbitron (or by changing a slogan if it is easily confused with the competition's). Before computerized systems became available, firsthand *diary reviews* (usually by specialist companies located near the diary warehouses) were standard procedure after each ratings book was published. Computer tape now permits the information to be examined anywhere if the appropriate software is purchased.

Most professionally managed stations continually conduct program and audience research in their market. They try to understand problems and interpret trends before they affect ratings. Many large-market stations spend hundreds of thousands of dollars each year to find out:

- How their programming is perceived
- Which on-air personalities are liked and disliked
- How other competing stations/channels are perceived
- How the station image can be improved

Programmers use this research to head off problems before they become serious.

Broadcast stations and cable services of all sizes routinely use microcomputers in all their operations, including programming. Television ratings and syndicated program reports are available on disc (in several formats). Local station programmers use computer software to schedule shows, print daily, weekly and annual program logs and keep track of competitors' program purchases, in the same way as reps track purchases for many markets (see Chapter 3).

In addition, some local programmers use microcomputers to keep track of local **program availabilities** (syndicated programs not yet under contract in their markets) and their own station's program inventory, including contract details, plays and amortization schedule. Television programs are introduced, launched, bought and withdrawn constantly. Keeping tabs on the daily changes in the program market involves constant record keeping based on information from the trade press and reports from reps and distributors.[6] At present, only the largest stations (and reps) have the resources to track this crucial programming information and keep timely records. In 1987 NATPE, the trade association of both programmers (buyers) and syndicators (sellers), began developing a national computerized program database. NATPE's goal is to supply accurate, up-to-date facts on syndicated program availabilities for simultaneous use by all its members—at small as well as large stations and at rep firms and distributors. This innovation should substantially improve the quality of program decision making over the next five years.

Arbitron radio data also comes on discs in the IBM-PC format, an option called Arbitrend. Arbitrend reflects only the continuously measured markets and contains only a few demographics. Programmers for music radio stations can also purchase (or write) software to accomplish most of the tedious work involved in developing a station's music playlist. (See Chapter 15 on creating music wheels.) One widely used software program on the market accounts for 50 different characteristics of a song in selecting its position and rotation.

Using microcomputers in broadcasting and cable may be the single most important programming development since the invention of magnetic recording tape. Microcomputers are altering program evaluation, purchase and scheduling across the country, and those entering the programming field today need microcomputer experience.

RADIO REPORTS

Audiences for radio stations are more fragmented than broadcast television audiences (although the spread of cable is altering that condition for television). The largest radio markets such as Los Angeles have more than 80 stations, dividing the audience into tiny slivers per station. In general, radio stations compare their share of the audience and their cumulative audience to that of other stations with similar formats in the same market. The most popular stations use shares and the least popular use cumulative audiences— although formats lending themselves to tuning in and out (such as all-news) use cumulative audience ratings even when they are popular. This subject is examined in Part Four in detail. The top 100 radio markets correspond closely to television ADI/DMAs, but because some areas of the United States have radio but no television (largely in the West and South), the total number of radio markets is larger than the $210\pm$ television ADI/DMAs. Arbitron measures about 275 radio markets.

Ratings books for radio are organized differently from those for television. An Arbitron radio ratings book contains Share Trends, followed by Demographic Breakouts, Daypart Averages, Cume Estimates, Hour by Hour Estimates and a few smaller sections. The age and sex categories used in radio differ from those used for television because radio stations target their programming to more precisely defined demographic groups. Thus, age ranges for radio are smaller than those used in television, typically just ten years, as in 25–34. Most classification groups end in "4" for radio (24, 34, 44, 54); the groups used for television (18–49, 25–54) are broader, reflecting the more heterogeneous nature of television audiences and thus television advertising sales.

Metro Audience Trends

The Metro Audience Trends section reports a station's Metro shares for five ratings books—the current survey and the previous four surveys, covering, altogether, a period of about a year. These data show a station's share pattern (its "trend") over time for four separate demographic groups: 12+, 18–34, 25–54 and 35–64. A hypothetical example for the demographic category of Total Persons 12+ is shown in Table 2-5. A programmer can get a quick overview of all stations' performance in the market from the Metro Audience Trends section.

Consider the Mon.–Sun. 6 A.M.–MID period in Table 2-5 as an example. It shows that from Spring '85 to Spring '86, WCCC clearly led the market and continued to have climbing shares and cume ratings in the last book. WBBB was the number two station and had an upwardly trending cume. WDDD was at the bottom of the market with flat ratings. WAAA's 12+ share declined from 3.3 to 2.6, but the drop is less than a full ratings point, and the station's cumulative rating remained at 10 percent of the market (near the bottom of the hypothetical market). Up and down data tell a program director that the music probably needs some fine tuning in the Mon.–Sun. 6 A.M.–10 A.M. slot. WAAA's programmer needs to examine additional pages in the book, however, before making any major decision.

Demographic Breakouts

Pages from Arbitron's Specific Audience (Table 2-6) and Listening Locations (Table 2-7) sections illustrate different ways of displaying ratings and share data serving different purposes. Table 2-6 shows Metro and TSA AQH ratings for several ten-year age groups broken out by gender (and Men 18+ and Women 18+), with Persons 12+ and Teens 12–17 listed separately. Table 2-7 shows Metro AQH population estimates for three different places people hear radio (At Home, In-Car and Other) for drivetime and three other time periods. These data are reported separately for Persons 12+, Men 18+ and Women 18+ (Table 2-7 shows only Men 18+). These Specific Audience and Listening Locations data help programmers see which dayparts draw which audience subgroups and where listeners most use the station. In combination with other tables provided in an Arbitron book, they suggest how different programming (or additional promotion) can improve audience composition (and therefore salability).

Table 2-5 Arbitron Radio Market Report, Metro Audience Trends

Metro Audience Trends
Persons 12+

	MONDAY - SUNDAY 6AM - MID					WEEKEND 6AM - MID				
	Spring 85	Summer 85	Fall 85	Winter 86	Spring 86	Spring 85	Summer 85	Fall 85	Winter 86	Spring 86
WAAA										
SHARE	3.3	3.7	••	3.2	2.6	3.0	3.7	••	2.9	2.1
AQH(00)	168	187	••	163	133	128	163	••	125	96
CUME RTG	10.7	11.6	••	10.8	10.0	5.9	5.9	••	6.2	5.1
WBBB										
SHARE	3.6	3.7	••	3.5	4.4	3.0	3.2	••	3.0	3.4
AQH(00)	183	187	••	179	228	128	143	••	129	150
CUME RTG	11.7	11.1	••	11.6	13.2	5.6	6.4	••	5.8	6.8
+ WCCC										
SHARE	8.0	7.6	••	7.8	9.4	7.5	7.0	••	7.8	9.5
AQH(00)	404	385	••	395	488	324	315	••	331	426
CUME RTG	16.7	14.9	••	15.7	17.1	10.4	9.5	••	10.0	11.1
WDDD										
SHARE	2.5	2.7	••	2.1	2.3	3.2	3.4	••	2.3	2.5
AQH(00)	124	140	••	108	120	136	150	••	97	112
CUME RTG	7.4	8.4	••	6.4	7.1	4.7	5.5	••	4.3	4.7

Footnote Symbols: •• Station(s) not reported this survey.
+ Station(s) reported with different call letters in prior surveys - see Page 5B.

Source: Arbitron Ratings Co. (1986), used with permission.

Table 2-6 Arbitron Radio Market Report, Specific Audience

Specific Audience
Monday - Sunday 6AM - MID

	AQH (00)													
	Persons 12+	Men 18+	Men 18-24	Men 25-34	Men 35-44	Men 45-54	Men 55-64	Women 18+	Women 18-24	Women 25-34	Women 35-44	Women 45-54	Women 55-64	Teens 12-17
WAAA														
METRO	174	55	8	15	21	8		112	28	35	30	6	12	7
TSA	186	55	8	15	21	8		124	39	35	31	6	12	7
WBBB														
METRO	322	142	18	68	43		6	177	39	69	41	13	9	3
TSA	370	167	18	78	56	1	6	200	42	87	42	13	9	3
+ WCCC														
METRO	636	269	12	23	36	47	59	366	22	19	51	44	88	1
TSA	667	281	12	23	36	53	60	385	22	27	51	46	95	1
WDDD														
METRO	135	55	9	8	18	4	8	69	5	11	19	7	13	11
TSA	135	55	9	8	18	4	8	69	5	11	19	7	13	11
WEEE														
METRO														
TSA														

Footnote Symbols: • Audience estimates adjusted for actual broadcast schedule.
+ Station(s) reported with different call letters in prior surveys - see Page 5B.

Source: Arbitron Ratings Co. (1986), used with permission.

Table 2-7 Arbitron Radio Market Report, Listening Locations

Listening Locations

Men 18+

	METRO AQH (00)											
	MONDAY-FRIDAY COMBINED DRIVE			MONDAY - FRIDAY 10AM - 3PM			WEEKEND 10AM - 7PM			MONDAY - SUNDAY 6AM - MID		
	At Home	In - Car	Other	At Home	In - Car	Other	At Home	In - Car	Other	At Home	In - Car	Other
WAAA	18	26	13	9	27	21	12	8	6	14	18	11
%	31	46	23	16	47	37	46	31	23	33	42	25
WBBB	36	43	57	27	31	92	25	17	18	30	27	43
%	26	32	42	18	21	61	42	28	30	114	34	56
WCCC	129	49	77	122	33	140	118	29	14	56	17	27
%	51	19	30	41	11	48	73	18	9	24	17	5
+ WDDD	29	26	7	19	22	6	22	10	4	52	37	11
%	47	42	11	40	47	13	61	28	11			

Footnote Symbols: * Audience estimates adjusted for actual broadcast schedule.
+ Station(s) reported with different call letters in prior surveys - see Page 5B.

Source: Arbitron Ratings Co. (1986), used with permission.

Arbitron also reports an hour-by-hour analysis that includes 8 demographic groups by AQH for the Metro area. A programmer can track a station's performance hour-by-hour from 6 A.M. to 1 A.M. to isolate particularly strong or weak hours during the broadcast day. Other sections of the Arbitron radio book include ADI data by demographics and daypart, both of which help radio programmers understand how listeners use radio.

Time-Spent-Listening

Programmers are rarely content with the bare facts reported by Arbitron (or Nielsen in the case of television), and so they use all these various ratings to make many different computations. For example, radio programmers generally want to know how long their audience listens to their station, known as *time-spent-listening* (**TSL**). TSL is computed by multiplying the number of quarter-hours in a daypart times the rating and dividing by the cumulative audience.

To illustrate, assume we have the Los Angeles *Arbitron Radio Market Report* and want to compute the 18+ TSL for KABC-AM. We can pull the AQH and cume from the book to produce the TSL. The TSL for adults 18+ for this station, Mon.–Sun., 6 A.M.–MID., is calculated using the following formula:

$$TSL = \frac{AQH \text{ in Time Period} \times AQH \text{ Audience}}{Cume \text{ Audience}}$$

Therefore, the TSL for KABC-AM is:

AQH in Time Period $= 504*$

AQH Audience $\quad = 872\ (00)**$

Cume Audience $\quad = 9{,}875\ (00)$

$$TSL = \frac{504 \times 872}{9875} = 39.9$$

*There are 504 quarter-hours from 6 A.M.–MID., Mon.–Sun.

**Zeros indicate that these numbers are in thousands, i.e., 87,200.

Therefore, the programmer concludes that the average length of listening to KABC for an adult 18+ is 39.9 quarter-hours during a given week, 6 A.M.–MID. A high TSL indicates that people (who listen) are listening for long periods of time, not that a lot of listening goes on. TSL refers only to the amount of listening by those who do listen. Television programmers also calculate time-spent-viewing using the same formula.

Turnover

Another calculation, **turnover,** indexes the rate at which an audience changes, or turns over, during a time period. Turnover is calculated by dividing the cumulative audience by a quarter-hour rating:

$$Turnover = \frac{Cume\ Households\ or\ Persons}{AQH + Households\ or\ Persons}$$

A low turnover rate indicates a loyal audience, and high turnover means a station lacks "holding power." Television stations, on the other hand, *expect* more turnover than radio stations and go after greater *reach*. Turnover is calculated for public broadcasting and cable as well as commercial radio and television. Tracking the amount of turnover over time on a graph provides a quick clue to changes in audience listening or viewing patterns for an individual station.

CABLE RATINGS

Nielsen reports cable network ratings data separate from broadcast network data for the larger basic and premium cable services. Services are included in Nielsen's *Monthly Cable TV Status Report* when they achieve a 3 percent share of audience. Half of its 4,000 peoplemeter sample are cable subscribers, and Nielsen issues monthly cable reports covering the **national** audiences for the largest services drawn from peoplemeter data.

On the **local** market level, greater discrepancies exist. Both Arbitron and Nielsen measure cable service audiences along with broadcast station audiences in the all-market sweeps (using diaries or meters or both). But cable line-ups differ from franchise to franchise within one market, and accurate tracking of channel attributions ("I watched Channel 3") has been difficult. In consequence, ratings for the smaller services have not been stable even within a single market. To qualify for inclusion in the standard television sweep reports, a cable service must reach 20 percent of net weekly circulation (in other words, 20 percent of the market's television households must view it for at least five minutes during the survey week). In the first year of reporting (1982) only HBO, WTBS-TV (the superstation now called TBS), Showtime and ESPN qualified. By 1988, however, a dozen more top cable networks qualified in all markets, including Cinemax, The Movie Channel, CNN, USA, CBN, MTV, TNN, Lifetime, Nickelodeon and C-Span I. Other cable services, such as WGN and WWOR, easily qualify in some regions of the country. However, cable networks appearing on only some of a market's systems have more difficulty meeting the minimum viewing level, even when they are regularly watched by the cable subscribers able to receive them.

In general, the introduction of peoplemeters has benefited cable services far more than most broadcast stations (they also aid some independent stations). Viewers tend to fill in diaries at the week's end, losing track of where VCR recordings came from and forgetting the names of the many (relatively new) cable networks; so the more familiar-sounding networks tend to get undeserved diary entries and consequently high ratings. Peoplemeters, however, record the exact channel viewed and length of viewing (as did audimeters) and the composition of the audience. However, the audimeter sample was frequently criticized for lagging behind the national rate of cable penetration. Peoplemeters more accurately record national and major market cable channel viewing and provide the demographic breakouts so desired by advertisers. *Most* local markets, however, continue to be measured with diaries.

Premium Services

The pay movie services have special measurement problems. Movies, the largest element in their programming, appear in repeating and rotating patterns to attract large cumulative audiences for each feature. This contrasts with the broadcast television pattern of scheduling a movie or series episode only once in prime time (typically) and seeking the largest possible audience for that one showing.

Indeed, viewers shift the times they watch pay cable so much more than they do broadcast television (by recording movies on home VCRs) that it becomes problematic to use the same measurement criteria. And the greater number of basic and pay-cable television networks split up the ratings much as radio stations do in major markets. Cable programmers use the ratings information available to them to judge individual program popularity and channel popularity, but as yet cable networks win only specific time periods in competition with broadcasters. Frequently, however, the cumulative audiences for all showings of a top-notch movie on HBO equal the size of a television network's audience.

Table 2-8 is a sample page from Nielsen's *Pay Cable Report*. Its terminology differs from that of broadcast ratings books. For example, MAFF refers to the combined ratings of stations with more than one affiliation ("multiaffiliates"). DIST refers to distant independent stations that are not transmitted by satellite, whereas SSS refers to satellite-transmitted independents (**superstations**). CBLE refers to all cable-originated programming except pay net

Table 2-8 Nielsen Ratings for HBO, July 1987

II-14

NIELSEN MEDIA RESEARCH SPECIAL REPORT
HBO NATIONAL ESTIMATES

DAY TIME STATION	NETWORK	HH RTG	HH SHR	HH CUM %	ADL 18+	WOM 18+	WOM 18-24	WOM 18-34	WOM 18-49	WOM 25-54	WOM 50+	MEN 18+	MEN 18-24	MEN 18-34	MEN 18-49	MEN 25-54	MEN 50+	TNS 12-17	CHD 2-11
SUN-SAT																			
8.00PM-11.00PM MON-SAT &																			
7.00PM-11.00PM SUN																			
HBO		9	16	59	6	6	6	7	7	7	4	6	5	5	7	7	4	6	6
ABC	A	4	7	29	2	3	2	3	3	3	2	2	2	2	3	3	2	2	3
CBS	C	8	15	65	5	6	5	6	6	6	7	4	3	4	4	4	5	6	3
NBC	N	8	15	62	5	6	5	5	5	6	9	4	3	3	4	4	7	3	2
MAFF	A-C-N	13	23	76	8	9	7	8	8	9	10	8	5	7	7	8	9	8	6
IND	I	<	<																
DIST		6	11	42	4	4	2	3	3	4	6	4	2	3	3	4	5	2	2
SSS		1	2	9	1	1		1	1	1	1	1	1		1	1	1	1	
CBLE		3	5	26	4	2	1	1	1	2	3	2	2	1	2	2	3	1	1
PBS	P	7	12	51	1	4	2	3	3	3	6	4	2	1	1	1	6	2	2
HUT & PUT	*	2	3	21	1	1				1	2	1			1	1	2		
		55			38	41	32	37	38	40	49	36	24	32	34	37	43	29	26
11.00PM-11.30PM																			
HBO		6	14	30	4	4	4	5	4	4	2	4	4	4	4	4	2	4	2
ABC	A	3	6	14	2	2	2	2	2	2	1	2	2	2	2	2	1	2	1
CBS	C	9	21	29	6	7	3	6	6	7	11	6	3	4	5	9	9	2	1
NBC	N	9	19	28	6	7	3	5	5	7	10	5	2	3	4	5	8	2	1
MAFF	A-C-N	11	24	39	7	7	4	6	6	7	10	7	3	6	6	7	10	3	1
IND	I	<	<																
DIST		4	8	15	2	2	3	3	2	2	3	2	1	2	2	2	2	2	1
SSS		1	3	3															
CBLE		3	3	8	1	1	1	1	1	1	1	1		1	1	1	1	1	
PBS	P	4	9	20	2	2	2	2	2	2	3	2	2	2	2	3	3	2	1
HUT & PUT	*	2	2	4							1						1		
		46			31	33	22	28	30	33	41	30	18	25	27	31	37	19	9
9.00AM-12.00MD																			
HBO		4	12	73	2	3	3	3	3	3	1	2	2	3	3	3	1	3	3
ABC	A	2	5	39	1	1	1	1	1	1	1	1	1	1	1	1	1	1	1
CBS	C	6	17	84	4	4	3	3	4	4	6	3	2	2	2	3	4	3	2
NBC	N	6	15	81	4	4	3	3	3	4	7	3	2	2	2	3	5	2	2
MAFF	A-C-N	7	19	88	5	5	4	4	4	4	6	4	2	3	3	3	5	3	2
IND	I	<	<																
DIST		4	12	63	2	2	2	2	2	2	3	2	1	2	2	2	2	3	3
SSS		1	2	20															
CBLE		2	6	52	1	1	1	1	1	1	1	1	1	1	1	1	1	1	1
PBS	P	5	15	77	3	3	2	2	2	2	4	2	1	2	2	2	4	2	3
HUT & PUT	*	1	3	38	1	1			1	1	1	1				1	1	1	1
		36			21	24	19	21	21	22	32	19	13	16	17	18	25	19	19

Source: A. C. Nielsen Co. (1987), used with permission.

Table 2-9 Directions for Reading the Daypart Section of Nielsen's Pay Cable Report

HOW TO READ THE DAYPART SECTION

DAY TIME STATION CH	NETWORK	HH RTG	HH SHR	CUM %	ADL 18+
SUN-SAT					
8:00PM-11:00PM					
HBO		12	25	64	8
ABC	A	10	21	67	6
CBS	C	10	21	64	6
NBC	N	8	17	61	5
MAFF	A-C-N	<<			
IND	I	3	6	25	2
DIST		2	4	16	1
SSS		2	4	21	2
CBLE		2	4	22	1
PBS	P	1	2	17	1
HUT & PUT	*	47			33
8:00PM-11:00PM MON-SAT &					
7:00PM-11:00PM SUN					
HBO		11	24	65	8
ABC	A	10	22	67	6
CBS	C	10	22	66	7
NBC	N	8	17	61	5
MAFF	A-C-N	<<			
IND	I	3	6	26	2
DIST		2	4	16	1
SSS		2	4	22	2
CBLE		2	4	22	1
PBS	P	1	2	17	1
HUT & PUT	*	47			33
11:00PM-11:30PM					
HBO		8	21	37	5
ABC	A	9	23	33	7
CBS	C	8	21	28	6
NBC	N	7	18	25	5
MAFF	A-C-N	<<			
IND	I	3	8	12	2
DIST		2	5	7	1
SSS		1	3	7	1
CBLE		2	5	9	1
PBS	P	1	3	3	
HUT & PUT	*	39			28
9:00AM-12:00MD					
HBO		5	16	74	3
ABC	A	7	23	82	4
CBS	C	6	20	82	4
NBC	N	5	16	79	3
MAFF	A-C-N	<<			
IND	I	3	10	44	1
DIST		2	7	32	1
SSS		2	7	43	1
CBLE		2	7	38	1
PBS	P	1	3	31	
HUT & PUT	*	31			18

An estimated 10 percent of HBO households were tuned to ABC during the average quarter hour Sun-Sat 8:00PM-11:00PM.

An estimated 17 percent of HBO households using television were tuned to NBC during the average quarter hour Sun-Sat 8:00PM-11:00PM.

An estimated 33 percent of all adults 18 years or older in HBO households viewed their television during the average quarter hour Mon-Sat 8:00PM-11:00PM & Sun 7:00PM-11:00PM.

An estimated 37 percent of HBO households viewed one quarter hour or more of HBO Sun-Sat 11:00PM-11:30PM.

An estimated 39 percent of HBO households were using their television during the average quarter hour Sun-Sat 11:00PM-11:30PM.

An estimated 4 percent of all adults 18 years or older in HBO households viewed CBS during the average quarter hour Sun-Sat 9:00AM-12:00MIDNIGHT.

Source: A. C. Nielsen Co., used with permission.

works, including basic cable networks transmitted by satellite and local origination. Table 2-9 shows how to read the Daypart section of the report. This report is the equivalent of Nielsen's national broadcast television ratings. Notice that specific titles of programs appearing on the broadcast network affiliates are omitted.

Cable Penetration Measures

Using figures supplied by Nielsen and the industry itself, the industry regularly updates cable statistics, reporting how many households have access to cable at the present time—called **homes passed** or **HP** (see Table 2-10). As of 1988, nearly 80 percent of U.S. households were passed by cable wires. **Cable penetration** is the percentage of television households subscribing to *basic cable service*. In Table 2-10, basic cable penetration is shown as nearly 42 million, which is 47.5 percent of TVHH. (As of 1988, cable penetration exceeded 50 percent.) Projections for 1990 anticipate 54 percent penetration for cable or higher. In Table 2-10, the number of pay-cable subscribers appears both as a percentage of total television households (most common usage) and as a percentage of basic cable subscribers (important to the industry as those are the homes actually able to sign up). For example, just over 27 percent of U.S. television households subscribed to pay cable in 1988, but over half (57.6%) of basic cable subscribers took one or more pay channels.

Like radio, cable services are also concerned with audience turnover. In cable, turnover is the ratio of disconnecting subscribers to newly connecting cable subscribers (the number of **disconnects** divided by the number of **new connects**). The common cable industry term for turnover is **churn**. The problems associated with a high rate of churn are described in detail in Chapter 9.

The audiences for many advertiser-supported networks are too small (at any one time) to show in Arbitron and Nielsen ratings books, although the largest services appear in both local market reports and national peoplemeter

Table 2-10 *CableVision's* Cable Barometer

CABLE BAROMETER	1988	1990 ESTIMATES
Television Households (TVHH)	87,800,000	93,900,000
Homes passed by cable (HP)	69,632,000	81,783,000
Percent of TVHH passed by cable	**79.3%**	
Basic cable subscribers	41,772,000	50,706,000
Percent of TVHH with basic cable	**47.5%**	54%
Percent of HP with basic cable	59.9%	
Pay cable subs	24,101,000	32,959,000
Percent of TVHH with pay cable	27.4%	35%
Percent of HP with pay cable	36.6%	
Percent of basic subs with pay cable ...	**57.6%**	

Figures are as of January 18, 1988

Source: CableProFile Data Base, International Communication Research, reprinted in *CableVision.*

reports. Therefore, the smaller basic cable networks estimate their audiences on the basis of customized research. Advertiser interest in cable ratings leaped ahead once the top five services (ESPN, TBS, CNN, USA and CBN) reached half of all television homes in late 1987. Especially for narrowly targeted cable services, advertisers want detailed demographic breakouts. This has fostered the growth of customized cable research at the local level.

RATINGS LIMITATIONS

Although many broadcast programmers are aware of the limitations of ratings, in practice these limitations are rarely considered. This result is not one of ignorance or carelessness so much as of the pressure to do daily business using some yardstick. Programmers, program syndicators, sales staffs, station reps and advertising agencies all deal with the same numbers. In any one market, all participants—those buying and selling programs, those selling and buying time—refer to the same sets of numbers (Arbitron and Nielsen reports), and they have done so for decades. The "numbers" for any single market usually show a consistent pattern that makes sense in general to those who know local history (such as changes in power, formats and ownership). Although broadcasters and the ratings companies know that the "numbers" are imperfect, they remain the industry standard. In practice the numbers are perceived as "facts," not estimates.

Occasionally a gross error will require a ratings company to reissue a book, but, for the most part, small statistical inequities are simply overlooked. To eliminate as much error as possible, the major ratings companies use advisory boards that suggest how to improve the ratings estimates. However, a change in ratings methodology always means additional costs passed on to broadcasters—a fact destined to create a conservative rate of change now that the shift to peoplemeters has been accomplished.

The major limitations can be briefly summarized. Readers interested in further information should consult the references listed at the end of this chapter. The following five practical and theoretical problems limit the validity, reliability, significance and generalizability of ratings data:

1. *Sample Size.* Although each company attempts to reach a sample that represents the population distribution geographically (by age, by sex, by income and so on), occasionally a shortfall occurs in a market. In these instances, certain demographic groups have to be weighted to adjust for the lack of people in the sample (such as too few men between 25 and 49). Weighting by large amounts makes the estimates less reliable. In this case, the responses of too few individuals represent too many other people/households.

2. *Lack of Representation.* The major ratings companies refuse to sample from group living quarters such as college dormitories, bars, hotels, motels, hospitals, nursing homes and so on. The problem with measuring such viewing is that the number of individuals viewing varies, sometimes greatly, making it nearly impossible to determine how many diaries or peoplemeter buttons

need to be provided. The rating services argue that such viewing accounts for only a small percentage of total national television viewing and is therefore not worth going after (that is, not cost-effective for broadcasters to pay to measure). On the other hand, cable services such as ESPN, watched in nearly every bar in the country, suffer from the omission of these audiences.

3. *Ethnic Representation.* Estimates for ethnic groups are one of the most hotly debated aspects of broadcast audience estimates. Ratings companies have long grappled with the difficulty of getting randomly selected minority households to cooperate with the ratings company by filling out a diary or having a meter installed. Critics argue that those minorities who agree to go along with prescribed procedures are most like white sample participants and are most atypical of the ethnic group they are intended to represent. Thus, for example, a participating black family may not be like the vast majority of black families in a given viewing area. Many minorities remain apathetic to the needs of ratings companies, even though financial incentives are offered. Ethnic populations may thus be undercounted, and those who are counted may often be unrepresentative of their ethnic group.

4. *Cooperation.* All ratings companies use accurate and statistically correct sampling procedures: People are selected at random to represent (within a small margin of error) the population from which they were drawn. For representativeness to occur in practice, however, the *people originally selected* must cooperate when the ratings company invites them. Cooperation was not much of a problem when Nielsen used the older television audimeters, which required little or no action from the participants. But **cooperation rates** for peoplemeters and diaries fall short of 50 percent, and participation differs among key demographic and lifestyle groups. Moreover, long-term cooperation from all viewers may be a problem. Using a diary requires participants' willingness to train themselves to fill it out as they view or listen and to learn how to fill it out correctly. Peoplemeters require pushing buttons every 15 minutes as on-screen reminders interrupt viewing. They also require assigning spare buttons to casual guests.

    When cooperation rates are low, for whatever reason, the participating sample probably differs from those who declined. Those who accept typically demonstrate a highly favorable view of the medium and use it more often than those who refuse to cooperate. Refusals may indicate a lack of interest in the medium or, at the least, too light a use to warrant learning a fairly complicated—but infrequently applied—process. It is easy to visualize a single person or a young, childless couple who says to the ratings company, "No thanks, I'm (we're) *almost never home. I (we) hardly ever watch TV at all.*" Thus, those who view more or use the medium more are probably overrepresented in the sample, resulting in correspondingly inflated viewing estimates and unrealistic measures of the total television audience's preferences.

5. *Definition of Viewing/Listening.* No one seems to be entirely sure precisely what "viewing" television or "listening" to radio means. They sound simple, but for those using the peoplemeters to be counted as "viewers," household members must activate the computer with the hand-held device only while in the room where the television set is on. Some peoplemeter systems even have sensors to detect the presence of people in front of the set, setting off on-screen messages to "push your buttons." In all systems, however, the sole criterion for being a viewer is being in the room. Viewers can very easily be reading magazines, talking, thinking, playing a game—in short, paying little or no attention to the picture or sound—but are still counted as viewers. Conversely, a viewer might be in a nearby room doing a menial task and listening intently to a program's sound. This person is normally not counted as a viewer. In short, being there may or may not constitute "viewing." What the ratings services measure, therefore, are potential viewers with the option of letting television (or radio) occupy their attention. To date, no commercial techniques measure viewing as a function of the attention paid to what is on or to the way that content is used.

Peoplemeter Limitations

After 30 years of depending on one ratings system, Nielsen's abrupt change in 1987 from audimeter- and diary-based national television ratings to peoplemeters created an uproar. The shift happened all in one year, and many in the industry felt unprepared with too much at stake. One objection to peoplemeters centers on what happens when the *hand-held devices are not correctly operated*. When mistakes are made, as is inevitable, viewing is invalidated and not counted in the ratings. Given the high likelihood that people will have occasional mechanical difficulties and that children and teens will "fool around" with the meter, much legitimate viewing may be lost. Nielsen argues the necessity of omitting figures where the device was misused, claiming that such inclusions would produce unrealistic figures. Nielsen further claims that in a national sample of 4,000 households, occasional omissions have only a negligible impact on ratings.

Another peoplemeter problem occurs with *sample composition*. The issues discussed above concerning who chooses to become part of the sample and who refuses and why is worsened, not resolved, by peoplemeters. Nielsen's own studies show that peoplemeter cooperators differ from noncooperators in that the former are younger, more urban and have smaller families (they may also differ in other, unreported ways). Older people and those living in rural areas are underrepresented in the peoplemeter sample, in part because of many people's reluctance to learn to use "another new technology." However, it is recognized that Nielsen's previous national sample overrepresented older viewers and that post-1987 sample composition more accurately represents the country's overall population.

A third limitation centers on a new form of resistance to allowing Nielsen (and AGB) to install the *peoplemeter hardware*. Installing the older audimeter involved little or no hassle for participants. Peoplemeters, however, require a substantial amount of wiring and hole drilling. For many people, allowing workers into their homes to do such work is an intolerable intrusion. And of course, if households allowing the installation do so in part because they are eager to be part of the television sample, they thus do not represent

the overall population, probably producing inflated viewing estimates and dis-
tortions in program preferences.

A fourth and final limitation occurs because peoplemeters transform
generally *passive viewers into active viewers*. Every time a participant enters the
television room or leaves, the hand-held device must be activated. Such behavior involves more conscious decisions to view, what to view and when to stop
viewing than the usual television behavior. Research shows that most viewing
gets done with little self-awareness on the viewer's part. Now, viewers with
peoplemeters must actively record their behavior, and the results are probably
atypical viewing. Nielsen, however, maintains that peoplemeter users rapidly
become accustomed to them and "normal" viewing habits soon return, similar
to the way viewers become accustomed to using **remote controls** (hand-held
channel changers).

Peoplemeters present a new list of measurement limitations, while at
the same time removing some problems that plagued the older ratings system,
principally those caused by the diary process—which had lost much credibility
with the advertising, cable and broadcast industries. At the same time, some
old problems continue, such as cooperation rates and sample composition.
Whether a ratings system uses peoplemeters, infrared sensors recording the
presence of viewers in a room, diaries, the old audimeters or some yet-to-be-
developed variation on these methods, ratings remain *estimates* of audience
preferences, always subject to a certain margin of error. Some television programs, and radio formats, will not receive a true or completely fair rating regardless of which system is used—or even from a combination of measures.
Children's and very light adult viewing will probably always remain uncertain.

Standard Error

The concept of standard error is not a ratings limitation, but rather a
part of a mathematical model whose use reduces some of the problems associated with rating procedures. In practice, however, very few people using audience ratings ever take standard error into consideration. The "numbers" are
seen as factual; sampling errors and other errors or weaknesses in research
methodology are not considered in any way.

In essence, using the standard error model compensates for the fact
that ratings are produced from a sample of people, not a complete count of an
entire population. For whenever researchers project sample findings into the
general population from which that sample was drawn, some error necessarily
occurs. A standard error figure establishes the range around a given estimate
within which the actual number probably falls. The range suggests how high or
how low the actual number may be. The formula for **standard error** is:

$$SE = \sqrt{\frac{p(100 - p)}{n}}$$

where SE = standard error
     p = audience estimate expressed as a rating
    n = sample size

For example, suppose that a random sample of 1,200 people produces a rating of 20. The standard error associated with this rating is computed as:

$$SE = \sqrt{\frac{20(100 - 20)}{1200}}$$

$$= \sqrt{\frac{20(80)}{1200}}$$

$$\sqrt{1.33}$$

$$= 1.15$$

A rating of 20 therefore has a standard error of plus or minus 1.15 points—meaning that the actual rating could be anywhere from a low of 18.8 to a high of 21.1. Another difficulty in calculating error is determining *how confident* we want to be of the results. It is possible to be very confident (with, say, a 95 percent probability of being right) or somewhat confident (with only a 65 percent probability of being right). Nielsen and Arbitron ratings are generally calculated to the lesser standard. Most social science research uses the higher standard. Both Arbitron and Nielsen include standard error formulas in all their rating books for those wishing to calculate error in specific ratings and shares, but of course printing the range for each rating/share would make rating books unusable. Nonetheless, the range is the most accurate version of each rating or share, given its data base—which may itself introduce a great deal more error.

SUMMARY

Program and audience research splits into qualitative investigations of audience reactions and preferences and into quantitative ratings information on audience size, age and sex. Television, cable and radio programmers in nearly all markets need a thorough understanding of ratings. The data provided by Nielsen, AGB, Arbitron and Birch are the "thermometers" for judging the success of programming decisions. The two widely recognized estimates of viewing are ratings and shares, and both figures can be calculated for a whole network, for a particular station, for a whole daypart, for a specific program, for a wide geographic area, for a metropolitan area, for a whole demographic group, for a subset of women or men and so on. In addition to ratings and shares, the other major measurement tools television programmers use are homes-using-television (HUTs) and persons-using-television or radio (PUTs and PURs). Television programmers use syndicated program reports, AID and other specialized analyses to select and schedule programs. Radio programmers often use microcomputer software to help them analyze their demographics and schedule their music. Radio programmers look at computations of average quarter-hour persons (AQH), cumulative audience (cumes), time-spent-listening (TSL) and turnover. Reach and frequency are tools for radio, cable and public television programming (as well as advertising sales). All rating or share numbers are only estimates of viewing and listening. They contain significant amounts of error because they are based on samples of the total audience. Unfortunately, for a variety of reasons, ratings data are treated as more reliable than they actually are. Qualitative research methods interpret ratings information; they tell programmers what ratings information means. Focus groups, microcomputers and peoplemeters are changing the program decision-making process.

Notes

1. James E. Fletcher and Roger D. Wimmer, *Focus Group Interviews in Radio Research* (Washington, D.C.: National Association of Broadcasters, 1981). See also Dennis S. Howard, "Don't Believe Everything You Hear on Focus Groups; Follow These Guidelines in Evaluating the Sessions," *Marketing News*, 28 January 1977, pp. 20–21.

2. James E. Fletcher and Roger D. Wimmer, *Call-Out Research in Managing Radio Stations* (Washington, D.C.: National Association of Broadcasters, 1982). See also "Use of Call-Out Research for Radio Expanding as Stations Employ More Sophisticated Techniques," *Television/Radio Age*, 31 May 1982, pp. 40–41.

3. James P. Forkan, "TvQs Complement Prime Time Ratings," *Electronic Media*, 16 June 1983, pp. 10ff.

4. Hugh M. Belville, Jr., "Cable Ratings Methodology Must Employ Common Parameters to Those Used by Broadcast Television," *Television/Radio Age*, 17 January 1983, pp. 70–73.

Gale D. Metzger, "Cable Television Audiences: Learning from the Past and the Present," *Journal of Advertising Research* 23, August/September 1983, pp. 41–47. See also George Swisshelm, "Need Seen for Expanded Meters, Different Diaries to Measure Cable," *Television/Radio Age*, 28 March 1983, pp. 37–39.

5. The final two-hour episode of *M*A*S*H* garnered 77 percent of the audience using television on the night of February 28, 1983. That rating exceeds by seven points the previous all-time high rating for the "Who Shot J.R.?" episode of *Dallas*. "News Update: *M*A*S*H* Sets Ratings Record," *TV Guide*, 12 March 1983, p. A-2.

6. David E. Wilson, "Program Buyers and Sellers: Can They Compete Together?" *Programmer* (NATPE trade magazine), October 1986, pp. 6–8.

Selected Sources

Belville, Hugh M., Jr. *Audience Ratings: Radio, Television and Cable.* Hillsdale, N.J.: Erlbaum, 1988.

Fletcher, James E. *Handbook of Radio and TV Broadcasting: Research Procedures in Audience, Programs and Revenues.* New York: Van Nostrand Reinhold Company, 1981.

Fletcher, James E. *Music and Program Research.* Washington, D.C.: National Association of Broadcasters, 1987.

Fletcher, James E. *Broadcast Research Definitions.* Washington, D.C.: National Association of Broadcasters, 1988.

Hiber, Jhan. *Winning Radio Research: Turning Research into Ratings and Revenues.* Washington, D.C.: National Association of Broadcasters, 1987.

Inside: Nielsen Station Index, 1982–83. New York: A.C. Nielsen Company, 1982.

Lindlof, Thomas R., ed. *Natural Audiences: Qualitative Research on Media Uses and Effects.* Norwood, N.J.: Ablex, 1987.

Radio & Records. *R&R Ratings Report.* Los Angeles, California: Radio & Records, Inc., semiannual special reports.

Research Guidelines for Programming Decision Makers: A Programmer's Guide to the Dynamics of Radio. Laurel, Maryland: Arbitron Radio, 1977.

Webster, James. *Audience Research*. Washington, D.C.: National Association of Broadcasters, 1983.

Wimmer, Robert D., and Dominick, Joseph R. *Mass Media Research: An Introduction*. Belmont, California: Wadsworth Publishing Co., 1987.

The New Arbitron Ratings Radio Market Report. Laurel, Maryland: Arbitron Ratings Company, 1985.

How to Read Your Arbitron Television Market Report. Laurel, Maryland: Arbitron Ratings Company, 1987.

CHAPTER 3 \ STATION REPRESENTATIVES' ROLE IN PROGRAMMING

John von Soosten

A Guide to Chapter 3

John von Soosten is vice-president and director of programming for the Katz Television group, the largest television representative firm, having over 200 client stations. The Katz Programming Department provides clients with programming research and advises stations on programming decisions. Before joining Katz in 1984, Mr. von Soosten was vice-president and program manager for five years at Metromedia's WNEW-TV (now WNYW-TV) in New York. Prior to that, he was production manager at WNEW-TV for eight years. Earlier in his career, Mr. von Soosten taught television production at the college level and was a production technician at WOR-TV (now WWOR-TV) in New York. Mr. von Soosten holds a B.S. degree from Ithaca College and an M.S. from Brooklyn College. He has been president of the National Association of Television Program Executives (NATPE), vice-president of the International Radio Television Foundation (IRTF) and secretary of the NATPE Educational Foundation.

THE REP PROGRAMMER'S JOB

Blair, HRP, ITS, Katz, MMT, Petry, Seltel, Telerep—you've undoubtedly seen these names in trade publication articles, in advertisements, on research materials, in directories and even on television station letterheads. All of these companies (and several smaller companies) are **station representatives**—national sales organizations selling commercial airtime on behalf of local market television stations.

Reps sell commercial airtime on local stations to national spot advertisers. As the advertising agency represents an advertiser in buying commercial time, the station rep represents the station in selling the time. Local stations are well equipped in their hometowns to sell commercial time to local merchants and other advertisers, and all commercial stations employ a local sales force for this purpose. However, it is not economically feasible for a single station to employ its own sales force to sell commercial time to national advertisers across the country; there are far too many advertisers and advertising agencies in too many cities to be covered by a station's sales force. That's where the rep comes in. Reps employ sales people in many cities to sell on behalf of the local station to advertisers based in those cities. (Several reps have offices in over 20 cities.) Because reps sell on behalf of many stations, they can afford to maintain sales forces of hundreds of people across the nation selling on behalf of dozens of stations. The largest station representatives have client stations in as many as 200 markets. The rep receives a negotiable commission from its client stations for the commercial time the rep sells.

While the station representative is primarily a **sales** organization, reps provide additional services to client stations: *marketing support, sales research, promotion advice* and *programming consultation*. Through these support services, the reps seek to help client stations improve their programming performance in terms of audience delivery, which will in turn lead to increased advertising rates and presumably, increased profitability for the station and the rep. (However, although revenues may go up, profitability for the station sometimes does not.) The eight major rep firms have such programming staffs, working with programmers at client stations to shape and guide the stations' programming schedules. Rep programmers seek to guide their client stations toward the programs that will attract the most viewers in the demographic groups most desired by advertisers. At the same time, rep programmers must consider each station's programming philosophy, the mores of the community and the quality of each program.

The rep programmer works closely with the general manager, program manager and other station or station group executives to determine each station's needs and philosophies. The rep programmer makes specific recommendations regarding syndicated programming purchases, scheduling and strategy. The rep provides detailed, comprehensive research information incorporating both a national perspective and specific local market data. And the rep programmer keeps client stations informed of national and regional trends, programming successes in other markets, the latest syndication information and competitive network and local station programming news.

But the rep's role is primarily that of a *consultant*. The rep programmer does not actually purchase syndicated programming, make the programming decision or determine station policy. As a licensee, the station has the ultimate responsibility for all programs it broadcasts. The rep programmer's role is that of an advisor.

The Rep Programming Department

A rep firm's programming department is comprised of knowledgeable, experienced programmers who act as consultants to anywhere from as few as a dozen stations to as many as forty stations. Rep programmers usually have prior experience as program managers at television stations. Some gained their experience at syndication companies, at the networks or at ratings research firms like Arbitron and Nielsen. Some rep programming departments have program researchers who keep the programmers and the clients informed of the latest ratings performances of networks, stations and programs. Most rep firms have sophisticated research tools and computer software available to their programmers and researchers. Much of the research information available to the reps is unavailable to local stations because either the expense is too great for a single station or the information is generated for all markets, a needless and expensive excess for a single station. Also, the reps can invest in sophisticated and expensive computer systems, because they are dealing with many stations. Finally, the reps maintain close contact with all three networks, enabling them to supply an affiliate with competitive information regarding the other two networks.

The reps disseminate generic national research information on a regular basis. They publish ratings results of new programs, and they provide exhaustive ratings information after each rating sweep period. Because of their national overview of programming and their own experience, combined with the opinions of their colleagues, rep programmers are often able to look at programming decisions with a perspective not available to a local station's general manager or program director.

Syndicated Program Acquisition and Scheduling

Syndication is the arena in which rep programmers and the majority of station programmers spend most of their energies. And with good reason. For most stations, the amount of money spent annually on the acquisition of syndicated television shows is the single largest budget expense for the station. The station that buys a syndicated program that later turns out to be a dud, or the station that overpays for a syndicated show, may be in for economic worry for years to come. And the station that makes several "mistakes" (not uncommon) has serious problems.

The rep provides the station management with programming advice supported by research and experience-based opinion. The rep suggests to the station which shows should be acquired, provides rationale for the acquisition and recommends the placement of the program on the station's program schedule. Although reps spend most of their time dealing with syndicated programming, and therefore work closely with syndicators, it is critical to understand that the reps *do not work for* the syndicators. The rep works for the stations, since the rep firms are paid commissions by the stations based on advertising sales.

The rep programmer spends a good deal of his/her day meeting with syndicators, listening to sales pitches by the syndicators and watching videocassettes of sales pitches, research information, excerpts of the program or actual pilots of the show. In the pitch, the syndicator tries to convince the rep programmer of the merits of the program and that the program, if scheduled on the rep's client stations, will help the stations improve their ratings performance. Although the reps do not actually purchase the program, and although the syndicator must still pitch the station programmers directly, a rep's support in the form of a positive recommendation to the station paves the way for the syndicator when he/she contacts the station. Most syndicators maintain close and frequent contact with the reps. They keep the reps informed of ratings successes, changes in sales strategy, purchases of the program by leading stations or station groups, and any other information the syndicator feels may be helpful in winning support from the rep. Syndicators often try to enlist the rep's support for a show in a specific time period on a specific station represented by the rep. Frequently, syndicators inform the reps of programs during the nascent development stage, often as a trial balloon to gauge the rep's reaction prior to beginning a sales campaign or shooting a pilot of the program.

Syndicator contacts with reps do not take the place of contact between syndicator and station. Rather, syndicators take a calculated risk to gain support for a program, for if a rep dislikes the show or does not feel it suits a station's needs, the rep's advice to the station can damage the syndicator's efforts. Many syndicated shows have not been bought by stations because they did not receive the rep programmer's endorsement.

THE SYNDICATION PROCESS

Let's look more closely at the syndication process. **Syndicators** (also called *distributors*) supply programming on a national scale to local stations. Unlike the three major broadcast networks, syndicators do not have a single "affiliate" in any market. Instead, syndicators can and often do sell their programming to any and all stations in a market. Depending on the nature of programs offered by the syndicator, certain stations in a market may be more frequent customers than other stations. For example, some affiliates build programming blocks of game shows while other affiliates build blocks of talk shows. And independent stations are more likely to air movies and children's animated programs. Although the syndicator may have more than one customer in a market, only one station is licensed to carry any particular program at a time. Thus, one station may buy syndicated reruns of *The Cosby Show* from Viacom, while another station may buy the rights to *I Love Lucy*, also from Viacom. And a third station may purchase *Perry Mason* from Viacom. Each station will have exclusive right to all episodes of the series it bought during the term of the license.

Syndicators "sell" the broadcast rights to a program to the station. More accurately, the syndicator or the producer of the program actually owns the rights to the show. Some syndicators create, produce and distribute (to local stations) their own programming while other syndicators merely distribute (for a commission) programs created and produced by others. The syndicator licenses ("rents") the program to a station for a specific term or period of time. During the license term, the syndicator grants the station the *exclusive* right to broadcast the program. At the end of the license term, the broadcast rights revert to the syndicator, who may now license the program all over again to any station in the market.

When the syndicator approaches the station or rep programmer, he or she outlines the terms and conditions of the offering. Most "deals" include the following:

- *Title.* In the case of programs entering syndication after a network run, the syndication title may be different from the network version. Thus *Happy Days* became *Happy Days Again* in syndication.
- *A description of the program.* This would include whether it is first-run or off-network, the storyline or premise, and other pertinent information.
- *The cast, host or other participants.*
- *The duration.* The program may be 30-, 60- or 90-minutes long, or another length entirely.
- *The number of episodes,* including originals and repeats. Sometimes a minimum and maximum number are offered.
- *The number of runs.* The syndicator indicates the maximum number of times the station may air (**run**) each episode.
- *The starting and ending dates.* Programs are sold by specific lengths of time, such as six months, one year, three-and-one-half years, five years, seven years.
- *The commercial format.* Each show is sold with a fixed number of commercial spots. For example, a typical half-hour program will be

formatted for (1) seven **internal minutes** of commercial time in two breaks of two minutes each and one three-minute break within the program plus (2) an **end-break** (external) of 92 seconds following the program.

- *The method of payment.* Programs are sold for cash, for barter or for cash-plus-barter.

- *Down payment.* In cash or cash-plus-barter deals, the syndicator might request a down payment (typically 10 to 20 percent) at the time the contract is signed, sometimes several years before the station receives the rights to the show.

- *Payout.* The remainder of the cash owed by the station to the syndicator must be paid when the program begins to air. Typically, the balance is paid in installments over a period of time. This is similar to mortgage or auto loan payments.

A Pitch

Using the hypothetical syndication offering of the equally hypothetical *The Bill Smith Show* as an example, let's look more closely at the syndicator-rep-station relationship:

About 9:30 one morning, the New York–based rep programmer's telephone rings. The voice at the other end of the phone line is that of a Los Angeles–based syndication salesman (calling at 6:30 A.M. Pacific time from his home) with whom the rep has developed a professional friendship/relationship. After a minute or so of how's-your-family chatting and two or three minutes of exchanging trade gossip ("Did you hear Pete Green is out as general manager of WBBB? Do you know who's going to replace him?"), the syndicator tells the rep that he's coming to New York next week and would like a few minutes to tell the rep about his company's latest offering, *The Bill Smith Show.* And how about lunch, too? The rep agrees to see the syndicator next Tuesday at 11 A.M., followed by lunch.

Tuesday morning arrives and so does the syndication salesman, shortly before the appointed 11 A.M. With him is the syndication firm's research director. The rep and his/her several colleagues join the two syndicators in one of the rep firm's conference rooms. There's amiable conversation about the syndicators' rough flight into New York, the hot, rainy, humid weather New York has been experiencing for a week, and the good weather the syndicators have left behind in Los Angeles. The salesman asks the reps about the sales of one of his competitors' off-network programs, trying to ferret out competitive information. A rep asks about the status of one of the syndicator's somewhat shaky first-run programs, to which the syndicator replies that the program is stronger than ever, but, after a few minutes of verbal fencing, acknowledges it is still not performing up to expectations.[1] Finally, at about ten minutes past eleven, the "pitch" begins.

The syndicator removes several glossy, expensively printed, full-color sales brochures from his briefcase. Bill Smith's smiling face and the title of his show are on the cover of the brochure. The salesman guides the reps through the first few pages, elaborating on the printed descriptions of the show's plot, characters and leading stars. He makes reference to the show's "outstanding" network history, "the best since *Cosby* or *M*A*S*H*," but he offers no research to support his claims. (That will come later in the videocassette and from the researcher.) The reps take the following notes:

TITLE: *The Bill Smith Show*

DESCRIPTION: Off-network sitcom about a zany recluse and the lovable neighbors in his apartment building.[2]

CAST: John Jones as the zany but sensitive Bill Smith
     Jane Doe as Bill's amorous neighbor, Helga
     Max Brown as the bumbling building superintendent, Sam

DURATION: 30 minutes

The syndication salesman suggests that the reps watch a short, 15-minute videocassette presentation. As they watch, the reps see a succession of hilarious *Bill Smith Show* highlights, followed by clips of several tender, emotional scenes, designed to show Bill Smith's range of talent. Although *The Bill Smith Show* has been on network television for two years, the producer of the tape is taking no chances that the reps may not have been viewers of the show. The presentation's producer has also put together many of the show's more memorable or funnier scenes, hoping to create a highly favorable impression of the show.

Now the focus of the tape shifts to the program's network performance. The presentation shows that *The Bill Smith Show* has taken a previously moribund time period on the network and has increased the network's household audience share in the time period by 50 percent over the previous occupant's performance, despite a weak lead-in program and strong competition from the other networks.[3] In fact, in its first season, *Bill Smith* has single-handedly taken the network from a weak third place to a strong second place. As a result, the network moved *The Bill Smith Show* in its second season to a different night and time, where the results have been similarly impressive. The research focuses on similar gains made by the show in the women 18–34, 18–49 and 25–54, children 2–11 and teen demographics. It omits all mention of male viewers over age 17.

In the tape's final several minutes, the enthusiastic announcer stresses the usefulness of *The Bill Smith Show* in syndication as a lead-in to an affiliate's early newscast (typically 5 P.M. or 6 P.M.) or an independent station's 6–8 P.M. schedule. The tape also compares the show's writing, cast of characters and network performance to such perceived network and syndication successes as *M*A*S*H*, *The Cosby Show*, *Three's Company* and *Who's the Boss?* The tape ends with several additional hilarious scenes and the syndication company's logo.

Now the syndication company's research director goes to work. She hands each rep programmer a packet containing research studies. Much of the research mirrors the research shown on the videocassette, but it is presented in more detail. A copy of last week's overnight ratings in the metered markets is included showing *Bill Smith* to have finished in first place for the fourth week in a row. The rep programmers and the syndicators discuss the research data. The reps question the obvious omission of data for the male demographics, which they deduce is a shortcoming for the appeal of *The Bill Smith Show*. The researcher claims that lack of male appeal is not a shortcoming, because the time periods in which the program will play in syndication have relatively few male viewers available and because women and children control the television set anyhow. The reps continue to question the point, and the researcher promises to provide additional information to show that males also like the program. And so it goes for about half an hour, with the reps questioning research data and making counterarguments based on their own research. Finally, the reps are satisfied that the syndicators' data is generally accurate as far as it goes.

Now the discussion turns to the deal itself. In a presentation punctuated by frequent questions and requests for elaboration, the syndication salesman outlines the rest of the offering. The reps take notes:

> EPISODES: Minimum of 96, maximum of 168 if the program runs seven years on network.
> RUNS: 6
> YEARS: $3\frac{1}{2}$ to 5 (depending on number of episodes produced)
> START DATE: Fall 1993
> FORMAT: Cut for 7 minutes
> PAYMENT: Cash
> DOWN PAYMENT: 15%
> PAYOUT: 36 equal monthly installments
> ASKING PRICE: Not stated to reps

(Generally, the asking price is not discussed with the rep, since the syndicators are pitching the reps on all markets at one time and since the syndicators would prefer to quote the price directly to the customer, the stations.)

Finally, the syndicators have made all their points, and the reps have asked all their questions. It's now time for lunch. (Most syndicator meetings do not involve lunch, but when they do, it's a chance for less formal discussion of the program and other issues.) The reps and the two syndicators walk to a nearby restaurant for lunch. During the meal, the salesman discusses half a dozen major markets where *The Bill Smith Show* will be offered during the next few weeks, trying to gauge (through the reps) need or interest by the reps' stations in each of those markets. The syndicator suggests specific spots in each station's schedule where the show might fit and tries to get a reaction from the reps. The reps play it close to the vest.

Eventually the discussion turns to other topics. The reps and the syndicators touch on renewals of one older show in several markets. They discuss the syndication company's plans for future **first-run** shows (the reps may be able to alert their stations to a potentially hot new show or trend through such advance information). At one point, the salesman says he'll be back in town in a few weeks with a new package of 30 movies his company is about to unveil. The reps manage to pry out of him three "typical" titles, possibly the three most popular films in the package.

Finally lunch is over. The syndicators go to their next appointment, at another rep firm, and the reps return to their offices, possibly for another meeting with another syndicator.

Rep/Syndicator Rules

The relationship between rep programmers and syndicators is generally friendly and mutually dependent. The reps need to get programming information from the syndicators, and the syndicators need the rep's support. Yet the relationship must also be guarded. Because the reps are agents of their client stations, they must maintain an independence from the distributors with an impartiality befitting the trust placed in the reps by the stations.

Therefore, certain "rules" govern the relationship between syndicator and station rep. Reps rarely make blanket program recommendations, and they do not endorse any particular program or syndicator. While reps may often support or take a stance against a particular genre or programming trend, they are generally quick to point out that not every station in every market necessarily can be included in their assessment. No program will have equal appeal in every market, and the competitive needs of stations differ greatly from market to market.

Another unwritten rule is that rep programmers do not supply syndicators with privileged client-rep information. As an extension of the station, the rep programmer does not want to supply information to syndicators that would aid the syndicator in negotiating against the station. Privileged information includes prices the station would be prepared to pay, prices the station already paid for other programs, other programs the station is considering purchasing, future plans and strategies, contract expiration dates and any other information that might be harmful to the station's negotiating position.

Rep/Station Consultation

The rep programmer speaks regularly with the general manager and the program manager at each client station. There is also contact, albeit less frequently, with station sales management and research directors (if any, since most stations do not have a research department). The rep programmer occasionally meets face-to-face with clients, either by visiting the station or when station personnel travel to New York to meet with the rep sales management and with advertising agencies. Most reps endeavor to meet with as many clients as possible at the annual conventions of **NATPE** (National Association of Television Program Executives), **INTV** (Association of Independent Television Stations) and **NAB** (National Association of Broadcasters).

A good working relationship between station and rep programmer is important. Consultation is not a one-way process; reps do not presume to be an all-knowing authority dispensing wisdom from a skyscraper in New York.

Instead, the consultation provided by a rep programmer is very much a give-and-take exchange of ideas. Just as the rep has a national perspective, enabling him/her to draw upon experiences in other markets, the station programmer generally knows better than almost anybody else his/her market, the viewers' attitudes and lifestyles and the station's successes and failures over the years.

How well is the station's current schedule performing? Has there been audience growth, slippage or stagnation since the previous ratings report? Since the same period a year ago? Two years ago? Are older shows exhibiting signs of age? Has the competition made schedule changes that have hurt or helped the client station? Does the client own programs that can be used to replace weak programs, or must the client consider purchasing programs for weak spots? These are just a few of the considerations that become part of rep/station consultations. Generally, a station seeks audience growth from previous ratings books. Of course, in order for one or two stations to experience audience growth, other stations in the market must lose audience. The rep programmer seeks to help the station stem audience erosion and instead create growth.

The rep also helps the station programmer analyze the most recent ratings report. Both parties look for trouble spots. If a program has **downtrended** (shown a loss of audience from several previous ratings periods), the programmers may decide to move it to a different, perhaps less competitive, time period. Or they may decide to take the show off the air entirely, replacing it with another program. Sometimes a once-successful but downtrending program can be **rested** or "put on hiatus" for a period of time, perhaps three months minimum to a year maximum, or for a part of the year, such as the summer. When the program returns to the air from hiatus, it often recaptures much of its previous strength and may run successfully for several more years.

The programmers may note that a certain daypart is in trouble over a period of several hours. A wholesale revision may be in order. They may need to rethink a station's programming strategy to decide if the current form of programming is viable or if the station needs to switch to another genre. For example, if a two-hour game block is not working, should the station switch to court shows or sitcoms or talk shows? A change of this magnitude is quite difficult to accomplish, for the station usually has contractual commitments to run its current programming into the future. Also, most viable programs of other genres are probably already running on other stations in the market. It is usually easier to rearrange the order of the existing shows to see if a different sequence will attract a larger audience. It's also easier to replace a single show than an entire portion of a schedule.

Beyond household ratings, the programmers look at the audience demographics, for even if a program is not number one or two in household rating and share, a strong performance in a salable demographic may make the program acceptable despite the rating. For example, the program may be number two or three in household rating/share but may have very strong appeal to young women, making it number one in the market in women 18–34 and women 18–49. These are attractive audience demographic groupings for many advertisers. Thus, the program might be acceptable for the station's needs despite its ratings performance.

In another example, the program might be the number-three rated show in the time period but may have exhibited significant ratings growth over previous ratings books. Thus the programmers may decide to leave the program in place, since it is **uptrending** rather than downtrending. They may decide to change the lead-in show to try to deliver more audience to the target show. They may also decide to give the show more promotion to build audience.

Programming is usually purchased far in advance of its actual start date. In November of any year, stations are already planning for the following September, even though the current season has barely begun. Off-network programs are frequently sold two or three years before they become available to stations in syndication. Once purchased, the station is committed to paying the agreed-upon license fee to the syndicator regardless of the program's continued network performance. It is not uncommon for a once-popular network program to fade in popularity in the two or three years between its syndication sale and its premiere in syndication. Although the station may be "stuck" with a program of lesser value than originally perceived, the syndicator does not waive or offer to drop the license fee. A deal is a deal. Conversely, some network shows increase in popularity as their network history continues, meaning that the station that bought early may enjoy paying a smaller license fee than if the program had been purchased a year or two later when its popularity was greater. Reps and their client stations thoroughly research, analyze and plan acquisitions carefully in order to purchase wisely.

RESEARCH DATA

Much of the rep programmer's time consulting for stations is spent preparing information, researching program performance and formulating a programming strategy. Since the stations receive the same Nielsen and Arbitron ratings books as the rep, the rep must be thoroughly familiar with both the current and past performance of each station in each market that he or she represents. Many hours are spent analyzing this information.

The reps also have available to them additional Nielsen and Arbitron ratings information not generally purchased by stations because of its cost. These reports include:

- *ROSP.* Nielsen's *Report on Syndicated Programs* provides a complete record of all syndicated programs. The ROSP aids in the selection, evaluation and comparison of syndicated program performance.
- *SONR.* Nielsen's *Syndicated and Occasional Network Report* provides national NTI audience estimates for programs distributed by subscribing syndicators and/or occasional networks, including barter specials, syndicated sporting events and barter movie packages.
- *SPA.* Arbitron's *Syndicated Program Analysis* provides data on all syndicated programs.

- *NTI. Nielsen Television Index,* based on peoplemeters, is the daily rating performance on a national basis of all network programs and provides household and demographic delivery.
- *NAD.* Nielsen's *National Audience Demographic* report, published eight times a year in two large volumes, provides comprehensive estimates of all network program audiences across a wide range of audience-type categories.
- *PTR.* Nielsen's *Persons Tracking Report* tracks program performance in terms of household audiences and viewers per 1,000 viewing households. The PTR includes "specials."
- *HTR.* Nielsen's *Household Tracking Report* tracks program performance by individual network within half-hour time periods.
- *NCAR.* Nielsen's *Cable Activity Report* compares all basic and pay cable and broadcast audience levels.
- *NPA.* Arbitron's *Network Program Analysis* provides audience data for network programs in each ADI (market).
- *Network Programs by DMA.* Nielsen's reports provide audience information by station within each DMA (market) for network programs.
- *DMA Test Market Profiles.* These Nielsen reports provide marketing and media information for all markets.

In addition to these reports, which are also purchased by syndicators and some station groups and large market stations, some reps pay Nielsen and/or Arbitron to prepare special research reports exclusively for the individual rep's clients. By developing such reports in conjunction with the ratings services, these reps are able to tailor the available information to their own needs and the needs of their clients. They are also able to provide an exclusive research tool unavailable through any other rep. One example of such customized ratings research is the Katz Comtrac system, which has become an industry-standard research tool because it provides easy-to-use comprehensive overviews of station and program performances (see Figure 3-1).

Katz's first Comtrac page for M*A*S*H (Figure 3-1, one of several Comtrac pages, continuing until all markets are covered) tracks the shares obtained by the show in syndication in a condensed format. It shows *which stations* in which markets purchased M*A*S*H and *when* they scheduled it. Then it lists the shares for M*A*S*H in the *three previous ratings books* (May '86, November '86 and February '87 in this example), also telling what *kind of lead-in* it had and the *lead-in's shares.* Next it shows the program's *current lead-in and shares* in each market, and then M*A*S*H's *own shares and ratings* (including some abbreviated demographics) and its *lead-out.* Finally, the Comtrac page shows M*A*S*H's *two main competing programs* in each market and their audience *shares.*

Figure 3-1 Example of a Comtrac Page

Source: Copyright 1987 A. C. Nielsen Company. Used with permission.

Computers for Program Analysis

In recent years, rep programming departments have invested heavily in high-end personal computer systems with large storage capability. The personal computer (PC) has given the reps the ability to create sophisticated research tools for their own use and for dissemination to stations. Many reps are now routinely turning columns of numbers into easy-to-comprehend pie charts, bar graphs, line graphs and other formats. With the Nielsen or Arbitron numbers as a backup, the visual displays of information are extremely effective in analyzing the performance of both a client's and the competitors' programming. The reps also use PCs as information storage/retrieval systems. For example, a PC can list for any given market all programs in syndication, the name of the syndicator, cash or barter terms, number of episodes, runs, years, start date in syndication and, most important, the call letters of the station in the market owning the syndication rights to the program, with a blank space indicating that the program is unsold and therefore available. (This is similar to the national syndication data base NATPE is creating for all shows, described in Chapter 2.)

Audience Flow Graphs

Some reps have invested heavily in large mainframe computers. The complete Nielsen and/or Arbitron data tapes for all markets in each rating sweep can be loaded into a mainframe computer. Once in the rep's in-house computer, the data can be transformed into customized research data. For example, the flow of audience from one program to the next can be graphically delineated in audience flowcharts. Bar graphs can show, for each station in a market, the amount of audience retained by the target program from the lead-in program, the amount of audience tuning into the program from other stations, the new audience turning on their televisions, the amount of audience lost to other stations, and the number of sets turned off from each station in the market (see Figure 3-2).

THE STATION'S DECISION

The syndicator has visited the station and made his or her pitch to either the general manager or the program manager or both. The rep has consulted with the station, providing research support combined with experience and judgement resulting in a recommendation regarding the program. The terms of the deal have been analyzed by the rep and the station, and the programmers now must determine how they might utilize the program.

Each programming decision is different than any other. Each show is different; each deal is different; markets and competitive situations differ; corporate philosophies and needs not only differ but may also change over time. The personalities and opinions of the syndicator, the station general manager and program director and the rep programmer all enter into the decision. Although innumerable permutations and combinations exist, the basics of the decision-making process involve an assessment of need and an analysis of selection options.

Figure 3-2 Katz Audience Flow Graph

PROBE *PLANNING*

AUDIENCE FLOW ANALYSIS

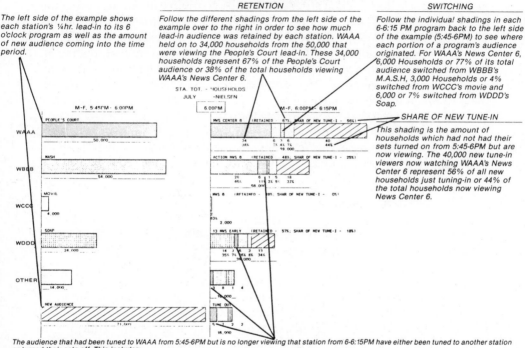

RETENTION

The left side of the example shows each station's ¼hr. lead-in to its 6 o'clock program as well as the amount of new audience coming into the time period.

Follow the different shadings from the left side of the example over to the right in order to see how much lead-in audience was retained by each station. WAAA held on to 34,000 households from the 50,000 that were viewing the People's Court lead-in. These 34,000 households represent 67% of the People's Court audience or 38% of the total households viewing WAAA's News Center 6.

SWITCHING

Follow the individual shadings in each 6-6:15 PM program back to the left side of the example (5:45-6PM) to see where each portion of a program's audience originated. For WAAA's News Center 6, 6,000 Households or 77% of its total audience switched from WBBB's M.A.S.H, 3,000 Households or 4% switched from WCCC's movie and 6,000 or 7% switched from WDDD's Soap.

SHARE OF NEW TUNE-IN

This shading is the amount of households which had not had their sets turned on from 5:45-6PM but are now viewing. The 40,000 new tune-in viewers now watching WAAA's News Center 6 represent 56% of all new households just tuning-in or 44% of the total households now viewing News Center 6.

The audience that had been tuned to WAAA from 5:45-6PM but is no longer viewing that station from 6-6:15PM have either been tuned to another station or turned their sets off. This includes:
— 6,000 Households now viewing WBBB's Action News 6, representing 11% of the total Action News 6 audience.
— 3,000 Households now viewing WCCC's 13 News Early, representing 7% of the total 13 News Early audience.
— 3,000 Households now coming from other station's outside the market.
— 5,000 that have turned their television sets off.

Source: Katz Television Group.

Need

Perhaps the most important part of making any programming decision is establishing a need for the program and determining whether the program in question is the best for filling that need. Sometimes this is very easy. The need may be quite obvious. For example, a first-run program may fail to attract a large enough national audience and be cancelled by the syndicator. It therefore needs to be replaced on all the stations carrying it. In another example, despite increased promotion and a strong lead-in, a particular program on a given station may exhibit a continued downtrend in several successive books and from year-ago performance in the time period. It needs to be replaced.

At other times the need may be less obvious. A show may perform reasonably well but show no audience growth and finish second or third in the time period. Is there a need to replace it? Will a replacement show perform as well, better, or not as well?

When a syndicator is pitching a station, he or she tries to identify or create a need for the station to buy the particular program being offered. While the syndicator may be quite correct that an existing program needs to be replaced, he/she is looking at it strictly from the perspective of selling a program in the market. The syndicator's need to sell a particular show may not be the same as the station's degree of need (if any) to replace an existing program.

The rep approaches the determination of a need by first looking at the performance of the existing program schedule, identifying trouble spots including individual programs and entire dayparts. (For example, three out of the four programs from 4 to 6 P.M. may be performing quite well, but one may be a weak link and therefore a candidate for replacement. In another situation, the entire 4 to 6 P.M. schedule might be performing poorly and need to be replaced, perhaps including a switch from one program type to another, such as from talk shows to court shows.)

Selection Options

Once a need to replace a program has been established, a replacement must be selected. The programmers have four basic options. Think baseball, for the alternatives are analogous in both television and baseball:

- *Do nothing at all.* If the station or baseball team is trailing, it's sometimes best to leave the lineup unchanged, hoping for an improvement in performance or a mistake by the competition. Sometimes there's no alternative, since the bench strength is either depleted or no better than the current players, and no stronger players or programs can be bought.
- *Change the programming or batting lineup.* Swap the lead-off hitter with the cleanup batter, or swap a morning program with an afternoon show, or reverse the order of the two access shows. (There are many more examples.)
- *Go to the bench* for a pinch hitter or go to the inventory of programs "on the shelf" (already owned by the station but not currently on the schedule) for a replacement show.
- *Hire a new player* or buy a new show.

Let's look at each area in greater detail.

1. *Do Nothing.* Although a time period may be in trouble, there's sometimes nothing to be done. The station may not own any suitable replacement shows. While other shows already on the air might be swapped, the station and rep programmers might feel that such a swap would be harmful to another daypart (perhaps a more important daypart) or that the other program(s) might not be competitive in the target time period. Then, too, the potential replacement shows available from syndicators may be perceived as no improvement over existing programming, or they might be too expensive. Finally, the programmers may decide to leave the schedule intact, hoping the program will "grow" or attract additional viewers. Often, increasing promotion can help. Sometimes the only choice is to do nothing at all.

2. *Swap Shows.*   The second alternative is to change the batting order. Generally, the station and rep programmers look first at the station's entire program schedule to see if the solution might be as simple as swapping time periods for two or more shows already on the air. Often a program originally purchased for one time period can improve an entirely different time period when moved.

For example, the *Oprah Winfrey Show* premiered in syndication in September 1986. It was positioned by its syndicator as a morning program (9–11 A.M.), meaning a reasonably low risk and low purchase price to stations, since morning HUT levels are low. After *Oprah*'s dramatic and very strong ratings performance in the November 1986 and February 1987 ratings books, many stations moved the program to the more important and more lucrative early fringe (4–6 P.M.) daypart to improve their performance in early fringe. *Oprah* quickly became a dominant early fringe program, vastly improving the time period performance of many stations and increasing audience flow into affiliate early newscasts. In some cases, the program *Oprah* replaced was merely moved to the morning time period previously occupied by *Oprah;* in other situations, stations needed to purchase a replacement morning show to fill *Oprah*'s vacated time period.

In most cases, syndicators are delighted when a station moves a show from a lower HUT level time period to a time period with higher HUTs. A higher HUT level means a higher *rating*, even if *share* stays the same or drops slightly. For syndicators selling barter time in a program, higher ratings in individual markets contribute to a higher national rating, which in turn translates to higher rates charged by the syndicator to the barter advertiser.

But for a station, such a move may also mean higher license fees paid to the syndicator. Primarily in the case of first-run programs, syndicators often make *tier* or *step deals* with stations. At the time the deal is made, stations and syndicators often agree on price levels for different dayparts. One price is agreed upon for morning time periods, another higher price for early fringe and perhaps a third still higher price for access. A *four-tier agreement,* which may also include late night, is not uncommon. Moving a program from one daypart to another triggers a change in license fee. It is to the station's advantage to negotiate a step deal to avoid a potentially expensive program playing in a low-revenue time period.

Step deals are relatively rare for off-network programming, which generally has a single license fee level and which is generally priced by the syndicator based on the revenue potential of the daypart in which it is presumed the program will play. Thus, when a station buys an off-network sitcom or hour action/adventure show for access or early fringe, the price the station pays remains the same over the life of the contract. If the show is a ratings failure in access or early fringe and must be moved to a less lucrative morning or late-night time period, the station's financial obligation to the syndicator remains unchanged. Thus, a station can find itself with a very expensive "morning program," a daypart of significantly lower revenue potential than early fringe or access (meaning that the program may turn out to cost the station far more than the time period can generate in sales income).

If the station buys an expensive off-network show that later moves to a time period with lower HUT levels, the station may experience some discomfort in its bottom line (low profitability), but the consequences are generally not disastrous. However, if the station buys several expensive shows that do not perform and are moved to lesser time periods, the economic impact can be quite serious. Due to the relatively long license terms of off-network shows (typically three to four years), a station can take years to recover when several "mistakes" are made.

3. *Substitute Shows.* The third alternative is to go to the bench for a pinch hitter. Programmers have a responsibility to manage existing product while at the same time remaining competitive. It's not always necessary to spend more money to buy a new program. Sometimes the solution to a problem is already owned by the station. A simple swap of programs already on the air may not be the best answer. A station with strong bench strength may have enough programs "in the dugout" to replace a failing show in a competitive manner. Corporate accountants like this sort of a solution, because it does not add expense to a station's budget while it does effectively utilize existing product that must be expensed (paid for) whether or not it airs.

The rep and station programmers look at the strengths and weaknesses of the shows on the shelf. Generally, they have aired before. How well did they work? Have they been *rested* long enough to return at their previous performance level, and if not, is that level superior to the current program's performance? Are the shows dated? Will they look "old"? Are the potential replacement shows suitable for the time period? Are they compatible with the other programs in the daypart? Are they competitive? Are they cost-effective? Do they appeal to the available demographic?

4. *Buy New Shows.* Having examined the first three possible solutions, the programmers at the rep and the station generally consider purchasing a program. Since an added expense is involved whenever a purchase is made, the programmers must determine whether a new program will be superior to an existing show, and if so, will it be a stronger performer to the extent of offsetting the additional cost.

While expense is always a consideration in any programming decision, programmers and corporate and station managements should always keep one very important factor in mind: They must keep the station competitive. Remember, their job is to deliver the largest mass audience with the strongest demographics. Although they must always keep an eye on the bottom line and therefore program in a cost-effective manner, a false economy results from trying to avoid expense if the result would be to lose even more revenue. If ratings decline, eventually revenue will also decline.

Instead, programmers must balance expense against returns, determining the ratings potential and the projected revenue in order to determine whether a new purchase is practical and if so, how much the station can afford. The rep's research is often very helpful in projecting the future performance of a program, whether already on a station's schedule or a future acquisition. Anticipated performance naturally plays a large role in determining the purchase price.

CALCULATING REVENUE POTENTIAL

Based on the projected rating of a program and the sales department's estimate of *cost per point* (the number of dollars advertising agencies are willing to pay for each rating point delivered by the station), the programmers can determine the amount of money the station would be able to pay for a show. It works like this:

A rating point equals 1 percent of the television households in a market. If there are 500,000 television households in market A, a rating point represents 5,000 households. A show that receives a 15 rating in market A would deliver 75,000 households.

Advertising agencies are willing to pay a certain amount for each thousand households, called *cost per thousand or* **CPM.** Let's say the agency assigns a five dollar CPM. A 15 rating in market A would be valued at $375 for a 30-second commercial ($5 CPM × 5,000 households per rating point ÷ 1,000 = $25/point × 15 rating = $375).

Let's say the station is considering a half-hour off-network sitcom cut for six commercial minutes and sold with six available runs over four years. Six commercial minutes in each episode translates to twelve 30-second spots per day. The revenue potential is calculated by multiplying the projected rate per spot at the anticipated rating by the number of minutes to give a gross revenue potential. The gross is now netted down (reduced) to allow for commissions paid by the station to salesman, reps and advertising agencies. At a 15 percent commission rate, the station nets 85 percent of the gross. The net is now netted down again to a projected **sellout rate** (the number of spots actually sold over the course of a year is generally less than the number available in the show). Most stations use an *80 percent sellout rate* for planning purposes in order to be safe; if they actually sell out at better than 80 percent, that's all to the good, and the bottom line. This final revenue figure is called the *net net*. The calculation per episode would look like this:

$ 375	rate
× 12	30-second commercials
$4,500	gross
×.85	net revenue level (after 15% commission)
$3,825	net
×.80	sellout rate
$3,060	net net

The $3,060 is the amount of income the station can expect to generate during the current year for each run of the program. To compute what the show would generate when it goes on the air, the station and rep sales managers would inform the programmers of the potential rate for all future years the show will be available. A typical increase in cost per point from year to year might run from as low as 3 percent to as high as 12 percent depending on inflation and local market economy. Using figures supplied by sales, the programmers use the formula shown above to project the net net revenue potential of the program over the life of the show. In this calculation, they must also revise the rate based on the rating delivery of the show. A program that produces a 15 rating in its first run might be moved by its fifth and sixth runs (since it can be expected to weaken as it is repeated) to a time period with lower HUT levels, such as late night, and may only generate a 5 rating. Therefore, although CPMs are increasing, the lower rating will bring down the spot rate, lowering the revenue potential for the program in that run.

Let's look at a simplified example of the complete calculation. We'll assume the program is available two years from now. There will be 130 episodes, six runs each (780 total runs) over four years. The station plans to trigger the episodes as soon as the contract starts, running five episodes a week for three years, with no hiatus, until all 780 runs are exhausted. Coincidentally, this will take exactly three years (5 days/week × 52 weeks = 260 days per year divided into 780 total runs equals 3 years).

The various calculations of the revenue potential of *each individual episode* are shown in Table 3-1. The percentage rate increases are estimated by sales. This year and next year are the two years between the time the station buys the show and the time it goes on the air. Years 1, 2 and 3 are the years of usage before all runs are taken. The years are not necessarily calendar years; often they begin in September with the start of the new season and the availability date of the program.

Now that we've figured the *revenue potential per run* of each episode as shown in Table 3-1, it's easy to compute the *total revenue potential* for each episode over the life of the contract based on projected usage.

Run 1, Year 1	$ 3,439.44
Run 2, Year 1	3,439.44
Run 3, Year 2	1,945.34
Run 4, Year 2	1,945.34
Run 5, Year 3	1,313.76
Run 6, Year 3	1,313.76
Total revenue	$13,397.08 Net Net

But wait, we're not done. Now, let's figure how much the station can **pay per episode**. Stations assign percentage ranges in three areas: *program purchase cost, operating expense* and *profit*. Program purchase cost may run as low as 30 percent of total revenue for an affiliate, which gets most of its programming from the network, to as high as 50 percent for an independent, which must

Table 3-1 Calculation of Revenue per Episode

$ 5.00	current CPM	Year 1: Runs 1 & 2 of each episode in access at
×1.05	(5% increase estimate)	15 rating.
$ 5.25	CPM next year	
×1.07	(7% increase estimate)	Year 2: Runs 3 & 4 of each episode in early
$ 5.62	CPM Year 1 of show	fringe at 8 rating.
×1.06	(6% increase estimate)	
$ 5.96	CPM Year 2 of show	Year 3: Runs 5 & 6 of each episode late night at
×1.08	(8% increase estimate)	5 rating.
$ 6.44	CPM Year 3 of show	

YEAR 1		YEAR 2		YEAR 3	
$ 5.62	CPM	$ 5.96	CPM	$ 6.44	CPM
× 5000	households	× 5000	households	× 5000	households
1000		1000		1000	
$ 28.10	cost per point	$ 29.80	cost per point	$ 32.20	cost per point
× 15	rating	× 8	rating	× 5	rating
$ 421.50	rate	$ 238.40	rate	$ 161.00	rate
× 12	commercials	× 12	commercials	× 12	commercials
$5,058.00	Gross	$2,860.80	Gross	$1,932.00	Gross
× .85	Net revenue	× .85	Net revenue	× .85	Net revenue
$4,299.30	Net	$2,431.68	Net	$1,642.20	Net
× .80	Sellout	× .80	Sellout	× .80	Sellout
$3,439.44	**Net Net per run**	$1,945.34	**Net Net per run**	$1,313.76	**Net Net per run**

purchase or create all of its programming. Let's use a median figure of 40 percent for our example.

With a total revenue projection of $13,397.08 per episode, the station using a 40 percent program cost figure would estimate the *price per episode* at $5,358.83. Since nobody figures so closely, to the exact dollar, a range of $5,000 to $5,500 per episode would be a reasonable working figure. Multiplying these figures by 130 available episodes would indicate a total investment of $650,000 to $715,000 for the program. The station would certainly try to negotiate a lower cost for the show but might be willing to go higher, even considerably higher, depending on how badly the station needed the program or the perceived importance of the show to the station's image (to viewers and advertisers) and competitive position.

Unfortunately for the station, the syndicators can and do perform the same calculations. They generally quote a purchase price significantly higher than the station wishes to pay. In our example, knowing that the station could expect to make as much as $20,000 in the access time period if all six runs of each episode ran in access but not knowing that the station might plan to take some runs in early fringe and late night, the syndicator might ask $10,000 to $15,000 per episode. The station might want to pay $3,000 to $4,000 but expect to pay $5,000 to $6,000 per episode and go as high as $7,500 if it really needed the show.

Obviously, the two parties have to reach a middle ground or the show will either be sold to another station in the market or go unsold to any station. And now the fun begins: negotiation.

Negotiation

Most programs are sold by syndicators to stations through good old-fashioned negotiation. Generally, the syndication company "opens a market" by pitching the program to all stations in the market. The pitch will be the same to all stations in the terms of the deal (episodes, runs, years, availability date, price) but may differ subjectively depending on the stations' needs, strengths, weaknesses and programming philosophy. The syndicator will try to determine or create a need at each station with the hope that several will make an offer. In this ideal situation, the syndicator will be able to select which station receives the show on the basis of highest purchase price offered, size of down payment and length of payout, ability to make payments, best time period, strength of station, most compatible adjacent programming and other similar factors.

Often the syndicator receives no offer from any station but may have one or two stations as possible prospects. Negotiations may continue for weeks or even months, with syndicator and station each making concessions. The station may consider paying a higher price than originally planned or may agree to also purchase another program. The syndicator may lower the asking price or may increase the number of runs and years. The station may raise the percentage of down payment, and the syndicator may allow the station to pay out over a greater length of time. Negotiation is basic horse trading.

Bidding

Some syndicators of hit off-network programs have opted to sell their programs by confidential bid to the highest bidder in the market rather than through negotiation. In 1986/87, Viacom sold the megahit *The Cosby Show* at mega prices, shattering records in all markets. Shortly thereafter, Columbia-Embassy sold *Who's the Boss* at astronomical prices, in some cases eclipsing even *Cosby*'s prices. Both *Cosby* and *Boss* were bid rather than negotiated.

Here is how bids work. The syndicator opens half a dozen or so markets in a week. Each station receives a complete pitch, including research data, terms and conditions. Only the financial terms are omitted during the pitch. After several days, when all stations have been pitched, the syndicator sends telexes simultaneously to all stations revealing the syndicator's lowest acceptable price and certain other financial details. Stations are given a few days, perhaps 72 or 96 hours, to bid on the program. The syndicator analyzes the bid price, the amount of down payment offered and other financial terms to determine the highest bidder. The highest bidder wins the program, pure and relatively simple.

The rep programmer usually becomes involved in advising client stations during the bidding process. The syndicators notify the reps of the markets coming up for bid, and the reps immediately notify their respective client stations. The reps provide their usual research analyses of the program's performance, coupled with their subjective views of how well the show will play in syndication and in the client's lineup. The reps advise the stations whether or not to bid. The reps frequently project the rating and help clients determine the amount of the bid if a bid is to be made.

Perhaps most important, the reps keep track of *reserve* (asking) *prices* and reported or estimated *selling prices* in other markets. The rep programmer informs the client of these pricing trends in order to help the station determine a *bidding price*. The rep also informs the client of down payment percentages and payout terms in other markets, serving as a guide to successful bidding.

Bidding is a fairly simple, clear-cut procedure for syndicator and station alike. There is no messy, drawn-out negotiation. The syndicator makes only one trip to the market, not repeat visits over many weeks or months. The sale is accomplished quite quickly. An atmosphere of competition between stations is established, often turning into a frenzied escalation of prices by stations reaching ever deeper into their piggy banks to be sure they acquire the must-have program. And the syndicator generally achieves prices far in excess of the amounts that might be realized through negotiation.

But bidding only works for the must-have shows that are truly megahits. An atmosphere of anticipation has to pre-exist and stations have to have a strong desire to own the program.

Stations generally dislike bidding. It forces them to pay more than they normally would. In a negotiation, station management usually gets a feel for the amount of competing interest and the syndicator's minimum selling price. In a bidding war, stations get no sense of the competition for the show. A station may be the only station to bid, in which case it bids against itself. It may also bid substantially above any other bidder, a waste of money. In this situation, each station works in the dark, which can be unsettling. However, stations realize that if they want to be in the ball game for a bid show, the syndicator not only owns the bat and ball, but also makes the rules.

PAYMENT

Payment for programming takes one of three basic forms: *cash, barter* or *cash-plus-barter.* Pay-out arrangements vary and are usually negotiated.

Cash and Amortization

As the name implies, **cash** license fees are paid as money by check. In most cases, cash deals are like house mortgages or auto loans. There is an initial down payment, generally made at the time the contract is signed, followed by installment payments over a period of time. The down payment is generally a comparatively small portion of the total contract amount, perhaps 10 or 15 percent. The remaining payments are triggered when the station begins using the program, or at a mutually agreed-upon date, either of which may be a month or two or several years after the contract is signed. If the contract is for a relatively short amount of time or a low purchase price, the payments will be made over a short period of time. A one-year deal may have 12 equal monthly payments, and a six-month deal may be paid in only two or three installments. On the other hand, a five-year contract may be paid out over three years in 36 equal monthly payments, beginning when the contract is triggered; no payments would be due in years four or five of the contract.

When stations buy programs for cash, whether negotiated or bid, they pay out the cash to the syndicator on a schedule as agreed in the deal, but they allocate the cost of the program against their operating budget via an amortization schedule. **Amortization** is an internal bookkeeping scheme used by stations to control and apportion the expense of operating the station so that a profit margin can be maintained. Amortization does not affect the syndicator or the amount paid to the syndicator.

Amortization schedules differ from station to station, depending on the company's policy. Some stations use different schedules for different program types or planned usage. The two most widely used amortization schedules are *straight-line* and *declining-value.*

Straight-line amortization places an equal value on each run of each episode. If a program cost a station $10,000 per episode for five runs of each episode, the straight line amortization would be computed by dividing the five runs into the $10,000 cost per episode, yielding an amortized cost per run of $2,000, in this case equivalent to 20 percent of the purchase price. If the station had negotiated more runs at the same per-episode license fee, the cost per run would decline. For example, had the station purchased eight runs for $10,000, the straight-line amortized cost would be $1,250 per run. The lower amortized cost would reduce the station's operating budget by $750 each time the show is run. On a five day a week strip, over 52 weeks, or a total of 260 runs in a year, the $750-per-run saving would total $195,000, a sizable amount. (You can see why it is important to negotiate well and get as many runs as possible.) Despite all this, the station would still pay the syndicator the full $10,000 per episode, multiplied by the total number of episodes.

Under the **declining-value** method of amortization, each run of an episode is assigned a different value on the premise that the value of each episode becomes less each time the same episode airs. Thus the first run is expensed at a higher percentage of total cost than is the second run, and the second run is expensed higher than the third run, and so forth. A typical declining-value amortization schedule for five runs of a program might be:

First run	40%
Second run	30%
Third run	20%
Fourth run	10%
Fifth run	0%

Comparing the same program under both the straight-line and declining-value amortization systems would show the following regarding the operating expenses of running the show:

	Straight-line	Declining-value
First run	$2,000 (20%)	$4,000 (40%)
Second run	2,000 (20%)	3,000 (30%)
Third run	2,000 (20%)	2,000 (20%)
Fourth run	2,000 (20%)	1,000 (10%)
Fifth run	2,000 (20%)	0 (0%)
Total	$10,000 per episode	$10,000 per episode

In both schemes, the total amortized amount over the five runs is the full per-episode cost of the program. In the straight-line method, the station expenses each run (or "charges" itself) equally, even though the performance of the show may decline as more runs are taken of each episode. An advantage of this method is that the initial run or runs are comparatively inexpensive, especially if the show performs well. A disadvantage is that the final run is just as expensive as the first run, even though the show's popularity may have faded and the ratings declined.

Under the declining-value method, the bulk of the amortization is taken on the first two runs, when the ratings would presumably be at their highest, and relatively few dollars would remain to be expensed in the final runs. In our example, 70 percent of the cost of the program is taken in the first two runs under the declining-value system, but only 40 percent is taken for the same two runs straight-lined. If the show falls apart in the ratings after two or three runs, the declining-value station has most of its financial obligation behind it while the straight-line station still has the bulk of the expense to look forward to. Note that using declining value amortizes all the expense of each episode over the first four runs. Since stations sometimes fail to use all the available runs of a program, the fifth run at no charge can be quite helpful to a station since if the run is not taken, there is no charge against the run as there would be in the straight-line system.

The straight-line system is frequently used to amortize *first-run* shows, which are expensed on a weekly basis and which generally run no more than twice per episode. The declining-value system is often used for *off-network* programs and *feature films,* which are generally expensed on a per-run basis and which generally are sold with five to ten runs per episode or film.

Finally, amortization is only an internal allocation of dollars against usage. It does not change the payout of the license fee to the syndicator. The program may be fully run and amortized before the payout is completed, or the station may continue taking runs of the show for years after the payout to the syndicator is complete, with the amortization of the episodes allowing the expense against the operating budget to be delayed until the programs are actually run. When all episodes are fully amortized and all payments made to the syndicator, the final dollars expensed in both amortization and payout will be identical.

Barter and Cash-Plus-Barter

The second payment method is **barter.** Barter is a fairly simple payment system. The station agrees to run national commercials sold by the syndicator in return for the right to air the program. No money actually changes hands. The syndicator makes all of its money from the sale of commercials to national advertisers, and the station gives up some of the commercial time that it or its rep would have had to sell.

From the station's perspective, barter can be more attractive than cash. In some cases, especially for untried and unproven first-run shows, stations may be more willing to give up commercial airtime than to spend money. If a syndicator takes three minutes of commercial time within a show, and the station receives three minutes, the syndicator has received 50 percent of the available commercial time and the station retains 50 percent. As we saw earlier, stations generally figure 30 to 50 percent of their revenue goes to programming expense, so barter may seem expensive. But when you consider that stations are rarely 100 percent sold out and may average only an 80 to 90 percent sellout over the course of a year, the barter time the station gives up really represents only 30 to 40 percent of the revenue potential.

Barter tends to be used primarily for the sale of *first-run* programs, especially animation and weekly shows, because it is an effective way for syndicators to maximize revenues to fully cover their production and distribution costs. The production of first-run shows is generally expensive, and stations are often unwilling to pay sufficiently high license fees for untried first-run programs. However, the syndicator can generally cover production and distribution costs by bartering a program.

The syndicator must clear (sell the show to) stations in enough markets to represent at least 70 to 80 percent of all U.S. television households. Based on this minimum of the total United States reached by the program, the syndicator projects a national rating and, using a national cost per point, determines a rate for each 30-second commercial. The syndicator then attempts to sell all the national time in the show to national advertisers at, or as close as possible to, the determined rate. The syndicator tries to clear the show in the strongest time periods on the strongest stations in order to achieve the highest rating. The ratings from all markets clearing the show are averaged to produce a national rating, which will, it is hoped, equal or exceed the projected rating. If the syndicator can get the 70 to 80 percent national clearance, sell all the spots at or near rate card, and deliver the rating promised to advertisers, the syndicator will make money, and the show will stay on the air. If not, the syndicator is likely to lose money and the show may not be renewed for another cycle.

Cash-plus-barter means exactly what the name suggests. Part of the license fee is paid in cash, albeit a lower cash license fee than if the show were sold for straight cash, and part of the license fee is given by the station to the syndicator as commercial time, which the syndicator sells to national advertisers. A typical cash-plus-barter deal for a half-hour show might be a cash license fee plus one-and-one-half minutes of commercial time (1:30 national) for the syndicator, with the station retaining five minutes (5:00 local) for its own sale.

SUMMARY

Although the primary job of the station representative is to sell client stations' time in the national spot market, the major rep firms also advise on programming, especially on syndicated program purchases and the scheduling of new purchases. Rep programmers spend most of their time meeting with program syndicators to stay informed of new syndicated program opportunities, researching program performance, devising programming strategies for client stations and, their most important function, consulting with the station managements they represent. Interactions between reps and syndicators are governed by ethical guidelines protecting the rep's client stations. Rep programmers have advantages over local station programmers because they purchase all the expensive rating reports, have a national perspective on programming practices and have contacts at all three broadcast networks. Moreover, they use sophisticated computer software for program analysis. Rep programmers calculate revenue potential using cash, barter or cash-plus-barter for potential purchases. They also advise on negotiation and bidding and aid clients in determining the best methods of pay out and amortization. Because more money is at stake in programming decisions today than just a few years ago, and the pressure to perform well is higher, station management relies even more heavily than before on the input of the rep programmer.

Notes

1. Many programs are created specifically for syndication, with no prior network or cable exposure. Often, these programs are sold to stations on a straight barter or a cash-plus-barter basis. Unlike off-network shows, which are sold for a number of years with a certain number of runs per episode, first-run programs are generally sold one year at a time with a predetermined number of weeks of original programs and repeat programs. For example, a 52-week deal might include 30 weeks of original programs (150 shows) and 22 weeks of repeats (110 of the original 150 shows). Each year, the contract is renewed (often at a higher price) and fresh episodes are produced.

2. Programs that were created for prime-time network run, and that have actually run on a network, are called *off-network*. Generally, a bare minimum of 65 episodes (three seasons) is considered necessary for *stripping*, allowing 13 weeks of Monday–Friday stripping in syndication before repeating an episode. Between 100 and 150 episodes are considered optimum for stripping while 200 or more episodes can be a financial and scheduling burden to a station.

3. Programmers try to schedule successive shows in a sequence that will maximize the number of viewers staying tuned to the station from one program to the next. The shows flow from one to the next, with each building on its predecessor (see Chapter 1). Theoretically, the audience flows with the show. Additional audience may flow into the program from other stations and from new viewers just turning on their television sets. This is *audience flow,* a combination of (1) retention of existing audience, (2) dial switching from other stations and (3) attraction of new tune-in viewers.

Selected Sources

Brotman, Stuart N. *Broadcasters Can Negotiate Anything.* Washington, D.C.: National Association of Broadcasters, 1988.

Friedman, Wayne. "Turbulent Times for TV Reps," *View* (1 September 1986): pp. 40–44.

Heighton, Elizabeth J., and Cunningham, Don R. *Advertising in the Broadcast and Cable Media.* 2d ed. Belmont, California: Wadsworth Publishing Company, 1983.

"Many Came, But Few Were Chosen," *Broadcasting* (2 February 1987): 50–63.

Station Representatives Association. *The Station Representative: His Role in National Broadcast Advertising.* New York: Station Representatives Association, September 1980.

CHAPTER 4 \ GROUP OWNERSHIP AND PROGRAMMING

Lewis Klein

A Guide to Chapter 4

Lewis Klein is president of Gateway Communications, Inc., a group owner of four television stations: WBNG, Binghamton, New York; WTAJ, Altoona-Johnstown, Pennsylvania; WLYH, Lancaster-Lebanon, Pennsylvania; and WOWK, Huntington-Charleston, West Virginia. Gateway Communications is a wholly owned subsidiary of Macromedia, Inc. Before Gateway was formed, Mr. Klein was the director of television programming for Triangle publications from 1967 to 1972, supervising the program activities of Triangle's six stations and serving WFIL in Philadelphia from 1950 to 1972 in various program department functions. He was executive producer of the award-winning *Frontiers of Knowledge* series as well as *American Bandstand* and *College News Conference*. He served on the faculty of the University of Pennsylvania and has been an adjunct professor of Radio-Television-Film at Temple University in Philadelphia for over 35 years. Mr. Klein is past president of the National Association of Television Program Executives, the Television and Radio Advertising Club of Philadelphia and the Delaware Valley Chapter of the Broadcast Pioneers; and he became president of the NATPE Educational Foundation in 1979. In 1982 he received the NATPE President's Award and in 1983 was made the Broadcast Pioneers' Man of the Year.

TYPES OF GROUP OWNERSHIP

Most broadcast stations and the larger cable systems belong to companies owning more than one station or system. The profitability of broadcast and cable investments attracts corporate buyers, who gain important economies of scale from multiple ownership. Because they can buy centrally in large quantities, they can get reduced prices for many kinds of purchases, including programs. FCC and Justice Department permissiveness also encourages the formation of multimedia companies and very large, diversified conglomerates, making group ownership a growing trend within the industry. In broadcasting, the owner of two or more stations of a given type (AM, FM, TV) is called a **group owner,** while in cable television the owner of several systems is called a **multiple system operator (MSO).**

Broadcast Groups

Broadcast group ownership involves a wide range of owner and station types. Stations may be owned by a network or a nonmedia corporation; groups may combine network-affiliated and independent, UHF and VHF, AM and FM stations; the stations can be in small markets or large. Some group owners control only radio, others only television, and some have combinations of radio and television stations. In the top 100 markets in 1987, more than a hundred group owners controlled nearly 80 percent of all television outlets (485 stations) and 90 percent of the VHF (that is, the more profitable) stations.[1] And over three-quarters of all television stations in all market sizes are under group ownership. As for radio, group owners also control more than three-quarters of all 10,000 or so commercial stations. New groups continue to emerge (36 more television groups were formed in 1986); thus group ownership plays a major and increasing economic role in the broadcasting industry and has, in turn, characteristic effects on programming.

Group ownership of the right stations in the right markets can be remarkably profitable. The three traditional national television networks' **owned-**

and-operated (O&O) stations constitute the most prominent group-owned constellations. Of the network O&Os, those in each of the top three markets *alone*—WABC, WCBS, and WNBC in New York; KABC, KCBS, and KNBC in Los Angeles; or WLS, WBBM, and WMAQ in Chicago—gross more revenue than any other groups.

Limitations on broadcasting group ownership changed drastically in 1985 when, in one of its many deregulatory initiatives, the FCC liberalized the ownership rules. The new rules increased maximum total ownership from 21 (old 7–7–7 rule) to 36 stations (12 of each type—12 AM radio, 12 FM radio and 12 television), if the potential aggregate television audience of any one owner does not exceed 25 percent of the national population.[2] As a concession to the lower coverage potentials of UHF television stations, only half of a UHF's potential market is counted in adding up the 25 percent maximum. The new ceiling on group ownership led to a buying spree in the 1980s as corporations sought to take advantage of the opportunity to carve out bigger slices of the national market. For example, shortly after adoption of the rule, Taft Broadcasting Company's purchase of another television group brought it to the 12 maximum (later reduced to 7).

However, with one exception, no owners reached the maximum of 36 stations, counting all types. The sole exception was the combination resulting from the purchase of the American Broadcasting Companies Inc. (the ABC networks) by Capital Cities Communications Incorporated in 1985. The 12 stations of each type owned by the merged companies violated several FCC ownership rules: The television stations could potentially cover more than 25 percent of the nation (**25-percent rule**); some stations violated the **duopoly rule** (against owning stations with overlapping coverage areas); the **one-to-a-market rule** (against acquiring both television and radio stations in the same market); and the **cross-ownership rule** (against ownership of both daily newspapers and broadcast stations in the same market).[3] In the end, Cap Cities/ABC reduced its list to 8 television, 10 AM radio, and 9 FM radio stations, with the television stations reaching just under the 25 percent coverage ceiling, as shown in Table 4-1.

Note that most of the leading television groups listed in Table 4-1 owned fewer than the maximum number of stations (although Gannett owned 13 in 1988—one minority controlled), and all still fell far short of the 25-percent rule's coverage ceiling. The failure of most owners to take full advantage of the **12-12-12 rule** arises from several causes, among them the facts that desirable buys among stations are hard to find and that regulatory barriers persist, such as the 25 percent coverage limitation.

Moreover, the localized nature of modern *radio* makes group ownership of AM and FM stations less attractive than owning *television*, so few companies show interest in reaching maximum ownership in both television and radio. In 1987 Infinity Broadcast Corporation was the *largest* radio-only group owner, with 14 stations, including outlets in the ten top markets. With its purchase of 5 NBC radio stations and previous holdings, Emmis Broadcasting became one of the dominant radio group owners in 1988. In addition to Capital Cities/ABC, the other major groups in radio are CBS and Westinghouse.

Table 4-1 Leading Television Group Owners, 1988

GROUP	NO. OF STATIONS	% PENETRATION[†]
Capital Cities/ABC	7 VHF, 1 UHF	24.20
NBC (GE)	7 VHF	22.32
Fox Television Stations	3 VHF, 4 UHF	19.38
CBS	4 VHF	19.04
Tribune Broadcasting	4 VHF, 2 UHF	18.47
Home Shopping Network	11 UHF	18.25
Gillett Group*	11 VHF, 2 UHF	13.08
ChrisCraft/United	5 VHF, 2 UHF	10.70
Gannett	8 VHF, 2 UHF	9.86
Westinghouse	5 VHF	9.66
Cox Enterprises	6 VHF, 2 UHF	9.29
Hallmark Cards	6 UHF	8.90
Telemundo Group	1 VHF, 5 UHF	8.35

*Gillett includes Busse Broadcasting and SCI Television.
[†]Penetration = Aggregate television homes reachable (with UHF stations discounted by 50%).

Source: "The 20 Largest Station Groups (by Coverage)," *Channels,* April 1988, p. 46.

Fox, with the fourth largest potential *television* reach, close behind CBS (see Table 4-1), is owned by the latest candidate in a long list of would-be "fourth [commercial] network" owners, Rupert Murdoch. His Fox Broadcasting Company (**FBC**) is linked with program production (Hollywood's 20th Century–Fox). Founded in 1986, FBC owned seven television stations in 1988 (the former Metromedia group). Independent (that is, nonnetwork-affiliated) television stations welcomed the chance to join the new Fox network to escape from the constant battle to buy an adequate schedule of syndicated programs that independent status entails. Nevertheless, FBC has only 130 affiliates, against over 200 for each of the three traditional networks, and it offers only a part-time service as yet. FBC planned to build its programming schedule gradually. (One of its earliest offerings, a much-publicized hour of late-evening comedy by Joan Rivers, proved a futile attempt to challenge Johnny Carson's long-running leadership in that field.) FBC had to expect many programming setbacks, but Rupert Murdoch, an international media magnate with deep pockets and a reputation for taking on long-shot projects, seemed prepared to withstand several years of heavy losses.

Meanwhile, other television group owners such as Tribune Broadcasting, Westinghouse (Group W) and Post-Newsweek began to increase production and programming activities as they expanded their station lineups. In the long run, as group owners build up their television holdings to the maximum coverage, they will begin to approach the power of the traditional networks in their ability to underwrite major, original prime-time program series.

Table 4-2 Ten Largest Cable Multiple System Operators (MSOs), 1988

MSO	SUBSCRIBERS	SYSTEMS
Tele-Communications Inc. (TCI)	9,516,200*	1,500
American Television & Communications (ATC)	3,700,000	615
Continental Cablevision	2,169,000	106
Comcast	2,094,000	90
Cox Cable	1,441,800	24
Warner Cable Communications	1,343,500	101
Newhouse Broadcasting	1,098,000	65
Viacom Cable	1,080,000	48
Cablevision Systems	1,042,500	40
Jones Intercable	1,012,600	38

*TCI owns about 52% of United Artists Entertainment.

Source: *Broadcasting*, May 2, 1988, p. 36, and "Cable Television Tightens Its Grip," *Channels*, May 1987, p. 47.

Cable MSOs

No rules limit multiple ownership of *cable* television installations, and about 500 MSOs own three or more cable systems. Multiple system operators control about 90 percent of the over 8,500 systems, and the largest MSOs actually dominate the cable market by virtue of owning most of the major-market and more profitable systems, while also having financial interests in cable program services. Cable systems vary greatly in size, from the largest, Cox Cable in San Diego and Cablevision's Long Island Cable in New York each with upwards of 300,000 subscribers, down to systems with under a hundred subscribers. Table 4-2 shows the top ten MSOs, led by Tele-Communications Inc. (**TCI**) and American Television & Communications Corp. (**ATC**), each with millions of subscribers and hundreds of systems. Broadcasters have an interest in about a third of the cable systems, but the FCC does not allow broadcast licensees to own cable systems within their own broadcast coverage areas. National Amusements, Viacom's parent corporation, for example, owns five television stations, eight radio stations and 18 cable systems, scattered through a dozen different states across the United States, and is looking to buy a movie studio. Program producers have ties with about 20 percent of cable systems and newspapers with nearly 20 percent.

GROUP CONTROL OVER PROGRAMMING

Because broadcast stations have a legal obligation to serve their specific communities of license, group owners must necessarily give their outlets a certain amount of latitude in programming decisions, especially decisions that affect obligations to serve local community interests. Beyond that, broadcast group owners have no common method or standard for controlling programming at their stations. Most employ a headquarters executive to oversee and coordinate programming functions with varying degrees of decentralization.

Some headquarters closely supervise local program budgets and program-related decisions. Typically, a group headquarters allows the individual station to initiate program purchasing decisions but reserves the right of final approval. On the other hand, some group owners retain the initiative by purchasing programs jointly for all their stations, thus centering most of the programming strategy within the home office. For example, Cox Broadcasting and Fox Broadcasting exercise this tight ownership control, usually requiring home office approval of any major program purchase by an owned station. CBS and NBC closely monitor programming decisions, as does Westinghouse (Group W). Cap Cities/ABC stations have local autonomy in the program realm, though the owner retains ultimate control by closely tracking the profit margins of individual programs through analysis of detailed financial reports. An executive of the Gannett Broadcasting Group was quoted in 1987 as explaining why his firm does not buy programs as a group: "Our feeling is that local management has a better understanding of the needs of its marketplace. That's been Gannett's philosophy, starting with its newspapers."[4] In general, most group owners rely on local program directors to make scheduling decisions and to assume day-to-day program responsibilities, but the headquarters play a role in stations' major program-purchasing decisions, key program personnel hiring and overall program department budgeting.

As for cable, by the late 1980s, the largest MSOs appeared to focus more on adding subscribers to their existing systems than on adding new systems; they also had begun giving slightly more autonomy to their local managers as they sought to trim headquarters budgets to reduce overhead.[5] Nevertheless, cable group owners tend to centralize programming more than broadcasting groups because cable has no special *local* responsibilities under federal law (as does broadcasting), and many of the largest MSOs also own several cable program networks. Tele-Communications Inc., for example, controls all programming decisions for its hundreds of cable systems. The local system executives serve largely as passive intermediaries for the headquarters staff, collecting local information and subscriber complaints and forwarding them to headquarters for action. Local TCI managers lack the authority to make program changes or even to extend wiring to uncabled areas. American Television & Communications, on the other hand, allows its system managers to individualize their channel arrays and to retain considerable control over local scheduling. In all cases, however, the MSO headquarters negotiates contracts to obtain licenses for the carriage of the national cable networks.

GROUP OWNERSHIP ADVANTAGES

The main programming advantages of group ownership are the cost savings in program purchases, equipment buys (such as computers and cameras) and service charges (such as by reps and consultants) that accrue from buying at wholesale, so to speak. Insofar as groups produce their own programs, they also save because production costs can be divided among the several stations in the group—a kind of built-in syndication factor. Moreover, group-produced programs increasingly are offered for sale to other stations in the general syndication market, constituting an added source of income for the group owners.

Broadcasting

Group buys often give the member stations first crack at newly released syndicated programming as well as lower cost per station. Distributors of syndicated programs can afford such discounts because it costs them less in overhead to make sales trips to a single headquarters than to call on widely scattered stations individually, and the larger groups can deliver millions of households in a single sale.

Large group owners can also afford a type of negative competition called **warehousing.** This term refers to the practice of snapping up desirable syndicated program offerings for which the group has no immediate need but which it would like to keep out of the hands of the competition by holding them on the shelf until useful later (see Chapter 3). Also, group executives have a bird's-eye view of the national market that sometimes gives them advance information, enabling them to bid on new programs before the competition even knows of their availability. For their part, producers often minimize the risk of investing in new series by delaying the start of production until at least one major group owner has made an advance commitment to buy the series. Many promising program proposals for first-run access time languish on the drawing boards for lack of an advance commitment to purchase.

In addition to enabling member stations to realize savings on program buys, group-owner headquarters staffs can be helpful in many practical ways to local programmers—in preparing commercial copy, designing sets, helping to run contests, recruiting staff members, dealing with the FCC, settling legal problems and working up budgets. The headquarters can sometimes even help in covering for illnesses in the local program-production staffs. Some groups hold periodic training or brainstorming sessions for their program directors and production managers to improve their skills and freshen their inspiration. Many group headquarters arrange for exchange of videocassettes, program activity reports and station visits. Program directors of individual stations within a group can strive for promotion within the organization, thus retaining tenure when moving on—a boon for both employees and group owners.

Network O&Os as a Special Case

The stations in the top four markets that are owned and operated by the national television networks exercise extraordinary power by virtue of their group-owned status. Each such **O&O** group reaches about a fifth of the entire U.S. population of television households, making their collective decisions to buy syndicated programs crucial to the success of such programs. Thus these few group-owned stations influence national programming trends for the entire syndicated program market.

Although O&O stations remain legally responsible for serving their individual local markets, they naturally also reflect the common goals and interests of their networks. As an example of a rather subtle network influence, consider the choice of the prime access program that serves as a lead-in to the start of the network's evening schedule. An ordinary *affiliate* (that is, one bound to its network only by contract rather than by the ties of ownership) can feel free to choose a program that serves its own best interests as a station. An *O&O* station, however, must choose a lead-in advantageous to the network program that follows, irrespective of its advantage to the station. O&O stations also must take great care in choosing and producing programs to protect the group image, especially in New York, where they live next door to company headquarters.

As the main center of the advertising agency business, New York stations have more influence than other stations in the network, even other O&Os. The New York O&O stations, by virtue of being the ones most seen by advertising agency executives, have a disproportionate impact on network affiliates as a whole.

The casual viewer makes no distinction between networks and network-owned stations. In the 1987–88 season, WNBC (the New York NBC O&O) promoted a 7:30 P.M. checkerboard of off-network shows as if they were hot new network programs, purposefully trying to sell viewers on the illusion that network time on WNBC-TV began at 7:30 instead of 8 P.M. It also leads off its local news with the network NBC chimes, and WCBS-TV opens local public affairs programs with the familiar CBS eye logo. Such practices lend prestige to local and syndicated programs but obscure the difference between station-originated (or purchased) and network-originated programs. Viewers lose sight of the stations' local identities. To overcome this absorption into the network image, some O&O stations make a special effort to assert their own separate identity, generally by means of conspicuous community-oriented programs, on-air support of community public-service projects, and even explicit image-building campaigns centered on such themes as "your community-minded station."

The 19 O&O stations of the three traditional national networks earn tremendous profits for their networks as stations, making even more money than the networks as such (bear in mind that the networks have to use part of their advertising income to *pay* their affiliates for carrying commercial programs).[6] In 1986 and 1987 the O&O stations of the three networks had operating margins more than double that of NBC, the most profitable network, illustrating just why broadcast groups compete to buy major-market television stations. The O&O stations also perform an invaluable function in assuring that top-market network stations will provide **clearance** for network programs, setting a precedent for the remaining 200 or so affiliates in the rest of the country.

So important to the success of programs is their exposure in the top markets that some syndication companies offer special inducements to get their wares on the prestigious prime access slots on network O&O stations. These inducements can take the form of attractively structured barter syndication deals (see Chapter 8) or, amazingly, even payment of outright cash to ensure carriage.[7] The latter type of deal, known as a **compensation incentive,** occurs primarily in New York, the country's premiere market.

Cable Television

MSOs have much the same advantages as broadcast groups. However, cable systems normally obtain licenses to carry entire channels of cable programming (*cable network services*), rather than individual programs or program series (a distinction between broadcasting and cable programming that is discussed in detail in chapters 9 through 11). Major MSOs, negotiating on behalf of hundreds of local cable systems, gain enormous leverage over program suppliers. Indeed, a cable network's very survival depends on signing up one or more of the largest MSOs.

Like broadcast group owners, MSOs plan regular meetings for their local system executives. In the 1960s and 1970s these meetings concerned technical and marketing problems almost exclusively, but increasingly programming strategies came to the fore as the early technical problems were shaken out and marketing practices became more standardized.

GROUP OWNERSHIP DISADVANTAGES

Nongroup program directors (at the minority of independent stations and cable systems) enjoy more autonomy and can move more aggressively and rapidly than their group-controlled counterparts. Group headquarters programmers and their sometimes extensive staffs impose an additional layer of bureaucracy that tends to slow down local decision making.[8] Local program executives know their local markets best and can adapt programming strategies to specific needs and conditions. A group-acquired broadcast series or cable network that may be well suited to a large market will not necessarily meet the needs of a small-market member of the group. When a huge MSO such as TCI makes a purchase for hundreds of different systems, not every system will find the choice adapted ideally to its needs. Thus group ownership imposes some inflexibility as the price of the economies of scale it can realize.

GROUPS AND COMMUNITY PROGRAMMING

As noted earlier, group-owned stations and, to a lesser extent, major-market cable systems tend to be conscious of obligations to do some programming for the benefit of the local markets they serve. The high visibility of broadcast groups, the factor of absentee ownership (regarded as lessening a licensee's ideal ability to serve its local community), and the necessity of making a periodic case for station license renewals make them inviting targets for consumer groups that might have reason to oppose renewal. To offset possible unfavorable publicity, the largest group owners tend to encourage their stations to be especially sensitive to the politics of their respective markets, to respond to consumer interests, and to emphasize public service programs concerning local issues. For example, when Gannett Broadcasting Group, part of the newspaper-owned multimedia corporation, acquires a station, it (1) spends lavishly on developing its news programming and (2) "promotes the station as the one that solves community problems."[9] Of course, single-owner stations usually cultivate their images with similar programming efforts, but it is not easy to make such programs broadly attractive; however, the larger resources and collective experience of group owners can assist their stations in overcoming the difficulties of producing good public-service programming.

Not burdened in the Communication Act of 1934 with the public service obligations of broadcasters and virtually guaranteed renewal of the franchises issued by municipalities under the liberal terms of the 1984 cable law, MSOs feel less vulnerable than broadcasters. Nevertheless, some groups encourage their systems to produce local programming in the hope both of reducing **churn,** the debilitating subscriber turnover that reduces cable profitability, and of stimulating *local advertising sales* (see Chapter 12). And despite the liberal renewal law, cable systems often find it expedient to use local productions as a means of cultivating goodwill in their municipalities, smoothing the way for negotiating improvements in franchise terms and, eventually, franchise renewal.

PRODUCTION BY GROUP OWNERS

Commonly owned broadcast groups and cable MSOs increasingly produce programs for sale in the syndication market. In an obvious step, given the ever-increasing demand for programs, groups that produce series for their own use decrease their cost by also making them available to other stations, cable systems or ownership groups.

Broadcast Groups

The syndication market comprises all program needs not satisfied by network feeds (carried by affiliates) and the programs produced by stations or cable systems for purely local consumption. Network-affiliated stations get an average of about **70 percent** of their programs from their *networks* and produce about **10 percent** of their programs *locally*. The remaining **20 percent** they lease from syndicated program *distributors*. Independent (that is, nonnetwork-affiliated) stations rely, of course, **almost totally** on *syndicated* programs to fill their schedules (see chapters 7 and 8).

An important segment of the syndicated program pool also comes from network sources, known as *off-network* programs—those that have completed their contractual network runs and reverted to their producers. In recent years, production costs for off-network series rose sharply, their numbers decreased (as the networks cut back on the number of original episodes by using more reruns), and the demand for such programs grew (because of increased numbers of stations and cable services). These developments encouraged group owners to organize their own production arms that could not only cut their programming costs but also bring in additional profit from other stations via the syndication market.

Group W led in the development of group syndication in the early 1970s with its daily *P.M. Magazine*. It started as the local *Evening Magazine* at its owned station in San Francisco, KPIX-TV; then the five Group W television stations began to share in producing the series, each contributing its own local material around a common core. Eventually Group W syndicated the idea to over a hundred stations, providing the core segments but requiring each participating station to set up its own special production team to prepare exclusive local inserts and to introduce and close the show. Other, more straightforward, syndication offerings came from such groups as Multimedia (*Phil Donahue*), Blair (*Divorce Court*) and Tribune (*Geraldo*).

A similar trend emerged in radio (see Chapter 13). For example, a group owned by the Church of Jesus Christ of Latter-Day Saints (the Mormons) owns Bonneville International Corporation, comprising five AM, seven FM and two television stations. That group has taken the lead in moving from regional to national syndication, distributing 24-hour beautiful and easy listening music formats across the country.

Cable Groups

When it comes to MSO production of programs, the parent companies tend to develop or purchase separate program-producing subsidiaries, most commonly in the form of **cable networks.** In addition, the largest MSOs have increasingly purchased **equities** (part-ownership) in basic cable services that want to be carried by them (especially newly developed services needing space on systems). Equity participation has improved the financing base for many services, spurring much expanded production of *cable-exclusive* programming in the late 1980s for many basic services. At the same time, the pay networks need to supplement the feature films they license from Hollywood with their own cable-exclusive programs (see Chapter 11), also encouraging the growth of original cable production.

Three of the major MSOs have dominating interests in cable programming, and almost all of the top 25 MSOs have minority shares in at least one service. **TCI,** for example, owns part of American Movie Classics, The Discovery Channel, The Fashion Channel, Tempo TV, Black Entertainment Network and Cable Value Network. At the same time, it also controls Netlink USA, which markets packages of pay and basic services to owners of backyard earth stations (**TVROs**). **ATC** is owned by the magazine publisher Time Inc., which also owns HBO, Cinemax and Festival; ATC has a part-interest in Home Premiere (a PPV service), The Fashion Channel, Cable Value Network and Black Entertainment Network—nine services in all. In addition, both TCI and ATC have minority shares in WTBS, CNN and Headline, controlled by Turner Broadcasting. **Viacom,** owned by National Amusements Corp., is a cable programming giant, owning outright Showtime, The Movie Channel, Viewer's Choice I and II (PPV), MTV, VH-1, Nickelodeon and Nick at Nite, and with part-interests in Lifetime, The Fashion Channel and Cable Value Network. Unlike broadcast group production, which is normally limited to a single series or some specials, cable program services usually must fill 24-hour schedules year round, requiring a much larger scale of original production to complement syndicated material. A few successful cable programs have even been syndicated to broadcast stations, a reversal of the usual direction. Viacom's *Bizarre* is an example.

Owners of cable program networks naturally also license their network services to cable systems outside their own group of systems (no problem of competing with themselves arises because, in virtually all markets, each cable system has a monopoly within its franchise area, even though very large metropolitan complexes may be broken down into several local francise areas). Broadcasters and others criticize the monopolistic trend in the cable industry represented by co-ownership of both cable systems and cable program services. They allege that MSOs discriminate against other program providers (such as television stations) in favor of their parent corporations, just as the network O&Os favor (and therefore clear for) all network programs. In fact, in recent years, the federal government has actually supported increased **vertical ownership** (owning both program outlets and program suppliers) as economic and efficient in domestic and international trade.

FUTURE TRENDS

The full effects of liberalized broadcast ownership rules have yet to be felt, but other aspects of deregulation, such as repealing of **trafficking** (station resale) rules, reduced emphasis on local ownership of stations and favorable rulings on the creation of very large conglomerates with extensive broadcasting interests, encourage the group ownership trend.

The Gannett Company illustrates the growth of conglomerates. It is the largest newspaper group in the country and owns the Gannett Broadcasting Group, comprising eight AM, ten FM, and ten television stations. When Grant Tinker, the enormously successful and creative president of NBC (and before that head of MTM Productions) left NBC in 1987, the Gannett group promptly made a deal with him to underwrite new program series that he would produce through a production house called GTG Entertainment. (By 1988, Tinker had moved into producing prime-time shows for CBS, the lowest-ranked network.) Thus large group owners enter into domestic co-ventures among several stations, groups and independent producers to underwrite and produce ambitious series too big for any one group to handle alone. This trend extends the practice of **coproduction,** a long-standing method used in the international program market to share costs. Major motion picture and broadcast producers from different countries get together to pool their fiscal and talent resources for production of major feature films and television series.

Viacom International Inc. is another example of a huge conglomerate, **vertically integrated**. In addition to owning all or part of seven cable program networks, it also owns five television stations (four VHF and one UHF), Viacom Productions and a large MSO (Viacom Cable). Still another example is

News Corporation/20th Century–Fox, owned by the international media magnate, Rupert Murdoch. His U.S. holdings include the Fox Broadcasting Network, seven television stations, Metromedia Producers Corporation and 20th Century–Fox production and distribution divisions, producers of dozens of movies and television series and syndicators of hundreds of programs produced by smaller companies as well as its own.

The broadcast networks have entered cable programming as a hedge against further erosion of their network audiences. ABC in particular has profited from owning 80 percent of ESPN, allowing the two services to share the large number of hours of live and taped sporting events resulting from ABC's huge investment in sports rights and the 1988 Winter Olympics in Calgary. ABC also owns 33 percent of Lifetime and Arts & Entertainment. NBC produces for The Disney Channel and also owns 33 percent of A&E. In 1988 it investigated buying into Turner Broadcasting (owners of WTBS, CNN and Headline News) and other cable programming suppliers. CBS formed the ill-fated CBS Cable and owned part of Sportchannel, but eventually sold off all its cable program and system interests. But in the long term, closer ties between the broadcast networks and cable program suppliers are inevitable to spread out the immense cost of television program production.

Distribution via satellite is another development likely to affect group-owner programming activities. Satellite relay facilities have reduced the cost and trouble of sharing programs among small as well as large groups of users (see Chapter 13). Satellites also impact on news-gathering practices, making possible a great proliferation of specialized news-agency services. Group W, for example, operates The Newsfeed Network, which delivers current news, sports and weather material to subscribing stations. Conus Communications, a subsidiary of group–station owner Hubbard Broadcasting Inc. (one AM, one FM, six television), bypasses the large national and international video news agencies by enabling individual station-satellite linkages for news distribution. Thus Conus helps stations achieve their own unique coverage of distant news and sports events, either as individual contracting stations or as parts of ad hoc groups.

The ultimate effect of satellites, high definition television (**HDTV**) and other new technology will lessen dependence on the traditional national networks for television (and radio) programming, both as sources of original material and off-network syndicated material. HDTV is beginning to attract top-notch production talent. At the same time, the networks find themselves less able to invest in high-cost programming because of cable's erosion of the network audience. Contributing to this erosion is the increased difficulty of persuading affiliates to clear time automatically for network schedules. At one time the networks had considerable leverage over affiliates because the networks leased the coaxial-microwave relays that were the sole real-time program distribution system. Now, however, satellite dishes, installed by virtually all stations, give affiliates many alternate sources of instantaneous delivery at reasonable cost. All this encourages the emergence of new program providers. Nonnetwork group owners will play a prominent role among them.

SUMMARY

Ownership of broadcast outlets by group owners and of cable television installations by multiple system operators (*MSOs*), dominates the broadcasting and cable television markets. FCC rules limit broadcast group owners to 12 AM, 12 FM and 12 television stations and imposes other curbs on concentration (25-percent rule). MSOs have no concentration limits, and the top two MSOs control many hundreds of systems. Economies of scale and efficient use of resources favor group ownership, enabling centralized purchasing of programs and other equipment and services at a discount. The network O&O stations, as a special case of broadcast group ownership, exercise great influence over the syndicated program market and over the working arrangements of networks themselves. Broadcast groups, and to a lesser extent MSOs, tend to encourage local production by their owned stations or systems in order to cultivate goodwill in their communities of license or franchise. Programs produced by broadcast groups for common use by their owned stations have become a growing source for the general syndicated market. Groups have also begun to form cooperative ventures among themselves to underwrite high-cost programs, challenging the dominance of the traditional broadcast networks in this field. MSOs tend to be held by media conglomerates that also own basic and pay cable program services. The urgent need for cable-specific programs to supplement feature films on pay-cable channels has stimulated owners of these channels to become new sources of program production. A favorable regulatory climate encourages the growth of group ownership and vertical integration. Four factors—the increasing need for programs as stations, cable systems and cable networks proliferate; the weakening of the traditional networks as a program source; the loosening of the ties that bind affiliates to their networks; and the convenience and low cost of program distribution by satellite—suggest that group ownership will play an ever-increasing role in program production for both broadcast stations and cable.

Notes

1. For lists of group owners and MSOs and their properties, see *Broadcasting-Cablecasting Yearbook*. See also "Family Ties," *Channels 1987 Field Guide*, pp. 24–25, and "Who Owns Broadcasting?" *Channels*, April 1987, pp. 47–56, and April 1988, pp. 28–46.

2. Note that the 25 percent maximum coverage refers not to any group's actual audience (its "reach"), but to its *potential* audience; of course, in practice stations never reach 100 percent of their potential. The FCC bases coverage measurement on Arbitron's Areas of Dominant Influence (ADIs), which omit households a station may cover in fringe areas beyond its immediate market (such as distant cabled areas).

3. The FCC has exempted some owners from some of these rules ("grandfathered"). Other rules affecting ownership include *nationality* (a foreign owner can hold only a small percentage of the stock in a station-owning company), and *minority status* (the FCC allows members of minority groups valuable tax deferrals to encourage minority station ownership and also allows a group to own 14 stations of one kind if minorities control 2 of them). Buyers often seek either temporary or permanent exceptions to the ownership rules. In 1987 an ingenious entrepreneur managed to buy control, at least temporarily, of 17 television stations, 12 of them in a single year. He planned to comply with the FCC rule by setting aside 5 of the 17

in trust for his children, a stratagem the FCC appeared ready to approve. Rinker Buck, "George Gillett's Private World," *Channels,* September 1987, pp. 29–34.

4. Jean B. Grillo, "Hey, Big Spender," *Focus,* February 1987, pp. 54–57.

5. Ellis Simon, "The MSO Game," *Cable Marketing,* July 1986, pp. 14–19; "In Focus: Cable— Who's Got the Power and How They're Using It," *Channels,* March 1986, pp. 39–56; Meryl Gordon, "Colossus of Cable," *Channels,* October 1986, pp. 26–33; "The ABCs of ATC," *Broadcasting,* 8 November 1982, pp. 48–58; "In Focus: What's Driving Cable," *Channels,* May 1988, pp. 60–78.

6. In very basic terms, network economics work as follows: The network obtains programs, sells time within those programs to advertisers and arranges for the programs, including advertising, to be delivered to affiliates for broadcast, to the extent that each affiliate has "cleared" time for its network's programs. The network pays each affiliate an agreed-upon rate of **compensation** for airing network programs in keeping with network-affiliate contracts, renewed every two years. Because affiliates have the legal right to reject (fail to clear time for) programs, the O&O stations play a vital role in ensuring *clearance* in the top markets and in setting an example of clearance for the rest of the affiliates.

7. *Barter syndication* refers to an increasingly common method of providing syndicated programs to stations: an advertiser, rather than a station, buys the rights to a given syndicated program. After incorporation of the advertiser's own commercials in some (usually half) of the commercial breaks in the program, the advertiser offers the program to stations at no charge. The station gets a "free" program and has the chance to profit by selling the remaining open spots. An advertiser particularly anxious to place a program in a particular market and/or a particular station may sweeten the deal by offering the station more than half the spots.

8. "The Programmers Speak," *View,* March 1983, pp. 53–58.

9. Jeri Baker, "Grant's Back & Gannett's Got Him," *Channels,* July–August 1987, pp. 40–43.

Selected Sources

Channels Field Guide. Annual report on television, cable, radio and new media technologies, published in January since 1980.

DiSante, Evelyn. "Who will Survive?" *Multichannel News* (19 July 1982): 9 ff.

Howard, Herbert H. *Group and Cross-Media Ownership of Television Stations in 1987.* Washington, D.C.: National Association of Broadcasters, annually in January.

Regulatory Trends in the 1980's: More Owners—More Stations. New York: Station Representatives Association, Inc., 1980.

TV Facts, Figures and Film. Twice-monthly trade magazine on the business of television, published by Broadcast Information Bureau.

"Who Owns Broadcasting?" *Channels,* April 1987, pp. 47–56, and April 1988, pp. 28–46.

PART TWO / BROADCAST TELEVISION STRATEGIES

Part Two has four chapters addressing commercial broadcast *television* programming. Each television chapter looks at the main components of programming strategy—evaluation, selection and scheduling of programs. The first two chapters consider **network** programming and the second two look at **station** practices. The television chapters come before commercial cable and radio and noncommercial broadcasting in this book because broadcast television dominates the audience's and industry's thinking about programming. Because of the huge sums of money involved in television programming decisions, the commercial television networks and major-market stations set the patterns for the rest of the industry. In the 1950s, broadcast television forced radio out of its leading position; eventually, radio found its more specialized programming niches. Later, cable copied many broadcast television strategies.

As the programming strategies of the three commercial broadcast television networks—ABC, CBS and NBC—differ more by time of day than they do from network to network, the first two chapters in Part Two subdivide programming by daypart rather than by network. The next two chapters analyze program strategies for different market sizes. Markets ranked 1 to 25 by the ratings companies are the **large markets**, 26 to 100 are the **mid-markets**, and 101 to 210 + are the **small markets**.

The first chapter in Part Two, Chapter 5, examines the high-visibility entertainment programming of **network prime time.** These programs generate a network's image in the public eye, and their ratings define a network's commercial value in the minds of advertisers. Chapter 5 therefore has special importance. It covers the competitive strategies the three national networks use in pilot selection, program renewal and cancelation. It looks at the distinctive scheduling styles of the three established networks and the role of the new Fox network. It analyzes recent trends in program genres, including specials, spinoffs, sports and movies and looks at costs for prime-time entertainment programs.

Chapter 6 deals with **nonprime-time** programming. It considers program acquisitions and ratings for early morning, daytime, late night, overnight and weekend network programs. The author analyzes the constraints operating on network news and the major nonprime-time formats of all three broadcast networks: talk shows, soap operas, game shows, children's programming, evening newscasts, weekend sports and public affairs, describing the roles of time clearances, program development and scheduling for each format. Chapter 6 provides an insider's perspective on commercial network television programming for the nonprime-time dayparts.

Chapters 7 and 8 examine television strategies from the station perspective. One chapter deals with network affiliates, the other independent stations. Affiliates dominate television. Of the just over 1,000 commercial television stations (1,019 in 1988), the 632 network affiliates typify television in the eyes of the general public. In 1988, 215 stations were affiliated with ABC, 210 with CBS and 207 with NBC. Viewers associate network names more than station call letters with affiliates because they air about 14 hours per day of high-visibility network programming, leaving few hours in which to develop local identities. Chapter 7 introduces the professional programming language station managers and programmers use. The author writes from the viewpoint of major and mid-sized market **affiliates,** and spells out the competitive options for the station programmer for each daypart. The chapter analyzes the specific decisions an affiliate programmer must make in each time period and examines ratings strategies for an affiliate competing with two rival affiliates and at least one independent station.

Chapter 8 looks at station programming strategy primarily from the vantage point of the nearly 400 **independents** competing with network affiliates for audiences and advertising revenue. The top 25 markets typically have three or more independents. The three-affiliate versus two- or one-independent pattern occurs in most markets between 25 and 75. The smallest markets may not have a local independent. Only in the late 1970s did independents become truly competitive—upsetting two decades of three-way market monopoly by affiliates. Even after major inroads on affiliates' market shares, independents still must settle for a smaller portion of revenues per station. Nevertheless, the independent station programmer, not the affiliate programmer, has the full range of television programming options, filling the entire schedule with purchases or locally produced programs. On the whole, independents have become profitable by counterprogramming their affiliate competitors. The options the author describes apply to small- and large-market UHF and VHF independents, including such giants as superstations TBS, WGN and WWOR.

Part Two, then, covers commercial broadcast television programming. It focuses on the evaluation, selection and scheduling of programs from the separate perspectives of networks and television stations.

CHAPTER 5 \ PRIME-TIME NETWORK TELEVISION PROGRAMMING

Robert F. Lewine

Susan Tyler Eastman

William J. Adams

A Guide to Chapter 5

Robert F. Lewine is president of the Academy of Television Arts and Sciences Foundation, an office he assumed in 1964. He has the distinction of having served as a vice-president of programming at all three networks—ABC and NBC in New York and CBS in Hollywood—and as vice-president of television at Warner Brothers. His background includes commercial production, program research, advertising and program production. In addition to founding *Television Quarterly*, Mr. Lewine has been actively involved in the development of the Emmy awards since their inception and the establishment of the ATAS/UCLA television archival library in Los Angeles. He often teaches at the University of California in Los Angeles, the University of Southern California, Columbia College and California State University at Northridge. While serving as trustee of Columbia College and of the American Women in Radio and Television Foundation, Columbia College awarded him an honorary doctorate of Humane Letters in 1982.

Susan Tyler Eastman, editor and author of other chapters, supplied sections on program evaluation, seasonal strategies and recent trends in network scheduling and program renewals. See Chapter 9 for biographical information.

William J. Adams, assistant professor at Kansas State University in the Department of Radio-Television since 1986, completed his Ph.D. at Indiana University in 1988. His dissertation research on network programming trends was funded by the National Association of Broadcasters. He holds an M.A. from Ball State University in journalism and a B.A. from Brigham Young University. He has published extensively as a journalist and scholar, especially focusing on network prime-time programming. He contributed original historical data on program cancelations and renewals to this chapter, describing program theories, reporting on network audiences and decision-making styles, and analyzing trends in prime-time program formats. Together, these three authors examine the three broadcast networks' procedures for selecting, evaluating and scheduling prime-time programs.

PRIME-TIME NETWORK AUDIENCES

Network television's visibility makes it an inviting target for critics. Its national popularity focuses public attention on its strengths and weaknesses. Of the almost 15,000 hours the three commercial networks program each year, about one-fifth is singled out for special critical attention—the *weekly 22 hours* of **prime-time** programming. That figure multiplied by 52 weeks and again multiplied by three networks equals 3,432 hours of prime-time network programs a year.

The 32 weeks from late September to mid-May form the main viewing year. The remaining 20 weeks (off-season) of summer are filled largely with reruns, unused pilots and tryouts for potential series. In the early 1980s the networks began using the summer for testing new program ideas in short runs. This practice accelerated partly to counteract the loss of audiences to independent stations and cable television, and partly to satisfy affiliated stations that were worried about the extreme ratings drop occurring during the July sweeps. Also, summer tryouts give the networks *first-run* programs to promote to audiences (as opposed to the traditional summer *reruns*) and an extended period for testing audience reaction to these proposed fall shows. But the period from September to May still has the largest audiences and therefore warrants the networks' most strenuous programming efforts.

Audience ratings throughout the day are important to the networks, of course, but the ratings in the 22 prime-time hours are absolutely vital. A failure in prime-time programming may take years to remedy. NBC's ten years in third place is a case in point. Low ratings affect viewer and affiliate loyalty and public image as well as advertising revenue. The prime-time hours—from 8 P.M. to 11 P.M. (EST) six days each week and from 7 P.M. to 11 P.M. on Sundays—constitute the center ring, the arena in which each network's mettle is tested. Prime-time programs are the most vulnerable because low ratings in these valuable hours lead to devastating losses in advertising revenue. Both advertisers and networks expect the highest return from prime-time hours.

Demographics to Peoplemeters

Some advertisers are interested mainly in tonnage—the sheer, raw size of an audience, as measured by the ratings for a program. This scattershot approach, aiming at all ages and both sexes, best suits advertisers of soaps, foods and over-the-counter drug products. Other advertisers prefer targeting a specific segment of the audience by its **demographics** (age and sex). Demographic measurements have been part of broadcast ratings since the 1960s, but Paul Klein of NBC and Mike Dann of CBS introduced the concept of **"ideal demographics,"** the theory that all prime-time programming should aim at one consumer segment of the audience. That ideal audience consists of 18–34 year old, white, middle-class, urban women. They, the programmers claimed, both control most consumer purchasing and succumb most easily to televised advertising messages.[1]

As a consequence of adopting this theory, the three major networks canceled a large number of entertainment programs in the early 1970s because they appealed to a predominantly older demographic group, even though they attracted sizable audiences. The networks canceled about half of the thirty top-rated programs in 1970 and 1971, replacing them with prime-time series aimed at the younger adult audience.[2] ABC took the lead in this new demographic targeting. CBS and NBC followed along but also tried to retain some older people in their audiences as well.

While the networks continue to support ideal demographics as the basis for program decisions, as do most advertising agencies, their use has been attacked by media critics and marketing researchers who say that demographic traits should fit the product. As a *Los Angeles Times* television critic wrote, "You can't sell bubble gum to ballet fans or Xerox copiers to teenagers."[3] The so-called ideal demographic fails to target audiences for electronics manufacturers, retailers of big-ticket items such as high-priced cars or top-of-the-line appliances, and manufacturers such as Geritol or Levi. By the mid-1980s the age demographics of a particular program or night were considered more crucial than a network's overall age demographics. Programs appealing to audiences 25–54 or to men drew advertisers who wanted that particular demographic breakdown rather than the demographic average of all a network's programming. In the late 1980s, for example, *Golden Girls* and *Murder, She Wrote* succeeded through skewing toward older viewers, while *Monday Night Football* succeeded by targeting men.

In 1986 David Poltrack, head of CBS Research, claimed that the ideal demographic group continued to represent the single largest segment of the prime-time audience; the group had simply aged as the baby-boom generation had grown older. It now consisted of white, urban women, aged 24–44, but by the 1990s, the ideal audience would be women 34–50 + years (all races).[4] Critics, however, argue that there are more people in the other demographic divisions than in the so-called ideal group, and so any network or advertising campaign concentrating solely on Poltrack's ideal demographic could lose more audience than it would attract. Indeed, an excessive emphasis on youthful female viewers may have contributed to the erosion of broadcast network audiences during the 1970s. Research shows that targeting the ideal group led to a decline in program variety and much complaint about the "sameness" of programs on all three networks.[5]

As an alternative to demographic targeting, **psychographics** or lifestyle research analyzes audiences in terms of their likes/dislikes, political and social attitudes, hobbies, consumption habits and so on. However, gathering psychographic information has proved extremely expensive; moreover, the results are often difficult to interpret and generalize. In the 1980s, easily gathered demographic information was combined with distinct lifestyle divisions within the television audience, creating several product-targeting systems.[6] The widespread popularity of such marketing tools helped force the broadcast networks to switch from the traditional rating methods to peoplemeters in 1987. As explained in Chapter 2, peoplemeters keep track of an individual's television viewing, and some versions of the peoplemeter supply a laser pen to record the pricing bars found on most consumer products. Such systems provide information on both demographics and purchasing behavior to programmers and potential advertisers.

Least Objectionable Programming

Unfortunately, the quality of programs, aside from their ability to attract viewers, has rarely seriously concerned most advertisers—at least not enough to affect their practices. There are notable exceptions. A select roster of advertisers (Firestone, Hallmark, IBM and Xerox, for example) insist on prestigious programs as vehicles for their advertisements and therefore tend to sponsor entire programs, rather than merely buy participating spots. In contrast, most advertisers care little about program quality, seeking only vehicles for reaching appropriate markets for their products.

Indeed, overly strong audience support for a program may actually discourage the renewal of a prime-time series. Prime-time network television strives to provide the largest possible audience (overall or within a demographic group), not necessarily the most satisfied audience. Many programmers believe that prime-time series that generate strong reactions among viewers may in fact split the audience into two groups: those that "love" and those that "hate" a show. A show that generates only *moderate* liking, but is liked by everyone, may get the biggest audiences.[7]

NBC programmer Paul Klein called this idea the theory of **least objectionable programming (LOP)**. He assumed that viewers of the three networks would choose the one of the three programs that created the least outcry among co-viewers, whether anyone actually liked the program or not. LOP has been a major consideration in prime-time programming since the early 1960s. The difficulty with the theory is that it assumes a limited number of program options for viewers. If there are only three shows to watch, two may be so strongly disliked by some people that the third show gets most of the audience. But by 1988, over 85 percent of Americans could receive nine or more television channels, and half of homes had 20 or more (typically 36) channels on cable. Moreover, over half of homes had videotape recorders (and 40 percent used remote controls). Under conditions of vastly increased program supply, prime-time programmers face the difficult task of satisfying advertisers' demands for large, well-identified audiences, and viewers' demands for programs they really want to see. The networks are being forced into increased targeting of specific segments of the audience, rather than the traditional mass appeal, in prime-time programming.

RATINGS

Regardless of whether an advertiser wants sheer tonnage or a specific audience segment, commercial spot costs depend mainly on the absolute ratings (total estimated audience) of the programs in which the ads occur. A television advertiser, unlike a radio advertiser, must pay for all viewers, whether or not they fall within the desired target audience. Program *ratings* alone determine the cost of a commercial spot.

However, ratings lack precision. As pointed out in Chapter 2, network ratings *estimate* the number of viewers, on the basis of viewing by a few thousand families, representing nearly 90 million television households. It is very unlikely that most estimates are exactly right. In fact, statisticians often claim that no real difference exists between the fifth-rated and thirtieth-rated shows in prime time; the differences in their ratings could be due to nothing more than inevitable **sampling errors.** But because advertisers (and ad agencies) have agreed to base the price of a commercial spot on the absolute rating numbers, they ignore their inability to measure small differences. A program with an 18.5 rating will generate millions of dollars more in advertising revenue, over the course of a season, then a program with an 18 rating, even though the difference between the two is statistically meaningless.

The treatment of ratings as absolute numbers by both advertisers and networks has led to fights over unmeasurable fractions of a ratings point and demands for more measurements, produced more often. These demands have led to ratings being reported in a number of different ways. For prime-time programming, the most common of these are the *sweeps, overnights, pocketpieces* and *MNA reports.*

Sweeps and Overnights

Four times each year (November, February, May and July) a highly controversial rating event occurs—the **sweeps.** This subject was discussed in Chapter 2. The results of sweeps rating periods directly affect the rates network-affiliated and network owned-and-operated stations charge for their advertising time. The stations, therefore, demand that the networks' display their highest-quality merchandise during the sweeps periods to attract the largest possible audiences and maximize ad revenues. The practice of **stunting** (the deliberate shuffling or preempting of the regular schedule for specials, adding celebrity guests and extraordinary hype) makes the four sweeps periods highly competitive and, at the same time, not always the most valid indicators of a network's or station's real strength.

As described in chapters 2 and 3, national ratings take several different forms. Aside from the sweeps, the **overnights** (available only in the biggest cities) are the most avidly monitored of ratings data. Overnights provide only total numbers of prime-time viewers, without demographic breakouts such as age and sex. They are used to monitor overall urban audience reaction to such "program doctoring" as changes in casts, character emphasis and plot line. The overnights also indicate immediately whether a new program has "taken off" and captured a sizable audience in the urban markets. Continued low ratings in the overnights during the first few weeks of a newly introduced program's run spells cancelation unless the ratings show a hint of growth—or unless the program is expected to have stronger rural than urban appeal. *Little House on the Prairie* and *Dolly Parton* are examples of rural-appeal shows that initially "died in the cities."

Pocketpieces and MNA Reports

The ratings report of greatest interest to the creative community is published every other week in a small booklet known as "The Nielsen Pocketpiece." It includes ratings/shares and the all-important demographics for both prime time and daytime, plus general information such as average ratings by program type, number of sets in use by days and by dayparts, comparison of television usage between the current season and the one preceding, and other details. Figure 5-1 shows a sample **pocketpiece** page.

Programmers also find Nielsen's *Multi-Network Area Report* (MNA) very useful. The statistics in the MNA cover the seventy leading population centers in the country—all markets with at least three commercial television stations. Since the seventy markets represent about two-thirds of total television homes nationally, only two-thirds of the national Nielsen sample is involved in the MNA measurements. The networks use **MNA reports** to compare the performance of the three networks without the distortion caused by one- and two-affiliate markets included in the national Nielsen reports. The MNA reports include the so-essential demographic breakouts.

Audience Flow

Aside from a program's demographics, the networks look for its **flow**. Does the audience "flow through" to the next program? As explained in chapters 1 and 3, each network hopes to capture and hold the largest possible (young adult) audience, especially from 8 P.M. until midnight or later. Network strategies are usually directed at achieving *flow-through* in prime-time programs. Network analysis shows that, on average, the audience representing

Figure 5-1 Facing Pocketpiece Pages

A-16 *Nielsen* NATIONAL TV AUDIENCE ESTIMATES

EVE.SUN. JAN.3, 1988

TIME	7:00	7:15	7:30	7:45	8:00	8:15	8:30	8:45	9:00	9:15	9:30	9:45	10:00	10:15	10:30	10:45	11:00	11:15
HUT	66.8	68.4	68.6	69.2	69.8	71.0	71.9	71.9	69.9	69.4	68.6	67.1	65.4	64.1	61.7	58.7	53.3	47.9

ABC TV ←DISNEY SUNDAY MOVIE→ FLIGHT OF THE NAVIGATOR, PT.1 ←SPENSER: FOR HIRE→ ←DOLLY (PAE)→ ←BUCK JAMES (PAE)→

AVERAGE AUDIENCE (Hhlds (000) & %)	12,140 13.7	12.3 *	15.1 * 11.0	10.7 *	9,750 11.4 * 11.0	10.4 *	11.6 * 10.2	10.0 *	10.3 *		
SHARE AUDIENCE %	20	18 *	22 * 15	15 *	16 * 16	15 *	9,040 17 * 16	15 *	17 *		
AVG. AUD. BY 1/4 HR %	11.6	13.0	14.6 15.6	10.6	10.9 11.3	11.4 10.0	10.8 11.6	11.6 9.9	10.1 10.1	10.5	

CBS TV ←60 MINUTES→ ←MURDER, SHE WROTE→ ←CBS SUNDAY MOVIE ONCE UPON A TEXAS TRAIN (PAE)→ CBS SUNDAY NEWS

AVERAGE AUDIENCE (Hhlds (000) & %)	19,490 22.0	18.6 *	22,330 25.4 * 25.2	25.0 *	18,780 25.4 * 21.2	22.6 *	21.6 *	21.3 *	19.6 * 2,570 2.9	
SHARE AUDIENCE %	32	28 *	37 * 35	36 *	35 * 32	32 *	32 *	33 *	33 * 6	
AVG. AUD. BY 1/4 HR %	17.7	19.5 23.9	26.9 24.9	25.1 25.7	25.1 22.8	22.4 22.0	21.1 21.4	21.2 20.8	18.3 2.9	

NBC TV (1) ←OUR HOUSE (7:37-8:37)(R)(PAE)→ (2) MY TWO DAD'S (9:07) 9:37(PAE) ←NBC SUNDAY NIGHT MOVIE AN OFFICER AND A GENTLEMAN (9:37-12:06)(R)(PAE)→

AVERAGE AUDIENCE (Hhlds (000) & %)	12,400 29.0 * 14.0	11.2 *	17,190 15.6 * 19.4	17,280 19.5	16,210 18.3	17.6 *	18.5 *	18.4 *	18.3 *
SHARE AUDIENCE %	44 * 20	16 *	22 * 27	28	32	26 *	28 *	30 *	35 *
AVG. AUD. BY 1/4 HR %	29.1 28.9 11.9	10.8 15.2	16.0 17.0 18.6	19.9 19.3	17.4 17.7 18.8	18.3 18.2	18.6 18.3	18.3	

INDEPENDENTS
(INCL. SUPERSTATIONS)

AVERAGE AUDIENCE	10.4	11.5	10.3	10.7	9.0	8.7	8.2	6.7	4.0
SHARE AUDIENCE %	15	17	15	15	13	13	13	11	8

SUPERSTATIONS

AVERAGE AUDIENCE	2.6	3.0	3.1	2.9	2.9	3.0	2.8	2.2	1.0
SHARE AUDIENCE %	4	4	4	4	4	4	4	4	2

PBS

AVERAGE AUDIENCE	1.8	2.6	5.3	5.1	3.2	3.1	2.4	2.0	1.4
SHARE AUDIENCE %	3	4	8	7	5	5	4	3	3

CABLE ORIG.

AVERAGE AUDIENCE	3.9	4.2	5.5	5.4	5.9	5.9	4.6	4.0	2.6
SHARE AUDIENCE %	6	6	8	8	8	9	7	7	5

PAY SERVICES

AVERAGE AUDIENCE	2.6	3.0	4.0	4.0	5.4	5.8	5.7	3.9	3.5
SHARE AUDIENCE %	4	4	6	6	8	9	9	6	7

U.S. TV HOUSEHOLDS: 88,600,000
(1) NFL PLAYOFF GAME-SUN.,SEATTLE VS HOUSTON,(PAE),NBC,(4:00-7:37),(S)
(2) FAMILY TIES,(PAE),NBC,(8:37-9:07),(R)

For explanation of symbols, See page 8.

A-17

four out of every ten points in a lead-in program's ratings will flow through to the succeeding program.

Is it any wonder, given demographics and flow-through considerations, that the selection of ideas to be developed and entered into program line-ups seems as risky as the turn of a roulette wheel? (Roulette, however, would in fact pay off more often!) Recent estimates of the aggregate costs of program development for the three networks in a given year range up to $500 million. This staggering sum does not include the overhead costs of maintaining the departments and individuals who make these decisions. The salaries of top programmers reach the six- to seven-figure level, reflecting the substantial rewards for picking a winning schedule. The entire process of prime-time programming breaks down into three major phases: deciding to *keep or cancel* already scheduled series, developing and *choosing new programs* from the ideas proposed for the coming season, and *scheduling* the entire group. To understand program evaluation, selection and scheduling, the changing concept of a *season* needs to be spelled out.

NETWORK SEASONS

During the 1950s and 1960s, the season lasted a minimum of 39 weeks each year. By the mid-1970s, high per-episode costs had cut back the usual number of episodes produced for a series to 32, also dropping the normal length of the season to 32 weeks. But further cost increases combined with a high mortality rate forced an end to the pattern of ordering 32 episodes of a program, dropping the episode orders to 26. Now the networks typically contract for just **6 to 11 episodes** of new shows with two or more intended for repetition, and contracts say "cancelable any time." To fill out the 32 weeks of the regular (ratings) season, a program may be renewed and another 11 new episodes ordered, or another program may be substituted. Specials, miniseries and brief series tryouts fill the remaining weeks. By the late 1980s, the networks were ordering more episodes of established hits, however, carrying highly visible series through May and even into summer to create the illusion of a longer season. The 1987–88 year was ballyhood as the first 52-week season, although most summer network programs still were reruns. The competitiveness of the three networks has thus greatly altered the concept of the television season, breaking it into two phases beginning in September/October and January/February and varying the viewing season's length from year to year.

During the 1980s, March and April became tryout months for **limited-run** series. The production fee paid to license a prime-time series limits the networks to only two runs of each episode. Because of the few episodes usually ordered in the 1980s (typically 22 or fewer), the networks were threatened with running out of episodes before the 32-week season ended. To prevent this, the networks began taking popular series off the air for six to eight weeks, usually in March or April, and trying out a new series in the time slot. This off-and-on method of scheduling allowed the network to test a new program under the best possible conditions for the May sweeps, while saving the reruns for the summer months.

Whether this scheduling method improved a new series' chances for long-term success is debatable. The new show usually got highly inflated ratings while in the popular time slot, but these ratings seldom held up the following season when the new show moved into its permanent slot. In consequence, many limited-run series picked up for a second year were quickly cancelled when their ratings failed to live up to expectations. By the 1987–88 season, the networks were reconsidering this strategy.

Fall Premieres

Traditionally, the networks premiered their new series during a much-publicized week in late September. However, during the late 1970s, the traditional September **premiere week** slowly spread out. In the fall of 1987, it took five weeks to actually get the season started. Series now premiere in scattershot fashion throughout September and October.

The disappearance of a uniformly recognizable network premiere week can be linked to the actors' and writers' strikes of 1980 and 1981. In those years, the networks were forced to delay series' premieres until the strikes were settled and production on the individual series could resume. No strike occurred in 1982, yet the fall introductions still stretched for seven weeks. In 1985 ABC even premiered one series in August. Clearly, the networks had a new strategy: As the numbers of new fall premieres rose in the late 1970s, some programs got lost in the clutter of the crowded fall promotional bang. The strikes showed the networks the value of a long premiere period. They now spread the fall introductions to give each program some room. The length of time devoted for premieres fluctuates from year to year as the three networks (and Fox) jockey for best starting position.

But all of this juggling has not improved the *success rate* of new programs. The decline in network audience shares continues. By 1988 the networks commanded less than 75 percent of prime-time viewing (the remaining 25 percent shared among basic cable, premium television, superstations, independents and public television).

Although many new programs and new episodes of returning programs still start in September, some new network programs begin their runs in January or February, thus creating a **second season**. By late fall the fate of most prime-time programs already on the air is clear. Holiday specials usually preempt those destined for cancelation or restructuring, so that by January or February the networks are ready to launch their second season—with almost the same amount of promotion and ballyhoo as are accorded the new season premieres in September.

But even the two-season pattern eroded over the years. In 1974–75, the number of new entertainment series introduced other than at the start of either season (during September/October or January/February) jumped from three to eight. In 1976 they leaped to 16. The number of such introductions continued to climb until, by 1983, they equalled the number of new series offered in September (and showed a third peak in March). See Table 5-4 later in the chapter to trace this evolution. Odd-month starts are now almost double the number of new series begun in January/February. As a strategy, this is called the **continuous season** approach.

Summer Schedules

Traditionally, the summer has been exempt from the ratings race (although two local sweeps are always conducted in May and July). It has been an arena for *reruns* (often of weak series episodes), *tryouts* of questionable new series intended for the next fall, and *leftover pilots* and episodes of never-scheduled or canceled series. The networks' neglect of the summers made them a gold mine for the pay-cable movie networks and independent television stations. By the early 1980s, cable and independent stations had captured a substantial share of the summer audience.

Although there are fewer total viewers in the summer, an overall decline in their collective audience share forced ABC, CBS and NBC to begin budgeting millions of dollars for new summer programming. ABC started the trend in the summer of 1983, and NBC rapidly followed suit; in 1987, NBC's *Molly Dodd,* for example, aired in the months once reserved for summer reruns. CBS has been slower to take full advantage of the summer season. With the advent of summer schedules, the July ratings book takes on more importance as a measure of network and pay cable pull and as a vehicle for prefall testing of programs. In the summer, the networks can air several episodes of a proposed new series and gauge audience reactions over a period of weeks.

PROGRAM RENEWAL

Evaluation of on-air shows goes on all year. The final decision on whether to return a program to the schedule the following fall is usually made between March and May because the networks showcase their fall lineups at their annual affiliates meetings in May. However, last-minute changes occur right up to the opening guns in the fall. The critical times for new programs starting in September are the four or five weeks at the beginning of the fall season (September/October) and the November sweeps. Traditionally, programs surviving the waves of cancelation at these times and lasting into January or February were safe until May—although a network might decide, as a result of the February sweeps, not to renew some programs for the next season.

Program Lifespan and License Contracts

In the 1970s the **lifespan** of a popular prime-time series grew ever briefer. In the 1950s and 1960s, shows like *The Ed Sullivan Show, Gunsmoke, What's My Line* and *The Wonderful World of Disney* endured for more than 20 years. These records for longevity will probably never be matched again. By 1980, a program lifespan of ten years was regarded as a phenomemon. By the late 1980s, five years had become the standard run for a successful series.

Several factors account for this shortened lifespan: the increased sophistication of the viewing audience; the emergence of action/suspense series (a seemingly less durable format than the traditional family sitcom); the constant media coverage of television shows and stars (as in *Entertainment Tonight*), wearing each episode and series idea out quickly; the practice of syndicating a series while it continues its network run; and the scarcity of outstanding program forms and fresh, top-rated talent. Actor boredom with stereotyped roles also may shorten a program's run. Many stars tire of repetitive characterizations and fail to renew their contracts even when ratings are still high. *Dallas* developed a revolving door for cast members, epitomized by the famous dream episode in 1986, in which the producers reintroduced the character of Bobby, after having killed him off a year earlier; they accomplished this by pretending the entire previous year (22 episodes) had been a dream. A total of 16 characters were introduced and then eliminated on *Dallas* between 1979 and 1986.

The shortened lifespan of prime-time series also reflects the complexity of program **license contracts** that generally run for five years. When a series first makes it to the air, the network controls the contractual situation and usually requires several concessions from the producer. At this time, the producer has traditionally had to sign over such rights as creative control, spinoff rights, limitations on syndication and scheduling control. The producer also agrees to a specific licensing fee for the run of the five-year contract, regardless of the program's success (after all, most shows fail). Typically, this licensing fee is substantially less than actual production costs and makes no concession for sharing the profits should the program become a hit.

Producers practice **deficit financing** (paying more to produce a series than the network pays in license fees) because the potential profit from off-network syndication can run into the hundreds of millions of dollars. After the 1971 **prime-time access rule** barred the networks from taking a share of the syndication profits, all three networks demanded that the producers shoulder a large portion of the production cost. The networks argued that because only the producers get syndication profits, they should also accept more of the risk involved in prime-time production. When a script idea is first proposed, its producer is in no position to argue with this type of network reasoning.

However, at the end of the first contractual period, normally five years, the tables are turned. Now the producer enjoys the advantage. The series has a **track record** and enough episodes in the can for syndicating as a stripped show. In short, since the producers no longer need the network as much as it needs them, producers may demand the return of many of the concessions granted in the original contract. Moreover, a hit series' stars, directors and other executives now seek much larger salaries and concessions. Under renewal conditions, the network can often profit by dropping a popular show with a marked-up price in favor of an untried newcomer. Both the *Mary Tyler Moore Show* and *Barney Miller* went off the air when agreement on renewal contracts could not be reached.

Pivotal Numbers

Of the three phases of planning a fall schedule—evaluation, selection and scheduling—deciding which programs already on the air will continue and which will be pulled is perhaps the easiest. The decisions are based squarely on the network's profit margin—in essence, subtracting cost-per-episode from advertising revenue. And normally, revenue is directly related to ratings. Until the 1980s, a weeknight rating below 20 (or an audience share of less than 30) almost always resulted in a program's cancelation on any network. But because of steady network audience erosion, by the late 1980s, the target numbers dropped to a minimum weekday prime-time **rating of 15** and a **share of 25**. They will drop even further if the three networks' share of viewers drops more.

Entertainment programs stalling in the bottom 10 percent of the Nielsens are almost always cancelled as soon as possible. The most difficult decisions for network programmers involve the borderline cases, programs that (1) show signs of fatigue but are still holding their own or (2) are only just beginning to slide in the ratings or (3) are highly rated but draw the wrong demographics. Occasionally, the personal preferences of a top network executive or advertiser may influence a decision, but the prevailing view is that *cancelations had far better come too soon and too often than too late.*

Until the 1980s, the three networks differed little in their attitudes toward cancelation of long-running programs on the decline and were weakly committed if at all to **slow builders** (programs that acquire a loyal audience only after months of patient nurturing). In the mid 1980s, however, NBC showed slightly more patience with slow builders. Nonetheless, generally only series with borderline ratings benefit substantially from a longer introduction and promotional period. A proven exception to this rule is *60 Minutes,* which was on the bottom of the ratings charts for several *years* before catching fire, largely as a result of its move to Sundays at 7 P.M. Programs such as *Dallas, All in the Family* and *Simon & Simon* had much worse than "borderline" ratings for several months before the mass audience discovered them. Today, ratings strategy is basically the same at ABC, CBS and NBC; cancelation comes quickly at the first sign of weakness.

Program Costs

In addition to ratings, *profits* left after subtracting licensing costs from advertising revenues influence program cancelation. Two prime-time programs of the same length, on the same network, with identical ratings will, ideally, produce identical amounts of revenue for that network. But if one of them has slightly higher per-episode licensing costs (say, $425,000 versus $400,000) over a season, that difference may reduce net profit by a half-million dollars. The number of ad minutes remain the same for each program, and advertising rates are based on **cost-per-thousand,** no matter how much it costs a network to get a thousand viewers. Further complicate the situation by mixing in borderline ratings, and it's clear that *the program with the higher licensing cost will be cancelled before the lower-cost series.*

The **production fee** (license networks pay) varies with cost factors such as sets, costumes, special effects, stunt work, whether the show is taped or filmed, the amount of location versus studio shooting, cast size, the producers' and stars' reputations and so on. Since 1971, all three networks have concentrated programs into three basic formats—**situation comedies, crime dramas** and **movies**. The more expensive genres—such as science fiction, military, variety shows and westerns—have almost disappeared. These changes make comparing production fees over the years somewhat problematic. However, the 1978–79 season provided an unusually wide variety of programs for comparison, as shown in Table 5-1.

As Table 5-1 shows, the fees vary enormously according to program type. This variation explains why the networks rely so heavily on situation comedies and crime dramas, both among the cheapest types of programs to produce. Movies, although expensive, fill large amounts of time and therefore tend to be useful for plugging temporary night-long holes in the schedule until more sitcoms and crime dramas can be developed as replacements. As a result, movie nights come and go very quickly in prime-time schedules.

The news/documentary formats are by far the cheapest to produce, most being **in-house** productions. But with few exceptions, such as *60 Minutes* and *20/20,* such programs earn very low ratings. For example, in 1987 *Our World,* though it won critical acclaim, rated in last place for most of the season. In 1988, *West 57th* and *48 Hours* suffered the same fate.

Table 5-1 Production Fees by Program Type (1978–79)

PROGRAM*	GENRE	FEE PER 60 MINUTES
Supertrain	Action/adventure	$850,000
Battlestar Galactica	Science fiction	$750,000
NBC Novel for TV	Weekly miniseries	$750,000
CBS Saturday Movie	Theatrical movie	$600,000
How the West Was Won	Western	$600,000
BJ and the Bear	Action/adventure	$400,000
Paper Chase	School drama	$400,000
Eddie Capra Mystery	Crime drama	$390,000
WKRP in Cincinnati	Situation comedy	$380,000
Life Line	Documentary	$200,000
Real People	Public participation show	$190,000
Weekend	News magazine	$175,000

*All programs above were new to the year, and the cost represents the license fee paid for a 60-minute program. One exception, *Supertrain*, was produced by the network itself (**in-house** production), so the price listed is the actual cost of an episode, not a production license fee.

Source: *Variety* and other trade publications.

Table 5-2 shows how much production fees increased throughout the 1970s and 1980s. Moreover, advertising rates did not always keep up with production cost rises; network profits declined drastically in the mid-1980s before regaining strength in the late 1980s. During the mid-1980s, the networks introduced severe cost-cutting measures, including cutbacks in personnel and departmental budgets. CBS added one or two extra commercial spots to some of its most highly rated programs, in essence letting production fees influence the amount of time devoted to commercials.

NEW PROGRAM SELECTION

Phase two in planning a new fall season—the selection and development of new program ideas—poses more difficult problems than ongoing program evaluation. The three networks consider as many as 6,000 new submissions over a year. These submissions come in forms ranging from single-page outlines to completed scripts. Decision makers favor ideas resembling previous successes and quietly agree that almost all so-called original successes are in fact patterned after long-forgotten programs.

Concepts

The three networks invite submissions from established **independent producers** that enjoy substantial track records, such as MCA-Universal, Tandem, Spelling, MTM and Lorimar. Studios, other independent production companies and individuals are also sought out if some of their prior output ranks high in the ratings. These companies or individuals must have financial

Table 5-2 Average Cost per Hour for Prime-Time Programs

SEASON	PER-HOUR COST
1970–71	$205,523
1971–72	$222,217
1972–73	$227,136
1973–74	$232,829
1974–75	$227,075
1975–76	$253,174
1976–77	$322,674
1977–78	$360,778
1978–79	$443,454
1979–80	$449,663
1980–81	$571,395
1981–82	$594,034
1982–83	$660,063
1983–84	$702,841
1984–85	$757,439
1985–86	$801,628
1986–87	$858,446

Source: Data taken from estimates provided by *Variety* each September and February.

stability and the know-how required for dealing with network pressures and red tape. It is a given that long-established organizations have the most accepted writers under contract and have the clout to hire exceptional talents, making their submissions more persuasive than those from less experienced sources.

Many program **concepts** are dismissed out-of-hand; others are read and reread, only to be shelved temporarily. A few get a favorable nod with dispatch. Decision makers look for a program with staying power—that elusive combination of elements that makes a series continue to fascinate viewers over several years of new episodes using the same basic characters and situations.

Of the thousands of submissions that land on the networks' desks, roughly 500 are chosen for further development at network expense. At this point, the parties sign a **step deal,** contracts providing development funds in stages to the producer and giving the network creative control over the proposed program. The networks also get **first refusal rights,** preventing the producer from taking the idea to anyone else until the network has actually turned down the show. This provision allows a network to hold onto an idea for years.

As a rule, step deals authorize scripts or, in some cases, expanded treatments. The approved concepts often take first form as special programs, made-for-TV movies or miniseries. If a concept was submitted initially in script form, a *rewrite* may be ordered with specific recommendations for changes in concept, plot or cast (and even writers). Until recently, ABC had traditionally supported many more program ideas at this stage than CBS or NBC. However, ratings shifts have led CBS and NBC to allot more money to develop new program ideas. Most new program ideas are for half-hour comedies; concepts for one-hour dramas are far fewer, even though more prime-time programs are one hour in length. Half-hour sitcoms target the much desired demographic group of women 18–49 and, if successful, may hit the syndication jackpot. They are also the cheapest to produce and can be used as mid-season replacements and summer fillers. Consequently, the networks tend to order sitcom pilots more readily.

Scripts

Before authorizing a pilot, the program executive will first order one or more **scripts.** Although in the early days of television, certain program ideas received immediate pilot funding and even guaranteed places on schedules, such decisions usually depended on the use of a mega-star personality or big-name participation in the production. Generally, however, this practice has been abandoned as too risky. As of 1987, average expenditures at all three networks ranged from $20,000 for a half-hour comedy script to $40,000 for a one-hour drama script. Exceptional (read successful) writers demand even higher prices. Before a pilot reaches production, a second or even third script for proposed series may be called for to test the versatility of the series' idea.

Pilots

A **pilot** is a sample or prototype production of a series under consideration. Pilots afford programmers an opportunity to preview audience reaction to a property. Each network orders between 45 and 50 pilots to fill just over a dozen anticipated gaps in its new season lineup. Once a network decides to film or tape a pilot, it draws up a budget and advances start-up money to the producer. The *budget* and *advance* may be regarded as the third major step in the program development process. As of 1988, depending on whether videotape or film is used, half-hour pilots cost from $650,000 to $750,000, with one-hour dramas costing more than twice that amount.

The very practice of "piloting" creates an artificial situation. More money, more time and more writing effort go into a pilot than into subsequent episodes of the series. All the people involved put their best feet forward, trying to make the pilot irresistible to the network decision makers. The producer pulls out all the stops and spends more money than the network agreed to pay.

Because of its incredible expense and abysmal success rate, the pilot system has been denounced by some producers. Instead, they recommend five- to ten-minute presentation films in the place of full-blown pilots. About 150 pilots are produced annually to fill the three- to four-dozen newly opened slots on the networks each year. Series failing to make the final selection list for the fall season are held in reserve in anticipation of the inevitable cancelations. The networks also "short order" backup series from some of the pilots. They authorize production of 2 to 6 episodes and order additional scripts instead of the usual 11 episodes. With the probable network investment of over a million dollars in any pilot (considering overhead), necessarily every pilot, as well as all other episodes, will be broadcast sometime—high ratings or not. As a result of increases in pilot expenses, the networks now turn increasingly to made-for-TV movies to try out ideas.

Most contracts require delivery in early spring. When received, pilots are tested on special audiences as described in Chapter 2. Although **pilot-testing** research is admittedly inconclusive, it exerts considerable influence. The pilots are also repeatedly screened by committees of programming experts. The decision to select a pilot for a series may take into consideration (1) current viewer preferences as indicated by ratings, (2) costs, (3) resemblance between the proposed program and concepts that worked well in the past, (4) projected series' ability to deliver the targeted demographics for that network and its advertisers and (5) the types of programs the competing networks air on nights when the new series might be scheduled. Of secondary weight but also relevant to a judgment are (6) the reputation of the producer and writers, (7) the appeal of the series' performers (the talent), (8) the availability of an appropriate time period and (9) the compatibility of the program with returning shows. These considerations and others are juggled by the chief programmer. Fred Silverman, for example, was said to make the performer appeal his number one consideration; William Paley traditionally supported updated forms of older ideas; other programmers such as Brandon Tartikoff weigh counterprogramming considerations more heavily.

Those pilots not satisfactory for regularly scheduled series are usually saved for summer, when they provide the spice of original programming within schedules of tedious reruns. Often programmers group leftover pilots and promote them as weekly specials. Grouping provides scheduling continuity and makes promotion easier. In 1987 CBS added a new element to the summer pilot formula with the *CBS Summer Playhouse*, enhancing rejected pilots with the gimmick of asking the audience to call in to "vote" on whether the pilot should become a regular series.

If a pilot passes final muster and gets into the network's prime-time lineup, subsequent episodes of a half-hour series will cost between $450,000 and $500,000 (or about $800,000 to $950,000 for one-hour episodes). These are average costs (see Table 5-3) since each property differs as to the number of sets, size of cast and salaries paid. Made-for-TV movies cost from $1.3 million to $1.6 million, depending on ingredients; long miniseries such as *Winds of War* or *Amerika* cost tens of millions of dollars but, unlike most made-for-TV movies, sometimes provide a potential motion picture for eventual theatrical distribution (especially abroad).

PRIME-TIME SCHEDULING

At the end of the opening week of the 1979 fall television season, Les Brown, former *New York Times* television columnist and present editor-in-chief of *Channels* said, "For the opening week of the new season, Mr. Silverman [Fred Silverman, former president of NBC] mounted a potent schedule of programs that trounced both rival networks and broke a long losing streak for NBC-TV."[8] He went on to say, "Mr. Silverman scored his coup essentially by

Table 5-3 1987 License Fees for 12 Hit Programs

HALF HOURS	COST PER EPISODE	ONE HOURS	COST PER EPISODE
Cosby	$550,000	Dallas	$1,200,000
Cheers	550,000	Dynasty	1,200,000
Family Ties	500,000	St. Elsewhere	1,000,000
Golden Girls	450,000	Moonlighting	1,000,000
ALF	350,000	Miami Vice	1,000,000
		L.A. Law	950,000
		Cagney & Lacey	950,000

Source: *Variety*, 1987.

putting NBC's best movies forward—*Coming Home* and *Semi-Tough*—which had been originally scheduled for the crucial November sweep ratings." This lineup, not representative of NBC's regular programming schedule, was a successful move to lift NBC from its (then) last-place position even if only for a brief time. Mr. Brown quotes a rival network's spokesperson in the same article: "Silverman bought himself some time and a winning week by 'stacking' the schedule. Now let's see what he does for an encore." This example singles out one scheduling strategy networks employ: swapping regular programming for movie specials (a form of **stunting**).

Prime-Time Strategies

Six strategies dominate prime-time scheduling: lead-off, hammocking, blocking, tent-poling, counterprogramming and stunting.

1. *Lead-Off*. All schedulers use the strategy of beginning an evening with an especially strong program. Known as the **lead-off**, the first prime-time network show sets the tone for the entire evening. This maneuver can win or lose a whole night and thus affect the ratings performance of a full week.

A strong lead-off is considered so important that all three networks routinely move popular established series into the 8 P.M. positions on every weeknight. Moreover, the networks often shift strong series to provide a powerful lead-in to other weaker programs. No show is safe in any schedule position. (*M*A*S*H*, for example, occupied almost a dozen different time slots during its long run.) During the 1987–88 season, NBC moved the second-highest rated show on television, *Family Ties*, to provide a "lynch pin" for Sunday nights to counter CBS's *Murder, She Wrote*. While moving popular series may be commonplace in network strategy, it is an extremely risky practice. In 1987 CBS moved *Kate & Allie, Scarecrow and Mrs. King* and *Simon & Simon* to create strong lead-offs for several nights. The result was an immediate loss of almost four points for *Simon & Simon*, a two-point loss for *Scarecrow* and a one-point loss for *Kate & Allie*.

2. *Hammocking*. Although scheduling strategies can help bolster weak programs, it is obviously easier to build a strong schedule from a strong foundation than from a weak one. Moving an established sitcom to the next later half-hour and inserting a promising new program in its slot can take advantage of audience flow from the lead-off program to the rescheduled familiar sitcom, automatically providing viewers for the intervening program. This strategy is known as creating a **hammock** for the new program—a possible audience sag in the middle will be offset by the solid support fore and aft.

Late in 1986–87, for example, NBC moved *227* from its 8:30 time slot to 8:00 to provide a hammock for *Me and Mrs. C* between the popular *227* and *Golden Girls* at 9:00. Earlier in the season NBC had moved *227* from 9:30 to 8:30 to create a hammock for *Amen* between *Golden Girls* and *Hunter*. NBC also moved the highly rated *Night Court* to create a hammock for *Molly Dodd* between *Cheers* and *L.A. Law*. NBC's move of *Family Ties* to Sunday lead-off aided Sunday nights and also opened up a highly desirable space (a hammock) between *The Cosby Show* and *Cheers* on Thursday nights. While hammocking is among the best strategies for supporting new series, it can be risky for the established series being moved to create the hammock.

3. *Blocking.* The network may also use the hammock within **block programming**—placing a new program within a set of similar dramas or sitcoms filling an entire evening, a venerable and respected practice. In using this strategy, the programmer accepts the risk that the new comedy may lack the staying power of its "protectors" and so damage the program that follows. In effect, however, surrounding a newcomer with strong, established programs ensures the best possible opportunity for it to rate as high as the established hits.

The theory of blocking is that an audience tuning in for one situation comedy will stay for a second, a third and a fourth situation comedy (if of the same general type). The first show in a group usually aims at young viewers or the general family audience. Each ensuing series then targets a slightly older audience, thus taking advantage of the fact that as children go to bed and teenagers go out or do homework, the average age of the audience goes up. Blocking works best during the first two hours of prime time but typically loses effectiveness later in the evenings.

Examples of blocking are easy to find in prime-time schedules every year on all three networks. During the 1987–88 season, for instance, NBC formed a sitcom block on Saturday nights with *Facts of Life*, followed by *227*, followed by *Golden Girls*, followed by *Amen*. In the same season, CBS formed a crime show block on Wednesdays with *Mike Hammer!*, followed by *Magnum P.I.*, followed by *The Equalizer*. ABC, in turn, built a movie block on Sundays with the *Disney Movie*, followed by *The ABC Sunday Night Movie*. During the 1970s and 1980s, most of the highest-rated nights were built using the **stacking** strategy, including the most effective grouping of all—*The Cosby Show*, *Family Ties*, *Cheers* and *Night Court* in the mid-1980s.

4. *Tent-Poling.* Instead of splitting up successful half-hour adjacencies to insert an unproven half-hour show, in many seasons ABC and NBC turn to **tent-poling**—an alternative to the hammock. Each network focuses on a central, strong 8 or 9 P.M. show on weak evenings, hoping to use that show to anchor the ones before and after it. This strategy is particularly useful when a network has a shortage of successful programs and consequently cannot employ hammocking.

5. *Counterprogramming.* The networks also schedule programs to pull viewers away from their competitors by offering something of completely different appeal than the other shows, a strategy called **counterprogramming**. During the 1980s, for example, CBS successfully countered the strong, action-and-youth-oriented series offered by ABC and NBC on Sunday nights with *Murder, She Wrote*, a series providing continuity for the more sophisticated viewers tuning in to *60 Minutes* while appealing as well to older viewers. Much of NBC's success in the mid-1980s relied on counterprogramming with series such as *Highway to Heaven* and *Golden Girls*, which targeted underserved segments of the audience at particular hours.

In many ways, counterprogramming is the opposite of the "ideal demographics" approach. The former relies on finding a large, ignored group of viewers and scheduling a program for them. Most other strategies are intended to hold viewers who are already watching (flow strategies); counterprogramming *interrupts flow* to gain different viewers. This characteristic makes counterprogramming an effective scheduling option, especially for the network facing a superhit program on another network.

6. *Stunting.* The art of scheduling also includes maneuvers called stunting— a term taken from the defensive plays used in professional football. **Stunting** includes scheduling specials, adding guest stars, unusual series promotion, shifting a half-hour series to long form and otherwise altering the regular program schedule at the last minute. In the late 1970s the networks began deliberately making last-minute changes in their schedules to catch rival networks off guard. These moves were calculated, planned well ahead of time but kept secret until the last possible moment. NBC's surprise movement of its **blockbuster** movies from the November sweeps into the opening week of the 1979 fall season illustrates stunting. These moves are intended to blunt the effects of competitors' programs. Generally these maneuvers are one-time-only because their high cost cannot be sustained over a long period.

Scheduling hit films, using big-name stars for their publicity value and altering a series' format for a single evening are the common attention-getting stunts. They have high promotional value and can attract much larger than usual audiences. Of course, the following week, the schedule goes back to normal, and so these efforts generate sampling but rarely create long-term improvements in series ratings. Creating unusual program **crossovers** is a related stunt that affects ratings only so long as the crossover continues.

The Effects of Schedule Churn

Stunting during the 1970s resulted in a continual shifting of prime-time schedules. This scheduling **churn** constituted one of the major differences between 1960s and 1970s programming. (Here the term *churn* refers to the continual shifting of programs within the network schedule, and should not be

Table 5-4 Prime-Time Churn: Numbers of Time Shifts
and New Program Introductions from 1971 to 1986

YEAR	SEPT.	OCT.	NOV.	DEC.	JAN.	FEB.	MAR.	APR.	TOTAL	OUTSIDE OF SEPT./JAN.
1971	24	—	3	3	14	—	—	—	44	14%
1972	19	—	—	3	13	1	—	—	36	11%
1973	20	—	1	—	20	2	2	—	45	11%
1974	25	2	—	3	13	3	6	1	53	28%
1975	29	4	7	6	17	1	4	—	68	32%
1976	20	—	15	4	21	6	10	—	76	46%
1977	22	7	2	12	13	8	7	12	83	58%
1978	25	5	11	1	20	14	19	4	99	55%
1979	24	8	2	16	11	2	25	8	96	64%
1980	7	4	8	10	13	6	13	8	69	71%
1981	6	13	15	4	13	5	18	20	94	80%
1982	15	10	2	—	12	10	20	9	78	65%
1983	16	5	4	11	17	3	19	5	80	59%
1984	21	7	4	10	12	2	14	12	82	62%
1985	22	2	5	6	13	5	15	12	80	56%
1986	26	2	17	2	11	8	23	8	97	62%
Totals	321	69	96	91	233	76	195	99	1180	

Source: *Variety* listings, prepared by William J. Adams, Indiana University.

confused with subscriber *churn* as it is used in cable and pay television.) The 1960s represented a period of extreme stability in television schedules. New series were introduced during late September; second season changes, consisting only of a handful of time shifts and new series, always took place in late December and early January, and virtually no series were cancelled in less than 16 weeks. Preemption of regular series was held to a minimum and concentrated in particular time periods such as Christmas or Easter when the holidays provided a natural season for specials. The 1960s were also marked by stability within the audience and within the networks' comparative overall rankings. During the entire decade, CBS came in first, NBC second and ABC third.

During the 1970s, this stability vanished—the combined result of a closer ratings race, pressure from advertisers for "proper" demographics, increased cable penetration, pressure from public interest groups and declining network audience shares (toward the end of the decade). The number of time shifts, the moving of series from one slot to another, for example, went from less than a half-dozen in 1969–70 to over 40 by 1981–82. Table 5-4 illustrates the altering rates of time shifts. The number of shows cancelled in less than five weeks went from 1 in 1969 to a peak of 24 in 1978; early cancelations have held at about 20 per year since then. The number of series frequently preempted (more than one-third of their scheduled times) went from 0 to over 20. The 1970s also saw the collapse of the seasonal system for introducing time shifts and new programs and the end of ranking stability for the three networks.

Table 5-4 shows the number of series introduced or moved into new time slots during each month from 1971 to 1986. The September/January figures represent the traditional first- and second-season starting points. Therefore, series introduced in other months represent changes in the schedule that took place while the season was in progress. The chart shows the schedule churn caused by moving established series into new time slots (program shifting) and the introduction of new programs (requiring the cancelation of old programs). Included are figures for the first and second seasons only (32 weeks, excluding summers) because they represent the networks' main programming efforts. As can be seen, the mid-1970s saw a massive increase in schedule churn that has continued into the late 1980s. The September 1980 and 1981 figures reflect the effects of the actors' and writers' strikes that delayed the start of those seasons.

A program that a network wants to get rid of can be cancelled outright or *manipulated* (time shifted or churned) until its ratings fall. Manipulation sometimes makes good public relations sense when a show is critically successful and widely popular, although not quite popular enough among the desired demographic group. Examination of the results of program churn show that an individual program's ratings almost always fall when it is moved two out of three weeks (especially when moved in the second season). Other prime candidates for excessive schedule manipulation include those with higher-than-average production costs but which would cause managerial problems if abruptly cancelled (because they are supported by a highly placed executive or advertiser). *Paper Chase* on CBS is a clear example. Once low ratings or even a downward trend is achieved, network programmers can point to low ratings to justify cancelation (on the public occasions when some justification seems useful).

Cancelations

To attract and hold young viewers in large numbers, the networks now introduce nearly four dozen new programs into their prime-time schedules each year. Discounting movies and specials, during the 1980s the networks offered an average of 48 new programs, added to the average of 50 established ones returning to the air. Which new entries will beat the odds and survive this critical sweepstakes each year is the key question. Typically, *three-quarters of new series fall by the wayside*. Some are pulled within a few weeks; other may last until early spring if a network believes that too few viewers sampled them in the fall; some are kept on the schedule only until their replacements are readied.

From January 1974 to December 1978, the three networks cancelled more than a hundred series. This number of cancelations excludes temporary substitutes used during the year and does not disclose how many series struggled for only a few months and how many made it through the entire year. From 1984 to 1987, 150 series were cancelled, more than two-thirds of them one-hour programs, reflecting the fact that *one-hour series greatly outnumbered other formats*. For example, in 1985, 62 series were 60 minutes long while only 36 series were 30 minutes in length.

Table 5-5 New Programs Cancelled (Fall and Spring Combined)

SEASON	NUMBER AND PERCENTAGE OF NEW SHOWS CANCELLED*						Total Cancelled
	ABC		CBS		NBC		
1970–71	12	75%	7	78%	7	64%	26
1971–72	8	73%	7	58%	7	47%	22
1972–73	7	58%	4	36%	9	64%	20
1973–74	9	75%	6	60%	12	86%	27
1974–75	11	61%	8	73%	8	50%	27
1975–76	10	50%	9	53%	15	79%	34
1976–77	13	65%	12	71%	12	60%	37
1977–78	11	61%	17	81%	14	70%	42
1978–79	9	60%	14	70%	22	79%	45
1979–80	13	72%	11	58%	14	70%	38
1980–81	6	55%	9	69%	9	50%	24
1981–82	13	72%	8	67%	13	65%	34
1982–83	13	87%	13	81%	8	50%	34
1983–84	11	73%	9	64%	17	85%	37
1984–85	15	94%	8	80%	15	75%	38
1985–86	11	73%	14	82%	11	79%	36
1986–87	12	67%	17	89%	10	59%	39
Aver. % cancelled 1970–1984:		69%		69%		67%	
Aver. % cancelled 1984–1987:		78%		84%		71%	

*These figures are for new series, including movies, tried between September and May. They show the actual number of new prime-time programs *cancelled* and the percentage of all new series they represent. The apparent decline in the total since 1979 is misleading since the three networks increased March introductions beginning that year, and many of these shows, though not cancelled during that spring, were gone by November of the following year. These programs did not survive for long but are counted as survivors for their first season.

New Program Deaths

New programs have a higher cancelation rate than programs overall—because the latter includes the few hits that go on from year to year. The long-term average failure rate for all three networks exceeds 68 percent and, since the mid-1980s, *78 percent of new shows have failed*. The network enjoying the highest overall ratings naturally cuts the fewest programs, and conversely, the one with the lowest average ratings naturally scissors its schedule most drastically. What the network in the middle does varies from year to year. Consider Table 5-5 listing just the numbers of **new** programs **cancelled** after each season had begun.

During the 1986–87 season, for example, the ABC network scheduled 17 new programs altogether—seven one-hour dramas or adventure shows, a one-hour historical news magazine, eight half-hour comedies and one new movie night. Of these, twelve failed to finish the year or be renewed for another year (see Table 5-5). CBS fared even worse, having scheduled 19 new programs of all types. Seventeen of these failed to return the following year—

Figure 5-2 New Television Network Program Cancelations, 1970–71 to 1986–87

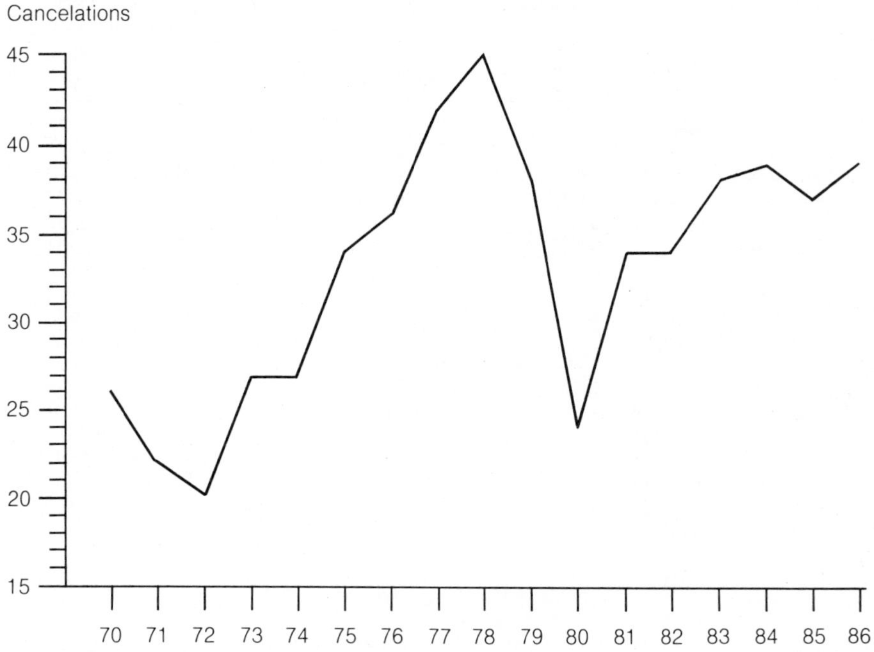

Cancelations

seven one-hour and eight half-hour comedies, and two new movie nights. Only a one-hour adventure, *Houston Knights*, and one magazine, *West 57th*, carried over to the 1987–88 season.

The 17 new shows NBC presented during 1986–87 had the best record by far. Of its seven new one-hour series, only two failed, although six of its eight half-hour comedies and both movie nights were killed. Of the 17 new NBC programs, then, seven survived—an exceptional percentage.

Totals from Table 5-5 and Figure 5-2 show cancelation of new programs peaked in 1978–79, forcing the networks to hold more series for the next season, which explains the drop in cancelations in 1980–81. Since 1980, the networks have given some programs a slightly longer tryout, but the total number of cancelations of programs new and old was rising again in the late 1980s.

Promotion's Role

All three networks use **on-air promotion** to introduce new programs. Beginning as early as mid-July and continuing through November (after especially heavy season-opening salvos), they intensify the promotion of their programs and their overall image. In addition, networks use newspaper and television guide announcements to list offerings for particular evenings. *TV Guide* magazine is so important to network television that programmers sometimes delay schedule changes so that the changes can make *TV Guide*'s deadline for affiliate program listings. The promotional value of *TV Guide* is essential both locally and nationally.

On-air promotional announcements play a significant role in the ratings success of a program. Not until a program is safely past the rocks and shoals of its first several airings (or until it becomes clear that nothing can help to get it past these early trials) does promotion let up. On-the-air promotions plug every program scheduled to appear in a season lineup. Weak or doubtful offerings needing extra stimulus get extra exposure. On-air program promotion continues all year around, with extra efforts devoted to sweeps periods. New slogans and symbols extol the virtues of overall network offerings and accompany all promotional announcements.

NETWORK DECISION MAKING

Few program decisions precipitate as much controversy as cancelation of programs. Since commercial television is first of all a business with tens of thousands of stockholders and hundreds of millions of dollars committed for advertising, the networks' overriding aim is to attract the largest possible audience in the ideal demographic range at all times. They always aim at the number one position. Ratings most influence prime-time programming strategy, and the networks make many controversial decisions each year: (1) cancelling programs favored by millions of viewers, (2) countering strong shows by scheduling competing strong shows, (3) preempting popular series to insert special programs and (4) falling back on reruns late in the season. Each network has exhibited a somewhat different pattern over the years in scheduling and risk-taking.

Programming Styles

The three networks do have distinctive scheduling "styles." For example, ABC tends to keep its schedule intact for as long as possible when it leads in ratings. It has traditionally used more spinoffs than the other two networks, and it typically aims new shows more directly to the young adult (16–34 years) audience.

CBS budgets heavy promotional blitzes to give new programs many chances of being sampled by viewers. But when CBS recognizes program weaknesses, it pulls the slow starters off the air, replacing them with specials during salvage operations. During the 1970s, however, CBS made exceptions. *Simon & Simon* and *Dallas* became late successes, but *Square Pegs* failed, despite persistent network support. CBS also developed a reputation for moving strong new series around even more than the other two networks. Rescheduling of strong new series in new time slots combined with quick cancelations of weak series led to public relations problems for the network in the mid-1980s, eventually forcing the reinstatement of such cancelled series as *Cagney & Lacey* and *The Cavenaughs*. In 1987 CBS went so far as to apologize to fans for the frequent shifts of *Designing Women*.

In the mid-1970s and early 1980s, NBC had dozens of program failures. Unable to extend patience then, it yanked unproductive entries before they could endanger the overall ratings of a night. NBC hit bottom in 1978 and 1979, starting the 1978 season with only eight established series (compared to 18 for ABC and 15 for CBS). During the year, four more of NBC's eight series failed, while only five of its new series held on. But frantic schedule manipulation may, in fact, have increased rather than decreased NBC's ratings difficulties. Realizing it could no longer afford the luxury of quick cancelations at the first sign of weakness, NBC reversed this strategy in the 1980s, holding on to their almost-successful series. A program such as *Hill Street Blues* illustrates the strategy of leaving a show alone as long as possible to afford the maximum opportunity for audience exposure. It had a disappointing start during the 1980–81 season, but NBC had confidence that ratings would improve as the audience "discovered" the show. That confidence was rewarded in the next broadcast season when *Hill Street Blues* climbed slowly from an average rating of 13.3 to a respectable 18.4 (and an average share of 31) for the 1981–82 broadcast season. Encouraged by the success of this scheduling strategy, NBC further distanced itself from the other two networks in the mid-1980s by holding on to a high percentage of its low-rated new series, demonstrating a more patient style.

NBC also defied conventional programming wisdom by diversifying into program types that most experts (especially at the advertising agencies) claimed had only a limited appeal at best. For example, *The Cosby Show*'s producer first offered the show to ABC, which rejected it in the belief that the audience of the 1980s would reject traditional values embodied in light family comedies. NBC also took a chance with *Golden Girls*, even though experts said a young audience would reject a program starring older women. Similar moves toward program diversity can also be detected in series such as *ALF, Miami Vice, Amen* and *L.A. Law,* which helped make NBC the leader in programming innovations in the late 1980s.

Following NBC's lead, ABC also attempted its own diversification in the late 1980s with series such as *Moonlighting, Max Headroom, Sledge Hammer!* and *Dolly Parton,* capitalizing on an expected "yuppie" bias in the new people-meter ratings method.

The move toward program diversity should *not* be overrated. In most cases, seemingly innovative programs merely vary the established situation-comedy and crime-drama formats that dominate prime time. None of the networks expect to revive such once-popular formats as variety shows, science fiction or costume drama (except in specials). NBC, for example, cancelled *The Big Show,* a vaudeville variety series, *Bret Maverick,* a western, and *V* (a big-budget science fiction series) in spite of strong audience approval and good ratings. In a 1986 interview on *Entertainment Tonight,* former network programmer Fred Silverman suggested that revival of such offbeat formats were designed to fail as part of a strategy of offering expensive, unusual series to bring in new viewers; once people have grown used to tuning in, however, the network cancels the expensive series, replacing them with cheaper, more conventional series, assuming that many viewers will continue to watch out of habit.[9] Critical approval and the extraordinary promotional opportunity that public acclaim provides also figure in decisions to cancel or hold low-rated new programs.

Critical acclaim usually has some effect only in the absence of other rating successes. The kudos for *Hill Street Blues*, for example, bolstered NBC's image at a time when it was in sore need of prestige, persuading programmers to stick with the show even in the face of low ratings. That Grant Tinker was both head of NBC programming and producer of *Hill Street Blues* may also have been a contributing factor. Under Tinker's direction in 1982–83, slow starters such as *Mama's Family*, *Cheers* and *St. Elsewhere*, which might well have been cancelled during Fred Silverman's earlier NBC tenure, remained in the prime-time schedule.

Despite such exceptions, the industry depends almost totally on early ratings to determine a show's fate, because the major advertising agencies use these figures as the primary basis for buying network time. As of the late 1980s, a single rating point translated into an estimated 874,000 homes. Over the course of a year, this one point represents about $60 million in network pretax profits (if the point comes from one of its two broadcast competitors). Small wonder then that ratings rule the networks, public irritation with the process notwithstanding.

Risk and Competition

All three networks prowl for the breakthrough idea—the program that will be different but not so different as to turn away audiences. *The Cosby Show* was one such show during the 1984–85 season, as was *ALF* during 1986–87. Network programmers can only guess what the next hit will be and why it succeeds. A program failure is easier to analyze: It can result from the wrong time period, the wrong concept, the wrong writing, the wrong casting, poor execution of a good idea, poor execution of a bad idea, overwhelming competition, the wrong night of the week and a dozen other factors.

Playing it safe with formats known to satisfy audiences is a normal reaction on the part of network executives. Considering the high stakes involved, program executives naturally resist any program that can be described as a trailblazer. Those programmers who dare to depart from the formulas, however, may occasionally enjoy the fruits of such standout hits as *Moonlighting* or *M*A*S*H*. Indeed, the current rate of program failure suggests that the unusual might be less risky than sticking to copies of old series. But given the rapid turnover in network presidents and vice-presidents of programming during the 1980s, iron nerves are required to allow a really new idea to remain on the schedule long enough to attract a significant following.

The Fox Threat

A growing array of competitors offers first-run syndicated programs to broadcasters in the battle for prime-time audiences. One of these competitors has ambitions to become the fourth major commercial television network: **Fox Broadcasting Company (FBC)**. While other prime-time program suppliers such as Operation Prime Time (OPT) and Group W predated Fox, FBC introduced a new angle by adopting network scheduling strategies. Until Fox came

Figure 5-3 The Three Commercial Broadcast Networks and Fox, Which in 1987 Launched Its Campaign to Become the Fourth

along, most syndicators merely produced programs and sold them to stations who aired them as it suited each individual station. (OPT, for example, was unable to compel simultaneous airing of its shows.) In 1987, Fox offered a complete program lineup for Sunday nights in competition with the three major networks' programs. Stations wanting the Fox programs had to agree to show them in order at the exact times Fox specified, thus providing the kind of nationwide stability in scheduling and promotion that prime-time syndication had previously lacked. Fox also expected to allow each series a full year to build an audience and to continue to supply original series episodes from September until July, long after ABC, CBS and NBC begin reruns. Fox slowly expanded its lineup to other nights of the week and to the late-night hours. Its occasional successes may inspire other television syndicators to adopt *uniform scheduling strategies,* thus duplicating one of the major advantages hitherto held exclusively by the three major broadcast networks.

CHANGING FORMAT EMPHASES

The late 1970s saw several major changes in the kinds of **formats** dominating prime time. One was the increased use of **specials**—a term encompassing one-time entertainment programs, sporting events, docudramas and

documentaries. Other changes included increased use of book adaptations, foreign television series and spinoffs or clones of existing series.

Specials

Although the situation comedy and crime dramas remain the mainstays of nighttime series schedules, other popular formats have won audience affections. In 1953 Mary Martin and Ethel Merman, luminaries of the Broadway stage, made television history when they joined in a song festival that enchanted their audience on *Ford's 50th Anniversary Show*. The setting consisted of a plain backdrop, and the only props were two bookkeeper stools. It was straight, delightful entertainment for 90 minutes and remains one of the medium's highlights—a breakthrough. This program was the first *special*.

Of the approximately 700 specials a year since that time, more than 500 have been *entertainment specials* for adults (live, film, or tape) or children, such as the Charlie Brown Christmas specials. About 100 each year are *sports specials*, including the Super Bowl and World Series games. The remaining 100 divide among *magazines* (including interviews such as those by Barbara Walters), *docudramas* and *documentaries*.

Entertainment specials often attract superstars (such as Dustin Hoffman and Katharine Hepburn) whose regular motion picture work or performing schedule (or health) prevents them from participating in series programs. Star-studded specials can invigorate a schedule, encourage major advertiser participation, provide unusual promotion opportunities and generate high ratings and critical approval.

Because of their popularity, the number of specials steadily increased each season, peaking at the end of the 1970s with the beginning of the economic recession. In the 1980s, specials changed format: Increasingly they became *long-form episodes of regularly scheduled series*, presented in their usual time slot. For example, the record-breaking final episode of *M*A*S*H* (77 share) was an extended episode of the existing series. Since 1983, one-fifth of the 500 or so entertainment specials each year were in fact long-form episodes of regularly scheduled series. Network programmers had awakened to the possibility that too many specials differing sharply from the regular programming might interrupt carefully nurtured viewing habits beyond repair—hence, the trend toward long-form episodes of regularly scheduled series. Such shows also have the advantage of being relatively inexpensive to produce.

Variety Programs

Variety shows were a mainstay of prime-time television from the 1950s through the early 1970s. Network programmers divided the genre into three subformats: (1) **vaudeville** shows, such as *Ed Sullivan* or *The Big Show*, built around a host introducing unrelated acts—ranging from animal acts to grand opera arias; (2) **comedy variety** shows, such as *Carol Burnett* and *Red Skelton*, built around a single comedian in a series of comic skits, perhaps with some music added; and (3) **musical variety** shows, such as *The Kraft Music Hall* and *Perry Como*, built around a musical star, with music or dance numbers and a little comedy for contrast.

Variety series had a much higher failure rate than most other program genres, but once a variety series captured an audience, it tended to hold it much longer than did other program formats. The normal wear-out cycle did not seem to apply. As a result, by 1971 nearly all variety series on network television had lasted at least ten years. All of these series, except for *Carol Burnett*, disappeared in 1971 as part of the networks' "demographic cancelations." Subsequently, each of the major networks reintroduced youth-oriented variety shows, typified by *Sonny and Cher*, *Donny and Marie* and *Barbara Mandrell and the Mandrell Sisters*. Some of these series started out with high ratings, but they lacked the staying power of the traditional variety formats and, by the late 1970s, all variety series had vanished from network prime time. Their disappearance may have resulted as much from high costs as from low ratings. Several variety shows aired since 1971, such as *The Big Show*, did well in ratings but were cancelled anyway. Between 1980 and 1988, the networks attempted only two new variety series, *The Steve Allen Show* and *Dolly Parton*. *Steve Allen* lasted only two episodes, and *Dolly Parton* sits in the cellar of the ratings. The variety format has only been successful in recent years as an occasional special on the broadcast networks.

Prime-Time Sports

During the 1950s and 1960s, boxing, roller derby, professional wrestling, football and basketball filled major chunks of the prime-time schedule. In the mid-1960s, however, the networks phased out most sports, concluding that costs were too high for the limited appeal in prime time. As a result, sports on CBS and NBC were relegated to the weekends and specials. Nowadays, **network prime-time sports** consists of ABC's *Monday Night Football* (and lower-rated baseball), occasional basketball games on CBS and NBC and special events such as playoff games, the Olympics, or network-created specials like the *Iron Man Competition*, *Battle of the Network Stars* or *Main Event* wrestling.

ABC, however, placed great emphasis on sports specials in prime time and successfully scheduled football and baseball games at night. From the mid-1960s through the 1970s, ABC led in sports programming, controlling the television rights to most major sporting events in the United States, and is credited with generating the huge popularity of the Super Bowl and Super Sunday.

By the mid-1970s, CBS and NBC were attempting to outbid ABC for the most profitable sporting events. Rivalry for NFL football, college bowls, NBA basketball and Olympics resulted in bidding wars that escalated the prices for sports television rights to previously unimagined heights. *Monday Night Football*, for example, went from a per-game fee of about $700,000 in 1977–78 to about $2,500,000 per game in 1986–87. The cost for special sporting events increased even more dramatically. The network acquiring exclusive rights to the 1988 Summer Olympics in Seoul, Korea (NBC) paid more than a half-billion dollars when all expenses were considered. Such costs cannot be fully recovered from within-program advertising sales, but the prestige and promotional value that attach to airing the Olympics and the benefits to affiliates in local ad sales drive the networks to seek such special events (see Chapter 6 on sports).

Extraordinarily high costs in the mid- and late 1980s, accompanied by ratings disasters such as Ted Turner's 1987 Goodwill Games, and increased competition from cable services for sports rights, made the broadcast networks reluctant to continue competing among themselves for sports programming, and they cast about for alternatives. One response was to eliminate some competition by agreeing to produce one unified network offer for some large events (such as future Olympics) and to schedule them on each network on a rotating basis. Whether this type of pool agreement would be viewed as legal or even practical remains to be seen. But the broadcast networks must continue to compete for the very top U.S. sporting events—the Super Bowls and World Series—because the public relations losses from letting cable services capture them would outweigh most direct cost considerations.

Magazines, Docudramas and Documentaries

The unexpected ratings success of the **magazine-format series** *60 Minutes* starting in the late 1970s led ABC and NBC to imitate it with *20/20* and *Prime Time Saturday,* starting in 1979. The success of all three of these programs encouraged the development of other nonfiction forms for prime time, such as *Real People* (1979), *That's Incredible* (1980), *Amazing Animals* (1980), *Believe It or Not* (1982), *Monitor* (1983), *West 57th* (1985), *Our World* (1986) and *48 Hours* (1988). While the more recent news/information magazine series generally win high praise from media critics, few have been ratings successes. But they cost less than half the average entertainment series, so the networks continue to try new information/public affairs shows, hoping for another *20/20* or *60 Minutes*.

Our World is a case in point. At $450,000 per hour-long episode, the series was well below the average in 1986; it won critical acclaim and made money for the network, even though usually last in the ratings. ABC intended to renew it in 1987, only to find its affiliates, who did not share in the network's profit, refusing to clear the time without better ratings. Unable to improve the show's ratings sufficiently, ABC ultimately cancelled *Our World*. CBS introduced *48 Hours* in 1988 to showcase anchor Dan Rather and bolster the sagging morale of its news department following massive staff layoffs in 1987. Clearance by its affiliates remained problematic as the ratings stayed low. Information formats, however, generate favorable publicity and easy profit for the networks, suggesting that they will remain among new prime-time offerings, even if most are quickly cancelled.

The **docudrama,** a dramatized version of historical fact, became popular in the 1970s. *Washington: Behind Closed Doors* (based on Watergate events), *Missiles of October* and *Roots* are perhaps the best known of the 1970s docudramas. In the 1980s, docudramas included *At Mother's Request* and *Nutcracker: Money, Madness, Murder* (both based on the same famous modern murder case), *Escape from Sobibor* (based on a 1943 Nazi death camp escape), *George Washington* and *Huey Long*. These docudramas tend to play fast and loose with the facts, leading to some criticism, but generally high ratings indicate that the docudrama will remain a popular format with networks.

Less noticed by the critics but steadily rising in popularity in the 1970s were long-form **documentaries.** Out of 809 specials broadcast in the 1978–79 season, 93 were documentaries, many of which did remarkably well in prime time. On ABC on March 4, 1979, *The Ordeal of Patty Hearst* gained a 34 share. NBC received a 30 share for *The Sea Gypsies* on January 7, 1979, and in 1982, ABC's *Ronald Reagan: At Home on the Ranch,* a "personality documentary," also got a 30 share. In 1983, the highest-rated documentary—*Vietnam: A Television History*—appeared on PBS rather than commercial television and in 1986, PBS again garnered high ratings and critical praise with its $9\frac{1}{2}$-hour documentary, *The Holocaust.* The success of these programs in prime time exploded the myth that public affairs programs are necessarily ratings losers.

Adaptations

The networks often adapt successful theatrical motion pictures into series formats. Perhaps the foremost example is *M*A*S*H,* derived from a feature picture by 20th Century–Fox. Many adaptations use only the feature title on the assumption that it alone will attract audiences. Frequently, the adaptation waters down the original film's story to make it more palatable to television audiences. From feature film hits came series like *Mr. Deeds Goes to Town, Blondie, Peyton Place, Hondo, Tarzan, Daktari, Twelve O'Clock High, Shane, Mr. Roberts, Dr. Kildare, Seven Brides for Seven Brothers* and *Down and Out in Beverly Hills.* Few of these mutations ever enjoyed real success.

Several British television series, however, have been successfully rewritten for American commercial television. Such **adaptations** include the hits *All in the Family* and *Three's Company,* two failed 1983 series (*Foot in the Door* and *Amanda's Place*), and the faddish, short-lived 1987 series, *Max Headroom.*

Spinoffs and Clones

Certain supporting characters in a series often become so popular they justify a **spinoff** program—a new series typically using the same actors in the same roles in another setting. This practice makes stars of supporting players who demonstrate a potential to carry their own shows. TvQs, the ratings that measure a performer's likability and recognizability, give programmers clues to the most promising candidates for spinoffs. Strong performers in lesser roles led to such spinoff series as *Maude, Rhoda, The Jeffersons, Mork & Mindy, After MASH* and *Benson.*

As much as 10 percent of prime-time entertainment in 1979 consisted of spinoffs from situation comedies or adventure/dramas. Because the original writers and directors generally also handle a spinoff series, they can continue their successful teamwork. They bring an experienced production staff from the parent program to support the new series, people familiar with the stars' personalities and the characters they play. Fresh program ideas, on the other hand, typically involve new combinations of producers, directors, writers, technical staff and actors, requiring lengthy adjustment periods. But the overriding advantages of spinoffs is the ready-made audience they bring from the parent program. Well-known characters such as Shirley and Laverne brought personal followings to their spinoff series from *Happy Days,* just as Lou Grant brought a following from the *Mary Tyler Moore Show* (though from any other perspective, his two series had very little in common). A spinoff succeeds best when it begins its run while the parent program is still in the schedule. Delay in getting a spinoff off the ground can ruin its chances for success.

A **clone** is a related idea. It copies an existing program, but generally on a competing network. Whereas a spinoff uses the same characters, a clone uses new characters in a plot and setting that closely resemble aspects of the original program. For example, inspired by CBS's success with *Dallas,* ABC cloned *Dynasty,* and when it too succeeded (after evolving in its own direction), NBC cloned *The Beringers,* which did not succeed. More recently, several clones of *The Cosby Show* have come (and gone).

MOVIES

Three types of productions regarded as movies fill prime time on the broadcast television networks: (1) **theatrical feature films,** those made originally for release in theaters; (2) **made-for-TV movies,** similar to feature films but made specifically for network television airing (containing commercial breaks); and (3) **miniseries,** multipart films made especially for broadcast airing in several installments. All three types share three major advantages for the networks: They fill large amounts of time with material that usually generates high ratings; they make it possible to air topical or controversial material deemed inappropriate for regularly scheduled network series; and they permit the showcasing of actors and actresses who would otherwise never be seen on television. The popularity of superstars such as Tom Cruise, Robert Redford and Molly Ringwald can be tapped by casting them in movies. Like many other stars who would never agree to star in a TV series, they are happy to be showcased in a miniseries or made-for-TV movie.

The three kinds of movies also share one major disadvantage—exceptionally high cost for the networks. Miniseries are typically the most expensive, and theatrical movies the second-most costly; both are more risky in ratings than made-for-TV movies, but all three remain widely popular.

Theatrical Movies

The **theatrical film** or motion picture has been a mainstay of prime-time programming since the mid-1960s, but cutbacks in Hollywood production during the late 1960s and early 1970s caused severe shortages of features. At that time, many critics predicted a phase-out of theatrical films in television prime time. The 1980s, however, saw a revitalization of Hollywood filmmaking. In 1980 only 120 theatrical motion pictures were made, but by 1985 the number rose to 320, reflecting four fundamental changes in the motion picture business: changes in *release dates, sequels,* expanded *content targeting* and *release cycles.*

1. *Release Dates.* Instead of the traditional head-to-head summer/winter release schedule, in the 1980s Hollywood studios began juggling release dates, providing a continuous flow of new films into the market (thereby lessening the effects of strong competition on other movies). For example, *Beverly Hills Cop 2, Harry and the Hendersons, Roxanne, Space Balls* and *Dragnet,* all major comedies produced for an early 1987 summer release, would, in the old days, have all been released at the same time, causing the inevitable box-office casualties. The new strategy separated their release by a few weeks, allowing each movie to dominate entertainment news during its initial week, a factor crucial to theater owners.

2. *Sequels.* During the last decade, Hollywood also began investing heavily in sequels such as *Superman II–IV, Star Trek II–V, Rocky II–IV, Karate Kid II & III* and so on. Such sequels benefit from built-in audience interest and involvement with the characters, as well as self-perpetuating promotion and reduced production costs.

3. *Expanded Content Targeting.* In spite of endless complaints about the quality of movies today, a comparison of the film subject matter in the 1950s and 1960s with that of the 1980s reveals much greater diversity in film topics today. By mid-decade, motion picture subjects ranged from sex films like *Bolero* to mad-slasher films like the *Friday the 13th* series to propaganda films like *Red Dawn.* At the same time, Hollywood thrived on big budget action/adventures like *Top Gun,* melodramas like *Platoon,* sophisticated comedies like *Hannah and Her Sisters,* science fiction like *Inner Space,* slapstick comedies like *Dragnet* and even innovative children's features like *Benji the Hunted* and *He Man.* Instead of narrow targeting to teenage moviegoers, the producers began designing films appealing to a broad audience base (12–44 years). This change made more of feature film output useful to the television networks.

4. *Release Cycles.* Perhaps most important of all, theatrical motion picture producers shifted to a new sales structure in the 1980s, allowing them to expand their financial base. During the 1960s, the average theatrical movie had a four-stage sales structure: first, release to the theaters, then removal to storage; about two years after the first release, an offer to the broadcast networks; after first run, individual sales to affiliated stations; finally, sale to independent stations, usually to become part of their permanent libraries. Considering that seven of ten theatrical movies lose money at the box office, this traditional sales structure yielded too little profit to justify expanding movie production.

By the 1980s, however, this structure had been transformed. Movies continue to be released first to **theaters**, but when box-office receipts begin to fall off (often in a couple of weeks), a movie is usually shelved for several months, then rereleased for a second theatrical run. In the meantime, it may have appeared on **pay-per-view** television. About six months after the final theatrical release, movies now appear in the **videocassette** market, first primarily for rental (at a high price), then several months later at a much lower price for sale to collectors. At about the time videocassette movies go down in price, they are licensed to the **pay-cable networks.** After a pay-cable run, they are offered to the **broadcast networks**; then, after a couple of years, they become available to **affiliates** and **independent** stations. **Foreign release** also expanded in the 1980s, allowing American films to draw in huge sums from foreign markets. Agreements among producers and distributors, primarily with England and Australia, for wider distribution of foreign-made films in the American market also increased movie competition—to the advantage of television programmers.

This multipart release pattern may shift again in the 1990s, however, as advertisers seek to get into the game. The videocassette of the 1986 feature film *Top Gun* contained a built-in Pepsi commercial. This addition permitted an unusually low initial price for the cassette. In spite of the commercial, *Top Gun* enjoyed the largest sale by a cassette up to that time. This success story may open up a new arena for advertisers, signaling an end to the initial high price for cassettes. The addition of commercial advertising to videocassettes, even at the start (no interruption of the film), might cancel part of their advantages over broadcast movies.

Motion pictures pose other problems for the broadcast networks. Their popularity on network television is unpredictable. *Star Wars*, for example, got lower ratings than a competing made-for-TV movie. Also, many theatrical films contain violence or sexual content that must be removed before broadcast television airing. Several scenes had to be shortened and lines redubbed before *Risky Business* met network continuity standards for prime-time broadcast. Such editing often destroys the flow of a film and may anger viewers. The theatrical film, even if it became available in unlimited supply, would not be a panacea for the shortage of network programming.

Made-for-TV Movies

Many viewers and critics bewail the disappearance of the **dramatic anthology** format, sets of single-episode television plays presented in an unconnected series. But in reality, the anthology format went through a style change in the late 1960s and returned as the **made-for-TV movie**. During the 1955–56 season, the very peak of the anthology era, dramatic anthologies made up about 526 hours of prime time. By 1981–82 made-for-TV films surpassed that total. The best of these movies compare favorably with the best of the dramatic anthologies of the earlier era. For example, *Marty* and *Requiem for a Heavyweight* were classic plays in anthologies, while *Bitter Harvest* and *Unnatural Causes* were made-for-TV movies of the same caliber, filling the equivalent role in programming fare.

In the later 1970s, the made-for-TV movie replaced the pilot as the major method for testing out new series ideas. Programs such as *T.J. Hooker* and *Seven Brides for Seven Brothers* succeeded as television movies before becoming series. Such pilots pay their way whether or not the concept ever becomes a series. And even when such a series later fails, the networks usually have made a healthy profit on the made-for-TV movie's initial run and on the normal advertising revenues from the run of the weekly series. Moreover, the made-for-TV movie has the advantage of being made-to-order to fit within a network's existing schedule. It can target a specific audience to maintain a night's flow and avoid the disruptions that theatrical movies often cause.

As a result, the made-for-TV movie-pilot has become very popular with networks and, fortuitously, with audiences. The ratings for some of these films equal and even surpass those for feature films shown on television. Of the top ten movies shown on network television during 1986–87, for example, all ten were made-for-TV movies. Such movies often command high ratings in syndication and sell well as videocassettes. Many have been sold as theatrical films in foreign markets. This flexibility, their popularity, their precise targeting and revenue advantages over regular videotape pilots, and the fact that the average made-for-TV movies cost about half what an average Hollywood theatrical movie costs, have established this format firmly in the economics of network television. In 1987 made-for-TV movies shown on network television outnumbered theatrical feature films by 268 to 216. CBS, which traditionally developed more movies than its competitors (50 in 1987–88), reduced its commitment for 1988–89 because television movies began costing nearly a million dollars an hour, more than one-hour series.

Miniseries

The success of specials and limited series on PBS's *Masterpiece Theatre* led the commercial networks into the production of multipart series presented in three to six episodes on successive nights or in successive weeks. Called **miniseries,** they ran for as long as ten or more hours. The best known of recent miniseries include *Holocaust, Shogun, The Blue and the Gray, Centennial, The Thorn Birds, North & South* and *Fresno.* In 1983 ABC presented *Winds of War,* a miniseries seen on six successive nights during the February sweeps for a total of 18 hours. *Winds of War* cost $38 million for production plus an estimated $25 million for promotion. The show, however, captured half of the total viewing audience (53 share). ABC sold all of its commercial spots at $350,000 a minute, earning the network revenues in excess of $30 million for the one showing.

Miniseries typically begin and end on Sunday nights, the night of maximum viewing. Shorter miniseries tend to be scheduled on sequential nights while longer series, such as *Winds of War,* stretch over two weeks, skipping the evenings on which the network has its most popular programs. Because of their exceedingly high cost, miniseries are usually only created for sweeps periods.

Both *Roots* (1975) and *The Thorn Birds* (1983) were produced at enormous cost and both gained unusually large audiences and high revenue. *The Thorn Birds,* for example, averaged a 41 rating and an extraordinary 59 share, making it the second-highest rated miniseries, just behind *Roots* (average 66 share over eight consecutive nights). Aside from winning high ratings and beating the competition, the networks derived considerable prestige and critical acclaim from these programs, which helped to justify the heavy investment. Some miniseries, such as *Rich Man, Poor Man* and *How the West Was Won,* have been turned into regular series, further reducing the financial risk involved.

By the 1980s the costs for **long-form miniseries** (10 hours or more) had skyrocketed to the point that the 30-hour *War and Remembrance* was estimated to cost over $100 million. At the same time, ratings for such long-form series dropped sharply. *Hollywood Wives, A.D., Robert Kennedy and His Times, Peter the Great* and *Amerika* all performed below network expectations, losing tens of millions of dollars without bolstering the network's overall ratings position. As a result, in the late 1980s the networks had switched from long-form to short-form miniseries (4 to 6 hours). Shorter series reduced the networks' financial risks and limited the damage that failures could cause to the overall ratings. However, networks value the prestige that comes from successful long-form miniseries such as *North & South* and *Love and War*, and when planning the next year's special schedule, some concepts always sound like winners. Consequently, though the long form may be limited to one or two projects a season, both short-form and long-form miniseries are here to stay.

THE CENSORS

The broadcast **Standards and Practices Department,** a behind-the-scenes group, exercises total authority over all network programming. Cynically and often angrily called "censors," this department at each network has absolute approval rights over every program—whether a single episode of a half-hour series, a two-hour special, a miniseries or a movie. The department acts as policeman and judge for all questions concerning acceptability of material for broadcast. It often finds itself walking a thin line between offending viewers or advertisers and destroying imaginative programming that may pull in high ratings. It decides between the imaginative and the objectionable. Members of the department read submitted scripts, attend every rehearsal, filming or taping, and often preview the final products before they are aired. If, in the department's judgment, a program fails to conform to network standards in matters of language or taste, it can insist on changes. Only appeal to the chairman or president of the company can overturn its decisions.

Over the years, the department's criteria for acceptability have changed. In the early 1920s one of the hottest issues was whether such a personal and perhaps obscene product as toothpaste should be allowed to advertise over the radio airwaves. By 1983 the hottest question was whether or not NBC's censors would permit a new series, *Bay City Blues,* to air a locker room scene that included nude men photographed, as the producer put it, "tastefully from the back." By the mid-1980s, child abuse, abortion and homosexuality were the problematic topics, while the late 1980s brought the thorny questions of AIDS, condoms and, as always, how explicitly sex could be shown.

The Standards and Practices Department decides acceptability on a show-by-show basis. While decisions may seem arbitrary, the censors normally follow certain guidelines. For example, a program's perceived audience is an important factor. A show appealing to children (or scheduled before 9 P.M.) will be regulated much more heavily than one aimed at adults and scheduled later. The program's daypart is also a major consideration. Traditionally, the censors have been much easier on series run during the morning or early afternoon (most notably, the soap operas) than on programs run during prime time. Also, censors tend to be more liberal with specials, miniseries and made-for-TV movies than with regular weekly series.

A network's implied position regarding controversial material, however, is the most important factor. During the 1980s, CBS tended to be the most conservative of the three networks, particularly regarding sexual content, while NBC was the most liberal. For instance, during the early 1980s, CBS censors reviewing scenes from *Capitol* came to the conclusion that a man in briefs was not acceptable while the same man in boxer shorts was. At about the same time, NBC's department cleared *Honeyboy,* a made-for-TV movie having scenes in which the star appeared clad only in bikini briefs. It also permitted a prime-time series called *The Shape of Things* to feature male strippers. By 1987 CBS was willing to allow *Cagney & Lacey* to do an episode encouraging the use of condoms but did not allow the use of "the word" on the air and did not consider paid ads for condoms acceptable.

During the mid-1980s, broadcast standards and practices departments increasingly found themselves fighting organized audience objections to what some perceived as an overly permissive network attitude toward sex. Indeed, content analyses of TV programs showed that the sexual intercourse mentioned on television occurred mostly outside of marriage as a result of one-night stands, and that abstinence was depicted either as a physical impossibility or a sign of mental illness. Gay liberationists, feminists, religious fundamentalists and other groups denounced this portrayal of sex without love or consequences. The networks' future battles over moral standards may be with viewers rather than with producers.

SUMMARY

Network prime-time television programming remains a high-risk undertaking. Large amounts of money, prestige and public interest are at stake. For all of their dollars, their care, their studies, their testing, their research, their meetings, their professionalism and their strategies, the networks' high hopes for most new programs are repeatedly dashed in a matter of weeks each new season. Cancelation often irritates audiences, but networks point to inadequate ratings (translating into inadequate profits) and swing the ax anyway. On the other hand, the networks also ensure low ratings for some programs by scheduling them against runaway hits or established series or by excessive churn (time shifts). Nine factors affect a proposed program's selection from among the hundreds of concepts, scripts and pilots. Among them, resemblance to past successes weighs more than originality; costs weigh more than the talent's appeal; competitiveness weighs more than compatibility. Scheduling strategies such as leading off with a strong program, hammocking, blocking, tent-poling and stunting are intended to bolster newcomers and create audience flow within a single network's prime-time schedule, whereas counterprogramming's goal is to interrupt flow to attract the competitors' audiences. Although annual program introductions shifted from all-in-the-fall to a two-season and then to a continuous-season sequence, program formulas remain much the same from year to year (in the 1980s) and from network to network. The only major prime-time programming innovation has been the miniseries. The dramatic anthology was revived as the made-for-TV movie. But the variety that once characterized prime time has disappeared. Three formats—sitcoms, crime series and movies—dominate the schedule. Network prime-time programming uses conservative strategies because of the enormous risks to individuals and revenues. Continuing audience defections and mounting program failure rates suggest that viewers are hungry for modest amounts of originality and for scheduling stability. Scheduling practices based largely on mass audience complacency, habitual viewing or repeating what works for another network may be outmoded in a television environment of VCRs and dozens of cable channels. Audience targeting and viewer satisfaction may become the keys to future nationwide broadcasting.

Notes

1. Paul Klein, "Programming" in Steve Morgenstern, ed., *Inside the TV Business* (New York: Sterling, 1979), pp. 11–36.

2. William J. Adams, Susan Tyler Eastman, Larry J. Horney, and Mark N. Popovich, "The Cancelation and Manipulation of Network Television Prime-Time Programs," *Journal of Communication* 33, Winter 1983, pp. 10–27.

3. Jerry Krupnick (syndicated columnist for Newhouse News Service), *Los Angeles Times*, Spring 1979.

4. David Poltrack, "New Technologies, Audience Behavior and Changing Network Audiences," paper presented at the Broadcast Education Association convention, Dallas, Texas, 12 April 1986.

5. William J. Adams, "Patterns in Prime-Time Network Television Programs from 1948 to 1986: The Influences of Variety, Churn and Content, with Models for Predicting Nightly Ratings" (Ph.D. diss., Indiana University, 1988).

6. F. W. Winter, "Match Target Markets to Media Audiences," *Journal of Advertising Research* 20(1), February 1980, pp. 61–66; A. Mitchell, *Social Change: Implications of Trends in Values and Lifestyles*, Menlo Park, Calif.: SRI International, January 1979; "A New Way to View Consumers," *Dun's Review*, August 1981, pp. 42–45; William Meyers, "What's New in Consumer Research: Of Belongers, Achievers, Survivors et al.," *The New York Times*, 5 December 1982, pp. 3–29.

7. "The Daydream Machine: A Survey of Television, All by Numbers," *The Economist*, 20 December 1986, pp. 72–79.

8. Les Brown, "'Stacking' the Schedule Put NBC-TV in Top Spot," *New York Times*, 27 September 1979, p. C19.

9. Fred Silverman, "Discussions of the New Season," interview on *Entertainment Tonight*, 13 September 1986.

Selected Sources

Bedell, Sally. *Up the Tube: Prime-Time TV and the Silverman Years*. New York: Viking Press, 1981.

Blum, Richard A., and Lindheim, Richard D. *Primetime: Network Television Programming*. Boston: Focal Press, 1987.

Cantor, Muriel G. *Prime-Time Television: Content and Control*. Beverly Hills, California: Sage Publications, 1980.

Levinson, Richard, and Link, William. *Stay Tuned: An Inside Look at the Making of Prime-Time Television*. New York: St. Martin's Press, 1981.

Newcomb, Horace, and Alley, Robert S. *The Producer's Medium: Conversations with Creators of American T.V.* New York: Oxford University Press, 1983.

Reel, A. Frank. *The Networks: How They Stole the Show*. New York: Charles Scribner's Sons, 1979.

Variety. Weekly trade newspaper of the television and film industry.

CHAPTER 6 NONPRIME-TIME NETWORK PROGRAMMING

Squire D. Rushnell
Mitchell E. Shapiro

A Guide to Chapter 6

Squire D. Rushnell, vice-president of long-range planning and children's television for ABC Entertainment, has been responsible for all of ABC's children's programming since 1974 and was in charge of *Good Morning America* during its climb to the number one position in its time period—1978 to 1981. Mr. Rushnell is widely recognized for his achievements with the multi-award-winning ABC *Afterschool Specials* series and *Schoolhouse Rock.* He has led ABC's long-range planning division since 1982. He started by serving in various management and program-producer positions with Group W Broadcasting after attending Syracuse University; then in 1969 he joined WLS-TV, the ABC-owned station in Chicago, as an executive producer and assistant program manager, later becoming program manager. Subsequently, he became vice-president of programming for the ABC-owned television stations before moving to the network headquarters.

Mitchell E. Shapiro, associate professor in the School of Communication at the University of Miami, Florida, has coordinated the school's telecommunication and broadcast journalism programs since 1982. Prior to that time, he was an assistant professor at Illinois State University. He earned a B.A. from the University of Miami, and an M.S. and Ph.D. from Florida State University. He regularly consults for television stations and teaches courses in programming and audience measurement and analysis. In addition, he has published articles dealing with programming in scholarly journals and presented papers at professional association meetings. In this chapter, the authors explain the development of ratings winners in each daypart and delineate the constraints operating on different types of nonprime-time programs at the network level.

NONPRIME-TIME NETWORK DAYPARTS

For the broadcast television networks, **nonprime time** generally describes *entertainment* programming in every daypart other than prime time excepting *news* and *sports,* which are handled by separate divisions at all three networks. Specifically, the three commercial networks program the following entertainment **dayparts** (compare to the corresponding list from the affiliates' perspective in Chapter 7, which differs slightly):

late-late night and early-early morning	1 A.M. to 7 A.M.
early morning	7 A.M. to 9 A.M.
daytime	10 A.M. to 4 P.M.
children's	Saturday and Sunday mornings
late night	11:30 P.M. to 1 A.M.

In addition, this chapter examines the state of the evening network *newscasts* and discusses the selection, scheduling and evaluation of *weekend* network programming. Although the audience level in any of the nonprime dayparts is considerably lower than in prime time, each contributes competitively, economically and in terms of prestige to a healthy network performance. Moreover, the network program executives in charge of weekday and weekend dayparts are just as dedicated to competing for available viewers as their prime-time counterparts. Everything is relative: A 4 rating can spell victory for an early-morning weekday program, but in daytime or on Saturday morning, an 8 rating represents success. Compare that to prime time: A program executive generally feels secure only with 17 or more rating points.

Clearances

Another difference between prime-time and nonprime-time programming is the considerable variance in **clearances.** When a network makes a new series available or decides to make a change in the scheduling of an existing series, an affiliated station has three options: clearing the series, not clearing the series or asking permission to air the series at a later time.

If an affiliate agrees to *clear a series,* it commits itself to carry the program in the time period that the network specifies. On the other hand, an affiliate may decide, for a variety of reasons, that it does not want to carry a specific network offering, and so it does not clear its schedule. The decision to clear or not clear a network offering usually must be made within *two weeks* (or a minimum of 72 hours for certain programs). **Preemption** occurs when an affiliate decides not to carry a specific episode in a series that has already been cleared.

An affiliate might want to carry a particular network offering but, because of prior commitments, have a full schedule and be unable to air the program in the specified time period. When this occurs, the affiliate can request permission to carry the series in a later time period. While this option erodes the size and changes the nature of the national audience for the series, the network usually prefers **delayed carriage** to **nonclearance.**

Most affiliates clear about 90 percent of their network's total schedule. Nonclearance of any show in only three or four of the top 20 markets, however, significantly lowers the show's average in the national Nielsen ratings. Unfortunately for network nonprime-time programmers, affiliates refuse to clear nonprime-time much more often than they refuse to clear prime-time programs, making clearances a major variable in national nonprime-time ratings. For example, all three networks stopped offering programming from 4:00 to 4:30 P.M. on Monday through Friday because large numbers of affiliates refused to clear their network offerings in that time period.

Parity

The three broadcast television networks constantly struggle for **parity,** a perfect match among themselves as to numbers of affiliates and total audience reached. Achieving parity is complicated by the fact that the three networks each have slightly different numbers of affiliates. The total number of affiliates is not the only measure, however, for affiliates within the same market differ as to audience potential. The number-one station usually commands larger viewership across the board. Moreover, some small markets have only one or two stations, which then have multiple affiliations. Ideally, a network seeks affiliation with the top-ranked station in each major market and assurance that the station will clear its programs.

The long-standing ratings war between *Today* and *Good Morning America* exemplifies the twin influences of clearances and number of affiliates: In 1975, ABC had only 183 primary affiliates, compared with 218 for NBC and 212 for CBS. But by 1983 ABC had 210 affiliates clearing *Good Morning America,* while about the same number (209) cleared NBC's *Today* and *The CBS Morning News.* An increase to about the same number of affiliates probably led to ABC's early-morning success in the 1980s; a loss of affiliates was a factor in NBC's ratings weaknesses in the same period. As of 1988 all three networks had audience parity in most time periods.

Demographics and Advertisers

Notwithstanding the effects of clearances and numbers of affiliates, programming strategies for different segments of the day do not vary greatly from network to network. For each daypart, the networks give primary consideration to the *demographics* of available audiences, *competitive counterprogramming* and *economic viability*. A network determines which segment of the available audience it will target, mindful of its competitors' programming and influenced in some degree by advertiser support for its programming.

The network programming executive's task is to put together a schedule of programs that will, at the lowest possible cost, (1) capture the largest possible audience, (2) attract the most desirable demographic groups, (3) maximize audience flow-through and (4) build viewer loyalty. In general, the audiences for nonprime-time dayparts are more *homogeneous* than the audience for prime time. In consequence, networks often schedule the same program types head-to-head, creating fierce internetwork competition.

Although advertising cannot be dismissed as an unimportant aspect of television programming, it should not be construed as the primary concern of television programmers. Network executives assert there is little direct association between what happens in any given network program and the advertiser. Rarely, if ever, does a direct line of influence exist between an advertiser and people or policies of network programming. Networks are similar to newspapers in this regard. Editorial departments and advertising departments tend to operate independently of each other.

One network program executive, when asked about advertising influence, said, "My job as a programmer is to spend as much money as I can get away with to attract the largest possible audiences and do programs which make us proud. Whether my company makes a million more or a million less is the responsibility of another department entirely." Of course, if the program executive failed to attract the largest possible audience, the sales department would find the programs less attractive to advertisers, and his employment would, in consequence, be jeopardized.

Moreover, indirect influences on programming practices can be as effective as direct ones. Most producers know better than to propose scripts that deal with subjects such as tampering with painkillers or rat hairs in cereal, since daytime television is largely underwritten by drug and food companies.

EARLY NEWS AND TALK

Late-late night and early-early morning, consisting of the hours from 1 A.M. to 7 A.M., have tiny audiences; homes-using-television (HUT levels) range from 3 to 5 percent of total television households. For this reason, broadcasters once tended to neglect these time periods. But the increasing competitiveness of the 1980s awoke interest in the revenue potential of these hours. For the most part, the networks have turned to their **news** departments to fill them. News is *first-run* programming of growing interest to audiences; it can be produced at low cost because overhead is low and the network can air leftover tapes and stories not used in previous newscasts.

Early-Early Morning

On the same July day in 1982, ABC premiered *ABC World News This Morning* and NBC premiered *Early Today*. A few months later, CBS joined the early-early crowd with the *CBS Early Morning News*. All three programs, scheduled Monday through Friday from 6 to 7 A.M., served as lead-ins to the national early-morning programs. The networks hoped to bolster sagging 7 A.M. ratings by getting flow-through from the preceding programs.

ABC World News This Morning, an early-early one-hour newscast, emphasizes hard news. Although relatively small, the 6 to 7 A.M. adult audience is predominantly male and professional people. Because little domestic news occurs during the night, the program draws heavily on stories from overseas. The anchor of this program crosses over to *Good Morning America* to read the news segments. By 6:15 in the morning, ratings shares run about 1.4/13 for ABC, a very slight favorite before 6:30 A.M.

In 1987, CBS's *Morning News* was moved back to 6 A.M. and expanded to 90 minutes, then cut back to 60 minutes as *CBS This Morning* took hold at 7 A.M. Like *ABC World News This Morning*, the CBS program emphasizes hard news and focuses on capturing the predominantly male audience at this time of day. At 6:30 in the morning, CBS's ratings run about 1.4/12.

NBC's *Early Today* combined news and interviews in two half-hour packages, hosted by the *Today Show* personalities. However, within a year, its pattern of low ratings and low clearances forced NBC to alter the format to two 30-minute hard newscasts, changing their names to *Before Hours* and *News at Sunrise* and changing to anchors with news credentials. The shows run about .8/10 at 6:15 and 2.1/20 at 6:30 A.M. Since 1983, NBC has offered affiliated stations the option of carrying either one or both of the half-hour segments (at 6 and/or 6:30 A.M.), in accordance with their own local news schedules. Clearances for all early-early shows remain low.

The *Today Show*

Early-morning programming on the three commercial television networks has followed consistent patterns over the years. Generally, the networks have offered magazine format programs or children's shows between 7 and 9 A.M. NBC's pioneer *Today Show* went on the air in 1952 with an information-oriented magazine format, eventually becoming one of television's longest running programs. Not far behind in longevity was CBS's *Captain Kangaroo Show*, a program tailored for preschool children, which began in 1955, ending only in 1982. The great age of these two programs, relative to the rest of television, gave them the status of classics of the medium. Twenty years passed before ABC's *AM America* (now *Good Morning America*) came on the scene in 1975.

Today's structure eventually became known as the **magazine format** because of its resemblance to print publications containing a series of articles bound together within a common cover. A television magazine contains a series of segments bound within a common program framework; one or more central personalities in a single setting provide the sense of continuity. *Today* succeeded in part because during the first twenty years of its reign, it had only three full-time hosts. Dave Garroway, bespectacled, bright and articulate, whose memorable sidekick was a mischievous monkey named J. Fred Muggs, was the first. Muggs made faces at the passers-by who peered into the ground-floor studio window (the New York *Today* studio had been an RCA product display showroom). Newsman John Chancellor was *Today*'s second host (1961 to 1962), followed by Hugh Downs, who remained NBC's early-morning greeter until 1971.

Moreover, relatively little turnover in backup personalities occurred: Barbara Walters, who launched her on-camera career as one of America's best-known women reporters on *Today*, lasted 9 years. Newsman Frank Blair stayed on the show longer than anyone else—22 years. Others who served as hosts or co-hosts were Frank McGee, Jim Hartz, Tom Brokaw, Jane Pauley and Bryant Gumbel. Consistency of personalities, on a program that offered more national exposure each week than performers could expect in other programs, helped entrench *Today* as a solid habit.

Today's format has changed even less than its cast. News and weather come on the hour and half-hour, with opportunities for stations to cut away to local news and weather. *Today*'s focus has remained on interviews with entertainers, authors and newsmakers.

CBS Efforts

CBS went head-to-head with *Today* using a magazine format hosted by Will Rogers, Jr., in 1956. Failing, it returned to a news block from 7 to 8, the CBS *Morning News*, followed by *Captain Kangaroo*. In 1973 CBS made another attempt at a live morning magazine with Hughes Rudd and Washington reporter Sally Quinn. Six months later, they returned to CBS *Morning News* and *Captain Kangaroo* and, eventually, in 1982 dropped the children's program altogether in favor of an expanded news program.

Faced with the inability of its **news division** to compete effectively with ABC and NBC in the morning, CBS took a leaf from ABC's book. Ever innovative in its strategies, ABC had given its **entertainment division** responsibility for its morning show. Accordingly, CBS kicked CBS *Morning News* back to 6 A.M. and turned over to its entertainment division the program that followed, which emerged as a 90-minute magazine show called *The Morning Program*, scheduled from 7:30 to 9 A.M. It used non–news hosts introducing light features in an informal setting, with inserted news updates by news personnel. However, this shift in emphasis and responsibility failed to improve the ratings as expected. CBS continued to trail ABC and NBC in the morning time period during 1987 and soon cancelled *The Morning Program*. The time period was returned to the news division. CBS then hired Kathleen Sullivan, a substitute host on *ABC's Good Morning America*, to co-host a new program, *CBS This Morning*. The new effort tried to strike a middle ground between news and entertainment.

CBS has thus shown little patience in the morning time period. Within only a few years, the network tried many different anchors and several executive producers, all failing to compete effectively with *Today* and *Good Morning America* in a short time frame. Some critics have blamed this failure on the constant change. ABC and NBC, in contrast, maintained relative stability in both on-air personalities and formats in their morning programs over the years, and consequently each developed a loyal following.

Good Morning America

Before 1975 ABC did not offer network service until 11 A.M. In 1975, it began to compete more vigorously in other dayparts, including prime time, but its station lineup of only 183 primary affiliates compared unfavorably with 218 for NBC and 212 for CBS. **Primary affiliates** are stations that have a regular affiliation contract with one of the three major broadcast networks, serving as that network's main outlet for programs in the market and carrying most of the network schedule. In markets with fewer than three commercial television outlets, one station usually becomes a **secondary affiliate** of the missing network(s). Stations with two affiliations choose to carry the most popular programs of both networks, though the affiliate will clear much less of the secondary network's schedule. To woo away primary affiliates from its competitors, ABC had to compete with a full network service, including early-morning programming.

As might be expected, in many small and medium markets with only one or two television stations, primary affiliations usually went to the older and stronger networks. Station managers who might be impressed by ABC's gains in prime time and daytime would still think twice about switching affiliation because they would have to fill the 7 to 9 A.M. period with local programming at added cost: NBC and CBS were both filling the time period and compensating their affiliates. Table 6-1 reveals early-morning viewing patterns and ratings prior to ABC's entry into early-morning competition.

ABC targeted NBC's *Today* as it launched a competitive morning news and information program. But with a twenty-three-year head start, *Today* had become entrenched with early-morning viewers. Research showed that the older the viewers, the firmer their viewing habits.

However, as in other dayparts, ABC aimed for a younger early-morning audience, particularly women 18–49. Women in this group were less habituated viewers than the over–50 group and thus more easily diverted to a new morning television alternative. Moreover, these women were also the audience segment advertisers most desired to reach.

Thus, in launching *AM America* in January 1975, ABC tried to offer a clear alternative to NBC's *Today*, targeting younger women. With Bill Beutel as host, the program had a uniquely informal style, using a living room set with easy conversation and brief feature vignettes. Nevertheless, nine months after *AM America* began, *Today* remained the unqualified leader, leading ABC executives to reevaluate (see Table 6-1).

ABC recast *AM America* as *Good Morning America* in November 1975. Instead of a seasoned journalist, ABC chose actor David Hartman as host be-

Table 6-1 Early-Morning Network Program Ratings, 1974 and 1975

FOURTH QUARTER, 1974		THIRD QUARTER, 1975	
	Rating / Share		Rating / Share
7:00–8:00 A.M.		7:00–8:00 A.M.	
NBC *Today*	5.5 / 37	NBC *Today*	4.2 / 39
CBS *Morning News*	1.7 / 16	CBS *Morning News*	1.5 / 21
ABC local programs		ABC *AM America*	0.9 / 8
8:00–9:00 A.M.		8:00–9:00 A.M.	
NBC *Today*	5.5 / 36	NBC *Today*	4.1 / 34
CBS *Captain Kangaroo*	3.7 / 23	CBS *Captain Kangaroo*	2.8 / 22
ABC local programs		ABC *AM America*	1.2 / 10

Source: NTI, December 1974, September 1975. Used with permission.

Table 6-2 Early-Morning Network Programs, 1980 and 1983

FEBRUARY 1980		FEBRUARY 1983	
	Rating / Share		Rating / Share
7:00–9:00 A.M.		7:00–9:00 A.M.	
NBC *Today**	5.2 / 27	NBC *Today*	4.5 / 21
CBS *Morning News*†	3.0 / 18	CBS *Morning News*	3.4 / 16
ABC *GM America**	5.5 / 28	ABC *GM America*	6.0 / 28

*7:30–8 and 8:30–9 A.M. average
†7:15–8 A.M. only

Source: NTI, February 1980, 1983. Used with permission.

cause of his warm, caring style and his ability to ask the questions that the viewer at home might ask. Well-known contributors included Erma Bombeck with humorous reports; John Coleman, the friendly weatherman; Jack Anderson with "Inside Washington"; Howard Cosell on sports; attorney F. Lee Bailey on law; and Rona Barrett with reports from Hollywood.

Good Morning America adopted a framework similar to *Today*'s: news on the hour and half-hour, time and weather services, and interviews with interesting people. By early 1980, some four and one-half years after ABC's quest began, *Good Morning America* overtook *Today* in overall ratings, with impressive gains among its primary target audience of young women (see Table 6-2). *Good Morning America* had captured a place for itself at the breakfast table.

The Recent Early-Morning Race

In January 1982, two other significant changes took place in early morning television. NBC promoted *Today*'s amiable host, Tom Brokaw, to the *NBC Nightly News*, replacing him with a sportscaster, Bryant Gumbel. This choice continued the trend away from journalism toward personality in early-

Table 6-3 Early-Morning Network
Programs, January 1988

	Rating / Share
ABC *GM America*	4.5 / 22
NBC *Today*	4.4 / 21
CBS *This Morning*	**2.1 / 11**

Source: NTI, January 1988. Used with
permission.

morning programming. Second, CBS made a bold move back into early morning, pushing *Captain Kangaroo*, on since 1955, back to the 6:30 A.M. time slot, later showing it on weekends only. Although CBS would deny any connection, some critics felt that the deregulatory attitude of the then-new Reagan administration in Washington gave CBS the courage to tamper with such an American institution as *Captain Kangaroo*.

CBS moved decisively. It replaced Charles Kuralt, the host of *CBS Morning News*, with Chicago news anchor Bill Kurtis, and expanded to a morning news and information service fully competitive with NBC's *Today* and ABC's *Good Morning America*. These events, along with CBS's hiring away *Good Morning America*'s executive producer, George Merlis, put *CBS Morning News* onto the competitive fast tract. Table 6-2 shows that by 1983, CBS was gaining, NBC was fading, and ABC was number one.

But by the late 1980s, the picture had shifted again. NBC's *Today* was back in first place and ABC solidly in second place. David Hartman left *Good Morning America* in 1987 and was replaced by Charles Gibson, who maintained the show's close second place. Faced with sagging ratings and abysmal clearance levels in 1987, CBS decided on a radical new strategy: displacement of the hard-news *CBS Morning News* with *The Morning Program*, a light talk-oriented show. However, *The Morning Program* could climb no higher than a 2.2 rating/10 share, so once again, this time after only a few months, CBS replaced *The Morning Program* with *CBS This Morning*, another news-oriented show (light this time around). In its first few weeks, it did about the same as its immediate predecessor in ratings, and NBC and ABC stayed on top.

Big money is at stake in the early-morning time period, both for the networks and for their affiliates. While CBS's early-morning programs have usually lost money because of low clearances and ratings, NBC reported that the profits for *Today* were approximately $20 million in 1986–87, and ABC reported about $12 million in profits from *Good Morning America*. In addition, the networks give between four and five commercial spots to their affiliates, which generate substantial station revenue. The history of early-morning competition illustrates the crucial role of audience parity in the big-time battle for revenues. A winner in early morning also supplies prestige and, if the show is truly a hard news program, builds news department morale, an increasingly important consideration in a era of biting cutbacks. CBS has made about 20 (so far unsuccessful) attempts at programming the early morning since the 1950s, and the reasons for trying again remain powerful.

DAYTIME PROGRAMMING

The magazine formats of *Today* and *Good Morning America* have rarely been successful in network **daytime** programming—the period between 10 A.M. and 4 P.M. Two syndicated programs—the *Phil Donahue* and *Oprah Winfrey* shows, using audience participation/talk formats—have provided stations with successful daytime counterprogramming to conventional network offerings. However, *daytime talk/variety* shows launched by three commercial networks have repeatedly died.

In October 1962, NBC tried *The Merv Griffin Show* during the early-afternoon hours and cancelled it in March 1963 (however, when Westinghouse reintroduced this program in syndication, it reached impressive audience levels). In April 1968 ABC scheduled the *Dick Cavett Show* during late morning, cancelled it in January 1969 and rescheduled it in late night. In July 1978 NBC made another attempt with *America Alive* during the noon hour. It lasted six months. With this record, it is little wonder that network programmers have stuck to the more successful formulas for network daytime programming: *soap operas, game shows* and *reruns* of popular prime-time series.

Soap Operas

Successful **soap operas** build loyal constituencies that last for decades. Few television series have lasted as long as *Search for Tomorrow;* it was launched on CBS in 1951, shifted to NBC in 1982 and finally cancelled in 1987, after a total of 35 years. *The Guiding Light,* started on CBS in 1952, was still going strong in 1987. CBS remained dominant in daytime soaps for most of four decades. ABC launched *General Hospital* in 1963, *One Life to Live* in 1968 and *All My Children* in 1970. In 1986 and 1987, *General Hospital* was the top-rated daytime soap opera and a hot fad with college students. This one hit soap brings ABC more revenue and does better at delivering women 18 to 49 than many of that network's prime-time shows. NBC's *Another World* began in 1964 and *Days of Our Lives* in 1965, but despite these long-running classics, NBC's daytime shows generally rate lower than its competitors'. CBS introduced another hit in 1973, *The Young and the Restless*, a relative newcomer as soaps go. But by 1988, it had recaptured top position for CBS. In 1988, CBS had five of the top ten soaps, while ABC had three and NBC two (see the top ten daytime shows in Table 6-4). The topics of these programs have become very "mature," but they operate within strict guidelines imposed by network program practices departments.

Establishing a new soap opera demands a long-range commitment. It takes years to achieve audience identification with new characters and involvement with their affairs.[1] The development begins with an independent producer providing the network programmer with a basic **concept** for a new series. If it seems promising, the network will commission a **treatment,** sometimes called a *bible*, analyzing each of the characters and their interrelationships and describing the settings in which the drama will unfold. For a treatment, the writers

Table 6-4 Network Daytime Ratings, 1988

	Rating / Share
The Young and the Restless (CBS)*	**9 / 29**
General Hospital (ABC)	9 / 27
One Life to Live (ABC)	8 / 26
Days of Our Lives (NBC)	8 / 26
All My Children (ABC)	8 / 25
The Price Is Right (2nd half)	8 / 24
The Guiding Light (CBS)	8 / 24
The Price Is Right (1st half)	7 / 22
Wheel of Fortune	7 / 21
Another World (NBC)	6 / 18

*CBS also carries *As the World Turns,* the *Bold and the Beautiful* and *Loving;* ABC also has *Ryan's Hope;* NBC has *Santa Barbara.*

Source: NTI, January, 1988. Used with permission.

receive development dollars or "seed money." The final step is to commission one or more **scripts**, advancing more funds to pay the writers. The entire **development process** can take one to two years and an investment of up to $50,000. Usually, several development projects are abandoned each season; only a very few get a chance on the air.

Once a network picks up a soap opera, **casting** begins. Casting the appropriate, charismatic character for each role is seen as crucial to a soap's success. To this end, CBS, ABC and NBC maintain their own casting directors to work with producers.

Most other network television is videotaped on the West Coast, where producers contend they can produce programs for less money than in New York, partly because of more favorable weather conditions for exterior shooting. Soap operas, however, continue to be shot in New York because nearly all of the shooting is interior and the Broadway theater provides a large pool of actors.

When a new soap opera is ready to go on the air, the daytime program executives schedule it to maximize audience sampling of the new show, frequently slotting the new program opposite the competition's weaker programs. Promoting a new entry is also vitally important. Once a soap is on the air, the day-to-day task of the daytime program executive is to constantly scrutinize scripts to see that they retain high levels of dramatic conflict and suspense.

Game Shows

Game shows such as *Wheel of Fortune* and *The Price Is Right* are another mainstay of daytime programming. Game shows are among the most profitable network programs, mainly because they can be produced fairly inexpensively, with several episodes taped in a single day. Aside from salaries, the ongoing cost of producing game shows is minimal: Every program uses the same set, and in exchange for on-air announcements, advertisers provide the prizes and cash awarded to the contestants.

The networks seldom invest in pilot programs for game shows because they cannot recoup their investment by airing pilots, as they do with pilot prime-time episodes. Game shows are developed somewhat differently from soap operas. Usually, a game show producer presents a **concept**, and if the network likes the idea, it commissions a **run-through.** The producer then rehearses the show's actors and participants, and network executives are invited to see the run-through. At this stage, a network may commission a **semi-pilot,** allowing the producer to videotape various versions of the game show with a studio audience and appropriate production elements such as music, without going to the expense of an elaborate set.

Like soap operas, game shows have strong appeal among female viewers, but the networks generally schedule them during the morning, as opposed to the afternoon, because games do not attract many teens and children, who make up a large portion of the afternoon audience. *The Price Is Right*, the longest-running game show on network television, started on NBC in 1956. After ten years on NBC and runs in prime time and syndication, *Price* returned to morning television in 1972 on CBS. In 1987 *Price* remained the highest-rated network game show, doing better than some soap operas and bringing CBS enormous profits (see Table 6-4).

In the later 1970s, several morning game shows airing on the networks were simultaneously being produced as first-run shows for syndication (mainly to be used in the 7 to 8 P.M. access hour). Episodes of series such as *Wheel of Fortune, Family Feud, $25,000 Pyramid* and *The Price Is Right* appeared in the morning on a network, while a different episode appeared in the early evening on the same or different stations all across the nation, sometimes even syndicated with the same host.

Reruns

Beyond game shows and soap operas, networks rely on the **reruns** of their own successful nighttime programs to fill out their daytime schedule. Usually, **situation comedies** such as *Who's the Boss?* or *Facts of Life* have performed admirably in daytime, as have such prime-time hits as *Love Boat*. But to strip the programs five times a week for at least 26 weeks before repeating, upwards of 130 episodes must have been accumulated, and the networks perennially lack enough sitcom episodes suitable for daytime airing.

Situation comedies have not been developed for original play in daytime for a simple reason: The best comedy writers are already working in prime time where they can demand higher incomes. And a prime-time series needs only 22 new episodes per year. For stripping in daytime, 22 programs scheduled five times a week would last for little more than a month. The top producers and writers are therefore too busy (and too expensive) for daytime programs for the broadcast networks.

Comparative Costs and Revenues

Daytime is one of the most lucrative dayparts for television networks. Its profit margin often challenges that of prime time because its program costs are substantially less, generating such programming labels as the "golden soaps." Producing the average game show or soap opera is far cheaper than making the average prime-time show. While a half-hour sitcom in prime time costs between $350,000 and $500,000 an episode (see Chapter 5), a soap episode averages about $60,000 to $70,000, and game shows can cost even less.

Moreover, there is a tradition of allowing more commercials in daytime. The National Association of Broadcaster's television code (disallowed by agreement with the Justice Department in 1982 but still loosely followed by the networks), allowed $9\frac{1}{2}$ nonprogram minutes in a prime-time hour and 16 minutes during daytime. In practice, the networks generally schedule about 14 minutes of commercials per hour in Monday through Friday daytime. (Prime time now averages $9\frac{1}{2}$ to 10; in addition, 1 to 2 minutes per hour are allotted to local station breaks.) Despite drawing much smaller audiences than do prime-time programs, daytime occupies more hours per day, has more advertising time for sale and has lower program costs, resulting in large profits for each network.

It follows that a successful daytime schedule is vital to a financially sound network. Extraordinary program investments in other dayparts, such as ambitious prime-time specials, children's dramas or Olympic coverage, tend to cost as much or more than the advertising revenue they generate. Traditionally, documentaries at the networks have been loss leaders, providing the viewers with important services, yet produced at a financial loss. Daytime programming supports these efforts by providing consistently large profits.

CHILDREN'S PROGRAMMING

Network children's programming has become a television battleground, not only because of network competitiveness but also because of increased public concern about the quality of programming designed for children. Children are perceived to be more vulnerable to television's impact than adults. Preschoolers, who cannot read and often watch alone, are the most susceptible to advertisers' messages and may confuse the program content with the sales pitches. Moreover, researchers do not know how clearly preschoolers distinguish between reality and fantasy. Adults do know children readily learn to use television content in games and as conversational referents; they may also adopt television personalities as role models, and copy the behavioral patterns they see on television.

Historically, Saturday morning has been the time period reserved for network children's programs. From a programming perspective, children tend to be the most fickle of all viewers. Their attention span is shorter, they have fewer loyalties, and they tend to sample more new programs. As one programmer put it, holding his hands a foot apart, "It's more convenient for them to change the dial—they only sit this far away from the TV." And today, in the 40 percent of homes with remote controls, children quickly learn to switch channels at will—and often.

Until the early 1970s, children's programs tended to look alike on all three commercial networks. Saturday morning consisted of wall-to-wall cartoons, each striving to present more visual action than the other, which usually translated into violence.[2] Story lines were thin, dependent on action rather than on plots. One writer said of the early days of children's programming, "In the old days the premise for a Saturday morning cartoon was, 'They're coming over the hill' . . . and it was biff-bam, zoom-zoom from there on."

ACT and Other Pressure Groups

Action for Children's Television (ACT), a pressure group formed in 1968 and led by Peggy Charren, has raised network consciousness about children's programs. ACT insisted the networks and stations could do a better job than they had been doing. As public interest in children's programming grew more vocal, ACT was joined by the PTA, National Christian Television and other groups on some children's issues. ACT took its campaign to Washington in 1969. There the Federal Communications Commission of that day lent a sympathetic ear and decided to do some investigating of its own.

At about this time, the **Public Broadcasting Service** (PBS) introduced an ambitious new series, *Sesame Street*. It featured a regular cast of likable characters who taught youngsters how to count up to 10 and then 20, using a format similar to commercials, already so familiar to children. The producer, Children's Television Workshop (CTW), had offered the program to all three commercial networks, but they saw the series as too costly, and some programmers even claimed children would not watch it.

At an FCC hearing in 1972, ACT posed these questions among others: Why was violence necessary in children's programs? Why was it necessary for there to be more commercials—nearly twice as many—in children's programs than in adult programs in prime time? Such questions were hard for network executives (many of whom were parents) to respond to adequately.

Pressed by ACT, the FCC's echoing of its concerns, and *Sesame Street* (whose immediate and widespread success embarrassed the networks), the networks adopted new standards for children's programming. Then ABC president Elton Rule, at the Washington hearing in 1972, pledged that ABC would no longer carry children's programs that contained violent "action devoid of comedy." During subsequent years, aside from slapstick comedy and cartoons, violence was all but eliminated on network children's programs. By the mid-1970s, all three of the commercial networks had named a vice-president in charge of children's programs. Before that, children's programming had been the last thing on the priority list for daytime vice-presidents, whose attention was largely on the more competitive early-morning talk shows, soap operas and game shows.

Commercials and Content Changes

Responding to ACT's complaint and that of parent-teacher associations and other groups that commercials in children's viewing hours were as culpable as the programs, the NAB issued new guidelines in 1976. The stipulations cut commercials from the allowable 16 minutes to $9\frac{1}{2}$ minutes; hosts and program characters were prohibited from presenting commercial messages; and vitamin commercials aimed at young people were eliminated. The NAB also developed advertiser guidelines for the presentation of toys, cereals and other products to children, and mandated clear breaks between program content and commercial content. Although the industry code has since been abandoned by the NAB, the networks still follow these general guidelines for children's programs and commercials.[3]

During the early 1970s a new term crept into the jargon of broadcasters: **prosocial.** Violence in children's programs was considered largely antisocial; the new approach to programming for young people aimed at integrating prosocial elements. These included (1) portraying constructive role models in story lines, (2) communicating respect for the feelings of others and (3) providing youngsters with positive messages.[4]

CBS recruited a panel of experts, mostly educators and psychologists, to assist in reviewing scripts. One of the first programs the CBS panel worked on was *Fat Albert and the Cosby Kids*, an animated program starring Bill Cosby, featuring prosocial themes woven into a highly entertaining half-hour.

ABC engaged Bankstreet College, noted for its experimental teaching programs, to review all of its children's scripts. The Bankstreet advisors, in concert with ABC's Program Department and Broadcast Standards and Practices Department, issued guidelines on sex roles, role models and age appropriateness for all scripts. They include concepts and policies similar to those advocated at CBS and NBC. An extract from the ABC script guidelines on children's programming follows:

> The best way to sum up our approach is a list of qualities that we should strive for in our programs. It is keyed to the word "respect," and it includes: "respect for the individual; respect for differences; respect for religious beliefs and ethnic qualities; respect for all animal life and for the environment; respect for private and public property; respect for moral values; respect for the feelings and sensitivities of others; and, not least, respect for oneself."

> In short, a program designed for the 2–12 age group must be one in which members of that age group can directly relate or identify with (not passively) but in a positive or pro-social manner. In this regard, having children and/or animals in featured roles is strongly encouraged.

> The portrayal of reprehensible or dangerous acts by children's heroes is particularly risky. Boyhood heroes and teenage idols fall hard, and sometimes carry a number of youngsters with them like toppling dominoes. Accordingly, the portrayal of untoward, imitatable behavior by such recent teenage favorites as rock-and-roll stars (including the far too celebrated predilection of a few of them for hard drugs) carries far greater temptation for imitation by youngsters than would the portrayal of similar behaviors by actors with whom they identify in a less hysterical fashion.

Bankstreet College was also commissioned to comment on all scripts for the *ABC Afterschool Specials*, a series of high-quality dramas for teen viewers that commenced twice-monthly broadcasts in the postschool hours in 1972. They won awards for their sensitive treatment of issues such as parental divorce, death of a sibling, appreciation of the handicapped and traumatic disease or alcoholism in the family. During the same season, ABC began telecasts of *Schoolhouse Rock,* a series of 3½-minute programs, scheduled each hour during weekend children's programs. The first ten programs taught youngsters the multiplication tables through animation and music. These were augmented with *Body Rock* on nutrition; *Grammar Rock,* the subheading for ten programs on the parts of speech; and *America Rock* on U.S. history, describing, for example, the story behind the Declaration of Independence and how a bill goes through Congress. Later, *Science Rock* was added, along with a computer literacy series called *Scooter Computer & Mr. Chips.* A decade and a half later, these same 3½-minute animated sequences continue to challenge new generations of youngsters in the intervals between Saturday and Sunday morning children's programs. In 1986, ABC aired *Kingdom Chums,* a religious special for children combining live action and animation; in 1987, it introduced *The Health Show,* produced by ABC News, and Alan Thicke's *Animal Crack-Ups,* featuring wildlife footage and guest celebrities.

Meanwhile, CBS augmented its weekend programming with *In the News,* shown every half-hour of Saturday and Sunday mornings. Each miniprogram was a two-minute explanation of a significant news story, so as to make it comprehensible to young viewers. As of 1984, about seven of these were aired every weekend, but they were dropped in 1987. During the mid-1970s, CBS also created the *Festival of Lively Arts for Young People,* periodic specials introducing viewers to various aspects of the arts, which ran several seasons. CBS continued these efforts with programs like *CBS Storybreak,* adaptations of popular children's books encouraging kids to read, and short segments like *Up to the Minute,* but in the late 1980s, however, major cutbacks in the CBS News Division, which produced *In the News* and *Up to the Minute,* ended these programs and made others like them doubtful. CBS also produces *Schoolbreak Specials* for teens, which, like *ABC Afterschool Specials,* focus on current issues in dramatic form, such as dealing with AIDS or other family traumas. A late-1980s hit, *Pee-Wee's Playhouse,* mixes live action with animated segments targeting younger children, and averages better than a 5.5 rating.

NBC, although slower initially to react to the critics, won praise in the 1970s with a live Saturday morning half-hour called *Go,* using children in the cast. For eight seasons, NBC produced *Special Treats,* dramas designed for telecasting in the after-school hours. As of 1984 NBC had financed 30 dramas in this series. Later, NBC shifted its efforts in quality children's programming to prime time, telecasting to a larger audience with *Project Peacock,* an anthology of children's stories. In 1986 NBC began *Main Street,* an award-winning 60-minute news-and-discussion show for teens, and in 1987, introduced *I'm Telling,* a brother-and-sister quiz show. However, cartoons generally command higher ratings than live action. In 1983 the top-rated children's show was NBC's *The Smurfs.* In 1987 CBS's *The Real Ghostbusters* shared the top honors, and in 1988, NBC's *Alvin and the Chipmunks* was number one (average 6.7 rating on Saturday mornings).

Cartoons

Cartoons are likely to remain the bulwark of Saturday morning programming, as opposed to **live-action** shows (film and tape programs portraying real people) because of cost as well as ratings. A half-hour of animation costs an average of $250,000 as of 1988, while a half-hour of live action can be as low as $15,000 in the case of *Mr. Roger's Neighborhood* or as high as $400,000 for an *ABC Afterschool Special* or *CBS Schoolbreak Special*. However, cartoons withstand rerunning better than live action, and—due to higher residual costs for on-camera actors than for off-camera voices—animation is less expensive to repeat. The studios have also reduced cartoon production costs by using computerized animating techniques using fewer drawings per second and less hand artwork.

The development of an animated children's series begins about 12 months before telecast, with pickups of new series exercised in February or March to allow producers 6 to 7 months to complete the order for September telecast. A producer—or in some cases a network itself—generates an **idea**. The next steps are an **outline** and **artwork**. The outline describes the characters and the setting; the artwork provides sketches of the characters in several poses and costumes. If a project passes these stages, the next step is to order one or more **scripts**, which usually go through many drafts before final acceptance.

Pilot programs are almost never commissioned for cartoons because of the long production time and high costs. Therefore, the decision to pick up a cartoon series costing over $3 million dollars for 13 episodes is based solely on artwork and scripts. Typically, a cartoon program's 13 episodes are aired by the network as many as four times each in a year, before going into syndication after enough episodes for stripping have been produced (buyers want at least a hundred episodes). As with other programs, networks produce few children's programs *in-house* (in the network's own studios with their own staffs). Instead, *independent producers* retain the rights to the programs, which they license to the network for a limited number of runs.

Live Action

Development of children's **live-action** programs is similar to that of animation programs but often substitutes a **casting tape** for animation artwork. The tape shows possible actors for the major roles. **Script** development for live-action children's programs follows the "writer's guideline" provided by the network. For example, the ABC guidelines explain that the *Afterschool Specials* always deal with problems that many youngsters can identify with; that the main character should be of the age of the target audience, 10–14; and that the story's dilemma should be resolved by the main character's own actions, not those of an adult. Moreover, there should be a happy ending that suggests to young people that they, too, can resolve their own problems. These guidelines are typical of those used at all three networks. CBS's hit, *Pee-Wee's Playhouse*, for example, follows this pattern at all times.

As with cartoons, independent producers retain the rights to most live-action children's programs, which they license to the networks for a certain number of telecasts (**runs**). This is in part because the networks are restricted by the **financial syndication rules** explained in Chapter 1.[5] In-house shows may also cost more money for the networks to produce because they have signed more restrictive union contracts than have many independent producers. However, when the network intends to air more than one or two runs of a program or series, it may make fiscal sense to produce in-house. Such was the case with ABC when it decided to build a library of quality half-hour children's dramas that could be repeated, like classics, for several years. The *ABC Weekend Specials* resulted.

The Issues Persist

Controversy over children's television programming continues. The networks walk a fine line between attracting youngsters, satisfying activist groups demanding better quality, and pleasing advertisers who want to expose young consumers to their toy and food messages. The topic returns periodically to the national spotlight in Congress and at the FCC. In 1983, despite public pressure, the commission took no action, but in 1987, the commission agreed to a fresh look. In the late 1980s, ACT turned its attention to the relationship between children's programs and toy merchandising, charging that many children's shows are designed solely as vehicles for selling a line of merchandise (toys, books, records, dolls and so on). It argued that these cartoons should be viewed not as programs but as program-length commercials and should be controlled as such. The makers publically acknowledge that cartoons such as *The Real Ghostbusters* and *Thundercats* were expressly developed as marketing tools by Kenner Parker Toys and LJN Toys. While this practice occurs at the network level, it is even more prevalent in syndicated programming supported by other major toy companies such as Mattel and Hasbro.

In 1979 Warner-Amex developed a children's service, Nickelodeon, that became one of the most popular basic cable networks (now owned by Viacom). Cable's ability to provide an entire channel dedicated to children's programming gives it the potential for defusing the public's concern over the paucity of broadcast children's programming and the FCC's refusal to regulate the field. Nickelodeon, however, can only program for one age-group of children at a time, leaving kids in other developmental stages without appropriate fare. Moreover, it programs many older off-network series, carries advertising and repeats portions of its schedule more frequently than the broadcast networks. Nevertheless, much of Nickelodeon's programming consists of original, live-action shows that compete with the best of network children's programming (for example, *You Can't Do That on Television* and *Pinwheel*).

EVENING NEWS

The evening newscast, the centerpiece of each network's television news organization, originally shifted from radio to provide a service to affiliated television stations, most of which had very limited news operations, if any. Network news departments were little better in the 1950s, each offering only 15 minutes of nightly news. Though extremely modest by today's standards, the expenses incurred by a network news operation during those early years were often far more than the network derived from within-news advertising.

Today, however, the three major network news operations are among the largest and most prestigious in the world. And they are profitable. Competition among the three for the evening news audience and advertisers has become intense.

Development

NBC and CBS introduced **nightly newscasts** to network television in 1948. These 15-minute presentations consisted of an anchor seated behind a desk reading news items to the camera, only occasionally relieved by a piece of film about an event that occurred some time previously. As television matured and the public came to depend primarily on it for news, the networks' news operations grew in size and prestige. In 1963, CBS and NBC expanded their evening newscasts to 30 minutes; ABC finally followed suit in 1967. However, the format changed little: It still featured an anchor or co-anchors reporting the day's events from behind a desk, though with increased use of film inserts. Live, on-location pictures of unplanned events were still out of the question because television cameras were too big to move readily and the logistics of transmitting the signal from a remote location too complex. Filmed reports of world events were possible, though the process of transporting, developing and editing film delayed reports, sometimes for days. Eventually, videotape recording, miniaturization of equipment and the availability of satellite transmission (both domestic and worldwide) liberated news operations from the studio and film camera. By 1980 most stations as well as networks used **electronic news gathering** (**ENG**), along with digital processing equipment for picture manipulation and graphic effects. New technologies thus transformed television news operations.

The same technologies, however, also enabled individual stations, despite their much smaller staffs and resources, to enlarge their scope and eventually pose a threat to the viability of the networks' huge investment in news operations. The following statistics give an idea of that investment: As of early 1987, the three television broadcast networks employed, in the aggregate, some 3,600 people, maintained over 700 news bureaus scattered across the country and around the world and spent over $600 million annually.[6]

CBS Evening News

In 1948 CBS became the first network to offer a regular evening newscast, *Douglas Edwards and the News* (later retitled *CBS Evening News*). Walter Cronkite replaced Edwards in 1962, serving as anchor until his retirement in 1981. During Cronkite's long tenure, the *CBS Evening News* expanded to 30 minutes, and by the end of the 1960s, it had regained the ratings lead it relinquished to NBC in 1957.

Cronkite became an institution. In time of crisis, more people tuned in to Cronkite than to any other newscaster; during the 1970s, polls repeatedly

Table 6-5 Network Evening News
Ratings, January, 1988

	1988
ABC World News Tonight	10.8
CBS Evening News	**11.9**
NBC Nightly News	10.7

Source: NTI, January 1988. Used with permission.

showed Cronkite as the most trusted source of news (and nearly a decade after his retirement, people still complained that they "missed him"). It had become evident that, all other things (such as news gathering, processing and presenting abilities) being equal, the one factor that programmers could manipulate was the *personality factor*. News program strategy became largely a matter of selecting news anchors with charisma and the right "chemistry" in their interactions with other members of the news team and the audience. These mysterious qualities seem to have little to do with professional news qualifications (though major news personalities usually do excel as reporters and writers). Thus the history of network television news has become largely a matter of tracing the succession of personalities who have occupied the key positions.

When Dan Rather took over the helm of CBS news on Cronkite's retirement, for example, Rather's credentials as a highly experienced journalist meant little if his chemistry did not match that of his predecessor. Not unexpectedly, after Cronkite's retirement, the ratings of *CBS Evening News* declined. Table 6-5 shows how close the three newscasts' ratings are, though CBS continues its lead.

NBC Nightly News

NBC first offered a regular evening newscast in 1949, the *Camel News Caravan* with John Cameron Swayze as anchor. Swayze was not an experienced journalist, but since all the anchor had to do was read the news, good delivery seemed more important than reporting skills. In 1956 NBC tried a new strategy, replacing Swayze with co-anchors Chet Huntley and David Brinkley, both experienced reporters. The renamed newscast, *The Huntley-Brinkley Report*, became the top-rated news program within a year, unseating CBS and remaining on top for most of the 1960s. When Huntley retired in 1970, NBC renamed the program the *NBC Nightly News*, and chose long-time journalist John Chancellor as sole anchor (though David Brinkley returned to the show from 1976 to 1979). Chancellor's shift to commentator in 1982 brought Tom Brokaw to the key slot. During the mid-1980s, *NBC Nightly News* expanded its background and analysis of events, cutting some of its hard-news reportage. This strategy worked, because by 1987 NBC had once again tied CBS in the nightly news race.

ABC World News Tonight

ABC started nightly newscasts in 1948, but because very few affiliates agreed to carry them, they quickly went off the air. It wasn't until 1953 that ABC tried again, using as nightly anchor John Daly, better known for hosting CBS's game show *What's My Line?* than for anchoring ABC's news. For three decades, ABC failed to pose a serious news threat to CBS and NBC. ABC's nighttime news had many anchors and co-anchors, including, among others, Howard K. Smith, Harry Reasoner, Frank Reynolds and Barbara Walters. None succeeded in lifting *ABC Evening News* out of third place.

In 1977, in a bold move, ABC surprised the industry by appointing the head of ABC Sports, Roone Arledge, to supervise both its news and sports divisions. Arledge had made ABC the number-one network sports organization with his unconventional strategies—introducing offbeat events such as gymnastics, ice skating, and track and field to network television, and building up the dramatic aspects of sports competition. Arledge brought this daring to the evening news, introducing an anchor quartet, rotating anchors and increasing the use of computer graphics. In 1983 he dropped multiple anchors in favor of Peter Jennings as sole anchor of *ABC World News Tonight*, and the ratings began to improve. By 1988 ABC ran neck-and-neck with NBC, tied for the second position, and the gap between these two and CBS had shrunk to a rating point (see Table 6-5).

The Outlook

Network newscasts have become powerful, prestige-producing programs for both networks and affiliates. Although direct profits range from low to nonexistent for the networks, the stakes are high, forcing intense competition among the three networks for the valuable evening news audience. In addition, Cable News Network (CNN) and other broadcast news services have captured part of the news audience. Many major-market affiliates have broadened their news coverage using ENG equipment and satellite transmission, employing regular Washington, D.C., correspondents and sending news teams to distant cities to provide extended coverage of events of particular local interest.

The networks also compete with their affiliates for airtime. The former have argued for years that they cannot do justice to the day's news events in only 22 minutes (the time left after commercials and credits). Cost-conscious management also wants greater use of extra footage, unaired news stories and facilities. Moreover, network news organizations have grown so large that high-salaried correspondents find themselves competing for a few seconds of airtime. All three networks have thus proposed expanding their nightly newscasts to one hour, and all have been refused by affiliates. The local stations prefer keeping that valuable 30 minutes of large-audience time to air their local news and syndicated shows, thus keeping all the revenue.

The networks probably will not be permitted to expand to 60-minute evening newscasts. In fact, some experts expect the 30-minute network evening newscasts to face clearance problems in the 1990s. Satellite signal relay from many domestic and international news sources (Headline, INN, Conus) has decreased the affiliates' reliance on their networks for world news. Stations can now subscribe to a combination of smaller services, providing news comparable to that of the major networks at reasonable cost.

Network news operations, facing intransigent, bottom-line-oriented parent companies, underwent drastic cuts in budget and staffing in the late 1980s. Cost-cutting managements looked for new ways to make news revenue-producing, and all three networks turned to **news capsules** and **summaries**, which immediately became revenue gold mines, and to **late-night newscasts**, a less successful strategy to date. On all three networks, prime-time news capsules reach larger audiences than even the top-rated network evening newscast.

LATE-NIGHT TALK AND NEWS

The period following the local stations' eleven o'clock news is the domain of **late-night programming**. NBC was most successful in developing new audience viewing trends in that time period. After launching *The Tonight Show* in 1954, NBC won that time period for the next quarter-century. NBC program executive Pat Weaver gets the credit for initiating the **talk/variety** format of *The Tonight Show* as well as for creating *The Today Show* two years earlier.[7]

The Tonight Show

Steve Allen was the first host of *Tonight*, followed by Jack Parr and then the inimitable Johnny Carson. Each show employed comedy, occasional singers and light conversation mixed with informal chats with show business personalities and miscellaneous interviewees. The basic concept is that at late hours viewers are not interested in serious topics. It was a premise that seemed to be right for NBC, but CBS and ABC were never very successful in executing late-night talk/variety formats of their own.

In 1979 Johnny Carson shocked NBC by talking about leaving the show. At the time, about 20 percent of NBC's income came from *The Tonight Show*. Low ratings for guest hosts had repeatedly demonstrated Carson's unique appeal. Losing Carson would have undermined the network's profitability for years to come. The next year, after lengthy negotiations, Carson renewed his contract (with a hefty raise to $5 million annually). NBC also agreed to cut the show back from 90 minutes to an hour and require Carson to host only four new shows a week, Tuesday through Friday (on Mondays, NBC aired reruns under the label "Best of . . ."). In 1986, 32 years after it premiered, *The Tonight Show* was still winning the late-night ratings race (see Table 6-6), despite determined efforts by competitors to oust Carson from the lead.

After Tonight on NBC

In 1973 NBC became the first network to offer programming in the **late-late time period** when it introduced *Tomorrow* at 1 A.M. The program used a **talk format** hosted by Tom Snyder, former local television news anchor. NBC captured part of the post–*Tonight* audience, and *Tomorrow* stayed on the air for almost ten years.

Table 6-6 Late-Night Network Ratings, Second Quarter, 1986

SHOW	NETWORK	RATING / SHARE
Tonight Show/Johnny Carson	NBC	**6.9 / 23**
Nightline	ABC	6.6 / 19
Saturday Night Live	NBC	6.3 / 20
Late Night /David Letterman	NBC	3.5 / 20
Friday Night Videos	NBC	3.4 / 17

Source: NTI, Second Quarter, 1986. Used with permission.

After guest-hosting frequently for Carson, David Letterman won his own daytime show on NBC in 1980 at 10 A.M. Because of low ratings and hence low clearances, the program lasted only four months, but NBC thought his off-beat style might better suit late-night audiences. Thus, in 1982, *Late Night with David Letterman* replaced *Tomorrow* in the hour following *Tonight* on Monday through Thursday. Letterman departed from the usual talk format by adding features such as pet tricks and elevator races to the standard guest interviews. *Late Night with David Letterman* developed a cult following among young viewers, especially college students who made up a large portion of Letterman's audience. By the late 1980s, the show regularly captured 20 percent of late-late viewers. On Friday nights, NBC successfully aired *Friday Night Videos*, a collection of music videos hosted by a different celebrity every week.

A New Challenger

In 1986 the Fox Broadcasting Company (FBC) put together a slate of programs for a lineup of independent television stations hoping to draw ratings away from affiliates of the three major networks. Fox's first offering was in late night, challenging the hitherto impregnable *Tonight Show.* Joan Rivers, a comedian who had regularly won good ratings when substituting for Johnny Carson, hosted *The Late Show Starring Joan Rivers.* Featuring big-name guests, the show started out well, but the ratings eroded quickly, and the frenetic Rivers was taken off the program the following May. In its second year, Fox's *The Late Show,* using rotating hosts, averaged about 6 percent of the late-night audience, and was finally cancelled in late 1987.

ABC Talk and News

Of all the networks, ABC tried the hardest to win a late-night audience. In less than a decade, it came up with four different approaches. After the short-lived *Les Crane Show, The Joey Bishop Show* gave *Tonight* a run for its money in the late 1960s in the Midwest but lagged far behind in the national ratings for late-night network programs (see Table 6-7).

In 1970 ABC gave the nod to Dick Cavett, who had earned enormous popularity among the critics despite poor ratings for a daytime show. However, the mass audience judged him too erudite, finding his topics heavy for the late-night time period.

Table 6-7 Late-Night Network Ratings at
11:30 P.M. 1981–1987

NETWORK	1981	1983	1985	1987
CBS	6.3	6.3	5.0	4.1
NBC	5.9	5.8	7.0	7.0
ABC	5.0	4.0	5.6	5.6

Source: NTI. Used with permission.

Admiring ABC's determination to offer *Tonight* some competition, many industry observers thought the network had staged a coup when it announced that Jack Paar would return to late-night television, alternating with Cavett and once-a-month specials starting in 1973. It had been some ten years since Jack Paar had stormed off NBC's *Tonight Show* set, yet when he returned, he looked almost exactly the same: the same style sports jacket, same hair length and the same tone of curious astonishment in his interviews. During the opening week, Jack Paar boosted ABC's ratings. Then they began to slide— back to Cavett's level. Jack was the same, but the audience was not. In ten years, apparently the viewers had become far more sophisticated and critical. The ratings stayed low, and Paar was retired for a second time in 1973.

In November 1979 ABC News seized on the American viewing audience's fascination with the Iran hostage crisis and began **late-night newscasts** summarizing daily events—the program that soon became *Nightline,* an innovative, in-depth news program using extended visuals relayed by satellite. Hosted by Ted Koppel, an incisive yet compassionate interviewer, *Nightline* emerged as a strong late-night competitor at 11:30 P.M. But as the late-night charts suggest, the viability of a news-oriented, late-night program varies with the condition of world events (see Table 6-7).

In spite of less than ideal ratings, ABC expanded *Nightline* to an hour in 1983. The network apparently felt that timely news programming made an appealing counteroffering to NBC's and CBS's entertainment fare. Moreover, ABC could fortify its news image in the public's mind. But in less than a year, ABC cancelled the second half-hour of *Nightline* when its ratings failed to improve. By the mid-1980s, *Nightline* had settled into second place at 11:30 P.M. against *Tonight* and the CBS lineup.

Looking for programming to follow *Nightline,* ABC brought back Cavett in *The Dick Cavett Show* in 1986, only to cancel it in a few weeks. ABC's next effort, *Jimmy Breslin's People,* suffered the same fate. The low ratings for both programs could be attributed to their late fall start-up, after most affiliates had already committed to syndicated programs to fill the time slot. Both *The Dick Cavett Show* and *Jimmy Breslin's People* lacked sufficient clearance to be competitive.

In 1987 ABC introduced *Monday Sportsnite,* a **late-night sports talk** show hosted by Al Trautwig, in the time slot following *Nightline.* Thus, ABC's next strategy was to retain the *Nightline* audience with light talk, consisting of soft feature stories about the people, places and events in sports. By mid-1987, this show was just hanging on in the ratings and was finally cancelled.

CBS Late Night

During most of the seven-year period in which ABC tried to go talk show against talk show, CBS was quietly garnering a respectable audience share by counterprogramming with **movies**. Except for its one crack at late-night talk/variety with *The Merv Griffin Show* for six months in 1972, CBS followed the strategy of scheduling movies 11:30 P.M. to 1 A.M.

By the end of the 1970s, CBS had captured first place in the late-night ratings race, but by the mid-1980s, had fallen again into third place (see Table 6-7). In 1986 CBS tried anew, this time with original **action-dramas** produced in Canada (*Adderly, Night Heat, Diamonds*) and reruns of recent prime-time action-dramas. CBS still finished in third place, largely because almost half of its affiliates either refused to clear the network offerings or delayed the broadcasts to very late hours when too few viewers were available. Even when offered an additional 30-second incentive (a local spot) in the first half-hour, many affiliates found they could make more money by airing syndicated product in the late-night time period.

Late-Late-Late News

In 1982 NBC introduced *Overnight*, a one-hour newscast aired from 1:30 to 2:30 A.M. Mondays through Thursdays (moving up to 2 A.M. on Fridays). It failed to catch on and was cancelled in 1983. About the same time, *CBS News Nightwatch* began, a four-hour **newscast** starting at 2 A.M., Sundays through Thursdays, cut back to two live hours and a taped repeat. Although many affiliates refused to clear this program, it consistently pulled a 1.5 rating, slightly higher than the competition, the syndicated *CNN Headline News*. CBS increased clearance for *Nightwatch* by offering it free to its affiliates at a time when they would either be off the air or purchasing heavily rerun syndicated programming (to keep the cost down).

WEEKENDS

Nonprime-time network television programming on weekends has remained much the same for decades. Saturday and Sunday afternoons have been dominated by **sports** appealing primarily to adult males who are more available at these times than any others throughout the week. Sunday morning, the time period with the smallest adult audiences, continues to be the choice for the networks' **public affairs** programs. Saturday morning is, of course, the domain of **children's cartoons** already discussed.

Sports

From television's earliest days, **sports** were a low-cost source of programming capable of attracting male audiences on Saturday and Sunday afternoons. During the 1950s, organized team sports owners identified television as a potential source of new revenue, and in the late 1950s and early 1960s, several major league baseball franchises moved to new markets (Los Angeles, San Francisco, Atlanta), lured not only by the prospect of additional gate receipts but also by the opportunity of operating in major television markets. By the mid-1970s, a strong interdependency had developed between sports and television, while the cost for sports rights skyrocketed. Today, the three networks provide a steady year-round diet of sporting events, mostly live, including NFL and NCAA football, major league baseball, NBA and NCAA basketball, boxing, golf, tennis, auto racing, bowling and horse racing. Each network carries about *600 hours of sports* annually.

ABC capitalized on the proven audience for sports by introducing its long-running *ABC Wide World of Sports* in 1961. A **sports anthology** program, it includes lesser-known activities such as gymnastics, figure skating and diving, as well as offbeat events such as wrist wrestling, iron-man competitions and celebrity competitions. The series, hosted by Jim McKay since its inception, was so successful that ABC added a Sunday afternoon version to the original Saturday show in the 1970s. CBS and NBC countered with their own weekend sports anthology series, *The CBS Sports Spectacular* (now *Sports Saturday* and *Sports Sunday*) and *NBC's Sportsworld*. These shows are essentially clones, and *Wide World of Sports* continues to lead in ratings.

In 1986 NBC introduced a 30-minute late-night weekend sports program, *George Michael's Sports Machine*. Airing on Sundays at 11:30 P.M., it provides sports highlights, a wrap-up of the week's sporting events and light features from the world of sports. It performed effectively against local programs in most markets. However, all three networks have lost a portion of the sports-news audience to ESPN, which supplies continuous sports updates, football (including NFL games), baseball, lots of fishing, golf, tennis and car and horse racing, and highlights of almost everything sporting to cabled homes.

The game of games is, of course, the Super Bowl, played on what is now called Super Sunday in late January and watched by 100 million people. It commands the highest ratings of any program, day or evening, and in 1988 captured an audience rating/share of 42/62 (lower than the 46/66 in 1987). The network having the Super Bowl usually follows it with a debut of new prime-time series to take advantage of the fact that five of the ten highest-rated programs of all time were Super Bowls. In recent years, all three networks have had the rights in rotating fashion and followed this strategy. The World Series is another super-event, running from four to seven days—though the games have moved into evening hours in recent years to capture more of the large prime-time audience. Ratings for Winter and Summer Olympics have been variable and lower for the Winter Olympics because winter sports are less widely popular as spectator sports in America. A potential U.S. gold medalist attracts big audiences in the summer, but events in which the U.S. participants have little medal chance drag average ratings down. Long segments of the Olympics usually appear in the daytimes and only brief highlights are scheduled in prime time. ABC changed this pattern in 1988, scheduling extended prime-time coverage of the 1988 Winter Olympics and lifting its ratings enough to put the network in second place overall for the 1987–88 season.

Saturday Night Live

In 1975 NBC unveiled *Saturday Night Live*, an innovative 90-minute **comedy/variety** program at 11:30 P.M. on Saturdays. Previously, NBC had scheduled *Tonight Show* reruns in this time period. On *Saturday Night Live*, a different guest star hosts each week, joining a company of regulars, many of whom have gone on to successful solo careers. *Saturday Night Live* graduates include Dan Ackroyd, John Belushi, Chevy Chase, Billy Crystal, Jane Curtain, Eddie Murphy, Bill Murray, Don Novello (Father Guido Sarducci), Joe Piscopo, Gilda Radner and Martin Short. *Saturday Night Live* features "Weekend Update," a humorous look at the week's news events, and satirizes current television programs. Although its audience share slipped to about 20 percent in later years (see Table 6-6), it continues to be renewed, and edited highlights of the show appear in syndication.

ABC tried to duplicate the success of *Saturday Night Live* on Friday nights at 11:30 P.M. with *Fridays*. Although moderately successful, the show was cancelled in 1982 when *Nightline* expanded to five nights a week.

In 1985 NBC adopted a fresh strategy for late Saturday nights, airing professional wrestling under the title of *Saturday Night Main Events* once every four to six weeks in the *Saturday Night Live* time slot. Delivering a large audience of 18–49 adults, wrestling has been competitive, with shares in the mid 20s.

Sunday Morning News and Public Affairs

All three networks have traditionally aired public affairs interview programs on Sunday mornings (start times vary). The format consists simply of a panel of journalists interviewing one or more recent newsmakers about current issues and events. In 1947 NBC began *Meet the Press*, network television's longest-running series, which was followed by CBS's *Face the Nation* in 1954 and ABC's *Issues and Answers* in 1960. The format of these shows changed little, and they stayed neck-and-neck in the ratings until ABC replaced *Issues and Answers* with the successful *This Week with David Brinkley* in the 1980s (see Table 6-8). Instead of grilling a guest, Brinkley's panel of journalists conducts a round-table discussion of the week's events with newsmakers, accompanied by feature stories on the events, and this format, combined with an 11:30 A.M. start, has given ABC the ratings lead.

In 1979 CBS extended its 90-minute early weekday news-magazine program to Sunday mornings, becoming *CBS News Sunday Morning*. Host Charles Kuralt brought a lighter version of the weekday program to Sundays, a strategy emphasizing soft features over hard news. In 1987 NBC launched a similar effort, *Sunday Today*, with Maria Shriver. Both shows earned shares in the 20s.

The Future of Nonprime Time

Significant changes in viewing patterns in nonprime time seem difficult to achieve. No early-morning effort, no daytime soap opera and no late-night strategy has ever met with instant success. Only in rare cases, as with

Table 6-8 Sunday Morning Network
Public Affairs Ratings, 1987

SHOW*	NETWORK	1987
Meet the Press	NBC	2.8
Face the Nation	CBS	2.8
Brinkley	ABC	4.0

*Start times vary from 9:30 A.M. to 11:30 A.M.

Source: NTI. Used with permission.

daytime game shows or children's programs, has a network been able to dislodge an established audience viewing habit.

With basic cable services, pay-cable channels and videocassette recordings competing with network television programming, the number of available viewers during all time periods has shrunk, making even more arduous the tasks of network programming. The new competitors not only seek part of the same audience but by competing for some of the same programs—especially movies and sports—they raise the network's cost of doing business. The cable networks' inroads on the broadcast networks' combined audience share have forced ABC, CBS and NBC to consider longer broadcast days. They have already moved into earlier weekday morning hours and later weeknight and weekend hours. Cable has also redefined the size of an acceptable audience in several dayparts.

SUMMARY

Nonprime-time dayparts can be more profitable than prime time because program costs are so much lower and the time span is longer, but gaining enough affiliate clearances to achieve audience parity is crucial to nonprime-time success and a problem for all three networks at different hours. Nonprime-time audiences also tend to be more homogeneous than prime-time audiences, so the networks usually program head-to-head rather than counterprogram. NBC and ABC dominate early-morning programming with the *Today Show* and *Good Morning America*. Daytime is the province of soap operas and game shows, and the development process differs for these two program formats. Daytime is important because its revenues balance the more expensive prime-time programming, and CBS has dominated in the soap ratings. The network evening news has become a tight ratings race among all three evening newscasts, with no sure winner from season to season. In late night, the *Tonight Show* has remained the classic, although *Late Night with David Letterman* became a recent hit on the same network, NBC. ABC's *Nightline* has also made a mark on the 11:30 P.M. time period, but CBS struggles, counterprogramming with action/adventure shows and shaky ratings. Weekend days contain Saturday morning cartoons, afternoon sports, Sunday morning public affairs and afternoon sports. Live action and cartoon programs for children follow script guidelines to ensure prosocial content, but animation dominates over live action in ratings and reusability. Competition in all dayparts grows increasingly hotter as program costs rise and HUTs go down.

Notes

1. For an overview of the literature on soap operas, see Bradley S. Greenberg, Kimberly Neuendorf, Nancy Buerkey-Rothfuss, and Laura Henderson, "The Soaps: What's On and Who Cares?" *Journal of Broadcasting* 26, Spring 1982, pp. 519–535.

2. See Surgeon General's Scientific Advisory Committee on *Television and Social Behavior, Television and Growing Up: The Impact of Televised Violence* (Washington, D.C.: Surgeon General, U.S. Public Health Service, 1972). See also Thomas E. Coffin and Sam Tuchman, "Rating Television Programs for Violence: A Comparison of Five Surveys," *Journal of Broadcasting* 17, Winter 1972–73, pp. 3–20; and Edward L. Palmer and Aimee Dorr, *Children and the Faces of Television: Teaching, Violence, Selling* (New York: Academic Press, 1980).

3. Although ACT originally contended that commercials should be eliminated from children's programming altogether, failing to make progress on this issue, ACT later redirected its efforts toward improving and expanding programs for children.

4. The difficulty in defining *prosocial* is illuminated by Dona A. Durham and Timothy P. Meyer, "TV and Prosocial Behavior: A Critical Review of Key Issues and Literature," a paper presented at the International Communication Association Convention, Dallas, Texas, May 1983. See also "Network Kidvid Programs and Advertisers Much the Same, with Subtle 'Prosocial' Growth," *Television/Radio Age*, 21 May 1979, pp. 40 ff; and "Networks' Efforts to Increase Educational Values of Kidvid Include Inserts' Specials, School Role," *Television/Radio Age*, 4 June 1979, pp. 44 ff.

5. The purpose of these financial syndication rules is to prevent the networks from controlling both the means of program production and the means of distribution (networking) within the United States. It is possible, however, for the networks to have a financial interest in foreign syndication.

6. N. R. Kleinfeld, "Making 'News on the Cheap' Pay Off," *New York Times*, 19 April 1987, p. 3-1.

7. Sylvester "Pat" Weaver, president of NBC in 1954 and 1955.

Selected Sources

Barcus, F. Earle, with Welkin, Rachel. *Children's Television: An Analysis of Programming and Advertising*. New York: Praeger Special Studies, 1977.

Fabe, Maxene. *TV Game Shows*. Garden City, New York: Dolphin Books, 1979.

Grossman, Gary H. *Saturday Morning TV*. New York: Dell, 1982.

Liebert, Robert M., and others. *The Early Window: Effects of Television on Children and Youth*. 2nd ed. Elmsford, New York: Pergamon Press, 1982.

Matelski, Marilyn J. *The Soap Opera Evolution: America's Enduring Romance with Daytime Drama*. Jefferson, N.C.: McFarland, 1988.

Mayer, Martin. *Making News*. Garden City, N.Y.: Doubleday, 1987.

McCabe, Peter. *Bad News at Black Rock: The Sell-Out of CBS News*. New York: Arbor House, 1987.

Metz, Robert. *The Today Show*. Chicago: Playboy Press, 1977.

Metz, Robert. *The Tonight Show*. Chicago: Playboy Press, 1980.

Turow, Joseph. *Entertainment, Education, and the Hard Sell: Three Decades of Network Children's Television*. New York: Praeger, 1981.

CHAPTER 7 \ AFFILIATED STATION PROGRAMMING

John A. Haldi

A Guide to Chapter 7

John A. Haldi, vice-president of programming for WBNS-TV, Columbus, Ohio, analyzes each daypart in an affiliate's schedule and suggests strategies for effective programming. He served on the Board of Directors of the National Association of Television Program Executives (NATPE) and was elected president of the organization in 1966. His honors include the 1966 Governors' Award from the Columbus chapter of the National Academy of Television Arts and Sciences and "Man of the Year" nomination from the National Association of Television Program Executives in 1972. Mr. Haldi is well known for his locally created program ideas, such as *High Road to Adventure, In the Know, War Movies with Woody Hayes, Name Droppers* and *The Judge;* this last program has been syndicated nationally by Genesis Entertainment since 1986. WBNS-TV has won numerous awards for broadcasting excellence under Haldi's leadership, demonstrating his status as a master of television programming strategy.

AFFILIATE-NETWORK RELATIONS

The three commercial broadcast networks program approximately 70 percent of their affiliate's schedules. The remainder consists of about 5 percent local programs (news, sports events and occasional entertainment programs); and 25 percent syndicated first-run shows (*Wheel of Fortune, Divorce Court, Jeopardy*) and rerun off-network properties (*The Cosby Show, Who's the Boss?, Murder, She Wrote*). Each program director blends the *network, local* and *syndicated* schedules to fill a particular station's needs. But the choices have expanded with the advent of satellite delivery from independent distributors, ad hoc networks, group-owned productions and, in 1987, the Fox network.

One of the affiliate's foremost obligations is to its network. The network accounts for approximately 10 to 30 percent in total station revenues. This figure includes income from **adjacencies** and spots sold within network programs and **compensation** ("comp") from the network on an hourly rate basis. Straight compensation from the network used to average 20 percent of a station's revenues in the 1950s; today, straight compensation accounts for about 5 percent. The amount of money derived from the network depends on the size of the market.

Large-market stations get more money, but the bigger the market, the less comp counts as a proportion of its total revenue. The smaller the market, on the other hand, the greater the percentage of station income coming from network compensation. Major-market managers often regard comp as spare change—it provides only 2.9 percent of revenue in the top ten markets. But comp is vital in markets 110 and smaller—it is a reliable source for more than 10 percent of station revenues. Without network compensation, many very small market stations would not be profitable to operate. Moreover, comp has intangible value—it is a key part of the basic network-affiliate deal.

In larger markets, some independents make even more in *gross* revenue than the affiliates in the same market. In the larger markets, stations can charge more for their national and local spots, and independents have more of them to sell; independents, however, also have higher programming costs, generally leaving the affiliate as the most profitable type of station (in *net* profit) in any market.

The affiliated stations are really paid by their network to carry the advertising contained in the network's programs (the reason for network compensation), a system spawned by the radio networks in the 1930s to gain wide exposure across the country for national advertising. According to *Channels* magazine, CBS pays out the highest total comp—$174 million, compared to NBC's $130 million and about $120 million at ABC—and there's a good reason why: CBS is defending the strongest affiliate lineup.[1] In the 152 markets where all three networks have affiliates, CBS stations held the top Arbitron audience share in November 1986. CBS affiliates were top-ranked in 51 percent of the markets, NBC in 36 percent and ABC in 22 percent. When the network's ratings slid in 1988, however, CBS affiliates dropped to second position in most markets. Moreover, the networks pay a premium for **VHF** stations. The sole "V" in one Midwestern market gets comp at three times the rate earned by the city's other two network affiliates, which have **UHF** channels, even though the VHF's audience is no larger.

According to the networks, comp rates have gotten out of line for dozens of affiliates, and many will be trimmed by the early 1990s. ABC has been the most aggressive in cutting compensation payments. In late 1987 they negotiated reduced payments by as much as 22 percent for at least 15 of their affiliates. Most of the stations affected were small- and medium-size outlets that were lured to ABC with hefty compensation premiums during the network's heyday in the late seventies and early eighties. NBC also cut comp rates for a few stations in the 1980s and worked with affiliates on reform of the rate structure by creating a standard index to set an NBC affiliate's hourly rate by market size, by audience share compared with the network's and by other specific criteria. The networks' comp payments have grown during the past decades, but not as fast as network or station ad sales.

Although the practice of paying network compensation is six decades old, it has faded to just a small amount in radio, and industry insiders see its demise in television within the next ten years. Two substitutes now are being debated: (1) Affiliates will pay for network shows, or (2) affiliates will pay cash and receive barter minutes to sell within each national program. In either case, networking as we have known it will diminish in importance. The family relationship between an affiliate and its network is disappearing, and soon one station could carry programs from all three networks. Nevertheless, a network franchise remains a valuable asset for any television station because of the popularity and visibility of network *programs,* the revenue from *compensation* and *adjacencies* (spots next to network shows) and the *savings* in local program outlay compared with filling an entire broadcast schedule.

Lack of **clearances** by the affiliate, on the other hand, jeopardizes the effectiveness and profitability of network programs (as discussed in Chapter 6).[2] If a particular affiliate consistently preempts network programs for its own local shows,[3] the network's Affiliate Relations Department will call the recalcitrant station in order to determine the problem and coerce that affiliate into the network's preferred clearance pattern. For example, CBS has a serious late-night clearance problem. Some stations delay the CBS late-night movie; others do not clear it at all. ABC cannot even depend on stations owned by its parent,

Capital Cities/ABC, to clear its weaker prime-time shows. Sometimes the partnership between network and affiliate becomes very strained, and very long, acrimonious meetings result. More often than not, compromise is necessary to keep the network/affiliate partnership affable and profitable. It takes more than a paper agreement to make the relationship work for both parties. In 1987 CBS and its affiliates locked horns over a CBS proposal to pay 40 percent to its affiliates for late-night clearances instead of the usual 10 percent. The catch was that CBS would then have dropped its prime-time rate from 32 to 30 percent. The incentive didn't work; both parties, after heated sessions, walked away from the issue and left things as they were. The long-range expectation of all parties, however, is that network compensation rates will drop sooner or later.

Network Agreement

Television **affiliation agreements** differ for each network but in general contain the following elements:

1. The affiliate has first call on all network programs.

2. Acceptance or rejection of network programming (*clearance*) must be made within four weeks of receipt of order, usually three weeks before the show airs. This is to get listings in *TV Guide* and newspaper television supplements, as well as to compile data to justify advertising buys. Presidential press conferences, general news conferences and news specials require a minimum of 72 hours clearance. Finally, breaking news stories, such as Senate hearings and fast-breaking domestic or international stories of great import could require same-day notification and clearance. Controversial episodes of entertainment series and/or movies are red-flagged by the network at least five weeks in advance so that the affiliate may screen and decide whether to carry the program. Upon receiving a program rejection, however, the network has the right to offer the rejected program to another television station in the same market.

3. The network's obligation to deliver the programs is subject to the network's ability to make arrangements satisfactory to it for such delivery (land lines, satellite or shipment of videotape).

4. The network agrees to pay the affiliate on the basis of an established affiliated station's network rate. This rate is based on a station's audience position (share of the market), size of the market and the station's contribution to the total network audience. The contract between network and affiliate always is renegotiated every two years.

5. Payment for each network commercial program broadcast over the affiliate station during "live time" is based on a percentage table similar to Table 7-1. Early evening and prime-time programs are clearly the most profitable to the affiliate because, of course, the networks gain the largest audiences at those times.

Table 7-1 Network Compensation Rates
(CBS Example)

	PERCENT OF AFFILIATE STATION'S NETWORK RATE
Monday through Friday	
7:00 A.M.–11:15 A.M.	7
11:15 A.M.– 5:00 P.M.	12
5:00 P.M.– 6:00 P.M.	15
6:00 P.M.–11:00 P.M.	32
Saturday	
8:00 A.M.– 9:00 A.M.	7
9:00 A.M.– 2:00 P.M.	12
5:00 P.M.– 6:00 P.M.	15
6:00 P.M.–11:00 P.M.	32
Sunday	
4:00 P.M.– 5:00 P.M.	12
5:00 P.M.– 6:00 P.M.	15
6:00 P.M.–11:00 P.M.	32
11:00 P.M.–11:30 P.M.	15

6. The network can reduce the affiliated station's network rates if market conditions change (after at least 30 days' notice, in which event the broadcaster can terminate the affiliation agreement within a predetermined time period). The networks retain staffs to reevaluate rates, who recommend varied compensation rates in different time slots in order to get a better clearance pattern from their affiliates. For example, late-night clearance for CBS stations (11:30 P.M. to 2 A.M.) eroded to new lows in the late 1980s, and this daypart will need repair (more clearances) in the early 1990s in order to recover as a network profit center.

7. The network agrees to make compensation payments with reasonable promptness within a monthly accounting period.

8. The broadcaster agrees to submit reports related to the broadcasting of network programs. These are in the form of affidavits.

9. The Federal Communications Commission (FCC) rules fix the term of this agreement to two years with prescribed periods during the agreement when either party may notify the other of termination. If each party concurs, the agreement is renewed automatically for another two-year cycle. (The two-year term was selected because that originally was the duration of a station license. Now the station license is for five years, but the affiliation agreement has remained on a two-year cycle.)

10. If a broadcaster wants to transfer its license to another party, the network can examine the new owner before deciding whether to accept the change.

11. The agreement also lists the technical conditions under which the affiliate will carry the network programs (when a broadcast standard signal arrives to ensure picture quality, for example). *Clipping* (cutting off the beginnings or ends of programs or commercials), *reselling* (including permitting noncommercial stations to re-air network programs) or *altering* any of the contents of network shows is expressly prohibited.

12. The rights of the broadcaster, derived from the Communications Act of 1934, also are itemized: (a) The broadcaster can refuse or reject any network program that is reasonably unsatisfactory or unsuitable or contrary to the public interest. (b) The broadcaster has the right to substitute programs in lieu of the network's if the substitution is considered in the broadcaster's opinion of greater local or national importance. The network, in turn, has the right to substitute or cancel programs as it feels necessary.

13. The network must tell the broadcaster of any money, service or consideration it accepted in the preparation of network programs. This condition is in response to Section 317 of the Communications Act of 1934 requiring this disclosure.

14. The network also agrees to indemnify the broadcaster from and against all claims, damages, liabilities, costs and expenses arising out of the broadcasting of network programs that result in alleged libel, slander, defamation, invasion of privacy or violation or infringement of copyright, literary or dramatic rights involved in programs the network furnished.

This list is a condensation of a CBS television affiliation agreement, reflecting the basic considerations involved in an affiliate-network partnership. The network connection is primarily a financial agreement. By carrying the network programs, the affiliate station automatically has unsold spot time around and within these network programs (*adjacencies*). The money received by an affiliate for the sale of these adjacencies is the affiliate's own and is not shared with the network. The more popular the network programs, the more the affiliate can charge for these spots. In addition, an affiliate receives compensation and popular programs and has the bulk of its schedule filled without a cost outlay. The relationship between an affiliate and its network may sound simple, but an affiliation is like a marriage or partnership. When affiliates are cancelled by their networks, by losing the franchise to a local rival, they are forced into independent station status and struggle, often ineffectively, to maintain a strong position in the marketplace. An affiliation is a valuable asset and usually is cherished and guarded with care.

Station Goals

The primary goal of network affiliate programmers is to wrap strong offerings around the national programming, preferably such strong programs that, even when the network is not the leader, the local station is still number one. Despite the current philosophy of deregulation by government, programmers always must be concerned with service to the public and programming for the needs of the station's community. A shift in philosophy by the FCC could bring back the stringent regulations of the late 1950s, 1960s and early 1970s. Programmers, beware. A generous attitude toward local involvement will keep a station's license secure.

The marketplace is becoming glutted with new television outlets. Some of the enemies:

- Distant signals (WTBS, WGN, WWOR)
- Local religious stations (UHFs)
- Sports networks (ESPN, USA, regional networks)
- Home shopping networks (CVN, HSN)
- The Nashville Network (TNN)
- Religious cable networks (Inspirational, TBN)
- Family and health networks (CBN, Lifetime)
- Nickelodeon (children's shows)
- Music channels (MTV, VH-1)
- C-Span I and II (carries Congress live)
- Pay movie channels (HBO, Showtime, Disney)
- News Services (CNN, Headline, FNN)
- The Weather Channel (TWC)
- Adult channels (and cassettes)
- Arts channels (A&E, Bravo)
- Local community access channels
- Videocassettes for home rental and sale.

Today's programmer faces more predators than at any time in the history of television. None of the aforementioned programming services has enough strength to do major damage by itself, but collectively they add up to shares of 10 to 25 percent in some time slots in the schedule. Table 7-2 shows markets of various size, listing sign-on and sign-off ratings and shares along with the missing ratings and shares ("Others") accounting for the fractured HUT level.

The television spectrum has become a carnival midway with barkers hawking for viewership. The station programmer faces a fractured market; still, an affiliated station will be a dominant factor in the advertising sales of its market if the programmer makes the correct choices.

Weekly Programming Dayparts

The local station goes on the air around 6 A.M. and off the air at about 2 A.M. (or 6 A.M. the next morning on weekends), which means 20 or even 24 hours of programming for seven days in each week. The broadcast weekday is

Table 7-2 Competition to Broadcasters in Five Markets, 4–8 P.M.

		RATING	SHARE			RATING	SHARE
Los Angeles				Detroit			
KCBS	(CBS)	4	13	WJBK	(CBS)	6	17
KNBC	(NBC)	5	16	WDIV	(NBC)	9	24
KTLA	(IND)	3	10	WXYZ	(ABC)	8	23
KABC	(ABC)	6	18	WXON	(IND)	3	8
KHJ	(IND)	2	6	WKBD	(IND)	4	12
KTTV	(IND)	3	10	WTVS	(IND)	1	2
KCOP	(IND)	3	11	Others		5	14
KMEX	(IND)	1	5				
KVEA	(IND)	1	2	Portland			
KCET	(ED)	1	3	KATU	(ABC)	5	18
Others		3	6	KOIN	(CBS)	6	24
				KGW	(NBC)	6	22
Boston				KPTV	(IND)	3	11
WBZ	(NBC)	7	22	KPDX	(IND)	1	5
WCVB	(ABC)	5	17	KOAP	(PBS)	1	4
WNEV	(CBS)	5	16	KWTV	(IND)	–	–
WHLL		1	2	Others		3	16
WFXT	(IND)	1	4				
WSBK	(IND)	2	6	Columbus			
WLVI	(IND)	2	5	WCMH	(NBC)	6	25
WQTV	(IND)	1	2	WTVN	(ABC)	5	20
WGBH	(PBS)	1	4	WBNS	(CBS)	7	27
WMFT	(IND)	–	–	WTTE	(IND)	2	7
WCVX		–	–	WOSU	(PBS)	1	3
Others		6	22	WTBS	(IND)	1	3
				Others		4	15

Note: Where the missing rating points and shares ("others") go is not revealed. Each programmer should request yearly reports from Arbitron and Nielsen to find out where these missing elements are going and determine why people are defecting.

Source: Arbitron, May, 1987.

made up of ten time segments (EST/PST), about 30 percent of which must be filled by the local affiliate programmer:

early morning	6	A.M. to 9	A.M.
morning	9	A.M. to 12	Noon
afternoon	12	Noon to 4	P.M.
early fringe (late afternoon)	4	P.M. to 6	P.M.
early evening	6	P.M. to 7	P.M.
prime access	7	P.M. to 8	P.M.
prime time	8	P.M. to 11	P.M.
late fringe (late evening)	11	P.M. to 11:30	P.M.
late night	11:30 P.M. to 2	A.M.	
overnight	2	A.M. to 6	A.M.

These **dayparts** are the standard for Arbitron and Nielsen in the eastern and western time zones, and shift one or two hours in central and mountain time. There are some pockets throughout the nation that accommodate for daylight saving time—Indiana is one of those states where the 11 P.M. news is at 10 P.M. six months of the year. Ratings researchers use these dayparts to measure audience viewing, and sales departments use them to sell commercial time throughout each day. Programming strategies differ according to the time segment involved.

In four of these dayparts (*morning, afternoon, prime time* and *late night*), the network provides nearly all the programs. In *early morning* and *early evening* the networks contribute part of the programming. *Early fringe, access, late fringe* and *overnight* are wholly local responsibilities. This chapter looks at the local affiliate programmer's options in surrounding or replacing network programming for each of these successive dayparts. The programmer's strategies include *targeting, audience flow, lead-in effects, local appeal* and *reuse* of expensive syndicated programs.

EARLY MORNING

	Estimated HUT Level*
7 A.M.–8 A.M.	8–15%
8 A.M.–9 A.M.	15–23%

The strategies for 6 to 9 A.M. can be very simple for the affiliate program director commanding first or second place: Change nothing—*stay with the web.* If an independent is beating the affiliate in this time period, however, surgery may be necessary. Six options exist:

1. *Children's Programming.*   If the market has enough advertisers who target children, theatrical cartoons and animated half-hours for young children may be the answer. *Bugs Bunny, Popeye* and *Tom & Jerry* are all available in library form. Animated half-hours such as *Voltron, My Little Pony, He-Man* and *The Flintstones* still manage to get 10 to 18 shares in most U.S. markets in early morning. A small added benefit to building a library of theatrical cartoons is that they can be utilized as fill material at the end of motion pictures in other dayparts.

2. *Off-network Syndicated Sitcoms or One-hour Drama/Adventure Programs.*   Early morning is a fine place for the fifth and sixth runs of such programming as *Mork & Mindy, Andy Griffith, Beverly Hillbillies* and *Happy Days Again.* One also can burn up the last runs of such properties as *Love Boat, Perry Mason, Bonanza* and *Eight Is Enough.* Advertiser interest in this category is more pronounced than for children's shows and evenly distributed throughout the year.

---

*The estimated **Households Using Television** (HUT) level was determined by averaging the levels in ten markets of different sizes from the November 1986/May 1987 season rating books. Only the lowest and highest figures were recorded. This method shows the way HUT levels vary from market to market.

3. *Syndicated Women-oriented Programs.* *Hour Magazine* with Gary Collins, *Geraldo Live, Donahue* and *Getting in Touch* with Dr. David Viscott are samples of syndicated shows targeting women. Many of these programs would appeal to the stay-at-home women's audience available during these hours.

4. *Expandable Combinations.* A ploy used in several markets has been to invest in a local women-oriented program starting as a one-hour entry and expanding the show to two hours (from 8 to 10 A.M.) when ripe. Such programming is most successful when directed specifically toward the female audience remaining alone after families have left for school and work. The 8 A.M. start is advantageous because it bridges the 9 A.M. slot that *Donahue* has managed to "own" throughout the United States. A women's show is also highly salable every week in the year. Women's programs also can have frequent community-oriented segments that apply to FCC commitments for public service programming. A good example of this option is WEWS-TV's *Morning Exchange*, 8 to 10 A.M., Monday through Friday. This Cleveland station's program follows the talk/information format but is wholly locally produced.

5. *Paid Religious Programming.* Religion will bring in money but dismal ratings with the demographics in the 50+ category. Nonetheless, an hour of Falwell or Oral Roberts can be quite expedient.

6. *Syndicated and Local News.* Some stations have utilized CNN's Headline service interwoven with their own local updates. The structure is most effective in the 6 to 7 A.M. time slot because the early, male audience is interested in information and turns over frequently. The 8 to 9 A.M. period should have more entertainment value since the majority of heads of households have gone off to work.

The 6 to 9 A.M. slot must be researched more thoroughly by organizations such as Arbitron, American Research Bureau, Magid, or McHugh-Hoffman. The HUT levels from 8 to 9 A.M. appear to be as healthy as the 9 to noon levels in most markets. Further study with positive results could elevate affiliates' revenues, which in turn would allow them to license better program properties for this early-morning period.

MORNING

	Estimated HUT Level
9 A.M.–Noon	20–25%

Syndicated hours and half-hours, sitcoms, network delays, children's programming, talk shows and local live programs—all have found comfortable positions from mid-morning to noon. The audience during this time consists mainly of preschoolers and homemakers, retirees, and people available at home as a result of an odd-hour work shift. Stations that schedule *Donahue* during this period have little problem. *Donahue* remains "king of the mornings" whatever the competition, attracting 30 percent shares of the morning audience. The networks only partly fill the 9 A.M. to noon period (ABC fills 11–noon; CBS and NBC schedule 10–noon), so this pattern leaves plenty of opportunity for local programmers to exercise one of the following options:

1. Write off the station's investment in **off-network syndicated properties** (after use elsewhere) by placing them from 9 to 10 A.M. or 10 to 11 A.M., then joining the network. Off-network properties such as *Facts of Life, Kate & Allie* and *Newhart* will most likely be scheduled here.

2. Purchase a **first-run early-morning syndicated talk show.** Some programs have been developed precisely for this time slot— *Oprah, Donahue, Geraldo Live* and *The Wil Shriner Show.* Both *Donahue* and *Oprah* are strong enough to move from morning to afternoon and flourish. The most recent entries, such as *Wil Shriner,* must prove themselves.

3. Develop a **local live show.** Rating books show many local live programs, such as *AM Pittsburgh, Midmorning, AM Philadelphia* and Cleveland's *Morning Exchange.* Each of the five ABC O&Os produce a one-hour local live program (for example, *The Morning Show, AM Los Angeles* and *Kelly & Co.*), the structure of which would be worth studying if a programmer is thinking of going in this direction.

4. Many markets have tried a **movie** from 9 to 11 A.M. This option has been modestly successful, depending on the competition. It is ideal for an independent station, but a third-ranked affiliate may want to consider it if the station's film library can support it.

5. Develop a **game show block.** CBS now schedules game shows from 10 to 11 A.M.; therefore, two half-hours from 9 to 10 A.M. would make a perfect fit for CBS affiliates or as a counterprogramming move for ABC or NBC outlets.

6. Many markets have found a **courtroom block** to be very successful in the afternoon. Why not try it in the morning? By linking *The Judge, Superior Court, People's Court* or *Divorce Court,* one could have a one- or two-hour period of time that would be the right length for morning use.

The 9 A.M. to noon time period is characterized by **passive viewing,** a condition where viewers often leave the room to perform household tasks. A programmer must find shows that do not demand **high-intensity viewing** for more than one hour at a time. That is why half-hours ideally suit the morning. Many local shows are yet to be born using the mini-cam, which has the great benefit of going into the community rather than being frozen in a studio on a make-believe set. Major market stations in Boston, Los Angeles and Cleveland have attempted this kind of morning programming. These shows contain a provincial flavor, making them desirable for the local market but unsuitable for syndication on a national level.

AFTERNOON

	Estimated HUT Level
Noon–4 P.M.	26–32%

Network **soap operas** dominate the *early afternoon* daypart (noon to 4 P.M.). Affiliates should not consider preempting soap operas because once the cement of the drama hardens, dedicated viewers are glued—some for as long as 10 or 20 years. Preempting a favorite soap for a presidential speech or a news special brings an eruption of ire from addicts (put the news specials someplace else if not from the network). But several alternative programming possibilities should at least be considered for part of this time period. Most programmers divide the afternoon daypart into two parts: the noon hour and the 1 to 4 P.M. time period.

1. **Noon news** is popular with the stay-at-home audience. The noontime pause in at-home and office activities creates an ideal slot for information. Noon coverage of world and local activities is a ritual, as much for stations as for the audience. Stations aspiring to leadership in news coverage cannot omit the noon news. Furthermore, it makes money in spot sales and recycles and updates the top stories from the previous night's 11 P.M. news, which helps spread the high news expenditures.

2. An **afternoon movie** was highly popular with audiences in the 1950s and 1960s, but today most affiliates have abandoned this programming option. The 1 to 3 P.M. period would be nearly ideal for movies were it not for the continued popularity of soap operas in that time period. But movies could be an option for a station from noon to 2 P.M. if its news commitment does not take priority.

3. Although most network affiliates would be committing hara-kiri if they preempted the soaps during this period, a few do manage to get away with substituting either a local or regional **talk show** or a **syndicated property.** Generally, they get no better ratings than the poorest soaps.

Lack of clearances for some of the dayparts by many affiliates has resulted in an accommodation by the three television networks. CBS, for example, makes the 12 to 12:30 P.M. time slot available to affiliates for local use. NBC experienced a lack of clearance from 3 to 4 P.M. when they started *Santa Barbara.* Many affiliates moved *Santa Barbara* to the morning; others didn't carry it at all. In its place they put talk shows (mainly *Donahue* and *The Oprah Winfrey Show*) and, frequently, syndicated spot carriers (shows for which the stations pay cash-plus-barter minutes in order to produce revenue). If an affiliate is going to refuse to clear the network, it is wiser to do it before a new series starts; once the public sees the show, cancelation becomes noisy and painful.

EARLY FRINGE

	Estimated HUT Level
4 P.M.–6 P.M.	29–35%

Two major changes occurred during the mid-1980s in the 4 to 6 P.M. time period. First, all three networks relinquished the 4 to 4:30 P.M. time slot because of a consistent lack of affiliate clearances. Second, many affiliates backed up their local newscasts to 5:30 P.M. and, in some cases, to 5 P.M. In the top five markets, several affiliates even begin their news at 4 P.M. Two stations in Los Angeles (KNBC and KABC), for example, start the news war at 4 P.M., and WLS in Chicago also begins its news that early. The advantage is that early local news releases the whole hour of prime access time (7–8 P.M. EST) for first-run syndicated programming such as *Wheel of Fortune, Jeopardy, The Newlywed Game, Hollywood Squares* and the like. Although this strategy leaves the 4 to 6 P.M. time period somewhat fractured, it is still fertile territory for the following options.

90-Minute Options
1. The first option for early fringe is a **motion picture.** The 90-minute movie format, designed by the ABC O&O stations, started four decades ago when theatrical product was very scarce. The ABC O&O film editor would shave theatrical movies to fit an hour-and-a-half time slot. This meant that a 100-minute or longer feature film could be edited to 78 minutes, in order to make room for 12 minutes of commercials. *The Early Show, Movies in the Afternoon* and *Million Dollar Movie* are all umbrella titles under which affiliates of all three networks have placed the thousands of films found in such libraries as Paramount, MGM, MCA, 20th Century–Fox and Warner Brothers.

   There is an apocryphal story about Fred Silverman, now an independent producer, who (when he was a novice film editor at WGN-TV in Chicago) solved the length problem for an Elvis Presley movie, *Jailhouse Rock.* He merely eliminated the musical numbers! Silverman, too, almost was eliminated.

   A newer adaptation of **shaved-movie editing** is the **speeded-up** movie. New projection processes can mechanically condense a film, cutting its length by a sixth or so, just by speeding up the entire film. It is now possible to pick up time for commercial use without leaving out anything of the original. Only experts can detect when this device has been used.

2. Another approach to the 90-minute format is using **made-for-TV movies (MFTV)**. They are ideal to fill a 90-minute window since these television-ready productions have a running time of about 75 minutes. They need no editing; they simply can be slotted and filled with commercials and promotional spots. Another form of MFTV movie is the two-hour version that runs approximately 94 minutes. Like the shorter form, these MFTV movies are scripted to have natural breaks, and they fit into a two-hour time slot with great ease. However, the quality of these products rarely matches the quality of theatrical film; the name value of the stars is slightly less; and the promotional support is usually weaker. Nevertheless, in recent years—because of cable and pay television—MFTV movies are not overexposed and can compete effectively with their oft-seen theatrical counterparts.

Stripping Off-Network Reruns

Because the **prime-time access rule** (de facto) prohibits affiliates in the top 50 markets from using network reruns in the hour preceding network time, affiliates typically use the sitcom in early fringe programming. Independent stations can now afford very high prices for off-network reruns to schedule against affiliates' newscasts between 6 to 8 P.M., forcing network affiliates to come up with large expenditures to control the early fringe time. Such shows as *The Cosby Show, Who's the Boss?, Growing Pains, Newhart, Kate & Allie, Cheers, Night Court* and *Family Ties* now typically appear in early fringe on affiliates. *Alf* and *Head of the Class* will soon join this group. Four half-hour series are ideal for filling the 4 to 6 P.M. period. If one of the four series is weak, the station can plug in another. Between 4 and 6 P.M., affiliates use a strategy called "aging your demos." The strategy requires starting with **kiddult** comedies around 4 P.M., phasing into **family** programs around 4:30–5 P.M., and following with **adult** programs as a lead-in to the 5:30–6 P.M. news.

Acquisitions for a two-hour comedy block are becoming increasingly expensive. For example, the cost of popular off-network reruns increased from a low of $600 to an extreme high of $26,000 per episode in the five years from 1982 to 1987 in the Columbus (Ohio) market, ranked 35th. *Who's the Boss?*, for example, went for $12,000 an episode in this market.

Competition has forced the affiliate stations to vie mightily for these high-priced network reruns, driving the prices up still further. Even though an affiliate (in one of the 50 largest markets) cannot run these programs in access time, record prices have been received for *The Cosby Show,* eclipsing any prior sale. Viacom was able to command more than double or triple the previous market high when it sold *Cosby* to stations. Moreover, Viacom included a clause in *The Cosby Show* syndication contract that gives the distributor the right to withhold one minute of commercial time for its use. (This is called a **barter spot** and must be figured in the cost of each episode as explained in

Chapter 3: It means the station gets 5½ minutes to sell, and the distributor gets 1 minute.) There are other peculiarities to the *Cosby* deal. Viacom's contract gives each station only one exposure of *Cosby* per day on a Monday to Friday basis. It also controls which episode is to be run. This contract started in 1988, and Viacom (not the stations) schedules the shows over the 182 weeks. Over a 3½-year period, some episodes will run as often as seven to eight times, while others will run only three to four times. In this manner, Viacom maximizes the value of its 1-minute barter time (all the viewers see the same episode and its ads at the same time) and also takes the most advantage of television and print campaigns. Other distributors, selling such products as *Who's the Boss?*, have come up with variations of the Viacom prototype. (In the traditional deal, the station retains all minutes and pays straight cash, thus gaining control of the scheduling and frequency of all episodes, distinct advantages for the cash-rich affiliate.)

The barter consideration seems to be here to stay. For some time now, game shows such as *Wheel of Fortune* and *Jeopardy* have included one minute of barter in each of their properties. King World's *Oprah* demands two minutes of barter time for the distributor, leaving the station ten minutes to sell (in this 60-minute show). The new "rule" of 60 seconds of barter time for every half-hour applies only to *first-run* syndicated programs such as *Oprah* at this time; there is no rule for off-network barter deals as yet. However, as stations negotiate for megahits, they increasingly are required to pay cash and give away barter time. Barter has become a major factor in many *off-network* and *most first-run* syndication negotiations.

Long-running network series have been scarce in recent years; in consequence, syndicated properties with the 130 episodes ideal to program on a Monday through Friday (**stripped**) basis are rare. There are actually 260 time slots per year to fill (52 weeks × 5 days). If the series has 130 episodes, each show can be repeated twice a year with a six-month rest between exposures. This cycle is ideal for a good show. If a syndicated series has fewer than 130 episodes, individual episodes must be rerun more often unless the station regularly schedules sports or election-year programming in that slot. If it has more than 130, fewer reruns are needed, or the cycle can be stretched to cover more weeks. Syndicated series with 160 or more episodes command very high prices in the major markets.

The catch is that, as of the 1980s, the networks began licensing only 22 or so new episodes of any series each year. (In the 1960s, as many as 39 episodes were produced for a prime-time slot; see discussion in Chapter 5.) A series now has to run for six years to amass 132 episodes—and very few programs have had that kind of longevity. When a show does stay on the network that long, most stations want to buy it, and the distributor jacks up the price to match the demand. Some shows that have hit the golden jackpot in recent years have been *Taxi*, *M*A*S*H*, *Little House on the Prairie*, *All in the Family*, *The Jeffersons*, *Cheers*, *Family Ties*, *The Cosby Show*, *Night Court* and *Who's The Boss?*

Programmers, beware of *hidden futures costs*. A recent network cancelation affected the syndicated sale and scheduling of *Webster*. This was an ABC property, placed on Friday nights at 8 P.M. during the 1986–87 season.

Paramount, the syndicator, sold futures on 100 episodes of *Webster* to dozens of stations with the understanding that it would deliver a minimum of 100 and a maximum of 150 episodes for stripping on a rerun basis beginning in the fall of 1988. *Webster* was presold to many stations two years before it became eligible to be aired (**futures**). But in mid-1987 ABC cancelled *Webster* on the network (with only 100 episodes produced), and the stations were suddenly faced with a contract clause giving Paramount the right to produce 50 original episodes over the two seasons following network cancelation. This brings to 150 the number of episodes available for syndication but greatly increases the cost of the show to stations. Originally scheduled for a fall 1988 start-up, stations now have the option of stripping the 100 off-network *Webster* episodes, starting in 1988, or televising just the new first-run episodes on a weekly basis. However, in order to assure enough episodes for stripping, all participating stations have agreed to "pony up" 25 percent of the license fee in cash (collectively) for each new *Webster* episode to cover the show's production costs. Because of ongoing contracts with the actors, writers and producers, the cost probably will stay close to the $450,000 per episode figure that was the license fee when it was on the network. Many programmers did not expect ABC to cancel *Webster* when they signed the contract. They knew of the clause but figured it was highly unlikely that ABC would cancel a program whose ratings were higher than those of most ABC shows that season. Most stations were not prepared to pay the extra money; they assumed the network would pay the bill for them by keeping *Webster* on the network for two more seasons. Paramount's *Webster* deal has been an industry eye-opener.

In addition to barter and futures deals, another method of obtaining strip product is the **front- and back-end deal.** This method required a station to run a property only once a week until enough episodes have accumulated for stripping, usually three to five years. The original syndication contract for *Star Trek*, for example, required the station to pay so much per episode on the front end and once again to pay at the back end when the show became available for stripping. The advantage of the deal is that it gives the station control of a once-a-week property that eventually will accumulate enough episodes to be stripped. If the property falters, the show gets cancelled; if it is successful for five to six seasons, the station then has a viable first-run property that it can play any place, including in access time.

Early Fringe Blocks

Four kinds of shows have characterized the early-fringe time period on affiliates. The current trend is to *counterprogram* by blocking several similar shows together, provided they make an effective lead-in to local news.

1. *Children's Programming.*   Most affiliates have turned away from children's programming in the 4 to 6 P.M. period for two reasons: First, deregulation by the FCC eliminated its intimidation factor, once forcing stations de facto to air children's programming somewhere in the schedule; second, the advertising support for this type of programming generally is only available in the third and fourth quarters (back-to-school and Christmas). Children's fare has found its haven on independent stations. Distributors have been able to barter children's programs or sell them for cash to independents, and they showcase such winners as *She-Ra; G.I. Joe; The Transformers; Silverhawks; He-Man, Master of the Universe; The Smurfs;* and such standbys as *Fat Albert, Woody Woodpecker, Popeye, Bugs Bunny, The Flintstones, The Jetsons, My Little Pony* and *Tom & Jerry.* Most stations place these children's programs from 6 to 9 A.M. and from 4 to 6 P.M. in most markets. Besides being a revenue source, children's programs get kids to turn on the set. Smart programmers start from that point and phase into more adult programming. This practice (*aging your demos*) characterizes many affiliates and most major-market independents in early fringe.

2. Court Shows.   Courtroom dramas have mushroomed: Available now are *The Judge, People's Court, Divorce Court, Superior Court, The Supreme Court* and other less well-known efforts. This type of programming is excellent counterprogramming against other genres, especially if three or four are strung together. By placing the strongest of the court shows first, the other two or three can follow the leader. This format was a staple in Detroit in the late 1950s, and then came to Columbus, Ohio, in the 1960s. It flourished there for many years under such titles as *Traffic Court, Juvenile Court, Municipal Court* and *The Judge* (this last was licensed for syndication nationally in 1986 by Genesis Entertainment). A court show block is particularly effective against talk shows and sitcoms.

3. Game Shows.   Many affiliates have been successful in developing a game show block. There certainly is an ample supply—*$100,000 Pyramid, New Card Sharks, Jeopardy, The New Hollywood Squares, Chance of a Lifetime, Lingo, Match Game, Super Password, The New Family Feud* and on and on. Game show shares range from 10 to 20 percent and have become an economical form of programming in early fringe (and access) for any size market.

4. Magazine Talk Shows.   The grandaddy of all magazine talk shows is *Donahue.* He proved he could get big ratings in the morning. Then along came *Oprah Winfrey* in 1986. She proved not only could win in the morning but dominate in the afternoon. Oprah is now called "queen of the afternoons," capturing shares of 30 percent in afternoons and reaching nearly 10 million viewers, most of them women. *Sally Jesse Raphael* has continued the tradition but in a half-hour format, and her program is especially effective if it is placed adjacent to a *Donahue* or an *Oprah,* establishing a carry-over factor. New entries in the talk format are *Geraldo Live* and *Ask Dr. Ruth.* The two heavyweights in this division remain *Donahue* and *Oprah;* if you can afford them (and your competitors failed to get there first), they are worth the franchise.

A non-issue-oriented talk form is the successful *Hour Magazine* with Gary Collins. He manages to blend interviews, information and music. Another entry is Group W's *The Wil Shriner Show,* which is lighthearted and breezy in style. These programs have been scheduled mainly in the mornings, and have done extremely well for audiences who prefer more of a magazine format in early fringe.

EARLY EVENING

	Estimated HUT Level
6 P.M.–7 P.M.	41–53%

The 6 to 7 or 7:30 P.M. time period usually is devoted to news on most affiliates. Each network provides 30 minutes of national coverage. Affiliates in markets below the top five adhere to one of two patterns: (a) precede or follow the network news with 30 minutes or one hour of local news, or (b) sandwich the national news between two local newscasts, a 30-minute one preceding and a 30-minute one following.

1. *Local News Block.* Some stations in the top five markets have instituted *two-hour local news* programs that start around 5 P.M. and stretch to 7 P.M., at which time they add the *network news,* for a total of two and a half hours of news. (In a few cases, this news block starts as early as 4 P.M.) This much news, of course, must utterly dominate the ratings or fall victim to counter-programming that usually wins in total audience preference. The total *news* audience typically skews old, so winning the key 18–49-year-old audience is more important to gaining some advertisers, and therefore the all-important revenue, than winning the ratings in the adults 18 + demographic group.

2. *Sandwich News.* For the average affiliate, *90 minutes of news* between 6 and 7:30 P.M. is all its market can handle. The most successful structure has been the **sandwich,** which splits the local news into two sections: The six o'clock unit carries the fast-breaking items, and the seven o'clock segment handles the follow-ups and feature material. Of course, sports and weather can be sprinkled through both portions. Many markets have added a 5:30 P.M. news section featuring hard news headlines and reports from sites in the ADI (area of dominant influence). ENG equipment, remote trucks, helicopters and mobile satellite dishes bring in events from the outlying reaches of a station's coverage (**remotes**), making local people, places and events more important in the overall news picture.

The affiliate with the strongest news team usually dominates its market. Local evening news is television's front page. Beginning in the 1970s, competition became so fierce that consulting firms sprouted everywhere to advise stations on presenters, content, format structure, set design, program pace and even the clothing to be worn by the on-air personnel. This has resulted in look-alike newscasts across the country, featuring Barbie-doll anchors and cloned news stories. An affiliate can avoid this by developing a particular style of presentation and employing on-the-air newscasters and reporters who depend on their journalistic talents more than they depend on their looks. The copycat news organizations are effective for a little while but are always vulnerable to the real professionals in the long run.

PRIME ACCESS

	Estimated HUT Levels
7 P.M.–8 P.M.	52–62%

Access time is that half-hour moat dug by Westinghouse to prevent the broadcast networks from further invading their affiliates' schedules (and as a self-serving device to strengthen Group W's syndication arm, which was producing first-run programs suitable for this time period). The hope that access time would stimulate quality programs has long since faded, and what remains is largely a nightmare of game shows and recycled quiz formats.

1. *First-Run Syndicated Half-Hours.* Once a bright flower bloomed in the access desert in the form of *The Muppets;* its popularity (ratings) had faded, however, by the early 1980s. As new properties faltered and old programs died from fatigue, the idea of stripping first-run game shows accelerated in popularity. If one episode of a show works once a week, why not five times a week? Consequently, television logs have become loaded Monday through Friday with such gems as *Wheel of Fortune, Jeopardy, Joker's Wild, Family Feud* and *Tic Tac Dough.* The anemia in suitable first-run programs for access is evident in Table 7-3, a list of the top ten prime access shows from late 1987.

Another syndicated property that has managed to hang on over the years is *Entertainment Tonight.* This is a magazine concept requiring no local station involvement. Slick, polished and timely, *Entertainment Tonight* combines some of the most successful elements of *PM Magazine* with fan magazine trivia. However, this program too has peaked and appears to have settled into third place (in access shares) behind the superhit games, *Wheel of Fortune* and *Jeopardy.* The newest entry with a magazine format is *USA Today,* copying the popular newspaper. It was expected to be so successful that it was purchased by stations in half the top 50 markets even before a pilot show was available.

2. *Local Access Shows.* Some stations, unwilling to wait for syndicators to develop a long-lasting new genre to fit the 7–8 P.M. time period, are doing it themselves. In the early 1970s the Group W station in San Francisco, KPIX-TV, applied its budget for prime access to an innovative local magazine show entitled *Evening.* This program reflected San Francisco's lifestyle, its people, its oddities and its beauty. The show proved such a success that the remaining Group W stations in Pittsburgh, Boston, Philadelphia and Baltimore adopted the pattern. Eventually, the group-owned stations started to exchange program segments, and it became apparent that other stations might be able to use this material if a show like *Evening* were begun in markets across the country. *Evening* went into syndication as *PM Magazine* in 1978, and it became the backbone of the access time period for nearly 140 stations for several years. However, the ratings for *PM Magazine* waned in 1985 and 1986, and finally in 1987, Westinghouse pulled the plug on its syndication. Some stations have made a deal with Group W to continue their season of *PM*

Table 7-3 Top Ten Prime Access Shows, 1987

	RATING / SHARE
1. *Wheel of Fortune*	16.0 / 32
2. *Oprah Winfrey*	11.0 / 32
3. *Jeopardy!*	10.0 / 27
4. *Entertainment Tonight*	9.0 / 19
5. *People's Court*	9.0 / 22
6. *Donahue*	8.0 / 22
7. *M*A*S*H**	8.0 / 19
8. *Family Ties**	7.0 / 15
9. *Dukes of Hazzard**	7.0 / 19
10. *Cheers**	7.0 / 15

*Off-network shows not available for access in top 50 markets.

Source: Nielsen Syndication Service, November 1987 Cassandra Rankings. Used with permission.

in their respective markets with help from Group W O&O stations. The *PM* concept often lacked balance between syndicated material and local stories. If the local material is downplayed, the entire show loses its local flavor and then depends entirely on the universality of the syndicated pieces for its appeal, a risky expectation. The Group W *Evening/PM* concept should lead other broadcasters to develop formats producible, at least in part, in their own markets rather than to continue depending on established programs from national syndicators.

3. *Blocks.* The year 1987 saw the return of **checkerboarding** (rotating several shows on different week days in the same half-hour) in access time, which had been on hiatus during the early and mid-1980s. It exploded with *The Newlywed Game* and *The Dating Game,* and *Family Feud* kept it rolling in the mid-1980s; *Win, Lose or Draw* joined this hit group in the late 1980s. Although *Wheel of Fortune* and *Jeopardy* remain the dominant programs in the 7–8 P.M. time period, competing stations have encouraged syndicators to produce more first-run, once-a-week sitcoms for checkerboarding against a game show block. Included in the current crop are *Charles in Charge, We've Got It Made, Suddenly Sheriff, Marblehead Manor, You Can't Take It with You* and *The Dom Deluise Show.* In some markets, these sitcoms were placed under a generic umbrella such as *Comedy Playhouse* or *Comedy Checkerboard.* Ratings for these programs have not been outstanding, but they have established themselves as an alternative. Stations are hoping that one or two first-run weekly situation comedies will survive long enough to be stripped Monday through Friday at some time in the future.

Syndicators still are trying to find the new winners of the future. Titles such as *Dreamhouse, Home Shopping Game, Secrets & Rumors* and *Truth or Consequences* are all possible contenders. King World has recently licensed a game in search of a television format: It will be interesting to see what producers create out of *Monopoly* for television.

PRIME TIME

	Estimated HUT Level
8–11 P.M. (EST)	58–66%

Prime time is the most highly viewed period of the daily schedule for affiliates. From 8 to 11 P.M., the networks pour on expensive and highly competitive programs, supported by arresting promotional campaigns on the air and in newspaper and magazine ads. Independent stations have been unable to bite into this time period with any consistency, and it remains the payload of the three national networks. The networks must get clearances by affiliates for this time if they are to maintain network parity. Any network riddled by a high percentage of nonclearances may damage its position as a leader simply because some of its programming is not being seen by the public. Each nonclearance becomes a zero when the ratings are being tabulated. Even a delayed broadcast of a program would count for something in the tabulation.

Preemption

From time to time, an affiliate may identify a section of the network schedule that needs repair but that the network cannot fix until later in the season. Under these conditions, an affiliate might "pick off" a weak night for a local movie special, a musical-hour special or a program having some significance to the local community. Networks tolerate these **preemptions** if they do not happen too often, and the station need only convince its viewers that a preemption is justified. When the public is not convinced, phone calls, letters and the press scold the affiliate for its defection.

It is best to preempt on *different* days rather than pick off the same time slot week after week because regular preemptions irritate viewers who are robbed of certain shows.

Judgment must be exercised when bumping a *new* network show that appears to be doomed in the New York or Los Angeles overnight ratings. Many a programmer has been burned by preempting a big-city loser only to find that it became a hit in local markets, and that, with time, it also became a hit in the big city. This situation occurred with *Murder, She Wrote, 60 Minutes, Golden Girls* and *Little House on the Prairie*.

There are some stations located in university towns with outstanding national football and basketball programs. These hotbeds of sports often can cause a network much consternation. Seventy-five hours or more of network prime-time fare can be refused when regional and local sports bump network shows. When this occurs, the network does *not pay* its affiliate for nonclearance, and the affiliate *must pay* for this new programming. If the local team is hot, the ratings can be very high, but a losing season can make the affiliate wish the station had taken the network programming. It is always a risky choice unless the local team is a national contender.

Networks will, under some circumstances, offer an affiliate the chance to place a preempted program in a nonnetwork time slot (**delayed carriage**). The affiliate usually can find a suitable time slot for a preempted program in late night or on weekends. Seldom, if ever, will a network permit a preempted program to cover another network program.

In examining the track record of an affiliate, a network often studies the preemption ratio in order to determine how "loyal" a station has been over a period of time. The network will use this defection as a wedge, especially if the affiliate wants to increase its network's hourly compensation rate. A *good clearance record* is, more often than not, a valued chip to be used in network negotiations. A maverick station not only will be watched carefully but might be subject to *compensation cuts* if the station does not come into line with other affiliates in total audience delivery.

LATE FRINGE, LATE NIGHT AND OVERNIGHT

Late fringe begins with the half-hour directly following prime time and continues into the late- and late-late-night periods, eventually arriving at morning (6 A.M.) on some stations.

Late Fringe News

	Estimated HUT Level
11 P.M.–11:30 P.M.	32–45%

Affiliates traditionally reserve **late fringe,** the 11–11:30 P.M. time slot, for **late local newscasts.** A carry-over from radio, the eleven o'clock news is part of the ingrained tradition of affiliate programming. Only an independent can counterprogram with movies or other programming, and not many have been successful in the 11 P.M. to 1 A.M. zone. The affiliate has the edge, and a habit pattern is very difficult to break.

Independent stations have tried to break the 11 P.M. news hold for years with first-run shows. Only one show—*Mary Hartman, Mary Hartman*—dented the public's late news loyalty; this happened in most markets for two to three years, then the news regained its losses. The Fox Network had hoped to repeat *Mary Hartman*'s success at 11 P.M. with *The Late Show with Joan Rivers.* Unfortunately, the public did not accept the show, and after approximately 26 weeks, Fox blew the whistle and fired Joan Rivers. However, Fox programming on many independents continues to challenge affiliate news at 11 P.M.

Late Night Entertainment

	Estimated HUT Level
11:30 P.M.–2 A.M.	22–30%

The last weeknight segment most affiliate programmers must fill is the 11:30 P.M.–2 A.M. period, **late night.** NBC's the *Tonight Show* was untouchable in the ratings until Johnny Carson's 1979 contract allowed him to pretape two days a week (nonlive) in addition to having 17 weeks' vacation during the year (co-hosts required). Both ABC and CBS made gains against these irregularities on NBC. Carson's 1987 contract reduced him to three appearances a week and a one-hour show. This gives other affiliates and independents another chance to invade the Carson bastion.

The networks scheduled large numbers of reruns, mostly cop and detective shows, to fill this period in the late 1970s. By the early 1980s, CBS was trying adult action/adventure reruns such as *Hart to Hart* and *Magnum, P.I.* with some success. In the mid-1980s, ABC's *Nightline* got high ratings, but an in-depth news show usually demands a diet of political crises to survive. *Nightline* suffers from lack of live clearances; many stations delay its broadcast until midnight. This move cripples its chances of getting good ratings. NBC initiated its own late-late talk show (following *Tonight*), *Late Night with David Letterman*, with spectacular success for a while. Both ABC and CBS fell back again against NBC's onslaught (see Chapter 6).

There are several gambits that affiliates can employ at 11:30 P.M.:

1. Carry the Network.

2. Sitcoms and Movies.   Most affiliates program their movies from 11:30 P.M. to 2:00 A.M. A variation of this pattern is to place a half-hour off-network sitcom (*Taxi, Barney Miller, Cheers*) at 11:30 P.M. and start the movie at midnight. A third possibility is to use the 11:30 to 12:00 slot for sitcoms and follow with a delayed broadcast of the network, such as the *CBS Late Movie*.

3. A 60-minute Adventure Series.   The hour adventure show has found a home from 11:30 P.M. to 12:30 A.M. *Magnum, Simon & Simon* and (eventually) *The Equalizer* have gotten good ratings for their entire run, followed by a theatrical movie starting at 12:30 A.M. The first 60 minutes comes up with good ratings, but the nonmovie people defect at 12:30, wiping out the early gains. It appears that the long form, using an 11:30 movie start, is the most economical and wisest structure for most affiliates, especially since feature films also can be rerun in earlier time slots, maximizing the flexibility of theatrical and made-for-TV products.

4. Movies.   Scheduling feature films in alternative time periods became increasingly important in the 1980s as film syndicators sought to reduce the length of rental agreements. A **play** or **run** is one exposure of any part of a program or film on the air, and every airing constitutes a valuable property for both the station and the syndicator. Syndicators want to maximize the number of plays on pay television after a film has appeared in syndication (see Chapter 11), and short contracts allow a movie to return rapidly to the syndication market for resale. This practice forces an affiliate to use up all the runs the station purchased within a short length of time, as short as three years for many contracts (for three runs). Affiliates (and independents—see Chapter 8) had traditionally commanded contracts of six or more runs over a period of six years for movie packages but were forced to change their movie scheduling strategies in the mid-1980s.

Overnight Options

	Estimated HUT Level
2 A.M.–6 A.M.	5–8%

For some affiliate programmers, usually in urban markets, one time period remains to be filled, the **overnight** slot. In some markets, this daypart ends about 4 A.M. or whenever the movie is over. In other markets, stations program all 24 hours, concluding the overnight period at 6 A.M. just in time for early-early-morning programming.

1. *Movies.* Most stations program the overnight time period only on Friday and Saturday nights, but a slowly increasing number of affiliates have copied successful independents in their markets and counterprogrammed a second and even third round of movies during the weekday overnight period.

2. *More News.* CBS affiliates have CBS *News Nightwatch* available for part of this time (see Chapter 6). Stations can also license Turner's *Headline News* for the full overnight to feed the information-hungry.

3. *Experiments.* It would be interesting to see some station repeat its 4 to 6 P.M. programming in the 2 to 4 A.M. period. Sitcoms at 11:30 P.M. have proven successful. Why not string a bunch together, even though they are in the seventh and eighth runs, and see what happens? Another experiment would be to take the network's prime time and repeat it from 2 to 5 A.M. Research in the top five markets has indicated there are a lot of people still awake and watching television—third-shift workers, service workers and night people pop up in metered markets in surprising numbers. This is another time period badly in need of research, which could result in an untapped revenue center for affiliates. **Residual rights** (royalty payments for reuse of the shows), however, would make this programming difficult to arrange.

WEEKEND REALITIES

Saturday and Sunday create a different set of programming problems. Football, basketball, bowling, baseball, tennis, golf, auto racing, horse racing and boxing all take turns at capturing the adult male viewer. Cartoons draw children, and dancing captures the female teens.

Saturdays

On Saturdays, if a station schedules a **two-hour movie,** perhaps from 10:30 A.M. to 12:30 P.M., family viewing can be encouraged in a time period historically reserved for children. Scheduling a movie also can yield 52-week advertising sales contracts without depending on kid-oriented commercials, which usually are viable only during the third and fourth quarters (because advertisers buy time to announce back-to-school and Christmas sales). Careful selection of stars and titles can lure parents into watching the films along with the children. Elvis Presley, Jerry Lewis, John Wayne, Francis the Talking Mule, Ma and Pa Kettle, and science fiction titles are all sure-fire, split-level (**kiddult**) audience getters of this type.

Country-western and Nashville **music** also can be used for counter-programming. Saturdays from 2 to 4 P.M. or 4 to 6 P.M. are ideal time blocks for such programming. These shows usually cost little and easily can be promoted if the community likes the music.

The toughest hour on Saturday for the affiliate to fill is the 7 to 8 P.M. time slot, especially if the competition already owns *Fame* and *Hee Haw*. A good attack is to program a *Bugs Bunny* or *Tom & Jerry*–type house show against these giants. The **cartoon half-hour** will garner young demographics (18–34) and set up whatever is planned at 7:30 to complete the hour. Use the rabbit, mouse or cat to lead the way, and almost anything will work at 7:30 P.M.

The other successful option has been the **dance program.** Syndicated weekly shows like *Dance Fever* and *Solid Gold* draw predominantly female audiences with good numbers on early Saturday evenings. The number of new syndicated dance and music programs, following up on the success of MTV, the cable channel programming short **videos** (performance clips), dramatically increased in the mid-1980s, creating new, albeit untried, options for the adventurous affiliate with plenty of teens in the local market. By the late 1980s, dance and video popularity had faded, and the Saturday prime access is awaiting the development of new forms. Many affiliates just go with the sixth or seventh rerun of *Wheel* and *Jeopardy* and the like.

Late Saturday night traditionally has been programmed with **feature films.** NBC's *Saturday Night Live* arrived in the late 1970s, developing a large new audience, the college-age group. Their taste for **sophisticated comedy** relegated theatrical films to second place in most markets. A programmer must choose contemporary box office hits to stay within competitive reach of the syndicated first-cast version *Saturday Night Live* (the later cast has been much less successful). If recent movies fail to work, one can try classic films (*Citizen Kane, Rebecca, Casablanca*). A comedy block also could be tried from 11:30 P.M. to 1:30 A.M., made up of half-hours back-to-back in the genre of *M*A*S*H, All in the Family, Cheers, Three's Company, ALF* and *Who's the Boss?*

Sundays

The affiliate has very little room to maneuver on most Sundays. The afternoons contain season-to-season sports (network or regional), news from 6 to 7 P.M. and network entertainment from 7 to 11 P.M. The only period left for local development is the morning. This ghetto usually has contained network public affairs, religious and cultural programs, panel shows and some kids' shows—all of which spell low ratings and low income.

When scheduling Sundays, the affiliate programmer should consider "service people" who work evenings all week and never have a chance to see prime-time programming on workdays. The night people are out there; they just need something with mass appeal. And how about all those people who go to church early and all those people who do not go to church?

The most successful property one can schedule on Sunday mornings is a prime-time–type **feature film.** Name the 10 A.M. to noon period something other than "Atheist Theater" and watch the numbers roll in. With limited competition, the HUT level will explode, and advertising revenue will follow shortly. If success comes quickly, the station should consider backing up the start to eight o'clock for the fifth and sixth runs of **sitcoms** that are always tough to play off. A wasteland can be turned into a highly watched and lucrative programming period. Cable television imports such as CBN, TBN and independent stations have relieved most broadcasters of the obligation to provide televised religion on Sunday mornings, although that obligation was always more myth than reality.

Late Sunday night following the 11 P.M. news also remains a difficult time to program—it is the Siberia of the weekly schedule. If the community is large enough, a 60-minute **adventure series** or a **short movie** is the best a programmer can do because of the low number of homes watching television. Using HUT levels as a guide always raises the chicken-and-egg question, however. Perhaps HUT levels are down because little worth watching is ever scheduled in the late-late time period. Certainly, some independents in major markets draw a salable-size audience. It might be worth a gamble to try some better-quality films and promote them on Sunday nights.

THE PROGRAMMING WAR

By studying other markets similar to their own, programmers can learn a great deal from other situations throughout the country. It is not a foolproof system—what works in New York does not work necessarily in Peoria—but if one can align the home market with other similar markets, there is a lot to be learned.

The affiliate programmer must continue to scan the marketplace to find new forms that might reshape the late afternoon to the station's benefit. Programmers must read the trade magazines religiously and ferret out the unusual and untried, as hit programming sometimes comes from unexpected sources. There is no longer "a little guy" in programming. Many programmers have banded together to form screening committees, which meet before the NATPE annual conference and jointly view first-run pilots, verifying their collective evaluation of these efforts. This gives the lone affiliate programmer parity with the program teams of group-owned stations. It is most important to be able to screen and negotiate for all properties. That only can be done by monitoring what's being produced, knowing which outfit will distribute it, and understanding the likely contract terms.

Programming is war. You are a general. The object is to win—win in all time periods. Winning means high ratings. High ratings bring top dollars from the advertiser, and top dollars let you control the market for another season. If you can do this and still keep a balanced schedule reflecting community needs, cultural roots and the entertainment demands of your audience, then, indeed, you are a programmer.

SUMMARY

A program schedule must be analyzed hour-by-hour to take into account available options, the competition and the economic benefits of reusing already-purchased programs. Network affiliates are bound by contract and by financial advantage to their networks, and those in the top 50 markets remain more restricted by FCC regulation than independents and affiliates in mid-sized and smaller markets. A network affiliation supplies popular programs, adjacencies and compensation, but PTAR rules access. If an affiliate's options are few, however, its visibility is generally greater than an independent's (or a public station's), and one of the network affiliates holds top place in nearly every market in nearly every time period. The strategies that get them there include targeting a major demographic group that is unserved to build a new audience (local women's programs or off-network sitcoms for night workers in mornings) or providing a desirable lead-in to succeeding programs (stripped movies or reruns before evening news are an example, cartoons in weekend access is another). Audience flow is the prime consideration in early fringe in order to draw a male-adult audience for local news. Throughout the schedule, unused runs of popular syndicated series (off-network reruns) provide the fodder to build strong ratings.

Notes

1. Steve Behrens, "Will Temptation Undo the Tie That Binds?" *Channels*, May 1987, pp. 41–43. See also, "Compensation: Network Television's Costly Controversy," *View*, 2 March 1987, pp. 31–35.

2. **Parity** exists when all three networks reach approximately the same number of households in a given daypart. When too many affiliates of one network refuse to clear a particular time period (because a low-rated program is scheduled, for example), that network no longer has any chance of massive improvements in that program's ratings since ratings are a percentage of the *total* U.S. households. And of course, the network's overall rating is affected—which in turn affects its advertising rates and therefore its profitability.

3. Preemptions also allow the local station to charge national spot rates rather than local rates for its prime time, creating a strong incentive to preempt if other program options are available.

Selected Sources

Austin, Bruce A. "People's Time in a Medium-Sized Market: A Content Analysis." *Journalism Quarterly* 57 (Spring 1980): 67–70.

Boemer, Marilyn Lawrence. "Correlating Lead-In Show Ratings with Local Television News Ratings." *Journal of Broadcasting & Electronic Media* 31:1 (Winter 1987): 89–94.

Channels. Periodic reports on the new television season, syndicated shows and local television news.

"Journalism Special Report," *Electronic Media* (31 August 1987): J1–J19.

"Special Report: Journalism," *Broadcasting* (16 November 1981): 39–48; (26 July 1982): 39–91; (27 September 1982): 43–71; (25 July 1983): 37–84; (27 August 1984): 47–108; (17 December 1984): 47–62; (7 April 1986): 45–123; (28 April 1986): 46–65; (31 August 1987): 41–52.

Wakslag, Jacob J.; Agostino, Donald E.; Terry, Herbert A.; Driscoll, Paul; and Ramsey, Bruce. "Television News Viewing and Network Affiliation Changes," *Journal of Broadcasting* 27 (Winter 1983): 53–68.

CHAPTER 8 \ INDEPENDENT STATION PROGRAMMING

Edward G. Aiken

A Guide to Chapter 8

Edward G. Aiken is vice-president and general manager of WTOG-TV, Tampa–St. Peters-burg, Florida. He gained experience as producer/director and promotion manager at WBAY-TV in Green Bay, Wisconsin, before going to WNEM-TV in Saginaw, Michigan, as program director in 1970. He joined KPHO-TV in Phoenix, Arizona, in the same capacity in 1973. In the 1970s KPHO became a leading independent television station, winning against affiliate competition in several time periods and creating a programming model for other independents. In 1980 Mr. Aiken became vice-president/director of programming for Petry Television, Inc., one of the largest station representative firms in New York. He specialized in syndicated television programming, especially movies, for independent client stations, advising stations on syndicated purchases and scheduling, and representing the rep point of view as an industry spokesperson. In 1984 he became vice-president and general man-ager of Pappas Telecasting's KMPH-TV in Fresno, California. The following year, he was named senior vice-president of Pappas Telecasting as well as vice-president and general manager of a second station, WHNS-TV in Asheville, North Carolina. In 1986 Mr. Aiken joined Hubbard Broadcasting's WTOG-TV. This chapter shows his wide experience with television station strategies.

THE REALITIES OF INDEPENDENCE

An **independent** television station provides a stimulating challenge to its program director (in other words, a tough job!) since it has no built-in foundation for its schedule in a network feed. However, the nearly 400 inde-pendent television stations do not assume the posture of economic stepchil-dren. Although an independent will probably never rank number one in over-all ratings against competing network affiliates, it can lead in key dayparts in both households and the most desired demographic groups. Scheduling strong off-network series during prime access time and purchasing ratings-attracting shows from part-time networks have dramatically improved independent sta-tion audience shares. A professionally programmed and managed indepen-dent with an equally aggressive sales force can attain ratings and economic par-ity within most markets against affiliates. However, independent programmers must face two unhappy realities—*high programming costs* and *negative spot time-buyer attitude*—while learning to use the primary advantage that independents possess: *scheduling flexibility*.

It costs more to program an independent than a network-affiliated station; nearly half an independent's budget goes to programming. Virtually all the programs on an independent must be bartered, and these costs usually es-calate. Stations now pay as much for an individual program series, such as *Cheers* or *Family Ties*, as they did for an entire week's schedule not too many years ago. As of 1988, for example, reruns of the superhit *Cosby* cost a mid-market (between 20th and 30th) independent from $55,000 to $35,000 an epi-sode for several runs. Although prices declined somewhat in the late 1980s, many stations were still trapped by the need to pay for previously acquired expensive programs.

Some national and local spot time-buyers still look down their noses at many independents, making it difficult for these stations to earn their share of the advertisers' dollars. However, most ad agencies and advertisers changed their buying habits in the early 1980s as independents became more competitive. By that time, independents had demonstrated the resources to make top-notch program purchases and were employing competitive scheduling that improved their ratings. Moreover, the programming environment for commercials on an independent is similar to, if not better than, that of an affiliate scheduling the same client's advertising spot.[1] Independents air programs comparable to those of their affiliate competition but have less nonprogram clutter. During prime time, for instance, affiliates usually schedule local or national spot advertising at the hour or half-hour breaks, amid network spots and promos and station identifications (**IDs**). Independents can scatter their advertising throughout each hour, typically creating a less cluttered environment for each ad.

These considerations aside, the independent's most important programming reality is its greater scheduling flexibility: It is not tied to the program flow from a network. As a result, it can effectively *counterprogram* the other stations in a market by targeting specific audiences the networks are not serving at all or not reaching because their programs are inconveniently scheduled for the potential audience.

POSITIONING THE INDEPENDENT

Convincing the audience that a station is really different from its competitors is called **positioning** the station. Each station seeks a unique, positive image separating it from its competitors and giving the audience reasons for seeking it out. Experience teaches that independents establish their positions by creating "islands of success" using **counterprogramming, audience flow** and **promotion.** To develop counterprogramming, flow and promotional strategies, independent programmers must keep in mind what audiences the network affiliates or other independents in the market are reaching, what programs are popular and what position is viable for themselves.

Counterprogramming

Research continually points to a substantial audience that does not watch *news.* They may not care about what goes on, may want their news in capsule form or may prefer entertainment over news. The independent programmer, using the right kind of programming, can counter the early evening news block on the network affiliates and establish an "island of success" of at least an hour's duration. It can extend up to two hours, depending on how the competition schedules their programs. Independents in the top 50 markets capture top ratings because they are free to schedule *off-network reruns* during access time, while the affiliate competition is limited to *first-run* programming.

Although the news block and prime access time have proved an enormous boon to independents, many other dayparts present similar entree for independent programmers. Countering the late news and the plethora of weekend sports and public affairs on the networks with comedy/action/adventure programs or movies is also an effective strategy. Because independents have been so successful in countering news, some affiliates have cut back on news in favor of entertainment programs, heating up the competition for viewers. Countering adult programming with shows that appeal primarily to *children* in the morning and afternoon also works well, though the sliding **kidvid** audience in the key 3 to 5 P.M. daypart (accounting for as much as 25 percent of revenues on some mid-market independents) has caused stations to take a new look at local lifestyles. By 1988, increased use of child care, cable channels and VCRs had reduced the size of the total children's audience.

Flow Strategies

Additionally, the independent programmer must maximize the station's potential for **audience flow** just as networks and affiliates must—as described in preceding chapters. The goals of flow strategy are to maintain current audience while building on it to take advantage of the rising persons using television (PUT) levels of key demographic groups (such as men and women 18–49, 25–54, for example). The following list of programs shows audience flow that builds from one audience to another:

- 3:00 *Scooby Doo*
- 3:30 *Smurfs*
- 4:00 *Thundercats*
- 4:30 *G.I. Joe*
- 5:00 *Gilligan's Island*
- 5:30 *Brady Bunch*
- 6:00 *Happy Days*
- 6:30 *Facts of Life*
- 7:00 *Jeffersons*
- 7:30 *M*A*S*H*

In this illustration, the audience is slowly "aged" by targeting the programs first at children as school ends, at teens as the afternoon progresses, at women still later, and adding men while retaining the children, teens and women in the evening hours. Recall that **targeting** means selecting programs having especially strong appeal, as demonstrated by research, for a particular age group or gender group. More precise targeting is possible using psychographic program research and other qualitative evaluations of program appeals, as discussed in Chapter 2.

Promotional Images

An independent can also counterprogram by developing a program-identified image—as a **"sports station"** featuring local, regional, professional or amateur sports; as a **"movie station"** with feature films in every daypart; or as a **"local news station"** by scheduling news in nontraditional time periods, concentrating on local news and presenting local angles on national stories. In many large markets with more than one independent, a sports image may be the only open avenue, albeit a risky one. Sporting events attract a fickle audience, made up of a relatively small core of team loyalists and fleshed out by people who watch when the team is winning but who go away when the home team is losing. Their inconsistency and the probability that superstations and other sports-oriented cable networks have acquired the local team franchises (that used to "belong" to local independents) suggest caution in any shift to a sports image nowadays. Developing viewer loyalty and habit formation with more traditional *series* programming may be more effective for mid-market independents (and those in fifth or sixth position in large markets) than developing a narrow station image.

One new strategy is to become an **FBC affiliate.** More than 100 independents now carry the Fox schedule. Unfortunately, as of 1988 Fox was only able to supply a limited schedule of programs (Saturday and Sunday prime time and a late-night show), and initially, only Sunday nights were competitive in the ratings with ABC/CBS/NBC fare. StarCast, another programming network for independents begun in 1988 and based in Orlando, Florida, offers stations a weekly 18 hours of vintage off-network series, leavened with some sports and news. These services help independents but go only a short way toward a full 24-hour schedule.

Positioning an independent is a complex task. People watch *programs,* not *stations* (or Fox), so choice programming at the appropriate times is the most important factor to promote. Presenting shows in a high-quality environment is also important; a shoddy on-air environment creates a negative rub off that will be lasting and devastating. High-quality film prints and tapes, aired in a tight, professional on-air manner, will do much to create a lasting positive image for viewers and effectively position the independent.

THE PROGRAM SUPPLY

Regardless of the particular strategy for building "islands of success," programming requires money. In large markets with strong competition, it means a lot of money—because an independent does not have a magic button labled NETWORK supplying up to 15 hours a day of programming and revenue in the form of network compensation. Typically, network programming allows network-affiliated stations to operate with fewer personnel than are needed at independents (excepting news personnel). Since network compensation averages 5 percent of an affiliate's revenue, and networks fill up to 70 percent of the affiliate's schedule and promote those programs to audiences, many affiliates can focus wholly on sales and spend little staff time on programming and promotion. (The notable exceptions are those affiliates that dive into the news game to see who can outspend the other in people and equipment to gain a valuable rating point and image advantage.) The independent, however, has to pay cold, hard cash for almost everything it programs, fill an 18 to 24-hour schedule and promote and advertise every program itself.

Usually, the independent *licenses* programs from syndicators (off-network reruns, first-run syndication, movies) or *produces* them itself (e.g., sports, news, talk, children's). Increasingly, stations trade some of their spot airtime (*bartering*) to obtain program materials. And *ad hoc networks* supply another way to compete with the three major broadcast networks in entertainment programming. As pointed out in earlier chapters, Fox Television greatly increased its role as a supplier of high-quality entertainment programming to independent stations during the 1980s. However obtained, there are three basic forms of program material dominating independent programming: *syndicated series, movies* and *local programs.*

SYNDICATED PROGRAMS

Varying in length—30, 60, 90 minutes—syndicated programs range in cost-efficiency from the "bread and butter" to the "caviar" of an independent station. The bread-and-butter programs cost little, relative to their potential return on a per-run basis. All off-network syndicated series are bought on a *multiple-run* basis. As of 1988, an independent typically licensed a network rerun for six to eight runs over five years. Films are a different matter. Syndicators have reduced the length of performance contracts for feature films to three or four years, with a reduced number of runs (typically three or four), to remarket these films more quickly to pay-cable networks. (See Chapter 7 on series and movie contracts for affiliates because similar contract restrictions apply; see Chapter 11 on licensing movies for premium services.)

The most cost-efficient series are those that can be *stripped* (run Monday to Friday or Sunday to Saturday in the same time period). The most successful syndicated program on independent stations is the sitcom having *kiddult* appeal. Such a show appeals to both children and adults, especially women 18–34 or 18–49, and draws audiences that are not interested in affiliate news or sports.

Deciding which off-network shows will work in any given market is often highly frustrating for programmers. They must consider (1) the *rating* and share of a program while it was on the network—both nationally and in the market in which it will play when purchased; (2) the *time period(s)* in which the program will prove itself most cost-efficient; (3) whether the program will have *staying power* as a strip; and (4) whether the program will do better as a *strip*, a *single* or a *two-time-per-week* entry (**checkerboarded**). Many independents do not spend the money to buy the historical data needed to document each program in each market from Arbitron or Nielsen. National sales representatives, however, do buy this data and supply it to client stations. (See Chapter 3 on the role of reps in programming.) But even in the best of circumstances, and given the maximum amount of research and historical data, programmers sometimes must rely largely on market experience and intuition in making program decisions.

Kid Appeal

A number of programs whose primary appeal is to kids (2–11 years) have worked well for independents in both the early morning (6:30–9:00 A.M.) and early afternoon (3:00–5:30 P.M.) time periods. These include theatrical cartoons (*Bugs Bunny, Popeye* and *Road Runner*) and cartoons produced specifically for television and packaged in half-hour formats (*He-Man, Flintstones, G.I. Joe, Smurfs, Thundercats* and *Scooby-Doo*). The vast majority of children's programs today are marketed by the **barter** route. Stations pay no cash for the programs, instead giving up a portion of the commercial inventory in the program to the syndicator who, in turn, sells the time to national advertisers such as toy manufacturers, cereal makers and candy manufacturers.

Kids take control of television sets immediately after they come home from school. An independent station must entice as many children as possible into watching as early as possible, in order to hold them through the early-fringe viewing time.

Kiddult Appeal

Children and women dominate the early fringe/news block (4–7 P.M. or 5–8 P.M. audience, depending on the time zone) in which potential spot-time buyers look not only at household rating points but also at specific demographics, most often women 18–34 or 18–49. The kids in the audience provide the bulk of household rating points while the women in the audience give programs salability to advertisers. Programs such as *Brady Bunch, Happy Days, Little House on the Prairie, Gimme a Break, Jeffersons* and *Benson* have strong appeal in early fringe.

Adult Appeal

Five types of programs have been used to attract adult audiences. Game shows declined in audience appeal in the late 1970s and early 1980s but again became hot in the late 1980s. *Wheel of Fortune* is especially attractive to advertisers since it delivers a predominantly young adult audience (women/men 18–34 and 18–49); other game shows skew toward older demographic groups (adults 25–54 or adults 50 +). Action/adventure series such as *Charlie's Angels, CHiPS, Battlestar Galactica, Starsky and Hutch* and *Kung Fu* work well in early afternoon and early fringe (as strips) and on weekends as counterprogramming to network sports. On weekends, such shows attract women, countering male-oriented sports programming the network affiliates usually offer.

At one time, the talk/variety programs such as *Merv Griffin, Mike Douglas, Dinah Shore* and *Phil Donahue* were the bread-and-butter series for independents. All these programs except *Phil Donahue* had success stories in virtually every daypart. *Donahue* remains strong in the morning between 9 A.M. and noon in many markets (especially the Midwest, as discussed in Chapter 7). In the mid-1980s, however, most audience interest shifted to magazine-type programs such as *Hour Magazine*, the reality-based *People's Court* and soft-news feature programs such as *Entertainment Tonight* and *USA Today*. In the late 1980s, the *Oprah Winfrey Show* joined the exclusive club of hit talk shows, and independents were as hot to grab this show as affiliates. *Oprah* is usually scheduled in late afternoon.

Program Futures

In the early 1970s, Paramount Television Sales auctioned the off-network syndication rights to both *Happy Days* and *Laverne & Shirley* as **futures.** Stations in the same market bid competitively for these programs while they were still on the network. Since then, various syndicators have sold *Love Boat*, *Dukes of Hazzard, Taxi, Cosby* and *Who's the Boss?* as futures. These sales made Paramount a lot of money and defined an elite class of most desired programs, but the buying of futures is a strategy filled with danger for both the syndicator and the station.[2]

Futures buying works as follows: The syndicator has or purchases the right to sell a certain series for individual stations to air either after the series' network run or by a certain date, even though the series may continue in network first-run after going into syndication. Such a program has usually had a successful run on the network for four or five years—in some instances, only three or four years. The syndicator assumes the series will continue for a minimum of five years on the network in order to have enough episodes to make the series strippable (see *Webster* example in Chapter 7).

Until *Happy Days* was offered for syndication, series pricing was determined for the most part by a formula for each market, as applied to the entire country (times the number of dollars the syndicator paid out for the rights to distribute, and sales costs plus profit). Paramount changed all that with *Happy Days*. Seeing the potential for the program to generate not only large household rating points but also to reach key demographics (children, teens, women 18–34 and 18–49, men 18–49), they elected to market it on a supply-and-demand basis. Since *Happy Days* was the only series in the late 1970s with unique potential for attracting the kind of audiences stations could sell at premium prices and since several individual stations in many markets competed for the opportunity to program it, Paramount let the marketplace determine the price after setting a minimum starting point.

The strategy worked: *Happy Days* became the most successful program in terms of syndication revenue in broadcasting history at the time—sold at premium prices to be played two or three years from the time the commitment was made. Later, Paramount used the same marketing technique for *Laverne & Shirley*. The prices paid for *Laverne & Shirley* far exceeded those for *Happy Days* (as much as $100,000 per episode in the top markets), yet *Laverne & Shirley* did not equal *Happy Days* in syndicated ratings success, and *Happy Days* itself did not maintain as strong a ratings pull as many experts had predicted. Subsequently, both programs were substantially outperformed by *M*A*S*H, Three's Company* and *The Jeffersons*.

Many independent stations bid for an elite program to establish a franchise for themselves in access time. Affiliated stations in the top 50 markets are prevented from playing off-network programs in access because of the *prime-time access rule*. Independent stations can charge more for spot advertising within an off-network program or require an advertiser to take a less desirable program availability concurrent with a spot in a hit show.

In 1987, *The Cosby Show* became *the* megahit show for many stations to license (for a fall 1988 starting air date). Viacom, the syndicator, positioned the program not only as a success in its own right but as a key building block for a station in both early fringe and in access. Both independents and affiliates bid record high prices for the program, banking on it to "take" its own time period and also to flow that audience into the following program(s). The highest price was paid by WWOR-TV in New York: $350,000 per episode for up to 112 episodes in a $3\frac{1}{2}$-year contract.[3] Also in 1987, *Who's the Boss?* became a hot property, and again stations got caught up in bidding higher and higher prices for the right to *Who's the Boss?*

Many stations have gotten badly burned and still sting financially from earlier high-cost/low-yield program buying decisions. No single program can "make" a station's program schedule. A strong program can become an island of success; it must, however, be built on if it is to perform outstandingly.

Program Barter

Traditionally, the independent station's alternatives to purchased or locally produced programs were the relatively rare network programs it begged, borrowed or maneuvered (1) from network-affiliated stations when, occasionally, they preempted network programs; (2) from ad hoc networks such as the one Mobil Oil set up for high-quality programs and miniseries such as *Edward the King;* (3) from special networks set up for sporting events; and (4) from the Fox network. Fox's primary target audience is adults 18–49, with a skew toward women 18–34 years.

A fifth alternative is (5) bartered programs, which are supposedly "free" but in reality are not. Although no money passes from the station to the program supplier for bartered programs, something of equal and sometimes greater value is given to the supplier—advertising inventory.

Television stations have *two* customers—viewers and advertisers. Without the first, it is difficult, if not impossible, to attract the second. Assuming the station attracts a reasonable number of viewers to its programming, it can sell time in or adjacent to its programs to advertisers. Time in this context is **inventory.** A television station's advertising inventory (its salable time) acquires an arbitrary dollar value based on the rating each of its programs achieves (or is expected to achieve if it is new programming or in a new time slot). The station's ability to get this dollar value is based on supply and demand for the program itself, the station's overall inventory position and the condition of the market as a whole. If a station pays cash for a program, it can charge advertisers whatever it feels it can get for the inventory within or adjacent to that program, and the station keeps all the revenue those sales efforts generate. But if the station barters for the program, it must give up part of that precious commodity—inventory—to the program supplier.

As explained in Chapter 3, if the station, for example, pays a program supplier $1,000 per telecast for a program having an inventory of twelve 30-second commercial spots, and if the value of each spot (based on ratings and supply and demand) is $500, the total potential return to the station is $6,000 (or a program cost-to-potential-return ratio of 16.6 percent). In the barter case, the program supplier may say to the station, "I'll give you the program for no cash outlay. All I want is $2\frac{1}{2}$ minutes for my clients." Those $2\frac{1}{2}$ minutes cost the station $2,500 in inventory it cannot sell (or a program cost-to-potential-return ratio of 41.6 percent). Using a nonbarter program allows the station to keep the (potential) $6,000 in revenues. Over a 52-week period, using a barter versus a nonbarter program represents a potential return of $182,000 versus $312,000.

This situation compounds when a barter program does not perform in terms of audience delivery. The station is then faced with the dilemma of taking the program off the schedule or moving it to another time period. If it is moved or cancelled, the station is still obligated to air the syndicator's commercials in the original time period for the entire length of the contract.

The programmer must answer some rather critical questions concerning barter programming: Is the cost-to-return ratio too high? Do the program's potential ratings and lead-in value outweigh the cost ratio? Is barter the only way to obtain the program? How many barter programs can the station afford at any given time?

A number of programs that enjoyed successful runs on the networks became available to independent stations via the barter route in the 1970s, some of the most notable being *Hee Haw, Wild Kingdom* and *Fame,* in addition to a long list of game shows. In the early 1980s, many syndicators began asking for cash as well as barter minutes, particularly in the case of expensive, first-run syndication, beginning with *Mike Douglas* (now defunct) and continuing with *Donahue, People's Court* and *Family Feud.* By the mid-1980s, barter fever had spread to programs for major time periods and off-network series.[4] Off-network series like *Family, Switch* and the *Nancy Drew/Hardy Boys Mysteries* and some feature films were also added to the barter group. *How the West Was Won* became a barter program, and most first-run music programs go the barter route. By the late 1980s, more than 80 percent of *weekly* first-run programs were bartered, as well as many strippable first-run and off-network series.

This trend will probably continue for two reasons. First, stations that have purchased substantial amounts of off-network programming must acquire barter programs to operate within their budgets; their cash flow has been restricted by these prior, expensive program purchases. Second, syndicators have found they can make more money by selling all or part of the advertising themselves within programs stations want, and so the practice is bound to increase among syndicators.[5]

MOVIES

Considered the most cost-efficient form of programming available, feature films allow the independent programmer considerable flexibility at relatively modest cost. Dozens of distributors sell **movie packages** grouping "A," "B" and "C" movies for cash or, increasingly, for barter. Despite enormous prices for box-office hits (as much as $400,000 per title in Los Angeles, for example, though down to about $1,200 in very small markets), most independents constantly seek to upgrade their movie libraries and keep their titles fresh. A *movie library* normally consists of 1,000 to 2,000 or more film titles with unused runs. Movie licensing agreements now average **five** years (up from the three-to-four year contracts of the mid-1980s). *Overexposure* of films on cable prior to independent licensing remains a key problem.

Movie watchers tend to be women 18–34 or 18–49, especially for familiar titles or superstars. One successful movie strategy is to create **theme weeks,** heavily promoting "monsters-we-all-know-and-love" or "beautiful ladies week." Theme weeks are usually created by *horizontal scheduling* (stripping movies across the week at the same time).

Stacking

Movies can also be *vertically stacked* (placed sequentially on one day). **Stacking** allows a programmer to air many hours of the same kind of show in one day while varying the type every few hours. For instance, KPHO-TV (Phoenix, Arizona) aired a seven-hour block of movies on Saturdays for many years with great success by targeting four specific audiences:

9:00 A.M.	Saturday Morning	The movies selected for this particular showcase appeal to children (to lure them away from the traditional cartoon fare on competing network-affiliated stations). It also attracts young adults. Examples are *Tarzan* movies, *East Side Kids* and *Lassie*.
10:30 A.M.	World Beyond	Science fiction and monster films will attract kids, teens and men and women 18–34 (**kiddults**).
12:00 noon	Action Theater	Western, war, and sword-and-sandal films have been very successful in attracting men and women 18–49. Particular attention is given to picking titles with big-name stars, such as John Wayne or James Stewart.
2:00 P.M.	Adventure Theater	This is similar to Action Theater with the added dimension of thrillers and long-form science fiction. It has greatest appeal to adults 18–49 and draws an especially large proportion of men.

Stacking is most successful when used as a thematic showcase device. When purchasing movies, programmers can then select titles for specific showcases and further increase the cost-efficiency of the station's movie programming. In the mid-1980s, syndicators began selling "movie review" half-hours with notable critics such as Gene Siskel and Roger Ebert, Rex Reed and others. This practice capitalized on the large amount of time devoted to movies on independents and led to the strategy of packaging a **movie review** along with a block of feature films.

LOCAL PROGRAMS

Local programs may be as inexpensive or expensive as the station chooses and can take as many forms as syndicated programs or movies. They include (1) sports of a local or regional nature, (2) news, (3) public affairs, (4) children's programs, (5) talk and women's interest, (6) musical variety and, if the station is so inclined and well-heeled enough, (7) drama.

Sports

Some of the most successful independent stations in the country have a sports image: WGN, Chicago; WTBS, Atlanta; WWOR and WPIX in New York; and KTTV and KTLA in Los Angeles, to list a few. Independents have the scheduling flexibility to accommodate sporting events during every daypart, and sports events attract a desirable demographic target (men 18–34 and 18–49). Any number of advertisers are willing to pay premium prices to be identified with a televised sport because it sells their products. This fact makes sports programming a hot strategy for a number of independent stations.

There are three cost approaches to sports programming. In the first, a station purchases telecast rights from the team, produces each game (cost of talent, play-by-play, color) and delivers the signal back to the station (by AT&T Long Lines, satellite or a combination of both). Although very expensive, this route has the greatest potential for revenue because the station can sell all the advertising inventory. This approach does, however, have its risks. All the spots may not be sold, reducing the potential revenue; and the team's standing in the won/lost column most often determines ratings, which, in turn, determine advertiser support.

In another option, the team itself assumes all production and delivery costs and pays the station for the time. The team assumes all financial risk and sells the ads, but it will also reap most of the potential profits since there are no rights fees involved. The station is paid for the airtime (but less than if they sold it themselves) and, in the minds of viewers, gets the credit for bringing them the games.

In the third possibility, an outside producer/syndicator pays the team for the rights to telecast. The producer/syndicator sells part of the available time within the games and barters with the station for the time (or purchases it outright). This method is common with college basketball and football.

Prime time (8 to 11 P.M. eastern/pacific or 7 to 10 P.M. central/mountain) is ideal for sports programming on independents since that is when they traditionally face the toughest network competition (which seldom is sports) and revenue potential is highest. An independent carrying a lot of sports programming takes risks because the audience composition for sports skews to men both during the game and following, and men are generally not a loyal audience. Also, since women are the primary target of most advertisers, the station may lose out on potential sales. Sporting events also tend to break up audience flow, thus driving nonsports viewers to the competition.

News

One common independent practice is to program news in *nontraditional* hours. If the late news airs on competing network affiliates at 10 (CST/MST) or 11 (EST/PST) P.M., successful independents program their news first at 9 or 9:30 P.M. in the central/mountain time zones or 10 or 10:30 P.M. in the eastern and western time zones. This strategy allows viewers to see the news on the independent and allows the independent to position itself in two different time periods, initially counterprogramming affiliates with news against entertainment and then entertainment against newscasts.

News programs can be cheap or expensive to produce—the station decides. If the *rip-and-read* approach is used, cost is minimal (announcer rips copy from wire service printer and reads it on the air). A 60-second update every hour or two with a news reader giving details under a slide or series of slides creates few problems and costs little. The ratings, however, reflect the amount of effort and budget expended.

When an independent takes the expensive, sophisticated, and thus competitive approach, it must hire a full-time staff of at least a news director, an assignment editor/coordinator, a producer plus weather/news/sports anchors and reporters, photographers, editors and writers. Staff size will vary with the area to be covered and the depth of news treatment desired.

Equipment looms as the next cost consideration. If the station opts to go the **ENG** (electronic news gathering) route, thousands of dollars will have to be expended, especially if the station chooses to have "live" capability via microwave. Receiving the satellite-distributed national/international news services requires an earth station, which also adds to capital outlay. The cost for a dish varies according to the level of sophistication the station wants and needs. It can range from $25,000 (plus site) to $500,000. The station can select among many options, such as mechanical reorientations from one satellite to another, an uplink to provide transmit capability, reception of multiple transponders (channels) from each satellite and redundancy (backups for safety) in both **uplinks** and **downlinks.** Additionally, if the station is located in an area with heavy microwave signals, the satellite receivers must be shielded at yet further cost.

Although some VHF independent television stations have been relatively successful with news, especially when programmed at nontraditional times, few ever equal the total household rating points of network-affiliated stations. Audience perception is that independents cannot or do not do news as well as the affiliates, and it persists although analysis of an independent newscast is likely to show no difference from a competing network-affiliated newscast in reporting style, content or overall quality.

This audience myth has proven a stumbling block for many independents programming news head-to-head with affiliated stations. For example, the superstation WGN-TV in Chicago tried head-to-head news competition for several years. In May 1979, Arbitron ratings for 10 P.M. in Chicago were:

			ADI RATING				
Station			1979		1980		1988
WLS	(ABC)	News	20	News	17	News	19
WBBM	(CBS)	News	18	News	15	News	13
WMAQ	(NBC)	News	12	News	13	News	14
WGN	(IND)	News	5	*Soap*	6	*Soap*	5
WFLD	(IND)	*San. & Son*	5	*Joan Rivers*	6	*M*A*S*H*	3
WPWR	(IND)	—		*Dr. Ruth*	1	*Odd Couple*	2
WGBO	(IND)	—		—	—	*Bosom Buddies*	1

In response WGN moved its news to 9 P.M. (for one hour) and soon averaged a 7 rating for its news. However, in February 1980 and 1988, Nielsen ratings for the 10 P.M. time slot were no better with *Soap*.

As each ratings point is worth many thousands of dollars in revenue over a 52-week period, most independents have abandoned the *head-to-head* news strategy in favor of the *nontraditional* time period. Several news services, including Independent News Service (INS) and WPIX, provide a half-hour of national/international news to package with a local half-hour. Overall, the amount of locally originated hard and soft news grows steadily on independents.

Public Affairs

Public affairs programs give independent stations an opportunity to excel. As someone once said, "Public affairs need not be dull affairs." If management permits, an inspired and well-budgeted public affairs department at an independent television station can be television at its best. Superstations such as WGN produce excellent public affairs shows. But *cost* remains a problem. It is difficult to sell public affairs programs to advertisers, and most stations refuse to invest time, personnel and money in programs that don't make money.

The **documentary** and **magazine** formats best demonstrate a station's public affairs commitment. But few independents choose this route. Very few UHF independents do more than a bare minimum of public affairs, and much of that is done in election years. Local weather and other natural disasters, however, offer independent television stations the same opportunity as local radio stations for responding to community events in ways that attract substantial audiences. (See Chapter 15 on news radio for more on local news responsiveness.)

Children's Programs

From both revenue and ratings standpoints, independents have been successful with locally produced children's programming. During certain dayparts (*early morning* and *afternoon*), children usually control the television set. Although *live* programming eats away at the profit margin, some formats for local, live children's programs are workable. Identifying which *segment* of the children's audience the station wants to attract is crucial: preschool, grades 1 through 4, grades 5 through 8 or high school. High schoolers are the most difficult to reach since they are the most fickle in their viewing habits. Preschoolers require sophisticated, well-researched material, obtainable only at considerable cost. The age groups easiest to program for are grades 1 through 4 and 5 through 8.

Costs of locally produced programs vary depending on production complexity, but the major costs are talent and studio time. Care must be given to **continuity acceptance** standards (policies covering vocabulary level, pacing, intensity and type of sales pitches and so on) so as not to take advantage of the audience. Some long-running children's shows on independents are *Bozo* on

WGN, *Wallace & Ladmo* on KPHO and *Blinky's Club* on KWGN. Most independent stations, however, have abandoned the hosted children's show.

Talk and Women's Interest

Women make up most of the daytime audience in most markets, and a number of them want more from television than entertainment. They want to be informed, enlightened and challenged, and a stimulating local, live (or taped) program can do all three if properly produced (whether on an affiliate or an independent; see discussion in Chapter 7 on this same topic).

Local programs appealing to women are fairly easy to produce and in most instances not overly costly. Their most important ingredient is the *producer/ host or hostess*, who must be in tune with what is happening in the community that will be of interest to and challenging for area women. The least expensive way of producing such shows is in the studio with invited guests. More expensive is the *remote* (out-of-studio), using ENG equipment to relay (or tape) some or all of the material from wherever the activities occur. So far, few independents have seriously tackled *local* women's programs, but *syndicated* women-oriented programs, such as *Donahue, Oprah Winfrey* and *Hour Magazine,* have had success on independents.

The talk format can accommodate *off-length* time periods (following full-length movies and live sporting events), and it has community appeal and low cost, all of which point to its greater use in independents' local production strategy. The talk format always raises fairness issues (see Chapter 16), and, of course, the host/hostess is a crucial factor in success.

Musical Variety

These programs may be successful in some markets, although overall the **musical variety** format has declined in popularity. For every type of music an audience exists, although some music attracts very small audiences. In certain parts of the Midwest, for example, polka music attracts a loyal and rather large audience on television; country music draws enthusiastic audiences in the Midwest, South and Southwest. Jazz, on the other hand, usually appeals only to very small, urban audiences (and even smaller rural audiences).

Musical variety programs are fairly expensive even when local talent is used in the station's studio. The largest expense comes from the musicians' fees as determined by the local musicians' union. Other costs (sets, props) can be spread out and amortized over the run of the show, of course. (See Chapter 3 on **amortization.**) Except for major-market efforts, local musical variety programming suffers in comparison to syndicated and network fare. However, it can be scheduled in many time slots as its audience tends to seek it out rather than the station having to seek out the audience.

The latest version of the musical program emphasizes dance numbers rather than the variety format. For no cost, stations can copy MTV's video formula by using videos supplied by recording studios. This kind of program draws a large and loyal teen/young adult audience when it emphasizes rock music, and an older audience when it focuses on country music.

Drama

On a local basis, **drama** is a very ambitious undertaking, and productions should be examined in detail before cautiously proceeding. The most expensive items involved are *time* and *people*. Rehearsals take up a large amount of time; some personnel from the station must be present to block (position the actors) the play for television and rehearse the technical people (camera operators, lighting, sound). Although tackling drama can be professionally satisfying, it is very expensive, has a poor cost-to-return ratio, and is rarely attempted by independents (or by affiliates or the networks . . .).

PROGRAMMING AND SALES

Sales is related to programming. It is imperative for the programmer at an independent station to become familiar with, and involved in, sales. The programmer must know what budgets spot advertisers have, what target demographics each advertiser seeks and what effects local and national economics are likely to have on advertising budgets. Programmers must know which programs appeal to national advertisers and which to local advertisers. *Ideal* programs do both, of course.

An ongoing, working dialogue between the programmer and the sales manager must cover subjects such as rating potentials or projections, pricing for spots within programs, budgets for both national and local advertisers, advertiser resistance to certain programs or time periods, recommendations on spot versus bartered programs and methods of selling programs other than the traditional cost-per-thousand, cost-per-point and cost-per-person. Programming's escalating costs make it crucial for programmers to know a program's revenue potential before it is purchased. An open relationship with sales management and a program director who *understands* sales are essential.

Unsalable Programs

Obvious questions arise when a program cannot be sold by an effective sales team. For example, a program may be scheduled in a time period not meshing with an advertiser's planned marketing campaign. If an advertiser's marketing plan is to break during the middle part of the second quarter of a given year, but the television station schedules a program that would be an obvious "buy" for the advertisers in the first part of the second quarter, that advertiser is automatically eliminated. The marketing campaign does not correspond with the planned airing of the program. Buying or creating a program that demands a premium price from advertisers but that appeals to advertisers whose sales plans exclude premium prices can also create sales problems. Much time and effort, to say nothing of money, can be fruitlessly spent in seeking out, negotiating for and eventually buying the license rights to programming that later proves to be *unsalable*.

Access and Decision Making

Independent programmers must keep up-to-date on changing program possibilities if they expect to compete effectively within their marketplaces. Being *aware* of available product is only the first step, however; programmers must aggressively pursue and be willing to take a chance on programs their judgment says will work in their markets. Establishing ongoing, candid relationships with program suppliers and producers is quite important, for those without pipelines will find themselves out in the cold. Keeping in touch with the business also means reading about trends and tastes and learning what is going on in the production centers of Los Angeles and New York—though what is a *hit* in those two unique markets only *hints* at what might work in other markets and may mislead a station in another part of the country.

The short-term effect of program scarcity is that programs cost more, thus eroding profit margin. But an even worse tactic is scheduling programs that do not attract a *large* enough audience, further reducing advertising revenue and eroding the profit margin. The long-term effect of not having access to new programs is that the programmer cannot plan on a long-range basis. And without long-range planning, successful program purchases fade in value.

Programmers cannot operate in a vacuum. Program manager, sales manager and general manager working in concert create dividends in both audience shares and revenue. Often the perspective of one manager is 180 degrees from that of another. Then the effective programmer must communicate to the general manager and/or sales manager the rationale for programming decisions. Raw research data and extracted data become the tools for determining whether a program should be actively sought, what price should be paid and how the program should be scheduled. Monies must be set aside for research and program development so that fresh, innovative programming becomes an option.

PROGRAMMING AND RESEARCH

If effective *communication* with program suppliers is the lifeblood for the independent programmer, *research* is the nerve center. Chapters 2 and 3 review the research all stations should consider as they make programming decisions. Independent programmers, especially, must review every scrap of research material, particularly that indicating how an off-network program performed in a given market, most crucially the market in which the programmer operates.

Tracking an off-network program in similar markets is essential to learning how that program might perform in a given market. The programmer must check the Arbitron and Nielsen ratings books for the essential information on how the program performed in rating, share, total women, women (18–34, 18–49 and 25–54), total men, men (18–34, 18–49 and 25–54), teens 12–17, kids 2–11 and kids 6–11 through several ratings periods.

Although a program may perform very well on the national level, it will not necessarily have appeal in a particular market and vice versa. For example, *Little House on the Prairie* was cancelled on the network but outperformed local news when counterprogrammed in the Midwest. *Star Trek* was never a hit on the network but flourished as a staple on independents.

The independent programmer must track that kind of information. Rep firms, as discussed in Chapter 3, can supply ratings information to their clients, and syndicated program ratings are, of course, available through both Nielsen and Arbitron as well as from distributors—although the distributor's information should be taken with a spoon of salt (that is, it benefits their sales pitch to embellish a show's strong points and play down its weaknesses).

CONSTRAINTS AND SURVIVAL

Most programmers are vividly aware of the many constraints various individuals, groups and circumstances impose. Specifically, budget and equipment limitations may mean the programmer cannot buy and schedule a particular program because the station cannot afford it.

An independent's operating signal may be a major constraint on its ratings potential. **UHF** stations have traditionally had more disadvantages than VHF stations in the same market. Cable penetration, however, has made a significant difference, leveling out the technical characteristics of signals and introducing all channels on a more or less equal basis. When cable systems convert UHF channels to unoccupied VHF channels between 2 and 13 (**repositioning**), these independents have a big opportunity to win viewers. The remote control tuner also improves UHF viewing levels. Tuning all channels in a similar manner (all on consecutive numbers on the same dial or on a key-pad) gives underdog independents (and even public stations) frequent chances for viewer *sampling* and gives the independent *parity* in cable homes.

Community pressures are also of concern to the independent programmer. Organizations such as ACT, NOW, NAACP, Urban League, Chicanos Por La Causa and others have sought their "day in court" with the media. They represent viewers that independent programmers must be willing and able to address in their programming. Independent stations are no less responsible for addressing the needs of minority or pressure groups than are affiliated stations. In some respects, independents are even preferred vehicles because they have content flexibility and can make time available in nontraditional time periods.

The newest problem for independents arises from the end of the **must-carry** rules for cable systems. Some new UHF stations have been refused carriage on systems without empty channels, ruining their chances for capturing an audience. The potential for *carriage charges* is an even greater concern. Profitable independents worry that cable operators will auction off their channel space to the highest bidders, radically altering independent economics.

But the biggest problem independent programmers face is the dearth of *proven* off-network syndicated programming suitable for stripping. This has given new impetus to first-run syndicated programs. High production costs, coupled with network cancelations of programs that do not perform at a given national rating and share level, have diminished the supply of proven, strippable programs. Although some relief is available to independent stations from Fox and other first-run suppliers, the first-run market cannot meet the independents' insatiable program appetite. When stations find insufficient programming available, it creates a situation parallel to that of radio in the early 1950s: Radio stations then recognized that they could not be all things to all people all the time and, consequently, specialized in single formats. Many independent stations may be forced to become specialty stations such as "the movie station" or "the sports station" to survive in the 1990s.

SUMMARY

The independent television station must purchase, produce or barter programming to fill 18 to 24 hours every day. Syndicated series, movies and sports make up the bulk of independent programming. Licensing practices for key off-network series now commonly require the purchase of program futures, and contract lengths for feature films are shortening to fewer years and fewer runs. Although expensive, series programming can build loyal audiences, kiddult sitcoms generally attract the most desirable audiences. One of the primary jobs of independent station programmers is tracking the ratings of syndicated series. Movies fill large amounts of time and are more successful when thematically stacked. While sporting events also fill large amounts of time with highly visible programming, their male audiences are not loyal and dependable. First-run programs, on the other hand, are often cheaper but harder to get viewers to sample without a large amount of promotion; they also lack track records on which to base purchasing and scheduling decisions. Increasingly, off-network reruns and first-run series are being bartered, often to the station's financial disadvantage. Independents typically avoid head-to-head news competition with affiliates and are reasonably successful with nontraditional news scheduling. Counterprogramming, flow control and promotion are an independent's primary strategies, and scheduling salable programs is an overriding goal. The advent of cable has been a boon to most UHF stations since repositioning on the home receiver (especially on the lower numbers) allows the independent station (as well as the public station) to compete based on programming, not signal quality or reception difficulty. Programming an independent still remains risky and challenging.

Notes

1. This was first apparent in a major 1977 Arbitron study comparing affiliate and independent audiences in 23 markets; it was later substantiated in the 1980 Burke study comparing advertising environments, based on a survey of 200,000 viewers, and bolstered by several proprietary studies by rep firms. Burke Marketing Research, Inc., *The Effects of Station Environment on Television Advertising Communications: Independent Stations vs. Affiliated Stations, 1981* (New York: Association of Independent Television Stations, Inc., 1981).

2. As explained in Chapters 3 and 7, with the current network schedule of about 22 original programs each year, the syndicator has a minimum of 110 episodes to sell for stripping after five years (130 after six years). Since there are 260 exposures (Monday–Friday strip slots) per year on a station, 110 episodes will fill one year by running each episode 2.36 times. The more episodes produced beyond 110, the much more valuable the series becomes to both the syndicator and the purchasing stations. The series brings a greater dollar return to the syndicator, and it requires fewer repeats in a year's time, which the station can amortize for a better return on dollars spent.

3. "The 'Cosby' Numbers in Syndication," *Broadcasting,* 27 April 1987, pp. 58–59. Viacom sold *Cosby* as a cash-barter show in $3\frac{1}{2}$ year deals. Typically, off-network shows are sold per

episode; *Cosby* was instead sold for cash as 182 weekly shows, the way first-run series usually are sold. Stations successfully bidding for the 182 weeks can use the episodes once a day at any time; if stripped for $3\frac{1}{2}$ years, stations get 910 telecasts altogether. Viacom also sold two 30-second barter spots in each episode to advertisers. Stations buying the show are also required to purchase additional episodes in 26-week increments, if three or more seasons are produced. By 1988 stations in all but 25 markets had purchased *Cosby*, paying the highest prices to date for any show. "Round One of 'Cosby' Cash Sales Almost Completed," *Broadcasting*, 21 September 1987, p. 75.

4. Frank DiGiacomo, "The Dash for Cash," *View*, 20 October 1986, pp. 35–38, and Frank DiGiacomo, "Comping for Clearance: Barter Syndicators Pay to Play," *View*, 2 June 1986, pp. 33–35.

5. "Petry Looks at the Future," *Broadcasting*, 21 February 1983, pp. 59–62, and "Independents Taking the Ad Hoc Road to Success," *Broadcasting*, 28 March 1983, pp. 70–72.

Selected Sources

"Focus: Independent Television." *Channels* (January 1987): 35–53, and "Fortunes in the Future?" *Channels*, January 1988, pp. 61–74.

INTV Journal: The Magazine of Independent Television. Bi-monthly (7 times a year) trade magazine focusing on the business of independent television stations, published by View Communications since 1985.

Morgenstern, Steve, ed. *Inside the TV Business.* New York: Sterling Publishers, 1979.

"Special Reports on Independents," *Broadcasting* (25 January 1982): 47–56; (1 February 1982): 36–48; (17 January 1983): 55–70; (24 January 1983): 66–73; (22 October 1984): 54–82; (30 September 1985): 55–74; (5 January 1987): 90–94; (28 December 1987): 39–72; (11 January 1988): 35–41.

"The State of Independents," *View* (4 January 1988): 73–96. See also Frank DiGiacomo, "Independent Television: Today's Questions, Tomorrow's Answers," *View* (5 January 1987): 91–120, and Kathy Haley, "The Push for Local Production: Independents Lead the Way," *View* (16 June 1986): 45–51.

Reis, Al, and Trout, Jack. *Positioning: The Battle for Your Mind.* New York: McGraw-Hill, 1981.

Van Petten, Vance Scott, ed. *Television Syndication: A Practical Guide to Business and Legal Issues.* Los Angeles: Los Angeles Bar Association, 1987.

PART THREE / CABLE PROGRAMMING
STRATEGIES

Part Three turns to another aspect of television—programs and services delivered by cable instead of broadcasting. Cable's strategies differ from those of broadcasting because it is a multichannel, wired technology, and its programmers must consider both broadcast stations and cable-only networks in the same competitive arena. The cable industry has two very different types of cable programmers: (1) Some select among the available satellite-delivered and over-the-air services to program dozens of channels on a local cable system or group of systems; (2) others program a single channel (an ESPN, Disney or local access channel), or perhaps a pair of co-owned channels (such as HBO and Cinemax). Part Three begins with a chapter describing the programming constraints operating on multichannel programmers, cable system operators. Then the following chapters focus on single-service cable programming, covering basic and premium networks and local cable-only services. Each of these chapters follows the consistent structural pattern of this book by examining program evaluation, selection and scheduling within a particular programming context.

Chapter 9 analyzes strategies for programming the more than 8,500 **cable systems** in the United States. Law, technology, economics and marketing affect cable programming in ways that differ markedly from their effects on broadcast programming. This chapter shows how they constrain the system programmer (the cable operator) and then details options for selecting among premium services, basic cable-only networks and distant independent signals including superstations, while leaving channel space for the broadcast signals the system wants to carry.

Nonpay or **basic cable networks** occupy Chapter 10. Like the premium services, nonpay cable services provide a schedule of programs to cable "affiliates," the local systems, but most are supported by a mix of advertising revenues and per-subscriber fees paid by the cable operator. Because of their large number (more than 55) and their diverse and fluctuating programming strategies, this chapter concentrates on an overview of the major *national* services as of 1988 grouping them by content and target audience into ten subsets of direct competitors for access to cable audiences.

Chapter 11 examines the well-developed strategies of the **premium networks.** For an extra monthly fee or a per-program charge, most cable systems deliver to their subscribers one or more of a dozen nationally distributed channels of programming called *pay-cable* and *pay-per-view networks;* microwave program distributors (MMDS) also supply many of the same national services using another technology. The revenues—which the premium suppliers and the cable systems share—largely account for the resurgence of cable in the 1970s. Pay services remain central to cable marketing strategy. They program mostly theatrical movies so the author focuses on the evaluation, selection and scheduling of feature films but also looks at premium cable's specials and sports. Eight pay-cable networks and five pay-per-view services distributed their programming nationally as of 1988, and these are described in detail in Chapter 11.

Chapter 12 looks at cable systems' **local cable-only** programming and services, including local system-produced or purchased programming (LO), community access programming (access) and ancillary services. These three kinds of program content arise from diverse circumstances, but for the most part, they share the common feature of originating at the local cable system level as responsibilities of the local cable programmer. This chapter also examines syndicated programs packaged by the local programmer, interstitial programming, cable radio and subsidiary services indicating the direction of local cable programming for the next decade.

Part Three, then, focuses on the special programming circumstances of cable and the unique constraints that operate on different types of cable programmers. This part concludes the portion of this book on commercial television programming.

CHAPTER 9 CABLE SYSTEM PROGRAMMING

Susan Tyler Eastman

A Guide to Chapter 9

Susan Tyler Eastman, associate professor of Telecommunications at Indiana University, teaches, publishes and consults in cable programming. She edited and co-authored *Strategies in Broadcast and Cable Promotion* (Wadsworth, 1982) and the first and second editions of this book—*Broadcast/Cable Programming* (Wadsworth, 1981 and 1985). Both received Broadcast Preceptor Awards from San Francisco State University for their contributions to knowledge about the industry. She contributed the programming chapters in S. Head and C. Sterling's *Broadcasting in America,* 5th edition (Houghton Mifflin, 1987), authored chapters on cable programming for French and Spanish-language publications and recently co-authored *Teaching Writing in Every Course* (Allyn & Bacon, 1988). Before joining the faculty at Indiana University in 1981, she taught at Temple University in Philadelphia. She has a B.A. from the University of California at Berkeley, an M.A. from San Francisco State University and a Ph.D. from Bowling Green State University. In 1980 she was awarded a charter faculty internship by the National Association of Television Program Executives at WCAU-TV in Philadelphia. She served as chair of the Bloomington Telecommunications Council monitoring the local cable franchise and has many scholarly publications on cable television and sports programming. She also has producing and directing credits and regularly conducts seminars and workshops about programming.

THE JOB OF THE CABLE SYSTEM PROGRAMMER

Choosing among the nearly 70 satellite-delivered program and shopping services, numerous over-the-air stations and expanding numbers of local and regional services and then scheduling them are the main activities of the cable system programmer. Chapters 10 and 11 illustrate the range and variety of cable networks jockeying for position on America's 8,500 local cable systems, and the responsibilities of the cable programmer increase as the number of program services expand, while deregulation and technological advances remove old limits on choice. In the 1960s and 1970s, finding enough programming to fill all a large system's channels was a big problem. But the dramatic rise in the number of satellite-delivered program services in the 1980s redefined the programmer's job. The programmer now has to decide which national services to add or delete, how to promote and market cable-only services, which networks should share channel space, which local broadcast and access channels to carry, which syndicated programs to acquire or barter for, how to organize programs on locally programmed channels, and how to assess the impact of engineering improvements in cable equipment and picture quality, such as high-definition television, and competing technologies such as VCRs.

Responsibility for programming decisions varies greatly from system to system and owner to owner. More often than not, no matter what the system size, no full-time local programmer is employed. Nationwide, there may be as few as 500 cable system programmers—though accurate numbers are hard to obtain for the small systems.[1] Instead, programming decisions are usually made at the group level, by a management team of vice-presidents, directors of marketing and regional managers for dozens, even hundreds, of cable systems. Local system managers feed their recommendations into the group's decision-making process.

At the group headquarters level, programming is a broadly defined responsibility involving aspects of marketing and sales, advertising and promotion, technical and engineering matters and general management. The multiple system operator (MSO) may structure the programming of all its systems much alike, as does **Tele-Communications Inc. (TCI),** the largest cable MSO with about 8.3 million subscribers on owned and affiliated systems. At another extreme, it may encourage local decision-making about programming as does **American Television and Communications Corp. (ATC),** the second largest cable MSO with over 3.6 million subscribers. (See Chapter 4 for a discussion of group managerial styles as they relate to programming.) TCI, for example, developed a national program package supplying by satellite an identical array of advertiser-supported cable networks to most of its 1,500 systems. In contrast, ATC tends to individualize the array of services on its 615 local systems. However, within one broadcast market (an ADI or DMA), all cable operators now share the long-term goal of **common channel lineups** (having the cable-only networks on the same channel number on all cable systems). When achieved, standardization will aid market-wide advertising sales and on-air promotion. The Los Angeles ADI was the first major market in which several cable operators agreed on a uniform channel array, and in the late 1980s, newly constructed systems (**new-builds**) in Philadelphia and New York adopted uniform channel configurations. Technical considerations, however, limit the realization of such plans in many markets with long established systems, leaving considerable leeway for the skills of the cable programmer.

Cable marketing and programming are intimately connected, and managerial structures in the large MSOs reflect this situation. Programmers must have the skills of a market researcher and a business negotiator to license programming at a financial advantage that will have long-term appeal for sufficient numbers of subscribers and advertisers. They also need expertise in scheduling to locate channels in user-friendly and promotable arrays. Still another aspect of the MSO programmer's job is evaluating possible uses of new technologies and nonentertainment programming capabilities—such as security and alarm systems, interactive shopping and banking and data and computer services. Keeping one sharp eye on the competition and another on new revenue sources is part of the current programming game.

PROGRAMMING A MULTICHANNEL SYSTEM

The tasks of evaluation, selection and scheduling for cable and other multichannel nonbroadcast services such as **SMATV, MMDS** and **DBS,** reflect different conditions than those operating in traditional broadcasting.[2] Each of these **broadband** (multichannel video) services supplies many channels of programming obtained from varied sources. The rapid growth of competing cable program suppliers dependent on advertising sales, further **vertical integration** of MSOs with their suppliers and the construction of several previously unwired large markets, have increased the visibility of cable programming problems.

The Problem of Evaluation

Audience evaluation has been a persistent cable industry problem. Inadequate viewing data especially hamper national advertiser-supported networks in selling their commercial time. (The pay networks presumably face cancelation if their services fail to meet audience expectations.) Most nonpay services, however, depend on ad sales, and advertisers want to know how many people their messages reach (see Chapter 2 on this topic). Ad-supported cable services are usually packaged in the lowest level of cable service (**basic cable**) along with retransmitted broadcast signals and offered as a bundle to all subscribers for a single lump fee. On some large systems, a secondary group of ad-supported services may be offered to subscribers for an additional monthly fee (**tiered,** marketed at a second or even a third pay level). Although the total number of a system's subscribers is always known, more or less accurately, how many of them view the less popular nonpay channels cannot now be accurately measured on most systems.

Cable service now reaches over *half* of America's television households, but national audience shares for most advertiser-supported cable networks (*excluding* the top ten services) rarely exceed 1 percent of television households at one time. Even the very top services celebrate a 2 rating in prime time (the same as a 4 in cable households). Within many local markets, the cable-only audience is a small number of people—although in some mature cable markets, the combined audience for all *cable-only* channels exceeds that of the broadcast channels, and when all viewers of repeat showings of a program are summed, the audience for that one program may exceed a competing broadcast station's audience. Moreover, *combined,* all basic and pay cable networks often capture 20 or 30 percent of the national television audience, even in prime time. Cable viewing percentages really represent two audience measurements: One is the audience watching television at a given time (*AQH* ratings/shares); the other is the *cumulative* audience that watches a given program in all its showings (see Chapter 2). The adoption of *peoplemeters* in national viewing measurements has dramatically benefited the most popular cable networks by increasing their reported share of prime-time viewers but has contributed little to knowledge of the viewing of the less popular advertiser-supported and local-only services.

But the overriding problem in evaluating cable program audiences is that cable audience shares cannot be compared directly with broadcast audience shares (also discussed in Chapter 2). Cable **franchise areas** differ in size and shape from markets defined according to broadcast station coverage patterns (ADIs or DMAs). This prevents advertising time buyers from estimating cable's effectiveness in comparison to broadcasting and other media. Advertising **interconnects** within a single broadcast market (arrangements for the simultaneous showing of commercials on some ad-supported channels) are cable's main strategy for increasing the size of salable audiences, but interconnects generally occur only in and near the large markets, leaving thousands of cable systems with unsalable (too small and undefined) audience sizes. Cable has been forced to develop criteria other than ratings for selecting and scheduling national and local services and wooing advertisers.

The Problem of Churn

A second major problem for system programmers is audience **turn-over.** Subscribers who disconnect, even if replaced by new subscribers, cost the system in hookup time, administrative record changes, equipment loss and duplicated marketing effort. Initial marketing campaigns usually achieve penetration levels of 55 percent or higher, except in metropolitan areas where penetration runs as low as 25 percent in the first wave. But as many as 30 percent of the initial subscribers may cancel service within the first six months. Turnover on pay channels averages 5 percent of pay subscribers per month. The industry refers to such changes in the number of subscribers as **churn.**

The *churn rate* for any local system or specific cable network can be calculated for a year, or any other length of time, by dividing the number of disconnections by the number of new connections.

$$\frac{\text{disconnects}}{\text{new connects}} \times 100 = \% \text{ churn}$$

For example, a system having 200 disconnects while adding 300 new subscribers has a 67 percent churn rate. Usually, rates above 20 or 30 percent presage financial disaster. Not all cancelations can be prevented, of course; many occur because people move, children grow up and leave home, or because of general economic recession, unemployment and the like. Some cable operators even encourage a small amount of *content churn* for promotional purposes, adding and deleting channels to announce "new services" in hopes of keeping and gaining subscribers. But minimizing unproductive *audience churn* is one of the primary responsibilities a system's programming and marketing executives share.

Cable vs. Broadcasting

The programming problems of cablecasters differ from those of broadcasters. A broadcaster fills one channel all year around; a cablecaster must fill many channels—typically 36, but increasingly 54 or more (80 percent of systems now have 36 or more channels). A broadcaster purchases and schedules individual programs; only infrequently do cablecasters buy or produce specific programs (see Chapter 12). Instead, they obtain licenses to retransmit whole networks of prearranged and prescheduled programming. A broadcaster with a network affiliation fills up to 70 percent of the station's schedule with one network's programs, and generally a broadcast station's promotional efforts are closely linked to its network's image. The cablecaster, on the other hand, is connected with several networks—perhaps 30 or more—while also retransmitting the signals of local and distant over-the-air broadcasters. Its image comes from its total package of channels as well as its local origination programming, public relations, paid local advertising and on-air promotion. Lastly, broadcast stations receive most of their income from advertising spots sold within programs; cable systems are supported primarily by monthly fees paid by their subscribers (with growing advertising support in the larger cities).

Advertisers and cable operators have different—sometimes conflicting—goals. As one cable executive put it, "What drives advertising are eyeballs, while cable operators want perceived value. The more we [cable programmers] go for eyeballs, the lower will be the perceived value."[3] Thus the growth of local advertising sales creates a significant tension within the cable industry, adding to the pressure on cable programmers.

Although advertising practices are changing and economic conditions will differ by 1995, the programming strategies of cable systems will continue to be determined by four elements discussed in the next sections: a system's *legal* responsibilities, its *technology*, the *economic* factors affecting program selection and local *marketing* considerations. All constrain cable programming choices. All limit the system programmer's options because cable industry management makes programming decisions based on this entire complex of factors.

LEGAL CARRIAGE REQUIREMENTS

Since keeping a franchise once it has been won is an overriding operator's goal, meeting legal contract requirements has the highest priority. The first set are the channels or services stipulated in the local franchise contract. A second set of carriage restrictions may be imposed by the policies of the cable system owner—generally a corporate MSO.

Franchise Requirements

Under previous FCC regulations, every cable system had a legally defined number of local over-the-air signals that had to be placed on the system. These signals were the **must-carries,** defined as the "significantly viewed" broadcast stations. They included at least one local affiliate of each of the three major broadcast networks, any local independent stations and at least one local public station. See Chapter 1 for the details of the old must-carry rules. Recent rules did not require **redundant carriage**—having to carry multiple affiliates of the same network—because it excessively limited the cablecaster's options when a small-capacity system lay between two large broadcast markets and consequently had stations from both markets coming into the franchise area.

Broadcasters and cable operators generally hold opposing views on cable carriage of all local broadcast stations. Local *broadcasters* want all cable systems operating in the same market to carry their stations so they can remain competitive for the largest possible audiences. Without a legal requirement forcing cable systems to carry all local broadcast stations, cable operators can exclude some stations from easy access to cable viewers—since cable's very installation normally requires disconnecting over-the-air antennas, making broadcast-only reception more than a little inconvenient. In 1987 all must-carry rules were eliminated, leaving cable operators free to choose the most popular stations for carriage.

From the *cable operator*'s perspective, carrying local-market affiliates and independents remains important to supply local news and local advertising, but carrying major-market affiliates of the same networks also provides a popular source of news and information that probably will draw more viewers. **Distant independents** such as the **superstations** are consistently among the most popular cable offerings. Major-market stations (and the superstations) have higher budgets, greater technical expertise and larger professional staffs than smaller stations and, as a result, generally attract more viewers. In areas where a large-market affiliate or public station has high visibility, the viewing of small same-network stations has been minimal when both were available on the same cable system. Therefore, the cable operator wants to be free to select the most viewed stations. On the broadcasting side, however, removal from several local cable systems is likely to bankrupt some small UHF independents, additionally reducing audience and advertiser options. It becomes increasingly probable that broadcasters will eventually have to *pay* for carriage, especially those stations attracting very small audiences.

Although federally-mandated must-carry rules are gone (though public stations may get some protection from Congress), local **franchise agreements** often specify *nonbroadcast* signals that must be carried (public **access** and local origination channels) and *comprehensive local station carriage* (all stations licensed to serve the franchising city). Local contracts may even specify that channels be set aside for *leasing* to local businesses. Although federal law now prohibits local authorities from setting specific program or rate requirements, many cable operators promise specific carriage plans and other services in order to gain a **franchise agreement** (or negotiate a **franchise renewal**). The cable operator has then legally contracted to provide such services. Federal regulations no longer require any local access or leased channels nor, of course, do they require that cable systems carry pay channels or superstations or any other particular programming. But when a franchise agreement specifies particular services, the cable programmer must place them on the system before calculating the amount of channel space available for other services.

MSO Policies

Parent corporations frequently impose restrictions on what their local systems can carry, as discussed in Chapter 4 on group ownership's influence on programming. Some MSOs, for example, have policies freezing out adult programming; a few have policies favoring access and program guide channels—even when they are not legally stipulated in a franchise contract. TCI's standardized carriage policy for most optional channels obviously improves the MSO's position when negotiating contracts with basic and premium networks. (Basic networks that fail to be selected by some of the largest MSOs—TCI, ATC, Continental, Storer, Cox, Warner, Comcast, United, Newhouse, Viacom—stand little chance to survive.) At the same time, MSO pressure to carry one package of cable networks inhibits the programmer's local responsiveness.

Many cable companies are owned by corporations that emphasize bottom-line profits. When choices must be made between (a) access and specialized services for very small audiences or (b) channels likely to be widely popular, usually the least profitable services will be cut. From the financial point of view, small audiences should be sacrificed for larger ones because popular programming generates more advertising revenues. Such MSO priorities, then, limit the system programmer's options.

TECHNICAL CHARACTERISTICS
AFFECTING PROGRAMMING

A system's technical characteristics also limit the programmer's options. Cable's ability to carry many signals simultaneously results from its **broadband** capacity (a feature of **coaxial** and **fiber optic** cable), but the precise number of channels a system can carry is a function of the types of cables, traps and converters it uses and whether these are addressable, and if so, whether one-way or two-way. A system's technology determines which services are appropriate and which are not practical from an engineering perspective.

Channel Capacity

As of the late 1980s, most cable systems had a capacity of 36 channels, and major-market systems had 54 to 108 addressable channels. Small-capacity systems generally occur in small towns already having high levels of cable penetration, reducing any economic incentive to increase the number of channels. Nonetheless, upgrading from 24 channels progressed slowly even in potentially lucrative markets in the early 1980s. An economic vise trapped the winners of the urban franchises in markets such as New York, Boston, Philadelphia and Chicago; they were caught between their franchise promises and the unanticipated high costs of underground wiring in metropolitan areas (as much as a million dollars a mile). High interest rates and a shortage of conversion equipment, especially reliable addressable converters and the sophisticated computer software and hardware necessary to implement addressability, held down both **new-builds** and the expansion of established systems (**rebuilds**). But growth resumed in the middle and late 1980s, making likely that nearly 90 percent of television homes will have cable as an option by the early 1990s (the "homes passed" universe explained in Chapter 2).

In addition to the cost of capital, two other factors directly affect the rate at which cable systems are rebuilt: local contract negotiations with power and telephone carriers and the availability of experienced manpower for installation. The use of telephone poles and underground rights-of-way is generally shared with other utilities that seek to defend their market positions. Local telephone companies, viewing cable as a potential competitor for consumer and business services, are not always quick to respond in negotiations for pole and underground conduit arrangements. The other problem is that most cable installers are either free-lance or employed by a parent MSO and travel among many systems. A shortage of experienced installers persists, and new construction demands generally prevail over rebuilding needs.

The politically unstable relationship between **antitrust law** and **exclusive franchising** creates another restraint on system expansion. Cable operators have been reluctant to build high-capacity systems of 100 channels or more without legal assurance that cities will retain the exclusive franchise model perpetuating "natural" monopolies. The alternative, **multiple franchising** (having more than one cable operator wire the same geographic area, also called **overbuilding**), raises the specter of unbalanced competition: Later entrants might build more economical systems offering cheaper services. Early entrants with many nonrevenue-producing features demanded by franchising authorities could be forced out of business. To protect their investments by making quick, short-term profits, many cable operators renegotiated their franchise agreements in the mid-1980s, eliminating unprofitable features they had originally agreed to provide. Susceptibility to being overbuilt, however, is generally tied to poor service—low channel capacity, high rates and poor customer complaint response—and the threat of possible overbuilds spurred much improvement in system capacity and service in the late 1980s. To date, fewer than three dozen overbuilds have actually occurred (among nearly 8,500 systems).

Additionally, cable equipment manufacturers are another factor. They want to avoid over-expansion in their industry, which providing quick response to cablecasters' equipment orders would do. As more and more of the United States is progressively wired and upgraded, it is not hard to foresee a plateau in the demand for cable equipment. Pacing factory output is practical economics for cable equipment manufacturers. All these factors, then, affect the numbers of channels the cablecasters can program on established systems.

Then, a system's wiring, of course, sets limits on its capacity. In essence, coaxial cables carry one television signal on each of the VHF channels, 2 to 13. Nowadays, however, technology defeats this limit (of just 12 channels) two ways: by adding *extra cables* (a second coaxial or fiber optic cable to every house) or by adding *channel converters* on each television set. Current models of converters add the **midband** (between channels 6 and 7) and the **superband** (above channel 13) to the existing frequencies, raising capacity to a maximum of 54 channels per cable.[4] Adding an extra cable can then double capacity to 108 channels.

Midband and **superband converters** have permitted even the smallest systems to add four or more channels without totally rewiring the franchise. On average, programming fills only about two-thirds of the channels on systems with 54 or more channels, the remainder being held in reserve. Most systems have fewer channels available than there are competing cable networks, which gives rise to a shortage of **shelf space** (cable channel capacity), working to the advantage of large cable operators and the disadvantage of new program suppliers.

General economic, political and manufacturing conditions, then, as well as engineering arrangements, affect new construction and upgrading of existing systems. The total number of systems with more than 54 channels has remained tiny. On the other hand, systems with few channels serve very few people. As of 1988, the trade press reported channel distribution approximately as shown in Table 9-1 (figures vary).

Addressability

Addressable converters further alter cable programming strategies. **Addressability** refers to the capability of sending customized packages of signals to each home (such as with or without certain pay channels or a second tier). Most addressable systems are **one-way**, sending signals only from the cable headend to the subscriber. Without addressability, all services, including premium channels, pass every home and are mechanically **trapped** from entering

Table 9-1 Channel Distribution

	NUMBER OF SYSTEMS	PERCENTAGE OF ALL SYSTEMS	PERCENTAGE OF SUBSCRIBERS
54 or more channels	592	2%	15%
30 to 53 channels	3,549	42%	62%
20 to 29 channels	1,437	17%	14%
19 or fewer channels	2,028	24%	7%
No information	845	10%	2%
Totals	8,451	100%	100%

Source: 1987 *Television & Cable Factbook,* 1988 *Channels Field Guide* and 1988 *CableVision* data.

nonsubscribing homes (a practical limit of three trapped channels currently exists in most systems). With addressability, headend computers direct different sets of channels to individual homes, without any mechanical constraints on the number of scrambled premium services.

At present, one-way addressable technology provides strong advantages in accurate and low-cost hookup (or cancelation) and billing service. One-way addressability keeps churn costs to a minimum by cutting out service calls for adding or changing service (there are no traps to install or remove). Urban systems are usually 100 percent addressable today.

Two-way addressability, also called **interactive** cable, refers to more advanced systems in which the subscriber can also send information to the system's main computer. The best known of the interactive systems, Warner's **Qube,** permitted subscribers to respond to questions posed by live hosts on local program channels; to shop at home by entering personal account numbers; and to purchase pay-per-view programs by pushing buttons on a key-pad. The Qube system was installed in Columbus (Ohio), Cincinnati, Pittsburgh, Dallas and other cities but was copied only by few other cable operators. Because the cost of operation outweighed the financial return, in 1984 Warner Cable ended interactive entertainment on its systems, retaining only a series of pay-per-view channels.

The primary reason for investing in addressable converters to date is **pay-per-view (PPV).**[5] Its economics appear so favorable to cable operators over the long haul that its potential has become the major selling point for manufacturers of two-way addressable equipment. Consider a hypothetical $5 per household per week for pay-per-view events: That would effectively triple monthly system revenues, not counting revenues from multiple tiers or premium channels. For example, only four pay-per-view events selected by a household in a period of a month could add $20 *per subscriber per month* to the average $13 that comes in as basic service revenue and the $4 or so retained per premium channel. In spite of programming and technology costs, pay-per-view has the appearance of a gold mine. Many cable operators have built in two-way capacity, but marketing of pay-per-view services began slowly, awaiting 25 percent addressability on systems nationwide and easy-to-understand ordering methods. (See Chapter 11 for more details on pay-per-view programming and technology.)

For several reasons, the installation rate for multistrand addressable cabling has been very slow, even in large, wealthy rebuilt systems—partly because in the beginning the equipment tended to break down and supply inaccurate billing records. Another addressability issue is its lack of security. Devices inside homes are easily tampered with, defeated and stolen, reducing addressability's potential profit. In the early 1980s, Cox Cable shocked the industry at a cable conference by announcing the results of an audit of a newly installed addressable system: Nearly 90 percent of their converters showed signs of tampering; over half had been defeated. Nearly half of their subscribers were receiving free premium programming. Estimates of homes illegally receiving basic cable or pay signals range as high as 20 percent in some franchises. This figure suggests one reason many marketing campaigns achieve less than anticipated levels of penetration is that many subscribers targeted for the additional services are already enjoying them!

The problem involves more than purposeful cheating, however. Subscribers often inadvertently take the converter box with them when they move, a costly inconvenience for cable operators. Moreover, homes with multiple television sets find the monthly fees for two converters out of line with their expectations. This has led to a new generation of pole-top converters (intended for telephone poles, but which may be located outside the subscriber's home or in apartment building basements). Another solution has been to reduce or eliminate the monthly charge for second and third converters. Still another solution is a "converter deposit" to discourage casual theft or loss. Some highly sophisticated systems can even detect illegal converters by remote control. Unreliable billing and service records further compound the problem of theft in many systems, and many MSOs have chosen upgradable one-way systems to minimize their financial risk.

ECONOMIC FACTORS AFFECTING PROGRAMMING

The most powerful factor affecting carriage of most cable networks is their *cost* to the local system. Besides viewer popularity, cost is directly affected by whether the cable network is advertiser- or subscriber-supported, whether the MSO owns part of the service and what additional incentives the service offers.

Most advertiser-supported networks charge local systems a small per-subscriber fee to supplement their advertising revenue. These fees, ranging from 3 cents to 25 cents per subscriber per month (even more for former pay channels), become a sizable monthly outlay for a system carrying 15 or more advertiser-supported services to 10,000 or 20,000 subscribers.

$$\$.10 \times 10,000 \text{ subscribers} \times 20 \text{ services} = \$20,000 \text{ monthly cost}$$

Cable systems typically allocate a monthly budget of about $1 per subscriber to cover the cost of all basic programming.

On the positive side for cable systems, salable spot time on advertiser-supported channels (local **avails**) brings in revenue. Moreover, provisions for print advertising and promotional support from the program supplier *offset* per-subscriber fees. In other words, some fees paid to national cable program suppliers are, in effect, returned in the form of advertising avails, co-op advertising funds or prepaid ads in *TV Guide* and other publications that attract audiences to the local system. A further factor that must be weighed in the economic balance is which satellite delivers a network's signal since not all systems have the equipment to obtain signals from all satellites. These factors are discussed in detail in the following sections.

Licensing Patterns

From a local cable programmer's perspective, cable networks come in four varieties: those that the *subscriber pays individually* for (**premium** channels); those that the *system must license* for a small monthly or annual per-subscriber fee (most ad-supported services); those that are *free* to the system (highly specialized); and those that *pay the system* for carriage (unusual).

In the first case, the **pay-cable networks,** such as HBO or Showtime, require subscribers to pay a *monthly fee* (around $10 or $12 for movie services). A portion of that fee, negotiated by the cable system and typically around half, stays with the local system. For example, $6 of the approximately $12 that subscribers pay for HBO stays with the local system; the other $4 per subscriber per month goes to HBO. The fact that a pay-cable channel imposes no cost on the system (except for pickup) while actually producing substantial revenue has placed premium services at the heart of cable economics.

In the second and most common case, the **basic cable network** charges the local system a *fee per subscriber per month* while usually also carrying advertising. The most popular services make some spot time available for local sale as well. ESPN, WTBS, CNN, USA Network, MTV, The Nashville Network, Lifetime, Nickelodeon and others fall in this category. Services such as The Weather Channel come gratis when placed on the basic tier or when upper-tier penetration is very high, indicating a large number of subscribers, but otherwise charge the system a small monthly fee per subscriber. Other specialized channels such as the Reuters Financial Reports and C-SPAN I and II (live coverage of Congress) also charge the cable system a license fee but do not have advertising. Proposed new services are commonly offered free to cable systems for one year as an incentive to carriage. Since the per-subscriber charge is in cents per month, generally too small to bill individually, basic services charge the cable operator for carriage and are typically included in the lowest service tier. In large capacity systems, however, several ad-supported networks may be "bundled" on an upper **tier** for a small additional sum (typically $5) or offered as an **expanded basic** service, replacing the minimum basic array for a higher cost (typically $18 to $20 rather than the $13 average for minimum basic). A few franchise contracts prohibit **bundling** of channels, but most systems with 45 or more channels group channels on upper pay tiers in addition to basic and premium offerings. Typically, the local system charges subscribers a monthly fee for basic service (bottom tier) that reflects programming, administrative and engineering costs and system profits, commonly about $13 as of 1988. Upper pay tiers then usually add on $5 per month and pay channels run about $11 each. For example, Telecable Corp., a top-25 MSO operating many small systems, charges $11 for a 23-channel basic service and $18 for an expanded 35-channel basic, which includes such popular cable-only networks as ESPN, CNN and USA Network. In addition, it offers three or four pay services on each of its systems. Of course, individual pay services and upper tiers or expanded basic appear separately on the subscriber's monthly bill, but only if the subscriber agrees to the additional service.

Home shopping services are advertiser-supported, but the local system usually receives them *free of charge*, although often the contract specifies basic tier placement. Many of these services operate as barter networks, similar to the barter programs discussed in chapters 3, 7 and 8. Barter services usually offer *marginal* entertainment programming—less than top quality or frequently rerun—or highly specialized content (such as continuous product selling) on an exchange-for-time basis (**barter**) to cable operators. In this arrangement, most advertising spots are presold by the distributor, although a few local avails may be included as an enticement to carry the channel. The best known of these barter services is Home Shopping Network (Modern Satellite Network in another incarnation); it carries only shopping or other information its advertisers supply. Religious channels also typically come without charge and may come without explicit advertising, being supported by viewers' donations or the parent organization. Religious groups then buy time from the religious networks, in effect, using "program-length" advertising to reach their audiences. Locally originating services, such as local news or classified advertising channels, would not require a licensing fee (but would, of course, require production support).

Finally, in a few cases, financially powerful program distributors *pay the local cable operator* to carry their program channels at a rate determined by the number of subscribers. To compete with the well-established Cable News Network, for instance, ABC/Group W paid cable operators the equivalent of $1.50 per subscriber (one time only) to carry the newly introduced Satellite News Channel, and planned also to pay systems an ongoing *compensation* of 10 cents per subscriber per year (see Chapter 10 for an analysis of the demise of Satellite News Channel). To get its Spanish language channel carried, Univision (formerly SIN) pays cable operators a small amount per month per Spanish-surname subscriber (rates vary with the quarter of the year). Trinity Broadcasting Network pays operators monthly for carriage. More recently, most national shopping services began offering local cable systems a small percentage of their sales as an incentive to carriage. They use zip codes to assign sales to particular local cable systems.

Program content has no bearing on channel pricing method—with the exception of the premium movie channels. (Their revenues must cover the fees for licensing first-run movies as discussed in Chapter 11.) In the 1980s, smaller than projected advertising revenues forced nearly all basic cable networks into a similar economic pattern: *Charge a fee, sell advertising, make local spots available* and, if possible, *provide promotional support*. Those cable networks charging the largest per-subscriber fees face strong pressure to reduce or eliminate those fees when competition without fees surfaces. On the other hand, ESPN, one of the most popular services, dropped its fees only to reinstate them a couple of years later, and it continued adding cable affiliates despite high license fees.

Among financially weaker services or those lacking adequate shelf space on systems, a common strategy is to offer **equity holdings** (part-ownership) to cable MSOs. Many of the larger MSOs (TCI, Viacom, Continental) now have equity shares in several cable program networks, guaranteeing the networks shelf space and giving the MSO tax advantages. Cable programmers, of necessity then, schedule these program services in prime locations when possible.

Signal Importation Fees

The Copyright Act of 1976 originally specified such low **copyright royalty fees** for the importation of **distant independent signals** that royalty payments by cable systems had a negligible effect on programming decisions. The Act, however, contained the proviso that the Copyright Royalty Tribunal might alter the fee schedule if the FCC changed the carriage rules.[6] In 1982, the FCC altered the cable carriage rules, and the CRT raised copyright fees substantially. Much wailing from the cable industry and much cheering from program producers and distributors (rights-holders) ensued. Cable systems now pay 3.75 percent beyond their base **compulsory license fee** (see Chapter 1) for each distant signal they import. The new fees most affected the carriage of **superstations** since this extra copyright fee is paid above and beyond the mandatory copyright fee and the transmission fees charged by the common carrier. Copyright, then, adds yet another cost consideration to decisions about WTBS, WGN, WWOR and other satellite-transmitted independent broadcast stations. Despite the complaints, however, few cable systems dropped superstations they already carried, and superstation audiences continued to grow. WTBS, for example, reached 43 million homes by 1988. Superstations, programming live sports, older movies and older network fare, are highly popular drawing cards for cable systems.

Spot Availabilities

Local availabilities (**avails**) on the most popular advertising-supported networks are becoming more valuable to cable systems as they *interconnect* for simultaneous cablecasting of commercials. Offering spots for local sale is a major bargain point for the cable networks when renegotiating contracts with local systems. These spots are, for the most part, deducted from program time rather than network advertising time, so they cost the network little. There is, of course, a practical limit on how much a program can be shortened to allow for advertising. Moreover, infrequent interruption is one of the positive appeals of cable-only programming to subscribers. Most advertiser-supported services, in consequence, offer about two avails per hour and cluster all advertising spots in just a few program breaks.

Availabilities that cannot be sold, however, offer little advantage to a local system, though they can be used for system promotion. But not all systems are capable of local inserts. In mid-sized and large markets, however, unsold spots on the top cable-only networks may reflect weak local sales efforts and weak local economic conditions. In most metropolitan areas, however, profitable advertising **interconnects** have become the standard pattern. In the San Francisco Bay Area, for example, 32 cable systems use microwave to distribute local advertising on channels such as ESPN, WTBS, CNN, USA and MTV.[7] This means that the entire Bay Area cable audience (more than half of all television households) becomes the base for ad rates on those channels. This total potential audience is large enough to convince advertisers that a substantial number of viewers will watch their ads.

Promotional Support

When cable programmers are deciding which networks to carry, they also consider how much **promotional support** is provided. *On-air promotion* as well as *print advertising* and *merchandising* are especially valuable for gaining new subscribers, reducing churn and creating positive images in the minds of current and potential subscribers, local advertisers and municipal officials. Local systems have learned that they must identify themselves as the source of the most-wanted cable programming and convince the public that they supply valuable services and are responsive to community needs. Most national cable networks aid these efforts by supplying professional-quality consumer marketing and sales materials, including on-air spots, subscriber information kits, direct mailers, bill stuffers, program guides and other merchandising. When this material meets local needs, it offsets a small portion of the cost of licensing some advertiser-supported networks.

Moreover, those national networks purchasing large amounts of national broadcast television and print advertising (*TV Guide* especially) to promote themselves to consumers have an obvious advantage over their competitors. Their high visibility makes them popular with subscribers and therefore with cable operators. For example, Ted Turner charges one of the highest per-subscriber rates for CNN, Headline and WTBS, but his commitment to advertising and promoting them has kept his services popular with operators. Many networks also offer local systems cooperative arrangements, either at sign-up time or annually, for local joint promotion of the network and system. About half of non-pay cable networks provide start-up assistance, varying from 10 to 50 cents per subscriber (in some cases, the parties negotiate a lump sum) to share the cost of introducing a new service.

All pay-cable networks supply camera-ready materials to the local systems to use in local print ads for annual promotional campaigns, a significant aid because most local systems lack art departments and must hire outside art or advertising firms for all their print advertising. Among the premium networks, HBO dominates in market position in part because it has traditionally supplied far more on-air and print promotional aid than its main competitors. When competition for an especially lucrative market heats up, the largest cable networks come up with financial incentives such as million dollar promotional budgets to ensure carriage.

Satellite Placement

Which satellite carries a cable network (**satellite placement**) is also a financial concern to cable programmers. For cable, by far the most important of the domestic television satellites has been Satcom III-R, which handled the signals of the strongest cable networks—HBO in particular—through most of the 1980s. Today, four satellites carry mostly cable programming: Satcom III and IV (owned by GE) and Galaxy I and III, owned by Hughes. Most receive-only satellite **dishes** aim at these four dishes today. Although supplemented by other cable-programming satellites (Satcom I-R and V, Westar IV, V and VI-S, Comstar III and IV and Galaxy II), Satcom III-R is the sole cable satellite whose signals are receivable by all cable systems, with Satcom IV and Galaxy I and III the next most commonly received satellites.

Receiving signals from more than one satellite usually requires another receiving dish because older dishes pick up only a tiny portion of the satellite orbital arc. Cable systems must purchase multiple dishes or more expensive wide-reception dishes to pick signals off other satellites.

Program services using one of the **transponders** on Satcom III-R have been more widely carried than their less fortunate competitors, and they had a modest advantage in contract negotiations with systems whose receiving dishes drew only from Satcom III-R. Poor satellite positioning (especially on the Westar birds) initially slowed the nationwide distribution of many cable networks in the 1970s. Some anxious cable networks, unable to get space on Satcom III-R, even subsidized local purchase of an additional dish. CBN, for example, supplied a large number of dishes without charge to cable systems with the proviso that CBN be carried, as did Trinity Broadcasting Network (TBN), the superstation WWOR and GalaVision (the Spanish-language movie service).

However, cable operators face a new dilemma in the 1990s, rapidly affecting contract negotiations between cable networks and local systems. By 1995, three of the most widely used cable satellites, Satcom III-R, Galaxy I and Satcom IV, will have expended their useful life expectancy, and most cable program suppliers, and therefore local cable systems, will have to choose between continuing with **C-band** (the older, low-power satellites) or shifting to **Ku-band** satellites, the rapidly emerging high-powered satellites needing smaller receiving dishes. Most cable operators can use 10-foot dishes for Ku, compared to 16 to 20-foot dishes for C-band, although in some geographic areas (mostly the southern United States) large raindrops occasionally approximate the size of Ku radio waves (a humorous scientific oddity!), causing signal attenuation and necessitating larger dishes.[8]

A few satellite manufacturers will continue to launch C-band satellites (Hughes Communications will put up Galaxy IV in the early 1990s), but most new satellites will be either Ku-band or **hybrids** containing both C-band and Ku transponders. (The number and capacity of transponders determines the number of television channels the satellite carries, typically 24). According to industry estimates, three-quarters of the satellites launched in the next decade will use Ku-band technology. Although most cable program services will continue to transmit programming on C-band as well as Ku-band through the 1990s, their transmission costs will remain high until cable operators shift to the newer technology. Operators, on the other hand, remain reluctant to convert because Ku equipment is costly and their present C-band equipment is already paid for. HBO and GE, strong proponents of Ku transmission, began giving away Ku receiving dishes to cable operators in 1987 to encourage the technological shift.

Technical limitations, then, prevent cable programmers from freely choosing just any network that might appeal to their audience. They have to weigh the cost of shifting satellites (even technologies) or adding a supplementary dish antenna. In effect, then, the large numbers of services carried by satellites are not equally available to cable programmers. The ones the "dominant" satellites transmit are the most likely to be selected, perpetuating the advantageous market position of those cable networks that started early and had strong financial backing.

MARKETING CONSIDERATIONS

Cable programming seeks to attract and hold both the local audience and the local (or regional) advertiser. To achieve this goal, cable programmers must *maximize new subscriptions* and *minimize disconnections*. The nature of the local audience determines what programming has appeal. If sheer audience size justifies ad spot rates, then the exact audience demographics will determine whether and which advertisers will want to buy time—just as in broadcast television and radio.

Audience Composition

Research has established that, nationally, the cable audience has two persistent characteristics: It is younger and made of larger families than the noncable audience. In particular markets, however, subscribers to a system may differ from the national norm. The *demographic* and *psychographic* composition of a cable coverage area plays a major role in selecting a channel mix. A young, upscale, urban community, for example, probably wants several channels of sophisticated movies of recent vintage, whereas communities consisting of large families prefer "G" and "PG" movies, children's channels and information on such topics as cooking, gardening and health. Several channels of rock music and cultural programming seem appropriate for college towns; midwestern cities, having strong sports traditions, would probably like a heavy sports diet on cable television. These stereotypical expectations are not always fulfilled, however, when actual subscribers are examined. Families, for instance, often want mixes of channels to meet both adults' and children's needs.

Data collected at the time subscribers are initially signed and survey questionnaires included with monthly bills can provide insights into local subscriber psychographics, programming preferences and viewing habits. In addition, field surveys can supply information on nonsubscribers that helps programmers design advertising to gain new subscribers. Sometimes the local franchise authorities commission audience ascertainment research of value to system programmers, suggesting ways of reducing audience churn. The larger MSOs generally have research budgets; they typically collect systemwide data to aid in marketing decisions and employ their own or outside research staffs to develop and interpret audience data.

However, the gap between what people *say* they will or will not pay for and what they buy in practice creates considerable programming risk. Even the mere act of discovering what people *say they want* on cable has hazards. The difficulty occurs in composing questions of a hypothetical nature that seek to find out what someone "might do" under a variety of conditions. It is very human to say "no" to proposed services, the value of which is only dimly perceived, when monthly fees are involved. At the same time, it is very human to say "yes, I would watch or use that" to highly specialized services that involve no apparent cost. Later subscriber behavior has frequently differed dramatically from conclusions based on advance surveys.

And ratings data is often of little help to cable operators. Since cable franchise areas do not usually correspond to broadcast ADIs (or DMAs), broadcast ratings data fail to describe potential cable subscribers whose homes are passed. When funds for cable system audience analysis are absent, cablecasters fall back upon informal feedback and personal experiences. These data can be misleading and basing program decisions on them is risky.

Lift and Overmarketing

Another question cable programmers and marketing executives must ask is *how many channels* is the right number. Some evidence suggests that the mass audience is not yet prepared to deal with scores of cable channels, at least as of the late 1980s, and that two dozen might be sufficient to attract and hold subscribers—especially if one or two were changed periodically. Cable consultant Paul Bortz has even suggested that four or five satellite channels might represent a better value for the price in consumer's minds.[9] Unlike broadcast affiliates, cable systems can alter their affiliations among cable networks to always have a "new" service to market.

For newly built systems (**new-builds**), scheduling multiple pay channels is a widely adopted strategy. Marketing especially popular pay services along with basic service typically encourages more people to subscribe than might if only basic service were offered, a phenomenon called **lift.** Lift also operates in established systems when new pay services or highly popular advertiser-supported services (such as ESPN) are added on. Initially, lift may increase subscribership from 5 to 30 percent (estimates vary), and, of course, other marketing factors influence lift—timing, properly targeted appeals, promotion, competing services available and so on. At some point, lift diminishes as systems add more and more services, leading to *discounts* for multiple pay subscriptions in one household, a recent marketing strategy.

As with the credit card industry, one influence on marketing strategy is the degree to which subscribers have overextended themselves, committing to larger monthly fees than they can afford. On more sophisticated systems, many subscribers make total monthly commitments of $50, $75 or even $100 at the sign-up stage. When an appealing array of services is initially available or exciting new services are added to an established system, many subscribers overcommit themselves, resulting in nonpayment, late payments or disconnects. To mitigate **overmarketing,** cable systems set up alternate payment plans to aid indebted subscribers, who must then cut back on total services. Educating subscribers to budget more money for cable service is the long-term solution. In the short run, cable operators hold back some channels until subscribers gradually adjust to increased cable bills. Programming rollouts now occur in bite-sized increments to prevent too much, too fast for subscribers.

Content and Audience Appeals

Debate persists in the cable industry over which of two network concepts is more likely to survive: **narrowcasting** or **broad-based appeal.** The clarity of a particular network's concept has strategic value. Both subscribers and advertisers seem to feel more comfortable with sharply defined services; certainly, such services are easier to promote in on-air and print advertising and to market to potential advertisers. Defining sharpness, however, is more difficult than recognizing it, suggesting that a network lacking sharpness might also create a niche for itself by effective national promotion of multiple appeals over a long time period. Nonetheless, some cable networks—MTV and The Weather Channel, for example—have such clarity of concept; these embody narrowcasting at its simplest.

Defining cable program services requires separating two intertwined elements—the *content* and the *target audience.* The content may be chosen either from a restricted content pool or may represent a range of types and formats within one broad content area; the service may appeal either to the mass audience or only to a limited group of viewers (demographically or psychographically defined).

Figure 9-1 shows four possible combinations of program content and audience appeal. In one case, MTV, for example, combines both a restricted range of content (only rock music videos) and narrowly defined appeal (to teens and young adults); Financial News Network (FNN) follows this pattern, targeting financial information to business people. (**Slivercasting** is the term applied to services aiming at still more restricted groups of people—such as pork futures for commodity brokers or interactive games for personal computer users.)

By way of contrast, USA Network's content ranges from soaps to sports to movies to newscasts and appeals to the broadest possible mass audience (*dayparting* to the same audience the three major broadcast television networks seek). WTBS and CBN also fit this second pattern of broad content and broad appeal.

In a third model, Nickelodeon (NICK) programs a broad range of content, including off-network fare, movies, cartoons and original children's programs, but the service appeals mostly to young children and their families (about a quarter of cable households). Similarly, Univision (formerly Spanish International Television—SIN) programs mass-audience content, but it appeals only to Spanish-speaking people; Lifetime also schedules a wide range of health and exercise-related content, but appeals almost exclusively to women—half the total adult audience.

In the fourth pattern, The Weather Channel (TWC) has an extremely

Figure 9-1 Cable Service Content and Audience Appeal

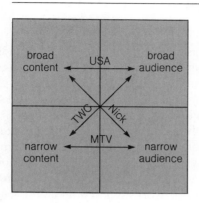

restricted type of content (all weather) but, like CNN and several other narrowcast services, may be useful to virtually all television viewers for a few minutes daily (broad demographic appeal).

Network concept becomes, then, one more element in the programming mix. The local programmer must gamble that the cable network selected for a system will (1) survive to provide programming for a reasonable length of time while (2) projecting a clear and marketable image to subscribers and advertisers.

Advertiser Appeal

Some channels interest specific types of advertisers. ESPN, the sports channel, an obvious case in point, strongly appeals to the male, beer-drinking, sports-loving audience. That appeal pinpoints a group of products that can be effectively advertised. Similarly, Lifetime appeals to manufacturers of patent medicines and exercise equipment, The Weather Channel to travel-related companies and so on. The mass-appeal cable networks are appropriate places for advertising many consumer products—although their relatively smaller audiences, in comparison to broadcast networks, keep their dollar value lower. Local cable programmers must choose cable services that draw the right demographics for local and regional advertisers to foster the sale of local avails. This consideration is especially important in small markets with only a few potential advertisers.

SELECTION STRATEGIES FOR SYSTEMS

Designing a system typically involves five steps, in this order: (1) assigning channels for the local origination and access channels the franchise requires or the MSO desires, (2) selecting local broadcast stations, (3) selecting premium networks, (4) selecting distant independent station signals and (5) selecting a composite of nonpay services to fill out the system. Systems with addressability can place highly targeted channels in the schedule, including pay-per-view, and very large systems with excess capacity may lease out some channels and reserve others for paced introduction of upper service tiers.

Sources of Programming

Nearly 70 national networks supply most of the programming that is designed explicitly for cable (*cable-only* programming). They package entire channels of programming for delivery by satellite relay. Thirteen of these are premium services, and the remaining 55 or so are basic cable networks. A few are hybrid broadcast and cable services such as Univision and the superstations, and about 10 are shopping-only services. As of 1988, broadcast network affiliates retained just over 60 percent of all viewing (when all dayparts are averaged), while the pay movie channels, superstations, local independents and public stations shared the remaining nearly 40 percent of viewing with a dozen of the most popular basic cable networks. Local origination, leased and access channels taken together represent only a fraction of 1 percent of cable viewing—by the most generous estimates.

The options open to a cable programmer after assigning channels to access and broadcast stations depend on the size of the system. Most find six or more channels immediately filled with local services. For marketing and economic reasons (to create *lift* and gain *revenue*) operators typically schedule from three to five premium channels. Generally, a superstation fills at least one channel because of the attractiveness of its sports and movies. If the system carries a program guide channel, about two-thirds of a 36-channel system remains open to fill with ESPN, CNN, Headline, USA Network, MTV, VH-1, Nickelodeon, CBN, Lifetime, Black Entertainment Network, C-SPAN I and II, Arts & Entertainment, The Nashville Network and other country music services, The Discovery Channel, The Nostalgia Channel, The Silent Network, The Weather Channel, FNN and other financial services, religious networks, home shopping services, regional sports networks, text news services and so on. Ideally, the demographic and psychographic composition of the local audience determines what goes on them, but in practice the choice is often guided by whatever provides immediate economic advantage. Cable MSOs such as Viacom and TCI have financial interests in many cable program services, favoring the selection (and advantageous channel placement) of their own program services on their owned and part-owned systems.

Channel Balance

The need to have **channel balance** further limits the cable programmer's choices. Although The Playboy Channel contains soft-core sexual entertainments rather than explicit sexual depictions, it generates protest in many conservative communities. Even hit movies on the highly popular pay services such as HBO and Showtime elicit occasional public outcry from some groups. Although a number of court decisions in the early 1980s supported the cable operator's legal right to show sexual (but not obscene) material, local public disapproval may be too high a price tag for some MSOs. In 1983, for example, Warner-Amex was sued for carrying R-rated material on The Playboy Channel and settled out of court, agreeing not to carry The Playboy Channel on any of its systems. The political contests for franchise renewal are potent corporate persuaders.

Cable programmers therefore protect themselves from extended criticism by **balancing** the services they offer. One way to balance a system is to bury controversial programming and create an overall image of responsible community service. Consumer promotional materials, for example, can stress the family-oriented content of many channels, even though the system contains adult-oriented programming on other channels. Cultural channels are often marketed more for their balancing effect than for any audience lift they create. News, public affairs and community access channels have a positive image effect. A further strategy, adopted by the industry as a whole, has been to locate adult programming only on pay tiers, which makes good economic as well as political sense because so many people are willing to pay extra for adult fare.

Piggybacking and Cherrypicking

Part-time cable networks also complicate the job of the local system programmer. Several services program only in the evenings or portions of the day and may share a satellite transponder (**satellite piggybacking**) because transponders are both expensive and were relatively scarce (in the early 1980s). Other part-time services may be delivered by microwave or originate locally. All part-time cable networks must be matched with time-complementing services (**channel piggybacking**) to keep the cable channels continuously programmed.

Cautious financial backers generally advise those planning new cable services to start with part-time rather than 18- or 24-hour schedules. But following this advice may be self-defeating. It violates the principle of continuousness, cancelling out the benefits of ready audience accessibility—important in encouraging sampling of any new service (see Chapter 1). Part-time availability also makes the network difficult to promote and lends itself to delivery problems.

One way around this dilemma is for the programmer to match part-time services for *content flow* so that subscribers perceive the pairing of two or more services as a natural unit. Many part-time cable networks, however, are stacked without regard for marketing effectiveness. Piggybacking a cultural channel (A&E, for example) in the evenings on top of a daytime shopping service interrupts audience flow and, more important for cable, makes the two services difficult for subscribers to remember. The channel they occupy will tend to lack position in the minds of many subscribers.

A further factor in piggybacking is the identity of the satellite that carries a network. Daily technical adjustments (for which cable systems generally lack staff) are needed when programmers pair networks that appear on different transponders. Signals coming from different satellites require an even more delicate engineering feat. Engineering inconvenience frequently causes local systems to steer away from part-time networks.

One way of creating a coherent identity for a channel is to cherrypick programs. Selecting individual programs from several cable services and syndicators and assembling them on a single channel is called **cherrypicking.** This practice is used in constructing some local origination channels, as discussed in Chapter 12. Some religious and sports networks encourage cherrypicking as a way of increasing the total audience for their most popular programs to impress advertisers. Other services license their programming for cherrypicking only by cable systems that lack the channel capacity to carry the complete service. Cherrypicking utilizes the full range of the programmer's skills in creating a coherently programmed channel, and like piggybacking signals from different sources, cherrypicking requires engineering support.

Four Selection Strategies

Four strategies summarize the preceding sections of this chapter. They operate in the programming selection process for local cable systems: (1) meet the contract, (2) match the system, (3) maximize the return and (4) maximize audience and advertiser appeal. These four overarching strategies encapsulate the legal, technical, economic and marketing considerations that cable programmers must weigh. When they are in conflict, legal and technical factors must predominate. The weight of various economic factors depends in large measure on the degree of "bottom-line" orientation of the system owner. Some MSOs greatly exceed others in their public commitment to local service, for example.

Meeting the contract refers to both federally imposed signal carriage requirements and franchise-imposed requirements such as providing access channels. *Matching the system* refers to engineering considerations such as channel capacity, addressability, satellite placement and hours programmed by part-time services. *Maximizing the return* means getting the greatest possible profit from the system while operating in accordance with the other three goals; this involves license fees and pay-back rates, spot time sales, promotional aid, reception costs and copyright fees. It also involves considering any corporate financial interests in specific program services. The most difficult principle to weigh is *maximizing the audience and advertiser appeal.* Programmers must estimate appeals before signing service contracts, and pilot tryouts are usually not an option.

Marketing considerations, therefore, become the primary arena for creative imagination and insight on the part of programmers. In the absence of hard data on audience desires and willingness to pay for and watch cable services, the characteristics of a local audience and advertisers are crucial factors in selecting which cable networks to place on a system and how to arrange them. Subjective analyses of network appeals and clarity of conception become the tools of the perceptive system programmer. The following chapter assesses the predominant appeals of the basic cable networks, one by one, and Chapter 11 looks at the premium services.

SCHEDULING STRATEGIES FOR SYSTEMS

Scheduling, on local cable systems, has a special meaning in addition to the usual sense of placing programs in an orderly flow. (The subject of scheduling locally originating or cherrypicked programs is discussed in Chapter 12.)

What is appropriate here are the strategies for placing whole channels of signals on the dials or digital displays of home television tuners, remote-controllers and cable converters—in other words, entire **lineups**. A related topic is that of switching from one network to another without irritating subscribers. Both these activities must be considered in light of maximizing *sampling* and *satisfaction*, primary goals of cable programmers.

Channel Lineups

Cable operators normally place the three nearest VHF broadcast-network affiliates on the same channels that they broadcast on (**channel matching** broadcast Channel 3 on cable channel 3, although they are not required to do so). Independent broadcast stations, public stations and distant broadcast signals are usually less fortunate since their numbers may be occupied by a local station or, more likely, by a basic or pay service of more direct value for the cable operator. As of 1987, cable operators were freed from restrictions on channel placement (unless agreed to in the franchise contract) and able to move both broadcast and cable-only services to their own best advantage.

For example, superstation WGN, licensed as Channel 9 in Chicago, appears all over the dial on cable systems outside its secondary Chicago coverage area, in part because the number 9 channel may be occupied by other Channel-9 broadcast stations, in part because programmers locate popular superstations higher in the lineup to encourage sampling of adjacent channels. More controversial, the **repositioning** of local broadcast stations from their traditional VHF channel numbers to higher numbers (20s and 30s and up) threatens station revenues by reducing the likelihood of audience sampling. TCI, however, has the announced long-term goal of locating all broadcast stations on the same cable channel as their over-the-air assignment, a strategy reassuring to VHF broadcasters but difficult to realize in the foreseeable future. Channel shuffling, of course, will in turn create short-term public annoyance, necessitating large amounts of on-air and print promotion.

Cable-only networks, both basic and premium, now appear in a variety of positions on cable systems across the nation. The lack of placement consistency makes national promotion and advertising difficult for the program supplier and the system (a local clarifying tag is always needed); it also makes embedding a fixed channel number in the public's mind impossible.

The primary constraint on channel placement is the number of channels a system has. Until the number exceeds a dozen, lineups are largely irrelevant—except as a benefit or irritant to over-the-air broadcasters that then must promote one or several channel numbers. After a dozen or so, viewers tend to become increasingly vague about the location of all except their favorite channels—generally the ones "most often viewed in the past." When systems have 36 or 54 or more channels, national research shows subscribers heavily viewing, on average, about a dozen channels. Systems using effective channel placement strategies, however, markedly increase the number of channels viewed in long stretches and the number regularly sampled. This fact has led the industry to the long-term goal of *uniform channel alignments within ADIs*. In the short run, this involves much channel shifting on many cable systems.

The cable industry has not yet reached consensus on how to determine the most effective **common channel lineup** for a market.[10] Various strategies have components of (1) clustering by content type, (2) clustering by demographic appeals or (3) mixing audience appeals. All three have goals of giving cable channels the best possible exposure (*parity* with broadcast services) while maximizing subscriber use (*sampling*) and satisfaction (to keep down *churn*). The systems that have been most successful in encouraging sampling among subscribers, accompanied by high satisfaction ratings for local cable service, group their networks and signals in meaningful sets, though the rationales for the groupings may vary from one tier to another.

One strategy is to place similar content on adjacent channels (*clustering by content*). Whether on basic or an upper tier, placing like networks next to each other makes a set that is easy to promote and easy for subscribers to remember. For example, placing news and information services such as CNN, Headline News, FNN, AP Newswire, UPI News, TWC and C-Span I and II together makes immediate sense to subscribers. Placing ESPN, WTBS, WGN and WWOR together has an apparent logic. Grouping a half-dozen music channels (rock, country and gospel) together seems an effective tactic. However, except in the largest and newest systems—generally in metropolitan areas—few cable operators carry more than three or four of any one type of network, excepting news. Yet most programmers need larger groups, sets of ten to line up from 20 to 29 or from 30 to 39, to package cable services effectively. The uniform lineups for major markets that have been developed to date do use this content clustering strategy for "news and information" grouping.

However, the idea of "similar services" may depend more on the *appeal* than the actual *content* (see "Content and Audience Appeals" earlier in this chapter). All music channels do not appeal to the same audience; nor do all news channels, for example. A strategy used by ATC and others is to cluster sets of cable and broadcast services that attract the same audience. This strategy links services having similar audience appeals (*clustering by demographic appeals*), maximizing *adjacent* channel sampling. For example, grouping a public television station, Arts & Entertainment and Financial News Network targets the mature, upscale viewer. Grouping Lifetime, Video Hits-1 and Cable Value Network provides a block for adult female viewers. Very small blocks of three or so channels can be linked by placing an appropriate pay channel between them. For example, Disney can link children's programming to women's programming; Cinemax fits well between young adult channels (such as old movie channels like AMC) and teen blocks (containing rock video channels).

The third strategy is to create tiers (say from channels 20 to 29) of varied programming—having something for everyone in the household within each tier (*mixing audience appeals*). When services are marketed in an expanded basic tier, cable specialists usually want to offer an array of channels with varied appeals for a lump monthly sum. This might include a package consisting of a children's appeal (Nickelodeon or Disney), a sports channel (national or regional), a teen-oriented music network and a women's appeal service (Lifetime or a shopping channel). Increasingly, cable marketers are dissolving distinctions between pay and basic services, mixing pay with basic in specific upper-tier pay packages. This third strategy, adopted by TCI among others, especially aids in gaining sampling for MSO-owned services, which are typically new (The Discovery Channel) or not yet widely popular (Black Entertainment Network). To encourage sampling, the MSO-owned service is placed on a channel immediately adjacent to one of the most popular entertainment services (a superstation, HBO, the most-viewed affiliates). Ideally, the new service also gets a VHF channel number or a very easy-to-remember position such as 20.

What defeats most of these and other easy subscriber-oriented channel logics are short-term marketing needs. Additional pay tiers can be sold to subscribers only if something on a tier strongly appeals to one or more members of a household. The channel capacity of most systems is too limited to make the marketing of several small pay tiers a reality for the foreseeable future. And the large systems are reluctant to encourage overmarketing. Therefore, most systems mix services to create a second tier with varied appeals, placing it adjacent to the hodgepodge offered as basic service. One problem comes from conceiving of tiers as *sequenced* rather than *concurrent* buys, a result of historical evolution of systems rather than long-term planning. A related problem lies in using *adjacent* rather than *scattered* elements to make up a tier. This practice has a technological rather than a marketing base. When established systems added midband and superband converters, for example, they added a set of four or six channels; these usually were filled with a mix of channels bearing no relationship to the rest of the lineup, just as second tiers may be logically unrelated (from the users' perspective) to basic tiers on large-capacity systems. A period of intense and widespread channel shuffling lies ahead, creating headaches for cable programmers and viewers alike. In the near future, upper tiers are likely to contain several, adjacent small groups of similar-appeal services with scattered services (especially pay services) filling in holes in the lineup.

Switch-Ins

Cable programmers often find it necessary to change from one cable network to another, for technical and economic as well as marketing reasons such as standardizing the channel lineup. An important marketing problem occurs when massive **switch-outs** are from one premium service to another. The largest switch-out to date occurred in the early 1980s when Times Mirror, Cox and Storer removed HBO and Showtime networks in favor of their jointly owned Spotlight movie service. Hundreds of thousands of subscribers were affected on systems owned by those three MSOs. Switch-outs also occur frequently among basic cable networks. The largest of these was when Group W and ABC introduced the Satellite News Channel (SNC), knocking Cable News Network (CNN) off hundreds of systems. (Later, ironically, both Spotlight and SNC were themselves switched out.) Numerous unplanned switch-outs also were forced when CBS Cable and The Entertainment Channel failed in the early 1980s.

Having a switch-out strategy will not eliminate subscriber complaints but can reduce disconnects. The first strategic consideration is *timing*. Switch-outs create maximum subscriber resistance when some big event is scheduled on the disappearing network. A switch-out during the middle of the month during nonratings periods (when no blockbuster movies or major sporting events are scheduled) best serves the cable operator dropping a well-known network. A second element in timing is the *length of notice* given subscribers. Very short notice, as little as one or two weeks, minimizes viewer complaints. What is simultaneously required is extensive advertising, on-air promotion and direct subscriber mailings during prior- and post-switch-out weeks ballyhooing new services.

Switch-outs turn from negative to positive events if they coincide with lagging subscriber interest in a cable network. When called **switch-ins** and used to stimulate interest among current subscribers, they may reduce unwanted churn and give lift. Effective switch-ins necessitate careful tracking of audience tuning behavior on a monthly basis in order to isolate weaker networks and time their replacement. Timing switch-ins for periods of channel realignment shifts attention away from services relegated to the upper tiers and focuses attention on new services. Switch-ins have rapidly become standard programming practice for cable systems—just as they presently characterize consumer product marketing in everything from toothpaste to cars.

MULTICHANNEL PROGRAMMING IN THE 1990S

The main goals for the cable operators in the 1990s are increasing advertiser revenues and minimizing churn. Major-market interconnects brought substantial revenues to some local systems in the late 1980s. Others now seek a share of the local advertising dollar. The top ten or so advertiser-supported networks became profitable in the mid-1980s, stimulating the launch of even more services. From the perspective of the local system, the fierce competition among program services means an active marketplace in which building a positive system image is difficult, lift is minimal, and churn is high. Subscriber turnover among pay channels can be expected to persist, and local systems must, in consequence, move toward addressability and improved system promotion. Customized promotion of basic services through program guides, consumer merchandising, on-air contesting and image promotion and external advertising of the cable system are tools for surviving in the **multipay** and **multibasic** environment of the early 1990s. Cable lineups in the larger markets will become more standardized, encouraging market-wide advertising sales and program promotion. As the cable subscriber base levels off in the coming decade, following completion of the wiring of the last major metropolitan markets, cable system programmers will begin altering their channel arrays as a marketing strategy, using new lineups and switch-ins to lure new viewers. Although operator-instigated churn may damage some national advertising and promotional campaigns and go counter to the strategy of market-wide uniform lineups, it will become a fact of life for new and marginal services in a stable cable universe. Program suppliers will respond to this development by offering stronger schedules of pay-per-view programming, speeding the introduction of addressability and the adoption of Ku-band satellite technology.

And on the immediate horizon lies a profusion of interactive shopping, banking, alarm and security, computer database and yet-to-be-named services that may provide new economic underpinnings for cable systems in the mid-1990s and beyond. For now, information and entertainment networks will continue to dominate cable programming, and the larger MSOs will use their ownership interests as leverage to gain favorable carriage fees and favored channel placement. Shopping services will be forced to buy their place in cable lineups by offering lucrative percentages of their sales to operators. Independent broadcasters may be forced into a similar pattern. Basic cable as a whole will reflect a pluralistic mass audience, while premium channels will target about one-third of homes, those upper-income families willing to pay for specialized programming needs. Mixed tiering of basic and pay channels will become standard practice on the newest and largest cable systems. Although much of cable programming borrows heavily from broadcasting, the largest basic services will offer more and more original programming, and unique programming forms will continue to develop on cable in the 1990s. Popular new ideas will then be recycled to feed the endless programming appetite of the established broadcasting and cable networks.

SUMMARY

The multichannel natures of wired (cable and SMATV) and wireless (MMDS and DBS) broadband television services are central to their programming strategies, but the industries are handicapped by audience measurement and churn problems. After placing the franchise- or MSO-required services on a system, the job of the programmer is to select among broadcast stations and the nearly 70 premium and basic cable networks to fill a system's channels. Two technical factors constrain the programmer's choices: channel capacity and the presence or absence of addressability. Several economic considerations also affect the selection process, chiefly the four different licensing patterns that exist: premium pay, pay by the system, free or barter and pay to the system. When salable, spot availabilities can alleviate programming costs by producing additional local revenue. Promotional support from cable services and equity arrangements also help to reduce costs and churn, but additional costs may accrue for satellite reception and distant-signal copyright fees for some services. Then there are marketing considerations such as the composition of the local audience, how to gain lift among new subscribers without overmarketing, and balancing audience and advertiser appeals. The keys to cable programming, from the perspective of the system operator, are selecting among the available cable networks and over-the-air signals to design a package that meets franchise obligations and special local marketing needs, is balanced in its appeal to subscribers and advertisers and is economically practical for the operator. Channel lineups that are readily marketable to subscribers, while maximizing sampling and minimizing churn, involve strategies for market-wide standardization and promoting new-service switch-ins. For the 1990s, cable systems will program for multiple audiences in a multipay and multibasic environment in which new services war for shelf space on local cable systems.

Notes

1. Cable programmers have annual salaries ranging from $15,000 to $35,000; most are college graduates, and about one-third have a year or more of graduate or professional school. About 60 percent of cable programmers had experience in production or program syndication (or other fields related to cable) before moving into cable programming. "*Cable Marketing* Survey: Not Many Full Time Program Directors But Their Value to the Management Team Increases," *Cable Marketing,* March 1982, pp. 14–17. See also Alan Radding, "Who Is the Cable System Program Director and What Does He Really Do?" *Cable Marketing,* March 1982, p. 31.

2. Five basic modes of receiving television coexist: (1) conventional broadcast stations transmit signals through the air that are received directly by home television sets; (2) cable systems use special antennas to receive satellite, broadcast and microwave signals and retransmit them to homes by means of coaxial cable mounted on telephone poles or buried under streets; (3) **SMATV** systems receive satellite signals by means of ground or rooftop satellite dishes and deliver signals to points within a building by wire; (4) **MMDS** is a modification of SMATV in which satellite (or over-the-air) signals are retransmitted by a microwave relay, picked up by the homeowner's receiving dish and then delivered to television sets by wire; and (5) **TVRO** (also **DBS**) requires no stations or intermediate companies (except for billing purposes) because each household receives signals through its own backyard dish and leased decoder.

3. Marc Lustgarten, president of Rainbow Programming, quoted in "Panel Looks at How's and Where's of Cable Growth," *Broadcasting,* 28 March 1988, p. 58.

4. Converters electronically shift special cable channels located on the frequencies between VHF channels 6 and 7 ("midband") and above channel 13 ("superband") to unused VHF channels on the home television set. Block converters allow a different set of channels (than those normally appearing in those positions) to appear on channels 7 through 13; tunable converters shift tuning from the set dial to a new dial or key-pad capable of tuning large numbers of channels. See Thomas F. Baldwin and D. Stevens McVoy, "Home Drop," *Cable Communication,* 2nd ed. (Englewood Cliffs, N.J.: Prentice-Hall, 1988) for more technical details.

5. Judith Topper, "The Changing Economics of Addressability," *Cable Marketing,* March 1986, pp. 36–39ff. Also, Judith Topper, "Addressable Converters Soar Again," *Cable Marketing,* September 1987, pp. 32–35.

6. The basic formula was set by Congress and cannot be altered by the Tribunal. "Copyright Royalty Tribunal—Reimposes Distant Signal Rules," *CATA Cable Newsletter,* November 1982, p. 1.

7. Interconnects vary between "hard" ones that are physically joined and "soft" ones in which an advertising representative is shared out there is no electrical connection. "Cable Interconnects: Making Big Ones Out of Little Ones," *Broadcasting,* 1 March 1982, pp. 59–61.

8. Judith Topper, "Cloudy Forecast for Cable Satellites," *Cable Marketing,* March 1987, pp. 18–21ff.

9. Jack T. Pottle and Paul I. Bortz, with the firm of Browne, Bortz and Coddington. *Cable and Its Competitors: An Analysis of Services, Economics and Subscribership; The Impact of Competitive Distribution Technologies on Cable Television* (Washington, D.C.: National Cable Television Association, March 1982).

10. Judith Topper, "Putting Channels In Their Place," *Cable Marketing,* January 1987, pp. 22–29ff.

Suggested Sources

Baldwin, Thomas F. and McVoy, D. Stevens. *Cable Communication*, 2nd ed. Englewood Cliffs, N.J.: Prentice-Hall, 1988.

Cable Marketing. Monthly cable industry trade magazine focusing on the marketing and promotion of cable television. New York, 1981 to date.

Cable Strategies. Monthly trade magazine concentrating on the operations and marketing of local cable services. Denver, 1986 to date.

Cable Television Business (formerly *TVC*). Biweekly trade magazine covering cable system management. Englewood, Colo., 1964 to date.

CableVision. Monthly cable industry programming magazine; includes monthly status report on cable penetration and subscriptions, the scheduling of feature films, top MSOs and top cable systems. Denver, 1975 to date.

Heeter, Carrie, and Greenberg, Bradley S. *Cableviewing*. Norwood, N.J.: Ablex, 1988.

Practicing Law Institute, Gary L. Christensen, chairman. *Cable Television: Retrospective and Prospective*. New York: Practicing Law Institute, 1985.

Rice, Jean, ed. *Cable TV Renewals & Refranchising*. Washington, D.C.: Communications Press, 1983.

CHAPTER 10 \ BASIC CABLE NETWORKS

Susan Tyler Eastman

A Guide to Chapter 10

Biographical material on **Susan Tyler Eastman** appears at the start of Chapter 9. She assembled this chapter from articles in trade periodicals, personal interviews and promotional materials, updated with the most recent statistics and background information in the
National Cable Forum's 1988 *Cable Programming Guide,* the 1988 *Channels Field Guide,*
View, Broadcasting and other trade reports. This chapter provides an overview of basic
cable services heading into the 1990s.

BASIC NETWORK CONTENT AND ECONOMICS

All satellite-distributed cable services other than the **premium** (i.e.,
pay-cable) networks are called **basic cable networks.** Most are advertiser-
supported and placed on a cable system's lowest tier. These services usually
come free to cable subscribers (as part of the cable system's basic service fee,
bundled for about $13), but the cable operator pays a monthly license fee to the
program supplier for most of them (see Chapter 9). So that large systems with
more potential viewers pay more than small systems, cable network license
fees are always structured as "*per subscriber per month*" charges.

This chapter describes most of the operational, basic, *cable-only* networks as of 1988 with an established subscriber base (generally over 5 million).
It distinguishes between the **foundation services** (first, best established and
most popular) and newer competitors. The reader can use this information to
track the growth of cable networks in the coming years and analyze changes in
programming concepts and scheduling strategies. It provides reference material that college libraries frequently lack and supplies a 1988 baseline for understanding the market position of the more than 55 basic cable services. (For comparison, see the 1985 edition of this book for its 1984 baseline.) Details on the
premium networks and local origination/access channels appear in Chapters
11 and 12.

This chapter clusters basic networks by *content* and *audience appeals*
because competition for shelf space on cable systems occurs largely among
similar services. About half of basic programming consists of broadly appealing
mixes of program forms similar to those of broadcast television; the other half
represents innovations in narrowcast content (all weather, all videos, all news,
all shopping) or adaptations from other media (teletext-type news and financial
information). In addition to licensing cost, operators consider the service's
position in their lineup, its national visibility, ad availabilities, promotional
support, satellite placement and other elements in selecting among competing
basic cable networks. The following ten groups encompass the competing programming of more than 55 basic-cable services:

- Sports
- News/information/public affairs
- Music
- Arts/film
- Children's/educational

- Full service
- Lifestyle
- Religious
- Shopping
- Program guides

Just as most premium networks compete for shelf space as movie channels, so basic services vie within these groupings for inclusion on cable systems. Basic cable networks usually have two revenue streams: *license fees* paid by cable systems and *network advertising*. Most basic networks offer some of their ad time to the local system (**local avails**) as an incentive for carriage. Many new services also offer minority ownership shares (**equity**) as an incentive for carriage. But the biggest incentive for pick up and basic tier placement is a schedule of original programming (**exclusivity**), distinguishing a service from its competitors (**differentiation**) and creating promotability. Basic networks much prefer to be placed on a system's lower tier. Placement on an upper or expanded tier reduces a network's total potential audience since not all basic subscribers pay for higher tiers. An upper tier position especially hurts advertiser-supported networks as they depend partly on measures of total potential audience size (**reach**) to sell spots.

Four basic networks have reached (or nearly reached) 44 million homes, the major success plateau of half of all U.S. television households: **ESPN, CNN, WTBS** and **USA.** This means these services are carried on nearly all of the country's 8,500 or so cable systems. Ten more successful services reach well over one-third of television homes (the 30 million plateau): **CBN, MTV, Nickelodeon, The Nashville Network, Lifetime, C-SPAN I** (nonprofit), **The Weather Channel, Headline, Arts & Entertainment** and **Nick at Nite.** Cable operators often use these widely popular services to lure subscribers to pay for upper or expanded tiers. Most broadly appealing services lured operators into carrying them by being *free* to systems for several years (though licensing fees were reinstituted by most networks in the relatively flush late-1980s when basic fees to subscribers rose). Less popular basic networks *must* charge a licensing fee because they do not attract enough national advertising to cover costs, placing them in the double bind of lacking shelf space while being too costly (to cable operators) to get more. At the same time, the most desired services, ESPN, CNN and MTV, for example, are able to charge relatively large licensing fees because operators especially want them and are willing to pay.

The number of competing services, however, continues to grow (witness the flood of shopping services in the late-1980s), and the cable/broadcast shakedown period will continue into the mid-1990s. Many forecasters predict mergers and buy-outs within the next few years until fewer than three dozen or so cable-only services remain. Generally, 10 million homes is considered the *minimum reach* to attract sufficient advertising for financial success. Figure 10-1 shows the comparative sizes of the basic networks' audiences, including superstations, as of the beginning of 1988. (Subscriber counts for premium services appear in the next chapter.) In reading the bar graph, keep in mind that pre-

Figure 10-1 Comparative Potential Audiences: Basic Cable Reach as of January 1988 (rounded to nearest million)

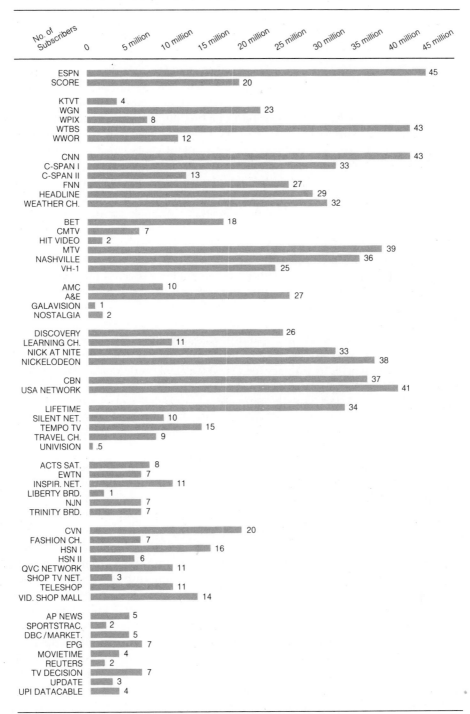

mium audiences are *paying* subscribers while basic reach refers only to *potential* audiences subscribing to the basic cable service but not necessarily viewing the channel.

SPORTS CHANNELS

Seven nationwide services supply most of the sports on cable: ESPN, SCORE, WTBS, WGN, WWOR, WPIX and KTVT. Of these, ESPN and SCORE are the sole sports-only networks. USA Network and HBO also supply a limited schedule of sporting events as part of a broader array of programming, as do some smaller services. USA Network (described later in this chapter) is known especially for its wrestling matches and HBO (described in Chapter 11) for its boxing events; Tempo TV carries some minor league events, and GalaVision has some sports popular with Hispanics. In addition, as many as a dozen *regional* cable sports services compete with the *national* cable and broadcast networks and broadcast television stations for the adult male sports audience.

ESPN

ESPN, the *largest* cable network reaching 51 percent of U.S. television households (about 45 million in 1988, and 48 million expected for 1990), is the dominant supplier of sporting events and sports-related programming to cable systems. A subsidiary of Capital Cities/ABC, with RJR Nabisco Inc. holding a 20 percent interest, ESPN has 8,478 cable affiliates—nearly every cable system in the country and U.S. territories and possessions. It is also widely carried in Central America, the Caribbean and Mexico and carried in scattered countries throughout the world. Its primary feed is on Galaxy I, with an alternate feed on Satcom III-R. ESPN was launched in 1979, soon becoming the first profitable basic cable network. More than 700 national advertisers place ads on ESPN, and it provides about 40,000 local advertising availabilities a year to its affiliates. ESPN costs cable affiliates 19 cents a month per subscriber for the main service, 25 cents with NFL football.

ESPN schedules a wide variety of sporting events, including *mass appeal sports,* such as NFL and college football, basketball, hockey, boxing, golf, tennis and auto racing, and *special interest sports,* such as soccer, billiards, skiing and track. It also carries a few instructional and lifestyle programs, such as *The Fishing Hole* and aerobics, and offers timely sports news coverage through *SportsCenter* and frequent score updates during daily programming. It also schedules a business news program on weekday mornings, sports interview shows and a sports-trivia game show. Its connection with ABC Sports makes many network sporting events available for extended cable carriage or replay at minimal cost, especially long superevents such as the 1984 and 1988 Winter Olympics in Sarajevo and Calgary.

ESPN's exclusive, original programming has clear vertical appeal to men of all ages interested in sports (but especially upscale men 18–49), although women comprise about 20 percent of its audience, according to ESPN research. Unlike broadcast networks, however, ESPN lacks the advantage of **"efficiency of scale."** The larger its audience grows, the more it must pay for the rights to sporting events. In addition, its production costs are high. For example, ESPN purchased a three-year $153 million package of National Football League (NFL) games (4 preseason, 8 regular season and the Pro Bowl) covering 1987 to 1990. The eight-game 1988 NFL football schedule brought an outstanding cable-only rating of 10.6 with a 16 share, delivering a cumulative audience of nearly all cable households. In addition to regular affiliate fees, ESPN charged cable operators 9.25 cents per subscriber per month for the NFL football package, sold out its network spots and still failed to do more than break even on the games, though the package boosted its visibility with the public and its credibility with advertisers.

ESPN's prime-time rating averages 1.5, and its share is about 3 percent of all television households (equivalent to a 3 rating and a 6 share in cable households). NFL football catapulted ESPN to 10 and 12 ratings on selected nights. Auto racing is, to the surprise of many programmers, among ESPN's most popular programming. Its sports scheduling follows the seasonal routine of national sports—which have become year-round for golf and tennis and increased in length for other mass appeal sports as television contracts became a primary source of income. Except for game highlights and rare special events, ESPN carries mostly live or taped first cable runs of sporting events, relegating reruns to the very late night or early morning hours.

SCORE

A part-time network co-owned with the Financial News Network, SCORE provides a continuous sports wire ticker, live half-hour updates and daily wrap-up reports in the evening hours. It reaches about 20 million U.S. and Canadian households with an 8 P.M. to midnight schedule on weekdays (5 P.M. to midnight on weekends). It is delivered by Satcom III-R and has over 1,000 cable affiliates in the United States and Canada.

Launched in 1985 and co-promoted with FNN (the Financial News Network), SCORE piggybacks on FNN after 8 P.M. weeknights and comes free to cable operators carrying both services. It carries national advertising and is also licensed to some broadcast television stations as a late night service. Among its most popular programs are its live call-in talk shows, featuring such sports celebrities as Lakers coach Pat Riley, fight promoter Don King and others. Shows such as *Ring Rap, Tennis Talk, Huddle Up* and *The Fan Speaks Out* generate thousands of phone calls weekly. SCORE also has the exclusive rights to some professional soccer games and tennis tournaments, Canada Cup Hockey, some horse racing and NCAA basketball and the NIT tournament. Like ESPN, it also carries a sports trivia game show. SCORE is a **slivercast** service (extremely narrowly focused), seeking to position itself as a unique offering of strong appeal to male sports buffs.

Superstations and Sports

The national superstations also program large amounts of sports in direct competition with each other, the broadcast networks and ESPN. Because of their popularity with viewers, most cable systems carry at least one of the five biggest national superstations: **WTBS, WGN, WWOR, WPIX** and/or **KTVT**

Figure 10-2 Cable Sports Suppliers for Cable Television

(see Figure 10-2). A **superstation** is, typically, an independent broadcast television station distributed (scrambled) by satellite (by a **common carrier** such as United Video or Eastern Microwave) to cable systems across the country. The common carrier charges the cable operator a fee for delivering the superstation (which does not go to the superstation). In addition, cable operators pay a semi-annual compulsory *copyright fee* for distant signal carriage (see chapters 1 and 9). The superstation gets its revenue from increased advertising rates based on both the over-the-air and cable audiences. Beginning in 1987, about a dozen *affiliates* were also distributed in scrambled form by satellite for sale to TVRO households; these include WABC-TV in New York, WBBM-TV in Chicago, WXIA-TV in Atlanta and several Denver and Detroit stations. But the affiliate-superstations are intended for backyard dish owners; it is the *independent* superstation with original sports and entertainment programming that has been so popular with cable subscribers.

1. *WTBS.* Turner Broadcasting's WTBS, now promoted as SuperStation TBS, was one of the first national cable networks (launched in 1976) and is today one of the very largest services, reaching over 43 million homes via Galaxy I and securely entrenched as a foundation cable service. Turner invented the term superstation for his Atlanta UHF independent and actively promotes

WTBS's nationwide audience, programming primarily for the national rather than local community. WTBS carries the teams co-owned by Ted Turner, the Atlanta Braves (baseball), Hawks (basketball) and Flyers (hockey), and actively contends for national basketball, baseball, football and hockey game rights, as well as auto racing and special superevents. Through 1989–90, WTBS has the national cable rights to 75 National Basketball Association (NBA) games and most Southeastern Conference college football games. Planned for every four years, Ted Turner's Goodwill Games have become a major international sporting competition. The first Goodwill Games (1986) were held in Moscow and had 3,000 entries from 79 countries. The 1990 Goodwill Games are scheduled for Seattle. Sports, however, occupies only a portion of WTBS's schedule; the superstation is better known for its family-oriented movies and off-network reruns, which are described later in this chapter under "full service" networks. Systems pay common carrier Tempo Enterprises 10 cents per subscriber per month for WTBS.

2. WGN. This superstation's main attraction is its live Chicago sports, popular throughout the Midwest and many other parts of the country. Owned by the Tribune Company, WGN reaches over 23 million homes on Galaxy I. It supplies exclusive carriage of the co-owned Chicago Cubs' baseball games and some college sports such as Big Ten conference games. WGN is a successful VHF independent in the third largest U.S. market, attracting large ratings in its broadcast coverage area by programming for its local market. But about half of WGN's total audience lives outside the Chicago area, attracted by WGN's live sports, original children's programming and theatrical and made-for-TV movies. For a fee of 10 cents per subscriber per month, WGN is delivered to more than 5,000 cable affiliates. Although WGN's penetration is greater in the Midwest than other parts of the country, it reaches about one-quarter of southern homes in the United States (while WTBS reaches about one-quarter of homes in the Chicago area). In 1985, major league baseball began charging teams whose games were carried on superstations an annual fee, dividing it among the league's 26 teams. Carriage of the Chicago Cubs costs WGN's parent corporation about $3 million a year.

3. WWOR. Formerly WOR-New York, WWOR-New Jersey is also a long-established major-market VHF independent with local economic strength. It reaches nearly 12 million cable and microwave households on more than 2,000 cable affiliates. In addition, a broadcast audience of 8 million New Yorkers can receive it. It is distributed mostly in the Southeast, Florida, Texas and California, available for 10 cents per subscriber per month from common carrier Eastern Microwave. Purchased from RKO in 1987 by MCA, Inc., WWOR carries mostly sports, movies and off-network reruns. It has traditionally carried *more sports* than any other independent in the country, including the games of seven professional teams: the New York Mets (baseball), the New York Rangers, New York Islanders and New Jersey Devils (all hockey), the New York Cosmos (soccer) and the New York Knicks and New Jersey Nets (basketball). It also carries Big East college basketball. But in the late 1980s, the station increased its off-network rerun lineup, licensing *Magnum, P.I.,*

Kate & Allie and *A-Team*. In 1987 WWOR bid for the rights to *The Cosby Show*, paying a record amount, estimated at nearly $350,000 per episode, for 125 episodes. At present, its schedule is about one-third sports, one-third movies and one-third syndicated series.

Both WGN and WWOR use their increased coverage by cable to increase their advertising rates. They need not alter their programming strategies to please audiences outside their local markets, however, because these independents already program for very large, heterogeneous local audiences.

4. *WPIX*.   A Tribune-owned New York independent, WPIX is a well-established New York station and, like WGN and WWOR, serves a huge broadcast audience as well as a national cable audience. WPIX reaches about 11 million homes, mostly in the eastern region of the country, about 4 million on cable and about 7 million off-air in New York. It programs a broadly appealing schedule of news, entertainment, movies and children's shows, in addition to the major league baseball games of the New York Yankees. WPIX pays one of the largest rights pacts in the industry for the Yankees. Like the other superstations, its carrier United Video charges cable operators 10 cents per subscriber per month for WPIX.

5. *KTVT*.   A Dallas-based independent owned by Gaylord Broadcasting, KTVT went up on satellite in 1984 (placed there along with WPIX and WGN by common carrier United Video and also available to cable operators for 10 cents per subscriber per month). Its audience of about 3 million homes lies mostly in the Southwest. Like the other superstations, it carries a package of hometown sports in addition to family-oriented movies and off-network reruns. KTVT supplies games of the Texas Rangers (baseball) and some college football and basketball games. Distribution by satellite to about 415 affiliates permits the station to sell its advertising time at much higher rates (for a larger potential audience) than the VHF station reaches by broadcasting in the Dallas area.

In 1988, Eastern Microwave added two more superstations to this select group—WSBK-TV in Boston and KTLA-TV in Los Angeles. Like those described above, these superstations have important sports rights; the Boston Bruins and Red Sox, the LA Clippers and the California Angels. Eastern Microwave markets these superstations mostly to TVROs.

Regional Sports Networks

Several regional cable sports networks compete with ESPN and the superstations to bring the games of favored professional and amateur area teams to communities where sports interest is strong. Many of these services are *premium cable* (pay or pay-per-view) and thus are mentioned only briefly here.[1]

Cablevision Systems, a large MSO, owns SportsChannel New York which has over a million paying subscribers. SportsChannel New York carries the Mets and Yankees, advertising that it has 175 games that cannot be seen elsewhere. Moreover, it is profitable, unlike many other regional sports services. Cablevision also owns one of the oldest regional sports services, Prism, which has provided live sporting events to bars and other public places in the Philadelphia area since 1977. Also profitable, it now reaches about 400,000 paying subscribers. Four other pay sports networks are Pro-Am Sport Systems, co-owned with the Detroit Tigers; Home Team Sports, carrying the Baltimore Orioles, owned by Group W and serving over 700,000 subscribers in the Washington-Baltimore area; New England Sports Network, co-owned by the Boston Red Sox and Bruins and SCI Television; and Home Sports Entertainment in Houston, reaching a half-million homes with the Houston Astros and Rockets, Texas Rangers and Dallas Mavericks. Some pay services carry just the games of a single hometown team, such as Giantsvision in San Francisco.

Cablevision is also the leader in basic (or tier) sports networks, owning SportsVision Chicago, SportsChannel New England and SportsChannel Florida. Of these, only SportsVision Chicago reaches a million homes. It advertises that it carries 81 live, exclusive White Sox games. None of these services as yet break even. Two larger services, Madison Square Garden Network (MSG), owned by Gulf & Western, and Prime Ticket in Los Angeles, owned by MSO Bill Daniels and another partner, reach 2 million homes each. Both became financially successful only after several years of operation. MSG carries the New York Knicks and Rangers to about 100 affiliates; Prime Ticket carries the Los Angeles Lakers, Kings and Lazers on about 40 affiliated systems.

Other regional basic cable sports networks include Pirates on Cable in Pittsburgh, owned by TCI, reaching nearly a million homes, and the Sabres Network, reaching a half-million homes in the Buffalo area. Smaller regional services include Utah Jazz, Arizona Sports Programming Network (carrying the Phoenix Suns, San Francisco Giants and San Diego Padres) and Trail Blazers in Portland. The *failures* in this arena almost outnumber the successes, however. Sportsvue Cable Network in Milwaukee and Sports Time in the Midwest both failed in 1985. Group W's attempt to create four regional sports networks blanketing the country failed to take off, leaving only its Home Team Sports in Washington-Baltimore. Even after several years of operation, many regional sports services struggle for a foothold in the cable market, delayed by inadequate shelf space and the slow wiring of several major metropolitan areas.

Local sports services have proved especially profitable for cable operators with several franchises within a region where a single team is popular. For example, Cox-San Diego has been very successful with its Cable Sports Network carrying the San Diego Padres and some San Diego Aztec football games to about 170,000 households on four adjacent cable systems. Syndicated broadcast programs such as *The Wrestling Network* are also available to cable systems for piggybacking or cherrypicking in cities without broadcast airings.

NEWS, INFORMATION AND PUBLIC AFFAIRS

Twenty-four-hour *all-news* was one of the most competitive of cable programming areas from 1982 to 1983. The battle between Ted Turner, owner of Cable News Network, and ABC and Westinghouse, co-owners of Satellite News Channel, illustrates most of the elements that influence survival or defeat in basic cable network programming.

CNN and Headline News

From its beginning in 1980, CNN led the basic cable services in audience popularity and wide distribution. Owned and strongly promoted by Turner Broadcasting System, Inc., owner of WTBS, CNN survived early red ink to become the only broad-appeal cable news service in the country. It operates 24 hours a day with in-depth news coverage and feature stories, matching the quality, breadth of coverage and reliability of the major broadcast networks. CNN is now distributed in Europe and Great Britain to homes and hotels and excerpted in China on China Central Television, the country's state broadcast service. In addition to its 20 news bureaus, CNN/Headline has 180 broadcast television affiliates in the United States also supplying news stories.

Headline News consists of cycling 30-minute summaries of the major national and international news stories, drawing on CNN's worldwide news-gathering facilities. Local operators can program local news within the last 6 minutes of each half-hour. Today Headline reaches 29 million cable viewers about 3,500 cable affiliates and is carried in various dayparts by 180 broadcast affiliates.

Although broadcast news tends to appeal to older demographic groups in the United States, cable all-news brings in a larger proportion of the younger and more upscale demographic groups that especially interest advertisers. CNN's scrambled signal reaches over 43 million homes on about 8,000 cable systems, carries both national and regional advertising and schedules two local avails per hour. Cable operators are charged an average of 22 cents per subscriber per month today for CNN and Headline.

The Satellite News Channel Story

Satellite News Channel (a joint venture of Group W and ABC Video) entered the cable news field in 1982, and for a year its entry clouded the outcome of the long-term race for news shelf space on cable systems. SNC provided a 15-minute, headline-only news service. Its combination of programming support from ABC network television news and sports plus use of the Group W facilities created an immediate programming challenge to Turner Broadcasting. CNN (in the person of Ted Turner) responded to the new competition by adding Headline News, a 24-hour service originally consisting of a 5-minute repeating cycle of news headlines (now a 30-minute cycle). Headline, marketed to broadcast stations as well as cable systems, was then offered free to systems subscribing to CNN, and for 5 cents per-subscriber-per-month without CNN, increasing to 10 cents when placed on a tier.

It was on this economic side, moreover, that the real news challenge lay. CNN charged cable systems 20 to 25 cents per-subscriber-per-month while SNC paid a system up to $1.50 per subscriber for inclusion in the basic cable lineup. (One-third of the total amount per subscriber actually came in promotional launch support.) After the initial payment, the Satellite News Channel came to systems without a payment in either direction. Thus, a financial advantage came with carrying SNC network, a strong appeal for many struggling cable systems in the early 1980s. To counter SNC's strategem, for a brief period,

Ted Turner paid new cable affiliates $1.00 per subscriber per year if they contracted to carry all three services—WTBS, CNN and Headline.

A third factor also had a part in the outcome of this all-news contest: satellite carriage. The industry's main cable satellite, Satcom III-R, transmitted CNN. Westar V carried the SNC network—requiring cable systems to use a second receiving dish (or a sophisticated one capable of drawing from both satellites). In addition, over $2,000 in special switching equipment was needed to use SNC's regional feed format that addressed varied news items, sports scores and the like, to different geographical regions.[2]

Of the three variables, journalistic quality, fee structure and satellite position, per-subscriber fees would seem to have had the most influence on negotiations between MSOs and CNN as contracts came up for renewal. CNN, however, retained its momentum: In 1984, Turner purchased the still struggling SNC and merged it with Headline, his struggling second service. Turner ultimately bought out the competition and survived, a pattern that is being followed among sports and shopping services in cable today. The quality of CNN and Headline newscasts continues to satisfy viewers and advertisers and, therefore, system affiliates.

Then, in the late 1980s, NBC contemplated beginning its own cable news service in competition with CNN, but soon reversed direction (perhaps remembering ABC's lesson, certainly finding shelf space difficult to attract) and attempted to purchase part-ownership in CNN. GE, owner of NBC, and Turner were unable to reach final agreement, and NBC withdrew, at least temporarily, from the cable news game.

The Weather Channel

The Weather Channel (TWC) is a unique 24-hour cable offering that competes with other information services for shelf space. Begun by Landmark Communications, Inc. in 1982, TWC supplies a continuous round of international, national, regional and local forecasts and weather features. National, international and regional forecasts and weather-related features are provided in full video, using morning and prime-time anchorpersons on camera and a large staff of behind-the-scenes meteorologists. For local reports, TWC divides the nation into about 700 weather zones for compiling local weather data; this information is then redistributed back to the appropriate cable headends through an addressable satellite technology called Weather Star so that cable homes only receive information from their own local weather zones. Local weather information appears in text form (alphanumeric displays).

TWC reaches about 32 million viewers on more than 3,000 cable systems. Typically, viewers tune in for only a few minutes each, making low AQH ratings (generally less than half a ratings point nationally), but a large number of people tune in reliably from day to day, making high cumulative ratings. During periods of severe weather, audience shares naturally go up. TWC carries national advertising and makes local spots and promotional aid available to cable operators, coming free to cable systems (if placed on the lowest level of service) on Galaxy III (previously from Satcom III-R).

TWC's hourly cycle includes local forecasts eight times an hour, travel weather four times hourly, and the long-range outlook and a feature report each twice hourly. It covers major weather stories such as floods and hurricanes in depth as extended feature material. Its hourly aviation weather reports provide a unique and valued service to pilots, and the general public tunes in especially for long-range weekend and holiday forecasts, ski and beach reports and travel advisories. TWC's highly specialized content and easily identifiable name generate immediate consumer recognition.

C-SPAN I and II

Cable-Satellite Public Affairs Networks I and II (C-SPAN I and II) are the only networks exclusively programming *national* public affairs. C-SPAN I provides live, gavel to gavel coverage of the U.S. House of Representatives. When the House is not in session, C-SPAN I carries tapes of House and Senate hearings, political interviews and live phone-in interview programs with public figures. It also supplies live public addresses (occurring in the Washington, D.C. area) by presidential contenders, cabinet members and other important political figures such as heads of congressional committees. In election years, it carries live remote coverage of caucuses and debates from all around the country. C-SPAN II carries live gavel to gavel coverage of the U.S. Senate. When the Senate is not in session, it provides live coverage of news conferences and congressional hearings such as Supreme Court confirmations.

Neither service carries advertising, but promotional aids are supplied. C-SPAN II comes free to cable operators carrying C-SPAN I, and systems are prohibited from cherrypicking one service with parts of the other. C-SPAN I is delivered by Galaxy III and reaches over 33 million homes on about 3,000 systems; C-SPAN II also comes via Galaxy III to about 13 million homes on 500 systems. A nonprofit cooperative of cable MSOs owns C-SPAN and supports the services with monthly dues (about 5 cents per subscriber). Their unique, nonpartisan public service image make the two C-SPAN services especially attractive to cable systems with sufficient shelf space to accommodate them.

Financial News Network

Another set of cable news sources are the specialized *business news* networks. Although all-news has vertically defined content, the individual networks differ in their targets (audience appeal). CNN seeks mass appeal while several business-oriented news networks slivercast to an upscale, business executive audience. The most widely distributed of these is Financial News Network (FNN) which reaches homes as a part of broadcast newscasts as well as on cable on Satcom III-R.

Programming only from 6 A.M. to 8 P.M. five days a week, FNN provides a cycle of business news headlines, a stock scoreboard, interviews with analysts and fund managers, a commodities segment, investors advice and general business news using live anchors and actualities. It uses a news *wheel* format (as does The Weather Channel), rotating five updated segments of news in each half-hour in the midday (see Chapter 15 for examples of news wheels). In addition, FNN schedules feature programs interpreting domestic and international news events in light of their impact on U.S. business interest, with international news scheduled in the early morning daypart (6 A.M. to 8 A.M.). Based in Los Angeles with studios also in New York, FNN carries daily live call-in programs with advice on business matters.

As with most news (and weather) services, crises and disasters increase ratings. For example, the 1987 stock market crash dramatically boosted the public's awareness of FNN, and its real-time stock index quotes and minute by minute updates of market information generated immediate credibility in the business community. FNN's coverage featured interviews with leading financial experts and was credited with providing a calming influence during the hectic days of plunging stocks.

A publically held company with Infotechnology Inc. as principal owner (owned in turn by Dr. Earl Brian and Merrill Lynch & Company), FNN reaches 27 million cable homes on about 1,700 cable systems. FNN has been especially active in seeking shelf space in *major markets* where business viewers are concentrated. It took about six years for the service to reach profitability, losing more than $17 million in the meantime, according to trade estimates. In order to make money, FNN sells blocks of time to advertisers hawking business advice during daytime hours, a practice that undermines its overall news credibility. During the 1987 stock market crisis, however, sponsored programs (long-form advertising) were preempted. Co-owned SCORE and Teleshop are piggy-backed with FNN on most cable systems. SCORE appears in the early evening, Teleshop in the late night hours.

Text News Services

Besides live news formats using anchors, moving video and graphics, cable systems can obtain **alphanumeric** news channels (text-only). They carry varying amounts of news, sports, features and stockmarket reports in a text-only or graphics-enhanced format. These services are teletext-like rather than true **teletext** (using a television signal's vertical blanking interval) or **interactive videotex** systems. (They are sometimes called *cabletext* services.) For cable operators, they have three important aspects: They are cheaper than some full video services (between $100 and $300 a month, depending on the system's subscribership); they provide a valued service to the hearing handicapped in the local community; and they can be easily piggybacked on other part-time services to fill a channel continuously.

AP News Cable, for example, is a fully automated, 24-hour cable news service without advertising, supported only by cable operators' fees (of about 5 cents per subscriber per month). It comes on Galaxy I, and operators must have special decoders to receive it. The text may be displayed in "page" or "roll" format. AP News Cable gains immediate credibility from its parent organization, the long established and respected Associated Press wire service, a major international news source for newspapers and broadcasting. Two cable variants are also offered: AP News Plus is enhanced by graphics, and AP Business Plus focuses on stock reports. Altogether, the three AP services reach about 6 million homes on 314 cable systems.

Other alphanumeric clones of AP include the UPI Data Cable, Reu-

Figure 10-3a Basic Cable Service Logos

ters News-View, DBC/MarketWatch, Cable SportsTracker and Update. United Press International's UPI Data Cable reached about 4 million homes on 450 or so cable systems; it carried local as well as national advertising. The parent organization, however, had financial and managerial difficulties for a decade, creating an unreliable—and expensive—service for cable operators. Moreover, UPI charged 10 cents per subscriber per month, about double the cost of other text services, so it died in 1988. Reuters, another international wire service, offers Reuters News-View to cable systems, a 24-hour all-news channel, emphasizing financial news and sports scores as well as world news headlines and highlights. It reaches about 2.5 million homes on 127 cable systems. Dow Jones Cable News was another similar service consisting of 24 hours of business, financial and economic news provided by the co-owned Dow Jones newswire, *Barron's* and the *Wall Street Journal*, but it ended cabletext service in 1987 because of insufficient system penetration for profitability. Currently, DBC/MarketWatch, owned by the Financial News Network, is picking up the slack on about 430 cable systems reaching 8 million viewers. Update, a TCI-owned text news service, reaches 3 million homes in the Denver area. Cable SportsTracker, as the name suggests, supplies continuous sports scores and sports headlines to less than a million viewers on 40 cable systems. These text-only services compete for shelf space only on the large capacity systems, so far

Figure 10-3b Basic Cable Service Logos

collectively attracting space on just over 1,000 cable systems. Like FNN, their biggest audiences occur in metropolitan areas, though they are far too small to show up in national ratings.

MUSIC NETWORKS

Borrowing from radio, cable programmers have created several *all-music* channels with rock, country and gospel formats. Of these, the 24-hour Music Television (MTV) from Viacom is the most widely distributed. It was the first to become financially successful and provided a model for other music networks (often direct clones). Nearly all of the almost 8,500 cable systems in the country carry at least one of these music networks, which one varying by region and system ownership interests.

Figure 10-3c Basic Cable Service Logos

MTV and VH-1

MTV (Music Television) and VH-1 (Video Hits 1) program a mix of video clips (**videos**) provided free by record companies promoting their rock groups, short live interviews with rock celebrities and special features. MTV uses host **VJs** (video disk jockeys) and a unique graphic look to package a zany, irreverent rock music service. It schedules music news, an 800-number request show, a daily music-trivia game show, "no repeat" Mondays and features such as summer concerts, a comedy miniseries and the annual MTV Video Music Awards ceremony. MTV maintains an active roster of about 1,000 videos, repeating the top four or five hits daily (except Mondays!) and adding to the playlist from about 40 new clips provided weekly by the record industry. Video Hits-1 (VH-1) follows a similar pattern but targets an older adult contemporary (AC) audience, ages 25 to 49, playing videos accompanied by celebrity interviews, original productions and animated material and lavish on-air contesting.

Most of their programming comes for free, though MTV created a big flap in 1984 by paying for Michael Jackson's *Thriller* video (and an associated documentary) to gain exclusive rights. But most videos come gratis because their producers seek exposure for the recording group to foster record and disk sales. MTV rotates its playlist weekly, playing the top hits (power videos) about four times a day (28 times a week) and giving fewer plays to less popular videos. MTV's playlist concentrates mostly on the current top-40 songs and the most popular rock groups; black performing groups appear more commonly on its sister service, VH-1.

Home viewers of MTV are urged to subscribe to cable FM service to receive its simulcast Dolby stereo sound. Without this addition, MTV's sound comes through the usual monaural tv set speakers. With this addition, a multiplexed pair of sound signals is decoded at the home FM tuner providing two channels of high quality stereo sound. VH-1 is also available to cable systems in stereo but few offer it to subscribers. Cable systems sometimes charge subscribers a monthly fee for FM service, typically $1 to 2 per month, and it generally includes several other cable FM signals.

In 1984, Ted Turner launched a competing rock video network, Cable Music Channel, that MTV soon purchased, ending the threat of a financially attractive CNN/WTBS/Headline/CMC package that might eat into MTV's shelf space. In 1985, Viacom, the broadcast and cable program supplier, syndicator and MSO, purchased the MTV Networks (including Nickelodeon) from originator Warner Amex, giving Viacom powerful interests in both basic and pay programming as well as system outlets. To capture the slightly older audience Turner's service had appealed to, MTV created sister service VH-1.

Viacom charges cable operators about 15 cents per subscriber per month for MTV (usually offered in a package with Nickelodeon and discounted with pay services Showtime and The Movie Channel). VH-1 comes free to systems also carrying MTV. Both music services carry national advertising and come to cable systems on Galaxy III (previously on Satcom III-R). In addition to 6 minutes of national advertising, MTV offers two minutes an hour for local sale and is commonly included in local cable advertising interconnects (along with ESPN, CNN and USA). For systems seeking a channel targeted to the 12–34 age group, MTV has clear vertical appeal. It reaches more than 39 million homes on about 4,600 cable systems. VH-1 is especially strong in urban areas. It also offers local systems 2 minutes an hour for local sale (in addition to 4 minutes of national advertising). VH-1 reaches nearly 25 million homes on about 1,700 cable systems. According to Viacom's research, there is about 25 percent crossover among the audiences of the two channels, though the amount is difficult to measure (except on peoplemeters) because of short viewing times and may be much higher in homes with teenagers who use remote control devices.

Because of their low cost (free videos) and high appeal to the target group, MTV's video-only format was promptly copied by dozens of competing national and local services. To continue as the dominant, pace-setting service, MTV was forced to broaden its content in the late 1980s into exclusive, original programming (interviews, games and specials). MTV normally commands ratings of only about 2 percent but has enormous visibility and strong appeal to its target demographic. It is considered a *foundation* music service in most markets.

The Nashville Network

Begun in 1983 by Opryland Productions (Gaylord Broadcasting) in conjunction with Group W, The Nashville Network combines country/western hit songs with music-oriented variety shows, celebrity interviews, comedy and game shows. Unlike MTV, The Nashville Network (TNN) mixes a wide range of programs in a varied format and programs only 18 hours daily (9 A.M. to 3 A.M.). Its top-rated shows, averaging a 2 rating in prime time, are *Nashville Now*, a magazine format, and *Fandango*, a made-for-cable game show about country music trivia. TNN became profitable in 1987 after four years of operation, and today it reaches more than 39 million homes on nearly 7,000 cable systems, largely in the South, Midwest and West. Targeting the country/western devotee ages 25 to 54, its main national competitor is Country Music Television (CMTV, described below) which programs only country music videos. TNN sells national and regional advertising and makes additional 2 minutes per hour available for local sale. It comes via Galaxy I and charges cable operators 10 cents per subscriber per month.

BET: Black Entertainment Television

Black owned and operated, BET has TCI, HBO and Taft Broadcasting as corporate minority shareholders (Bob Johnson has 51 percent ownership) and has surfaced as a successful narrowcast cable network. Although one of the earliest services (formed in 1980), BET grew slowly until the late 1980s, held up because of delays in cabling the big cities with the greatest density of black homes—Washington, Baltimore, Cleveland, Detroit, Philadelphia, Chicago and major parts of New York. Moreover, BET remained a part-time service until 1985, programming mostly music videos and was not marketed aggressively to cable operators, partly in response to a lack of interest in black viewers among some operators. However, the demonstrated drawing power of black programming among black households (shares of 5 or so in prime time) and the spending power of 27 million black Americans, combined with the marketing power of TCI, HBO and Taft, have given BET a unique and defined position among basic cable networks. Today, BET reaches about 18 million homes on 1,000 cable systems.

BET's programming comes at low cost since it draws on black talent not aggressively sought by other services. This includes taped black college football and basketball games, motion pictures featuring black performers and older off-network series such as the original *Bill Cosby Show* and *I Spy.* In addition, BET schedules some talk and how-to programs, mixed with music videos of black artists. During the annual Black History Month, BET adds discussion and feature specials on black issues. Programmed 24-hours a day, seven days a week, BET comes to cable operators for 3 cents per subscriber per month via Galaxy I.

CMTV and Other Music Services

CMTV (Country Music Television) follows the MTV model more closely than BET or TNN. Purchased by Caribou Communications from original owner Telestar, it reaches nearly 7 million viewers on 570 cable systems, mostly in the South and West. CMTV programs only country music with an urban emphasis, using videos produced by record companies and showcasing country music performers. Its national penetration was slowed by carriage on Comstar IV, a noncable satellite.

Hit Video USA, a 24-hour music service owned by Woldlinger Broadcasting, is produced by KO5HU, a low-power VHF television station serving Houston. The service carries advertising, offering 4 of its 8 hourly minutes to local affiliates. It charged cable systems 3 cents per subscriber per month in 1988, escalating to 5 cents in 1990. The service also has other low-power television station affiliates across the country. Hit Video USA targets the 18- to 35-year-old audience with rock videos in a contemporary hit format and includes a toll-free request line to the Texas studios. It reaches over 2 million homes on about 170 cable systems, largely in the West and South, and is carried on Satcom IV.

Gospel Music Network, another variant in the videos game originating in New Mexico, programs Christian music videos. Owned by Gospel Music Network Ltd., it reaches about 750,000 viewers on about 31 cable systems in the Southwest. Many religious cable networks, however, fill a large portion of their schedules with gospel music, placing them in direct competition for cable shelf space with this service.

These three services, each competing with each other and the larger services for a niche among cable subscribers, are only the iceberg's tip. Many large-market MSOs acquire music videos and program full or part-time services for their local subscribers—because the programming is so cheap (no licensing cost) and targets a salable audience in major markets. Going up on satellite generates costs, however, and several attempts at national video-only services have failed.

ARTS AND FILM SERVICES

The ABC and CBS television networks both jumped into arts/culture programming in the 1980s, the content area with the most spectacular failures in cable programming. Two large scale, well-funded efforts, backed by experi-

302 PART THREE/CABLE PROGRAMMING STRATEGIES

enced broadcasters, lasted less than a year. For example, CBS formed CBS Cable in 1981, an arts/culture network, consisting of drama, opera, music, variety, Broadway plays, cabaret performances and documentaries. These productions had especially high technical and performance quality. The programs were aired in three-hour blocks, repeated three times, making a twelve-hour daily schedule. This network reached 4 million homes but failed to sell its service effectively to advertisers, lost $30 million for CBS, and went out of business in 1982 after one year of operation.

The Entertainment Channel, launched in mid-1982 as a cultural pay channel and backed by Rockefeller money, failed by mid-1983. Announced as high culture programming, the network obtained the American rights to BBC productions previously unexposed on U.S. public television and moved rapidly into broader-appeal programming, hedging its bets with movies and British action-adventure series. Lacking a clear definition in the market, the service folded. Its rights to BBC productions were a precious commodity actively sought by the surviving cable culture networks, A&E and Bravo (a pay-cable service), and by PBS for distribution by public television.

A&E: Arts & Entertainment

A&E, an advertiser-supported joint venture of ABC Video and the Hearst Corporation, reaches about 30 million homes on 2,500 cable systems. Starting with 3 prime-time hours, it expanded to 20 hours daily in 1985. A&E programs the performing and visual arts, broadly defined to include comedy and variety specials as well as theater, classical music and dance. A&E produces very few programs itself, purchasing about 40 percent of its schedule from the BBC and most of the rest in the U.S. and Canada. In addition to drama such as BBC miniseries, opera and ballet, its program schedule includes literary works, sculpture, painting, photography and design. It competes directly with public television and Bravo to obtain programming from what has proved to be a limited number of sources, especially for original American programming. A&E succeeded where CBS and others failed by keeping programming costs low (purchasing rather than producing programs) and seeking broad rather than narrow appeal (comedy as well as opera, for example). Delivered by Satcom III-R, A&E charges cable operators 6 cents per subscriber per month, carries advertising and makes three minutes of spot time available per night to local systems; it does not supply co-op funds or launch assistance. It delivers an upscale audience of interest to a broad range of advertisers and has been successful since it went to a 20-hour daily schedule.

American Movie Classics and Nostalgia

These two services compete for viewers with very similar programming—mostly vintage Hollywood movies. Both strive for broad family appeal. Both began as pay networks, switching to basic services in 1987 when shelf space failed to emerge. Neither carries commercials. Both are available for a monthly fee to operators.

Co-owned by two powerful cable MSOs, Cablevision Systems and

TeleCommunications Inc., American Movie Classics (AMC) reaches about 10 million homes on 1,400 cable systems. It is offered to cable systems as either a basic service ($2.45 per subscriber per month) or as a pay service (at the same fixed rate). It rapidly increased its penetration when it became a basic service and expanded its program hours from part-time to a full 24-hour schedule. Distributed on Satcom IV and hosted by Bob Dorian, AMC carries classic movies in black-and-white and color, specializing in old musical comedies and accompanying them with brief biographies of Hollywood's superstars, excerpts of upcoming movies and old newsreels of historic footage. AMC repeats its daily cycle of films starting at 9 P.M. nightly. The movies are uncut and uninterrupted, and the service carries no advertising.

Owned by the Nostalgia Network Inc., with investments by Cooke Cablevision and Telecable, The Nostalgia Channel comes by satellite from Dallas, Texas. It programs a mix of pre-1960 movies, vintage off-network series (black-and-white), old newsreels, celebrity interviews and videos of pre-1960 music. It is advertising free and charges cable operators a monthly fee of $1.25 per subscriber. Nostalgia reaches over 2 million homes on 185 cable systems.

GalaVision

Also a recent shift from pay to basic cable, GalaVision is a 24-hour Spanish-language entertainment service. It carries mostly contemporary and classic movies and novellas (Spanish-language minidramas), with some children's programs, sports and music videos. Because its main program element has been classic films (Spanish-language or subtitled), GalaVision has been similar to AMC and Nostalgia but may turn to broader programming in coming years. At present, it offers five movies each day, plus other programs. Owned by Univisa and based in Los Angeles, it capitalized on the collapse of the Spanish International Network (SIN) in 1986, converting from pay cable to become one of two co-owned nationwide services targeting Hispanic households (the other is Univision). GalaVision carries no advertising and charges systems based on the percentage of Hispanic households in the market (fee varies). It reaches about 1 million homes over 300 cable systems and is expected to expand quickly in markets with large Hispanic populations.

CHILDREN'S AND EDUCATIONAL SERVICES

Public and independent commercial broadcasters have two main cable competitors for the children's audience: Nickelodeon/Nick at Nite and The Discovery Channel. These are basic cable services carrying advertising. (Nick at Nite piggybacks on the daytime-only Nickelodeon.) The Learning Channel narrowcasts with educational programming primarily for teens and adults. Broad-appeal services such as USA Network, WTBS and CBN also program for children (mostly cartoons and old off-network series) in some dayparts. HBO and The Disney Channel also target children with some programs, but both are pay services.

Nickelodeon and Nick at Nite

Until 1985, Nickelodeon was the sole basic-cable network exclusively programming children's fare. It supplies a 13-hour daytime service (7 A.M. to 8 P.M.) targeted toward young people (preschool through teen), focusing on the younger child in the mornings and teens in the late-afternoon and evenings. At 8 P.M., Nick at Nite takes over, using older hit television shows to create an irreverent, fun entertainment service for young adults. Both services are owned by Viacom, the cable programming giant, through its subsidiary MTV Networks, and piggyback on the same satellite, Galaxy III.

Nickelodeon's wide programming array includes animated series, comedy, adventure, rock music and magazine shows, with large amounts of original, made-for-cable children's programming. This service has won innumerable awards from parents' groups, public service agencies and the cable industry for the quality of its shows. Nickelodeon became an ad-supported service in 1984 and is offered separately or in packages with Nick at Nite and co-owned MTV and other Viacom program services. As a solo service, Nickelodeon can be licensed for 17 cents per subscriber per month. Nickelodeon reaches 38 million homes on 5,670 cable systems in the United States. Nick at Nite reaches 33 million homes (of Nickelodeon's 38 million) on 3,175 affiliates.

The Discovery Channel

Managed and owned by New York Life Company and Allen & Company, with equity interests on the part of four major MSOs (Cox, Newhouse, TCI and United) and other investors (including Group W), The Discovery Channel became the first cable network to concentrate on **documentary** entertainment. Launched in 1985, it now fills an 18-hour a day schedule with nature, science and technology, history, human adventure and world exploration programs. More than 60 percent of its programming is exclusive, and much of the rest (originating in Canada) has its first American television showing on Discovery. The channel carries national advertising and charges cable affiliates 5 cents per subscriber per month for carriage. It programs in five 2- or 3-hour blocks, repeated three times a week, to attract sponsors and foster recognition by viewers. Discovery carries an exceptional number of public service announcements especially designed to raise environmental awareness. It also sells, through its cable affiliates, a monthly program guide. As of 1988, The Discovery Channel reached over 27 million homes on 2,700 cable systems via Galaxy I.

The Learning Channel

Although self-instruction and educational programming make up a part of several services, only one cable network has concentrated on instructional programming. Begun as the Appalachian Community Service Network in 1980, now called The Learning Channel, this all-education network brings formal and informal educational programs, business and career information and hobby, how-to, self-improvement and personal enrichment series and specials to over 11 million cable homes. Only about 10 percent of its schedule is exclusive. To attract a broad audience, The Learning Channel carries *USA Tonight*, the Independent Network News originating from WPIX in New York. In its ad-supported general schedule, it includes shows on cooking, sewing and bridge to appeal to senior citizens, SAT review courses and science and math for teenagers and personal finance programs. In addition, it provides about two dozen telecourses annually for college credit to several million more adults through colleges and universities. It also supplies teleconferences and specials to schools, colleges and businesses. These are the source of most of its revenues (it does not carry advertising in telecourses or teleconferences, of course). Owned by Infotech and ASCN, The Learning Channel competes with public broadcasters, The Discovery Channel and Arts & Entertainment for much of its programming, drawing on sources such as the Annenberg/CPB Foundation and Agency for Instructional Television (AIT). Programmed from 6 A.M. to 2 A.M., The Learning Channel is picked off Satcom III-R by 930 cable affiliates for a licensing fee of 3 to 5 cents per subscriber per month.

In 1988, Jones International (parent of MSO Jones Intercable) launched another instructional network for adults, Mind Extension University. It carries ten telecourses offered for credit at Colorado community colleges and Colorado State University. As with The Learning Channel, students tape the courses on home VCRs, and if credit is desired, enroll at a local college. ME/U comes free to cable operators on Galaxy III, reaching 1 million viewers on 63 systems.

Other Children's Services

Games are an arena where the unique capability of cable contrasts with over-the-air broadcasting. Cable systems with sufficient channels can offer interactive and semi-interactive computerized games to subscribers who purchase the necessary home-end equipment. Most services that have been tested, however, are pay services, requiring a monthly fee in addition to a substantial equipment investment.

PlayCable was the first service to use cable to convey interactive games. Its games are varied every hour or so and must be coupled with a $200 Intellivision console. The subscriber pays a monthly fee of about $13. This system varies from the usual pay-cable arrangement in that the subscriber deals directly with the PlayCable company or a retail store to obtain the home decoder equipment. PlayCable does not require a fully-dedicated channel because the games are sent to the Intellivision console (downloaded) via an FM signal that can be multiplexed on any channel. As of the late-1980s, PlayCable reached only a few thousand homes.

Another games competitor, The Games Channel, was tested in California by Group W and eventually dropped. Like PlayCable, it required an extensive investment in headend equipment, and consumers had to pay a one-time installation fee of $50 and a monthly fee of about $15 for 20 repeatable games. Unlike PlayCable, The Games Channel required its own fully-dedicated video channel. Atari and other giant video game manufacturers are other potential games competitors, but the mass audience's decreased interest in computer games and the slow penetration of personal computers and fully interactive videotex keeps these services from being viable. An era of "multiplay" has been predicted when some homes will subscribe to several games channels just as they do to several premium movie channels today.[3]

FULL SERVICE NETWORKS

Four cable networks *daypart* in the same way the broadcast networks do, offering a broad array of programs targeting the mass audience. WTBS, USA Network and CBN are among the most established and most widely distributed of all cable services. They are usually considered *foundation* services and appear on almost *all* cable systems. TNT joined this group in 1988.

WTBS and TNT

Owned by Turner Broadcasting, WTBS—promoted as SuperStation TBS—carries a full range of programs and specials for every age, 24-hours a day in stereo. Committed to family programming, its schedule includes classic movies, original sitcoms, children's shows and sporting events. (Its sports programming was discussed earlier in this chapter.) WTBS airs 35 to 40 movies weekly, drawn from MGM, RKO, pre-1950 Warner Brothers and other studios. Its 6,000 film classics comprise one of the largest film libraries in the world. WTBS is distributed by common carrier Tempo Enterprises via Galaxy I to over 43 million cable homes on 12,700 cable systems worldwide (including virtually all cable systems in the United States).

Turner Broadcasting System's Turner Network Television (**TNT**) is the newest mass-appeal cable service, launched in 1988 with a reach of between 17 and 30 million cable households (less than one-third the reach of a broadcast network). Fees to cable operators were set at 15 cents per subscriber per month in 1989, 20 cents in 1990 and 25 cents in 1991 (with no discounts for volume). Like most basic cable services, TNT has two revenue streams: advertising and per subscriber fees, but TNT makes double the usual number of spots available to cable operators, offsetting its high subscriber fee: 6 minutes/hour are sold by TNT and 4 minutes/hour by local operators. TNT appears on Satcom III-R, the most widely available satellite. To compete with the broadcast networks, Turner plans an ambitious schedule of original programming and live sports in the 1990s, ultimately projecting as much as 80 percent of the service's budget for programming (the norm in cable is 50 percent). Initially, however, the service drew on Turner Broadcasting's enormous film library, and some sports—such as the 1990 Goodwill Games and most NBA basketball—moved from WTBS to TNT. An open question for cable programmers is the degree to which TNT will supplant WTBS. The new service may skim the cream of WTBS's movie and sports programming, and operators may substitute the new service for the older one, partly to avoid **syndex** problems. Since both services are controlled by Turner Broadcasting (along with CNN and Headline) and six major MSOs share a financial interest, however, TNT and WTBS may be programmed in complementary fashion and eventually be packaged as a unit to cable operators. TNT will attempt to compete with USA Network, CBN and the broadcast networks in programming, and may inadvertently compete with WTBS for shelf space.

USA Network

USA Network promotes itself as "America's 24-hour All-Entertainment Network." Owned by MCA and Paramount, USA reaches 42 million homes on 10,000 cable systems—most U.S. and Canadian cable systems and others. It divides its programming into five blocks—family, sports, women, children and teens—dayparting to appeal to the largest possible audiences at each hour in competition with the broadcast television networks (and WTBS). In one of the biggest off-network program deals, it scored exclusive rights to *Murder She Wrote* and *Miami Vice* (distributed by MCA). USA paid an estimated $300,000 an episode for *Murder,* more than any other cable service has paid for an off-network hour show. USA has also purchased off-network reruns such as *Airwolf* and *Riptide* and game shows such as *Tic Tac Dough, Jackpot* and *Candid Camera.* It has access to the Paramount film library and major sports rights in professional wrestling and college basketball. USA Network is scheduled like a broadcast network, with once-a-week and stripped daily programs of varied formats to mesh with at-home activities (**dayparting**). USA charges cable operators 8.5 cents per subscriber per month, sells national advertising and makes 2 minutes an hour available for local advertising. It is carried on Galaxy I and Satcom III-R.

CBN Cable Network

CBN, once called the Christian Broadcasting Network, now programs family entertainment and information in every daypart, targeting all ages and carrying nearly all types of programs. About 25 percent of its schedule is religious programming, reflecting a wide range of Christian perspectives. Best known is the prime-time *700 Club,* hosted by Pat Robertson until he ran for president. CBN airs reruns of *The Cosby Show, Remington Steele, Hardcastle & McCormick, Hell Town, Crazy Like a Fox* and *Father Murphy,* such expensive purchases increasing its visibility among advertisers and television viewers and its national ratings (between 1.5 and 2 in prime time). CBN also carries such quality series as *Paper Chase* and college sports, and it produces several original weekly series. The 24-hour network is supported by national advertising and viewer donations, coming to cable systems free with 2 minutes an hour available for local sale. It reaches about 39 million homes on over 8,000 cable systems via Galaxy I.

LIFESTYLE AND NICHE NETWORKS

Several networks target a population subgroup such as women (Lifetime), Hispanics (Univision) or older viewers (Tempo TV) with a broad array of programs. Other services (The Silent Network and The Travel Channel) narrowcast with a restricted range of content to a particular audience.

Lifetime

Formed from a merger of the Cable Health Network and Daytime, Lifetime has evolved into a dual entertainment and information network targeting women and doctors. Owned by Hearst, Capital Cities/ABC and Viacom (one-third each), Lifetime promotes itself as an *all-talk* network. Its programming consists of daily talk, self-help and lifestyle shows, supplemented by dramatic series and movies. Among its best known shows are *The Doctor Ruth Show*, *What Every Baby Knows* and *Regis Philbin's Lifestyles*, mostly live, originally produced programs. Lifetime also carries reruns of *Cagney & Lacey*, *Falcon Crest* and other off-network series appealing to adult women. On Sundays and early weekday mornings, Lifetime supplies the all-day *Doctor's Sunday*, providing physicians (and other viewers) with medical education programs and other features of interest to the medical community. Supported by national advertising (especially drug manufacturers) and charging a licensing fee of 6 cents per subscriber per month (and special fees to hospitals carrying the Sunday medical programming), Lifetime reaches over 37 million homes on over 3,600 cable systems. It makes 2 minutes per hour available to cable operators for local sale and is delivered by Satcom III-R.

A new competitor to Lifetime, YOU TV, debuted in 1988 on Satcom III-R. It carries about three-quarters original programming, most talk, and targets the same general audience as Lifetime. YOU TV programs fitness, leisure, lifestyles and appearances shows for women and medical and health shows for all adults 24 hours daily. It offered cable operators 15 cents per local subscriber for launch promotion (free for the first year), charging 5 cents and then 8 cents per subscriber per month in succeeding years.

The Silent Network

A very small cable player, The Silent Network programs two hours weekly on Saturday mornings (9:30 to 11:30 A.M.) for the deaf and hearing impaired. Its entertainment and information shows have *voice*, *sign language* and *captions*, making them appealing for family viewing in homes where not all members are hearing impaired. Owned by Sheldon Altfield and advertiser supported, The Silent Network comes free to cable systems across the country via Satcom IV. It reaches over 10 million homes on 380 cable systems.

Tempo TV

Purchased by NBC from Tele-Communications Inc. in 1988, Tempo TV is in the process of shifting from advertiser-provided programs to more standard advertiser-supported programs. Formerly the Satellite Program Network (SPN), 80 percent of Tempo's programming was supplied by advertisers who purchased blocks of time. Now the 24-hour service focuses on the 45 to 70 year old audience with four types of programs: broad-appeal international and travel programming mainly in prime time; women-oriented lifestyle (mild exercise and hobbies) and information/how-to shows on weekdays; entertainment, including a Broadway show-business talk show and a limited schedule of classic movies; and outdoor shows and sporting events. Tempo TV carries coaches shows on Monday evenings and a Tuesday and Wednesday night and weekend schedule of small college football and basketball, minor league baseball, wrestling and racing. About 14 hours spread through each week consists of informercials. The 45+ cable subscriber typically has large amounts of disposable income and represents an unserved cable niche. NBC plans to shift Tempo to live sports and business news by the early 1990s. It reached over 14 million homes on about 700 cable systems via Satcom III-R as of 1988.

Univision

Univision is only a shadow of the former Spanish International Network (SIN), its previous incarnation. Because it owned five major-market, profitable broadcast television stations, SIN had large amounts of original Spanish-language programming to distribute to cable operators and reached tens of millions of Hispanics in America. A forced sale of the broadcast stations in 1986 (because of a legal excess of foreign ownership) left a reorganized Univision with a small cable-only audience. Univision no longer produces much except a nightly Spanish-language newscast, purchasing its Spanish-language movies, **novellas** (soap-opera like dramatic series lasting about six months) and children's programming from Mexican and Latin American producers such as Mexico's Televisa and Brazil's TV Globo (though Globo is linked more closely with Telemundo, a broadcast-supply competitor to Univision). As of 1988, Univision had climbed back to over 4 million viewers on 31 broadcast stations and 435 cable affiliates. It is owned by Hallmark and competes directly with GalaVision for viewers since both are now basic cable services.

The Travel Channel

Begun by the Trans World Airlines in 1987, The Travel Channel at first programmed 50 percent shopping and 50 percent travel. A reorganization in 1988 followed an equity offering to ATC and other cable operators (TWA retains 63 percent of the stock). The service then shifted to travel-only programming. Now it carries travel information, tourist-oriented programs, travel opportunities (reservations and tickets can be arranged over 800 numbers) and a travel-oriented game show. It targets an upscale, older demographic group likely to be able to travel frequently. Although available for 24-hours a day, many operators carry only portions of the programming, piggybacking it on other part-time services. The Travel Channel reaches over 7 million homes over 220 cable systems and projects rapid growth to 22 million by 1990. Its revenues come from national advertising and the sale of merchandise. Cable operators also receive a cut (5 percent) of the telephone sales from their geographic area, an incentive for carriage even among those without an equity position.

RELIGIOUS NETWORKS

One of the earliest types of programming available to cable operators was evangelical religion, usually considered "long-form advertising," and often having a narrow, denominational appeal. Since the late 1970s, however, ecumenical networks have appeared, carrying messages from several mainstream churches as well as large fundamentalist groups. Many of these are local or regional services, not available on satellite nationally. Some others, such as National Christian Network (NCN) tried and ended satellite delivery. Following CBN's lead, nearly all religious-backed services promote themselves as "programming for the family" and devote only a portion of their time to overtly religious activities and interests. All these services come free to cable operators. Unlike CBN, however, the ones listed here do not sell spot advertising. Viewer donations and parent organizations support them.

The Inspirational Network

PTL (People That Love), the broadcast and cable arm of evangelist Jerry Falwell and the discredited Jim and Tammy Bakker, is one of the largest religious cable networks. Renamed The Inspirational Network in 1987 following several scandals, it now reaches about 11 million cable homes on 1,100 cable systems. Like TBN, The Inspirational Network pays cable operators for carriage (3 cents per subscriber per month), though it expects to begin charging 3 cents per subscriber as penetration increases. It sells time to religious programmers, carrying Baptist, Methodist, Presbyterian, Catholic, Jewish, Adventist, Lutheran, Reformed and Assemblies of God programming in a mix of current affairs, gospel videos, dramas, exercise, teaching and therapy shows, in addition to more formal preaching. Among its most popular programs is the *PTL Club*. The service also supplies 12 hours of local avails to cable operators throughout the week, reserving early fringe hours and prime time on Sundays for sale by the network. The service comes to operators on Galaxy I.

Other Religious Networks

Several other religious networks also mix sectarian and nonsectarian programming, four of them with a Christian flavor targeting the nuclear family. The largest, ACTS Satellite Network, reaches 6 million homes over 351 cable systems. Owned by the Southern Baptist Convention and programmed from Texas, ACTS carries about 25 percent religious and 75 percent family-oriented programming.

Trinity Broadcasting Network (TBN), a 24-hour nonprofit broadcast and cable service, reaches about 7 million homes over 523 cable systems with Christian-oriented health programs, talk shows, exercise, music, teaching and children's shows. Its flagship show, *Praise the Lord Program*, is stripped weeknights in prime time. In an unusual strategy, TBN pays cable systems a *cash incentive* to carry the network: 10 cents per subscriber per year (up to a $25,000 cap) and 25 cents per subscriber per year for promoting the service ($25,000 annual limit), with camera-ready advertising materials provided by TBN.

Eternal Word Television Network (EWTN) is a nonprofit, Catholic-oriented service from Alabama, carrying family programming and reaching about 9 million homes on 430 cable systems. EWTN is a part-time service, programming only in the evening hours (7 P.M. to 1 A.M.) and backed by donations from viewers. It comes on Galaxy III, a more desirable satellite position than some other religious services have.

Slightly smaller, National Jewish Network (NJN) reaches nearly 7 million people on 300 cable systems. It is a part-time, family-oriented service, consisting mainly of discussions of ways to live as a 20th-century Jew in America.

Finally, the Liberty Broadcasting Network, owned by the Oldtime Gospel Hour Inc. in Lynchburg, Virginia, is associated with evangelist Jerry Falwell and Liberty Baptist College. It reaches only about 1 million homes over 39 cable systems with Christian family entertainment. Even smaller, the Motivation Network, owned by Rock Christian Network (nonprofit) and programming large amounts of gospel music, reaches about 200,000 homes on a dozen systems.

SHOPPING NETWORKS

All-shopping networks appeared on the cable scene in the late 1980s, the latest innovation in cable programming. About a dozen are national, satellite-delivered services, coming free to cable operators and usually offering a percentage of sales and ownership equities as incentives to carriage. Most are live, not taped, and include games and hosted guest interviews. Although promoted generally as *discount* shopping, when fees for handling and postage are included, many products cost as much or more than in a retail store. Many of these services have already failed, including the Crazy Eddie World of Home Entertainment Shopping Network, Cox's American Catalog Shopper's Network and Tempo Galleria. Others such as Sky Merchant (owned by MSO Jones Intercable) were sold to competitors. New entries, such as The Sweepstakes Channel—offering discount subscriptions to magazines, books and audio cassettes— are announced almost monthly. The cable services also compete with similar programs on broadcast stations. Shopping services divide into three types: broad-appeal networks offering a wide range of *deeply discounted* products (CVN, CDN and HSN I); those with a mid-range, *upscale department* store look (QVC and HSN II); and a few *specialty retailers* targeting an upscale audience (The Fashion Channel).[4]

1. *HSN I and II.* First to capture shelf space as a national cable shopping service in 1985 and first to generate national excitement as a potentially lucrative innovation in cable programming, the Home Shopping Networks (HSN I and II) have faded somewhat as competitors have gained from their experience. Without MSO participation (publically owned by Home Shopping Network Inc.), these services lost out to services more profitable to the cable operators. To gain reliable outlets, HSN purchased nine broadcast television stations in the late 1980s. Nonetheless, Home Shopping I, a deep-discount service, reaches nearly 15 million homes on over 1,200 cable systems (and over 45 million when the broadcast audiences are included). Home Shopping II, an upscale service carrying higher quality merchandise in a broad array, reaches about 5 million of the same homes on 300 systems. (Operators must carry HSN I in order to carry HSN II.) Both networks offer operators 5 percent of telephone sales (via 800 numbers) coming from their geographic area (as identified by zip code). In addition to jewelry, electronics, hardware, toys, clothing and collectables, HSN retails pharmaceuticals and financial services. HSN I is distributed by Galaxy III, HSN II by Satcom IV.

2. *CVN.* Publically traded and backed by the largest cable MSOs (TCI, ATC and United), Cable Value Network (CVN) is positioned to become one of the most successful services. After two years of operation, it reached 18 million major-market homes on just 1,500 cable systems and is a foundation service for TCI, United and ATC systems. A 24-hour discount service offering the usual array of electronics, tools, toys, jewelry and clothing, CVN gained an exclusive franchise to market National Football League (NFL) merchandise (appearing with other sport products on Monday nights before football games on a show called *The Locker Room*). CVN pays cable operators 5 percent compensation and is distributed on Satcom III-R.

3. *CDN.* Consumer Discount Network (CDN) began strong and faded rapidly, overexpanding by beginning a sister service without adequate shelf-space commitments. Owned by Entertainment Marketing Inc. in Houston, Texas, CDN supplies mass market, low-priced electronics, sporting goods, clothes, jewelry, housewares and novelties. It reaches about a half-million homes on 68 cable systems and pays cable operators 8 percent on sales. CDN distributes K-mart products and seeks shelf space in urban areas where deep discounting is popular. It is carried by Westar IV.

4. *QVC.* QVC Network (once Quality Value Cable), a public owned service offering equity participation, has signed long-term agreements with most of the top 20 MSOs, positioning itself as a mid-range foundation service (to be offered alongside one of the deep-discount services). QVC distributes Sears products and pays 5 percent compensation. It retails the usual jewelry, electronics, appliances, toys, games and clothing but generally only the better product lines. QVC is a 24-hour service, reaching over 11 million homes over 800 systems on Satcom III-R.

5. *STN.* Shop Television Network (STN) is publically owned and backed by JCPenney. This service is the only interactive shopping service to date. It uses Teleaction equipment, requiring only a touch-tone telephone and TV set in the home (no special keypads or hookups needed). Cable operators, however, must install pole-mounted "frame grabbers" provided free by STN/Teleaction. STN is being rolled out only in major markets with particularly dense cable penetration, starting with Chicago, and necessitates the prior construction of microwave facilities. The 24-hour STN presently serves about 3 million homes in 60 markets via Satcom III-R. A mid-range service, it retails brand-name products touted by celebrity hosts such as Pat Boone, Juliet Prowse, Richard Simmons and others. STN pays operator-compensation on a sliding scale, and JCPenney handles all customer service and order fulfillment.

6. *The Fashion Channel.* Backed by United Cable Television and 66 other equity investors (including TCI), The Fashion Channel is a segmented service like a specialty shop. It retails only brand-name clothing in a mix of mainstay fashion and designer labels. The Fashion Channel reaches nearly 9 million homes on about 600 cable systems via Satcom IV.

7. *Teleshop.* Originally a late, late portion of Financial News Network's schedule, Teleshop is now a 24-hour stand-alone service seeking equity commitments from cable operators to gain carriage. Backed by FNN, it reaches about 11 million homes on 850 systems via Satcom IV and pays compensation on a sliding scale. At first a deep-discount service, the merchandise has been upgraded to brand-name items and travel services.

8. *Video Shopping Mall.* Publically held and backed by Goodway Marketing in Jenkinstown, Pennsylvania, Video Shopping Mall (VSM) is a part-time service (6 hours daily) intended for cable systems and backyard dish owners. It features home-study courses with a direct-marketing approach, mixed with self-improvement programs. VSM is piggybacked on The Discovery Channel on Galaxy I as an early morning feed. It reaches about 14 million homes on 600 cable systems (as many as 20 million including broadcast and TVRO distribution).

PROGRAM GUIDE SERVICES

In order to let subscribers know what is scheduled on these basic cable channels, cable systems with more than 30 channels typically provide a program guide. The major pay services also supply printed guides for their own channels.

Guides to a cable system's programming can be printed and mailed to subscribers or they can be electronically generated and placed on a dedicated channel. Printed guides permit fuller descriptions of program content and allow subscribers to plan their viewing as much as a month in advance. Electronic guides give easy-to-read summaries of what is currently on an array of channels or what is scheduled for the remainder of the day on a single channel. Both carry advertising and can be wholly or partially subscriber-supported, though the trend is toward advertiser support. The local system programmer supplies monthly information on specific programs to the guide's editor.

As of the mid-1980s, printed guides were more common than electronic guides, but in the largest MSO-owned systems electronic guides are supplementing print.[5] The costs of printed guides are rising rapidly, while electronic guides offer greater consumer convenience.

Printed Program Guides

There are three types of printed guides: single channel guides to pay channels, generic multichannel guides and customized guides. They vary in size from about five-by-six inches to tabloid-size, though small ones are more common. The paper varies from rough newsprint to glossy pages with high-quality four-color illustrations. Typography and layouts vary from cluttered and crowded to customized, artful designs.

HBO sells its guide, the most widely circulated *single channel* guide, to systems to mail to their subscribers with their monthly statements. It contains an illustrated, hour-by-hour listing of all shows on HBO, in a handy, colorful, easy-to-use format, without advertising. The Disney Channel distributes a similar guide for its programs. Both guides cost the cable system about 4 cents per subscriber, and versions for the four U.S. times zones are printed. *Nostalgia Monthly*, with glossy features and listings for premium channels, distributed by The Nostalgia Channel, costs subscribers $19.95 a year.

Generic program guides cover several cable networks, usually the most widely distributed premium channels, such as HBO, Showtime and The Movie Channel, and the top 20 basic cable networks. Generic guides carry advertising, and the same guide is sold to many systems. *TV Guide* now covers the most popular cable channels among its broadcast listings so that it functions as a generic guide to cable channels as well as to broadcast television stations. Generic guides do not cover all cable-only networks and emphasize prime time and late night while skimping on daytime listings; they of course omit all local cable programming. Some guides provide detailed descriptions of show content and include feature articles, while others are bare bones. *Cableview* and *Premium Channels*, two of the most widely available generic guides, have about 30 to 60 pages and cost the cable operator between 20 and 50 cents a copy (plus mailing costs). *Cablewatch* costs subscribers $1 a month.

As systems expand and carry more uniquely scheduled channels, an individualized guide to show just what that system carries becomes increasingly important. Market-wide guides such as *TV Guide* carry only a few cable-only channels, and not all of them are available to every cable subscriber; at the same time, *TV Guide* listings exclude whatever local cable programming subscribers do have. Without a localized guide, viewers have no way of knowing what many cable channels carry and cannot plan their viewing to take advantage of unusual programs. From the operator's perspective, much of the promotional value of having unique local channels, such as pay-per-view and LO, disappears if viewers do not know what can be seen on them. And their revenue potential is nil without viewers.

The inherent problem with *customized* printed guides to a whole system, however, is that more channels mean more program listings. To provide a complete information service, all programs on all channels must be listed half-hour by half-hour (or hour by hour). Guides to large systems are fat and awkward to use. To keep printing costs down, pages are crowded, and cheap paper and poor typography are the rule. The cable operator usually eliminates space for feature articles to run advertising to cover the costs of printing and mailing, further reducing the guide's appeal.

The operator is actually in a no-win situation. Systems that do not encourage sampling of their offbeat channels find subscribers reporting dissatisfaction with service. Customized guides do stimulate viewer sampling, provided they are clear and easy to use. At the same time, they are so expensive that operators generally charge subscribers for them, while subscribers who may be unconvinced of the value of the cable service in the first place are not likely to want to pay for a guide—creating ill will if the payment is required.

In one effort in 1983, Tele-Communications, Inc. (TCI) created *Cabletime*, a generic guide for all its cable systems—which were located in different time zones but carried the same cable networks, more or less. Instead of separate guides for each time zone, TCI distributed the same guide with an elaborate grid for deciphering when a program was scheduled in each time zone.

Subscribers quite naturally refused to learn the coding system and rejected the guide. This failure was expensive, and the company retreated to single-channel premium guides while "reformatting" *Cabletime*.

A tough question for creators of customized guides in large markets is whether to include the broadcast channels that are carried on the system. If they are not included, viewers must use *TV Guide*, newspaper supplements or other program guides to find out about the most-watched channels. On the other hand, including them greatly increases the number of listings, making the guides even more unwieldly, and they then duplicate much information available elsewhere.

Electronic Program Guides

Electronic guides may be the solution to many of these problems, but they tend to be supplementary rather than stand-alones. On most systems, program information appears in alphanumeric form (as text only) and has no graphics. Because the resolution of television screens is much lower than that of printed pages, individual words must be large and clearly separated to be readable; therefore, video screens display only 20 to 22 lines of copy at one time.

Some cable systems adopt a limited electronic format, placing the names of important films in a heading on text news channels. Only a very few titles can be promoted at one time, and such listings mention only premiere premium films and specials, rarely local services. In another option, electronic program listings are used as filler on access channels when there is no other programming to run. The disadvantages of this practice are that viewers cannot predict when they will find program listings, and the information is usually sketchy because this service is only offered part of the time and receives little attention from the cable programmer.

Some systems dedicate a full channel to alphanumeric listings of program titles that continuously page or scroll past the viewer. Twenty-four hours of programs, half-hour by half-hour, however, occupies a very large number of frames. Because of the immense number of program titles appearing on a system with 24 or more channels, listings typically include only the titles of featured films and specials on pay channels and exclude the descriptive addenda so popular with viewers. Figure 10-4 shows a page from one such electronic guide.

The most widely distributed electronic guide is called, naturally enough, Electronic Program Guide (EPG). It is a full-channel service, functioning like a basic cable network on a dedicated channel. EPG reaches more than 7 million homes on 320 cable systems. Besides the alphanumeric EPG, it comes in a simple text and graphics service now called EPG Jr. (on 153 systems) and an enhanced version using full-motion video called Prevue Guide (carried by 100 systems). Owned and distributed by common carrier United Video, EPG offers equity to cable operators and carries national advertising. Cable operators must have an Amiga computer at their headend to store ads for playback and can insert local ads. According to United's projections, the enhanced service needs at least 12 million homes to attract sufficient national advertising to be profitable.

Figure 10-5 Frame of an Electronic Program Guide

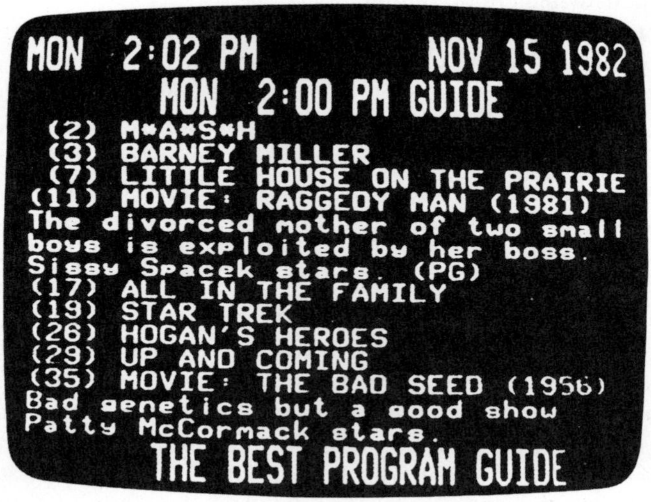

```
MON  2:02 PM           NOV 15 1982
       MON 2:00 PM GUIDE
   (2)  M*A*S*H
   (3)  BARNEY MILLER
   (7)  LITTLE HOUSE ON THE PRAIRIE
  (11)  MOVIE: RAGGEDY MAN (1981)
The divorced mother of two small
boys is exploited by her boss.
Sissy Spacek stars. (PG)
  (17)  ALL IN THE FAMILY
  (19)  STAR TREK
  (26)  HOGAN'S HEROES
  (29)  UP AND COMING
  (35)  MOVIE: THE BAD SEED (1956)
Bad genetics but a good show
Patty McCormack stars.
       THE BEST PROGRAM GUIDE
```

Source: Courtesy of TV Watch, Inc.

Several other listing and promotion services have been announced, but only a few are widely distributed as yet. TV Decisions, a customized (system-specific) text-only service, reaches 7 million homes on 177 cable systems. Movietime, a 24-hour service reaching over 4 million homes on 60 systems, programs a continuous round of theatrical and cable movie promos. Owned by cable operators (including ATC, Continental and Cox), a cable programmer (HBO) and a Hollywood Studio (Warner), Movietime is likely to achieve high penetration in the near future. Just getting started in 1988, The Preview Network supplies both listings and hosted Hollywood-style entertainment talk, including long-form previews of new series and movies and behind-the-scenes segments on television shows and movies. For the present, listing and promotion services seem appealing to operators with large capacity systems, and large MSOs continue to experiment with them, but small capacity systems lack space for a nonrevenue-producing service that supplements but does not replace printed program guides.

SUMMARY

Basic cable networks fit in ten broad groupings based on content (programming) and appeals (target audience). The foundation services usually can command per-subscriber/per-month licensing fees from cable operators. Most services carry national advertising and offer local insertions; many offer equity shares to operators as well, especially newer services. However, the most important incentive to carriage is exclusive programming. Four basic networks reach about half of all U.S. television households (over 40 million homes), and a reach of 10 million homes is considered the bare minimum for success. ESPN dominates the sports services and pays high prices for the most popular major sporting events, but the five superstations compete for the rights to important professional and college games, and several basic and pay-cable services carry less costly or highly specialized sporting events. Only a limited number of mass appeal sporting events have proved capable of attracting significant ratings, and the broadcast networks seek these too. CNN has become one of the top newsgathering services in the world, proving itself to journalists while finding popularity with audiences. It dominates the all-news cable-only services, having purchased its only serious competitor, but business news and other narrowcast information formats have proved viable for FNN, The Weather Channel and some text-only networks. MTV sets the pace among music networks and has been cloned by other rock, country and gospel services. A mix of exclusive and original trend-setting programming seems to be MTV's key to maintaining leadership among music networks. The arts and film services, led by A&E, have less visibility because they lack position as unique services. PBS and the premium movie services seek much of the same program material. A&E has succeeded where several competing services failed because it avoided costly original production, instead seeking exclusive rights to foreign programs. Among children's networks, Nickelodeon/Nick at Nite and The Discovery Channel have prominent positions, in part because of powerful owners and in part because of the scarcity of (nonmusic) broadcast programming for children and teens. SuperStation TBS, USA Network and CBN are foundation services, commanding huge audiences with broad appeal programming. They have been more successful, by and large, than narrowcast services. Among lifestyle services, only Lifetime has reached high penetration levels, supported in part by its unique medical programming. Dozens of national and local religious services compete for the Christian viewer, most programming more general family entertainment than overt sectarian content. The newest group of networks, the national shopping services, lack much shelf space as yet, especially in major markets. They typically offer equity positions and compensation as an incentive to carriage. They divide into discount, brand-name and specialty services, competing primarily among like services. Finally, electronic program guides supply text-only or text-and-graphics program listings in generic or customized form to cable systems. The addition of full-motion video, color and feature material makes these services appealing, but only to operators with large capacity cable systems. What this chapter does not reveal are the yet-to-be-invented cable program forms that will emerge as competitors for shelf space in the mid-1990s.

Notes

1. Ellis Simon, "Regional Sports Webs Take On Growing Importance," *Cable Marketing*, September 1986, pp. 34–47ff.

2. Allen M. Charlene, "96 Hours of Cable News," *View*, January 1982, pp. 26–31, and "Turner the Victor in Cable News Battle," *Broadcasting*, 17 October 1983, pp. 27–29.

3. Mark Trost, "Waiting for Atari?" *View*, December 1982, pp. 29–31.

4. Chuck Moozakis, "Home Shopping: How's It Selling?" *Cable Television Business*, 15 No-

vember 1987, pp. 34–40, and Judith Reitman, "Cable and Home Shopping: Building the Connection," *Cable Marketing*, January 1987, pp. 30–34ff.

5. Midge Pierce, "Program Guides: New Directions," *Cable Television Business*, 15 November 1987, pp. 24–30; Fred Dawson, "What's On?" *Multichannel News* (insert), 19 July 1982, pp. 18–25; and Joseph Lisant, "Electronic Guides," *View*, February 1983, pp. 37–41.

Selected Sources

Cable Marketing. Monthly trade magazine covering cable services.

Cable Television Business. Semi-monthly trade magazine on cable operations.

CableVision. Monthly trade magazine focusing on cable.

1988 *Channels Field Guide*. Latest annual report on the cable and broadcast industries from Channels of Communication.

View. Monthly trade magazine on cable and broadcast programming.

CHAPTER 11 \ PREMIUM PROGRAMMING SERVICES

Jeffrey C. Reiss

A Guide to Chapter 11

Jeffrey C. Reiss, chairman and chief executive officer of Reiss Media Enterprises, Inc., founded Request Television and heads this national pay-per-view service. Before forming his own company in 1984, Mr. Reiss was instrumental in founding Showtime and also the Cable Health Network, which later merged with Daytime to form the basic cable network now known as Lifetime. Mr. Reiss served as president and a principal stockholder of the Cable Health Network. At Viacom International, Inc., he was executive vice-president of the Viacom Entertainment Group and president of Showtime (1976–1980). Mr. Reiss is credited with developing the concept of multipay marketing while with Showtime and was responsible for several original pay-cable productions, including the first made-for-pay series, *What's Up America.* Before joining Viacom, Mr. Reiss was director of feature films for ABC Entertainment (1973–1976), where he helped pioneer the two-hour made-for-tv movie. He joined ABC from Cartridge Television, Inc., the manufacturer of the first home videocassette recorder, where he directed program acquisitions and development. As a partner in Kleiman-Reiss Productions, he presented several theatrical productions; he earlier worked as a story editor for Norman Lear's Tandem Productions and in the literary department of General Artists Corporation. Mr. Reiss has taught at Brooklyn College and New York University. In this chapter, he details the programming sources, formats and strategies available to premium programmers.

PREMIUM TELEVISION SERVICES

Premium television is an umbrella term for the group of specialized entertainment services, which for an optional fee offer subscribers special or "premium" programming, primarily unedited movies and original productions in a commercial-free format. The premium television field divides into two distinct components: (1) monthly **pay-television** services requiring that viewers pay a monthly subscription charge, in addition to a basic service fee, and (2) **pay-per-view** services charging on a program-by-program basis, also in addition to a basic cable service fee.

Premium channels may be distributed to homes, bars and hotel rooms by a cable system (**pay-cable**) or satellite master-antenna television installation (**SMATV**), transmitted by a multichannel microwave distribution system (**MMDS**), broadcast in scrambled form over-the-air by a subscription television service (**STV**), or beamed directly (**DBS**) to a backyard satellite dish (**TVRO**) (see Figure 11-1).

The programming services described in this chapter are generally available in any of these distribution technologies but are most commonly delivered by cable operators to individual homes. The content of a cable system's offering of premium services derives mainly from *eight national pay-tv services* and *five pay-per-view services,* each distributing a program schedule to local cable systems by satellite. The home subscriber pays a basic fee with additional monthly charges for the pay channels and per-program charges for each pay-per-view event.

Shelf Space

One way to understand the cable programming business is to consider the wholesaler-retailer analogy: National cable programming services are like coast-to-coast *wholesalers* in that they sell their product—programming—to

Figure 11-1 Satellite Delivery of Pay Program Signals

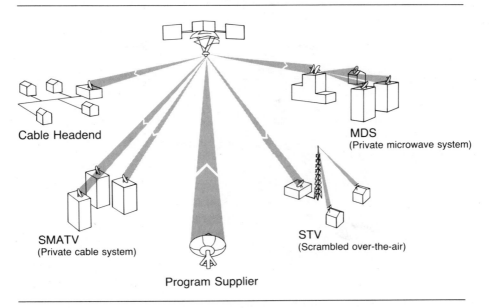

Cable Headend

MDS
(Private microwave system)

SMATV
(Private cable system)

STV
(Scrambled over-the-air)

Program Supplier

regional and local outlets, the cable system operators. Cable operators are like *retailers* because they sell their product—in this case, television programming services—to consumers, home by home and subscriber by subscriber. The wholesaler's functions are: (1) licensing existing shows or financing original programming created by Hollywood's studios, independent producers, or in conjunction with international joint-venture partners; (2) packaging that programming in a form acceptable to consumers (by providing interstitial promotions such as wraparounds, titles, on-air hosts, graphics); (3) delivering that programming—usually by satellite—to cable operators; and (4) supporting their products with national advertising and promotion and by supplying advertising materials and co-op dollars at the local system level.

The cable operator as retailer must decide how best to market the channels of programming in the local system's inventory (as discussed in Chapter 9). Just as a supermarket manager has to allot shelf space to products, deciding to display some more prominently than others, a cable system operator must decide which premium and basic cable services to offer and promote to subscribers. In making these marketing decisions, the local manager considers channel capacity, the demographics of the subscribership, the program distributor's pricing and level of promotional support and the number of local broadcast stations that are carried. As used in this book, **shelf space** is the term describing the amount of channel capacity each system has to fill, which varies greatly among the nearly 8,500 U.S. cable systems. Premium services compete with one another for a share of the shelf space on local cable systems by offering financial incentives as well promotion and advertising support. (Local systems promote their premium services extensively to increase revenue from

Figure 11-2 Comparative Subscribers: Pay-Cable
and PPV Reach as of January 1988

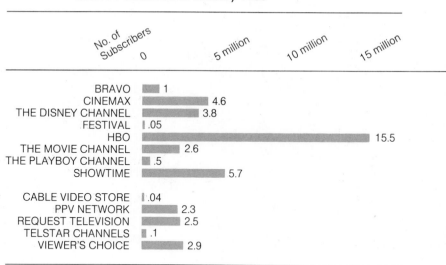

subscriptions; see the discussion of **lift** in Chapter 9.) Figure 11-2 shows premium subscriberships as of 1988. (These are not reach but actual paying subscriber rolls.)

Nearly every cable system in the United States carries at least one premium service, and over 90 percent carry two or more monthly pay services. Pay-per-view is the newest addition to the market, with national service available only since November 1985. It works best on systems with addressable technology (see Chapter 9). Far fewer cable systems, consequently, offer pay-per-view services (about 20 percent as of 1988), but this percentage is expected to double by 1990.

If a system has only one pay channel, the odds are very high that it is Home Box Office (HBO), since about 6,700 systems (out of nearly 8,500) carry HBO. Relatively few systems carry just Showtime or one of the other pay services. With HBO in the primary role, the competition among the others focuses on securing shelf space as the second or third (or even fourth) service provider on the local cable system's menu of premium offerings. The chief second place contenders are Cinemax, The Disney Channel, The Movie Channel and Showtime. Bravo, The Playboy Channel and Festival, the newest entry, play much smaller roles. The nationally distributed pay-per-view services as of 1988 were Cable Video Store, Request Television, Telstar Channels, Viewer's Choice and Pay-Per-View Network.

A period of intense jockeying for position in the early 1980s produced several casualties. Among those pay services no longer available are the Entertainment Channel, Eros, Home Theater Network and Spotlight. But some services have established strong local followings by tailoring their services to a particular region. These include two movie services—Z Channel and Prime Ticket in Los Angeles—and many regional pay sports networks already described in Chapter 10. Three services have recently shifted from pay to basic: American Movie Classics, The Nostalgia Channel and GalaVision.

Multipay Environments

The idea of *multipay subscriptions*—the sale of multiple premium channels to a single cable household—had its most rapid growth in the early 1980s, only to quickly level off in the face of consumer irritation over the duplication of film titles and the ready availability of videocassettes. A decade earlier, most cable experts thought subscribers would be willing to pay for one, at the most two premium channels. A ceiling effect on total cable bills was assumed. One view was that subscribers would resist paying more for cable than they did for their telephone bills (around $30 per month on average for upper-income families). However, in the early 1980s multipay arrived. When offered a varied selection of pay channels, a large percentage of pay subscribers signed up for two or more services—particularly in newly constructed cable systems (new-builds) where enthusiasm for cable was high and promotion strong. In one case, research for Showtime, the second largest pay-cable network, demonstrated that when HBO and Showtime were marketed together in a newly installed system (undergoing first-time sales), 98 percent of basic subscribers took at least one premium service. But the big news for the industry was that 70 percent of that 98 percent took *both* HBO and Showtime.[1] Similar research findings by other program providers confirmed that those offered a wide selection of premium services could be expected to subscribe to at least two, and maybe more. Thus encouraged, HBO launched Cinemax, a second premium movie channel, developed both as a companion to HBO and as a means of protecting its market share from competitors like Showtime and The Movie Channel.

The earliest pay networks offered a mix of movie programming with a small amount of sports and entertainment specials having broad appeal to a heterogeneous audience. The prospect of selling an array of pay subscriptions to a single household, however, stimulated the creation of even more specialized premium services that targeted their programming to attract narrowly defined (homogeneous) interest groups—for example, at male adults or children or culture buffs.

With increased choice, though, came increased volatility and churn for cable operators and programmers. In the late 1980s, industry reports show more than half of all homes subscribing to basic cable also subscribed to one or more premium services. About a quarter of those premium subscribers take a second premium channel when offered; a far smaller percentage take three or more premium channels.

Selling subscribers additional premium services has proven an easier task than keeping them. Three patterns in pay subscription were evident in the 1980s. By 1984, an increasing number of multipay subscribers had begun to cancel their second or third premium choices, and some dropped the pay portion of their cable service entirely (**churn**). This phenomenon grew at a rate of more than 33 percent in the mid-1980s. As the initial excitement of signing up for cable services wears off, some subscribers naturally decide to keep only those premium channels they watch and enjoy the most. Other subscribers, believing that the programming offered by the major movie services is too much alike, cancel those where the duplication of movie titles seems the highest or where the perceived value of the entertainment declines (**downgrading**).

A number of other subscribers migrate from service to service (**substitution**). When a new premium service is marketed in a cable system with a long established lineup of premium services, subscribers tend to cancel one service in favor of a new one. This happened in several communities when the adult-oriented Playboy Channel or, at the other end of the spectrum, the family-oriented Disney Channel was introduced. Many subscribers substituted them for their existing pay services rather than adding them to their current subscriptions.

Ultimately, the growth in new multipay subscription sales stalled, while churn accelerated in the mid-1980s, influenced by two external factors. Videocassette recorders became cheaper and more plentiful, and new home construction on a large scale virtually halted, changing what had been a flood of new cable subscribers to a mere trickle.

Pay-cable programmers have adopted strategies focusing on image and programming to combat churn, downgrading and substitution. They try to develop a unique identity or image for a service through advertising and promotion (**differentiation**) and they create unique, original programs and pay high prices to license the exclusive rights to movie titles (**exclusivity**). Those services competing with HBO—particularly Showtime—target their movies to more carefully defined audiences and directly counterprogram HBO's lineup. Differentiating their program content through the acquisition of exclusive rights to hit movies and developing appealing and promotable original shows have become the keys unlocking the subscriber's door.

In the late 1980s, cable systems began offering pay-per-view services to attract subscribers who had turned to videocassette rentals for their entertainment. The national pay-per-view services supply the latest movies, special events and sports programming on an a la carte basis, but without the inconvenience of traveling to and from a videocassette rental store.

The jury is still out on which multipay purveyors will succeed in securing second and third places on most cable operators' shelves in the long run. Despite some very high-profile, high-budget efforts at developing original programming, most subscribers continue to choose one service over another on the basis of the quality and quantity of movies it provides. That reality keeps Showtime, Disney, The Movie Channel and Cinemax locked in competition for second place after HBO, while nervously looking over their shoulders as videocassette recorders and pay-per-view further penetrate the entertainment marketplace.

Revenue Split

Economic considerations come strongly into play when a local system is deciding which premium networks to carry. As discussed in Chapter 9, cable systems charge their subscribers about $8 to $12 above the basic monthly cable bill to receive a premium channel. The local system operator sets the exact monthly charge, usually within a range negotiated with the program supplier. The revenue for a premium channel is distributed between the programming service, which licenses the programming and is responsible for delivering it to the cable system *headend* (its technical distribution facility), and the cable system operator, who receives the satellite signal, delivers it by coaxial cable to subscriber homes and then bills them for the service. Though subject to negotiation, about 30 to 40 percent of the monthly revenue usually goes to the program service while 60 to 70 percent goes to the cable operator.

Where Showtime, for example, typically costs subscribers about $10 per month, the operator keeps about $7, and Showtime receives $3; in an HBO deal, the operator more commonly keeps about $6, and HBO gets $4; Disney splits are usually 50/50. To gain carriage and achieve broad local acceptance, the premium programmers also offer cable operators discounts and financial incentives based on volume and/or market penetration, further altering this retail/wholesale pricing mechanism.

Pay-per-view services, which sell individual programs, operate somewhat differently. In general, the distributor and operator divide sales revenue either 50/50 or 60/40 (in favor either of the pay-per-view packager or the cable operator). However, the revenue split often varies from title to title, depending on the program licensing fee involved and the potential audience size. In the case of Request Television, the cable operators and the individual studio suppliers negotiate the revenue split directly, sometime resulting in a more favorable percentage for the system operator. This is possible because of Request's unique business model whereby the participating studios pay Request a fee, eliminating the middle cut in revenues. The other PPV services charge the system operator a monthly per-subscriber fee (going to the pay-per-view service) for handling scheduling and distribution.

Because of the favorable revenue splits, pay services have become important components of operators' revenues. In fact, revenues from pay services stimulated a cable industry resurgence in the late 1970s and made the difference between profit and loss for many operators. Between 1975 and 1986, pay programming was the top money-maker of the cable television business. By 1986, HBO had become the second most profitable television network in America, falling just behind NBC, but ahead of ABC and CBS.

With the coming of cable rate deregulation in 1987, however, the revenue balance at the local system level began to shift. Most operators lifted their basic cable rates, thereby deriving more of their income from basic service. In a strategy aimed at increasing sales volume and bringing their fees more in line with the total cable package, most pay-cable services encouraged cable operators to lower the retail price charged for their pay services. A spate of discounting, free sampling and extended free trials in the late 1980s boosted pay subscriber rolls, but at cut rates. Operators expected to lose some "budget subscribers" but keep most over the long run. Cable rate deregulation is likely, in the long run, to force the pay networks to reduce their wholesale price to allow a lower retail price and encourage a higher percentage of subscribers.

MOVIES

The staple of both pay-cable and pay-per-view remains the Hollywood feature film, aired soon after theatrical release. The rapidity with which a film can be offered to subscribers is central to establishing a premium service's viability and value. Speed is of particular importance to the pay-per-view services, which generally present top movie titles four to six months after their initial domestic theater distribution. In contrast, the usual *exhibition window* for the monthly premium channels is 12 months after theatrical release, with the broadcast networks following at 18 months to 2 years.[2]

None of the premium services as yet carry commercials. With rare exceptions, films are shown unedited and uninterrupted, including those rated PG-13 and R (containing strong language and behavior normally censored on broadcast television) or services that offer them.

Rotation Scheduling

Rotation scheduling is a major area of difference between pay-cable and broadcast television. The premium services offer a range of 20 to 50 programs per month, some first-run and new to the schedule (**premieres**), and some repeated from the preceding month (**encores**).

In the course of a month, movies are scheduled from four to six times on different days and at various hours during the daily schedule. Different movie services offer varying numbers of monthly attractions, but all services schedule most of their programs more than once. (Programs containing nudity or profanity, however, rotate only within prime time and late night on most networks.) The viewer therefore has several opportunities to watch each film, special or series episode. These repeat showings maximize the potential audience for each program. The programmer's scheduling goal is to find the various complementary time slots delivering the greatest possible audience for each attraction during the course of a month, not necessarily in one showing.

Unlike the monthly pay-cable networks, pay-per-view services rotate rapidly through a short list of top-name Hollywood hit films. The same movie may air as few as four or as many as ten times in a day. This occurs because pay-per-view programmers market *"convenience viewing."* Most pay-per-view networks rotate two to four major movie titles a day, some across multiple channels.

Broadcast television's scheduling practices, organized around the delivery of commercial messages, differ broadly, resulting in the weekly series, the daily soap opera, the nightly newscast. In most cases, an episode is shown only twice in one year, and the largest possible audience is sought. Some premium networks have adopted the short-length formats of broadcast television, such as 30-minute episodes of *Brothers* and other made-for-pay situation comedies on Showtime. Most pay programs, however, run to their natural lengths, ending when and where the material dictates, rather than occurring in fixed segments to accommodate commercials. Even with series programs, frequent repetition and rotation throughout the various dayparts set premium program scheduling apart from broadcast scheduling.

Though most premium services operate around the clock (24-hour), some specialized premium networks are part-time services. For example, the Playboy Channel programs from 8 P.M. to 6 A.M., and Bravo schedules from 7:30 P.M. to 6 A.M., targeting overnight or evening audiences. These specialized networks use rotation patterns within those particular dayparts, similar to those of the general movie services. Individual episodes, specials and films are repeated on different days and in different dayparts, permitting all subscribers multiple opportunities to view each program.

Monthly Audience Appeal

Another major contrast between broadcast television and the premium programming services lies in their revenue-generating strategies. To maximize ad revenues, the commercial networks and broadcast stations program to attract the largest possible audiences every minute of the programming day. Premium networks, as explained in Chapter 2, try to attract the largest possible cumulative audiences over the period of a month.

The lifeblood (read daily operating revenues) of a pay service is its direct subscriptions. Pay-per-view services must satisfy their customers movie by movie, night by night. Pay-television services must satisfy their subscribers month to month, throughout the year, forestalling disconnections. A premium service's success is not determined by the audience ratings of its individual programs but by the general appeal and "satisfaction levels" of its overall schedule. Insofar as quantitative measures such as ratings reflect that appeal, they are useful in gauging response. But in cable, where subscribers must be persuaded to pony up month after month, qualitative measures take on greater importance.

Another quantitative measure is subscriber *turnover*. Since both schedules and subscriber billings are arranged by the month, viewers tend to evaluate programming in month-long blocks. Subscribers will most likely continue the service for another month if they use their pay service two or three times a week and see benefit in (1) its varied viewing times, (2) commercial-free, uninterrupted program content and (3) unique entertainment programs and theatrical feature films.

Still relatively new, the pulse of pay-per-view success is measured by the number of sales per show title (the **buy rate**). Careful matching of buy rates and titles offers both the pay-per-view distributor and the system operator a tool for fine-tuning scheduling and promotion plans.

Discontinuing a month-to-month pay service seldom reflects dissatisfaction with one or two individual shows. When viewers **disconnect,** they feel the service as a whole is lacking. Customers repelled by violence, for example, may disconnect a movie service if a large number of a particular month's films contain a great deal of violence. A family may determine that its desire for wholesome, G-rated fare is not being filled by the programming mix of one particular movie service and so will cancel after a trial month or two. This process also works in reverse. Favorable word of mouth remains the most potent method of attracting new customers, particularly in nonurban communities.

As such, a handful of individual programs each month makes the difference between success or failure when a premium service is new in a community and the local operator lacks a large and stable subscriber base. Having one or two blockbuster films on the order of *Beverly Hills Cop* or *Indiana Jones and the Temple of Doom* undoubtedly attracts new subscribers to the service and holds current subscribers even if their reaction to the balance of that month's schedule is negative.

Movie Balancing Strategies

Selecting programs that will appeal to different target audiences through the course of a month becomes the challenge of the programmer. For example, if a particular month's feature films have strong appeal to teenagers and men 18 to 49, the obvious choice for an entertainment special is a show that appeals to women. Pay-television programmers break down their audiences according to urban-rural classifications, age groups of 18 to 24, 25 to 49, and 50+, and by sex.[3] By scheduling programs each month that will appeal to all these groups, the programmer creates a "balanced" schedule.

Films subdivide into five groups with overlapping appeals. The major audience attractions for that month are the **premieres**—that is, the films that were recent box-office hits and are being offered for the first time on that premium service. These films may be G-, PG- or R-rated by the movie industry.

The second group of films placed in the schedule are the major G- and PG-rated, to establish a strong pattern of **family and children's appeal** in the schedule. The third group of films have varied **adult audience appeals.** Films without notable box office success usually fall in this category. They are repeated slightly less frequently than premieres and G-rated hits.

Other films that were not major theatrical hits may still rate as important acquisitions for pay-television services. Viewers may value seeing a film on television that they might not be willing to pay three to six dollars to see in a movie theater. **Foreign films** fall in this group.

Encore films are repeat showings of films that premiered 9 to 12 months earlier and features that premiered in the latter part of the previous month's schedule. Late premieres are often aired once or twice the following month to assure an adequate number of plays and use up all the contracted runs.

Title Availability

Balancing the number of major films and lesser-known but promotable titles every month, then adding a handful of encore presentations, is one of the key challenges a premium movie programmer faces. A crucial factor in preparing the lineup is title availability. Most films with good track records at the box office are obtained from the major film distributors, but an increasing number can be purchased from a wide variety of independent distributors and producers.

Theatrical films distributed by major studios are typically available to pay services 6 (for PPV) to 12 (for pay cable) months after their initial theatrical release. This time period varies depending on the box office success of the film. Twentieth Century–Fox kept *Star Wars,* a huge box office success, in theatrical release for almost two years and then held off its theatrical rerelease for another year, substantially delaying its availability on pay television. In a similar situation, Universal rereleased its enormously successful film *Jaws* after introducing its sequel, *Jaws II,* postponing the pay television exhibition of *Jaws* for more than four years. Conversely, Irwin Allen's disaster epic *The Swarm* fell short of box office expectations, had a limited theatrical run, and was not rereleased. It therefore became available to pay television shortly after its initial theatrical release.

Time constraints on the use of films also affect steady product flow, including how long and when a film is available to pay services. Commercial broadcast television buyers, for example, have the financial clout to place time limitations on distributors' sales of films to premium services. The broadcasters seek early telecast of key films to bolster their ratings during Nielsen and Arbitron sweeps. This tactic shortens the period of time during which the films are available to premium networks. Since most top-grade films are released in time for theatrical showings in the summertime, and broadcasters often want those same films for the November and February sweeps, premium networks must use them at an accelerated rate in the early fall and in December/January. Because those same films might be useful to the largest pay-cable networks that also seek rating points in the sweeps, this practice operates to the especial benefit of broadcasters. On the other hand, some desirable films are unsuitable for broadcast sale altogether, which increases their pay television availability. A film such as *Emmanuelle* would require such massive editing for broadcast television that it would be destroyed in the process. Therefore, distributors allow premium networks to schedule them as many times as they like for as long as they like.

Most of Hollywood's film classics are licensed to broadcast television stations on an exclusive basis, but a limited (and growing) number are available to pay television. Exceptions to the standard pattern include independent productions and major studio films that are removed from syndication or network release from time to time. In the foreseeable future, such classic favorites as *Casablanca, Citizen Kane* and *Adam's Rib,* which would be enhanced by being shown on premium services without editing, commercial interruption or inconvenient scheduling, may become available to pay television.

Occasionally, the major pay movie services disagree about whether or not to schedule a movie *after* it has already had a commercial broadcast network run. Some theatrical films, such as *Animal House* and *The Godfather,* played on pay services after they aired on the broadcast networks. Indeed, HBO and Showtime have found a pay-cable following for these movies when they are shown unedited and without commercials. Some survey research even demonstrates viewer support for the reshowing of films that have been badly cut for commercial television presentation or that have exceptionally strong appeal for repeat viewing. Almost all pay services show selected off-network movies, often drawing sizable audiences.

Exhibition Windows

Distributors create a distribution window for a film's release when offering it to the premium services. In this arrangement, premium programmers negotiate for a certain number of *first-run* and *second-run plays* during a specific time period, generally 12 months. For example, a given film may be made available to a pay-cable service from April to March. It might premiere in April, encore in August, and then be rescheduled as a G-rated of adult-appeal film in February, possibly encoring in the following month to complete the run. Programmers must project ahead to see that the scheduled play periods for similar films from different distributors do not expire at exactly the same time. Otherwise, viewers could be treated to five blockbusters or four westerns or three Paul Newman films in the same month, an inefficient use of scarce resources. Ironically, inadvertent clustering of films sometimes can be packaged and successfully marketed as a "festival" or "A night of _____," thus turning a potential problem into a promotable benefit.

Film Licenses

Feature films are licensed to pay-television networks in one of two ways: **per subscriber** or by **flat fee.** Per subscriber means the film's producer or distributor negotiates a fee per customer for a specific number of runs within a fixed period. Such a fee is based on the actual number of subscribers who had access to the film (though not necessarily the number who actually saw it). In a flat fee arrangement, the parties negotiate a fixed payment regardless of the number of subscribers who have access to it.

In the 1970s, the per-subscriber fees were small compared to theatrical distribution revenues and broadcast license fees and suited the rapid growth of the premium-network subscriber base. The film distributors were satisfied to get a share of every subscriber household receiving the premium network's programming. But once the pay-cable networks grew large enough to have to pay substantial amounts for the pay-television rights to a movie under that method, they usually abandoned the per-subscriber formulas and negotiated flat fee arrangements with the program suppliers. The flat fee method is also used for acquiring originally produced programming. A key element of pay-per-view is the per-subscriber fee paid by the cable operator to either the studio or PPV service provider.

Film Placement

General rules of thumb for film scheduling include beginning weeknight programming at 8 P.M. and starting final showings (of major offerings) as late as 11:30 P.M. to 12:30 A.M. Those networks concentrating on the overnight daypart employ still later final-showing schedules. For most of the premium movie services, an evening consists of three to five programs, depending on individual running lengths. Entertaining short subjects, elaborate animated titles and promotional spots for other attractions fill the time between shows. All-movie networks especially favor movie-oriented shorts such as interviews with directors or location tours. Most movie services operate for 24 hours, but for the short-schedule services, Saturday, Sunday and holiday schedules generally begin at 2, 2:30 or 3 P.M. and may include as many as six programs up to the final show that begins at 11:30 or as late as 12:30 A.M.

The premium services no longer **front load** their films (that is, schedule most of them at the start of the calendar month). Using 20 or more new films each month (not counting final encores of the previous month's premieres) usually means scheduling four premieres each week, gradually integrating first-, second-, third-, and up to sixth-run presentations week by week so that the viewer has a constantly changing lineup of material from which to choose, and new movies appear every week.

Counterprogramming broadcast network schedules is another strategic consideration. For example, on Monday nights, when *Monday Night Football* is a strong ABC attraction, premium networks tend to schedule films with female appeal. Preceding or following a popular broadcast network show with a program of the same genre creates a unified programming block (requiring channel switching, an easy move in cable homes with remote control keypads). Beginning programs on the hour as often as possible—especially during prime time from 8 to 11 P.M.—makes it convenient for viewers to switch to and from pay cable.

Films and specials containing mature themes are usually scheduled at later hours than G-rated films, even though pay television is not bound by broadcasting's traditions. PG features are offered throughout premium schedules. Monthly program guides encourage parents to prescreen all films rated PG or R early in the week to decide which are appropriate for their children to watch on subsequent airdates.

ENTERTAINMENT SPECIALS

In addition to feature films, several of the monthly pay-cable services offer series and high-gloss specials created expressly for their subscribers. Entertainment specials typically feature Broadway shows and popular Las Vegas nightclub acts, carried in their original, uncensored form. Other programming formats include made-for-pay-TV movies, original documentaries, television magazine series and blends of entertainment and documentary styles. A few made-for-cable series employing soap opera or situation comedy formats have been created, and a rare few former broadcast series (off-network) have been licensed to premium networks.

In recent years, the specialized pay-television services have sought to differentiate their image and audience appeal through a mix of fresh, original programming targeted to a narrowly defined base of viewers. This includes a mix of live action and filmed material for which they feel those consumers will pay. The Playboy Channel and Bravo have found niches by scheduling large amounts of original entertainment, including specials.

Selecting performers to star in original pay-cable specials and choosing properties to adapt to the television medium requires an in-depth examination of subscribers' expectations. Because the major broadcast networks frequently offer opportunities to see leading entertainers, either on specials or daily talk/variety shows, premium programmers are forced to seek out fresher, more unusual entertainers and material. Among their options are: (1) using performers who are well-known, but who appear infrequently on broadcast network television; (2) using performers often seen on broadcast television, but who rarely headline their own programs; and (3) developing programs and artists unavailable on broadcast television.

Premium programming must also satisfy a difficult-to-measure price/value relationship in the minds of subscribers. Here, the pay-cable and pay-per-view networks have made a major asset of taping shows on location, offering subscribers a front-row seat at theaters, nightclubs and arenas around the world. For instance, a Las Vegas nightclub special provides the cable subscriber with the same performance that costs $40 to 60 per couple to see in person. A telecast of a rock concert from New York's Central Park or a country music festival from West Virginia makes the viewer in Cleveland, Ohio, or Agoura, California, a part of that one-time event.

Unlike the typical broadcast network special, every effort is made by pay-cable producers to preserve the integrity of a complete performance, without guest stars, dance numbers and other window dressing used to widen the audience base of most broadcast network variety shows. At their best, these shows are vivid reproductions of live performances. Pay-television's time flexibility also permits nightclub acts and concerts to run their natural lengths, whether 1 hour and 11 minutes or 1 hour and 53 minutes. The private nature of pay-television viewing also allows for the telecasting of adult-oriented comedy and dramatic material unsuitable for airing on broadcast television.

By the close of the 1980s, original programming (including made-for-pay movies, series and specials) made up as much as 50 percent of some premium networks' monthly schedules. Showtime's annual budget for original programming grew from $6 million in 1979 to nearly $35 million in 1985. HBO, as of the mid-1980s, spent about $100 million annually on original programming, while its sister service, Cinemax, invested an additional $20 million.

SPORTS

The third major component in pay programming is sports. HBO and Showtime schedule major, big-ticket, national sporting events in prime time. Sports programming creates a divergence of opinion, however, in the pay-television community, with some programmers arguing that sports blur a movie service's image. In consequence, neither The Movie Channel nor Cinemax carry sports. HBO, however, has carried sporting events since its beginnings, while Showtime became a devotee in the 1980s. Austin Furst, former vice-president of programming at HBO, argued that two-thirds of HBO's subscribers watch sports and that those subscribers were "more pleased" by HBO than those having no interest in sports.[4]

Because of the broadcast networks' financial strength and audience reach, ABC, CBS and NBC still manage to outbid and acquire the rights to most major sporting events. Premium networks often have to settle for secondary rights or events of lesser national interest. Nevertheless, an audience can be found for some sports that broadcast television does not adequately cover, such as light and middleweight boxing, regional college sports, track and field, swimming, diving, soccer and equestrian competitions. In recent years, HBO has aggressively sought and won the rights to a long string of top boxing and tennis events.

Big-ticket boxing and wrestling were a programming staple for pay-per-view packagers in the first half of the 1980s. The relatively small number of headline events and the relatively small universe of pay-per-view equipped homes took PPV out of contention for major events. Rapid expansion of the number of homes with pay-per-view in the late 1980s, combined with the success of such events as *Wrestlemania* and championship boxing, rekindled cable operator and subscriber interest in pay-per-view sports. In addition, several of the regional pay-per-view sports channels, such as Dodgervision in Los Angeles, have become successful as PPV technology and marketing improved.

A number of already discussed regional pay-television operations have had success with month-to-month sports (see Chapter 10 on sports). The premium networks' advantage in sports programming is that they can emphasize sporting contests as entertainment rather than cover events in journalistic fashion. New program formats are emerging that focus on sports personalities and dramatize memorable sports events of the past. Such approaches broaden the appeal of sports, while offering intriguing programming possibilities not characteristic of broadcast television.

THE GENERAL PREMIUM MOVIE SERVICES

Home Box Office (HBO), the first of the national premium movie services, turned to satellite distribution in 1975 after operating for years via microwave relay and "bicycled" videocassettes. Its pioneering use of a satellite to beam its programming simultaneously across the nation sparked a revolution in television distribution and greatly speeded the growth of cable television.

In 1976, Viacom International, a major television program supplier and owner of cable systems, founded Showtime. Two years later that service, too, went up on the satellite. In 1979, Warner Cable joined forces with American Express and converted its in-house pay-television service, Star Channel, to an all-movie service, renaming it The Movie Channel (TMC). The following year, 1980, Time Inc. formed Cinemax as an all-movie service to complement HBO. In 1981, several major MSOs launched Spotlight, another movie-only service, only to disband it in 1984. As multipay marketing caught on, half a dozen other, more specialized pay services were launched between 1982 and 1984. However, the original top four—HBO, Showtime, Cinemax and The Movie Channel—together continue to represent nearly 90 percent of all pay-television subscriptions. (See Figure 11-3 for logos of some premium services.)

Cinemax

Time Inc. began Cinemax in 1980 in order to compete with Viacom's Showtime as a multipay alternative, both to protect HBO's subscriber base and complement its schedule. At the start, 99 percent of Cinemax subscribers also took HBO; that percentage eventually slid down to 85, showing that the service

Figure 11-3 General Premium Networks

had begun to find its own audience. Cinemax offers a differentiated selection of feature films geared to a younger audience than HBO's, especially urban professionals under 35 years—the affluent, contemporary crowd. Marketed jointly and scrambled since 1986, by 1988 Cinemax served over 5.1 million homes on 3,650 cable affiliates.

Beginning in 1983, Cinemax modified its programming from its all-movie start, adding entertainment specials and original comedy productions, such as *The Max Headroom Show,* to foster a personality distinct from HBO's. Although one of Cinemax's initial tenets was that it would not duplicate HBO's films within a given month, the smaller service sometimes premieres major movies such as *Aliens* at the same time as HBO. This permits Cinemax to take advantage of HBO's major promotional campaigns. Cinemax, however, schedules more movies every month than any of its competitors (85 films on average), more than The Movie Channel (78), HBO (50) or Showtime (55). About 10 percent of its schedule is original programming, mostly hip comedy and music. Cinemax is carried on two C-band satellites, Galaxy I and Satcom III-R, and a Ku-band satellite, Satcom K-1.

Festival

Launched in 1987, Festival is Time Inc.'s third pay-television service. "The Clean Machine," as it was once dubbed by Time Inc. insiders, targets subscribers who have *rejected* pay cable because of the presence of R-rated movies.

Festival's lineup consists mostly of G- and PG-rated movies, supplemented by a few heavily edited R-rated films, and about 25 percent of its fare does not appear on its sister services, HBO and Cinemax. In addition to hit movies, Festival will show some classic films, reruns of HBO specials and true stories/documentaries. It retails at about $6 to $7 monthly (two-thirds the cost of HBO, for example). The new service targets television viewers older than 50 and parents with very young children, especially those whose only pay service is The Disney Channel. Though Festival does not itself edit objectionable material out of the movies it exhibits, it does show films that have been pre-edited for airline use and other purposes. Its monthly schedule consists of about 70 titles, including 62 movies (one-third classic films) and 6 specials. By 1988, Festival was scrambled on Satcom K-1 and had several hundred ATC affiliates (owned by Time Inc.) serving about a half-million subscribers.

Home Box Office

As of 1988, Time Inc.'s HBO had 6,700 affiliates and over 15.9 million subscribers, making it by far the largest of the pay services (though with only one-third the reach of many basic services). It constantly fine-tunes its programming strategy, but its basic thrust is to license feature films from the major studios and independent distributors as soon as possible after their theatrical release, some on exclusive contracts. The service also programs originally produced specials with big-name entertainers (including Barbra Streisand, Liza Minelli and Kenny Rogers) "docutainment" series (*Time Was,* with Dick Cavett); comedy programs (*Not Necessarily the News*); children's shows (*Fraggle Rock, Seabert*); and big ticket sports (boxing, tennis).

Consistently popular, broad-based programming gives HBO nearly 50 percent of the pay market. With its sister service, Cinemax, it was the first of the pay-cable networks to scramble its satellite signal and market its service to backyard dish subscribers. HBO comes on Galaxy I, Satcom III-R and Satcom K-1. With the enormous financial resources of Time Inc. behind it, HBO can finance films during their early production stages in return for exclusive pay-cable exhibition rights (called **prebuying**).[5] It schedules about 50 movies a month, 18 of them new, and at least 7 new, exclusive entertainment specials.

In 1982 and 1983, seeking to further differentiate itself from competitors, HBO greatly accelerated its pursuit of exclusive titles. It produced a number of made-for-pay movies, designed to have their first showing on HBO. The first of them was *The Terry Fox Story.* HBO also signed exclusivity agreements with two motion picture studios, Orion and Columbia Pictures, obtaining first crack at films released by those studios (for a substantial price). In addition, the company raised $125 million in the investment community through a venture known as Silver Screen Partners for the production of a dozen or more motion pictures exclusive to HBO.

On another front, several international coproductions were begun with foreign partners. And in a 1983 coup, HBO signed an agreement with CBS and Columbia Pictures to create another major motion picture studio in Hollywood, Tri-Star. Each of these actions gave Home Box Office exclusive access to a considerable number of film titles. These movie exclusives proved to be highly promotable but very costly, particularly the blockbuster movies such as *Ghostbusters.* In 1984, the value of exclusivity appeared to wane, while programming costs continued to rise. HBO's management suddenly reversed course, renouncing exclusivity as harmful and sharing some of the titles it had earlier sought to corner. But its chief competitor, Showtime, began increasing the number of movie titles under its exclusive control, so in 1987, HBO once again embraced exclusivity, wresting away from Showtime the exclusive pact it had held with Paramount Pictures. HBO's agreement with Paramount left Showtime's planners scrambling in the late 1980s to fill the programming and promotion voids that HBO's $500 million deal created.

The Movie Channel

The Movie Channel, like HBO, Showtime and the other theatrical movie services, runs feature films as soon as possible after theatrical release. But unlike its competitors, TMC programs virtually no nonmovie titles, living up to its movie-only name. And because it airs no specials, it programs a greater number of movies than HBO or Showtime, often drawing on older features to fill the gaps. It shows an average of 78 uncut, first-run motion pictures each month, many of them unavailable on HBO and Cinemax. TMC uses hosts and packages its movies in highly promotable groupings under titles such as "Double Features," "Film Festivals" and "Movie Marathons." Its "VCR Theater" at 3 A.M. encourages subscribers to tape movies for later viewing.

TMC uses weekly (rather than monthly) scheduling, promoting 15 to 20 new films each week and then retiring them for several months. To further differentiate itself, TMC starts its prime-time movies at 7, 9 and 11 P.M. (rather than 6, 8 and 10 P.M. like most movie services).

In 1983, TMC's and Showtime's managements were merged, pooling their assets, including three transponders, in an attempt to increase their competitive stance relative to HBO. The two pay-cable networks, now wholly owned by Viacom, share financing, film licensing, production and distribution. In 1984, they concluded the exclusive licensing agreement with Paramount Pictures mentioned above, improving their competitive position but raising their costs, only to lose that pact in 1987 to HBO. Since then, Showtime/TMC have aggressively sought exclusive licenses to hit films. Carried on Galaxy I, TMC appears on 3,250 systems (including those owned by its parent, Viacom) with about 2.6 million subscribers as of 1988 (down from 2.9 the previous year).

Showtime

Showtime relies on feature films for a major portion of its audience appeal, but it has moved increasingly into dramatic and comedy series programming. Showtime regularly schedules family-oriented series starring big-name performers (*Faerie Tale Theatre*); taped musical performances; freewheeling comedy (*It's Gary Shandling's Show, Gallagher, Bizarre*); and Broadway musicals and dramas (*Broadway on Showtime*). In a more traditional vein are two original situation comedies (*Brothers* and *Hard Knocks*) and an historical drama (*Robin Hood*).

Through series programming, Showtime attempts to create the same kind of program loyalty that the broadcast networks generate with their soaps and their prime-time situation comedies. Original and exclusive programming, combined with active marketing, are its primary strategies. It carries more original series entertainment than any other pay-cable service. Showtime generally appears as the second or third premium channel on a system, not as the sole pay channel. Owned by Viacom and scrambled since 1986, it had 3,200 affiliates and over 5.7 million subscribers as of 1988. It participates in the joint production and licensing venture with TMC already described. Operating with TMC, Showtime has moved aggressively into packaging pay channels for backyard satellite-dish subscribers (TVROs) and for hospitals and other group-viewing situations.

THE SPECIALIZED PREMIUM SERVICES

Several premium services narrowcast to specific interest or demographic groups. Movies make up most of their schedules (with the exception of the regional pay-sports services already discussed). These services choose their movies for their strong appeal to a target group, rather than their broad appeal to a heterogeneous audience. Viewers targeted by the specialized premium services are variously defined by sex and age, as in the case of the Playboy Channel or the Disney Channel, or by common interests, as with Bravo.

Bravo
Bravo is a pay service operated by Rainbow Programming Enterprises. The network remains the last and most successful (although only modestly so) of the several "culture networks" launched in the early 1980s. Bravo's mix of hard-to-find foreign films, theater, jazz concerts and opera and dance productions regularly wins plaudits from the nation's television critics. Instead of mass advertising, it markets itself through local arts councils, disseminating promotional materials at cultural and artistic events. Cable operators see Bravo as a highly differentiated and "classy" service. Operators are charged $1.95 monthly per subscriber for the pay service ($3 if Rainbow's AMC/Bravo package is carried). Operators typically charge only $5 a month for Bravo, allowing $3.05 profit to the system for each subscriber.

Bravo, which went on the satellite in late 1980, programs *only* the prime time and the overnight period, forcing operators to piggyback it with daytime services. It airs unscrambled weeknights from 7:30 P.M. to 6 A.M. and weekends from 5 P.M. to 6 A.M. About 30 percent of Bravo's schedule consists of original performances produced by the network itself or the U.S. television premieres of foreign productions. About 70 percent of its schedule is international films.

The programming targets the affluent and sophisticated performing arts and foreign film buff and features internationally known performing companies such as the Bolshoi Ballet, the New York Y Chamber Orchestra and the Jerry Mulligan Jazz Quartet in concert. When the service first began in 1980, movies were much less prominent, but in an effort to boost subscribership,

Figure 11-4 Specialized Premium Networks

films now fill most of Bravo's schedule. The feature films presented on Bravo, however, differ sharply from those seen on the other premium movie services as some typical titles show: *Madame Rosa* (1977), *La Strada* (1954) and *Atomic Cafe* (1982). Starting in 1988, Bravo allocated certain nights to specific programming: Mondays for documentaries; Tuesdays for comedies; Wednesdays for great directors; Thursdays for profiles; Fridays for jazz; Saturdays for opera and stage (and cultural classics after midnight); Sundays for international premieres. At the start of 1988, Bravo had 350 affiliates, most belonging to Cablevision, and was purchased by 1.3 million subscribers. It is carried on Satcom IV.

The Disney Channel

The Disney Channel, launched in 1983, by the Walt Disney Corp., trades on that famous name. While its boosters say that no premium service has been launched with so much product recognition, it is equally true that no service has as much to live up to. The fastest growing pay-cable service in America in the 1980s, the Disney Channel has thrived in good times and bad. By 1988, the service had racked up affiliations with more than 4,300 cable systems with 3.8 million subscribers.

Anxious to preserve the box-office appeal of its animated classics, the Disney Channel trots out *Pinoccio* and *Sleeping Beauty* at rare intervals. Instead of its classics, the Disney Channel emphasizes original pay programs appealing to viewers of all ages. For the very youngest, it has *Welcome to Pooh Corner* and the *Mousercise* exercise show. For adults, Disney carries made-for-pay movies with broad family appeal and miniseries such as *Anne of Avonlea* with Colleen Dewhurst. Between movies, it uses unique animated and taped **interstitial** bits (shorts) hosted by Mickey Mouse. Though its original program content is relatively high, much of the schedule consists of nonclassic Disney library programs such as *The Love Bug*. Disney programs for children during the day, for the whole family in the early evening and for adults in the late evening. The 24-hour service appears on Galaxy I. Disney has also been successful in marketing its program guide, *The Disney Channel Magazine*, to systems and subscribers.

The Playboy Channel

The Playboy Channel, a premium service owned by Playboy Enterprises, publisher of the famous men's magazine, currently has 520,000 subscribers on 600 systems, down from a high of 800,000 subscribers in 1982. Like the Disney Channel, the Playboy Channel elicits instant brand recognition from consumers. Most people have a notion of what it is like before they see it.

In 1982 Playboy Enterprises bought into Escapade, an adult paytelevision movie service owned by Rainbow Programming Enterprises, and reformed it, introducing original programming bearing the Playboy stamp—such as *The News According to Playboy* and *Playmate Playoffs*. Playboy provides what it calls "a video magazine" of adult material targeted mainly at male adults 18+. Early Playboy research, however, demonstrated that subscribing couples tend to watch the programming together and that nearly half its audience was women. This research stimulated the inclusion of programming targeted specifically toward women in its schedule.

Though subscribers said they liked Playboy's original thrust, the part-time network has long suffered from one of the cable industry's steepest disconnect rates. Its 10 to 11 percent monthly churn means that the entire subscriber base has to be replaced every 10 months or so, just to maintain current levels. Various attempts to stem disconnects have led Playboy back to a mix that includes a high percentage of movies. The result is a service composed half of adult movies (e.g., *Fanny Hill*) and half of original specials, catering to an adult male audience. Now wholly owned and operated by the video division of Playboy Enterprises, the pay-cable channel operates nightly from 8 P.M. to 6 A.M. In addition, Playboy operates a limited pay-per-view service, as noted later, using portions of the same programming. Like the Disney Channel, the Playboy Channel is a highly differentiated, highly targeted premium service. But many large cable MSOs find the controversy associated with carrying the service not justified by the revenue it generates. By MSO policy, The Playboy Channel is currently locked out of three-quarters of cable homes.[6]

THE PAY-PER-VIEW NETWORKS

The dream of turning the television sets populating America's living rooms and dens into vending machines for the distribution of movies has been kicking around since the 1950s. It moved a giant step toward reality in the early 1980s when several local, stand-alone pay-per-view channels were launched.

But it wasn't until the rapid growth of home videocassette recorders threatened cable subscriber rolls and a new generation of addressable cable converters appeared that cable operators seriously began to make shelf space for pay-per-view.

Pay-per-view operates as the name implies. Subscribers select a program from an a la carte menu and are billed for each individual selection. For the viewer, the selection process may involve a telephone call to the local cable service to arrange for descrambling the signal (or a national 800 number) or may only require punching a code number on a remote control device (**impulse ordering**).

As with other premium services, the primary content is movies, though increasingly big-ticket sporting events and concerts are offered as well. For viewers, the key advantage to PPV is the *early availability* of major motion pictures, generally six months after theatrical release and six months or a year ahead of their first pay-cable appearance. The second major advantage is *convenience*. Though movies can be rented on videocassette (for slightly less) at the same time they first appear on pay-per-view, the PPV subscriber need not leave home to pick up and return a videocassette. In addition, there are no "late return" charges, and a movie's availability does not depend on how many copies of top films a store has stocked.

Several pay-per-view ventures were launched in the early 1980s. Among them was R.S.V.P., a sports-oriented service offered by ABC Video Enterprises and Getty Oil. It soon succumbed as a result of PPV's two key start-up problems: a shortage of suitable events, combined with a long delay in the installation of addressable set-top cable converters needed for pay-per-view order taking. In 1985, a second generation of pay-per-view services appeared as cable operators sought relief from a slump in the sale of new pay-cable subscriptions, the bread-and-butter of their business. About 25 to 30 percent addressability appears to be the "critical mass" for launching pay-per-view in most systems, and cable operators occasionally test different systems by offering a national PPV service and a local PPV channel side by side.

To be competitive with home videocassette rentals, most pay-per-view movies sell for $3.95 to $4.95 per viewing and are billed monthly along with the subscriber's basic and pay-cable charges. Since pay-per-view became available nationwide in 1985, manufacturers have started to develop more sophisticated impulse order-taking technologies to enable the subscriber easier access to pay-per-view. Order-taking equipment varies from cable system to cable system, depending on how much initial capital investment an operator wishes to make. Some systems use traditional customer service representatives to take individual orders by phone, while others utilize impulse technologies that allow a subscriber to order a pay-per-view program by pressing a few buttons on their cable converter or dialing a simple seven-digit telephone number. AT&T recently began offering cable operators a national 800-number service for PPV ordering. It can handle 35,000 PPV calls in five minutes.[7] Systems using these technically sophisticated but consumer-friendly order-entry technologies frequently have higher **buy rates** (number of purchases per event), but buy rates vary widely, ranging from about 10 percent to over 50 percent, depending

Figure 11-5 Pay-Per-View Services

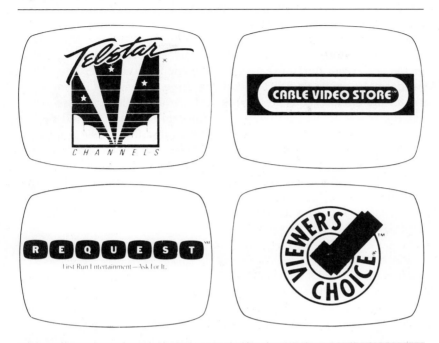

on the event, total pay channel offerings, marketing effort and type of event (live or movie).

Several major PPV service suppliers have also moved away from the term *pay-per-view* in their marketing, finding customers confused by it. Request Television, for example, markets itself as "The Rent-A-Movie Channel." Weekend nights, especially 8 P.M. movie starts, are the most popular with subscribers, and about half of PPV subscribers take one event per month, and about a quarter take two events, but only 10 percent or so take four or more events in a month. Industry estimates project a doubling of the PPV universe between 1988 and 1990. There are now (1988) about 6.6 million PPV homes out of 18 million addressable homes. By 1990, PPV homes will grow to at least 13.7 million homes. The total addressable universe is projected at over 24 million homes in 1990 and over 40 million homes in 1995.[8]

Request Television

Launched in late 1985, Request Television distributes via satellite a menu of four major motion pictures each week on a two-week cycle on each of two channels. Occasional special events such as wrestling are also offered. Request provides the distribution, marketing and promotional support for its movies, but negotiations for local system carriage of programming occur directly between the cable operator and the movie studios. Owned by Reiss Media Enterprises, Request delivers the films around-the-clock on two Galaxy I satellite channels.

As explained earlier, Request operates differently than the other PPV services. It handles movie scheduling and provides the satellite delivery of programming only *after* negotiations with the studios have been completed by each cable operator. Participating studios include Columbia, Lorimar, MGM/UA, New World, Paramount, 20th Century-Fox, Universal, Disney and Warner Bros. Operators pay nothing for delivery of the encrypted signal; the studios and event promoters pay the delivery cost. Revenue from local PPV sales are split between the operator and the supplier. However, cable operators rarely cherrypick the schedule, instead taking the program schedule offered by the suppliers in its entirety. Viewers may either telephone their cable service or push buttons on a key-pad to arrange to descramble the PPV movie or event. Each cable operator chooses the technology and creates the price structure for local viewing, varying them according to the operator's cost for installation and licensing each movie and local market conditions. In its first two years of operation, Request signed on over 160 cable affiliates serving 2.6 million addressable subscribers.

Viewer's Choice
Viacom launched Viewer's Choice on the same day in 1985 as Request Television began. This 24-hour PPV network provides a single movie airing continuously for one week (Wednesday to Tuesday) on each of the service's two channels. Subscribers can elect predictable, fixed times to view, for example the 2 P.M., 5 P.M., 8 P.M. or 11 P.M. showings, and movies are typically priced about $4.95 (retail). Like Request, Viewer's Choice occasionally offers specials such as the sports/entertainment extravaganza Wrestlemania II (costing $15 a home).

Unlike Request Television, Viewer's Choice licenses movie titles from the studio sources, much the way pay-cable networks do, and then sub-licenses them to the cable operator. Viewer's Choice sets the wholesale price for each movie, typically $2.00 to $2.50 for a movie and remits $1.80 to $2.25 to the film company. Viewer's Choice, the studio or event supplier and the cable operators split the revenue from subscriber purchases. By early 1988, Viewer's Choice had 75 cable affiliates and was delivered to 2.9 million addressable subscribers nationwide. Viewer's Choice I and II are carried on Galaxy III, shifted from Satcom III-R and Galaxy I. Both can be phone-in services using AT&T's 800-number ordering or can use impulse technology. In conjunction with AT&T and CableData, Viacom successfully tested the 800-number national turnkey system in Milwaukee in 1987, stimulating the growth of the entire PPV industry by making ordering simple, uniform and widely understood by customers, as well as making likely direct cost benefits to operators from nationwide marketing and promotion. Most cable systems with PPV services will eventually adopt 800-number ordering unless they use the more expensive impulse systems.

Cable Video Store
Unlike both Request Television and Viewer's Choice, which concentrate on the latest Hollywood hits, Cable Video Store (CVS) offers a broad menu of 50 to 60 movies a month, only a *few* of which are new releases (much

like a corner video rental store or supermarket booth). Operating since April 1986, this scrambled 24-hour, single-channel service telecasts classic films and older movie hits that may have recently appeared on the monthly pay-cable channels. It charges from $.99 to $3.99 per movie.

Owned and operated by General Instrument's Jerrold Division, CVS uses Jerrold's own impulse-ordering technology, requiring a special cable converter in each subscriber's home. Jerrold finds that impulse ordering more than *doubles* buy rates compared to phone-in systems. As of the start of 1988, CVS had 10 system affiliates serving 40,000 addressable subscribers.

Telstar Channels

Telstar Channels, launched in mid-1986, is a four-channel, movie-only system, with each channel operating 24 hours a day. Channels 1 and 2 each provide a single major motion picture, while Channel 3 rotates three titles. The fourth channel provides viewers with a menu for ordering (text only). The movies range in subscriber cost from $2.00 to $4.50. Telstar Channels acquired World Video Library (a short-lived PPV competitor) in 1986, substantially increasing its stock of films. As of 1988, Telstar Channels had about 30 cable affiliates and about 80,000 addressable subscribers nationwide.

Pay-Per-View Network

American Television & Communications (ATC), Cox Cable, Continental Cablevision, Newhouse Broadcasting and Telecable Corporation linked in 1987 to form Pay-Per-View Network, a cable operator consortium negotiating for product and distributing it via satellite to member systems. Pay-Per-View Network is the successor organization to Event Television, a pay-per-view attempt that was abandoned by its operator-owners in 1986 after failing to generate either programming or profits. This new venture, promoted as "Home Premiere," is carried on Galaxy III and reaches 2.3 million subscribers on its parent cable systems.

Part-Time and Regional PPV Services

Playboy Enterprises Inc. offers its adult-oriented The Playboy Channel programming on a night-by-night and/or weekend-long basis in a limited number of markets. Called Playboy on Demand, it comes on Friday to Sundays and can be purchased for just Friday night, just Saturday night or all weekend. The Playboy Channel comes on Satcom IV.

Several smaller pay-per-view operations also vie for niches in the premium television universe. Some telecast nationally on a part-time basis, others provide full-time service in a single market or group of markets. Warner Cable, for example, offers a variety of PPV options in its five largest systems and expects to offer addressable PPV service in all its markets within the next five years. Warner's predecessor company, Warner Amex Cable, pioneered the development of two-way addressable technology (the Qube technology) and has tested the PPV market longer than any other company (a decade in Columbus, Ohio). Warner created the first dedicated PPV channels with a five-minute delay before automatic billing as a method of enticing viewers to check out PPV channels. However, the large number of other channels on Qube systems (100 or more, including all monthly pay services) originally undermined the effectiveness of its pay-per-view marketing because Qube subscribers had so many other viewing options. Over the long haul, however, multiple PPV channels proved effective money-makers for Warner, and the MSO regularly purchases packages of films to schedule on all its systems, which then appear as local exclusives to subscribers.

The potential profitability of pay-per-view has encouraged many cable operators to launch their own in-house PPV services. Operators such as Cablevision and other MSOs negotiate directly with sporting event packagers and the Hollywood studios for a group of films, eliminating the middleman, much like Request Television. The advantage is that programming is controlled locally, both in selection and scheduling. The disadvantage is the high cost of building and operating a local videotape facility.

DIRECTIONS FOR PREMIUM PROGRAMMING

The decade of the 1980s contained dramatic changes in premium services. While HBO, the leading premium network, continued to dominate the marketplace, the number two service, Showtime, wrestled with strategies to build its market share. HBO turned to consumer marketing, further raising its profile with America's viewing public. Meanwhile, Showtime forged exclusivity of movie product into a primary weapon, only to lose that edge to HBO. Showtime further differentiated itself through substantial investment in original programming. Pay-per-view networks entered the picture in the late 1980s, offering movies and entertainment on an a la carte basis.

The wider availability of top-name movies on pay-per-view and rented videocassettes reduced the overall attractiveness of off-the-shelf film titles, pressing the movie-based pay networks into seeking even more exclusive and original product. HBO's competitors are likely to pursue stronger creative and financial links, perhaps even partnerships, with program suppliers and cable operators. Carrying advertising is another option for marginal pay services.

As cable systems continue to expand their program offerings, raising the price of basic service in the process, the cable customer's average monthly bill may approach $50 in the early 1990s. Even so, premium services will be under increasing pressure to reduce their retail prices to bring them better in line with customer expectations and spending patterns. A low-price, high-volume strategy seems likely to replace the retail pricing strategy that has been endemic to pay-television since its beginning.

As pay-per-view services increase their market penetration, offering the early release pattern for movies that was once the exclusive province of pay-cable, several pay-cable services may evolve into "super basic" channels on many cable systems, functioning to provide lift for a second or higher programming tier. By 1990, impulse technology will become standard for cable converters, opening a wide range of possibilities for cable operators and programmers alike. An increasing number of cable subscribers will be able to order a pay-per-view movie, concert or sporting event in an instant, and increasingly, they will avail themselves of the opportunity. Projections of 20 to 30 million PPV homes in the mid-1990s will entice Hollywood's studios to release movies to pay-per-view services close to their theatrical release date, truly creating a "home box office" bonanza for movie makers and event organizers. VCRs and PPV will continue in head-to-head competition through the early 1990s.

SUMMARY

Premium cable networks, for which subscribers pay over and above the cost of basic cable service, primarily provide theatrical feature films, with a large dollop of entertainment specials and sporting events. The services divide into 8 national, pay-per-month pay-television services offering a full menu of programming, and 5 national pay-per-view services charging per program for a movie, concert or sporting event. General premium services aim their movies at a broad-based audience. Specialized pay services target narrowly defined de-mographic or interest groups with cultural programming and classic film, adult programming or family-oriented programming (in addition to regional sports). In the multipay environment, HBO is number one, and the rest of the pre-mium services compete with one another for shelf space and for attractive cable channel positions by offering lucrative revenue splits to cable operators. All services suffer from the problems of churn, downgrading and substitution. The major strategies for combating these problems focus on differentiation and ex-clusivity. Pay movie networks rotate their program schedules to increase their utility to cable consumers, providing a balanced mix of premiere movies, fam-ily and children-oriented programs, adult-appeal shows, foreign films and en-cores on most services. The pay-per-view services take a more targeted ap-proach, Request carrying on a channel only four movies and special events chosen by affiliated cable operators, others such as Viewer's Choice repeating for up to two weeks only one movie selected by the PPV service. Premium pro-grammers must consider title availabilities, exhibition windows and licensing practices in selecting and scheduling theatrical motion pictures. Beyond that, they look for blockbuster events (such as wrestling superevents). The keys to PPV penetration are user-friendly technology, convenient scheduling and ex-clusive movies and events. Like pay-cable, pay-per-view will operate in a mul-tipay environment with addressable homes having several PPV channels, forc-ing both kinds of services into seeking more differentiated images. For both pay-cable and pay-per-view, the major strategies for the early 1990s focus on marketing, financing original product and balancing the retail price charged for premium services against the rising price of basic cable service.

Notes

1. Showtime research in 1980.

2. Sophisticated distributors have been extremely successful with several rounds of alternate theatrical rereleases and pay-television exhibitions. A pay "run" is a playing period of about 30 days in which an attraction is telecast three to eight times. This pattern applies to pre-mium networks, subscription television and other pay services.

3. Pay cable typically uses the age categories of 18–24 and 25–49 because these groups best

separate people with the most similar entertainment tastes, whereas broadcasters tend to focus on consumer buying habits. The 18–24 age group watches more films, for example, because the bulk of films are directed toward that age group, in part because their lifestyles permit easy attendance at movie theaters.

4. "Austin Furst on HBO's Programming," *Cablevision*, 26 February 1979, pp. 63–65.

5. Jefferson Grahmam, "Guess Who's Amassed a Fortune in Feature Films?" *View*, June 1983, pp. 2–36. See also Hoyt Hilsman, "The Price of Pictures," *View*, February 1983, pp. 56–59; and "Special Report: The HBO Story," *Broadcasting*, 15 November 1982, pp. 48–52.

6. In 1983, Warner-Amex Cable was indicted by a grand jury on charges of carrying two adult films that "pandered obscenity" on The Playboy Channel. Warner-Amex settled the case out of court, agreeing not to present programs that would receive an X-rating (if they were rated) or other sexually explicit materials in Hamilton County (Cincinnati), Ohio. See "Cincinnati System's Carriage of Playboy Brings Obscenity Charge," *Broadcasting*, 20 June 1983, pp. 74–75. See also Mark Frankel, "Can Playboy Save Its Skin?" *Channels*, November 1986, pp. 37–40.

7. *Cable Marketing*'s Special Reports, "Marketing Pay-Per-View," July 1987, pp. 46–49ff, and "Pay-Per-View: The Logistics," June 1986, pp. 20–33ff. See also Judith Reitman, "Pay-Per-View Inches Along," *Cable Marketing*, November 1986, pp. 18–20ff.

8. Patricia E. Bauer, "Young and Impulsive: Pay-Per-View Projected Growth," *Channels*, May 1987, pp. 50–51.

Selected Sources

Baldwin, Thomas F., and McVoy, D. Stevens. *Cable Communication*. 2nd ed. Englewood Cliffs, N.J.: Prentice-Hall, 1988.

Cable Marketing. Monthly trade magazine focusing on management, technology and the marketing and promotion of cable services. New York, 1981 to date.

CableVision. Monthly trade magazine covering the cable industry. Denver, 1975 to date.

Channels of Communication. Monthly trade and consumer magazine keeping a close track of developments in pay-per-view and new programming practices.

Childers, Terry L., and Krugman, Dean M. "The Competitive Environment of Pay Per View." *Journal of Broadcasting & Electronic Media* 31 (Summer 1987): 335–342.

Multichannel News. Weekly trade articles on national cable programming. New York, 1979 to date.

"Special Report: Cable." *Broadcasting* (24 March 1986): 52–87; (7 July 1986): 75–80.

View. Bimonthly trade magazine covering television programming. New York, 1979 to date.

CHAPTER 12 LOCAL CABLE PROGRAMMING

Donald E. Agostino

Susan Tyler Eastman

A Guide to Chapter 12

Donald E. Agostino, associate professor and chairman of the Department of Telecom-munications at Indiana University, was also chair of the Bloomington Telecommunications Council during a period of franchise renewal and regularly consults for the cable industry. After earning degrees from Gonzaga University (B.A.), the University of California at Berkeley (M.A.) and Ohio University (Ph.D.), he joined the Indiana University faculty in 1973. Since 1978 he has worked with the National Science Foundation, developing funding for radio and television programs about science and developing ways to measure the reach and impact of these programs. In addition to television producing and directing credits, he has published trade reports and scholarly articles about videotex, videodiscs, radio program management and cable access programming.

Susan Tyler Eastman is currently the chair of the Bloomington Telecommunications Council, which monitors fulfillment of the local cable franchise and supervises two community ac-cess television channels and community access radio. She has published and consulted on cable programming. The rest of her credentials appear at the start of Chapter 9. Together, these authors appraise local cable-only programming and special services on cable.

LOCAL CABLE-ONLY PROGRAMMING

Local origination programming (**LO**) by cable operators and **public access** channels operated by community groups or local public institutions de-veloped during the rapid growth of U.S. cable service in the 1970s and early 1980s, then adapted to the cable industry's radical changes during the late 1980s. In the very early decades, cable systems successfully marketed their ser-vices by delivering a "big city" complement of five or six television channels to communities with little or no local broadcast television. No additional services were needed then to attract subscribers. Widespread acceptance to two new possibilities changed all that: the chance for truly local television service for un-served communities and the potential for new revenues for the cable operator through advertising sales.

Today, about one-quarter of cable systems, mostly those located in larger markets and college towns, offer LO or access channels. In the major markets, operators generally have sufficient revenues to support LO chan-nels until, if ever, they become revenue-producing through advertising sales. Major-markets and college towns generally also have enough community vol-unteers to make access services viable over the long term. Federal regulation in the Cable Communications Act of 1984 supports the right of local franchising authorities to require public access service.[1] Moreover, cable operators view local cable-only programming, whether produced by the operator, the commu-nity or a local public institution, as an appealing service for subscribers and as coinage for winning and renewing a franchise.

Nationally, local cable-only programming ranges from *automatic dis-plays*—a fixed camera panning time/weather dials, a news/stock/sports ticker, a listing of programs on other channels (a **program guide**) or a listing of local events (**community calendar**) on thousands of systems—to a relatively com-plex *live* productions from cable headend studios or remote locations. This

Table 12-1 Estimated Access and
LO Channel Distribution

TYPE OF SERVICE	NO. OF CHANNELS
Public Access	716
Educational	464
Governmental	368
Operator Origination	250
Leased Access	136
Total	1,934 (estimated)

Source: National Federation of Local Cable Programmers, 1988.

chapter focuses on the "produced programming" on about 1,000 systems across the country.

Most hours of local production consists of live and recorded public meetings, such as the city and county council, school board and other open meetings (especially those dealing with controversial local issues). The purpose of extended live meeting coverage is to provide a unique service to the community that over-the-air broadcasters would find inefficient to program. In some systems local production includes fully produced high-school sports, community theater or nightclub music performances. A few cable systems even cablecast local newscasts specializing in community events. A few purchase syndicated movie packages or reruns to stimulate viewing of an LO channel. The purpose of such expensive programming is, of course, to provide an audience for local spot advertising.

Although local cable-only production divides most clearly into two broad types—*system operated* and *community run*—cable programmers recognize several subdivisions of cable-only service. Some of these grew out of the federally mandated access requirements of the 1970s (public, educational and governmental channels, called **PEG** channels), no longer a federal requirement by the 1980s but often now a local franchise requirement. Table 12-1 lists the best available estimates of the distribution of approximately 2,000 local cable-only television channels as of 1988, excluding another 2,000 or so automatic-only channels. As few as 1,000 out of the 8,500 systems in the United States actually have local channels. Many of these, however, have two or more channels.

Most *public access channels* are services provided by the cable operator or the community on a first come, first served basis. Program content is not controlled by the cable operator, but the system often supplies all the facilities, equipment and frequently the production staff to aid community members in preparing and recording programs. Many of these channels operate part-time. Other public access channels are leased by a community group and operated entirely by the community. Such *access centers* have some full-time employees,

Table 12-2 Estimated Weekly Hours
of Programming

TYPE OF SERVICE	TOTAL U.S. HOURS PROGRAMMING/WEEK
Public Access:	
New	4,436
Imported	1,552
Educational:	
New	2,122
Imported	2,388
Governmental:	
New	1,736
Imported	390
Total	12,624 (estimated)

their own facilities and equipment and train their own staff and community members in production techniques. The cable operator then supplies only the feed (a **backfeed line**) from the access studios to the cable headend and may supply some engineering assistance.

Educational and *governmental access channels* are those operated by local institutions—the schools or the municipal government. Educational channels are usually programmed by college or high-school students and carry a variety of news and entertainment programs produced by the students. They may also distribute instructional programs to elementary and secondary schools or around a college campus. Governmental access channels generally carry only public meetings and political debates. Typically, they are operated by a small paid staff who runs the equipment and schedules replays of the meetings.

Local origination channels are those programmed by the cable operator, generally as advertising vehicles as well as community services. These commonly contain entertainment programs, news or classified advertising. Lastly, *leased access channels* are primarily commercial operations, leased from the cable operator for local sports, classified advertising (run often by a newspaper) or other for-profit or not-for-profit purposes. Many leases are indeed part-time, allowing one channel to serve many functions at different hours.

Altogether, PEG, LO and leased access channels across the country supply nearly 34,000 hours of programming weekly (including replays). Of that total about 12,624 hours each week are newly produced programs or newly imported to the community (see Table 12-2). Sharing of programs ("importing") among access producers in different communities is widely encouraged. Of course, many communities lack all of such services while a few have several channels, and the amount of newly produced programming varies widely from service to service. Nonetheless, local cable-only programming has grown from an insignificant outlet for a few participants to something of value to many members of the community in the cities and towns where it has survived.

LO BY CABLE OPERATORS

In keeping with its principle of *localism* in the regulation of broadcasting, in 1972 the FCC issued regulations requiring cable operators to provide programming to the community of franchise. All but the smallest systems were required to provide local programming "to a significant extent." Many cable operators reluctantly provided facilities and originated programming—though most preferred to limit cable service to delivery of broadcast signals, superstations and national cable-only networks. In the 1970s, much LO programming therefore consisted of whatever could be acquired for the lowest cost per-screen-minute. Initially, cable operators saw no advantage to supporting production and sales efforts. Two factors altered this posture—franchise renewal and advertising revenue—and they continued to be important to cable operators even after the courts overturned this federal requirement in 1979.

Franchise Renewal and Public Image

LO has become a way large cable systems might *narrowcast*, that is, reach narrow, specific-interest groups within the community. As program quality improved, and LO producers and programmers learned what kinds of programs and approaches were successful, LO demonstrated that cable could originate programming that met needs not filled by other media. Some MSOs, such as ATC and Warner Cable, committed their systems to providing LO as a way of serving their franchise communities and defending against cable's technological competitors. STV, MDS and DBS services could not match the subscriber-orientation evident in effective LO programming.

The wave of *franchise renewals* in the late 1970s and early 1980s introduced a strong rationale for operator-supported LO and access services, especially where active challenges to the current franchisee occurred. MSOs could promise to upgrade their LO facilities and expand their programming in order to foster support for renewing their franchises. A few MSOs even promised financial and equipment support for public access channels (this occurred in some college towns such as Bloomington, Indiana, and major cities such as Boston, Cincinnati and Pittsburgh). Cable operators now make localism an asset. A daily schedule of six or more hours of LO, including some local production, is a visible commitment to the community appreciated by subscribers and local government. This image becomes especially valuable in markets where subscribers are angered by rapid rises in monthly subscription rates and deteriorated customer service. Nationally, then, the pressure to renew franchises and build positive public images aided in the survival of many LO and access services. Another impetus was the lure of advertising revenue.

Advertising Revenue

By 1988, the annual advertising revenue generated by cable systems offering spot advertising (mostly major-market **interconnects**) exceeded $5.50 per subscriber. Most ad revenue comes from spots on the popular *basic* cable networks (ESPN, MTV, USA and others), but about 20 percent of all systems also accept advertising on *local* origination channels. (Rates vary from as low as

$2 to as much as $250 for 30-second spot time.) The success of the national cable-only networks in gaining advertising indirectly benefited local cable-only services. It increased cable's general visibility with advertisers, encouraged advertisers to take advantage of cable's flexibility and low cost and improved local facilities where they were used to produce local spots. Local cable-only programming is now valued for providing the most flexible vehicle for local spot advertising and for creating close advertising ties between sponsor and community.

LO Production, Syndication and Networking

LO production copies many of the strategies of commercial broadcasting, albeit on a very small scale. For example, LO programmers tend to select programs that are *broadly* appealing so as to attract the largest possible audiences for advertisers (although these audiences remain miniscule by broadcast standards). Because cable networks with broadly appealing content get higher ratings than narrowly appealing channels (see chapters 9 and 10), LO programmers copy this strategy in hopes that it applies to LO channels. The number of hours programmed is also on the rise, with many LO channels going from half-day to full schedules of 8 to 12 or more hours. A regularly available and predictable service is more promotable and more likely to attract an audience than a sporadic and unpredictable one.

U.S. Cable of Lake County in Waukegan, Illinois, for example, cablecasts over 80 hours of LO per week. The most-viewed programs are a 30-minute sports talk show, an auto racing program, health programs and local sporting events. Cable 6 of San Francisco cablecasts "the only regularly scheduled prime-time television program dealing with arts and entertainment in San Francisco" and *Lovestyles,* a half-hour late-night show dealing with concerns of the gay community. In Oklahoma City, Cox Cable televises the local rodeo as well as the Stars' ice hockey games. The ad availabilities in both programs are sold out. In several systems, a video dating service is the most popular local-only program.

In two small southern California beach towns, ML Media (an MSO) supplies a highly popular channel combining LO, access and classified advertising. The access/LO programming appears in the evenings, piggybacked on the money-making classified ads in the daytime. The service operates on an annual budget of about $65,000 and attracts a constant stream of community and student volunteers and interested viewers. The channel is more viewed than many access/LO channels, in part because of nature of the towns and because it is assigned to Channel 10 (VHF), a position that encourages sampling.

Many cable operators produce a local comedy show or a "teen scene" program. Local news updates inserted into CNN or Headline and local weather forecasts inserted into The Weather Channel are also common forms of LO. The ATC system in Ithaca, New York, and American Heritage Cablevision in Council Bluffs, Iowa, for example, originate daily half-hour newscasts on weeknights. On Long Island, Rainbow Programming Enterprises (a division of Cablevision Systems Corporation, a large MSO) made one of the biggest investments to date in local cable-only programming. In 1986 it created the first

24-hour local cable news service, *News 12 Long Island,* investing $6 million in equipment, crew, reporters and studios in a cable-only news operation distributed only on Long Island. This advertiser-supported basic service concentrates on news events on Long Island, using a staff of 100 people and facilities rivaling nearby regional broadcast stations.

Such programs indicate that cable is easily and (relatively) cheaply adapted to serve the community in ways that other media cannot because their costs are significantly higher. Low-power broadcast television (**LPTV**), a new class of broadcast station with signal coverage of less than 10 miles, has the potential of becoming cable's only direct competitor, but as yet, few LPTV stations are operational. Cable programmers have learned to make localism an asset to both advertisers and subscribers. Production quality, however, affects audience appeal, and as with all television, well-produced LO costs money. To recover expenses, therefore, LO productions must have broad appeal, a characteristic often at odds with localism.

As with other mass media, popular LO programming is eventually "networked" to a larger audience. A fundamental media distribution principle holds that programming has the lowest per-unit cost when it reaches a *mass* audience. Some LO programs have been popular enough to follow this pattern. Coproductions by the Cox Cable System and the Grumbacher Paint Co., for example, were distributed over 62 Cox systems. The program was a six-part series on art instruction, and it included promotion of a paint kit available by direct mail (from the sales of which Cox received a percentage). Thus this cable programming reached a very specialized audience by *networking* and so multiplied its producers' profits. Shopping services, as described in Chapter 10, have followed this pattern, commonly offering a percentage of sales to cable operators as an incentive for carriage. Small-scale independent producers and manufacturers wishing to feature their products increasingly syndicate or barter programs to LO programmers who have access to regional networks of cable systems.

LO is on its way to becoming a more specialized version of a commercial independent broadcast station. It relies on the most popular entertainment forms such as sports and music; purchases and barters syndicated material of established appeal; produces some local programming of high visibility within the community; and builds an advertising clientel among local businesses. Syndication of LO programs has become another potential revenue source for some MSOs.

Program Shorts

A rising cable-related business concentrates on syndicating packages of very short programs, some as brief as 30 seconds, called **interstitial programming.** Used singly and in groups, these **shorts** serve as filler between odd-length programs to complete an hour. Although travel-related companies, tourist offices and the U.S. government (especially the Departments of Defense and Labor), supply some of this programming gratis, commercial firms are producing an increased number of shorts especially for cable television because the market is much greater than in broadcasting. LO programmers license large amounts of such interstitial programming when budgets permit. The appetite for off-beat, original shorts appears to be growing, fueled in part by the generally higher quality of professionally-produced programming over **in-house** productions. Shorts provide a breather for audiences as well as a national outlet for independent filmmakers. The content and style of shorts varies from silent, single camera walks in an autumn forest to zany cartoons using pinched-clay figures. Music videos are themselves a form of short programming.

Shorts of all kinds remain popular with audiences, however, so suppliers market them to cable systems. Sometimes shorts are sequenced together to form half-hour features on LO channels—much as music videos are linked to form full-length programming. The trade press publishes monthly lists of syndicated shorts available to LO and access programmers.

ACCESS CHANNELS

Cable's channel capacity provides an opportunity for "people's television," a way for relatively small groups to gain access to the nation's most popular entertainment and information medium. **Access,** in cable television, is both a means of giving a small group a sense of identity and a means for providing them with a channel of communication to the larger community. Television helps special interest groups reinforce their common interest and relate their purpose to others—in effect, to become a recognized entity in the information culture. The common bond of these access user-groups might be age, ethnic background, political cause, intellectual interest or hobby. Minority groups, environmentalists, antiwar activists, readers of Tolstoy, model railroad club members, off-road racers and a myriad of special interest groups all want to be on television.

A cable system can dedicate a whole channel to access or piggyback access on an LO channel. In practice, deregulation combined with scant program budgets and undependable volunteer staffs have reduced PEG channels to a *hybrid community access service* in most cities.

Community Access

The FCC's 1972 PEG rules dramatically enlarged the way local franchise authorities envisioned what cable service could do for their communities. They also elicited a flood of dull, amateurish television productions and set up an adversary relationship between cable operators and access groups that lasted well into the 1980s.

Classic public access channels made some cablecast time and equipment available free on a *first-come, first-served* basis. Production support and technical facilities were available at an at-cost rate for additional time, and most access operations also offered instruction in the rudiments of studio and field electronic video production. Thus, in the 1970s, candidates for local public office often used access channels because no requirements for equal time applied. Independent filmmakers and video artists used the channels for their productions though much of this work was essentially personal rather than public communication. Some individuals undertook regularly-scheduled series. The most notorious was perhaps *The Ugly George Show* on New York City's Manhattan Cable. Host Ugly George approached women on the street and asked them to take off their clothes for his camera. Enough did so to give public access a vulgar image among both viewers and policymakers.

Only about five percent of the public access airtime of the 1970s was actually planned, produced and scheduled programming. Most was material that might be best classified as home movies by local producers or lengthy rap sessions. Public access programming, in fact, was viewed mostly by its principal participants. For example, in one study, a videotaped replay of a senior citizens dance was shown to be viewed almost exclusively by persons who attended the dance.[2] This systematic study of the audience for a well-run and promoted public access channel in a small city with no local television broadcasting showed an average weekly audience share of less than two-tenths of 1 percent.

In short, the concept of *unstructured* public access really never took off. It failed to attract groups willing to submit to the organizational discipline necessary for success in any mass medium—clear purpose, cost and equipment control and a coherent plan of audience appeal. Without these, and with growing disenchantment among policymakers and cable operators, it was clear access had to take a different line of development.

In 1979, the Supreme Court forced the issue in the *Midwest II* decision holding that the FCC's 1972 PEG requirements violated a section of the 1934 Communications Act holding that broadcasters and, by extension, cablecasters are not common carriers.[3] Cable operators could not be required by federal regulation to carry programming over which they had no say. The 1984 Cable Act, however, left a loophole for local access requirements, and most franchise agreements negotiated in the 1980s make some provision for public access channels, now more broadly referred to as **community access channels.** Either the cable operator makes the facilities and equipment available (under the direction of an access programmer) or some nonprofit group in the community, such as the municipal public library, an appointed council of access users, the school or hospital board, leases a channel from the cable company and manages the access operation. These are commonly called **access centers.** Under either structure the users must abide by the operator's policies concerning use of cablecasting facilities and cable time. The access center management retains some discretionary authority over content and scheduling, but generally continues the tradition of first-come, first-served in requests for production aid and program replay.

Most community access channels and centers have strict policies prohibiting cablecasting of commercial or sectarian material. At the same time, all other access messages, however controversial or offensive, are protected by the First Amendment guarantee of free speech (if delivered in a nonviolent manner and not obscene or beyond local limits on nudity). By federal law, local cable operators and city officials cannot allow some shows on access channels and refuse others. This puts them on the hot seat when neo-Nazis, racists or, on the other side, antigovernment groups seek to use access channels to air unpopular views. Most cable access programmers rush to "balance" their offerings when they see controversial programs coming. Nonetheless, the public, irrespective of political and social views, has the right to speak openly on access channels.

Models for Access Success

As with LO, exceptionally successful examples of access programs and access operations suggest viable directions for the future in programming and operating models. Community access programming's singular characteristic is localism, often to the level of "neighborhoodism." A number of reports describe the organization, policies and programming of thriving community access operations, but as one might expect, they take on the particular interests and emphases of their communities.[4] Four general characteristics have emerged, however, that provide a model for community access programming:

1. *Broad Community Support.*   Viable access operations usually enjoy the backing of city officials, cable system officers, community institutions, volunteer groups and, most importantly, subscribers. This coalition quite often convinces the city to turn over a sizable portion of the cable franchise fee to the access channel and enlists the support of persons knowledgeable in the arts, business, sports and public service. This money and expertise, in turn, help the access channel operators cover local events and issues with reasonable technical and conceptual quality. Such programming does attract a small, interested audience and is recognized as a worthwhile public service. At its best, access television provides the clearest example of localism in the electronic media, and it benefits subscribers, user groups and the cable operator.

2. *Consortium Approach.*   Community access operators typically see themselves as facilitators of community interaction, not as imitators of low-budget independent television. The access operator prefers to provide live coverage of a public discussion on a local zoning issue, for example, rather than produce a documentary on zoning problems. Access channels tend to be communications resources for the community, not production centers. Thus, creating viable access programming involves (a) helping community groups form consortia and (b) helping them integrate television communication into their own quite specific activities and interests.

3. *Live, Involved Programming.*   Successful access operators accentuate their community service function by **live,** full-length telecasting of significant meetings of local legislative bodies, advisory councils, school boards, community groups and other such deliberations on community business. Recognizing the importance of such coverage in a democracy, some city councils allow persons watching at home to participate by phone in the televised public discussion or to make an appearance using split-screen presentation from a neighborhood access studio.

Such live, interactive community programming is not likely to be duplicated by any other media services and, during debate of important community topics, commands a measurable share of the cable television audience. Such programming gives access a clearly defined and positive image in subscribers' minds and becomes a selling point for basic cable service.

Conversely, programming generic how-to shows, frequent repeats and lengthy blocks of viewer-requested replays dilutes the subscribers' notion of access programming's value. Many community access channels are overly dependent on just such programming.

4. *Regular Programming Service.* Although the philosophy of access television includes the notion that individuals should, on their own terms, be able to address the television audience, sequences of unrelated, stand-alone presentations cannot build audience loyalty and often alienate drop-in viewers. Access programming builds support with coherent, thematic, predictably scheduled programs and video services. This approach may smack of commercialism to access purists, but the experience of *successful* access operations indicates that what works in commercial and public television broadcasting and cable networking also works for access. Regular, predictable service is crucial to obtaining listings in local newspapers and guides to help viewers find the programs they want to see.

A successful access operation also needs the same components—though perhaps in lesser measure—that an LO or instructional video facility has, and additionally, needs a staff that can work effectively with a wide range of community institutions. Such an operation costs money; a sizable amount of capital is needed just to begin operation. An adequately equipped, industrial-quality access facility needs about $300,000 in electronics and about 6,000 square feet of secure space convenient to the public and served by *backfeed* lines to the cable headend.[5] A well-equipped operation that can easily support multiple projects needs three times that amount of money and space.

Salaries, rent, maintenance, repair and expendables for a minimum access operation—one that is heavily dependent on *volunteers*—cost about $90,000 a year. More typical access facilities have about eight full-time employees and annual operating budgets of $350,000 a year. Many failed access centers tried to start small and then grow, not realizing that an initial *critical mass* of capital and committed personnel was needed. Others started successfully but could not develop sources of funding to replace grant monies used for initial equipment and operating funds. Video production, even by volunteers (and sometimes especially by volunteers) is expensive, and the most common way of holding costs down is to cablecast exchange or syndicated programming. Such programming, more and more tangential to the original idea of access, illustrates how access programming is growing indistinguishable from LO programming.

Access centers have been aided by other recent changes in the television industry. Portable equipment required to produce video recordings of acceptable quality cost $10,000 to $20,000 in the 1970s. Moreover, maintenance was expensive, and the equipment was cumbersome to use. This equipment was popular in educational institutions and industry but impractical and too expensive for consumer use. Someone wanting to record an event, therefore, went to an access center to use its portable field equipment, often for what were essentially private events. Then along came the VHS **camcorder,** a popular consumer replacement of the home movie camera in the mid-1980s. The camcorder is compact, cordless, easy to use and maintain and costs about $1,100. Video production with privately owned or rented camcorders has now become commonplace, so access centers no longer need to equip and train all one-time-only video producers. This development helped to free access programmers to focus on the needs of viewers and the community. It is still the case, however, that most access center volunteers need extended training to operate video equipment. Training remains, then, a major component of access service.

In addition, since 1976 the National Federation of Local Cable Programmers (**NFLCP**) has coordinated the efforts of access managers and users, circulating programs and information and providing leadership and training. The NFLCP conducts regional and national meetings and conferences, just as commercial trade associations do, though on a small scale.

Educational and Governmental Access

The terms *educational* and *governmental access* are also holdovers from the 1972 *Cable Television Third Report and Order* in which the FCC mandated such access (**PEG**) channels. As required in the 1970s, cable systems offered reserved channels (**dedicated**) to both local school boards and local government. In most cases these institutions did not utilize the channels. Public or community access groups rather than government itself cablecast government meetings; and school districts interested in using television in their classrooms had already developed distribution systems—by broadcasting, microwave or videocassette. The *Midwest II* decision legally confirmed the real situation in the schools and government offices—the availability of a dedicated access channel did not usually mean implementation of access television.

By the mid-1980s, however, in some cities where access had failed and LO service was poor, municipal governments had taken over operation of their own channels as a part of franchise renegotiation. These include several cities in southern California, such as Lakewood, Norwalk and Placentia, that now successfully cablecast public meetings. Columbus, Ohio, is another city with big-budget access operations. Subscriber fees support three public access services in Columbus, one a governmental access channel. It has a budget in excess of $250,000 and originates a full schedule of public forums, political debates and city and county business meetings.

Notable exceptions on the school side are worth mentioning too, because they illustrate the possibilities for educational narrowcasting. An impressively planned and engineered cable loop in Spokane, Washington, links classrooms, homes and headend, carrying a set of cable channels dedicated to instructional use.[6] Students at home are linked to the classroom, standardized in-class materials are cablecast throughout the unified school district's classrooms, and students can do assigned home viewing or view repeats of classroom materials during evening hours. Such a system provides a model reflecting a well-organized school administration, an enthusiastic faculty and a service-oriented cable operator. "Homework Hotlines" have proved so popular they now exist on many cable systems across the country, sponsored by local schools.

Medical schools have developed similar cable loops with hospitals and clinics to instruct both medical practitioners and patients. In general, however, few schools and colleges operate educational channels. They use cable as they use broadcasting, for distribution of specific continuing education courses or series programming such as *Civilization* that might be of value to classroom viewers.

Leased Access

A leased channel is one turned over to another entity to program, either as a subscriber service or as an advertising vehicle. Leased channels account for less than 10 percent of all cable channels and occur, in most cases, in the larger markets. Most systems provide *no* leased access, but large capacity systems often provide at least one channel for lease. Systems with a small number of channels lack space for leased channels, and franchise agreements only rarely require leased access. In addition to leased access centers, shopping, sports and *security* services, however, have shown positive audience reaction, making them viable leased channel concepts. *Classified advertising* is also proving a big success on some leased channels.

Leased access channels raise the issue of whether cable is a common carrier or a publisher with full First Amendment protections. The requirement of leased access suggests a common carrier model, and in consequence, the cable industry opposes it. Optional **commercial leasing** allows the cable operator to form joint publishing ventures on one or more channels, thereby establishing itself as a publishing entity, presumably with the same rights as newspapers or other retail businesses. Although a forced leasing contract can supply exactly the same content as an optional leasing arrangement, it is the optional arrangement that clearly establishes the cable operator's intention to be a publisher or retail business.

Access Syndication

Satellite-delivered programming (called **access syndication** or *imported* programming) is on the verge of becoming an option for most access programmers. Initiated by a volunteer group in New York called Paper Tiger TV, the *Deep Dish TV* project in 1985 and 1986 created the first public-access satellite network, available to local cable programmers without charge. Access programmers needed only to locate a local receiving dish (usually supplied by the local cable operator) to downlink the programs. *Deep Dish TV* consisted of a theme-oriented ten-part series, assembled from hundreds of videotapes made available by access programmers across the country. Although the network folded after a year or so of operation, it created an appetite for national syndication of access shows, increasingly being shared today through interest groups across wide regions, though mostly by "bicycle," not satellite so far. Paper Tiger TV was able to reactivate the Deep Dish TV network in 1988, supplying a weekly hour of access programming by satellite.

SCHEDULING LOCAL CABLE-ONLY CHANNELS

The programming goals of a local cable channel are similar to those of a broadcast station: to acquire and produce programs appealing to a target audience. Scheduling goals are also similar: to develop as broad, loyal and large an audience as possible. The challenge for cable programmers is to achieve these goals under franchise, economic and competitive constraints. Franchise contracts often require cablecasting programs of very limited appeal. Budgets, facilities and numbers of personnel scarcely compare to those of the smallest independent television stations. And the rest of the channel array offers programs of the highest quality and popularity with which LO and access must compete for audience attention.

Block Programming

Local cable's strengths, however, can overcome some of these problems. Because of its time flexibility, LO and access channels can carry live, local events such as public meetings and sports events of unpredictable length. The timing of *live* programming of course depends on the producers or authorities actually in charge of the event—the cable programmer cannot usually influence it. But the audience such coverage draws can be maintained by scheduling related, pretaped programming *before* or *after* the live event, using a **block** programming strategy. Cablecasting of a school board meeting might be preceded by a documentary on local school planning or a syndicated program dealing with education. In the same manner, a football coaching film might follow a live high school football contest. These related, taped shows can easily be repeated with the repeat cablecast of the originally live event and promoted jointly.

Repeat Scheduling

Repeat scheduling is an essential narrowcasting strategy for LO and access as well as the national cable networks—and even public television as explained in chapters 17 and 18. On local cable, Friday night's game, for example, should be recablecast at a fixed, predictable time and promoted on the air and in a program guide so interested viewers who could neither attend nor view the live coverage can watch the later telecast. LO and access scheduling practices seek *cumulative* rather than one-time-only audiences.

Cherrypicked Channels

When live coverage is a large part of the schedule, some cable programmers use another programming strategy. They schedule a potpourri of unrelated but individually interesting programs, similar to the format strategy of some public radio stations. (See Chapter 19 on eclectic radio.) Selecting among cable networks, syndicators and local programs is called **cherrypicking,** as described in Chapter 9. Such a channel offers a kind of curious surprise for the viewer, a jumbled toy-box of programs. Manhattan Cable in New York mixes sports, movies, inspirational and access programming into a single channel, and promotes the composite as "WWW," giving it a stationlike identity.

Instead, then, of programming an LO or access channel with a narrow range of programs giving it a distinct, uniform identity, cable programmers may schedule on the basis of individual program appeal, availability and community interest. Such an approach seeks *surprise* rather than *audience flow.* On-air graphics and promotional copy during breaks give such a local cable channel its visual identity. As Smith points out in Chapter 19, this program concept is quite difficult to master. It depends on great knowledge of the audience and greater sensitivity to nuances in program content than other programming strategies.

Program suppliers also have reservations about cherrypicking. They worry that their carefully targeted programs will be scheduled among incompatible shows, discouraging audience flow, or that viewers will not be able to find their offerings within the scheduling hodgepodge. Most local cable channel schedules are neither published nor listed on a menu channel. Moreover, networks offer co-op advertising, sales guarantees and other incentives usually only to those cable systems carrying the network's entire schedule without time shifts or preemption. In consequence, extended cherrypicking is rare on local cable.

EVALUATING LO PROGRAMMING

As with broadcast programming, peer recognition and viewer response indicate cable programming success. Public acknowledgments— through awards, for example—signal critical and peer approval and provide recognition for specific programs and channels. They are also useful ammunition for the cable system at franchise renewal time.

Ace Awards

The cable industry recognizes excellence in programming with its annual Ace Awards, presented at the Cable Software Symposium & Exposition, sponsored by the National Cable Television Association (**NCTA**). Like an Oscar (film), Emmy (broadcast television) or Clio (advertising), an **Ace** is awarded for superior effort to programs, actors or producers (or other behind-the-scenes talent) in numerous categories, including "community programming" and "excellence in local programming" as well as "national programming," "cable-television advertising" and so on. The National Federation of Local Cable Programmers (NFLCP) also acknowledges outstanding community programming with annual Home Town awards.

Subscriber Feedback

Cable systems want information on the number and characteristics of their viewers for two reasons: to program better for them and to aid in selling advertising spots. As pointed out in Chapter 2, Arbitron and Nielsen television rating services do not report audiences with an average overall rating of less than 1 percent of all the available television homes in the market. Typically, 50 percent or more of the homes in an NSI (Nielsen) or TSA (Arbitron) are cabled, but local cable programs practically never show up in the rating reports advertising agencies use, and commissioning independent audience studies to measure local cable audiences on nonaddressable systems is prohibitively expensive.

However, other measures of response can indicate the approximate size and interest level of a local cable audience. The viewer response to *discount coupons* or other *incentives* announced only on an LO channel is a fair gauge of the size and characteristics of that LO audience. The number and street addresses of respondents to per-inquiry advertising can be compared with responses to ads broadcast over radio or television. Local retailers can report the size of their store traffic before and after using LO advertising. Finally, old-fashioned "cards and letters" from supporters and critics offer unsystematic guidance about current programming. They can reveal what a local cable audience wants to see and how they want it scheduled.

Local cable audience measurement, then, is much like very small-market radio. Anecdotal and testimonial data must be sought out to convince advertisers to buy time. And both access and LO programmers must instigate direct feedback from the audience to get a sense of the community's program and schedule preferences.

ANCILLARY SERVICES

Cable operators are developing a wide range of ancillary services as supplementary revenue sources, adding to the monthly fees from cable television subscribers. In-house production of advertising spots and training tapes has been successful for systems with top-quality facilities. Leasing their production facilities is another option. In addition, systems are introducing ancillary program services—dividing into those intended for the general public (all cable subscribers) on a free or pay basis, and those intended only for closed user groups. Cable radio and teletext, for example, are for all who want them and are willing to pay for them; subsidiary services for businesses are private. Leased channels may be either type. For many of these extra services, the cable programmer serves as supervisor or administrator.

Although the economics of ancillary services are just developing, there are at present three payment models. In one pattern, the cable operator carries a service to increase basic subscriber rolls and returns a percentage of the monthly subscriber fee to the service supplier. Teletext follows this pattern. In another model, the cable operator leases a channel for a monthly fee, and the lessor programs the channel and promotes it among subscribers. Shopping services, newspaper headlines and classified advertising and security services usually follow this model. In a third pattern, an entity leases the channel for a monthly fee but does not market to the general public; it uses the channel to communicate private information (such as findings in the day's court hearings). If the system is not addressable, then this kind of information must be scrambled so that it can be used only by those people with decoders; if addressable, security is assured by sending the private channel only to those "drops" the leasing entity intends to reach. Ancillary services must be divided, then, according to their intended audience and according to their payment method. The cable programmer typically plays a central role in pay services intended for the general subscribership and a minor role in private services.

Cable Radio

Cable radio, also called **cable audio** and **cable FM,** resembles cable television. Program suppliers use relay satellites to distribute music networks to local cable systems. The cable operator installs cable outlets for home stereo receivers for an installation charge and, sometimes, a small monthly audio subscription fee, on top of the regular monthly fee for basic television service. When systems offer cable radio as part of the franchise agreement, they usually carry only local **FM** radio stations. (Carrying **AM** stations generates engineering costs higher than subscribers want to pay; they must be shifted in both frequency and modulation to fit within cable television frequencies.) A *cable FM hookup* is technically just an additional *cable television hookup.* Operators have no way of monitoring how hookups are used, and subscribers may switch back and forth between television and stereo connections at will. TCI, the largest cable MSO, dropped monthly fees for additional hookups in 1987 on most of its systems, retaining instead only initial installation and monthly converter fees.

When systems offer cable radio, local FM stations often must be shifted for technical reasons to slightly different reception frequencies. This annoys listeners and makes promotion and audience research difficult for the radio broadcasters. Some cable operators, however, draw from national cable-only audio networks to create a marketable service. The four primary influences on cable television programming—legal, technical, economic and marketing—apply in theory to cable radio as well. Cable radio, however, is much less well developed as of the late 1980s than cable television, but many observers expect a modest parallel development in the 1990s.

On the legal side, no **carriage rules** exist; the choice of channels remains entirely with the cable programmer. But if an operator has offered cable radio in franchise negotiations to win the overall cable contract (or as a renewal concession), then the agreement may specify local radio station carriage. If so, the local stations are usually cablecast as a single technical entity and imported signals added on unoccupied frequencies.

The technical side of cable radio is changing rapidly. Although many cable operators deliver over-the-air broadcast radio signals and taped, syndicated audio services, the national audio networks are shifting to the new digital technology. Satellites relay digital audio at low cost to cable systems who in turn deliver the very high-fidelity signal in digital form to home receivers. Home Music Store, for example, uses digital technology to distribute seven channels of stereo music, each in a different format.

The economics of cable radio operate somewhat differently from the economics of cable television. At present, most audio suppliers (nonbroadcast signal distributors) offer cable systems whole sets of audio channels, each with an identifiable musical format, so that the whole package can be marketed as a unit. Because the cost of producing audio is so much less than video, suppliers typically offer many channels, and cable operators purchase the whole package. Subscribers then pay the cable system a monthly charge for cable radio service. Some networks provide time for local advertising sales and offer some promotional support. Satellite placement and signal importation fees also affect the economics of cable radio networks.

Cable radio can be a basic or premium service, and superstations already exist. Altogether, 17 basic and pay audio services are available to cable operators as of 1988.

1. Basic Cable Radio.   Two of the largest suppliers of cable FM music are WFMT-FM in Chicago and Lifestyle. WFMT-FM, a hybrid broadcast and cable service, programs fine arts radio, largely classical music and arts talk, 24 hours a day. WFMT-FM is called a **radio superstation** because it is satellite-relayed to cable systems across the United States by a common carrier (United Video). United Video recently began distributing KKGO, a "SuperJazz" station. Lifestyle, an instrumental, easy-listening, music-only service owned by United Video, is a digital audio signal programmed only for cable systems and is satellite-distributed. As of the late 1980s, WFMT reached about 850,000 homes, and Lifestyle reached 2 million. Cable operators pay United Video a fee for affiliation.

Like television superstations, cable FM superstations increase revenue by selling their advertising time at higher rates because they reach huge audiences. And because subscribers usually pay extra to receive cable radio service, they can be expected to listen to it. When cable radio becomes an important revenue-producing service, cable radio networks will acquire the same audience evaluation problems characterizing cable television. These problems are discussed in Chapters 2 and 9.

MSO Jones Intercable recently launched Jones Galactic Radio supplying seven radio formats to cable operators for their FM subscribers. The service includes several rock, country and jazz variations and a reading channel. At present it is offered free to cable subscribers, but it may shift to pay at a later time. Jones sells a maximum of 4 minutes of advertising per hour (56 minutes of music), carrying only national ads. Galactic Radio comes on Galaxy III (as one might guess!).

A single-channel jazz service, The Jazz Network, supported by a combination of advertising and operator fees, began operation in 1983. In addition, at least four services provide satellite-delivered religious audio programming for free to cable systems. The audio to Cable News Network (CNN) is marketed (for a fee) as CNN Audio and can be placed on cable radio as a 24-hour news channel. Other competitors are expected to rapidly swell the number of cable radio networks—including broadcast radio stations seeking 24-hour stereo outlets.

2. Premium Cable Radio.   Beginning in 1983, the Home Music Store offered its seven music channels as a tiered pay service (all seven channels for one monthly fee paid by the home subscriber). Its varied formats are transmitted digitally and converted to analog by home decoders. This unusual service lets subscribers record very high-quality musical selections at home.

On the marketing side, cable operators must consider the lift potential of cable radio service—in other words, whether cable radio services will increase cable television subscriber rolls. Currently, cable operators do not market radio service independently; subscribers must pay for basic cable television to take cable radio. The cable operator structures radio as an ancillary service to television, but cable systems may eventually employ separate radio programmers whose responsibilities will be entirely separate from those of the television programmer. As with cable television, advertiser appeals and overmarketing will become important considerations. Unlike cable television, the over-the-air radio industry has settled the question of whether most stations will have vertical or broad appeal. Broadcast radio is strictly a **narrowcast** (vertical-appeal) operation.

Leased Channels

Optional leased channels, those not required by a franchise agreement but offered at the discretion of the cable operator, are potential revenue producers for large cable systems with channels to spare. Only systems with 36 or more channels lease channels, and most systems lease none of their channels. The difference between other cable networks and the leased channels is that the leasing company, not the cable operator, administers the channel. These administrative duties include marketing, billing, collecting, advertising, promoting and customer relations, in addition to programming content.

Pay leased channels operate much like premium movie channels and *nonpay* leased channels like basic services. Many leased channels requiring subscribers fees are pay-per-view sports services; typically, they provide the games of a single team. In order for the leased channel to go only to paying subscribers, the cable system must have special "box combinations" (like *traps* in reverse) distributed to subscriber homes or must have addressable technology. For example, in the state of Washington, the Supersonics lease time on one channel on cable systems throughout the Puget Sound area for showing their basketball games. Only addressable systems or ones providing "box combination" security can participate. The Supersonics sell the right to view the cable channel like a season pass, so they have no churn. Other operators of pay leased channels charge a monthly fee, sometimes providing seasonal sports of several teams (see Chapter 10 on regional sports channels) or a mix of movies, sports and other syndicated programming.

Channels that are supported by advertising or a sponsor like a newspaper are open to all cabled homes and appear as basic cable services. Basic leased channels typically carry either shopping or religious content, and these are increasingly national services such as described in Chapter 10.

In addition to *national* shopping networks, the **local shopping service** is becoming a popular variant of the basic leased channel. A local department store or retail chain operator rents a channel from the cable system and programs whatever content it desires, generally a continuous run of demonstrations of products for sale. But such local shopping services fight an uphill battle to gain shelf space because the national shopping networks such as Home Shopping Network (HSN) can generate greater revenue for the cable operator by kicking back a percentage of sales. Two other types of leased operations occurring widely throughout the country and intended for the general audience are **text news channels** and **classified advertising channels.** Both of these are basic, nonpay services, clearly intended for all who will watch. Many of these channels are jointly operated by a local newspaper and the cable operator. Newspapers serving cabled rural areas usually want to lease a channel for classified advertising. Increasingly, cable MSOs participate as part-owners in such arrangements because of the legal advantages publishing provides and because of potential revenue.

Although from the point of view of government and the public, two types of optional leased channels exist—those for everybody and those for restricted groups—from the point of view of the cable operator, *profit participation* versus a *flat lease fee* is the issue. Those leasing agencies that can offer the cable system increased revenue as subscriber rolls increase are likely to command much more of the optional channel space than those that require long-term, fixed leasing agreements.

Teletext

Teletext commonly refers to signals sent on the vertical blanking interval of broadcast television stations to subscribers who pay for **decoders** (and in most cases, pay a monthly fee for the service). Cable systems can create their own teletext service or license syndicated services. Teletext has advertising potential. The subscriber can switch from broadcast channels to teletext to get additional information on advertising appearing in the broadcast frame—or to find a classified advertisement. For example, car advertisers can purchase teletext ads amplifying their brief, 30-second on-air spots that would be of interest primarily to people wanting to buy a new car. Extravision, for example, was a local classified advertising service using teletext, reached by switching from the local CBS affiliate to the Extravision decoder. It was programmed by the affiliate (except for a minimum number of ads supplied by CBS). CBS's role in Extravision was largely to develop the technology, clarify the economics and market the service to its affiliates. However, Extravision was withdrawn in 1984 after weak affiliate and advertiser response.

Cable systems can also license national teletext services from syndicators such as Southern Satellite Systems (SSS). This common carrier distributes a teletext service by satellite relay on the vertical blanking interval of WTBS, the superstation described in Chapter 10. Teletext can be given a dedicated channel on a cable system, requiring no decoders, or decoders can be sold to subscribers so they can switch between WTBS and the teletext service. The future of teletext appears problematic to date as neither advertisers nor affiliates have rushed to participate.

Videotex

Videotex differs from teletext in that it is a fully interactive data service, requiring a full 6 mHz channel on a cable system and access to a personal or mainframe computer. Subscribers commonly interact with videotex via telephone lines; when received on an unoccupied cable channel, the term **cable-text** applies. Coaxial cable operates faster and more accurately than telephone lines, thus having a distinct advantage for computer users. On cable, videotex is typically a pay service that subscribers purchase directly from software suppliers such as CompuServe, Dow Jones and The Source, which program news and information databases intended for businesses and the general public. If a cable operator supplies a dedicated channel for such a videotex service, the supplier receives a portion of the subscriber's monthly fee (or charges an additional small fee beyond the videotex service operator's fee). More recently, XPress, Lotus' Signal and other companies began supplying data delivery for cable, with ownership participation by cable MSOs. XPress, for example, uses an FM frequency for downloading to IBM personal computers with specialized modems. It supplies text-only content in a broad range from news to specialized statistical databases. Tele-Communications Inc. (TCI), the largest cable MSO, has a financial interest in the service and supplies it on some of its cable systems. Generally, only systems with 45 or more channels can spare a channel for such a limited use, although as the number of homes with personal computers grows, services targeting these subscribers become another potential revenue stream for the 1990s.

Subsidiary Services

Other ancillary cable services are also for limited groups of subscribers. The difference between most videotex and other subsidiary services is that the latter are typically for private businesses or organizations, and their information has to be secure from unauthorized use. Chain retailers, for example, can lease cable channels to distribute information to their local outlets; Sears and J.C. Penney are considering this option. Large businesses can distribute information from their headquarters to local offices, related businesses and their subscribers, such as stock and commodity listings from Dow Jones to local brokers, farm wholesalers and farmers.[7] Corporations relying on common databases for sales or quick rate changes can also benefit from satellite relay from national headquarters to local offices and plants. Insurance agents, for example, need access to regional or national mainframe computers to determine rates and rapidly list new registrants; using telephone lines for this purpose is expensive and the service of low quality. Cable systems with enough capacity can afford to lease bandwidth for such private use.

TRENDS IN LOCAL CABLE PROGRAMMING

Though the technologies, users and policies affecting LO and access services are rapidly changing, current practices point the way to future developments. Local productions will improve in quality and increase in number; the expansion of advertiser-support and pinpointing of narrow target audiences will determine the kind of programming produced. Programs originating from access groups or centers will increasingly be intermixed with programming the cable operator produces locally. LO programmers will need to use sophisticated programming strategies to attract and hold a salable audience share against competition from local independent broadcasters, LPTV and cable network programming. One strategy will be to aggressively seek LO program listings in local newspaper supplements and guides. Independent producers and

advertising agencies will develop a variety of informational, interstitial and series programming for LO and some access services. Successful local cable programs will be networked among MSOs, regions and user groups. MSOs will
form subsidiary production companies for creating and syndicating LO programming. LO and ancillary services will be critically managed and evaluated
in terms of net profit to the cable system.

MSOs will shuffle the configuration of cable-based services based on
profitability. Deregulation of cable will allow more experimentation with new
forms of commercial messages, direct catalog sales, shop-at-home marketing,
co-production and barter arrangements on LO channels. This high level of activity holds the promise of large numbers of jobs for recent college graduates
with a willingness to participate in the development of new cable programming.

SUMMARY

Local cable-only programming divides into two broad types: that
produced by the cable operator (LO) and that produced by some community
group (access). The federally-mandated access channels of the 1970s (PEG)
have been transformed into local community access channels, some of which
are stand-alone leased access centers, but most are becoming hybrid LO/access
services. Today, the viewer can rarely distinguish the source of a program,
though the distinction between LO and access has historical and often ideological importance. Local cable-only programming is partly supported by advertising and provides cable subscribers with long-form and highly localized programming not available on other cable or broadcast services. MSOs generally
support local cable-only services to create positive local service images, aiding
franchise renewal, and to sell local advertising spots. Access programmers
have located four elements that characterize successful access services: broad
support, consortiums, live programs and regular scheduling. Scheduling of
local cable-only follows some of broadcasting's principles, including block programming, repeats and cherrypicking. Networking and syndication are processes driving local cable away from its roots in localism because of their efficiency. Ancillary services are a growing part of local cable, and in the 1990s,
services such as cable radio may follow the pattern of cable television. Optional
leased channels are increasingly providing a source of revenue participation for
cable systems through shopping channels and security services. Videotex and
other closed-user group services are finding places on the very largest cable
systems with spare capacity because they also generate revenue.

Notes

1. Cable Communications Act of 1984, Sec. 611. See the Practicing Law Institute's *Cable Television: Retrospective and Prospective* (New York: Practicing Law Institute, Gary L. Christensen,
Chairman, 1985).

2. Kenneth Ksobiech and others, *The Columbus Video Access Center: A Research Analysis of
Public Reaction* (Bloomington, Ind.: Institute for Communication Research, 1975), pp. 45–51.

3. *FCC v. Midwest Video Corp.*, 440 U.S. 689 (1979).

4. *Access Operating Rules & Procedures* (Washington, D.C.: National Federation Local Cable Programmers, 1983). See also C. J. Hirschfield, "An Innocuous Concept Becomes a Hot Issue: Leased Access," *View*, May 1982, pp. 131–132, and Judith Reitman, "Paying Back the Community," *Cable Marketing*, October 1986, pp. 28–34.

5. A backfeed line uses a separate coaxial cable between the point of video origination and the headend on one-way cable systems. Signals are carried to the headend on a frequency other than that on which they are cablecast in order to avoid interference. See also Midge Pierce, "LO: A Question of Balance," *Cable Television Business*, September 1, 1986, pp. 28–33.

6. Cox Cable TV in Spokane, Washington, is a 35-channel system with six channels set aside for educational access use.

7. Susan Tyler Eastman, "Policy Issues Raised by the FCC's 1983 and 1984 Subcarrier Decisions," *Journal of Broadcasting* 28, Summer 1984, pp. 289–303.

Selected Sources

Cable Strategies, a monthly trade magazine covering local cable operations and management, including community access services. Englewood, Colo., 1986 to date.

Community Television Review. Bimonthly newsletter covering access and local origination programming. Washington, D.C.: National Federation of Local Cable Programmers, 1979 to date.

Forbes, Dorothy, and Layng, Sanderson. *The New Communicators: A Guide to Community Programming*. Washington, D.C.: Communications Press, 1980.

Hollowell, Mary Louise, ed. *The Cable/Broadband Communications Book, Vol. 3, 1982–83*. Washington, D.C.: Communications Press, 1983.

Jesuale, Nancy, ed., with Smith, Ralph Lee. *The Community Medium, Vol. 1*. Arlington, Va.: Cable Television Information Center, 1982.

Oringel, Robert S. *The Access Management's Handbook: A Guide for Managing Community Television*. Boston: Focal Press, 1987.

Paper Tiger TV. *Deep Dish Directory*. New York: Paper Tiger TV, 1986.

Parsons, Patrick. *Cable Television and the First Amendment*. Lexington, Mass.: Lexington Books, 1987.

Shaffer, William Drew, and Wheelwright, Richard. *Creating Original Programming for Cable TV*. Washington, D.C.: National Federation of Local Cable Programmers, 1983.

PART FOUR / COMMERCIAL BROADCAST
RADIO STRATEGIES

Part Four of this book looks at radio. Although the nearly 11,000 radio stations far outnumber television stations, the combined revenues of the commercial stations fall far below those of television stations. As of 1988, listening levels, however, reached 3½ hours per person each day, just short of the average amount of individual television viewing. Radio is a local medium with lower production costs and correspondingly lower revenues. But the sheer number of stations gives radio programming a major industry role and creates thousands of jobs for programmers.

Part Four covers commercial programming strategies both from **network** and **station** perspectives but emphasizes the local orientation of most radio programming. It has chapters on national distribution, music, news and talk programming. Each author deals with the evaluation, selection and scheduling of radio programming. Although these chapters focus on broadcast audiences, it is important to recognize that over 40 percent of radio stations also reach listeners on local cable FM and as background to text-only channels.

Chapter 13 on **networks and syndicators** provides an overview of the radio broadcasting industry. Nearly 90 percent of radio stations pull in some programming from satellite transmissions. As the main sources of nonlocal material, networks play a major role as suppliers of information programming to music, news and talk stations. About 60 percent of commercial stations affiliate with a network to obtain national and international news items, and some networks act as feature resources to stations that otherwise originate most of their own content. Music format syndicators supply geographically scattered, automated-music stations with a complete programming schedule. Chapter 13, then, takes a national perspective on radio programming, covering the distribution, economics and contents of radio networks and syndicators. Some of the issues raised about national news and talk programs also apply to national television newscasts and public affairs programming; some of the issues raised about national program syndication also apply to cable.

Chapter 14 on **music programming** follows. Music format stations outnumber all other formats combined by a ratio of better than 90 to 1. Chapter 14 concentrates on rock music programming, but its strategies can also be applied to other music formats. To illustrate music radio programming strategies, the authors of this chapter create a hypothetical radio market into which they introduce a new station, step by step. Choosing a commercially viable format for any given market indicates how radio programmers are restricted and the methods they adopt for operating within those constraints. Chapter 14 continues the examination of the triple aspects of programming—evaluation, selection and scheduling.

Chapter 15 examines the locally programmed **all-news station.** Although this format occurs in its pure form only in very large markets, where a high degree of specialization can be supported economically, it occupies an important media role in times of local emergencies and national history-making events. All-news is advancing as an AM specialty in response to the shift of music formats to FM.

However, many of the concerns of the all-news programmer apply equally to five-minute hourly interruptions inside music formats as well as to more lengthy newscasts. Chapter 15 takes a local perspective on news programming on radio. Many of the issues raised in this chapter also apply to local television newscasts.

The last chapter in Part Four, Chapter 16, focuses on **talk radio,** another major-market specialty format varying from all-talk to news/talk mixes called information radio. From a programming perspective, talk radio differs from news radio because talk draws on audience members and guests to create large portions of the programming, whereas professional journalists occupy center stage in news radio. The typical talk format includes live celebrity interviews, but its most distinctive feature is the telephone call-in show. One talk station stands out from another primarily on the basis of the proportions of interviews, call-ins, conversations and news it uses. Chapter 16 discusses ways of structuring the talk radio format. The author also delves into the touchy issues of fairness and community pressure that operate in any size market and in any radio, cable or television format deviating from "canned" material.

Radio programming may not seem complex when compared to broadcast television or cable, but these chapters demonstrate that radio programming strategy is highly developed within music, news and talk formats and that radio networks and syndicators play increasingly important roles in an essentially local medium. Part Four completes this book's overview of **commercial** programming.

CHAPTER 13 \ NETWORK AND SYNDICATED RADIO PROGRAMMING

Jim Cameron

Rolland C. Johnson

Edward F. McLaughlin

A Guide to Chapter 13

Jim Cameron, president of Cameron Communications, Inc., has spent more than 20 years in the radio business. After earning a B.A. (cum laude) at Lehigh University in 1972 while working at WLVR-FM, he began his professional career as an air personality for WLIR, Long Island, and WQIV, New York, soon moving into radio journalism as news director for WHCN, Hartford, and WCOZ, Boston. In 1979 he became the founding news director of NBC Radio's The Source, also serving as correspondent and executive producer of *The Source Report,* a weekly newsmagazine. In 1981 he launched his own consulting firm, specializing in radio news and business/media relations. He has also served as East Coast editor of *Earshot: The Newspaper for the Radio Newsroom* and founded JForum, the Compu-Serve database for journalists. Cameron has served on the boards of directors of the InterCollegiate Broadcasting Service (IBS) and Audio Independents Inc. and received three Major Armstrong Awards and a George Foster Peabody Award for documentary excellence. He has taught at St. John's University and guest-lectured at SUNY at Stony Brook, Fordham University and Ohio University, also lecturing at the African Center for Journalism in Tunisia. His writings on broadcast journalism have been published in major media magazines.

Rolland C. Johnson, president of Duchossois Communications, a group owner of one television and nine radio stations and an MDS facility, is also president and a major stockholder of Indiana Communications, Inc., owner of three radio stations. Johnson began in radio in 1959 and has since been associated with it in virtually every capacity of local operation—announcing, programming, sales, management, ownership. He also consults on station acquisition, programming and management. His B.J. and M.B.A. degrees come from the University of Missouri and his Ph.D. from Ohio University. An associate professor at Indiana University, he chaired the Department of Telecommunications from 1981 to 1984. In addition to articles on network compensation rates in the *Journal of Broadcasting,* he was co-author of the 1975 NAEB "Book of the Year." He has also worked for the federal government at the National Science Foundation and was visiting Howard R. Marsh Professor of Communication at the University of Michigan in 1980.

Edward F. McLaughlin, president of EFM Media in New York, and formerly president of the ABC Radio Networks from 1972 to 1987, had a long history with ABC. Before becoming president, he was vice-president and general manager of KGO Radio, the ABC owned-and-operated station in San Francisco. He joined KGO in 1964, becoming general manager in 1967. Earlier, he had been general sales manager of KGBS in Los Angeles, office manager of Peters, Griffin and Woodward, and an account executive with KEWB, both in San Francisco. Currently, he is chairman of the Radio Network Association, a member of the board of governors of the North American Rock Radio Awards, and a member of the board of the International Radio and Television Foundation. He graduated from San Francisco State University and, in 1972, was named "alumnus of the year." EMF Media now consults in radio programming, especially for the ABC networks. Jointly, these authors analyze the evolving situations in radio network and syndicated programming.

RADIO PROGRAM DISTRIBUTION

Radio programming has undergone remarkable changes in the last 60 years. In the 1930s and 1940s, as the major electronic mass medium, radio broadcast live entertainment and information programs across the nation that all Americans could hear simultaneously. Radio supplied the primary national sales vehicle for consumer product brands such as Proctor & Gamble, Colgate and General Foods. Both entertainment and news programs provided by radio networks captured the devoted attention of Americans before and during World War II. The programs resembled what can be seen on television in the mid-1980s—dramas, variety shows, comedies and so on—and were called **long-form** programming. By 1950, network radio advertising represented over $215 million in total revenue—and that amount, given a much smaller and less developed economic environment in 1950 plus inflation since then, represents well over $1 billion in late-1980s dollars.

Television's Impact

But by 1953, network radio revenues had shrunk to less than $40 million because of television's inroads. Network radio was the first electronic medium to be nearly replaced by another medium. That replacement, in the 1950s, was swift, almost complete and nearly fatal. When television captured the bulk of the national advertising dollars, it also attracted the best talent and the biggest stars. It affected the revenues, the programs and the nature of the services that the radio networks provided. The percentage of stations affiliating with one of the four largest networks dropped from 97 percent in 1946 to 30 percent in 1955.[1] American families huddled in front of television sets instead of radio sets. National radio programs failed to draw significant, measurable audiences to sell to advertisers, and radio networks crumbled.

CBS, NBC and ABC radio survived in part because of revenues from their co-owned television operations. They eliminated more expensive entertainment programming and concentrated on the delivery of short newscasts—usually five minutes or less—or **short-form** programming. A fourth major network, Mutual, did not have a co-owned television operation but also changed from long-form to short-form programming. This was a profound change for the networks and brought about minor changes at the local level as well. No longer could radio stations look to their networks for the bulk of their programming. On the other hand, few stations, even in major markets, could afford to produce elaborate live shows. By 1960 recorded music had become the mainstay of radio programming because it was inexpensive to program, universally available and appealing to the younger listeners who increasingly constituted the bulk of the radio audience.

When networks provided less material, at the local station level a void appeared in nationally produced shows for radio. Program syndicators tried to fill this gap, producing features or short musical programs and making them available on tape or disc to stations throughout the United States.

The value of the radio networks dropped as their role diminished. To maintain visibility, they became news and sports suppliers, providing stations with services supporting their local identities. Rock and roll, the car radio, transistors, Elvis Presley and other music superstars, plus the maturation of the postwar baby boom, gave radio new life. But not until the 1980s did the national radio networks again begin to provide long-form entertainment programming. A major element in the recovery was the advent of satellite-relayed radio programming. The introduction of the satellite program relay dramatically affected the development of radio program *syndication* in the United States, just as it did radio *networking*.

Land Lines to Satellites

The major commercial radio networks in the United States originally based their operations in New York City. America's largest city was home for the new medium's advertising and talent resources, but more important, New York was where the telephone lines began and ended. Until the early 1980s, a network distribution map looked like a giant tree growing from a base in New York. All affiliated stations were fed by land line or telephone circuit from some branch of this distribution system, with stations in smaller communities often footing the bill for their electronic twig on this mighty oak, usually paying high prices for a hookup to the closest "branch" or city. Network distribution problems included greater demand for high-quality audio circuits than the phone company (AT&T) was willing to provide. The cost of constructing a link between a station and a network was often prohibitively expensive. At best, the audio chain was no stronger than its weakest link—often only 3.5 kHz, little better than a dial-telephone circuit. While this was adequate for spoken-word programming, such as news, it clearly inhibited network distribution of music programming, especially to quality-conscious FM stations.

The scarcity of national telephone circuits and the cost of creating new distribution webs effectively limited new networking efforts for decades. In the 1950s, one company attempted to distribute full-time radio formats on custom-pressed discs, but this proved expensive and inflexible and was soon abandoned. The answer to these problems arrived in the late 1970s with the introduction of relay communications *satellites*.

Network transmissions beamed from ground-based uplinks to satellites in geosyncronous earth orbit allowed affiliated stations to receive programs with high fidelity—and in stereo. Not only did satellite relay cut distribution costs for the networks, and thereby for their affiliates, it also made affiliation feasible for thousands of radio stations that previously could not afford the cost of connection to the network grid. Moreover, because all the major networks distributed from two major satellites, changing affiliation from ABC to CBS or from Mutual to United Stations became as simple as changing a circuit board at the station's satellite receiving end.

One initial problem for the networks was getting the satellite hardware into stations' hands. Some networks gave *receiving dishes* away; others arranged long-term leases or favorable financing packages for their affiliates. But by the mid-1980s, all networks made converting to satellite reception mandatory by dismantling their terrestrial distribution systems. Nowadays, ABC, CBS, NBC, United Stations, Westwood One and CNN Radio all use digital delivery on Satcom I-R.

Decentralization was a further advantage of satellite distribution to the networks. A program uplink can be located anywhere on the ground and still reach an overhead satellite. No longer limited by the realities of land-line distribution, several networks moved away from New York's high-cost sites. The Sheridan Network, for example, chose rural Florida as its base of operations; the Satellite Music Network chose rural Illinois. Other networks now originate programming feeds from several cities rather than just one. This was a welcome development for affiliates that often resented the East Coast bias they perceived in network offerings, especially in news. The conversion from terrestrial to space-based transmission systems also removed some traditional distinctions between the two rivals in radio program distribution—the networks and the syndicators.

Until the advent of satellites, one big difference between networks and syndicators was their *content*—resulting from their distribution technologies. A commercial **network** transmitted its programming, either live or prerecorded, simultaneously to all affiliates by way of its land-line distribution grid. Stations could carry the programs immediately as fed or tape them for later broadcast. A **syndicator,** on the other hand, lacked a live transmission capability and had to distribute all programs by tape or disc for airing at a later time of the station's choosing. The speed of delivery dictated the type of programming each producer could create. Networks, being able to feed an item instantly to all affiliates, used this technological advantage in news and sports coverage. Syndicators in turn developed expertise in non-time-sensitive programming such as variety entertainment, drama, artist profiles, feature shorts and music specials.

During the 1980s, however, many syndicators opted for satellite distribution of their programming, viewing such transmission means as more cost-efficient for small and midsized market stations. Deciding whether to feed a show "by the bird" or to distribute it on tape or disc now depends on two criteria: how many stations have contracted to air it and how time-sensitive it is. Some syndicators that rushed into satellite distribution soon regretted it. Bonneville, a firm that syndicated an easy listening music format for automated stations, went to a satellite feed only to abandon it as a result of subscriber pressure and economics: It remains cheaper for Bonneville to send tapes for **live assist** (mixed DJ talk and taped music) to its 150 already successful large-market affiliates than to feed them a live transmission of full-time music of no particular time-sensitivity.

The advent of satellites, then, blurred some traditional distinctions between networks and syndicators (see Table 13-1). Space-based transmission altered the speed of program delivery and therefore programming content. Networks soon started producing programs that traditionally had been the province of syndicators—providing short features and long-form entertainment programming—while many syndicators acquired live interconnection with their affiliates via satellites and could therefore distribute time-sensitive material such as advertising, sports and news. It was the arrival of cheap satellite distribution of programming that brought about these changes.

Satellites also allow the radio networks and format syndicators to overcome two distribution weaknesses that plagued them for many years: lack of program quantity and lack of technical quality in the distributed signal. Networks and syndicators can now provide several offerings simultaneously, and the signals that reach affiliates have the same quality as the originating signal. A program supplier can provide program A to one station and program B to another using the same satellite channel (*transponder*). High-fidelity and stereo are possible over long distances in space without significant quality loss, thanks to digital transmission technology. Stations can now mix locally produced,

Table 13-1 Traditional Distinctions

RADIO NETWORKS	RADIO SYNDICATORS
Mostly shortform	Mostly long form
Newscasts, sports, concert specials	Recorded music, features
National advertising	No ads
Live, satellite	Tape
Compensation paid	Licensing fee charged

network-originated and syndicated features or programs without unevenness in such audio characteristics as **presence, signal-to-noise ratio,** stereo and **dolby.** Moreover, the considerable cost savings achieved through satellite distribution effectively eliminated the major barrier to entry in the networking business—the expense of land lines. As a result, many new full-service and *ad hoc* radio networks appeared in the 1980s, increasing the competition among radio program services.

Demographic Targeting

Programming separates a station from its competitors and defines that station for its audiences and advertisers. Radio stations typically target a specific demographic group whereas the major networks, until recently, designed their programming for broad appeal across demographic groupings so as to integrate with a variety of affiliated-station formats. In addition to satellite delivery becoming a factor in the recovery of the networks, another important factor has been the development of demographically *targeted* network programming.

ABC launched a daring concept in radio networking in 1967: It created four separate networks—Contemporary, FM, Entertainment and Information—each targeting a different audience by delivering the news in a style appropriate for that audience. ABC programmed news that was written and delivered for specific demographic types ("cells" in ratings books) and specific affiliate formats. Its Contemporary and FM services were the first to clearly identify and attempt to fill the needs of youth-oriented music stations for news and other entertainment- or information-oriented features. Each of ABC's networks could affiliate with a different station in a single market without affecting exclusivity, and each network could also carry its own commercials, in effect quadrupling the revenue potential from a single newsroom. Eventually, ABC added two more networks—Direction and Rock—slicing the demographic pie ever thinner.

The nature of network signal distribution in the 1960s—by leased telephone land lines—influenced ABC's development of demographic targeting. At that time, it was cheaper for a network to lease land lines for 24 hours a day than to lease them for short segments of each hour. Full-time leasing also allowed the networks to cover breaking spot news as it occurred. Because a network typically used the lines for newscasts for only five minutes of each half-hour, for 50 or more minutes of every hour they were not in use. As might be expected, renting telephone lines throughout the country was extremely expensive.

To take advantage of the unused time on the lines, ABC created its four different networks by sending four distinct newscasts down the same line, staggering one after another during the hour. One station in a market could affiliate with ABC Entertainment, for example, and get news during the second quarter of each hour (which would be targeted to that station's demographics). A second station in the same market could affiliate with ABC Information and get news of interest to its audience in the first quarter of each hour; other stations could affiliate with ABC Contemporary or FM and get their newscasts at other times. This pattern allowed ABC to use its news personnel more efficiently while the cost of the land lines remained the same. And the network became attractive to a broader array of stations—potentially four times as many as when ABC had only a single news service. As a result, the number of ABC's affiliates jumped dramatically in the late 1960s.

Despite ABC's demonstrated success, surprisingly, the other networks did not copy this innovation until the late 1970s. In 1979, ABC gained head-on competition in demographic targeting when NBC Radio launched The Source (now part of Westwood), aimed at album-rock listeners in the 18–34 age range. Shortly after, the RKO Radio Network (now United Stations) was born, followed by CBS's RadioRadio network, both also targeting the same young-adult radio audience. Each of these new networks sought affiliation with previously unaffiliated stations, thus increasing each web's reach into thousands of additional stations.[2]

The desire to package programs that would appeal to audiences with certain demographic characteristics, in addition to the arrival of relatively inexpensive satellite distribution, resulted in the proliferation of radio networks in the early 1980s. But the one thing that satellite distribution and demographic targeting did not affect still separates networks and syndicators: their program economics, or *which way the money flows*.

RADIO PROGRAM ECONOMICS

Syndicated Sales or Barter

Radio stations airing syndicated programming usually pay for it in one of two ways: cash or barter. A station can make an outright *cash purchase* of the right to air a program, often with market exclusivity—meaning it will be the only station in a given city to air the show. The program's price is normally based on the purchasing station's own advertising rates. The more successful the station, the higher the rate it charges its advertisers and, in turn, the higher the rate it is charged by the program provider, the syndicator, because the program will be exposed to more listeners and bring the station more revenue through local ad sales.

Alternatively, a station may take a program on *barter*, trading the

right to carry the show for a commitment to air the commercials contained within it. (See chapters 3 and 8 for discussions of **barter** in television programming.) Westwood One's Earth News Radio, for example, is all barter. The syndicator takes on the job of selling the commercial time to national advertisers at rates competitive with radio network rates. Local stations also retain several minutes of commercial avails in each program for locally sold advertising. In either case, the syndicator sells or barters for only limited runs of a program, typically one or two airings within one year.

Network Contracts and Compensation

Networks use a much different system to receive their income, one based on affiliation by stations. An **affiliate** normally signs a contract with a network for the exclusive right to air its programming in a given market. The station pays nothing for this right, except its most precious resource—airtime. The affiliated station agrees to air whatever commercials the network feeds it and in return gets its choice of the network's programming. Westwood One, Mutual, ABC, CBS and NBC operate this way. In contrast, CNN Radio charges affiliates from $100 to $1000 per month depending on market size, and Transtar and Satellite Music Network typically charge $1,000 per month. Then, of course, they also sell 1 to 3 minutes an hour of national advertising.

Most network shows are fed with commercials within or adjacent to them. But many stations, because they do not air all the network programs, instead take their quota of network commercials fed in a weekly package and then air them throughout their broadcast day. The networks promote their services as being "free" to affiliates, while their competitors in syndication argue that giving up hundred to minutes of airtime each week in exchange for affiliation and access to programs is anything but free. For a station unable to sell its total ad inventory locally, the exchange of commercial time for network programming is rational. But in major markets where advertisers are plentiful, local rates are high and affiliates use few network programs, becoming a network affiliate can mean the loss of a great deal of revenue.

In many major markets, the networks sweeten the affiliation deal by offering stations **compensation** (see Chapter 7 on television compensation). In theory, compensation makes up the difference between what a radio affiliate's revenue actually is and what it would be if all network spots had been sold locally, factoring in the value of the network programs. The resulting payments differ greatly from market to market, but being a matter of public record in FCC filings, the networks try to keep "comp payments" at realistic and consistent levels. Still, it is not uncommon for important affiliates to be paid more than a million dollars annually for airing several dozen commercials each week, while the stations incur no obligation to air a single second of the network's programs. Satellite Music Network has been the most aggressive in getting major-market clearances by paying compensation. These types of affiliations, based solely on compensation and not programming clearance, put the networks against the advertising representation companies (ad reps) in the ongoing scramble to secure advertising money in the national marketplace.

Program Clearances and Exclusivity

In radio's golden days, affiliation with a network was essential for a local station's success. The networks provided programs the local stations simply could not produce themselves, especially the hourly newscasts so closely associated with the networks. Today, the reasons for network affiliation are different. The payment of **compensation,** for example, motivates major-market stations to affiliate.

While it used to be that the networks required their affiliates to *clear* almost all program offerings as a condition of affiliation, today that programming decision is left solely to the station. The network's only requirement is that the *commercials be aired*, and as these spots are fed in weekly packages in addition to their inclusion in network programs, it is often easier for affiliates to run the spots and air none of the shows—including the news. This leaves many networks with very impressive affiliate rosters but little or no airtime for their programs.

Another motivation for affiliation is one with a negative twist: to deny a network's offerings to a competitor in the same market. In such a case, Station A would affiliate, for example, with The Source, a young adult service, and would be given exclusive rights to all of The Source's programming in the city. Even if none of the shows were ever aired on Station A, its competitor, Station B, would be denied access to any of the shows, even if Station B *wanted* to air them and their adjacent commercials. For several decades, strong FCC prohibitions existed against such *exclusionary affiliations*, but FCC radio deregulation in 1982 eliminated them. (In contrast, these rules remain in force for television affiliates; see Chapter 7 on nonclearances in television affiliation contracts.)

NETWORK NEWS PROGRAMMING

The Communications Act of 1934 requires all broadcast licensees to "serve the public interest." Until deregulation in 1982, one of the ways the FCC measured such service was by requiring all stations to air news and public affairs programming. Until 1982, stations had to fill a "suggested" minimum percentage of their airtime with news and public affairs (otherwise, they ran the risk of being examined by the FCC at license renewal time). Once live entertainment ceased to be profitable for radio networks in the 1950s, the FCC's "suggestions" helped direct network attention to news. Most stations maintained local news departments to report on community affairs while leaving national and international news coverage to the networks. Clearly, this was what the networks could do best: pool resources around the globe to produce a high-quality, hourly news package for all affiliates' use. This remains one of the strongest program elements distinguishing networks from syndicators.[3] Indeed, some networks, such as *The Wall St. Journal* Radio Network, AP Network News and CNN Radio, offer affiliates nothing but news and information programs, leaving entertainment shows to syndicators or other network services.

After deregulation, the networking business changed dramatically. No longer required to air any news or public affairs, many stations cut back on such offerings. The timing of deregulation coincided with the recession of the early 1980s, and a few stations eliminated their local news departments completely in an effort to save money. Still other slashed their clearance of network news. Many music-oriented radio consultants argued that listeners, especially those in the most sought-after 18 to 34-year-old audience, did not want to hear news. Supporting this view, FCC officials argued that their deregulation policy would reflect market needs: If an audience exists for radio news, stations will provide it, and if no such demand occurs, stations need not air such programs.

Deregulation's Aftereffects

Diminished airtime for network news has had at least two serious effects, one psychological and the other pragmatic. First, with reduced exposure for their newscasts, the radio networks lost prestige at the time that their sister television networks were becoming Americans' medium of choice for news. Second, with fewer affiliates supporting a local news department, the network acquired problems in getting coverage of breaking local events. Network radio news editors have shaken their heads in disbelief when calling a major-market affiliate for information on a breaking local story only to be told by the station that it had no local news staff and that the caller should "call the network in New York" for information about the station's hometown news!

Those stations that continue to air newscasts usually do so for competitive reasons. Affiliates receive their news in short bursts, typically less than five minutes in each hour. All-news radio is still successful, but generally only in the top 20 or so markets (and most are owned-and-operated by CBS or Westinghouse; see Chapter 15). For talk-radio stations, news remains an important catalyst for controversy in their programming (see Chapter 16). While the radio networks continue to try to serve both of these information-intensive formats, they have had only limited sucess. In 1975, NBC Radio launched its "News and Information Service" (N.I.S.), a round-the-clock, all-news network format for radio; stations could air the network package en toto or interweave local news offerings amid the network feed. Though N.I.S. brought all-news radio to many medium and small markets for the first time, a lack of advertising revenue ended the venture in less than one year. This was a crushing blow to NBC Radio. NBC's three services continued to lose money in the 1980s, eventually being acquired by the California-based Westwood Radio in 1987, subsequent to Westwood's purchase of the Mutual Broadcast Network in 1985.

Identifying the Right Network

As the cost of covering world-ranging news events becomes greater, those local stations wanting news service become more dependent on the resources of the national wire services and networks. Most stations expend nearly all their news budgets in covering news in their local markets and cannot mount effective national and international coverage campaigns. Wire services provide copy, but usually it must be rewritten and delivered in a credible manner (with a variety of voices) to compete with top-line news productions. Stations have the alternatives of blending wire reports with local news (using local staff voices) or affiliating with a national network.

Once a station decides to affiliate with a network to acquire network news services, it must decide which network to approach. After eliminating the networks that already have affiliates in a given market, the station next considers which networks target the audience demographics the station is trying to reach. A rock music station aimed at the 18 to 34-year-olds, for example, might choose ABC's Rock Radio, CBS's RadioRadio, Westwood's The Source or United Stations I. A country music station might choose Associated Press's Music Country, which includes newscasts, or Transtar or Music Country Radio. A black-oriented station could choose National Black or Sheridan's black-oriented programming (see Table 13-2 later in this chapter).

NETWORK TALK AND ENTERTAINMENT

In the 1980s, the established networks returned to long-form entertainment programming—most notably **talk** shows. ABC's Talkradio, Mutual's *The Larry King Show* and NBC's TalkNet combine overnight long-form talk and interview programs, described in detail in Chapter 16. Most talk affiliates are AM stations, many having a long-time commitment to information/personality/sports, with strong talk images in their communities. In this area, any distinction between the programming provided by networks and by syndicators has blurred.

NETWORK SPORTS PROGRAMMING

Although a station rarely chooses an affiliation based solely on the sports coverage provided by a network, sports affect the amount of affiliation (hours of clearance) and the popularity of the entire service. ABC, CBS and NBC radio use many of their nationally known sportscasters who cover the same games on television. Most network sports programming, however, comes from regional networks set up to broadcast events of interest to people in particular geographic areas—such as the Indiana Basketball Network or the Nebraska Football Network.

Sports is a good money-maker for radio networks because it delivers a clearly identifiable audience, largely adult males, 18 to 49, with strong appeal to many advertisers. From the national network programmer's perspective, however, the difficulty with sports is that there are not enough attractive contests. Only games with national appeal are suitable for national distribution. And the cost of the rights to sports packages with wide appeal keeps climbing. Both news and sports are types of programs that networks will be expected to offer in the future and that distinguish them from fare typically supplied by syndicators.

NETWORK MUSIC PROGRAMMING

Music programming by networks was also reborn in the late 1970s. The success of syndicated services after the introduction of satellite distribution and the birth of new music-only networks, stimulated the established news and sports networks to expand their music services. Music programming divides into individual programs and series (**short-form**) and continuous formatted music (**long-form**). The major broadcast networks typically provided only the short-form programs, but during the early 1980s, some new networks began supplying long-form formatted musical programming via satellite.

For example, The Source was designed as a full-service network. In addition to offering hourly two-minute newscasts, it offers short-form features, comedy "drop-ins" and concerts—both live and pretaped. As with story selection for the newscasts, its music programming also focuses on the 18- to 34-year-old's lifestyle—in other words, rock and roll.

Concerts and Specials

The Source, RadioRadio and their rival youth-nets were latecomers to the networking of music-oriented programming. Syndicators such as DIR, producing the long-running *King Biscuit Flower Hour,* and Westwood One with its many concert series, have proven highly popular with both stations and advertisers, both of whom are willing to pay premium prices for exclusive access to top-ranked music in a concert setting. (Some syndicated acts cut across a variety of station formats, from soft rock to hard rock and even country, making clearances of some syndicated music shows easy to achieve on at least one station in most markets.)

On the networks, special music programs have grown from near zero revenues in 1975 to tens of millions in sales in the 1980s. They consist largely of live concerts or specials featuring star interviews intercut with songs. Access to these concerts and major performers has been, and still remains, beyond the reach of most local stations. Syndicators capable of recording such shows generally try to sell them to stations at prices ranging from $25 to $50 per hour in small markets to several hundred dollars per hour in large markets. Networks provide these music specials as portions of full-service networks programming news, sports and music, meanwhile syndicating them on a station by station basis as well.

Advertisers will pay a premium rate (above the normal network commercial rate) for music concerts and specials because the commercials in these shows are fixed, assuring clearance in advance within a specific program environment. Their commercials can therefore target the exact demographics of the affiliates clearing a music special, and often the advertiser enjoys the enhancement of being associated with a major musical event.

Concerts and specials can become a factor in compensation negotiations with affiliates. When a network supplies programming that many affiliates find desirable, the network gains leverage in the annual battles to set compensation rates. Even a slight diminution of compensation payments, en toto, balances increased production costs for special programs.

As with any other type of network program, the key to revenue for a music special is the size of its cleared audience. Fitting a particular concert or series of concerts to a demographic category matching a salable number of affiliates is more difficult than clearing a targeted newscast. Virtually any program targets either the youth demographic of roughly 18–34 years (it may include teens) or the adult demographic of 25–54 years. Each presents separate problems. In general, the youth demographic requires a more careful fit between programs and formats in the affiliate lineup than the adult demographic. The biggest distinction for networks, however, lies in programming for the pure and the mixed formats.

Pure and Mixed Formats

The album-oriented rock (**AOR**) format represents a pure **format.** It has an easily definable audience, predominantly males 18 to 24 and interested in varied, off-beat rock music accompanied by a laid-back DJ style. Country music, despite the rise of "urban country" over "country/western," is a relatively pure format appealing to a more adult audience (25–54). For both AOR and country formats, the list of acceptable artists, groups and even songs is generally agreed on by stations nationwide. For certain, stations agree on broad categories of musical exclusions from each of these formats.

Both formats also enjoy strong audience followings with salable demographics, making them ideal for network program series. What a network must supply is superior production quality, top artists, merchandising support and **protection** in the local market. (*Protection* means that the network will supply the program only to a single station, irrespective of the number of affiliates it has whose signals overlap, a form of exclusivity.)

The adult contemporary (**AC**), **Top 40** and contemporary hit radio (**CHR**) formats are mixed. Stations using them perceive a wide variation in acceptability. One station claiming to be AC may clear an artist that is totally refused by another station also claiming the same format. Thus, network programmers have difficulty identifying programs that will build audiences of salable size.

For a network seeking musical concerts and specials, three alternative strategies exist. The first is to produce many shows of varied appeal to capture fragments of the youth or adult audiences. The second is to concentrate on the relatively small number of stars that appeal across the broadest format spectrum. Neither of these strategies has the economic efficiency of producing programs directed toward the pure format groups, however. The third option is to buy or produce programs that have unique, broad appeals such as Dick Clark's *Countdown America* or special hosted shows. They succeed best as regularly scheduled features, and audiences seek them out. A broad range of affiliates will clear unique music programs, thus accumulating sizable audiences and potentially making them the most profitable of network programs, competitive with top-rated radio sports.

Full-Time Format Suppliers

Until the late 1970s, stations programmed their own music or purchased tapes from syndicators of long-form all-music programming such as TM and Century 21. Satellite delivery made possible a new type of syndicated service—the *full-time radio format, produced live.* Transtar and Satellite Music Network (SMN) began satellite delivery of complete formats with live DJs, newscasts and national commercials in the 1980s. Many stations carry their packages en toto, in effect acting as robot transmitters for these new network services. Other stations customize the programming by adding locally produced cut-aways, often including local news. Even these local elements could be pre-taped by affiliates and aired within the network feed using an automatic pulse-code system. Transtar affiliates receive an inaudible cue tone from the network that fires a cart machine, dropping in the local station's call letters and commercials. Both Transtar and SMN provide hourly news capsules, but their flexible format windows allow affiliates the option of covering those feeds with other programs of their choosing.

As of the late 1980s, the format networks supplied predominantly musical formats targeted at a defined audience, accompanied by minor leavening of news and, in some cases, a small amount of public affairs. The sole practical distinction between some networks and some syndicators now is that hourly newscasts are included in a music network service while separate network news affiliation is needed to accompany most syndicated formats.

From the beginning of radio until the very late 1970s, ABC, CBS, Mutual and NBC were the principal radio networks, due initially to the limited number of stations with sufficient power and, subsequently, to the expense of interconnecting stations via telephone lines. But by the mid-1980s, more than 30 networks blanketed the nation with long-form and short-form audio programming, and more specialized services may develop in the 1990s. Table 13-2 lists the most established networks as of 1988 and indicates the variety of content they make available to the local station programmer.

The Physicians Radio Network (PRN) is perhaps the ultimate in demographic targeting. Solely for doctors and supported by pharmaceutical advertising, it is a subcarrier service using Subsidiary Communications Authorizations (SCAs) on FM stations in all major cities. It requires special receivers (preset to a particular frequency) that the network gives away to doctors.[4] PRN programs an all-news one-hour show repeated throughout the day that is changed twice daily.

SYNDICATED PROGRAMMING

Syndicators fall in two distinct classes. One group produces *format* packages, typically a species of rock, easy listening, country, nostalgia or classical. They supply stations with tapes/compact discs or satellite interconnection for a monthly fee based on the size of the market. Another syndicator group produces special *features* such as weekly countdowns, religion or concerts, supplying stations with tapes, discs or direct interconnection for cash or barter.

Format Syndicators

Format syndicators can be distinguished from format networks because they typically supply only music, sometimes accompanied by music-related features, intended for fully automated stations. As shown in Table 13-1, format syndicators usually do not sell commercial time or produce newscasts. Table 13-3 lists ten of the major companies providing packages of formatted music programming in long-form for radio stations throughout the United

Table 13-2 Radio Networks, 1988

	NO. OF AFFILIATES[c]		NO. OF AFFILIATES
ABC:	**2,232**	Sheridan	**130**
Contemporary	251	Sun Radio	**71**
Direction	425	Transtar:	**1,008**
Entertainment	580	Format 41[a]	
FM	141	Adult Contemporary[a]	
Information[b]	619	Country[a]	
Rock Radio	92	The Oldies Channel[a]	
Talkradio[a]	124	AM Only[a]	
Associated Press:	**1,025**	Turner:	**177**
AP Network News		CNN RADIO[a]	
Music Country Radio		United Stations	
Network[a]		(formerly RKO):	**2,300**
Caballero (Spanish language)	**72**	US I	200
CBS:	**550**	US II	300
CBS Radio	400	US Program Network[a]	1,800
RadioRadio	150	UPI	**1,000**
Music Country Radio	**122**	Wall Street Journal	**85**
National Black	**150**	Westwood Radio Networks:	**4,832**
Satellite Music Network:	**890**	Mutual	700
Country[a]		NBC Radio	425
AC[a]		The Source	122
Black[a]		Talknet[a]	285
Beautiful[a]		Westwood One	3,300
The Wave[a]			
Gospel[a]			

[a] Indicates long-form or format networks
[b] Top-rated radio network, according to RADAR, in 1987
[c] Some stations affiliate with more than one service.

Table 13-3 Major Format Syndicators

SYNDICATOR	FORMATS
Toby Arnold and Associates, Dallas, Texas	Nostalgia, Contemporary, Soft Hits, Middle-of-the-Road, Country
Bonneville, Northbrook, Illinois	Easy Listening, Beautiful Music, Adult Contemporary
BPI, Bellingham, Washington	Easy Listening, Country, Adult Contemporary, Hit Rock, Middle-of-the-Road, Oldies, Classical
Century 21, Dallas, Texas	19 formats varying from Country to Religion
Drake-Chenault, Canoga Park, California	Country, Classic Rock, Soul, Beautiful Music, Adult Contemporary, Contemporary Hit Radio
Al Ham Productions, Huntington, Connecticut	Music of Your Life (nostalgia)
KalaMusic, Kalamazoo, Michigan	Easy Listening
Chas. Mickelson, Inc., Beverly Hills, California	Old-time radio shows
Musicworks, Inc., Nashville, Tennessee	Country, Adult Contemporary, Easy Listening
Programming Consultants, Albuquerque, New Mexico	Easy Listening, Hard Rock, Nostalgia, Country, Contemporary Gold, Contemporary Hit Radio

States. Besides these major suppliers, hundreds of regional syndicators market a package or two to a limited number of stations.

In the 1960s the FCC's *nonduplication policy* (limiting the amount of duplicated programming on co-owned AM and FM stations) spurred FM stations to find inexpensive programming. At this point, syndicators proliferated. They took advantage of the increasing desire among stations for narrow formats and of microprocessor technology to provide long-form automated packages. Consequently, the number of **automated** stations using format packages grew from a handful to over 2,000 in the 1970s. The syndicators select the music and suggest the order in which tapes should be played. Typically, this type of syndicator consults with individual client-stations about promotion, advertising spot placement, the length of the broadcast day, the role of announcers, the amount of news and so on. Using syndicated format packages, a small-market station can achieve a consistent "big-market" sound with recognized appeal to advertisers.

Feature Syndicators

The number of syndicators providing shorter programs or *features* also increased dramatically during the 1970s. Syndicated feature programs range from daypart packages, such as *Sports Shorts* or Sunday morning religious programs, to very brief inserts, such as 90-second interviews with star performers—for example, *Off-the-Record with Mary Turner* from Westwood One. Stations producing their own programming include short features to add spice and variety to a stretch of recorded songs and use the longer programming to fill unsalable time periods. Radio broadcasters also use features as a strategy for attracting a specific target audience, frequently subgroups of the station's overall demographic group that management wants to strengthen.

Syndicated features are as varied as their producers. Many of the companies that syndicate long-form format packages also supply short features that fit within their long formats. The shorts are also made available to other stations in the same market on a format-exclusive basis. (**Format-exclusive** means that the same short can be sold to more than one station in a market if their formats differ, but only one rock or one country or one talk station can license the program. This arrangement assumes non-overlapping listeners.) Drake-Chenault, for example, produces *The Weekly Top 30, The Great American Country Show, The History of Rock and Roll* and *The Golden Years,* and it produces format packages such as country, top 40, MOR, AC and Soul. Each program normally is sold to only one station in a market. Moreover, ABC purchased Watermark, Inc., in 1982, linking its network with a feature service to bolster the variety of the ABC networks' programming at low cost.

Weekly countdown programs are among the great strengths of the syndication field. One of the most successful short-form programs, a weekly two-hour program created by Tom Rounds and his Watermark Company in 1969, is *American Top 40* featuring Casey Kasem (until 1988). It targets young people, 12 to 25 years, and as of 1987, was heard on over 1,000 radio stations. Another long-time hit is Dick Clark's *Countdown America.* These programs are inexpensively produced and distributed but consistently command top-dollar

Table 13-4 Feature Program Syndicators

SYNDICATOR	SAMPLE FEATURES
The Broadcast Group, Los Angeles	*American Voices, In Depth Magazine*
DIR Communications, New York	*King Biscuit, Robert Klein Show, Supergroups in Concert, Direct News, The Rock Radio Awards*
Global Satellite Network, Tarzana, California	*Reelin' in the Years, Rockline, Country Live*
Mother Earth News, New York	*Mother Earth News*
Multimedia Broadcast Associates, New York	*Celebrity Corner, The Stan Martin Show*
O'Conner Creative Services, Universal City, California	*Kids Say the Darndest Things, Howard Ruff Commentary, More for Your Money*
Public Affairs Broadcast Group, Washington, D.C.	*American Voices*
Radio Arts, Burbank, California	*Your Hit Parade, Country Countdown*
Radio Works, Hollywood, California	*The Unexplainable, Line on Tomorrow, Stay Healthy*
Watermark, Inc., Los Angeles	*American Top 40, TV Tonight, Musical, American Country Countdown*
Weedeck, Inc., Hollywood, California	*Country Report Countdown, Inside Music, The Great American Spirit*
Westwood One, Culver City, California	*Live From Gilleys, Dr. Demento, Playboy Advisor, Off the Record with Mary Turner*

in advertising. Stations like weekly countdown shows because they provide quality programming at low cost for weekends, a time period when hiring air talent is rarely cost-efficient. Table 13-4 lists a dozen syndicators supplying primarily short-form or feature programming, giving samples of their most widely distributed features.

CRITERIA FOR NATIONAL DISTRIBUTION

In selecting programs for national distribution, the overriding factor is talent availability for writing, performing and producing the show. The original notion behind networking or syndication is that talent is scarce, and its cost can be most easily covered by pooling resources. Five interrelated criteria then guide network and syndicator choices. A first criterion is that a program must meet the network's or syndicator's standard of professionalism in writing, production and performance. A second criterion for national distribution is that the program must offer some element—be it location, star or budget—that the individual station cannot match. Once these two criteria are met, a program's third most important asset is its potential appeal. Whatever its precise demographic target, a program must capture the interest of *most* people in that target group.

A fourth evaluative standard is the uniqueness of the concept, style, talent or presentation. While star power draws radio audiences, the combination of top talent and a unique program format can give a network a franchise for a time in the competitive battle for affiliate clearance.

Trends or fads become a fifth consideration. Determining what is or will be "hot" requires intimate involvement with, and understanding of, the medium and its target audiences. Trends in other media often provide clues, and widely appealing subjects (celebrities) or forms (all-sports) jump to other media. The programmer must also know when something that is popular will lose its appeal. Periodic program revitalization and replacement is critical if a network or syndicator is to remain acceptable to both audiences and affiliates, and therefore salable to advertisers. The hallmark of the best network and syndicator programmers is how well they use these five criteria to evaluate programs and whole formats, irrespective of specific content.

NEW TRENDS IN RADIO DISTRIBUTION

Transmission technology changed radio programming by allowing dozens of new entrants into a business once dominated by a handful of companies. The original big-four radio networks (ABC, CBS, NBC and Mutual) once formed an oligopoly by controlling land-line distribution webs, but satellites opened networking and syndication participation. Today, producers of even a single show are able to place it on dozens of stations scattered across the United States, in effect creating their own network, thanks to low-cost time-sharing on satellite transmission channels. For stations, this represents a tremendous boost in the number of sources of new programming, allowing them to select among a smorgasbord of choices. It also offers program producers greater control over their creations by allowing them the option of selling or bartering their shows.

Another new avenue of communication afforded by satellites involves network-to-affiliate information transfer. Until the 1980s, the networks either used the U.S. mails to send program information, such as commercial schedules, to all affiliates, or "talked" to them on closed-circuit feeds on the network line between program feeds. Using instantaneous satellite communication, networks now send bursts of data to stations on a non-program-carrying channel for hard-copy reproduction, providing a competitive advantage to their affiliates.

Another trend in radio networking is a continuing de-emphasis on program clearance. Competition among networks for top-rated affiliates lessens their ability to demand mandatory airing of network program offerings. Thus, the major networks become more and more like spot advertising rep firms. This diminished emphasis on programming may eventually force cuts in their news/entertainment divisions, further reducing their command of airtime and shifting their efforts to other station services. Increasingly, networks will focus on supplying affiliates with market research, technological and program consultation and logistical support for local production of events having national appeal, such as political conventions.

Four other trends are likely to continue in radio programming. Traditional distinctions between networks and syndicators will further blur, and following the pattern set by cable television, the term *radio program services* will probably acquire general usage. The amount of long-form format programming produced at a single source will expand. The number of narrowly targeted music and information services will increase. And, finally, the number of automated stations using nationally distributed format packages will rise.

From the local station programmer's perspective, the source of programming is immaterial, of course, as is the method of delivery, just so long as the programming appears quickly, reliably and has high quality. The station programmer is concerned with the nature and quality of the programming itself, requiring innovative, trendy, timely and polished programming that will deliver an audience to advertisers. The expanded array of nationally available programming permits the station programmer to cherrypick—to select the best of what is available to accomplish the station goals. More and more, long-form formatted packages and short-form feature elements from both networks and syndicators will be blended at the local level to create precisely targeted services fitting the local program manager's needs.

SUMMARY

The business of nationwide radio programming has altered drastically since the 1950s. Defeated by television, the national radio networks abandoned most entertainment programming and turned to news and sports until the advent of inexpensive satellite relay and formatted radio in the 1970s. By the early 1980s, more than a dozen new satellite-distributed music or news networks had joined the traditional "big four"—ABC, CBS, Mutual and NBC. By the late 1980s, two of those entities had abandoned radio, while Westwood had become a new giant multinetwork supplier, competing with ABC's half-dozen targeted news services and its all-talk network. They have been joined by several other full-service entertainment networks. Stations affiliate with a network news service to get compensation and when they cannot afford their own national news staffs or need the prestige of the network sound to compete. They choose a network based on target demographics, cost and, increasingly, nonprogramming support services. Music networks and syndicators provide packages for automated stations and features to mix with locally produced material. The total number of both networks and syndicators greatly increased during the 1970s. Syndicators began supplying a portion of FM programming in the 1960s, and by the mid-1980s, they rivaled the old-line networks as major suppliers of feature materials, while also providing most packaged music formats. Both networks and syndicators face a period of intense growth in the 1990s because of their ability to respond swiftly to changing interests and fads. As the distinctions between the two continue to blur, they will come to be called *radio program services* rather than *networks* or *syndicators*, being distinguishable by whether they distribute timely material by satellite, carry nationwide advertising, pay compensation or provide news, and also by the type of content they supply.

Notes

1. Christopher H. Sterling and Timothy R. Haight. *The Mass Media: Aspen Institute Guide to Communication Industry Trends* (New York: Praeger, 1978), p. 47.

2. By 1970, half of all commercial radio stations were affiliated, the largest number with ABC; by 1988, the number had climbed to just over 60 percent. *Broadcasting Yearbook* (New York: Broadcasting, 1987).

3. In one of a series of six nationwide surveys in 1983 by Torbet Radio, half of station managers said *news* was the main reason they affiliated, followed by compensation, prestige, national sound, news actualities and features. The most preferred features were celebrity interviews appropriate for the station's demographics. The managers surveyed reported airing only somewhat over half of the network news feed, cutting it to shorter length, using only the actualities, or reducing the quantity of aired network newscasts as the day progresses. Mariann Deluca, *Survey of Radio Stations* (New York: Torbet Radio, 1983)—see 1 February, 7 April, 15 June, 25 August and 21 September Torbet press releases.

4. Desonne, Marsha L. *Radio, New Technology and You* (Washington, D.C.: National Association of Broadcasters, April 1982), p. 5.

Selected Sources

"Billboard Salutes Westwood One," *Billboard* (special insert 1987): W01–W043.

Bortz, Paul, and Mendelsohn, Harold. *Radio Today—and Tomorrow.* Washington, D.C.: National Association of Broadcasters, October 1982.

Keith, Michael. *Radio Programming: Consultancy and Formatics.* Boston: Focal Press, 1987.

McCavitt, William E., and Pringle, Peter K. *Electronic Media Management.* Boston: Focal Press, 1986.

Reymer & Gersin Associates. *Radio WARS I: How to Survive into the '80s* and *Radio WARS II: How to Push Listeners' Hot Buttons.* NAB Publications, Washington, D.C., 1983 and 1985.

"Special Report: Radio," *Broadcasting* (15 August 1983):47–52; (29 August 1983):47–94; (23 July 1984):49–89; (17 September 1984):39–80; (24 September 1984):42–75; (4 February 1985):51–59; (22 July 1985):43–79; (9 June 1986):49–119; (28 July 1986):46–79; (27 July 1987):45–64.

Webster, Maurice. *1987 Radio Survey.* New York: Radio Information Center, 1987.

CHAPTER 14 \ MUSIC PROGRAMMING

Edd Routt

Nick Alexander

A Guide to Chapter 14

Edd Routt, as general manager of several radio stations and writer on radio, brings a wealth of expertise in news, sales and station management to this chapter on music programming. He creates a hypothetical market in which the reader goes step by step through the process of selecting a competitive format. After deciding on rock music for this proposed station, he details a system for song classification and delineates the role of research. This chapter draws on the author's experience as a broadcast consultant and general manager of KSLM/KSKD, Salem, Oregon; vice-president and general manager of WKRG/WKRG-FM, Mobile, Alabama; general manager of KLIF, Dallas; general manager of WRR-AM/FM, Dallas; and sales manager of WFAA/KZEW, Dallas. In addition, he taught station administration for many years at Southern Methodist University and has written three books on broadcasting: *The Business of Radio Broadcasting* (TAB Books, 1972), *Dimensions of Broadcast Editorializing* (TAB Books, 1974) and *The Radio Format Conundrum* (with McGrath and Weiss, Hastings House, 1978). Mr. Routt and his son now own and operate two Class-A FM stations in Texas: KCKL at Cedar Creek Lake and KXAL in Pittsburg.

Nick Alexander, operations manager of KVIL-AM and FM in Dallas, began his professional career at KAND in Corsicana, Texas, becoming program director before moving to larger markets. He served variously as disk jockey and music director in stations in Tyler, Texas, Ft. Worth, Texas, and Fresno, California, eventually becoming operations manager of KYNO-FM for the Drake-Chenault organization. In 1976, he moved back to KLIF in Dallas working under Edd Routt, later joining him as programmer for WKRG-FM in Mobile, Alabama. In 1979 Alexander became production director of WFAA Newstalk 57 and KZEW in Dallas. After five years, he moved to KVIL where he supervises all commercial operations at the station and does free-lance announcing for advertising agencies. Mr. Alexander adds to this chapter current material on the strategies and practices of several popular music formats.

MUSIC FORMAT POPULARITY

Some stations play **country, classical, beautiful music, ethnic** or **nostalgia,** but **rock** is the prevailing genre in music radio. Rock music encompasses soft rock, hard rock and even country/rock, but it is most commonly classed as top 40, adult contemporary, album-oriented rock, contemporary hit radio, urban contemporary, soft rock and classic rock. More people listen to rock, in one form or another, than to any other style of music. There is no question that the passionate, relentless beat of rock is as firmly established in America as country, jazz and classical. Fueled by a resurgence of interest in the top-40 format, the early 1980s saw more format shifts than any years since the mid-1960s.[1] In all sections of the United States except the South, adult contemporary (AC) and contemporary hit radio (CHR) are the most popular formats, with country music, album-oriented rock (AOR) and beautiful music/easy listening (B/EZ) not far behind (see Figure 14-1).

CHOOSING A FORMAT

The first step in analyzing an unfamiliar market is to evaluate its stations and their current programming. This information can then be used to modify or replace existing program formats or to decide which property to buy and what to do with it after purchase. Such an evaluation takes into account:

Figure 14-1 Format Preferences by Region, 1987

AC—Adult Contemporary, **AA**—Alternative Adult, **AOR**—Album Oriented Rock, **BBnd**—Big Band, **BM/Easy**—Beautiful Music/Easy Listening, **CHR**—Contemporary Hit Radio, **Clas**—Classic, **Ctry**—Country, **Gold**—Oldies, **Jazz**—Jazz, **Misc**—Miscellaneous, **N/T**—News/Talk, **Rel/CC**—Religious/Contemporary Christian, **Span**—Spanish, **UC**—Urban Contemporary. Source: *Radio & Records*. Used with permission.

(1) the technical facilities, as compared to those of the competition; (2) the character of the local market; (3) the delineation of a target audience; (4) the available budget; and (5) the potential revenue. Once completed, this evaluation will determine which music format is commercially viable and can win in the ratings in a given market.

Comparing Technical Facilities

The best facility has the best chance to succeed. Thus, AM's power and frequency and FM's power and antenna height are important considerations. Generically, these elements determine signal quality. A clear, undistorted signal is less tiring to the listener than one that is distorted, faint or accompanied by natural or artificial interference. All other qualities of similar formats being equal, the station with the best signal will be the listener's choice. Emotional fatigue unconsciously sets in after a period of straining to hear a program with a noisy, uncomfortable signal.

An FM station with 100,000 watts of **effective radiated power (ERP)** with its antenna assembly mounted on a 1,000-foot tower is a much better facility than a station with the same power but with the antenna mounted on a 500-foot tower. The AM station with a power of 50,000 watts on a clear channel (820 kHz) is a much better technical facility than a station with 5,000 watts of power at 570 kHz. Usually the low-power station is at the mercy of the higher-power station. A 5,000-watt facility with a country or beautiful music format may be very vulnerable to a same-format station broadcasting at 10,000 or 50,000 watts.

This rule of thumb does not hold in all cases. For example, a 10,000-watt facility at 1600 kHz might easily fall victim to a 1,000-watt station at 710 kHz. In AM, both *power* and *dial position* are important. The lower the frequency, the greater the range of the AM signal. A 1,000-watt station at 710 kHz might easily reach a bigger population than a 10,000-watt station at 1600 kHz.

In FM, *tower height* and *power* are the principal considerations. A low-power (Class A) FM station with a 1,000-foot antenna might cover more territory than a full-power (Class C) station with its antenna mounted 200 feet above average terrain. Dial position is much less important in FM, although the center of the dial gets more sampling. An FM station at the fringe of the band needs an advertising and promotion blitz when altering its format. But always, having the best or one of the best facilities in the market is crucial to beating the competition.

In the AM versus FM competition, when music competes against music, the victories since the early 1970s have been going to FM. A beautiful music format on FM will win in ratings against a similar format on AM, simply because FM reproduces music with greater fidelity. This situation is true also of FM rock versus AM rock and FM country versus AM country. In fact, in recent years, FM has scored greater audience gains than AM in every music format.

The station's technical facility plays an important part in the initial decision to enter music programming competition. It would be aesthetically foolish and economically disastrous to pit, say, a daytime AM against a full-power FM in the contemporary rock field. Conversely, if the leading contemporary music station in a market is AM, and the new facility is a high-quality FM, the AM station will be extremely vulnerable to a programming assault.

Defining the Competitive Market

In deciding on a radio format, the programmer's essential first step is to review the competition thoroughly. Television, cable and newspaper competition can be ignored: Television and newspapers stay relatively stable media no matter what radio does; and cable companies compete principally for audience time, not for advertising dollars (though in major markets with advertising interconnects, cable is indeed an adversary and will become more so in the 1990s).

One of the prospective buyers' first steps toward a purchase decision might be to profile each station's demographics in a bar graph, to show what percentage of each of the six standard demographic groups each station has. The bars in such graphs display the age "leaning" of a station's audiences, suggesting the industry name of **skew graphs.** Arbitron is the principal source of the data; the 6 A.M. to midnight, Monday to Sunday page of a ratings book breaks out all individual demographic groups. However, any audience analysis service providing demographic separation has the necessary information. Table 14-1 shows skew graphs for two stations in the hypothetical market considered in this chapter.

With skew graphs of all stations laid out, program strategists can quickly analyze which age groups are best served by which stations and therefore which stations represent major competition. The examples in Table 14-1 show only age, but sex breakout would also be useful. For example, an AOR (album-oriented rock) operation might show 30 percent adults 18 to 34 years, but the males in the audience usually account for 60 to 70 percent of the total.

Identifying Target Audiences

It is not enough to study population graphs and other research data about a market's radio listeners. It is essential to go into the community to find out specifically what people are doing, thinking and listening to. It is helpful to observe lifestyles by visiting restaurants, shopping centers, gas stations, discotheques, bars, taverns and other places where people let their hair down.

The 40-year-old lawyer who dresses in dark suits during the week and has lunch at a stuffy club may be found in the evenings wearing jeans and a T-shirt in a favorite disco. He is hip, married, has two children and loves to go dancing with his wife. A potential listener to a new rock station? Absolutely! Are there more like him? They number in the thousands in most markets of the nation.

Formal research can supplement personal investigation. Most cities have research firms that can be hired to make special studies, and national firms such as Frank N. Magid Associates and McHugh-Hoffman specialize in broadcast station research. Other well-known radio consulting firms include Reymer & Gersen Associates, Jhan Hiber & Associates, and McGavern Guild Radio. A study assessing current formats using lengthy, in-depth telephone interviews might get interesting responses: too many commercials, bad commer-

Table 14-1 Skew Graphs for a Hypothetical Metro Survey

WMMM-AM

Age Group	Size of Group	Percentage of Total Audience									
		5	10	15	20	25	30	35	40	45	50
Teens	35,000										
18-24	29,500										
25-34	23,500										
35-44	11,400										
45-54	7,400										
55-64	8,700										
Total	115,900										

WNNN-AM

Age Group	Size of Group	Percentage of Total Audience									
		5	10	15	20	25	30	35	40	45	50
Teens	6,000										
18-24	7,000										
25-34	11,900										
35-44	6,300										
45-54	13,600										
55-64	20,000										
Total	64,900										

Source: Arbitron. Used with permission.

cial production, too much kinky music, too many contests, can't win contests, or jocks are idiots. As you can imagine, a station getting answers like these is ready for a major overhaul.

Many broadcasters employ university instructors and students to do summer studies that can be very beneficial. Later on, staff involvement in the community often provides feedback on how the community is reacting to the station's new programming strategies. DJ-manned student discos can provide an additional input channel.

As an example of the kind of findings that prove useful, a station in Dallas identified its typical listener as male, about 30 years old, earning $35,000 a year (in the 1980s), driving a Corvette, drinking a foreign beer, going out at least twice a week with a date to a good restaurant and playing tennis. The station sold this audience description to advertisers and to listeners. Promotional material stressed joining the "in" crowd who listened to this particular station.

Knowing the Available Budget

The usual hit-music operation requires six to eight disc jockies, along with a production director and, perhaps, a music director. In a market of 500,000, the program director may earn as much as $40,000 a year. The morning DJ probably gets $35,000, and the afternoon drive DJ may get up to $30,000. The production director's salary is probably between $20,000 and $25,000 per year, and the other five or six jocks fall in the same range. In the top ten markets, one may have to double or triple these salary figures to get the required talent.

In a medium-sized market (500,000), television and billboard advertising might run $15,000 a month for good exposure. It may cost five times that in a Dallas- or a Chicago-sized market. Not only are unit prices higher in large markets, but usually more territory must be covered. A set of billboards reaching the whole population in one market may require 35 billboards, for example, while a similar showing in Dallas would require 125 billboards.

Consultants are available to advise on every conceivable aspect of operations. Programming consultants find market voids, spot competitor weaknesses and frequently even assemble a staff to work up a specific format. One may employ legal, technical, management, personnel and sales as well as programming consultants—all of them may be useful at one time or another. Consultation is expensive, however. An engineer may charge $500 a day plus expenses; a programmer may charge $3,000 a month on a three-to-six-month contract; for a complete station overhaul, consultants range from $400 to $1,000 a day. In addition, a syndicated program service like Bonneville, depending on market size, could run as high as $10,000 a month. Nevertheless, a neophyte licensee may be literally unable to start up without using one or more consultants. A great deal of highly specialized knowledge and experience must be brought to bear immediately once the Federal Communications Commission has given the licensee authority to start operations.

Estimating Potential Revenue

In any area, advertisers *most* desire the 25- to 54-year-old audience (though most stations count all listeners over age 12). In radio, the audience subdivides into 10-to-15-year segments that specific formats target. Following Arbitron's pattern, most radio audience segments end in a 4. Most advertisers want ages 17–24, or increasingly, as the baby boom generation ages, 25–34 or 44–54 years. Rarely does an advertiser seek the audience aged 55 to 64. Advertisers assume older people are set in their buying habits; they are regarded as saving money rather than spending it, having bought about everything they are ever going to buy. But they see the adult market as having money, responding to advertising and as receptive to buying, even if it means going into debt.

Table 14-2 List of Stations, Types, Formats, Facilities

STATION	TYPE	FORMAT	PERCENT SHARE	FACILITY[a]
WAAA	AM day	Religious	1.0	1 K @ 1500 kHz
WBBB	AM day	Country	4.2	1 K @ 1600 kHz
WCCC	AM day	Talk	2.6	5 K @ 840 kHz
WDDD	AM day	Ethnic	4.8	1 K @ 900 kHz
WEEE	AM day	Local	0.9	1 K @ 710 kHz
WFFF	FM	Classical	1.1	100,000 @ 700'
WGGG	FM	Easy Listening	7.6	100,000 @ 600'
WHHH	FM	Beautiful Music	8.7	100,000 @ 540'
WIII	FM	AC(MOR)	0.8	3,000 @ 250'
WJJJ	FM	Ethnic	6.1	100,000 @ 540'
WKKK	AM	Country	9.9	5 KD/1 KN @ 970 kHz
WLLL	FM	Country	12.1	100,000 @ 700'
WMMM	AM	CHR	16.5	5 KD/5 KN @ 1480 kHz
WNNN	AM	News/Info	5.0	10 K @ 1010 kHz
WOOO	AM	CHR	0.6	1 KD/½ KN @ 1310 kHz
WPPP	FM	AOR	12.1	100,000 @ 540'
WQQQ	FM	MOR/Contemporary	4.9	100,000 @ 1,000'
Other	(Distant signals)		1.1	

[a] K = 1,000 watts; 5 KD/1 KN means that a station uses 5,000 watts in the daytime and reduces to 1,000 watts at night.

Increasingly, stations track the largest population group in the market and adjust their music formats to continue to appeal to this group as it ages. This has resulted in more play of 1960s music (oldies or classic rock), capitalizing on the hit songs of the baby boom's teen years. By the year 2000, however, the baby boomers may be too old to interest most advertisers—unless new products emerge.

STEP-BY-STEP SELECTION PROCESS

Format strategy can be examined by working through a hypothetical market—say, a metropolitan area of 500,000 inhabitants in which 17 stations are heard, licensed either to the metro area or to its suburbs. Further assume that a small group of radio enthusiasts is about to buy one of these stations and to design a program format from scratch. Table 14-2 lists the stations in the market.

All stations are licensed in the metro area in this example, except for two suburban stations. WEEE, the suburban AM daytimer, programs strictly for its local audience. WIII, the low-power FM station, block programs its schedule, running three hours of country music followed by three hours of rock, followed by an hour of gospel and so on. The station about to be sold is

WQQQ in the metro competition with a 4.9 audience share of the market—not bad, but well behind the leaders.

In going over the list of stations in the hypothetical market, the planners identify those with which they do not expect to compete seriously. The prospective facility is FM (a decided plus); it is full power (most desirable); and its antenna is on the highest tower in the market (bingo!). It is otherwise a dog. But the facility is superior to anything in the area.

First, the planners can scratch all AM **daytimers** as potential competition. That narrows the competition from 16 to 11. Next, they can knock out any good **classical** operations (one in the market, WFFF-FM) as most markets can accommodate only a single classical station. That leaves ten. It would be foolhardy to tackle two **beautiful music** easy listening operations with syndicated programming by Drake-Chenault and Bonneville (program consultants providing taped music and program counseling—see Chapter 13)—which is the situation with WGGG-FM and WHHH-FM. These two stations are among the most successful beautiful music stations in the country, and two beautiful music stations should be quite sufficient for this market. Scratching these cuts the field to eight. The FM suburban station (WIII-FM) can be eliminated since it will never be in competition with a high-powered metro FM; the latter certainly is not interested in duplicating WIII's limited and *suburban-oriented* format.

Two **ethnic** stations (WDDD-AM and WJJJ-FM) have a combined share of 10.9. The market shows a black population of only 25,000, or about 5 percent, and no other substantial ethnic population. It would appear that black-oriented radio is well represented by the two stations, showing a combined audience of twice the black population. Scratch one more (the FM ethnic WJJJ as well as WDDD, already counted out as a daytime AM). The field is down to six, plus the proposed buy.

The three **country** stations together have 26.2 percent of the market, and need to be considered. If country were adopted, WQQQ (the proposed buy) could easily defeat the AM daytimer with the country format (WBBB, already written off) and maybe even the AM full-timer (WKKK). But the FM country station (WLLL) would be a serious problem even with WQQQ's signal superiority and top-grade programmers. Although the country format targets an age and occupation group of great interest to many advertisers and is usually profitable, the planners estimate the market is already well served with country formats. Eliminating these two stations leaves four:

- A full-time AM rocker with a 16.5 percent share (WMMM)
- a 10,000-watt news/info AM facility with a 5 percent share (WNNN)
- A full-time AM **rocker** with a 0.6 percent share (WOOO)
- A full-power FM with an AOR format and a 12.1 percent share (WPPP)

Even if deciding how to program WQQQ is still not easy, at least the field of competition is much clearer, and the prospective new owners have weeded out the strong, effective stations from the also-rans. These circumstances surround the final four stations. The full-time AM **rocker** with the 16.5 percent share is an old-line, top 40 that has held top ratings for ten years, although in the last three years its shares have slipped from a high of 20 to the present level. As an AM, WMMM is vulnerable to attack by a well-done FM rocker, using basically the same formula: hit music, personalities, limited news, a few singing logos, games, contests and a lot of community involvement. But this rocker will be a fierce competitor! No new programmer can go into a market and knock off the number-one rocker without a long and costly fight, even if the competitor is an AM.

The 10,000-watt AM station is another old-line operation. WNNN affiliates with several **news** networks, has a heavy **sports** schedule, and generally attracts a 25- to 64-year-old audience, with the largest segment being 35 to 64 years. This station is not competing for the young audience, just the 25 to 54 age group.

WOOO, the full-time AM rocker with the 0.6 share, may be written off. It is poorly financed, and the staff is less than mediocre. It will not be a problem to WQQQ unless it is sold to someone with plenty of money and know-how. Even then, WOOO would be unlikely to reenter the rock field against high-powered FM (WQQQ), the other established rocker (WMMM), and the AOR (WPPP).

WPPP's full-power FM with the **AOR** format may be a problem but not as long as it holds onto its present formula. The AOR plan is a pure format, meaning that the DJs are very laid-back, and the music follows the traditional album line. The format is laced with the Who and Jethro Tull, and the audience has a much larger proportion of males than other music formats draw. New artists are introduced weekly, and new product from known artists is almost automatically sent to the station. WPPP might change formats if the new WQQQ (1) captures a substantial portion of the big AM rocker's audience and (2) cuts into the AOR station's predominantly male audience. Any programmer takes these chances: Sleeping giants are sometimes awakened when new people come to town beating drums to build audiences.

In the hypothetical market, counting both ethnic stations with disco formats, total contemporary listenership is about 45 percent. The AM rocker and the AOR-FM pull an inordinate portion of the audience, 28.6 percent. Three country stations combined have a 26.2 share of the market. There is only one news/information station, but a market of 500,000 will barely take care of one such station, much less two. Also people who listen to these adult-oriented, all-news or news/talk stations are much older and spend their non-news listening time either with the beautiful music stations or the country stations.

According to census data, the 18 to 49 age group represents 56.1 percent of the hypothetical market, and teens make up another 15.1 percent. Altogether, 71.2 percent of this market may be available to tune in WQQQ-FM, leaving a mere 28.8 percent potential for the adult-oriented stations. Advertisers should readily buy time on a new rock station, which clinches the decision to buy WQQQ and rock with a "new age" or "new wave" format.

IMPLEMENTATION

The program director's first step is to get the word out through personal contacts and the trade press that WQQQ is hunting top-40 jocks, a production manager and two people to handle the news. Since this station is going to rock, news will play a minor role. The program director will act as temporary music director to structure the music, and later one of the jocks can take over those duties and audience research. The music director works for the program director, doing research and preparing proposed additions and deletions to the **playlist.** The program director usually makes the final decision; the music director does the background work.

Getting records is fairly easy in larger markets. The program director makes contacts with friends in the record business (*promoters*) to get on their call schedules and mailing lists. This ensures that the station will receive all the current material immediately. Belonging to both **ASCAP** and **BMI** gives the right to play all the popular music, a necessary expense for virtually all music stations. (Classical stations also need to join **SESAC** to obtain foreign and other specialized music performance rights.) Small-market stations can improve their record service by reporting their playlist to trade publications who will place them on industry mailing lists. Developing rapport with record company promoters helps also.

Someone will have to dig for the **recurrents** and the **gold**—especially the latter. Because of their age, these records are scarce; distributors are often out of stock, and pressings are no longer being made. It may take months to build the gold library, and these recordings should be kept under lock and key to forestall avid collectors among staff members.

The program director may decide to "cart" all music—that is, to dub it onto audio cartridges. This enables the station to play its music inventory without damaging the actual discs, whether albums or singles. Carting also produces a control factor. The announcer who wants to play personal favorites will not have the opportunity, if all turntables are removed from the control room, if all music is carted, and if only the carts the program director wants played on the air are allowed in the control room. But carting is costly, time-consuming and risky, and some programmers believe that dubbing inevitably lowers quality. Digitally recorded compact discs, using laser-based technology, are improving the quality of aired recordings, but as of the late 1980s, the cost of the discs, along with technical difficulties in cuing and playing them on the air, makes them less popular with management than carts.

THE MUSIC

The music system that serves as a model for this chapter comes from a combination of systems used by leading radio stations across the country. This system represents one plan for programming an **adult contemporary** station designed to achieve maximum attractiveness to the 25–54 demographic target. The system has six major music categories in the system: power, current, recurrent, power gold, gold and oldies.

1. *Power.*   This category contains from 9 to 11 songs, played at the rate of 3 to 4 each hour. Rotation is controlled so that the same song is not played at the same time of day on consecutive days. Rotation time—the time that elapses before the cycle of 11 songs begins again—varies from as little as 1 hour and 45 minutes in a CHR format, to as much as 4 hours and 15 minutes in an MOR format. The exact rotation is decided by the program director. The songs in this category are the most popular of the day and receive the most airplay. They are selected weekly based on (1) their rankings in national trade magazines such as *Billboard* and *Radio & Records* and (2) local sales. Area record stores are contacted weekly for this information. Some stations also use telephone requests as a barometer of song popularity.

2. *Current.*   This category contains the remaining 15 to 20 currently popular songs. They are played at the rate of 2 per hour (and in an hour with no commercials, 3 might be played). Some stations subdivide this category by tempo, placing slow songs in one group and fast ones in another; other programmers subdivide by popularity, grouping those moving up in the charts separately from those that have already peaked and are moving down in the charts.

The powers and currents together form the station's current playlist of about 30 songs. This formula works on any popular music format, whether contemporary hit radio (CHR), adult contemporary (AC), country (C) or black/urban (B/U). It does not apply, however, to an oldies format, beautiful music, classical or news/talk.

3. *Recurrent.*   This category contains records that are no longer powers or currents, but that have been big hits within the last three years. They get played at the rate of 2 to 4 per hour, depending on commercial load. Some stations limit this category to 30 records played at the rate of once an hour; others may have as many as 100 songs, playing them twice an hour. Songs usually move into this category after being powers or currents, but a few would be dropped from the music list: novelty records that are burned out (see section on research) and records that "stiffed" (failed to become really big hits).

4. *Power Gold.*   This category contains records that were very big hits in the past three to ten years. There may be as many as 150 of these classics, and they are played at the rate of 2 to 3 per hour, depending on commercial load. The songs are replayed every two to three days and rotated across all day-parts. These are the "never-die" songs that will always be recognized by the target audience and immediately identified by them as classics. They greatly enhance the format because listeners get the impression that the station airs a broad range of music.

5. *Gold.*   The gold category contains the rest of the songs from the past three to ten years that are not in the recurrent or power gold categories. This group of 100 to 150 songs is played at the rate of 1 or 2 an hour, depending on commercial load. Songs in this group are carefully researched to make sure they appeal to the station's target demographic group. One source for many gold libraries is the *Miles Chart Display,* which lists every song by its national chart status over several weeks.[2]

6. *Oldies.* This category completes the record library. It is the largest group because it covers the greatest span of time—all the hit songs from the 1950s up to ten years ago. As many as 250 to 300 may be in the group, and they are played at the rate of 1 to 3 per hour. The commercial load and the number of older listeners the station wants to attract will determine how many oldies get played. Songs in this group had to be hits at the time they were released and must continue in popularity. Some programmers subdivide this category by years, as in songs from 10 to 15 years ago, 15 to 20, 20 to 25 and so on. Note that CHR format stations delete this category entirely.

Controlling Rotation

Regardless of format, music stations must control **rotation** (the frequency of play of different kinds of songs). Many stations still use the flip card system, in which each song is placed on a 3 × 5 card in a file box, and DJs are instructed to play the next available and appropriate song and place the flip card at the back of the stack. The gold book preceded the flip card system. The programmer listed all songs in a book, numbering the 31 days of the month beneath each song. When a song was played, the DJ marked out the number of the day on which it was played, each DJ using a different color marker for this. Since a new gold book was used every month, at the beginning of the month listeners often heard songs that had recently been played (even the day before).

Modern computers can be programmed with a host of restrictions to maintain exactly the rotation and balance among songs the music director desires. Computers provide daily or weekly playlists and prevent DJs from cheating; they, as well as the music and program directors, get printed lists of all the songs to be played. (It was easy to skip a 3 × 5 card or cram all the unwanted songs in on the last day of a gold book.) Computers can be programmed to follow a category rotation, avoid scheduling two songs by the same artist closely together, balance up-tempo and down-tempo songs, and much more, leaving control in the hands of the programmer rather than the on-air personality.

The Music Wheel or "Hot Clock"

When not busy interviewing potential DJs, talking to prospects on the telephone or obtaining music, the program director works on constructing **hot clocks** or **wheels.** A hot clock prepared by the program director (or consulting service) is a design, looking like a face of a clock, in which the formula for producing the planned station "sound" is visualized. It divides an hour into portions for music (by category), weather, news, promos and commercials.

Hot clocks tell the DJs where to place the elements that make up the programming for a given hour. The program director will devise as many hot clocks as are needed: one for an hour with no news, another for an hour with two newscasts, another for an hour with one newscast, another for an hour with 8 commercial minutes (or 10 or 12 or however many the station allows and can sell). Hot clocks are examples of **dayparting**—that is, estimating who is listening and what their activities are, and then programming directly to them.

Figure 14-2 Morning Drive Hot Clock

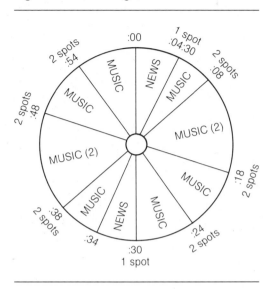

Typically, morning clocks include news, for example, but 7 P.M. to midnight clocks do not. In all, there may be as many clocks as hours in the day, with a completely different set for weekends.

Besides structuring the news, weather, promos and commercials, the hot clock also structures the music for a given hour. The music portion of an hour depends on the number of commercials to be aired. A commercial-free hour requires a lot more songs than a hour with 14 or so spots. Figure 14-2 shows a morning drive hour designed to handle two newscasts and 14 minutes of commercials. This leaves room for a maximum of 10 songs, depending on how much the DJ talks. The music for this morning hour would consist of 2 powers, 2 currents, 2 recurrents, 2 power golds, 1 gold and 1 oldie.

The clock in Figure 14-3 is intended for a late-night show that will not have any news. The music selection contains 16 songs, made up of 3 powers, 2 currents, 4 recurrents, 3 power golds, 2 golds and 2 oldies. This selection fits an adult contemporary format but would differ on a CHR station or an urban or country station. No single set of clock formulas will drive a station to the top in different markets. The key ingredients in designing a successful format are careful planning, ongoing local research and a willingness to adapt to changing audience tastes. Successful music programming is always market-specific.

Music Research

Most music stations employ one or more people to handle **call-out research** and assemble statistics. A rock station's music researcher compiles the list of the local top-selling albums, cassettes and compact discs based on local record store sales. The researcher also keeps tabs on records the station does not play but that are selling due to airplay on other stations and nightspot ex-

Figure 14-3 Nonnews Hours

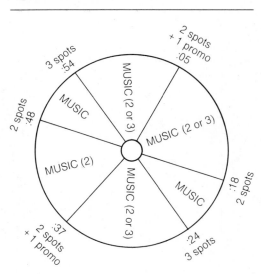

posure. The researcher may be employed full- or part-time and usually works for the music director.

Trade publications such as *Billboard* and *Radio & Records* are studied when adding new music to a playlist. Each week the researcher compiles a chart of the top 30 songs from each magazine and averages them to get composite ratings. Analysis of chart movements of newer songs and news regarding airplay in other areas are also helpful in choosing the "adds." In markets with a sizable black population, the researcher tracks the black/urban charts as well as pop in *Billboard* and *Radio & Records.* In markets where country wins in the ratings, the country music charts can suggest crossover songs. The *more* objective information the researcher gathers, the easier it is for the programmer to evaluate the record companies' advertising and sales. Record promoters will naturally emphasize their products' victories, neglecting to mention that a record died in Los Angeles or Kansas City. The station must depend on its own research findings to rate a piece of music reliably.

As explained in Chapter 2, call-out research gets reactions directly from radio listeners.[3] Two versions of the technique are used—"active" and "passive." In active call-out research, the names of active listeners are obtained from contest entrant lists. The passive version selects names at random from the telephone directory. In either case, respondents are asked to listen to excerpts from the songs being researched or to lists of titles and to rate them on a scale running from 1 to 7 as follows:

1 = "Never heard of it."

2 = "Dislike it strongly."

3 = "Dislike it moderately."

Table 14-3 How to Calculate Votes

TOTAL VOTES FOR	DIVIDED BY TOTAL OF	EQUALS A RATIO THAT MEASURES
6 + 7	sample	Positive acceptance
2 + 3	sample	Negative rejection
5 + 6 + 7	sample	Positive recognition
2 + 3 + 5	sample	Developed dislike
4	sample	Neutral
5	sample	Burnout
6 + 7	2 + 3	Acceptance
6 + 7	2 + 3 + 5	Tolerance
1	sample	Unfamiliarity
2 + 3 + 4 + 5 + 6 + 7	sample	Familiarity

4 = "Don't care."

5 = "Tired of it."

6 = "Like it."

7 = "My favorite record."

When a sample is completed (50 to 100 calls is typical), the votes for each number on the scale are tabulated. The various totals are then manipulated to obtain interpretations in terms of ratios or percentages (see Table 14-3).

For example, assume 50 contest winners are called within a week, and 25 records are discussed. Ten listeners say they like song number *five*, and fourteen say it is their favorite record. Twenty-four of 50 rate number *five* as a **6** or a **7**. For the "positive acceptance" measurement, divide *24* by *50*; the result indicates 48 percent of the audience want to hear number *five* played.

Compare the top 30 to 40 pieces on the current playlist to rankings in *Radio & Records, Billboard, Gavin* and *Record World*. If song number *four* is number one in *Radio & Records,* it gets 30 points. If it rates number *two* in *Billboard,* it gets 29 points; a rating of number *three* in *Gavin* gives it 28 points and so on. After charting each song against the four trade publications, the researcher divides the total by four to get the average ranking. Trade publication rankings are based on data supplied by hundreds of reporting stations. If the researcher finds from the call-out test that number *five* is burned out locally but was nevertheless still running in the top three or four nationally, the song would be retained but assigned a lower rotation position.

When doing caller research of any kind, it is crucial that the questions be asked in the right manner. Contest winners, for example, listen to your station and will tend to answer what they think you want to hear (after all, they are pleased with the station at the moment!). It is important to make them understand that they are being asked to shape the station's music selection. During a music interview, contest winners can also be asked to comment on other things they like or dislike about the programming. This requires a sympathetic ear on the part of the researcher.

When calling people randomly selected out of the telephone book, the first step in an interview is to *qualify* the person—that is, make sure the person is in your target demographic and listens to, or prefers, the kind of music the station plays. The second step is to ask about song preferences.

Another method of radio research, mentioned in Chapter 2, is **auditorium testing.** Several companies specialize in this kind of audience research. Typically, they bring a test group to a large room and ask them to evaluate music as excerpts are played. The tabulated results will be broken down demographically, usually providing valuable information to programmers on what songs to play in which dayparts. Additional questions can be asked such as "What station do you listen to most?" "Second most?" "Who has the best news/the best sports/the best personalities?" "What is the most irritating?" and so on.

NEWS

News has always been a problem on rock and roll stations. Many broadcasters do not want it, cannot afford it, feel their listeners are bored with it, but think they must provide news to satisfy unwritten FCC requirements. They dutifully promise in their license applications to program a certain percentage of news and are stuck with their commitments.

Do listeners want news on music stations? Frank N. Magid Associates, in a study of Los Angeles radio, found that a large percentage of rock listeners were "turned off" by news.[4] These same listeners also hated commercials, PSAs and anything else not related to music and fun. On the other hand, an Associated Press study found that everybody wanted lots of news on their music stations.[5] The Associated Press, which is in the business of selling news services to radio stations, is not likely to publish a study indicating young listeners do not want to hear news. Consultants, however, are in the business of finding out what is wrong with radio stations and have a vested interest in finding things wrong that can be fixed. A 1982 study by R. H. Bruskin Associates for CBS found that news and information make up eight of the top ten elements listeners say they listen for, on both AM and FM stations.[6] At any rate, radio network affiliations are up (see Chapter 13).

In any case, listeners expect to hear news on the hour and the half-hour, and the radio networks still schedule news at those times. Knowing this, some programmers schedule news at odd hours (20 minutes after and 20 before the hour, for example), hoping to pick up new listeners when competing stations schedule their news more conventionally on the hour and half-hour.

Some recent thinking on news scheduling hinges on the habits of some listeners and Arbitron's diary method of surveying listeners. The idea is to hold a listener for at least 5 minutes in any quarter-hour by playing some music (even on a talk/news station) so the station will get credit in a listener diary. On popular music stations, news is therefore buried in the middle of one or two 15-minute periods each hour. This strategy assumes listeners are turned away by news. Increasingly, stations targeting younger listeners are experimenting with eliminating newscasts except in morning drivetime.

Journalistic Content

Having decided where to put news, the programmer must then decide how to handle it, whether to go the low road or the high road. On the low road, jocks rip and read news wire copy as it comes out of the machine (for more on this, see Chapter 15). Some low-roaders satisfy the need for local news by simply stealing from the local newspaper (the news itself cannot be copyrighted, although specific versions of it can). Programmers who set higher goals for themselves do well to hire at least two persons to staff the news operation. One staffer does the air work in the morning while the other develops local stories, mostly over the telephone. The two news staffers reverse their roles in the afternoon. The morning person leaves **voicers** (stories recorded by someone other than the anchorperson) for use during the afternoon and evening newscasts, and the afternoon person leaves them for use early the next morning. This news operation would be relatively luxurious for a music station, however. The typical full-time news staff in radio stations throughout the country is only one person.

Nonentertainment Programming

The deregulation of radio has substantially eased FCC-imposed requirements for nonentertainment programming on radio stations. Minimum amounts of nonentertainment programming for AM and FM stations have been abolished as have the Commission's formal **ascertainment** requirements, although a licensee is still required to "informally" ascertain the problems, needs and interests of the community. On the anniversary date of license renewal, a narrative statement of the problems, needs and interests of the community and the programming the licensee has broadcast to meet those needs must be placed in the station's public file.

Section IV of the new FCC Form 301 requires, for radio stations, only a brief narrative description of the planned programming service explaining how the projected programming relates to issues of public concern in the proposed service area. Programming in general, for new applicants and for renewal applicants, has become progressively less and less an area in which the Commission intrudes.

However, programming representations to the Commission, once made, should be kept. A discrepancy between the amount of programming promised and that actually broadcast (a *promise versus performance* issue) may mean the Commission denies a renewal application (or, at least, instigates legal hearings). Moreover, if a competing application is filed against the renewal applicant, the licensee has an advantage over the competitor only if the FCC can find a "solid and substantial" service record. This record must include news and information programming, PSAs (public service announcements) and community-oriented programming.

News, public affairs and "other" nonentertainment programming create a flow or continuity problem for the formula format. The complaint is that "we have to shut down the radio station to air that junk." Junk, of course, is any programming not directly related to the music format. In stations with an information-oriented format featuring network news, local news, talk and sports, little flow problem exists, of course. Nonentertainment material may be effectively woven into this format. Public service announcements are both nonentertainment and community-oriented programming, and a station can make significant contributions to the community welfare with an aggressive PSA policy.

Radio will probably always be a service medium, and broadcasters will always differ on what constitutes community service. In a competitive major market served by a number of communications media such as newspaper, cable, television, radio, MDS, ITFS, LPTV and DBS, the FM radio station that plays wall-to-wall rock music is doubtlessly providing a service, even though it is merely a music service. In information-poor markets, owners may elect to mix talk shows with music, air editorial comments on community affairs and, in general, provide useful information to the community. The services provided should be based on competitive market factors, the owners' and managers' personal choices and a realistic understanding of the role a radio station can play in some market situations.

AIR PERSONALITIES AND DAYPARTING

In contemporary radio, there are SCREAMERS!!!, trying to wake the very young, and the **shock jocks,** the adult-male-oriented personalities courting FCC retribution daily. And there are very laid-back jocks who just talk conversationally when they open the microphone switch. Then, there are those "friendly" jocks who fall somewhere in between the screamers and the laid-backs. Once there was also the big-voice-boss who told the listener this was a Big DJ, a know-it-all, but this style faded in the early 1970s.

Dayparting is one of the major strategies of the music station programmer. The programmer's challenge is to make each daypart distinct and appropriate to the audience's characteristic activities and at the same time keep the station's sound consistent. The most important ingredient in making daypart distinctions is the personality of the jock assigned to each time period.

Morning

By and large, modern jocks are friendly or very, very laid-back. They "relate" to the target audience. Morning jocks, for example, probably will talk more than jocks on other dayparts, because their shows are service-oriented. They have lots of time and temperature checks. They may chat with the newscasters before the news, may bring the traffic reporter on and off the air, and, in fact, manage the morning team. Listeners preparing for work or school are keen on the time and weather conditions. And the larger the market, the more important traffic reports become. Reports of a pile-up on one expressway give listeners a chance to switch their commuter routes—and the stations a chance to earn a Brownie point.

On most stations the morning jock is the only performer permitted to violate format to any appreciable extent. The trend in the late 1980s was toward paired morning jocks, teams generally having a joker and a straight man or an upbeat and a sexy voice, frequently one male and one female. Normally, morning drivetime personalities are also the most highly paid. They have a greater responsibility than other jocks because the audience is bigger in the 6 to 10 A.M. period than at any other time of day. As the saying goes, "If you don't make it in the morning drive, you don't make it at all."

Midday

The midday jock is friendly, but the incidental services (requiring talk) during this daypart are curtailed in favor of more music. Although there is considerable out-of-home listening in the 10 A.M. to 3 P.M. period, Arbitron data show the majority of the listeners are at home. Many midday jocks capitalize on a large female audience by being sexy, using **liners** (brief continuity between records) having special appeal to women and by talking about what the listener might be doing at home. Some jocks even get off-color at times. In sum, the midday jock is more laid-back than the morning jock and tries especially hard to be warm and friendly.

Afternoon

The afternoon jock (3 P.M. to 7 P.M.) is more up-tempo, as is the music in this period if the station is dayparting. Teens are out of school, and adults are driving home from work, necessitating a delicate balance between teen-oriented music and music suiting the moods and attitudes of the going-home audience. Again, traffic and weather are important in this period but not as much as in the morning. The afternoon jock alludes frequently to evening activities—about how good it must be to finish work and to look forward to playing for a few hours, to taking your honey out, to being with your guy tonight or to doing whatever else people are planning. This jock relates!

Evening

Many contemporary stations program their 7 P.M. to midnight slot much differently from the other dayparts. The music may become heavily disco, heavily black or laced with teen-oriented pieces. Teens are more available to listen at night than the 18 to 49 listeners. Evening jocks may be screamers with a special appeal to teens. They may talk with teens on the phone and air some of the conversations. They may open the request lines and play specific records for specific people. In major markets, and even in many middle-sized ones, this practice creates problems for the phone company. In Mobile, Alabama, WKRG-FM asked the phone company to make a record of calls that did not get through to its four request lines. In one week, there were 65,000 such unsuccessful calls. Imagine what the number might be in Los Angeles or New York! In many major markets in the last decade the telephone company has appealed to station management to stop listener call-ins.

At some top-40 operations, the nighttime slot is regarded as a time for AOR music, but this stratagem has not been notably successful in highly competitive markets—mostly because such a drastic departure from format destroys consistency. A station should maintain basically the same sound in the 7 P.M. to midnight slot as it has in the other dayparts.

All-Night

In the all-night period, from midnight to 6A.M., the jock's attitude is usually one of camaraderie. "We're all up late tonight, aren't we? We have to work nights and sleep days." This jock must commune with the audience: the taxi drivers, revelers, police officers, all-night restaurant and grocery store workers, insomniacs, parents up giving babies two o'clock feedings, shift workers at factories, bakers and the many others active between the hours of midnight and 6 A.M. The commercial load is almost nil during this period, so the jock can provide listeners with a lot of uninterrupted music. Many stations use the period to beef up their PSA quotient, although this burying of PSAs in low-listener hours could be a problem if the owner is challenged at license-renewal time.

Under a strong program director, a kind of "sameness" can develop among all the jocks in a specified format—without the drabness or dullness normally associated with sameness. Sameness here means *predictability*. Listeners tuning in the station at odd hours hear the same "sound" they heard while driving to work in the morning or home in the afternoon.

ADVERTISING AND PROMOTION

The modern radio station pays almost as much attention to advertising and promotion as to programming. They are essential to keep a station from simply disappearing in the crowd. Nowadays stations use television, newspapers, billboards, bumper stickers, bus cards, cab tops and other graphic media. Promotional stunts are the special province of pop radio, involving the cooperation of programming personnel. A national group owner who went into the Dallas market in 1977 was rumored to have allotted a $600,000 budget solely for promotion. By the late-1980s, that figure would have tripled. Many hit music operations, seeking a general (mass) audience with emphasis on the 18 to 49-year-old group, might give away as much as $300,000 a year in cash!

Contesting

The traditional promotional stunt is the *contest*, but the industry favors the word *game*. Many people think they cannot win contests, but they like to play games. For many stations, a contest approach emphasizes a super-prize of $25,000 or more. Such amounts can be offered only once or twice a year (during the Arbitron survey sweeps). And because a station cannot afford to risk losing the big prize on the first day of the game, winning has to be made difficult.

People are more likely to think they can win a small prize than a $25,000 treasure hunt or open a safe containing $50,000. With a superprize, one person is made happy, but thousands are disappointed. Consequently, it is better to break up the $25,000 prize into $25 prizes and scatter them through the year. Direct mail contesting is now widely used to increase listening in specific geographic areas.

Currently popular games include **cash-call,** in which the jock makes one call-out per hour. The jackpot goes to the person naming its exact amount. This game involves a small prize, added to with each call until the correct amount is guessed. The DJs ballyhoo the contest before it starts to generate excitement, sometimes for days and days (*pre-contest hype*). Then they finally hold the contest.

Jock: Is this Mary Jones on Elm Street?*

Listener: Yes, I'm Mary Jones.

Jock: Well, this is Jocko at station WPPP, and if you can tell me the exact amount in our WPPP jackpot, you'll win!

Listener: Mmmmmm. Last I heard it was $485.

Jock: You win! You're right. Mary Jones, you've just won yourself 485 American greenbacks!!! You've ripped us off, you lucky lady you!!!

Listener: Oh, wow! I can't believe it.

The more exaggerated the winner's response to his or her victory, the better the programmer likes it. Later the station will air promos in which each winner's response is repeated and repeated (*post-contest hype*). Hyperbole is the element sought.

Cash-call is but one of many games. The "people's choice" gambit provides a variety of prizes and allows the contestants to identify ahead of time the prizes they want if they win. Magid's Los Angeles study determined that color television sets were very desirable prizes. A thousand dollars in cash was also popular, along with free trips to Hawaii. Prizes and contest rules should be carefully targeted to appeal to the exact age, sex and economic groups the station wants to listen.[7]

Exercise caution in recording and airing telephone conversations. The law requires that the person being called be informed immediately off-air, "This telephone conversation will be broadcast or recorded." Then the dialogue can begin: "I'm Jocko from WPPP." It is a troublesome law that ruins many such calls because once informed, the listener does not respond spontaneously. Management should seek legal counsel on this question and should write specific instructions to programming personnel on how call-out calls are to be handled.

Community involvement projects are as important as contests in programming a successful radio station. The station must be highly visible at local events to gain a strong, positive, local image. The following are community promotions benefitting both the station and the community:

- The station's van (complete with disc jockey, albums, bumper stickers and T-shirts) shows up at the entrance to the hall that features a hot rock group tonight.

---

* Avoid exact addresses and telephone numbers on the air.

- Two or three jocks take the van and disco equipment to the beach (or any public park) on the Fourth of July to provide music and "freebies" to listeners and friends.

- Jocks provide free music for high school and junior high school dances, local fairs and nonprofit benefits.

Commercial Load

More arguments arise over commercial load than any other aspect of programming a rock format. Before the 1970s, FM stations had few commercials because they had few listeners. Researchers began hearing listeners say, "I like so and so because they don't play commercials" or "because they play so much more music than other stations." Lights flashed and bells rang throughout the industry. Listeners hate commercials! Schulke and Bonneville, two of the early radio programming syndicators, began to employ the strategy of music sweeps and stop sets. A **music sweep** is an uninterrupted period of music; a **stop set** is an interruption of the music to air commercials or other nonmusic material such as news headlines.

Herein lies conflict. Sales personnel must have commercial availabilities (unsold spot time) if the station is to make money. Programmers rightfully argue that if the station is to score big in the numbers, it must limit its commercial load. The answer is compromise. Salespeople agree to raise rates, and programmers agree to provide 10 to 12 commercial minutes per hour instead of the 8 to 10 of other formats or the full 18 the sales department wanted. (In 1982, the FCC stopped expecting radio stations to adhere to the now-defunct NAB radio code that specified a maximum of 18 minutes of commercials per hour except during political campaigns and other local, seasonal events when increases were permissible.)

Not only do many successful rock operations run a reduced commercial load, but they also often program (and promote) *commercial-free* periods. Further, the quality of commercial production is critical. Commercial design must complement the format rather than clash with it. A typical commercial for a rock show coming to town indicates how to achieve relatedness: The commercial opens with a piece of the rock group's music, followed by a popular jock touting the show, and ends with more of the group's music. Many rock stations refuse to advertise funeral homes, intimate patent medicines such as hemorrhoidal creams and other products and services they believe will offend their listeners.

One key to understanding radio programming strategy is to compare stations in the number of commercial *spots per break* ("load") and the number of *interruptions per hour*. Too many spots in a roll creates clutter, reduces advertising impact and encourages listeners to twirl their dials (or push buttons). Too many interruptions, on the other hand, destroys programming flow and encourages listeners to migrate on their dials. Since advertising is necessary, management must establish a policy reflected in music wheels ("hot clocks") and stick to it.

In the past, stations have kicked off new formats with no commercial load whatever. They typically offer huge prizes to listeners to guess the exact time and date the first commercial will be aired. Another popular audience-holder is the two-, three-, four-, five-in-a-row concept, with the announcer saying, essentially, "We've got five in a row coming up *without* interruption." The longer the listener stays with the station, the more the station quarter-hour shares are improved. This programming technique is becoming commonplace in music-oriented formats. A tension will continue to exist between the number of commercials and the number of interruptions that can be tolerated.

Call Letters

Gordon McLendon, early innovator of the top-40 format, was one of the first broadcasters to recognize the value of *sayable call letters*. His first big station was KLIF, Dallas, originally named for Oak Cliff, a western section of the city. The station call was pronounced "cliff" on the air. Then there is KABL ("cable") in San Francisco, KOST ("coast") in Los Angeles, WWSH ("wish") in Philadelphia and KEGL ("eagle radio") in Fort Worth. These call letters are memorable and distinctive noms de guerre and get daily usage. Today, nearly every city has a "Magic" and a "Kiss." When the Belo Corporation in Dallas developed a new format for WFAA-FM, the historic letters were changed to KZEW, and the station is now known as "the zoo." (Gagsters used to try to pronounce WFAA, and it came out "woof-uh.")

In recent years, FM stations often combine their call letters and dial position in on-air promotion—especially if they are rock stations. WKRG-FM in Mobile is G100; the RKO station in New York, WXLO, calls itself 99X; in Indianapolis, an AOR station, WFBQ, calls itself Q95; a Bloomington station calls itself 97WB; another calls itself Power 92. This practice generally involves rounding off a frequency to the nearest whole number (102.7 as 103, or 96.5 to 97). The increase in stereo receivers with digital dial displays, however, has discouraged the use of rounding off. More stations now give their actual dial location on the air. Moreover, one undesirable by-product of cable radio's introduction is the need for cable operators to shift stations to new dial positions in cable-FM homes; another is the importation of competing distant radio signals. These factors may herald a return to call letter identification (instead of frequency).

Jingles

The day of the minute or half-minute singing jingle ID is largely gone. Nowadays, having a chorus of singers praise the station for a minute or half-minute is out of the question. That would take time away from popular music, which people tuned in for in the first place. Now most stations keep them very short and to the point. Automated stations sometimes effectively use jingles since they lack a live DJ to fill gaps in programming and repeat the station's name.

FCC AND OTHER CONSTRAINTS

Even with radio deregulation, a myriad of rules, regulations and guidelines exist of which radio broadcasters should be aware. To keep up with them, radio programmers read trade journals and join the National Association of Broadcasters (NAB) and the National Radio Broadcasters Association (NRBA). Programmers, too, have to be aware of legal constraints that may limit their ingenuity. Illegal or unethical practices such as fraud, lotteries, plugola and the like can cost a fine, a job or even a license.

Contests and Games

The principal point to remember about on-air contests and games is to keep them open and honest, fully disclosing to listeners the rules of the game. Conniving to make a contest run longer or to produce a certain type of winner means trouble. Perry's newsletter, *Broadcasting and the Law,* is useful for flagging potential difficulties.

The perennial problem with many brilliant contest ideas is that they are lotteries by the FCC's definition, and lotteries are explicitly and vehemently prohibited. If a contest includes "prizes, consideration and chance," it is probably a lottery. Consult the station's lawyers or the NAB legal staff if there is the slightest question.

Plugola and Payola

Announcers who "plug" their favorite bar, restaurant or theatre are asking for trouble for themselves and the licensees (**plugola**). Similarly, a jock who accepts a color television set from a record distributor in exchange for air play of a record is guilty of **payola.** But the big payola payoffs usually come in drugs, conveniently salable or consumable so they rarely leave evidence for the law. Nonetheless, such practices eventually surface, because talk gets around, leaving the people concerned subject to prosecution. Drugs make station management very nervous because the legal penalties can include loss of the station's license, a $10,000 fine and jail. Certainly any tainted jock's job is likely to disappear instantly. Most responsible licensees require air personnel to sign statements usually once every six months confirming that they have not been engaged in any form of payola or plugola.

Sounds That Mislead

Opening commercials with sirens or other attention-getting gimmicks (such as "Bulletin!") unjustifiably causes listeners to believe they are about to receive vital information. Listener attention can be gained in other more responsible ways that do not offend FCC rules or deceive listeners. Monitoring locally produced commercials for misleading production techniques is especially important.

Program Logs

Any announcement associated with a commercial venture should be logged commercial matter (CM), even though the FCC has done away with requirements for program logs per se. Program logs have many practical applications, aside from the former legal requirement, including billing for advertising, record-keeping, format maintenance and format organization. Common sense dictates a continuation of the old method. Advertisers demand proof of performance, and an official station log is the best evidence of whether and when spots were aired. If a station is challenged on the number of PSAs or nonentertainment programming it has aired, an official station log provides the best evidence of performance.

RADIO'S FUTURE

Music is the main course in radio, and FM does it better. FM will win over an AM facility whenever a showdown occurs. The exceptions occur among information and country music formats and then only for powerhouse AM facilities. A case in point is the sad story of the AM station in Dallas, KLIF, once the unquestioned national leader in rock radio. For 20 years KLIF held number one position in the market and was respected nationally as the station to imitate. Since the mid-1970s, however, Dallas has been an FM market. KVIL-FM is the leading station and shows no signs of weakening. KLIF no longer places among the top ten stations. Eight of the top ten in any market with more than twelve stations will probably be FM. KRLD (AM) and WBAP (AM) number in the top five in Dallas, but these are 50,000-watt stations on clear channels, programming news/sports and country music/baseball, respectively. The Dallas picture is being repeated in market after market across the country.

FM has become the home of adult contemporary and a whole package of rock formats. What lies ahead for AM radio? Not pop music, that seems certain. Oldies? Country music? Maybe. MOR music? Perhaps. But in no case can an AM stand up to a well-programmed FM station. One strong and recurrent view is that AM must program information to older audiences, even though doing so is expensive and complicated. So news and talk become viable alternatives for AM radio. Continued strength in the radio industry nationwide, however, suggests there is room enough for both AM and FM. Spot advertising revenues for radio continue to rise, and increasing numbers of new advertisers are learning radio is an effective medium for them. The programming problem is to locate a sizable audience not being served by a stronger facility in the same market.

For daytimers, religion has become a mainstay, along with limited-audience ethnic formats. However, the difficulties are illustrated by KKDA (Dallas), once a country music station. New owners launched a black-oriented format and quickly gained position in the market. When they then acquired an FM facility and duplicated their format, all of the AM listeners switched over to the FM station. The AM daytimer that once fared well was reduced to an also-ran. Frequently, an FM will show 7 and 8 shares in markets with more than 12 stations, while an AM daytimer plods along with 1s and 2s. AM stereo is mostly a gimmick, useful in promoting an AM station, but until a large turnover in receivers occurs, there will be few AM stereo listeners.

"New wave" was the latest and hottest thing in the music business in the early 1980s. It was a refinement of punk rock, but having more lyrical content and appealing to an audience with downscale demographics. By the mid-1980s, it was being called "new music" and showing Australian and British influence along with danceable, Americanized lyrics. AOR is now a one-per-market format, but most markets can support two easy listening stations.

The massive return to top 40 occurring under labels such as contemporary hit radio, hot hits and adult top 40 uses faster rotation times and top-rated songs, incorporating the new music in a flexible, trendy format, influenced by MTV, the cable music channel. In the late-1980s, stations were following the aging baby boom generation by increasing the proportion of oldies in their formats. "Classic Rock" had become the newest fad. Riding this wave, Transtar created "Format 41," targeting adults 33 to 48, with a median age of 41, hence the format name. Simultaneously, Z-Rock appeared, a hard rock format targeting the male-dominated 12 to 24 audience.

But many programmers overreact to fads in music. When disco first appeared, WKTU-FM in New York embraced it and zoomed to first place in one book, then faded. A few years ago, someone conceived of a solid gold format. One station in Detroit tried it, made good gains in the first book, then fell back into obscurity. Another station tried commercial-free radio for three months, soared in the ratings, then fell back into ninth place. Such formats are like the hula hoop: a craze today, forgotten tomorrow. What works is consistency—in service, in music, in technical quality, in station identity. The fast-buck artist does not stand a chance in the marathon race for big audience and big dollars.

This chapter has touched on only the more obvious strategies involved in the fascinating art of programming a modern music station. To the uninitiated, all radio music formats may seem much the same. In actuality, each is replete with subtle and not-so-subtle variations. To program a formula successfully in today's competitive market requires never-ending ingenuity, insight and professional growth. The name of the game is change, but it must be accomplished by consistency in the on-air sound. Radio programming is constantly evolving, and for those who enjoy innovation, it offers a rewarding challenge.

SUMMARY

Five factors determine which music format will win the largest audience market. Of these, the most influential is the quality of the technical facility. FM produces inherently higher-quality sound than AM, and that gives it an undisputed advantage in music competition. Among FMs, tower height and power give decided advantages, but among AMs, power and dial position matter. The remaining factors of market, target audience, budget and potential revenue indicate what programming is most competitive. Once a format has been selected, a staff must be hired and a record library created. The next big job is to program the music wheels for all the major dayparts and weekends. In broadcasting, dayparting means altering the programming at different times of the day to fit the audience's activities. Different styles of disc jockey patter match different dayparts on a popular music station. This chapter described a rock music rotation system composed of power, current, recurrent, power gold and oldies classifications. How to classify songs and rate them are the functions of the station's music research department and depend heavily on the radio trade press. The role of news and nonentertainment programming on a popular music station remains controversial, but once promises are given to the FCC, adherence must follow. Drug payoffs persist as a payola problem. The amount and kinds of on-air promotion and the number of commercials and breaks in programming also delineate stylistic differences among competing popular music stations. In the late 1980s, stations began returning to top-40-type formats.

Notes

1. Robert Sobel, "Top 40 Revival, New Artists Rock Music Radio," *Television/Radio Age,* 29 August 1983, pp. 25–27ff.

2. Daniel J. Miles, Betty T. Miles, and Martin J. Miles, *The Miles Chart Display of Popular Music* (New York: Arno Press, 1971 to date).

3. James E. Fletcher, and Roger D. Wimmer, *Call-Out Research in Managing Radio Stations* (Washington, D.C.: National Association of Broadcasters, n.d.).

4. KHJ-AM audience study by Frank N. Magid Associates, 1976, reported by Chuck Martin, program director, 1979.

5. "Radio News Listening Attitudes," survey conducted by Frank N. Magid Associates for Associated Press in 1977, abstract, 11b.

6. R. H. Bruskin Associates study, August 1982, commissioned by CBS Radio and presented to CBS Radio Network Affiliates, Phoenix, September 1982. See "AM and FM Listeners Have a Lot in Common," *Broadcasting,* 27 September 1982, pp. 81–82.

7. For a more detailed discussion of contesting and prize structures, see "Commercial Radio Promotion" by Harvey Mednick in *Strategies in Broadcast and Cable Promotion* by S. Eastman and R. Klein (Belmont, Calif.: Wadsworth, 1982; reissued Chicago, Ill.: Waveland, 1988).

Selected Sources

"Beyond the Ratings," monthly newsletter. Laurel, Md.: Arbitron Ratings Company, 1977 to date.

Billboard. Weekly trade magazine for the record industry, 1888 to date.

Bortz, Paul, and Mendelsohn, Harold. *Radio Today—And Tomorrow.* Washington, D.C.: National Association of Broadcasters, 1982.

Duncan, James H. *American Radio.* Kalamazoo, Mich.: Duncan's American Radio, twice yearly with supplements.

Lotteries & Contests: A Broadcaster's Handbook. Washington, D.C.: National Association of Broadcasters, 1985.

Radio In Search of Excellence: Lessons from America's Best-Run Radio Stations. Washington, D.C.: National Association of Broadcasters, 1985.

Shane, Ed. *Programming Dynamics.* Washington, D.C.: National Association of Broadcasters, 1984.

Sklar, Rick. *Rocking America.* New York: St. Martin's Press, 1984.

"Special Report: Radio." *Broadcasting* (4 February 1985):51–59; (11 November 1985):35–52; (28 July 1986):46–79; (27 July 1987):45–64.

"Radio: Special Report." *Electronic Media* (7 September 1987):R1–R8.

Routt, Edd; McGrath, James B.; and Weiss, Fredric A. *The Radio Format Conundrum.* New York: Hastings House, 1978.

Radio & Records. Los Angeles: Radio & Records, Inc. Weekly newspaper covering the radio and recording industries.

CHAPTER 15 \ NEWS RADIO

Don J. Brewer
Susan Tyler Eastman

A Guide to Chapter 15

Don J. Brewer writes of the day-to-day strategies of all-news radio. After more than 20 years with KYW News Radio, the nationally known innovator in the AM radio field owned by Group W Broadcasting, Mr. Brewer brings an extensive background in radio broadcasting to this chapter. He was regional affairs director for KYW as well as food and wine editor for all seven Group W radio stations for more than a decade. He was a station manager for a Department of Defense radio station in Germany after World War II, civilian director of the American Forces Network, Europe, and program director of Radio Free Europe before coming to KYW as an executive producer in 1970. He brings an insider's perspective to radio journalism.

Susan Tyler Eastman, one of the editor-authors of this book, provides a national perspective on news radio strategies and scheduling. Her background appears at the start of Chapter 9. Together, these authors review news programming options.

NEWS FORMAT PREREQUISITES

News radio holds a unique position in listeners' media behavior. In cars and offices and stores, nearly everyone turns to radio for news at times of disasters and historic events. Radio has a long tradition of bringing fast-breaking headlines to listeners more quickly than other media. This chapter looks at local *all-news* radio programming, a continuous source of news headlines and features.

Cost and Commitment

The all-news format strains the infrastructure of current broadcasting establishments—whether group-owned or independent—because the cost commitment is high. News cannot be automated, as so many other radio formats have been. Consequently, **all-news** is limited to major markets where sales revenue can match program outlay and where the potential news audience is large. And even under these conditions, the format is not likely to be very profitable. The same investment in another format would bring a much greater return both initially and once established. For the foreseeable future, all-news is a prestige format, practiced best by major network affiliates and group owners willing to absorb initial high costs and low ratings. Most all-news stations are stations owned by CBS or Westinghouse (Group W).

In the 1980s, several mid-market all-news stations moved to the **news/talk** format. This format is more flexible than all-news. For example, when a series of significant national events occur, such as hot events in the Near East, the stations shift to all-news; as the amount of hard news diminishes, they incorporate more talk and soft news features. The early morning television newscasts and overnight television news services now compete with radio all-news stations, forcing many to add original feature programming to their formats to remain competitive. However, flexible formats and popular features may threaten the news station's credibility. The farther the programming moves from journalism, the more it becomes an entertainment medium. And a gain in the entertainment column seems to mean a loss in the information column in the audience's long-term view. The basic caveat for any all-news programmer rests in one word: *credibility*. It must be maintained in every program element from headline to commercial; it goes a long way to ensuring an enterprise's success. It is the unique thing an all-news station has to offer audiences.

The news director of an all-news station lives with a very forthright credo: "Communicate credibility by commitment." The unspoken C in this dictum is *cost*. The resources needed to operate an all-news station are considerable. Attracting an audience of sufficient size and loyalty is a formidable task. Maintaining both journalistic standards *and* program innovation is constantly challenging. Management must be aware of these factors if the format is to survive. No format demands more management involvement. The heartening thing is that, once firmly entrenched, all-news programming commands a fanatically loyal audience. If creatively programmed, the all-news station can capture a broad range of listeners attractive to advertisers.

Founding Stations

In the mid-1960s, two major broadcast establishments laid the foundation for operating all-news radio stations as we know them today. The first was Group W, Westinghouse Broadcasting Company. It converted three AM stations—WINS (New York) and KYW (Philadelphia) in 1965 and KFWB (Los Angeles) in 1968—to all-news programming. CBS followed suit with WCBS-AM (New York), KCBS-AM (San Francisco) and KNX-AM (Los Angeles); later, WBBM-AM (Chicago) and WEEI-AM (Boston) were converted and in 1975, WCAU-AM (Philadelphia).[1] By the late-1980s, about 50 all-news stations were operating in major cities.

In 1974, NBC began an abortive experiment of providing an all-news network service called News and Information Service (see Chapter 13). Its demise in 1976 worked hardship on many of its medium- and small-market affiliates, most of whom subsequently dropped the all-news format or modified it to talk/news. The emergence of AP and UPI audio news services in the late 1970s, plus major network news and information divisions such as the ABC Information Network, gave heart to the survivors. But what was a tough, tentative format for many in major markets because an impossible, costly burden for stations on the economic fringe going it alone. As of the late-1980s, the national news networks played an important role in supporting local news gathering by providing headline services and national and international news stories. But all-news is essentially a locally programmed format. Network affiliation provides coverage most local stations could not supply; group ownership can provide shared features and investigative reports; but in the end, each station must support a full staff to fill the broadcast day.

INDEPENDENT AND NETWORK COMPETITION

A competitive pattern has emerged in the brief history of all-news radio stations: A well-operated, all-news station in a major market can count on a 5 to 10 percent audience share. It there are two all-news stations, they divide the audience share (given relatively equal effort and appeal). The format is not normally subject to radical ratings swings, perhaps because its audience is quite loyal.

All-news competition usually occurs between a network outlet and an independent station. The network-affiliated station programmer has the advantage of network resources but must air obligatory network news at key times. Thus, if the breaking story is local, the affiliate may be running behind the story, being forced to air the network feed that ignores a big local event. Added to that is the gnawing feeling among the staff that they are second-class citizens because the network voice automatically preempts their voices. The other side of the coin is that they must scramble to equal the network staff's professionalism to create a consistent sound. Although the independent does not have the same problems, it does have the entire burden of staffing and reporting national and local news, aided only by the wire services.

Aside from head-to-head combat, all news stations face a subtler form of competition arising from the *drivetime newsblock confrontation*—usually instigated by a well-established music station in the market with a fairly strong news department. To cope with the all-news station's intrusion into its market, a music station will often expand its news programming, particularly in morning drivetime. Since the music station can afford to compress its news staff effort into a two- or three-hour period, the facade of an important news effort can be erected. This tactic, coupled with a well-regarded local disc jockey, can be formidable indeed. Pulling away from such a station over a stretch of time is not too difficult, however, because sustained, tight utilization of news team strength will tell. Heavy use of well-researched and well-programmed series, made up of short vertical or horizontal documentaries in morning drivetime, is one of the most effective countermeasures. (**Vertical documentaries** are stories aired in brief segments throughout one day; **horizontal documentaries** occur in segments over several days, perhaps weeks.)

Programming the Coverage Area

Difference in signal strength among stations is often mentioned as a key advantage or disadvantage. For news stations, too strong a signal may lead to spreading its resources too thinly. For network-owned or affiliated news stations this is not a hazard because the network base is broadly appealing without the constant need for as much local backup as the independent programmer has to muster. Concentrating on the smaller metro-area audience can be more rewarding for the independent station in terms of audience loyalty than trying to be too many things to too many people at once. Such a situation exists in the Los Angeles area. There, listeners can tune (within the L.A. primary-coverage zone) to a 5,000-watt independent, while a 50,000-watt network outlet serves a much greater audience area. Power limitation, translated to audience limitation, is an obvious programming constraint. The programmer must be aware that many in the metro audience relate to outlying population groups and want to know, to some degree, what is going on "out there." Still, the metro-limited station cannot afford to cover the fringe audience too generously. Adding a metro-assignment reporter to the staff of the metro-only station tends to pay bigger dividends than making a spread gesture by setting up a suburban bureau in an area with few listeners. Suburban bureaus are for stations with wide-area signal coverage and adequate support budgets.

Setting up suburban bureaus, however, manned by outside reporters, ensures regional coverage. This strategy has its limitations—high cost in areas of necessary concentration—but it works to great station advantage. When economic factors dictate, **stringers** (free-lance reporters paid per story) can often cover an entire geographic area for the station, an especially useful approach for small- and medium-sized stations. The prime advantage of *full-time reporters* is their visible and audible station presence in the outlying areas. Serving the major-market bedroom communities nets the station their involvement and empathy. If, however, population is sparse or mainly rural, *stringers* are the cheaper alternative. A well-managed pool of stringers can add informed reporting of local issues without requiring local bureaus.

Sources of Programming

The all-news program manager has a multitude of programming resources available. If the station is a network outlet, most of the basic feature input is supplied, often by glamorous newscasters who lend a touch of extra authority. In most cases, these network features are line-fed at fixed times, and local program managers have little room for imaginative scheduling.

In the network wheel in Figure 15-1, the *N*s indicate live network feeds that usually restrict the local programmer's options. The letter *f* refers to features that may originate at the network or locally. If the features can be tape-delayed, local news directors have space to develop their own matrices, shuffling the tapes to fit around local news items. In either case, feature handling is usually a mix of advantages and disadvantages for the programmer. The main network support comes in the form of network personalities, often from the television side, reinforcing "name" prestige through features, promos and special series production.

The programmer connected with a group or chain of stations will probably have major cross-feeds from sister stations and possibly a Washington or New York bureau on which to draw. A bureau provides stories, analyses of national political and economic news and coverage of special events such as press conferences, U.N. developments and personality interviews. Added to these highly professional programming sources is the freedom to develop local staff and resources. The degree of station independence varies considerably among group-owned stations, but scheduling is normally left to the local manager.

FORMAT DESIGN

The news wheel, or programming infrastructure, forms the skeleton on which hang the sections of hard news, features, sports commentaries, editorials and so on. News is repeated in 20-, 30-, 45- or 60-minute sequences. Cycle length affects spot and headline placement, time, traffic, weather and

Figure 15-1 Network Affiliate All-News Wheel

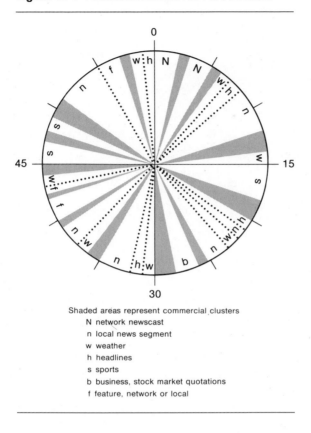

Shaded areas represent commercial clusters
N network newscast
n local news segment
w weather
h headlines
s sports
b business, stock market quotations
f feature, network or local

sports scheduling, major news story development and feature scheduling. As illustrated in the following sections, advantages and disadvantages accrue to all lengths; *which* a programmer chooses depends on local market conditioning to the format, staff capability, editorial supervision and content elements.

Spot Placement

The initial task of the all-news programmer, in company with other department heads, is to create the wheel (see Figure 15-1). The **wheel** is a pie chart of an hour divided into segments denoting points for insertion of commercials and public service announcements, normally clustered to minimize clutter. The general, sales and program managers start by agreeing on just how confining or flexible the wheel is going to be.

Typically, each hour contains 12 to 16 minutes of spot announcements spaced out in 18 interruptions (see Figure 15-2). Frequent breaks in the flow for commercial spots create less interruption in news than in music formats; voice shifts accompanying content changes are typical of news delivery and, in fact, contribute to its appeal. Commercial spots are usually less out of

Figure 15-2 Commercial Spot Spacing

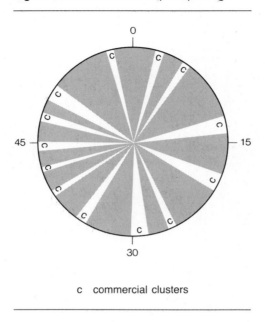

c   commercial clusters

place in an all-news format than in an all-music format. Restricting each spot break to one or two minutes of commercials and returning quickly to news content is important.

Headlines

Headlines are the handle to the news wheel. Normally programmed at the top of the hour and at the half-hour (see Figure 15-3), their presentation style and substance must be determined carefully. If they tease or bear only a slight relation to the stories that follow, credibility suffers. The program manager who fails to define headline policy carefully and fails to oversee how the staff applies it has a stuck zipper in the format.

For example, a **tease** headline might be written, "And, in Salem, Oregon, today, a wife who cried rape got an answer." This tabloid approach is damaging sensationalism. The ethical headline for an all-news format is more closely approximated as, "A jury in Salem, Oregon, has ruled against a husband, charged by his wife with rape while they were living together." If listeners are teased by the first kind of headline and distracted from hearing the follow-up story in detail, they have been deprived of valid information and will resent the station that "half-informed" them.

Sound beds (music backgrounds), gimmicky writing or flashy delivery weaken credibility and the cycle's rhythm. One common practice that works is to repeat a single, top story headline at the quarter- and three-quarter-hour points, usually as a prelude to weather, sports or some other format basic. As a subtle form of audience-attention reinforcement, it has wide acceptance.

Figure 15-3 Headline Placement on the Wheel

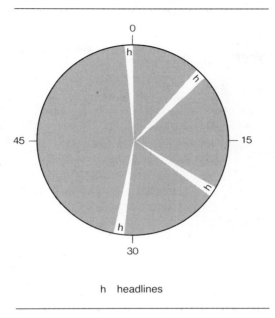

h   headlines

Time and Traffic

Once the wheel's spots and headlines are set, **personal service** components such as *time, traffic, weather* and *sports* can be keyed in (see Figure 15-4). Time and traffic announcements gain in importance during certain dayparts, especially morning drivetime. Determining their length is a pivotal decision, as is their frequency. And when time lags occur between on-site observation and actual broadcast, inaccurate traffic information seriously undermines the all-news station's believability.

Weather

The arrangement of *personal service elements* should be extremely flexible within the wheel. At times, of course, weather and sports become hard, major stories in and of themselves, such as during a major blizzard or when a local team wins a championship or fires its coach.

Weather is a key to an all-news station's prime programming periods. If a professional meteorology service is used, the station gains a special kind of credibility. Even in-house use of National Weather Service wires, area airport reports, Coast Guard data or standard wire service reports can be mixed to fit local audience needs. It is desirable, however, for the announcer to supplement wire reports by looking out the window.

Drivetime weather reports are usually short, covering only immediate-area conditions. An occasional forecast can be added to tell commuters what to expect going home and for the night to come. When a significant number of boaters, private pilots or farmers occur in the audience, special weather reports

Figure 15-4 Weather and Sports on the Wheel

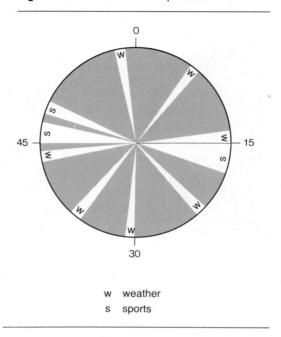

w   weather
s   sports

are useful at intervals. And the long-distance business commuter should get at least a spot check two or three times a day on weather in major cities the local airport serves.

Special weather reports can run from 30 seconds to 2 minutes and can be tied to a hard news story if conditions warrant. In general, weather is increasingly important as it becomes extreme (affecting commuting), during holidays (affecting travel) and as the weekend nears (affecting leisure plans).

Sports

Sports is generally granted the quarter- and three-quarter-hour slots, with local interest, volume, time of day and pressure from other news features determining its length. Sports reporting is anchored to scores and area team activities, but sportscasts are normally expanded on weekends to cover many more games or contests at distant points—after all, in the farthest reaches of Maine and California, Notre Dame alumni associations persist. Although weekday sports segments are usually held to about 2 minutes at the quarter- and three-quarter-hour marks, weekend sportscasts are easily expanded to 10 or 12 minutes.

In both weather and sports reporting, accuracy and timing are critical. A careful study of the market for various kinds of weather and sports information will dictate if segments should expand or contract. As in all other news areas, being right is more important than being first. The programmer who neglects a sizable special interest group will find the competition filling the gap.

THE NEWS PROGRAMMING

The station news programmer can creatively mix the elements of news programming within the format limits. The major elements—news, editorials and features—fill about 75 to 80 percent of an all-news wheel. Commercials, public service announcements and promotional announcements make up the balance.

Hard News

Typically news occupies about 75 percent of airtime. Within this general category fall **hard news** copy; recapitulations of major stories (**recaps**); question-and-answer material from outside reporters via mobile radio or telephone (**actualities**). These elements form the bulk of radio newscasts. To them, stations add in-studio *interviews, news conferences, round-table discussions,* and special *remotes* to balance coverage and add local flavor and variety.

Editorials

Most stations use an editorial director as writer, and the general manager often "voices the copy" (reads the material on the air). The most common schedule for editorials, running a minute or slightly longer, is a "26 Plan," entailing 26 plays per week for a given editorial occurring in all dayparts.[2] Depending on the number of **editorials** produced in a given week (usually two to four), they are salted throughout the schedule, Monday through Saturday, and each is repeated no more than once in each daypart.

For editorial content, most stations stick to local issues, avoiding national controversies and unresolvable social problems. Station management credibility is strained if the issues are too large, too unresolvable or require credentials management lacks. Widely reported local problems on which closure will occur in the coming months are especially suitable; they fit easily into the very brief format used for most editorials since listeners already know a great deal about the subjects. Issues that will be resolved by coming elections or events of moderate interest are usually safe for editorial comment. Also those problems about which all listeners agree (public safety, drunk driving, utility rate hikes, the dearth of children's television, violence in the streets) provide targets for numerous editorials.

Some stations take their editorial responsibility seriously, seeking to shape community opinion on controversial issues. But in the early 1980s, a new wave of tough-talking copy urged public action. Many editorial subjects raise fairness issues, and despite the end of the FCC's fairness doctrine, station owners usually have policies favoring airtime for opponents to respond. Even so, some editorials have stimulated legislative action and public awareness because of their hard-hitting content.[3]

Editorials are best scheduled in a section of the wheel farthest from the top stories, assuming that the news items are mainly local and that the editorials deal with local issues. Such scheduling means editorials appear toward the end of a 60-minute cycle. Local editorials and syndicated or network commentaries can be easily confused in some listeners' minds because they come from "strange" voices and are both persuasive statements, seeking to alter the listener's point of view. Separating editorials and commentary by at least 15 to 20 minutes is best, but one of each can fit into a 60-minute cycle. In any case, features, including editorials, should never be clustered, causing the listener to lose identification with the station as a hard news voice.

Features

Features are the salt and pepper in the format. In most cases, the reports or miniprograms are between 1-1/2 and 2 minutes long. Independent all-news stations either hire their own commentators and feature editors or purchase syndicated material from production houses or network sources without market presence. Group all-news stations usually do both; network affiliates, of course, share in the popularity of established news personalities. Public affairs, 7 to 8 percent of the mix, usually falls into one of six categories:

1. *Cultural segments* review local theater and films, food and wine shows, or report on local galleries and major museum exhibitions.

2. *Features* on science and medicine are well received, particularly those on personal health matters. This subject is handled either by a recognized local authority prominent in the medical community or by a national authority, who usually gives a lay summary of new material from leading publications for the professions.

3. *Business commentary* is another category frequently aired, going beyond stock market reports (basic news). A local brokerage house, a regional stock exchange or a syndicator such as AP or UPI provides them.

4. *Religious features* normally dwell on area judicatory meetings, plus church news of a social nature. But occasionally an all-news station will add a national commentator, usually syndicated, such as Norman Vincent Peale with his series of short homilies.

5. *Educational features* are an important building block in the format, particularly since so much hard news erupts from the school system nowadays. This area is a delicate one. The programmer obviously can get burned by a controversial commentator. Still, the material has to go beyond a recital of PTA meetings and social notes to be meaningful. Some risk-taking is necessary.

6. *Commentary* is authoritative personal opinion, as distinguished from station editorials reflecting management policy and opinion. Commentaries and commentators are delicate balancing acts. Many all-news stations shy away from local commentary because it is easily confused with the station's editorial policies. But, once a given format has matured, there is no real reason to steer away from local commentaries as long as they are not placed too close to the editorials and have a distinctive character of their own.

Figure 15-5 Network and Local News on the Wheel

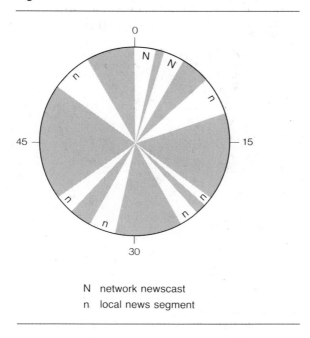

N   network newscast
n   local news segment

SCHEDULING CONSIDERATIONS

In a full-hour cycle after playing *commercial clusters*, *headlines* and *basic format elements* (time, traffic, weather, sports), eight fairly stable sections for news are left. The first and fifth sections contain the *hard news* (see Figure 15-5). The second and sixth segments normally deal with *news stories* of less immediate importance. The remaining sections incorporate some *soft news* and a mix of carefully selected *features* and news of local value. The fourth or eighth section often includes a station *editorial*—meticulously identified as management opinion. This pattern gives the listener headlines, hard news, more news, soft news and features in a repeating hourly cycle although the sources and specific content always vary.

Priorities

Within the basic format design, programming priorities should be explicitly recognized. First, programmers must disabuse themselves of the idea that earthshaking news developments on a global or national scale are uppermost in the audience's notion of what is news. Since the morning drivetime is the peak period of audience interest for most stations and, therefore, the most viable period commercially, it is then that personal services should be most frequent and varied. Schedule in this way: Time announcements at least every 2 minutes; weather information (of the moment and forecast) no more than 10 minutes apart; traffic information every 20 minutes (as accurate and close to the

Figure 15-6 Independent All-News Station Wheel

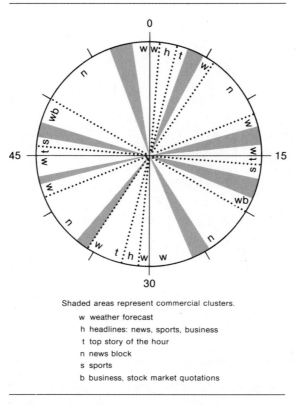

Shaded areas represent commercial clusters.

w weather forecast
h headlines: news, sports, business
t top story of the hour
n news block
s sports
b business, stock market quotations

Source: Prepared by Don J. Brewer, KYW-News Radio.

flow as humanly possible although the ideal will vary from market to market); plus, interspersed, allied information such as school closings, major area sports events and so on. In other words, the top priority in any all-news format is local, personal service programming. Item repetition slows during the day and is stepped up during evening drivetime (4 to 7 P.M.).

Flexibility

Although the mechanics of the format formula vary, its strategy is closely constrained. Many outside forces dictate the degree of a manager's flexibility within the format around the wheel. If the station is network-affiliated, the program manager must work around prior commitments to network segments; consequently, local discretion diminishes. If the all-news station is an independent, choice is wider (see Figure 15-6). Other sources of program material, however, often dictate placement. For example, sponsored segments may be sold as fixed positions in the wheel.[4]

Live-feed items also interrupt the cycle's rhythm. Adjusting program elements within the fixed dimensions of the product base is a continual process. The programmer must guide the process, but those decisions are strongly influenced by cost considerations, staffing patterns and the like.

News Repetition

Next to credibility, *predictability* demands primary consideration in news format construction. The programmer may wrestle a long time with this issue because program elements such as time, weather and sports are usually fixed within the cycle for audience access. But too many predictable items reinforce the canard that all-news is little more than endless repetition.

Programmers must remember that they and their staffs are *handling,* not manufacturing, the product. The placement and rotation of its basic elements become important, in a sense, inversely to momentum. In time periods in which local, national or world news creates a **critical information pile,** the cycle almost moves itself. When an event dominates all news sources, the editor has many opportunities to choose among wire services, external story angles and a variety of reaction sources. In effect, the story runs itself. In the slow news spaces, product management becomes crucial. The news programmer then controls the story, planning a measured release of information on the air, affecting the news event's very real impact on the audience. News management means carefully watched story placement, creative rewriting of leads and precisely calculated lifespan for individual stories.

Feature Repetition

Scheduling features is the fine art of format structuring. Beware of three pitfalls: scheduling repeats too frequently, scheduling material requiring more listener retention than they find convenient or including irrelevant non-local material. For example, if a feature segment is aired on a Wednesday at 10:40 A.M., then aired on Thursday and Friday at the same time or within an hour either way, chances are the audience will be largely the same. Scheduling the repeat of a morning drive feature in evening drivetime merely causes resentment in many drivers that catch both broadcasts.

The important question is how much soft (as opposed to hard, fast-breaking news) material is available? When? How often? What kind? Most soft material based on an audience's natural interest in medical and health information, the entertainment industry or hobby material, finds a catholic reception. Local audiences vary, of course, in what they need and will accept. The lesson from the consumer reporter fad of the 1970s was that when a special feature blurs into the normal flow of news, the program manager should take a hard look at its value as a separate program item.

COST AND QUALITY

In a 24-hour period the average all-news operation takes in about 400,000 words from all sources, including teletype; telephone; line-feeds from network, group or contract services; stringers; and its own beat reporters. Of this data, less than half will be aired. Control of product vis-à-vis control of cost requires a finely honed strategy. Cost-control cuts in many directions, but it counts most when the opportunity arises to "own a story." A lack of budget reserve at those crucial moments leaves a manager unable to capitalize on strength and gives competition an audience edge hard to overcome.

Original Reporting

The shrewd all-news programmer will be keenly aware of news themes that are being "ridden" in the market—a tendency among radio reporters and editors to follow on a story a local newspaper or television station generated, such as series on child abuse or auto repair swindles. If a radio news reporter picks up such a theme and converts it to a series of reports, it is not only duplicative (even when new material is exposed) but also drains budget. Rather, the prudent programmer hoards a portion of the operational budget for other opportunities—a local disaster, major storm or an original investigative project by the station staff—and then goes all out to swamp the story from every possible angle, thus "owning" it compared to the competition. One dividend of this maneuver is that such coverage is very likely to be an award winner is one of the several national or regional competitions that wire services, universities and professional associations sponsor. The station not only owned the story but picked up some prestige along the way. Corporate management likes to see awards on the wall as visible proof of station status and enterprise.

Reporting Assignments

In building audience and meeting competition, one crucial decision is selection and assignment of outside reporters. If there is any one place for a programmer to spend money on the grand side, it is with this group. The determination of station outreach is critical, but merely advertising the station's coverage is quickly pegged as public relations sham if actual beat coverage is slighted or faked. Listeners are acutely (if often subliminally) attuned to their environment, especially the sound of it. Cold handouts, studio copy, voice cuts and sound effects cannot replace the presence of a live reporter. The programmer should study the community's needs to define an appropriate geographical extent to the station's commitment. Political centers such as city halls, statehouses or county seats should get staffing priority. Beats in education, transportation, health, crime, urban affairs (ethnic concentrations), suburban centers and any special regional or local priority deserve close attention. A **correlator** (inside or telephone reporter), creating an actuality, often adds a local dimension to a story. The quick taping of a phone call can make the difference between a vaguely pertinent off-wire rewrite and a story with a local angle that has local audience impact and appeal.

Boilerplate Programming

One trap for the programmer is **boilerplate** programming—the purchase of canned generic features. These are packaged, syndicated features such as *One Moment Please*, a boilerplate in the form of short morality talks. Since they have no local association, they usually dilute the station's commercial momentum and should be avoided by large-market all-news stations having better alternatives. The programmer at a well-financed station should generate local feature segments on health, personal finances, local cultural activities, leisure time activities and entertainment—prepared and announced by station talent.

Commercial Copy

If union contracts permit the prerecording of announcement material, rather than requiring it to be aired live, the programmer has a distinct advantage in achieving voice change and more efficient staff utilization. If contracts do not permit it, the anchorperson suffers from the constant stress of changing gears from hard news copy to often widely disparate, even frivolous, commercial copy. A highly skilled announcer-reader can manage this feat, but many come off badly in the process, and credibility takes a beating. The ideal tactic is to have the anchorperson totally involved in news preparation as well as in delivery and accompanied by supporting announcers at the microphone.

Another problem is that many feature contributors come from the print media and are not accustomed to writing material to be read aloud. A radio listener's attention span is shorter than a print reader's, and there is no rereading on radio. Each all-news segment must be as brief as possible; the giving of involved directions, recipes and the like is an irritant.

Union Contracts

In most major markets union rules govern production personnel—a very real constraint for management. Most unionized radio stations have contracts with the American Federation of Television and Radio Artists (AFTRA), although many stations also have Newspaper Guild writers in-house. Union contracts set work rules, pay provisions and exclusivity that can manacle all-news programming. These elements are all tied to working conditions in the various union contracts. Contracts exist in which the repeat of a story in later shifts or dayparts carries a **residual payment** to the original reporter, writer or anchorperson. Sometimes this kind of provision is designated a "within-shift" rule allowing the story's use within the individual's scheduled shift, but adding a fee when used outside the particular shift. Added to that may be special tape **reuse fees** or added cost for use by another station in the network or group. When reporters cannot edit tape, write their own extraneous wraps or do simple editing because of contract constraints, delay becomes handicap. And handicaps create daily dissension and threaten cost-control.

News breaks; it doesn't wait. If management cannot afford a story because complex costs surround its on-air repetition (from matching to union labor shifts, taped amplification and extension or multiple-fee burdens of one kind or another), the story gets short shrift, if any attention at all.

Staff Size

As is immediately obvious, expecially in a union shop in which AFTRA or the Newspaper Guild controls most positions, personnel costs take a big budget chunk. The average all-news station in a major market has a news team of 25 to 35. Format evolution and union negotiations in the past several years have tended to tighten the staffing pattern, but all-news remains a labor-intensive format. Round-the-clock operations, living up to the slogan "All News All the Time" (KYW, Philadelphia), leave little room for staff economies without compromising the format's promise.

During the average shift, the "product communicator" is on the air between two to three hours and does some writing, collating or ancillary production work in the off-air period. Using taped segments on the overnight daypart (1 to 4 A.M.) is widely practiced, and curtailed staffing on the slower weekend shifts works reasonably well. Other options depend on availability of free-lance talent, overtime budgets, technical maintenance requirements and a basic assessment of market needs. For example, if an appreciable audience exists for the wee hours, then live newscasting becomes appropriate; if the audience is miniscule, then taped repeats become an option to preserve the budget for important news events. This choice faces all news programmers.

NEWS AUDIENCE DEFINITION

Most all-news stations have a relatively easy time with the 50+ age group and generally build strong cumulative audiences (cumes). Attracting and holding the 18 to 49 group and women present the greatest problems. The AQH (average quarter-hour) span is another tough block in audience-building schemes. Listeners tune in and out of all-news stations. In contrast, music stations may hold some listeners over long periods, giving them a leg up on total time spent listening (long TSL). (These measures were described in Chapter 2 under radio ratings.) The countermove is not to cater to random pressures but rather to choose the news mix in as catholic a fashion as possible and "be there" with a steady diet of quality reporting at all times.

Strategic use of audience research by the all-news program manager is important, but only if it is regarded as *one* factor in judging format suitability. It cannot be the governing force. Most stations subscribe to the monthly audience assessments of *Mediatrend,* now a feature of The Birch Report, and to Arbitron's highly detailed quarterly reports. Other services fall between these two in the details they provide. One of the most important research tools is The Birch Report, based in Coral Springs, Florida. As described in Chapter 2, it relies solely on telephone research rather than diaries and now has subscribers in most major markets. From time to time, new services arise, but they emerge slowly and tend to be marginally useful.

The sales keys are the October/November Arbitron reports on which most annual buys are made and on which most advertising agencies rely for guidance. A newspaper strike, severe storms, major sustained disaster stories and so on can "wobble" a report book in an all-news station's favor. Such measurement devices as **ESF** (expanded sample frame that culls new and unlisted telephone respondents) may hurt or help from book to book (see Chapter 2). Format changes in the market, such as a new talk station or FM proliferation, can alter audience measurements remarkably.

THE STRAINS AND PAINS

All-news radio presents an almost Kiplingesque "if" situation: If the general manager is interested mainly in short-term corporate tactics; if the sales manager musters a sales force that sells only numbers rather than the all-news product; if the promotion manager has no appropriate promotional strategy; if the chief engineer sees fit not to apply maximum special support requirements; if, in other words, management regards the format as an ideological loss leader and insists on "yo-yo" format deviations to compete in the ratings scramble—then the all-news programmer is in deep trouble. All-news demands complete support from all parts of the organization.

Problems Inside and Out

Here are a few internal problem areas with which programmers must be prepared to deal:

1. *The incompatible commercial:* Many advertisers think it is just the thing to submit copy that sounds like a fake news bulletin (that contains verbiage that seems interwoven with hard news copy) or that requires an anchorperson to do ethnic dialects. Erosion of credibility is obvious.

2. *The jingle jokers:* Many in promotion and, sadly, even in programming feel that the all-news format is inherently dull and repetitious and, therefore, needs hyping. They frequently insert jingles unrelated to the basic format sound package. They recommend promos that tease, non-news-related contesting and sensational headlines. They become especially frantic with promotional distractions during periods in which ratings firms are known to be gathering their listening data.

3. *The tech wreckers:* The demands of processing a heavy daily load of tape material, extra production requirements and sudden, awkward remote broadcast assignments have forced more than one technician to retreat to the sanctity of the transmitter. The chief engineer then announces sharp increases in "obligatory" meter readings and adjustments. Engineers will make themselves inaccessible if they feel they are being asked to do more than they think fair.

4. *The bottom line is all there is:* "You've blown the budget on the snowstorm, and we'll have to cover the capital hearings off the wire." Programmers often hear such talk from general managers. Programmers have to challenge poor-mouthing, perhaps their most dangerous confrontation with management. Many have fought with too little, for too much, at the wrong time, and over the wrong issues. The successful programmer finds out where the land mines have been placed before rushing into the fray.

Piling onto internal constraints are the ones coming from the audience. A programmer without a disciplined philosophy about how to deal with external complaints has an uphill struggle from the start.

1. *Repetition:* The initial cry from listeners when the format is introduced is "repetition." What the audience is really saying, however, is, "The way I listen to and use radio is not comfortable any more. You demand full attention, but I hear the same stories over and over." It takes a fair span of time before the audience begins to understand how all-news radio works.

2. *Bad news:* The need to convey "bad news" creates another external pressure. All-news never provides calming background music for the routines of the day, nor will it offer a stimulating, continuous round of exciting rock music or spirited talk and debate.

3. *Bias:* Audience mail will complain that the station promotes horrid fascist ideals and reprehensible communist plots. If the volume of letters on each side is about even, the station must be doing about right.

4. *Pressure groups:* Another powerful external pressure comes from civic groups and consumer bands bent on attacking the station's license. These attacks can trigger enormous legal expense and create much inconvenience. However, the station that practices ethical journalism and uses sound broadcasting management has little to fear from these onslaughts.

Promotional Effectiveness

An important key to successful competition is well-thought-out promotion. Clever slogans, jingle packages and spot promotional efforts are not enough; good promotion requires the sustained use of a valid theme underlying major programming *and* staff recognition of it. If the newsroom staff does not identify with a station promotion "theme," it will not be communicated to the audience. Amazing as it sounds, management often fails to convey its short- or long-range thinking behind a promotional theme or campaign to the news staff. Although overuse of cute promos dilutes the effectiveness of news material, programmers and promotion managers can work closely to judge the value of in-house promotional themes and external campaigns to the benefit of the entire format.

Another great weakness in most broadcasting is lack of on-air communication. Sometimes programmers forget to tell the audience what comes next in the program. The solution is called "promoting off the desk," meaning that the editor (with backup from writers, correlators and anchorpersons) must be foresighted enough to create audience expectations for an upcoming special series, phone interview sequence or other special item. This sort of promotion can be formalized to some extent.

Program Monitoring

Another aspect of maintaining a competitive edge is close monitoring of what goes on the air. A monthly review of script packages will show which writers and anchorpersons are "dogging it," that is, either using excessive paste-up of wire copy (necessary and permissible within reasonable limits on stories outside the station's coverage area) or simply using carbon copies of stories from previous news segments. Repetition of exact copy is an insidious tendency that may eventually bore the audience and drive it away. Many program managers have neglected this syndrome to their later sorrow. Keeping on top of script packages is a prime responsibility, and the competition will be quick to notice if a station fails to do so.

Last, programmers should not find themselves forced to play catch-up. They must listen to the competition regularly for the same reasons the competition listens to them.

FANATICS WERE YESTERDAY

Many practitioners of all-news radio remind one of Winston Churchill's definition of a fanatic: "He not only won't change his mind, he won't change the subject!" All-news programming tends to suffer from two extremes: those programmers who periodically want to revolutionize the format and those who are so locked into a format they will not consider change. All-news, in fact, is an evolutionary service, used by many different types of listeners at one and the same time. The programmer who does not dare to "dump the format" for an event that lends itself to another obvious form of coverage will lose crucial ratings battles. The judicious use of format openings such as massive team reporting efforts from remote locations, proper invocation of telephone programming and even the airing of play-by-play sports can have creative benefits. Little touches the life of any major audience group that is not compatible with the meaning of the word *news.* Conversely, there are very few things an all-news station can attempt into which a satisfactory amount of straight, hard news coverage cannot be inserted.

Despite the increase in news networks and syndicated news programming, all-news only became profitable in medium-sized markets when the FCC lifted its limit on the number of stations one group could own creating *economies of scale.* Without sufficient personnel and money (such as group ownership usually provides), all-news operations are almost bound to revert to the old rip-and-read practice of earlier days. They then collapse in the ratings and lose advertising support. To be sure, technology is cutting costs—slowly. ENG (electronic news-gathering) equipment is widening the audience's appetite for information that broadcast television alone cannot satisfy, ironically because of its own slavery to the old network radio formats and, of course, its own cost problems tied to the personality cult. The day of the self-transmitting remote reporter has come and the computer with audio-speech capacity is not far down the road. And satellite-distributed audio signals are reducing the cost of radio networking. But cable news networks are filling much of the public's news appetite, and all-news radio is likely to remain most competitive in major markets.

SUMMARY

The all-news format is costly and demanding, but, if given time to build an audience, it can command a highly loyal audience—although the demographics skew toward older listeners, and it is most successful in major markets. Six key content elements make up the fundamental structure of the news wheel: commercial spots, headlines, time and traffic, weather and sports. Once these elements are placed, the remainder of the open spaces in the wheel are divided among hard news (including remotes and recaps), editorials and features. In scheduling, the highest priority should go to those items (whether hard or soft news) providing local personal service such as time, traffic, weather and local events, especially during morning and afternoon drivetime. Flexibility in restructuring the news wheel for highly unusual events creates an image as a responsive and professional station that, in turn, fosters loyalty and strong cumes. Misplaced or too frequent repetition of hard news and feature elements encourages listeners to dial away. To remain competitive a news station requires a high budget and a high level of commitment from management. With a large budget, a station can provide original reporting, quality features and extensive beat reporting. Union contract limitations affect day-to-day programming, and news programmers must understand how contracts work. Both the public and higher-up management contribute to the constraints operating on news programmers, but the successes provide immense personal rewards. The future will hold greater competition from cable all-news services and an increasing number of network and nationally syndicated news suppliers. Some cost relief will come from new technological developments.

Notes

1. WCAU's format was modified to news and information in December 1978.

2. The number 26 is an arbitrary one, a hangover from traditional 13-26-52 week programming cycles; editorials could be run as readily in 18- or 30-unit schedules, but 26 is most common.

3. Edwin Kiester, Jr., "Bull's Eye! Those Editorials Are Now Drawing Blood," *TV Guide*, 17 September 1983, pp. 18–21.

4. Some all-news stations sell five- or six-minute blocks of news time to a single advertiser, allowing identification of that sponsor with a certain feature or news segment.

Selected Sources

DeMaeseneer, Paul. *Here's the News: A Radio News Manual.* Kuala Lumpur, Malaysia: Asia-Pacific Institute for Broadcasting Development, 1982.

Fang, Irving E. *Television News, Radio News.* Third edition. Minneapolis: Rada Press, 1980.

Kierstead, Phillip O. *All-News Radio.* Blue Ridge Summit, Pa.: TAB Books, 1980.

Kirkley, Donald H., Jr. *Station Policy and Procedures: A Guide for Radio.* Washington, D.C.: National Association of Broadcasters, 1985.

Routt, Edd. *The Radio Format Conundrum.* New York: Hastings House, 1978.

"Special Report: Journalism and Radio" *Broadcasting* (27 August 1984):47–108; (3 December 1984):47–90; (17 December 1984):47–62; (4 February 1985):51–59; (11 November 1985): 35–52; (28 July 1986):46–79; (27 July 1987):45–64.

CHAPTER 16 \ TALK RADIO PROGRAMMING

Bruce W. Marr

A Guide to Chapter 16

Bruce W. Marr is president of Bruce Marr and Associates, a broadcast consulting firm specializing in news, talk and information radio programming. He introduced the talk radio format to many client stations across the country. From 1975 to 1981, he was director of news and programming at KABC, Los Angeles, one of the creators of the all-talk format. Before joining KABC, an ABC-owned station, Mr. Marr worked for KFWB, a Group W–owned AM station in Los Angeles. He has lectured on radio programming at the University of Southern California (USC) and the University of California at Los Angeles (UCLA) and served as a director of the National Leukemia Broadcast Council. His chapter looks at many related formats ranging from all-conversation at one extreme to half-news/half-talk at the other, the format often called information radio. Since nearly all stations at some time include elements of talk, the discussions of fairness and public pressure in this chapter have relevance for all programmers.

THE BEGINNINGS OF CONTEMPORARY TALK

The term *talk station* was generally adopted when KABC in Los Angeles and a few other major-market stations discarded their records around 1960 and began airing nothing but the sound of the human voice. KABC started with a key four-hour news and conversation program entitled *News/Talk* from 5 to 9 A.M. KGO in San Francisco later adopted that designation for its overall format. KGO used news blocks in both morning and evening drive-time and conversation programs throughout the balance of the day. KABC focused on live call-in programs, interviews and feature material combined with informal and formal news coverage.

Though KABC originally promoted itself as "The Conversation Station," **news/talk** stuck as the generic industry term for stations that program conversation leavened with news during the drive periods. News/talk radio includes some half-and-half formats as well as *all-conversation* programming.

During the latter half of the 1970s, radio broadcasting changed drastically. At that time the hares of the industry—the AM broadcasters—paused to look over their shoulders at the tortoises—the FM stations. When they did so, they found themselves being overtaken. When they glanced forward toward the finish line, they saw that some of the FM tortoises were already leading the race. By 1977 an entire generation of listeners had grown up with their radios permanently locked on the FM dial.

In 1978 a number of AM broadcasters assessed the situation and recognized that FM had become the music medium of choice for a large part of the radio audience. To retain their audiences, several notable AM stations counter-programmed: They shifted their formats away from music to the spoken word. *Information* programming proliferated.

FLEXIBLE STRUCTURE

The talk format is fluid *and* stable. Its framework is fixed, but flexible enough to respond to issues on a day-to-day basis and quickly reflect changing community moods. Good broadcast personalities can sense audience moods and respond accordingly. Talk hosts, unhampered by a music rotation list and the like, can alter the tone of on-air talk more rapidly than announcers working in other formats.

When an issue or news event is significant enough to color the outlook of an entire community or even the entire nation, the sound of the talk station will reflect the audience temper. Coverage of significant events preempts the regular schedule and previously booked guests. Like most broadcasters, a talk station responds to major news events on the air; but talk and all-news stations respond to events more *rapidly* with on-hand personnel and equipment resources, and when appropriate, can devote all of the station's airtime to the event.

Because the news/talk format generally presents information, the audience readily accepts a news break. The interruption may be a network bulletin or a casual sounding "visit" from a member of the station news staff who joins the talk host in the studio to break a story fresh from a wire service or a local reporter. The newsperson's presence in the studio on such occasions provides the opportunity for questions and answers or conversation between the host and the newsperson. Assuring the audience that the station's news staff will follow the story and keep listeners informed as the story develops will keep them from shifting to an all-news station.

Local News Responsiveness

News department resources and personnel vary substantially from station to station. Certainly, mobile radios, helicopters and station cars make possible live, exciting, on-the-spot reports as an event is happening, but even a small station with a tiny news staff can cover a breaking story using the primary tools of electronic journalism: the telephone and enterprising production people. With a little ingenuity, a few credible contacts and a reverse telephone directory (arranged by addresses instead of names), studio assistants can put the talk host in touch with officials, eyewitnesses and other involved parties even before a news crew can reach the scene of a story. During periods of disaster, the news/talk station can become a vital clearinghouse for information.

When wide-ranging brushfires swept through thousands of acres of southern California in 1978 and again in 1987, KABC dealt with the disaster continuously throughout the day and evening—through news staff reports and through the liaison it established between those in need and those willing to help. One caller pleaded for safe pasture for his threatened livestock, and another listener responded with an offer. Other listeners, unable to reach their homes in the fire areas, heard neighbors call in to report on the fire-fighting efforts. Temporary housing offers were relayed on the air to evacuees. People who had lived through other devastating fires in the brush country around Los Angeles called with tips on how to protect homes and property. Beyond such valuable services, the station also delivered to its entire audience the story of the fire in very human and personal terms. Fortunately, this type of event is rare, but when it happens live coverage adds drama to the news/talk format. When preparing a budget, metropolitan market programmers should anticipate three or four events a year requiring live coverage.

Role of the Program Director

A special kind of partnership, involving a great deal of mutual trust, grows up between on-air personalities and their program directors in talk programming. Program directors establish station policies that ensure not only high journalistic standards but also take into account the bounds of good taste, Federal Communication Commission rules, libel laws and industry codes. Having established and communicated such policies, an individual program director must recognize that day-to-day errors and deviations will occur. The individual on the air has to make instant decisions and respond immediately. A conversation host interacts with phone callers for two, three or four hours a day. Callers can be assertive, aggressive, even belligerent. And no format is easier to second-guess, after the fact. Program directors should therefore avoid impulsively calling air personalities to task; in almost every case, the personality is the first to know when something has gone wrong.

In fact, talk radio is radio waiting for something to go wrong. When things do go wrong, the first approach of the program director should leave an opening for the personality to say, "I know it was bad. The reason was . . ." Although program directors are responsible for determining that the air talent understands what happened, they must then act as intermediaries and arbitrators between management and on-air personnel.

NATIONAL PROGRAM SOURCES

Music programmers can turn to a large number of outside music syndicators to augment their locally produced programs or to program their entire broadcast day (see Chapter 13). Talk radio programmers, however, were largely on their own until the early 1980s. Syndicators offered short features of five minutes or less, but only the Mutual network offered a major, long-form program, *The Larry King Show*. This program first aired from midnight to dawn in January 1978 on a 28-station network. The demand for such live **call-in** programming was so great that by 1987, 310 affiliates were clearing the *King* show.

By the late 1970s, the other major radio networks were exploring their affiliates' (and potential affiliates') need for long-form information programming. In November 1981, NBC launched TALKNET, which delivered continuous nighttime programming from 10 P.M. to 3 A.M. By 1988 it had 285 affiliates. Meanwhile, ABC also tested the appeal of network talk programming and, in May of 1982, began delivering 18 hours of talk daily over TALKRADIO, reaching 124 affiliates by 1988. In 1985 the Mutual network was purchased by Westwood, a Los Angeles-based syndication and production company that had previously serviced music stations with live music concerts, specializing in rock and country music programs. In 1987 Westwood also acquired the NBC Radio Networks, including TALKNET, and thus became the dominant producer and syndicator of network talk programming.

Both the Mutual network and NBC's TALKNET developed long-form talk programs specifically for network broadcast. These included the *Larry King Show* and TALKNET's *Bruce Williams Program*, dealing with personal finance

Figure 16-1 TALKNET Logo

and similar matters, and the *Sally Jesse Rafael Program*, a personal advice pro-gram, both aired from New York. On these participation shows, audience members call in to the network studio to ask questions, deliver opinions, re-spond to comments and so on.

ABC, on the other hand, took a different approach. Because it owned two well-established talk stations, KABC in Los Angeles and KGO in San Francisco, it utilized those stations' programs and personalities to launch its TALKRADIO network. The original TALKRADIO schedule included KABC's psychologist, Doctor Toni Grant, generalist Ira Fistell and the overnight pro-gram of Ray Briem. The *Owen Spann Program* originated from KGO until 1984 when it began airing from ABC's New York studios.

As these talk radio networks matured, their programmers evaluated the appeal of their programs to affiliates and listeners. Maurice Tunick, execu-tive producer of TALKNET before joining TALKRADIO, frequently pointed out that original ideas are worthless if they fail to meet the needs of stations. A reasonable number of stations must express interest in clearing a program *be-fore* it can go into production. Thus many original program ideas never make it into the networks' schedules.

In the early 1980s, affiliates began requesting additional program-ming to fill weekends when they generally operate with minimal staffing. All three networks responded. ABC and NBC begin to deliver "advice" programs featuring experts on gardening, car care, child rearing, law and so on, while Mutual added the late-night *Jim Bohanon Program* on Saturdays. Mutual also found another niche to fill: the early-morning commute hour, and it produced *America in the Morning,* a one-hour weekday program of news and features, airing from 5 to 6 A.M. local time and featuring Jim Bohanon.

In 1988 a new talk service emerged, Sun Radio Network, targeting small and mid-sized markets with 24-hour barter programming. Originating from WMCA-AM in New York and Tampa (Sun Radio's headquarters), it carries consumer/legal advice shows, celebrity interviews, a call-in psychologist show and the audio feed of *Donahue,* the television talk star. Like most major radio networks, Sun Radio appears on Satcom I-R but is also carried on Westar IV and Galaxy III. No matter where its 71 affiliates' dishes point, Sun Radio is available (see Table 13-2 in Chapter 13 for additional information on talk networks).

At the present time, a station clearing programs from two or more national radio networks could fill 15 or more hours of each broadcast day. However, some broadcasters feel that such network dependency deprives the local audience of programs dealing with local issues. Others point out that national programming has big budgets, extensive resources, major talent and access to nationally known guest experts that no single local station could expect to acquire. Former president of ABC Radio, Ben Hoberman (who as general manager had created KABC's talk format in 1960), said in an interview, "The very nature of radio is changing, but not for the first time. Much of the radio was networked until the 1950s when it had to adapt to the advent of television. Radio virtually became an exclusively musical medium, and the best way to deliver music was with local disc jockeys playing records. But now, as we enter the information age, there is a clear need for the kind of programming the networks can do best." Hoberman calls talk radio "foreground listing," a format requiring the audience to become actively engaged. Its special intimacy and power give commercials within the format added impact, making it popular with advertisers.

The national networks recognize that news/talk stations must program key dayparts locally. The networks structure their programming so that morning and afternoon drivetime can be all or mostly local, and stations can present individual local programs. One major structural difference between music and news/talk programming is that music forms a continuous, never-ending single program, while talk and news break into discrete units that can be added, deleted or reassembled into customized program structures.

LOCAL TALK PROGRAMS

To complement nationally distributed talk programs, programmers schedule local talk programming that provides an opportunity for local listeners to call in. As of the early 1980s, trendy local shows targeted specific demographic groups with *participation formats* focusing on services, not issues. Radio flea markets and swap shops in which callers describe something they have for sale on the air have broad audience appeal. By capitalizing on fads and hobbies, these specialized programs try to attract new groups of listeners to talk radio. The key element is that the listener contributes to the program within a highly controlled structure. ("Tell the audience what you have for sale, what's special about it, what your price is, and how they can get in touch with you . . .") In some markets, these programs have succeeded in attracting new groups of listeners.

TALK HOSTS

Conversation program hosts are often generalists, as are most broadcast journalists. They have developed the ability to grasp a subject's essence. The host of a general interest talk program will discuss world and local affairs, politics, medicine, economics, science, history, literature, music, art, sports and entertainment trivia—often on a single program. Talk hosts typically are inveterate readers: Some even find speed-reading courses helpful.

In the view of David Graves, former general manager of Chicago's WIND, a good talk host, like a great author or filmwriter, creates a vehicle that operates on more than one intellectual level. "The great talk show host," said Graves, in an interview, "uses humor, pacing and interesting phrasing to create a program that works as a pure audio entertainment form which will appeal to a large segment of the audience. On the other hand, the well-educated, sophisticated listener should not be offended by the level of the conversation."

Bias

The best of talk radio is either *broadcast journalism* or closely akin to it. Much of it, however, stresses *entertainment* over completeness of information and opinions over facts. As the talk format matured, it embraced more of the journalistic tradition, introducing a content conflict. Professional newspeople filter out their own biases as they write and prepare stories. In live talk radio, the on-air person cannot always keep personal points of view in check. Many talk hosts do not see themselves as journalists but as entertainers. When a station adopts a live talk format, management has to admit that the members of the on-the-air team have individual biases and must be allowed to express their viewpoints on issues discussed on the air. Management can, however, expect program hosts to treat guests with respect when the guests represent opposing sides of issues. This philosophy has grown from the experience of finding it fruitless to ask on-air personalities to be unbiased. Program hosts are often investigators, sometimes advocates, and biases are doubtless part of their stock-in-trade. Some talk hosts represent the listeners' own opinion or cases of "the man you love to hate." Others, popularly called **shock jocks,** advocate radical positions to capture audience attention.

Another new trend, however, stresses presentation of factual information in expert interviews rather than the volatile, listener call-in format. Experience has shown that angry, screaming hosts with call-in programs rarely get more than a 5 audience share, while informative, content-oriented programs using expert-guest interviews, if witty or otherwise entertaining, can draw substantially higher audience shares in many markets.

Turnover

When a newcomer takes over an on-air slot on a talk station, a certain amount of audience turnover occurs. Many listeners and callers go elsewhere; new ones find and accept the new personality. Initial reaction is usually negative when a host is removed and replaced, a natural response to a change that disrupts the listening habits of regular listeners. Even when ratings and other indicators confirm the need for a change, the followers of the departed personality will react vigorously enough to make programmers question their own judgments. The new host's first programs will find callers responding timidly, as they would with a new acquaintance. This newness will color the tone of the program for a time since the audience is an integral part of any conversation program.

Structuring Issue Debates

The discussion of controversial issues is a central part of talk programming. In structuring programs on controversial subjects, a key question arises: Is it wiser to invite representatives of each point of view to a single program and structure a debate or to invite individuals to express their points of view separately on consecutive hours of a single program or on successive programs?

Answers differ by station, but the common denominator is how to maintain control. Program producers cannot manipulate what individuals will say, but they can design program segments so that listeners perceive that the content is "under control." At a minimum, two persons participate in a telephone talk program: the host and the caller. A program guest adds a third presence. If two guests appear on the program, there are now four voices. Because it is radio, listeners have no visual reference and can easily lose track of who is speaking when there are more than three voices. If a debate gets out of control, listeners hear a cacophony of voices, one speaking over the other. As a rule of thumb, have few voices on a single show and keep them easily identifiable. The host can do the latter by referring to guests by name when prefacing their statements or asking them questions. Three guests are plenty for most debates, and too many for most call-in programs.

AUDIENCE

The talk format appeals to an older audience than most music formats attract. The most frequent talk target is the 25–54 group. Even when directed at this demographic group, the format will usually attract a substantial proportion of those 55 and over.

During the 1960s and 1970s, these demographics were a disadvantage: Most advertisers were trying to reach that large segment of the population that fell into the 18–34 category. During those years, programmers tried to lower the average age of their audiences, but with little success. KABC, for example, experimented on more than one occasion with youthful program hosts to appeal to the younger segment of the market. Each time the effort failed. Moreover, not only did the attempts fail in drawing young listeners, they also alienated the older, hard-core listenership.

By the early 1980s, that inordinately large population segment that once fell into the younger demographic groups had moved into the 25-years-and-over bracket that talk radio effectively reaches. The format therefore became more attractive to advertisers (who in turn had raised their demographic target and begun cultivating the older audience). Even so, programmers should keep the audience from skewing toward the top age demographics.

The typical *caller* does not represent the typical *listener* to talk radio except that both tend to be older. Some studies show that callers tend to fall in the lower income groups and be lonelier than radio listeners in general, some forming an unnatural bond with the station and a personality. However, callers represent a very, very small fraction of the audience, and they differ from one another depending on the nature of the program; most important, they are very different from listeners to the same programs. Unlike *callers*, talk *listeners* have higher than average spendable income and savings account balances; they take more than the average number of trips by air, buy more luxury cars and so on. *Callers* do not reveal an accurate profile of listeners, but frequently, station personnel become so focused on calls that they forget about the audience—which should be their prime concern. Switching the emphasis to the listening audience usually makes ratings go up.

Targeting the Content

Programmers can manipulate a demographically top-heavy talk audience downward by rigidly controlling subject matter. The program manager and the on-air staff must construct each programming hour to appeal to the target demographic group. *Freeform* (sometimes called open-line) programs in which callers set the agenda must be severely limited or entirely prohibited.

KTRH (Houston), for example, aired a significant amount of freeform programming when it began its talk format and found that it reached a predominantly older audience. Moreover, the older listeners added to the problem since they dominated the call-in airtime. They felt free to dial the station at any time and discuss issues that were of interest to them but not to younger listeners. Then the station imposed controls on the on-air subject matter and markedly reduced the average age of its audience.

One stratagem for forcing down the median age of an audience is the *sports conversation* show. Aired in late afternoon or evening, such a program will attract a significant audience younger than the normal 25+ target group without relinquishing males 25–49 that are the backbone of the station's potential evening drive audience.

Call-in psychology programs also have broad demographic appeal, reaching both men and women of all ages. The key to such programs is the nature of the subject matter itself. When properly produced and controlled, the on-air therapist is dealing with the most absorbing subject possible—the audience members themselves. In general, casual surveys of listener habits and opinions during the call-in portions of such programs are effective ways of targeting specific audience demographics.

Impact

If a talk station is sufficiently involved in the community it serves, it attracts influential civic and business leaders, political figures and intellectual leaders from all walks of life. It is not unusual, even in a radio market the size of Los Angeles, for public figures to call an ongoing program in response to the mention of their names on the air.

The talk audience is as active as the station itself. Conversation stations are foreground stations, designed to involve listeners. Seldom do listeners use conversation radio as a background the way they may a beautiful music station. This attribute represents an important sales advantage. Commercials are particularly effective within the conversation environment because they reach an audience that tuned in *to listen.* A commercial read live by an authoritative talk host has added impact.[1] The talk audience is also above average in education, spendable income and many other attributes that attract a broad range of advertisers.

GUESTS

Effective guests for talk radio come from all walks of life. They range from well-trained actors and politicians to unknowns on the air for the first time. A good guest must have something to communicate that interests the audience—unsuspected facts, offbeat experiences, unusual opinions or a unique mode of self-expression—and that usually generates argument. The most popular shows investigate issues and explore the facts, using guests who can supply a strong informational component.

Interviews

Every talk program director receives hundreds of **audition tapes** as part of the job applications of aspiring talk hosts—on which they interview nationally known celebrities. It follows that the applicants must think these interviews are their best. Too often, however, celebrities have nothing new to say. (Aspiring interviewers must feel that some of the "celebratedness" rubs off onto them.) The *best* audition tapes are those that give the program director an opportunity to hear how the host probes substantive issues, to learn how well the individual prepares and how agile his or her mind is. Celebrity interviews rarely offer such opportunities. Most of them include a few brief, pat questions from the host and lengthy answers from the interviewee. The person who stands to gain the most recognition from the interview is the celebrity.

Too often talk stations and hosts pursue well-known names as guests, people who will bring "star value" to their programs. But often the best guest will be a local person whose name is unknown to the listeners. The local station in the small community can program relevant topics without looking beyond its own coverage area for guests. Stations quite distant from the "talk show circuit" need not avoid locally produced talk programming for lack of interesting guests. An hour spent with a major movie star might better be spent with a mayor, school superintendent, game warden, newspaper publisher, football coach or auto mechanic. Many movie actors have plenty of eye appeal but are of little interest as voices. Good radio conversation requires ideas and opinions, not good looks. Public relations firms representing nationally known figures deluge major-market stations with offers for celebrity appearances. Those responsible for scheduling guests on such stations should consider carefully the relevance of every guest's contribution to its listeners' needs or desires, not merely the impact of the person's name.

Stations can interview by telephone guests that otherwise would never be available, and a conference call permits local callers to participate in the conversation. Programmers still prefer to have guests in the studio when possible.

Commercial Interests

Of all radio formats, the talk format is the most vulnerable to unscheduled commercial matter. The terms *payola* and *plugola* have been associated with the music industry, but the talk format offers the greatest opportunities for such abuses. An hour of friendly conversation presents endless opportunities for the on-air host to mention a favorite resort or restaurant or to comment on a newly acquired automobile. Moreover, the program host is often in the position of booking favored business acquaintances as guests. The on-air personality therefore receives many offers, ranging from free dinners to discounts on major purchases. Policies aimed at preventing violations must emphasize that management will severely penalize violators. Most stations require their on-air talent and producers to sign affidavits showing that they understand the law on these points, and some stations hire independent agencies to monitor programs for abuses. More than one station has reinforced this message by billing on-air performers for time if their casual conversations become commercials.

However, guests representing commercial enterprises may certainly appear on the station. It is appropriate, for instance, for a local travel agent to discuss travel in mainland China or for the proprietor of a health food store to present opinions on nutrition. And, obviously, many personalities on the talk show circuit have something to sell—a book, a movie, a sporting event, a philosophy and so on. Some mention of the individual's reason for appearing is appropriate because it establishes the guest's credentials. An apt reference might be, "Our subject today is solar energy, and our guest is John Smith, author of a new book entitled *The Many Uses of the Sun.*"

To summarize, two criteria should govern the booking of all guests:

1. The guest must contribute to building or maintaining audience.

2. Neither the station nor any individual in the station's employ may benefit from the appearance of the guest unless the remuneration is properly accounted for and commercial references are logged and announced.

ON-AIR TECHNIQUES

Call-in programs are the backbone of talk radio. The **call screener** (or producer) is a vital part of the talk radio staff because this person serves as the center who delivers the ball, in the form of the telephone call, to the on-the-air quarterback.

Telephone Screeners

Screeners add substantially to station budgets, but only through careful screening can a station control its programming. Airing "cold" or unscreened calls can be compared to a disc jockey reaching blindly into the music library and airing the first record that comes to hand. Few programmers would relinquish control in that manner. Telephone calls represent the playlist of talk radio.

The screener constantly manipulates the lineup of incoming calls, giving priority to a more appropriate caller and delaying or eliminating callers of presumably lesser interest. The situation changes constantly as new calls come in, and the good screener orchestrates them to provide the most appealing program for the listener. If, for instance, the subject under discussion is the city fire department, and ten callers are standing by when the fire chief calls, the chief's call obviously should move to the front of the pack and air at the first opportunity.

The screener filters out the "regulars" that call the station too frequently as well as drunks and others unable to make a coherent contribution. Callers thus dismissed and those asked to hold for long periods often complain of unjust treatment, but the screener must prevail, insisting on the right to structure the best possible sequence of talk. Effective screeners perform their jobs with tact and graciousness.

When screeners must dump a caller, they say something like "I'm sorry, your call doesn't fit into the programming we're doing at the moment, but thank you for calling." Most stations prohibit the use of the caller's full name to forestall imposters, callers identifying themselves as prominent people in a community and then airing false statements to embarrass the individuals they claim to be.

When a program depends on callers, what happens in those nightmare moments when there are none? For just this emergency, most talk show hosts maintain a clipping file containing newspaper and magazine articles they have saved from their general reading to provide the background for monologues when no calls come in. Another strategy is the "expert phone list." A list of ten or twenty professionals with expertise in subjects of broad appeal should yield at least one or two able to speak by phone when the host needs to fill time to sustain a program.

Screening Systems

Various systems are used for the screener to signal to the on-air host which incoming call has been screened and is to be aired next (see Figure 16-2 for call screener's equipment). Most talk stations now utilize computers, and some stations have even developed their own software for this function, al-

Figure 16-2 Call Screener's Equipment

Photo courtesy of David Graves, WIND Talk Radio 56, Chicago.

Figure 16-3 Screen of a Host's Computer Display

```
MIO:56 LAK:59 O'HRE:56 GOING UP TO 67
HUMIDITY: 53% WINDS: 15-S
- - - - - - - - - - - - - - - - - - - - - - - - - - -
1) JIM BOUTET ON NEWS AT 10:00
- - - - - - - - - - - - - - - - - - - - - - - - - - -
1-(DEBBIE)-WHAT TO LOOK FOR (IS AN
INSTRUCTOR AT TRITON) IN A SCHOOL;
CLYDE HIMSELF IS HEADED IN THE WRONG
DIRECTION

2-(JOE)-TRIES TO APPLY EDUCATION TO
PRACTICALITY

4-(ED)-IF A PLANE COMES INTO AMERICAN
AIR SPACE, IT SHOULD BE SHOT DOWN TOO

5-(NELLIE)-WOULD WORRY IF RUSSIAN
BOMBER WAS NOT SHOT DOWN

  (BOB)-AGAINST PANNING OF LIBERAL ARTS
EDUCATION
```

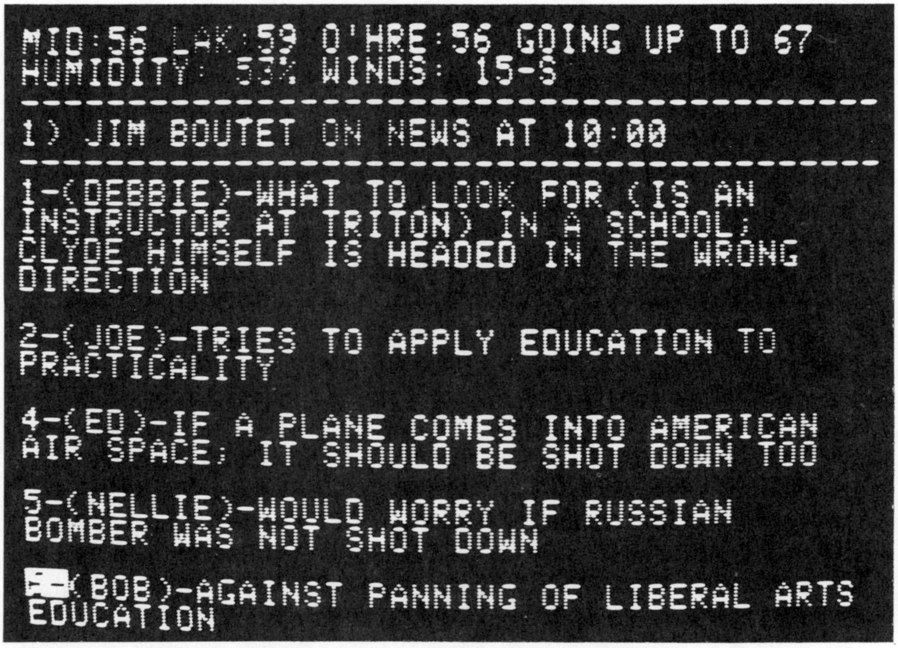

Photo courtesy of David Graves, WIND Talk Radio 56, Chicago.

though appropriate programs are now sold commercially. Using computers places greater control of the program in the hands of the on-air host. The computer display indicates the nature of the calls prepared for airing so the host can alter the complexion of the program by orchestrating the order of calls. Usually the information displayed for the host includes the first name, approximate age and sex of the caller, and may specify the point the caller wishes to discuss. Frequently the display includes material of practical conversational value such as the current weather forecast. (See Figure 16-3 for a host's computer display.) Hosts often use a timer to monitor the length of calls. Many hosts cut a caller off, as politely as possible after 1-1/2 to 2 minutes (3 minutes tops).

Delay

All talk stations use a device (usually an electronic **digital delay unit**) to delay programming a few seconds between the studio and the transmitter to "dump" profanity, personal attacks and other unairable matter. The on-air host generally controls a "cut button" that diverts offensive program material, although the engineer should have a backup switch.

Because the program is delayed (generally four to seven seconds before it reaches the air), the screener instructs all callers to turn off their radios before talking on the air. Failing this, callers hear their voices coming back at them after some seconds delay and cannot carry on a conversation. Listening only on the telephone, they hear the real-time program material and can talk normally with the host.

Electronic Logs

Most talk stations consider a round-the-clock, **tape-recorded log** a necessity. Such a log allows the station to retrieve and reconstruct precisely what was said on the air in the event of threatened legal action. These tapes are made on special slow-speed monitoring recorders running at 15/32-inches per second; a tape then lasts for 12 hours. The program can be recorded on one track while a telephone company time check is recorded on the second track, thus providing the exact time of all on-air events. Such tapes were recognized as official FCC master logs and, although the FCC no longer requires them, should be kept for at least three years.

Access to these log tapes by outside parties should be limited to those with a bona fide need. Many stations require a written request that is examined by the station's legal counsel before the station complies. Such tapes have been requested as evidence in litigation not involving the radio station but concerning guests that have appeared on the station. In such cases, many stations require the tapes be subpoenaed. Law enforcement agencies may also request access to log tapes. The Los Angeles Police Department once requested KABC's aid in establishing the exact time a play occurred in a baseball game it aired, which helped them pinpoint the precise time of a crime. The station, of course, granted access to the tapes for that purpose.

CONTROVERSY, FAIRNESS AND PRESSURE

Although talk radio programmers get many opportunities for creative expression, they also must devote considerable time to administration. Because the station deals almost constantly with public affairs issues, its programmers spot-monitor the station's programs for compliance with FCC rules such as *equal time* for political candidates, and to avoid legal pitfalls such as *libel*. A programmer, however, having many other duties as well, rarely knows as much about the minute-by-minute program as heavy listeners. Therefore, backup systems must be established.

Fairness Doctrine

Until the FCC repealed the Fairness Doctrine in 1987, the doctrine had more impact on talk stations than on any other format. Talk stations deal with controversial issues throughout every broadcast day. Talk broadcasters were therefore required to keep careful track of the time devoted to the various sides of controversial subjects and to schedule the presentation of views not previously covered. Since the demise of the doctrine, the legal need for such record-keeping has been eliminated, but talk programmers will continue to take steps to ensure that the station's overall programming reflects a fair presentation of controversial issues. They will do this because overall *balance* is part of talk radio's tradition and audience expectations, and because management will want to point to a history of overall fairness at license renewal time and whenever there is public outcry.

Public and Private Pressure

Talk stations frequently find themselves the targets of pressure groups, activist organizations and political parties trying to gain as much free access to the station's airtime as they can. Although most partisans deserve some time on the station, management must turn away those seeking inordinate amounts of time.

Political parties are well aware of the impact of talk stations and have been known to organize volunteers to monitor programs and flood the incoming phone lines with a single point of view. Politicians seeking airtime have sometimes misused the idea of fairness, confusing it with the equal-time provision for political candidates—sometimes through ignorance, at other times to confuse the program executive.

Because an effective talk station frequently deals with controversial issues, its management can expect threats of all kinds from irate audience members. A provoked listener will demand anything from a retraction to equal time and, on occasion, will support such demands with threats of legal action. Such threatened lawsuits usually vanish, however, when management explains the relevant broadcast law to the complainant. When the station is even slightly in the wrong, it is usually quick to provide rebuttal time to an overlooked point of view.

Often the issue that draws the audience's wrath is not a serious, controversial subject but a frivolous one. One recent statement that drew many shouts of righteous indignation was a Los Angeles sportscaster's opinion that Notre Dame's basketball team was superior to UCLA's. That remark drew phone calls and letters demanding the statement be retracted and the sportscaster discharged. Such teapot-sized tempests, although not serious, make demands on the time of talk programmers.

THE COST AND THE REWARD

By the mid-1980s, many stations had shifted from limited-appeal talk to broader audience appeal by switching from a *caller* orientation to a *listener* orientation. Talk radio programmers realized that listeners would tune out a poor phone call just as they would a weak record on a music station. Station programmers therefore began controlling the on-air subject matter and the flow of program material in preference to letting callers dictate the programming. Nationwide, the talk stations with the highest ratings adopted the strategy of focusing on the needs of the listeners, not the wants of the callers. The talk host who in the past had generated telephone calls because of an argumentative personality or an "over-the-back-fence" nature was replaced or redirected toward informational radio programming. Interviews with knowledgeable people replaced random phone calls, and programmers targeted specific demographic groups when choosing subject matter and determining the amount of time to devote to each topic. The strategy, then, became listener orientation through informational programming. At its best, talk radio now focuses on content quality and depth of coverage, not on stimulating outrageous comments.

A primary ingredient in the recipe for success in any talk format is commitment at the top—at the station management level. A timely and innovative music format can catapult a station from obscurity to the number one ranking during a single rating period. Talk stations and all-news stations, however, generally take years to reach their potential. But once success is achieved, the talk station enjoys a listener loyalty that endures while the more fickle music audience shifts from station to station in search of the hits. High figures for time-spent-listening and long-term stability in cumulative ratings demonstrate audience loyalty. (See Chapter 2 on radio ratings to review these measurements.)

The talk station producing a significant amount of local programming generally is more costly to operate than a music operation. Good talk personalities are often higher paid than disc jockeys, and they must be supported by producers, call screeners and, frequently, extra administrative personnel. Salaries of talk hosts vary a great deal, of course, from city to city. Some, in smaller markets, earn $20,000 to $30,000 while major-market personalities are paid as much as $200,000. Screener and producer positions are often entry-level jobs paying the minimum wage or just above, but they offer an opportunity to enter the industry and acquire experience.

The talk radio station of the 1990s combines news and conversation formats in a blend of programming characterized by live interviews, telephone actualities and on-air audience feedback. It has great journalistic flexibility and local responsiveness but will continue to be known best for its colorful host personalities.

SUMMARY

Talk radio varies from station to station in the proportions of live call-in programs, on-air interviews, network or syndicated advice shows, feature material and news. In addition to the now classic *Larry King Show* Mutual distributes, local stations have recently acquired national programming from such sources as TALKNET, TALKRADIO, Sun and other networks and syndicators. One key to effective, live talk programming is the on-air personality who may introduce journalistic bias into programs but stimulates loyal listening. Most talk radio targets an audience of prime interest to advertisers, although the station must rigidly control content to avoid attracting too large a proportion of older listeners. In-person and telephone guests and callers supply the content for talk radio, and the screener plays a pivotal role in structuring the flow of call-in programs. Talk radio has become listener rather than caller oriented, striving for a broad appeal through general informational programming, but any controversial coverage will always generate public and private pressures on the station. In such cases, detailed, written station policies and electronic logs provide the best offense and defense for the talk programmer.

Note

1. Station policies differ on the degree to which hosts can be involved in commercials. Many individuals fear losing their journalistic credibility, and personalities known for their balance want to avoid a persuasive role. Ironically, it is the outspoken advocate host who often makes the most appealing salesperson.

Selected Sources

Broughton, Irv. *The Art of Interviewing for Television, Radio and Film.* Blue Ridge Summit, Pennsylvania: TAB Books, 1981.

FCC Sensitivity Training Guide for TV Program Directors. Washington, D.C.: National Association of Broadcasters, 1979.

King, Larry. *Larry King.* New York: Simon and Schuster, 1982.

Levin, Murray B. *Talk Radio and the American Dream.* Lexington, Mass.: Lexington Books, 1987.

"The Many Faces of Format," *Religious Broadcasting* (September 1982):24–26.

Shapiro, Mitchell E. "The Changing Nature of AM Radio in the 1980s: Talk, Ethnic and Religious Formats." A paper presented to the Speech Communication Association, Boston, November 1987.

Sterman, Art. "A Look at KABC/ABC TALKRADIO," *Broadcast Engineering* (July 1982):51–59.

Tramer, Harriet, and Jeffries, Leo W. "Talk Radio—Forum and Companion," *Journal of Broadcasting* 27 (Summer 1983):297–300.

PART FIVE / PUBLIC BROADCASTING STRATEGIES

Part Five steps away from the *commercial* perspective on programming to examine the strategies operating in national and local *noncommercial* broadcasting. The term **noncommercial** refers to 325 television broadcasters and 1,301 radio broadcasters. Of the 325 television stations, 319 are **public** broadcasters and the balance operated by nonprofit groups such as religious broadcasters. (Most religious television broadcasters hold commercial television licenses.) Of the 1,301 noncommercial radio stations, about 350 are **public** broadcasters and the balance low-power religious, college or community stations. Part Five focuses on the *public networks and stations* who play the leading roles in noncommercial broadcasting. Because the contributions of five national organizations (CPB, PBS, NAPTS, NPR and APR) are central to understanding what these authors say about public broadcasting, the organizations are briefly described here.

First of all, there is the **Corporation for Public Broadcasting (CPB)**, a private, nonprofit corporation created by Congress in 1967. CPB distributes federal funds (tax dollars allocated by Congress) through **Community Service Grants (CSGs)** and **interconnection grants** to 319 public television stations; it distributes federal funds through CSGs and **National Program Production and Acquisition Grants (NPPAGs)** to 255 radio stations (as of 1988—not quite all public stations qualify from year to year for CSG grants). CSGs are matching grants tied to local fundraising; interconnection grants cover satellite transmission costs for television; NPPAGs are for the production and acquisition of radio programming. A 10-member board appointed by the President and confirmed by the Senate governs the Corporation.

Then there is the **Public Broadcasting Service (PBS)**, the television network. Nearly all public television stations (319 of 325) are members of PBS, which is owned by the member stations. It acquires and distributes programs but does not produce any. It is governed by an elected 35-member board. Similar to trade associations in the commercial industry (such as NAB and INTV), the **National Association of Public Television Stations (NAPTS)** handles representation, research and planning for noncommercial television stations.

Public radio has two network services. **National Public Radio (NPR)**, a private nonprofit corporation, produces and distributes programs for its member stations. NPR is governed by a 15-member board and has two classes of membership: *full members*—about 255 stations qualifying for CPB's CSG and NPPAG funds—and about 100 *associate members* purchasing NPR programming but not qualifying for Corporation grants. Then, an additional two-dozen stations receive CSG grants but dropped their membership in NPR. **American Public Radio (APR)** is the competing public radio network. It is an independent, nonprofit corporation serving 318 members, most also having membership in NPR. Governed by a 14-member board, APR acquires programming and distributes it by satellite.

In addition to having *membership* organizations (rather than affiliations), public stations differ from their commercial counterparts in their lack of a uniform means of support (such as advertising sales). This *varied support* affects both national network programming and individual station strategies. As with commercial broadcasters and cablecasters, how the station pays its way limits the programmer's options even as technological advances expand them. The chapters in this section follow the pattern of considering evaluation, selection and scheduling of programs as the major elements of the job of the programmer.

Chapter 17 introduces the **national television network** perspective on noncommercial television. The author examines the philosophical contradictions operating within the Public Broadcasting Service and the means for resolving them in a national schedule of promotable prime-time programs. The chapter shows how the national schedule of satellite-delivered programs is achieved and how national commercial ratings are adapted to meet the purposes of public broadcasting. Public television's audience characteristics are discussed in light of its philosophical goals and financial needs. This chapter raises many of the controversial issues affecting noncommercial programming and shows how economic pressure is forcing public broadcasting to make use of many commercial strategies.

Chapter 18 turns to the local **public television station** to analyze the programming impact of different types of public licensees. It shows how the philosophies of the 325 public stations arise from their means of economic support and how these philosophies in turn affect their programming. It analyzes how public station programmers learn about their audiences. The authors then describe the various program resources used by public station programmers and consider their main scheduling priorities. It concludes by examining competing perspectives on counterprogramming strategy for public television.

Chapter 19 deals with **public radio station** programming strategy. Out of nearly 11,000 total radio stations (1,301 noncommercial), about 350 are public licensees—nearly all FM broadcasters. Public radio occurs in six basic formats, and stations may be affiliated with one or more networks or independent. Satellite transmission has changed public radio's structure by making new networks possible and stimulating program syndication. The author shows how the technological changes that have profoundly affected commercial radio syndication are affecting public radio networking. The author then uses the example of KUSC's rise as a case study illustrating station programming strategy for public radio. The chapter considers the sources of public radio programs, the effects of various methods of placing programs in the schedule and the procedures for evaluating public radio programming.

Part Five, then, examines the noncommercial side of broadcasting. It draws analogies with the commercial world and points out distinctions and similarities in programming strategies.

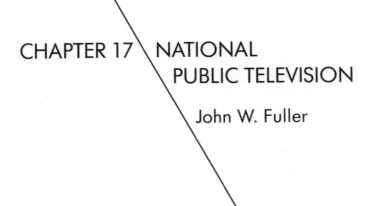

CHAPTER 17 \ NATIONAL PUBLIC TELEVISION

John W. Fuller

A Guide to Chapter 17

John W. Fuller, director of research at PBS, came to the national noncommercial network in 1980 from the position of research project manager at Arbitron in Laurel, Maryland. He started in television as studio director of WJKS-TV in Jacksonville, Florida, in 1966, moving to promotion manager in 1968. He then became research director for WTLV-TV in Jacksonville, and then served as program manager as well at the same station from 1972 to 1976. From there he went to Arbitron. He holds a B.A. in radio-television from Florida State University and an M.A. from the University of Florida in communications research. This chapter shows his intimate knowledge of recent changes in noncommercial broadcast programming from a national perspective.

THE NONCOMMERCIAL ENVIRONMENT

Programming the national **Public Broadcasting Service (PBS)** is a little like trying to prepare a universally acclaimed gourmet meal. The trouble is that a committee of 168 plans the menu, and the people that pay the grocery bills want to be sure that the meal is served with due regard for their images. Some people coming to the dinner table want the meal to be enjoyable and fun; others want the experience to be uplifting and enlightening; still others insist that the eating be instructive; and the seafood and chicken cooks want to be sure the audience comes away with a better understanding of the problems of life underwater and in the coop.[1]

The analogies are not farfetched. A board of 35 appointed and elected representatives of its member stations on 3-year terms governs the Public Broadcasting Service. The board is expected to serve 168 public television licensees operating 319 public (PTV) stations all over the country and in such remote areas as Guam, American Samoa and Bethel, Alaska. Since PBS produces no programming, it uses a host of program suppliers and tries to promote and schedule their programs effectively. In addition, constituencies ranging from independent producers to minority groups constantly pressure public television to meet their special needs. And, of course, the program funders have their own agendas too.

THE NETWORK MODEL

A national, commercial, American television network, as generally understood, acts as a centralized programming, sales and distributing agent for its affiliates, program suppliers and clients (advertisers). A commercial network supplies about 70 percent of an affiliate's entire program service, and the affiliate gets paid for the time it makes available. Commercial affiliates have little voice in choosing the network programs they air or the way they are scheduled. The commercial network's great strength lies in its ability to program some 200+ television stations simultaneously with a lineup of popular programs that the network itself either produces or, more commonly, commissions for production, usually under its close supervision. As important as the network programmers' choice of individual programs is their expertise in melding them into a sequence that holds the attention of national audiences.

How closely does the Public Broadcasting Service conform to this model? In commercial television, programming and money flow *from* network headquarters *to* affiliates. Production is centrally controlled and distributed on a one-way line to affiliates, paid to push the network button and transmit what the network feeds. Most of the economic incentives favor affiliate cooperation with the network, placing tremendous programming power in network hands.

In public television, money flows the opposite way. Instead of being paid as loyal affiliates, member stations *pay PBS dues.* PBS in turn supplies them with programs sufficient to fill prime time and much of the daytime hours. A station's remaining broadcast hours are typically filled with leased syndicated fare (movies, off-network reruns, made-for-syndication series and instructional programs for local schools), local productions and programs supplied by regional public television networks.

Four regional networks are headquartered in and serve the eastern, southern, central and western sections of the United States. One, the Eastern Educational Network, formed the **Interregional Program Service** in 1980 to distribute its programs nationally. It now serves a large group of stations in all regions, functioning as a second major PTV distributor. The parallel between the regional networks and PBS is strong: Member stations *pay a regional network dues,* and it then delivers programs to them (see Chapter 18). PBS, however, delivers its programs in a *prearranged schedule* whereas the regional networks distribute their programs during off-hours via satellite for local taping and scheduling (see Figure 17-1a).

Clout with PBS, then, rests with the stations. They spend their revenues as they see fit, expecting to be treated fairly and with the deference due any consumer. PBS, as a consequence, has a limited ability to get stations to agree on program scheduling. Quite naturally, local station managers display considerable scheduling independence. After the multi-transponder satellite system was phased in during 1978 and as low-cost recording equipment became available to the stations, they carried the PBS schedule less and less frequently as originally programmed. Until a networking agreement (the **common carriage** agreement) was worked out with the stations in 1979, no two station program schedules were alike. National promotion, publicity and advertising placement were, if not impossible, extremely difficult to achieve.

Implementing the common carriage agreement in October 1979 partially ordered this networking chaos. The nonbinding agreement established a **core schedule** on Sunday, Monday, Tuesday and Wednesday nights. During the hours of 8 to 10 P.M. (with delayed feeds for the central, mountain and pacific time zones), PBS fed those programs most likely to attract the largest audiences. In turn, stations committed themselves to airing the PBS core offerings (1) on the night they were fed, (2) in the order fed and (3) within the prime-time hours of 8 to 11 P.M. Some flexibility remained in station hands; if desired, stations could tape and air the two-hour core feed from 7 to 9 P.M. instead of 8 to 10 P.M.

For several years the common-carriage arrangement worked well; the typical "core" program received *same-night* carriage of 80 to 82 percent. Core slots thus took on a premium quality; underwriters and producers, looking for most favorable treatment for their programs, began to insist they be assigned a time slot within the core period—maximum carriage meant maximum audience size. With more core-quality programs on their hands than available hours in the core period, PBS programmers were forced to move some long-standing core programs (e.g., *Mystery, Great Performances*) outside the core period to make room for others and hope that the stations would still carry them on the feed night.

This move was partially successful; even though same-night carriage for the rescheduled programs fell, it was only to 50 to 55 percent. But station programmers took these moves by PBS as a sign that core programs could be moved around at will. Station independence began to reassert itself. By the 1985–86 season, same-night carriage had slipped to 73 percent. PBS, concerned with complaints from national underwriters that "their" programs were not receiving fair treatment, moved to bolster same-night carriage. In fall 1987, PBS announced a new policy of **"same night"/"same week"** carriage by which programs offered to the stations would be designated either for carriage the night they were fed or for carriage any other time within the feed week.

Programs *not* designated for same-night (or **core**) carriage have tended to receive pre-1979 treatment. Program managers commonly *tape-delay* programs with limited appeal and air them outside of prime time, using the vacated evening slots for station-acquired programming. Same-night carriage has averaged less than 40 percent of the stations for programs considered to have narrow audience appeal. Nearly all stations adhere to the same-night requirement, however, for programs PBS so designates (see Figure 17-1b).

PBS RESPONSIBILITIES

Since its founding, PBS has had two undisputed responsibilities: *to carry or reject programs* offered for national distribution and *to schedule* available programming. The program acceptance/rejection responsibility is grounded in the technical and legal standards the membership voted during the 1970s. The technical standards protect stations from Federal Communications Commission violations and maintain high levels of video and audio quality. By their very nature, they can be applied with reasonable consistency. The legal standards protect stations from libel and rights infringements and alert them to equal time and fairness obligations that may result from PBS-distributed programs. As the steward for underwriting guidelines, PBS's legal department also established the form for *on-air crediting* of PBS program funders.

Program Scheduling Task

Scheduling responsibility rests with PBS's **Program Department,** which develops strategies, and **Program Operations,** which manages the daily details of the national schedule much as a traffic department would at a commercial station. Program Operations must plug all the pieces of the jigsaw puzzle into place across the three satellite transponders, seeing to it that when an 11-episode series ends, another is ready to occupy its slot; when a drama has profanity, an edited feed of it is available; when the Saturday morning

Figure 17-1a PBS Fall '87 Projected Schedule

Week-at-a-Glance

Time	SUNDAYS	MONDAYS through FRIDAYS	SATURDAYS	
9:00 / 0900	SESAME STREET	SESAME STREET	THE AMERICAN ADVENTURE	
			THE AMERICAN ADVENTURE	
10:00 / 1000	MR. ROGERS' NEIGHBORHOOD	MR. ROGERS' NEIGHBORHOOD	FRENCH IN ACTION	
	SQUARE ONE TV (rpt)	SQUARE ONE TV	AMERICAN INTERESTS	FRENCH IN ACTION
11:00 / 1100	SESAME STREET	3-2-1 CONTACT	ComputerWorks	
		SESAME STREET	ComputerWorks	ECONOMICS USA
12:00 / 1200	MR. ROGERS' NEIGHBORHOOD		THE BUSINESS OF MANAGEMENT	
	3-2-1 CONTACT	MR. ROGERS' NEIGHBORHOOD	THE BUSINESS OF MANAGEMENT	
1:00 / 1300	THE WRITE COURSE	PBS SOFTSERVICE	THE FRUGAL GOURMET	THE NEW LITERACY
	THE WRITE COURSE		THE VICTORY GARDEN	THE NEW LITERACY
2:00 / 1400	THE MECHANICAL UNIVERSE		WOODWRIGHT'S SHOP	ECONOMICS USA (R)
	THE MECHANICAL UNIVERSE		THIS OLD HOUSE	ECONOMICS USA (R)
3:00 / 1500	FRENCH IN ACTION	PBS SOFTSERVICE	MOTORWEEK '88	THE BUSINESS FILE (R)
	FRENCH IN ACTION	SESAME STREET	MADELEINE COOKS	THE BUSINESS FILE (R)
4:00 / 1600	ComputerWorks		AMERICAN GOVERNMENT SURVEY	
	ComputerWorks	MR. ROGERS' NEIGHBORHOOD	AMERICAN GOVERNMENT SURVEY	
5:00 / 1700	PBS DARK	SQUARE ONE TV	FOCUS ON SOCIETY (R)	
	TONY BROWN'S JOURNAL	3-2-1 CONTACT	FOCUS ON SOCIETY (R)	
6:00 / 1800	AMERICAN INTERESTS	THE MACNEIL/LEHRER NEWSHOUR	GROWING A BUSINESS	THE AMERICAN ADVENTURE
	ADAM SMITH'S MONEY WORLD		INNOVATION/ NEWTON'S APPLE	THE AMERICAN ADVENTURE
7:00 / 1900				

Source: Public Broadcasting Service. Used with permission.

Figure 17-1b Prime-time Lineup for One Week

PBS FALL '87 PROJECTED SCHEDULE
Week-at-a-Glance

	SUNDAY	MONDAY	TUESDAY	WEDNESDAY	THURSDAY	FRIDAY	SATURDAY
7:00 / 1900	THE CONSTITUTION: THAT DELICATE BALANCE	THE MACNEIL / LEHRER NEWSHOUR (rpt)					DEGRASSI JUNIOR HIGH / WILD AMERICA
8:00 / 2000	NATURE	AMERICA BY DESIGN / THE FIRST EDEN / MAKING OF A CONTINENT	NOVA	SPECIALS	THE ADAMS CHRONICLES (R)	WASHINGTON WEEK IN REVIEW / WALL STREET WEEK	WONDERWORKS
9:00 / 2100	MASTERPIECE THEATRE	OIL / SPECIALS	WE THE PEOPLE / THE RING OF TRUTH	SPECIALS	MYSTERY!	GREAT PERFORMANCES	HEIMAT
10:00 / 2200	ONLY ONE EARTH	THE HEALTH CENTURY / TRYING TIMES / SPECIALS	THE STORY OF ENGLISH	SPECIALS	UPSTAIRS, DOWNSTAIRS	SPECIALS	
11:00 / 2300	SILK SCREEN / MAKE PRAYERS TO THE RAVEN						

Shaded area is designated for **same night** carriage.

Source: Public Broadcasting Service. Used with permission.

schedule of how-to programs runs short, a forgotten cooking series is resurrected to fill out the summer; and so on.

Public broadcasting faces a decision similar to the cable industry's regarding *new* satellites: whether to shift to high-power **Ku-band** or stay with low-power **C-band** (see Chapter 9). Westar IV, the public broadcast satellite serving both television and radio during the 1980s, exhausts its fuel by 1992, necessitating either purchase or lease of a new bird. Another crucial decision is whether to move into **high-definition television (HDTV)** for its advantages in creating a powerful visual aesthetic for live performances. Many public broadcasters consider noncommercial television better able to adopt HDTV now than commercial enterprises, because public broadcasting is not so tied to ratings—directly affected by the number of homes able to receive a new technology like HDTV. The issue of how to cover the cost of a shift to Ku-band and/or HDTV remains thorny: All stations would need new receiving equipment and/or studio equipment; PBS would need costly new distribution equipment.

A senior vice-president heads the PBS Program Department and is concerned with the long-range development of major program series and supervision of the PBS national program service. Other executives concerned with program scheduling, development and acquisition assist this vice-president. Subdivisions within the department concentrate on news and public affairs, children's and cultural programs and fund-raising specials. Other departments within PBS deliver, on a *user-pays* basis, programs for adult at-home college education, in-school instruction for children and corporate on-site training programs and materials. PBS Encore! provides stations with a menu of previously aired PBS programs (reruns) for supplementing local schedules.

PBS Fund-Raising Assistance

Through it all, one enormously successful PBS activity is its **Station Independence Program (SIP)**, a division in PBS's Development Department, that helps stations conduct on-air fund-raising appeals in which they solicit dollar pledges. The stations pay PBS dues for this fund-raising assistance. A key SIP function is consulting with the PBS Program Department on the acquisition, funding and commissioning of special programs for use during local station pledge drives. Mass-appeal programming with emotional payoff—such as heavy dramatic impact, warmly received performances, emotionally charged documentary subjects—seems to work best.

PROGRAM SOURCES FOR PBS

PBS has developed its own pattern of dramatic miniseries and anthologies, science and nature documentaries, concert performances, public affairs documentaries and a few other types—none of which the commercial networks offer on a regular basis. British programs such as *Masterpiece Theatre* and *In Search of the Trojan Wars* appear on American public television because they are available, high-quality programs at one-tenth the cost of producing comparable fare in the United States. But they, along with other foreign productions, occupy only a small fraction of all PBS programs (see Figure 17-2).

Figure 17-2 PBS Distributed Hours, by Producer

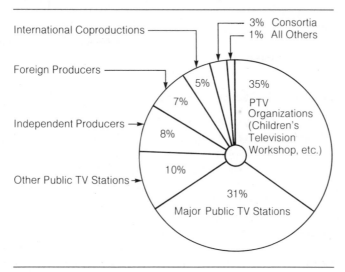

Source: Corporation for Public Broadcasting, *Public Television Programming Content by Category* (1984), unpublished.

PBS programmers face a special problem when assembling a schedule. Unlike the program chiefs at ABC, CBS and NBC, executives at PBS cannot simply order pilots, choose those with promise, then send production companies scurrying to produce what has been chosen. PBS does not produce or order up programs. Instead, they have from the beginning had to work with whatever was made available by others. Thus, attempts to inject balance into the national schedule to prevent, say, too many symphony concerts and too few investigative documentaries, have always been labored and, ultimately, frustrating.

Most programs PBS has distributed over the years have been someone else's idea and creation. Producers, not bound by any sense of national priority, produced whatever they chose (so long as funding could be found). Major producers in fact have portfolios of program ideas they constantly shop around to potential funders. A few get funded and, provided they pass PBS content and technical standards, receive a slot in the national schedule. A very large portion of PBS's schedule comes from series produced by or in conjunction with the *major producing stations*—WGBH, Boston; WNET, New York; WETA, Washington, D.C.; WQED, Pittsburgh.

In recent years PBS has moved to assert some control over the otherwise serendipitous *program development process*. With contributions from the stations, the **Corporation for Public Broadcasting (CPB)** first established the Program Development Fund for providing producers with seed money for projects PBS wanted in the national schedule. Then, in cooperation with CPB and the stations, PBS inaugurated the multimillion dollar Program Challenge

Fund, its purpose being to ensure the production of at least two major new prime-time series each season. Finally, to better regulate the flow of new productions into the national schedule, PBS established the Public Television Pipeline, a management system for monitoring and coordinating all program development activity from the proposal stage through delivery to PBS.

STATION PROGRAM COOPERATIVE

One important program source that has always been under PBS's control is the **Station Program Cooperative (SPC)**, a marketing system employed by the stations to cooperatively finance national, PBS-distributed programming. PBS administers the SPC, which supplies one-half of the national program service (some 900 hours of new programs annually). Station participants meet every October at the PBS **Program Fair** to screen some 50-odd programs, many of which are program pilots, and to hear producers of long-running series plead the case for refunding their shows. In the following months, several rounds of voting are held to winnow out the most desirable programs, the final round occurring in late winter (usually February). The "winning" producers are notified, and the rush begins to complete episodes in time for the fall PBS premieres.

Out of this process evolves a slate of some 25 to 30 programs paid for by the stations themselves.[2] The eventual cost of a program to any station is determined by the number of other stations committing to purchase the same program. The beauty of the SPC process is that it funds programs unattractive to or too controversial for underwriters—investigative news documentaries, children's series, minority programs—and so provides some counterbalance to the fully underwritten shows in the national program schedule. The SPC, however, uses a democratic election process and, in consequence, chooses conservatively, tending to refinance *long-running series* again and again, and often bypassing untried program ideas.

CONSTRAINTS ON THE NATIONAL SCHEDULE

The PBS Program Department thus receives programs from two major sources: the *stations* and independent *producers*. The results of the SPC determine most of PBS's options. And with program selection comes pressure from producers for the best scheduling positions. This sometimes comes even from SPC program producers, whose creations were fully paid for by the stations; these producers worked hard to make the program, and, understandably, they want it to receive the best possible treatment. But the most obvious pressure comes from corporations who underwrote a program with specific marketing goals in mind.

Corporate Pressure

Most programs PBS distributes enter the system via a station that develops, produces and finally delivers its program to the Alexandria, Virginia, PBS headquarters (hence, a variety of station credits appear fore and aft PBS programs). Local station producers often have *corporate underwriters* that actively participate in program production or purchase programs outright. Corporate executives in charge of underwriting invest not only prodigious sums from corporate treasuries but also personal effort and reputation, and they feel entitled to choice slots in the prime-time schedule—invariably, during the core period. Of course, PBS cannot fit in all such programs and maintain a balanced schedule.[3] A fully funded series must be played off, however, within and only within the underwriting corporation's fiscal year irrespective of audience response and schedule needs if the corporation is to receive a tax break. Because money flows into PBS rather than out, PBS program executives wield almost no power and usually must acquiesce to corporate demands.

The *major producing stations,* too, attempt to influence program decisions at PBS; for some, financial stability depends on preserving the income from their underwriters. **Underwriter** funding pays for salaries, equipment loans and other production expenses for turning out programs seeking system-wide distribution. Were a major underwriter to withdraw support, the financial effect on the station might be devastating.

Member Pressure

Other programming pressures occur. Many stations, for example, may *refuse* to telecast a program at the time fed because they feel it (1) does not deserve a prime-time slot, (2) contains too much profanity or violence to air in early evening, (3) will fail to attract contributors at fund-raising time, (4) occupies a slot the stations want for their own programs or syndication purchases or (5) has no appeal for local viewers. PBS program executives assembling a schedule must anticipate these problems to minimize defections from the live feed.

Program Rights and Delivery

PBS programmers must also wrestle with two problems common to both commercial and noncommercial programming: *program rights* and *late delivery.* In public television as in commercial television, standard program air-lease rights are set by contract with the producer, who owns the rights. PBS has traditionally negotiated with producers for as many **plays** as possible so that by airing the same program several times the typically small (per-airing) PBS audience snowballs. Extra plays also fill out the program schedule. At the same time, the program syndicator seeks as few airings as possible over the shortest time period to retain maximum control and revenue potential for a program. A compromise between various producers and PBS permitting **four** program plays within **three** years is now the standard rights agreement in public television. To fully amortize an underwriter's investment, PBS must therefore shoehorn programs into fewer seasons (three) than airplays (four).

Late delivery has obvious troublemaking possibilities. So many productions were behind schedule in 1981 that the fall schedule premiered without a single new series. As a consequence, in that extraordinary year, the "second season" premieres in January 1982 were so choked with overdue new programs that the popular *Mystery!* series had to be popped out and shelved until the following fall!

NATIONAL SCHEDULING STRATEGY

How, with so many conflicting interests and confounding considerations, can a national scheduling strategy emerge? In truth, none can, at least not in the fashion of commercial broadcasting, which allows network programmers to assemble their schedules, program by program, for maximum audience impact. In spite of the PBS program department's herculean efforts to hammer out schedules for fall, for winter and for summer each year, what finally emerges is a monument to compromise and appeasement. Agreeing on program schedules requires a round of marathon meetings with the research and program operations departments, accompanied by meetings with producers, meetings with station executives, countless phone calls and assorted conversations over lunch and dinner. After all interested parties have been heard from, one or two programs may actually remain where the programmers had initially scheduled them.

Nowadays, PBS programmers want to **maximize** audiences. Gone are the educational television days when paying attention to audience *size* was looked upon as "whoring after numbers." The prevailing attitude at PBS recognizes that a program must be *seen* to be of value, and that improper scheduling prevents full realization of a program's potential. Member stations now recognize that bigger audiences also mean a bigger dollar take during on-air pledge drives.

Still, opportunities occur throughout the year when the programmers and research people can put their heads together to solve scheduling problems one at a time, removed from the charged atmosphere attending fall scheduling meetings. The PBS Program Department does act alone sometimes, adding or subtracting from the schedule, reversing program order and so on; and at those times, scheduling strategies come into play.

Counterprogramming the Commercial Networks

Competition, of course, is a key consideration. The three ways of responding to it are *offensively* (attempting to overpower the competitor), *defensively* (**counterprogramming** for a different segment of the audience than the competitor's program is likely to attract), or by *ignoring* the competition altogether and hoping for the best. PBS has never been able to go on the offensive; its programs lack the requisite breadth of appeal. Prime-time PBS shows in midwinter, for example, average a **3 rating.** ABC, CBS and NBC regularly collect ratings of 15 to 25 and sometimes higher. (NBC's *The Cosby Show*'s 1986–87 season, for example, averaged 35 rating points.)

PBS, then, must duck and dodge. By studying national Nielsen data, programmers learn the demographic makeup of competing network program audiences so they can place their own programs more advantageously. For example, a symphony performance that tends to attract well-educated women over 50 living in metropolitan areas would perform well opposite *Knots Landing* and *Highway to Heaven,* having **downscale** (lower socioeconomic) audiences. Similarly, in searching for a slot for the investigative documentary series *Frontline,* PBS did not consider for a moment the 8 to 9 P.M. slot on Sundays because football overruns frequently push *60 Minutes* into this slot.

PBS tries to avoid placing a valued program against a hit series in the commercial schedules. Pressure to avoid these situations frequently comes from individual program producers. PBS also has traditionally avoided placing important programs during the three key all-market audience-measurement periods (**sweeps**) in November, February and May—times when commercial television throws its blockbusters at the audience. Recently, however, PBS has revised this strategy, acknowledging the value of ratings. Since the public television stations are also measured during the sweeps for all time periods and for the all-important cumulative audiences reached over a week (**cumes**), the major public stations demand priority programming (a form of **stunting**). As one PBS programmer put it, "When they announce the start of the contest, that is hardly the time to head for the sidelines." Ratings periods now display PBS's best— not weakest—programs, and this fresh approach has paid off. Recent audience figures show a rise in public television viewing.

Bridging

Another competitive strategy PBS uses is **bridging.** Most viewers stay with a program from start to finish. A lengthy program prevents an audience from switching to the competition's programs at the time where one network's programs end and others begin (crossover points). This strategy can be applied offensively or defensively. PBS generally defends. For example, all three commercial networks air one-hour programs in the 8 to 9 P.M. period every night, thus bridging any PBS show scheduled at 8:30 by eliminating the 8:30 crossover point. Were PBS to schedule a pair of half-hour shows in the 8 to 9 P.M. period, the 8:30 program would draw away very little of the network audience. Viewers of the hypothetical 8:30 PBS program would have to flow out of the lead-in program or come from homes where the television set had just been turned on at 8:30. At times, PBS successfully *avoids* being bridged. For example, in the fall of 1987, all three commercial networks began shows at 9:00 P.M. every night of the week. PBS's drama series *Heimat* started at this time too on Saturdays, but bridged NBC at 9:30 and all three networks at 10 P.M. (see Figure 17-3).

Otherwise, PBS counters the commercial networks simply by scheduling according to their general scheduling patterns. If two of the commercial networks have **long-form nights** (nights with two-hour movies or specials running 9 to 11 P.M. EST), PBS may schedule its own long-form programming opposite. The theory holds that when two of the networks tie up audiences from 9 to 11, no viewers are released to come to public television for a program starting at 9:30 or 10. Since all of the commercial networks break every night at 9, the PBS schedule does too, in the hope that if any dial twisting occurs at 9, some of the viewers might come to public television.

Figure 17-3 Illustration of Bridging at 9:30 and 10:00

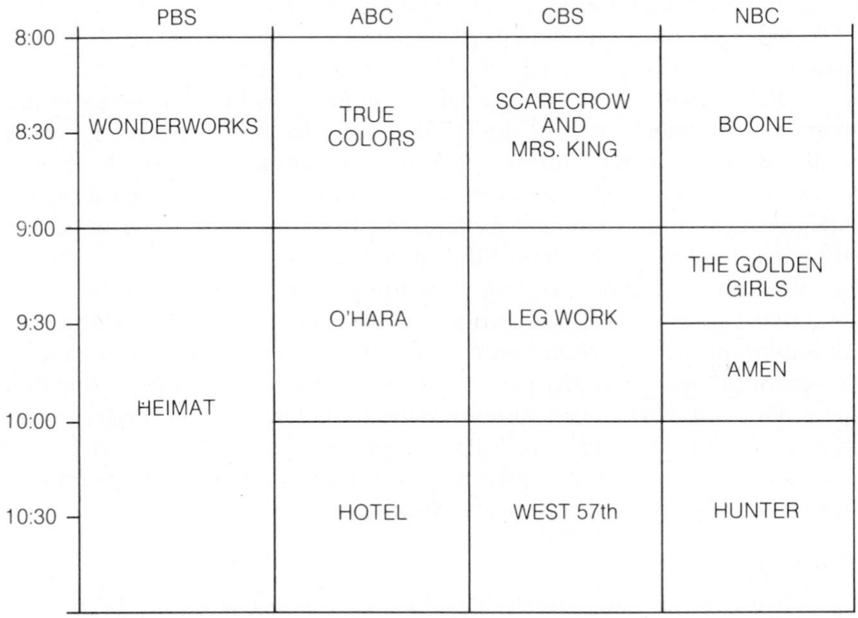

	PBS	ABC	CBS	NBC
8:00				
8:30	WONDERWORKS	TRUE COLORS	SCARECROW AND MRS. KING	BOONE
9:00				
9:30		O'HARA	LEG WORK	THE GOLDEN GIRLS
				AMEN
10:00	HEIMAT			
10:30		HOTEL	WEST 57th	HUNTER

Audience Flow in the Core Schedule

Certain PBS series are especially dependent on **audience flow** from a strong **lead-in.** The new six-part series on the scientific method, for example, *The Ring of Truth,* was not expected to build a loyal following the way a predictable series such as *The Wall Street Week* has. Thus, it was placed following an established, healthy science series, *NOVA*, which regularly draws large audiences (large, that is, for public television) and itself has no need for a powerful lead-in.

PBS gains an advantage on nights or in periods in which commercial television is not at its competitive best. One such night occurs every two years in November during national elections. While ABC, CBS and NBC are busy seeking every last ratings point from their simultaneous election coverage, public television and independent stations have a rare opportunity to score with counterprogramming.

National Promotion

A fledgling program needs help for viewers to discover it. Two forms of help, *advertising* and *promotion,* can alert potential viewers to a new program and persuade them to try it. Unfortunately, public television budgets rarely permit advertising, although major underwriters now include some promotional allotment in most program budgets. *National Geographic Special* is one such case.

Still another PBS strategy is to carefully schedule on-air promotion announcements for a particular program in time slots where potential viewers of that program (based on demographic profiles) are likely to be found in maximum quantity. Such on-air promotion is crucial as it reaches known viewers of public television. But its effectiveness is somewhat hampered by public television's limited prime-time reach. In one week, a massive on-air campaign promoting *one* program could hope to reach at best only 20 to 25 percent of all television households.

NATIONAL AUDIENCE RATINGS

Careful scheduling is necessary because public television must always demonstrate its *utility*. Many contributed to its continuance—Congress, underwriters, viewers. If few watch, why should contributors keep public television alive? Programmers have come to realize that critical praise alone is insufficient; they need tangible evidence that audiences feel the same way. The most meaningful evidence comes from acceptable ratings.

Nielsen Data

PBS obtains *national* audience data from Nielsen's *peoplemeter* service. Nielsen's *local* market service, the **Nielsen Station Index** (**NSI**), provides the individual-market data for PBS (see Chapter 2). Arbitron does not supply ratings data to PBS because they lack a national sample and because Arbitron's corporate policy does not allow public station program-titles to be collected and published in their rating books. (Arbitron books show ratings data, but without program identification.)

PBS's research funds only cover the cost of *one* national audience survey *week per month*. Forty weeks go unreported. The commercial networks, as described in previous chapters, purchase continuous, year-round national data. A newspaper program listings service, TV Data of Glens Falls, New York, compiles public station lineups from published station program schedules for the 52 weeks in a year. TV Data then calls all 320 public stations to collect last-minute program changes from the previous week. The resulting *carriage data* are delivered to PBS on tape, which the network analyzes to understand station usage of PBS programs. Once a month, PBS ships carriage data for a single week to Nielsen, which marries it with meter viewing data to produce the national PBS ratings.

Public television stations use the same Nielsen local station **diary** surveys during the four sweeps as do the commercial stations. Nielsen surveys a few large markets in October, January and March, and public stations in those markets can also purchase these reports.

Commercial network programmers, much to the irritation of advertising agency time-buyers, try to inflate affiliates' ratings by *stunting* with unusually popular specials and miniseries during the sweep weeks (see Chapters 1 and 5). These higher ratings provide the local affiliates with an opportunity to raise advertising rates. PBS programmers lack enough top-notch programming to stunt for an entire four-week period. PBS does, however, try to schedule a *representative mix* of PBS offerings during each of the national survey weeks. No more than one opera is permitted, for example, nor are too many esoteric public affairs programs scheduled during that week. Furthermore, PBS programmers are not above allowing an occasional *National Geographic Special* to drift into a national survey week.

PBS indulges in unabashed stunting during its 16-day fund-raising Festival every March. Just as networks stunt for economic reasons, so too does public television. The difference is structural: Rather than raise revenue by selling advertising time on the basis of ratings, PBS stations raise revenue by direct, on-air solicitation of viewer contributions. In general, large audiences mean large contributions. Hence, programs scheduled during a fund raiser must deliver large audiences.

Cumulative Audience Strategy

At all other times, PBS strives for maximum variety in its program schedule to serve as many people as possible at one time or another each week. Unlike commercial network programs, not all public television programs are expected to have large audiences. Small audiences are acceptable so long as the weekly accumulation of unduplicated households is large. PBS's programming success is therefore assessed largely in terms of its weekly *cumulative audience data* or **cumes.**

As explained in Chapter 2, Nielsen defines a cumulative household audience as the percent of all television households (in the United States for network ratings or in a local market for stations ratings) that tuned in for at least six minutes to a specific program or time period. The public television national cumes for prime time (8–11 P.M., Mon.–Sun.) averaged **35 percent** of U.S. households in 1986–87. This measurement is based on the number of U.S. television households that watched public television programs in prime time for at least six minutes during the survey week. Cume ratings for prime-time programs have ranged from under 1 to over 19 percent, the higher figure earned by a *National Geographic Special* on sharks. When all times of day are included, the weekly cume rises to nearly **60 percent** of the country's households, a respectable figure for the impecunious fourth network.

Based on prior experience, PBS programmers apply informal guidelines for what rating levels constitute adequate viewing. Nature and science programs are expected to attract a cumulative audience of 5 to 10 percent of U.S. households, dramas 4 to 5 percent; concert performances should attract 3 to 4 percent, public affairs documentaries 2 to 4 percent. Because of the way PBS programs are funded, failure to meet these levels does not mean cancelation. But failure to earn the minimum expected cumes could lead to nonrenewal by the Station Program Cooperative.

Loyalty Assessment

PBS researchers also study *audience loyalty* to evaluate program performance. Nielsen's overnight reports (based on data from the on-line metered sample homes in the top markets) permit detailed audience analysis station-by-station and quarter-hour-by-quarter-hour in these markets. If the audience tires quickly of a program, the overnight ratings will decline during the telecast (a fate to which lengthy programs are especially susceptible). If the audience weakened to the appeal of network competition, such as a special starting a half-hour or more later than the PBS show, the **overnight ratings** suddenly drop at the point where the competing special began. This information tells the programmers (roughly, to be sure) the extent to which the program engaged viewers. Noncompelling programs are vulnerable to competition. Shows failing this test have to be scheduled more carefully when repeated, preferably opposite soft network competition.

Demographic Composition

Still another concern researchers address is who is watching. Households tuning to public television each week are, as a group, not unlike television viewers generally. Many, in fact, use television heavily and, in search of variety, frequently turn to public television. Research has revealed, however, that audiences for individual programs can vary widely in demographic composition. Intellectually demanding programs such as *The Story of English* or *Great Performances* or *Masterpiece Theatre* attract older, college-educated, professional/managerial viewers. Because these "demanding" shows are scattered throughout the prime-time schedule, the cumulative prime-time audience exhibits an upscale tendency. Many programs, though, have broader-based followings, among them *Nature* and *Wonderworks*.

Public television's audience grew dramatically in the late 1970s and early 1980s. Audience figures reached nearly 100 million viewers per week. Viewing per week reached 3-1/2 hours, and public television's demographics mirror the nation's in education, income, occupation and race composition.[4] (See Figure 17-4). The growth of cable television has been a major contributor to this trend. Local cable systems make UHF public stations as easy to tune in as VHF stations and of similar picture quality—resulting in much greater use of PTV channels. But the end of cable must-carry rules in 1987 left several public stations without cable carriage (as many as 200 were dropped from some cable systems). Public television, because it cannot compete on the same footing as commercial stations, especially needs the reach and tuning parity afforded by cable.

THE AUDIENCE ISSUE

Public television representatives frequently are called upon to explain a seeming paradox: How can public television's audience duplicate the demographic makeup of the country when so many of its programs attract the **upscale** viewer? The question is second in importance only to that of how many people are watching; it is often tied to charges of elitism in program acquisition, implying PBS is not serving all the public with "public" television. PBS replies that it consciously attempts to provide alternatives to the commercial network offerings; to do so, the content of most PBS programs must make demands of viewers. Demanding programs tend, however, to be less appealing to viewers of lower socioeconomic status. The result is underrepresentation of

Figure 17-4a U.S. Population and PTV Audience Composition

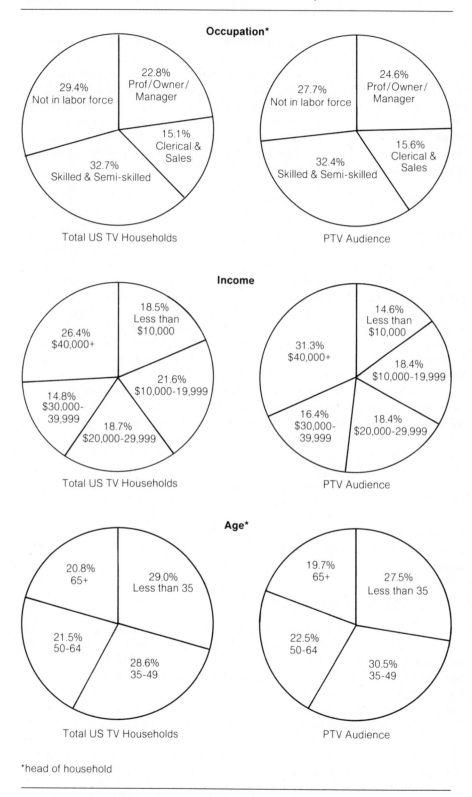

Occupation*

Total US TV Households

22.8% Prof/Owner/Manager
29.4% Not in labor force
15.1% Clerical & Sales
32.7% Skilled & Semi-skilled

PTV Audience

24.6% Prof/Owner/Manager
27.7% Not in labor force
15.6% Clerical & Sales
32.4% Skilled & Semi-skilled

Income

Total US TV Households

18.5% Less than $10,000
26.4% $40,000+
21.6% $10,000-19,999
14.8% $30,000-39,999
18.7% $20,000-29,999

PTV Audience

14.6% Less than $10,000
31.3% $40,000+
18.4% $10,000-19,999
16.4% $30,000-39,999
18.4% $20,000-29,999

Age*

Total US TV Households

20.8% 65+
29.0% Less than 35
21.5% 50-64
28.6% 35-49

PTV Audience

19.7% 65+
27.5% Less than 35
22.5% 50-64
30.5% 35-49

*head of household

Source: PBS Research/Nielsen TV index. Used with permission.

Figure 17-4b U.S. Population and PTV Audience Composition

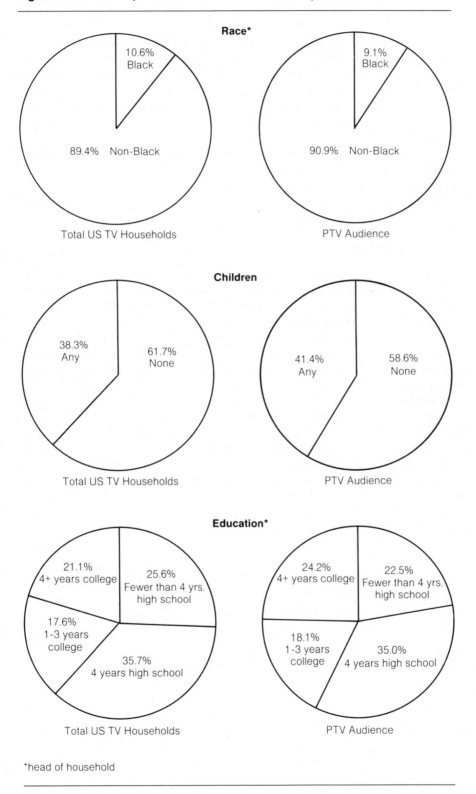

Race*

10.6%
Black

89.4%   Non-Black

Total US TV Households

9.1%
Black

90.9%   Non-Black

PTV Audience

Children

38.3%
Any

61.7%
None

Total US TV Households

41.4%
Any

58.6%
None

PTV Audience

Education*

21.1%
4+ years college

25.6%
Fewer than 4 yrs.
high school

17.6%
1-3 years
college

35.7%
4 years high school

Total US TV Households

24.2%
4+ years college

22.5%
Fewer than 4 yrs.
high school

18.1%
1-3 years
college

35.0%
4 years high school

PTV Audience

*head of household

Source: PBS Research/Nielsen TV index. Used with permission.

such viewers in certain audiences. But this underrepresentation is, on balance, only slight, being offset in the week's cumulative audience totals for other programs having broader appeal. Critics often overlook that underrepresentation does not mean no representation. *NOVA*, for example, is watched each week in some 1.4 million households headed by a person who never finished high school. Even operas average over one million such downscale households in their audiences.

The kinds of audience statistics just cited serve a unique function: justification of public television. Commercial broadcasters justify their existence when they turn a profit for their owners and investors; public broadcasters prove their worth only when survey data indicate the public *valued* (i.e., viewed) the service provided.

SUMMARY

PBS operates in a more constrained environment than the commercial networks. Its member stations pay dues, and PBS serves them with programming. Corporate underwriters, independent program producers and member stations exert pressure on PBS in the selection and scheduling processes, constraining PBS's programming strategies. The SPC process also favors programs popular with stations in the largest markets as votes reflect market size. Counterprogramming, bridging and audience flow operate as major scheduling strategies in the prime-time core schedule. Promotion builds ratings, but funds for it are often lacking. SIP provides stations with special fund-raising programs and assistance and is among the most successful of PBS's services. While PBS uses the Nielsen ratings, it focuses on cumulative audiences and measurements of loyalty. A long-standing controversy in public broadcasting is whether its programming is elitist; analysis of audience demographics shows that the composite schedule has broad appeal. Although specific programs may draw largely upscale viewers, all programs capture some viewers from all demographic groups. Cable television has significantly increased the pool of available viewers for public broadcasting.

Notes

1. S. Anders Yokom, Jr., *Broadcast Programming*, 1st edition. Belmont, Calif.: Wadsworth, 1980.

2. Some programs arrive at the Fair with partial corporate funding, accompanied by requests to SPC to make up the difference. Failing SPC support, the producers must either persuade their corporate funders to fully underwrite the programs or turn elsewhere (usually to additional corporations) for the balance.

3. "Not Much Schedule Juggling at PBS," *Current*, 12 July 1983, p. 4.

4. PBS Research/Nielsen Television Index, 1986–87.

Selected Sources

Agostino, Don. "Cable Television's Impact on the Audience of Public Television." *Journal of Broadcasting* 24 (Summer 1980):347–65.

Attracting Minority Audiences to Public Television. Washington, D.C.: Corporation for Public Broadcasting, 1981.

Current, weekly Washington newspaper about public broadcasting, 1981 to date.

Frank, Ronald E., and Greenberg, Marshall G. *The Public's Use of Television: Who Watches and Why.* Beverly Hills, Calif.: Sage Publications, 1980.

Fuller, John W. *Who Watches Public Television?* Alexandria, Va.: Public Broadcasting Service, 1986.

Mahony, Shiela; Demartino, Nick; and Stengel, Robert. *Keeping PACE with the New Television: Public Television and Changing Technology.* New York: Carnegie Corporation, 1980.

A Report to the People: 20 Years of National Commitment to Public Broadcasting, 1967–1987 and 1986 Annual Report. Washington, D.C.: Corporation for Public Broadcasting, 1987.

Witherspoon, John, and Kovitz, Roselle. *The History of Public Broadcasting.* Washington, D.C.: Current, 1987.

CHAPTER 18 PUBLIC TELEVISION STATION PROGRAMMING

James Robertson
Bruce L. Christensen

A Guide to Chapter 18

James Robertson recently retired as the president of Robertson Associates, Inc., an independent consulting firm focusing on public broadcasting. He was its principal consultant to more than thirty clients in the last nine years. Prior to this time he had been successively employed (from 1954 to 1973) as director of programming for WTTW, Chicago; vice-president for network affairs for National Educational Television (NET), the predecessor of PBS; vice-president and general manager of KCET, Los Angeles; director of broadcasting for the University of Wisconsin's WHA; and executive director of National Educational Radio for the National Association of Educational Broadcasters (NAEB). His role as president of Robertson Associates involved the evaluation of the effectiveness of existing stations, planning for new ones, and research and community surveying preparatory to the development of statewide public broadcasting plans for public radio in Ohio, Nebraska and Virginia and for public television in Indiana and Illinois.

Bruce L. Christensen, president of PBS and formerly president of the National Association of Public Television Stations in Washington, D.C., represents public television's legislative, regulatory and planning interests in the nation's capital. Prior to joining NAPTS in 1982, he was director of media services and general manager of KUED-TV and KUER-FM at the University of Utah in Salt Lake City and taught classes in public broadcasting as an adjunct associate professor in the department of communications. Before moving to the University of Utah, Mr. Christensen served as director of broadcast services for Brigham Young University and general manager of its radio and television facilities. He holds a master's degree in Journalism from Northwestern University. He was elected to the board of directors of the Public Broadcasting System in 1979 and has also served on the boards of the Pacific Mountain Network and Rocky Mountain Corporation for Broadcasting. Together, these authors bring wide-ranging experience to this discussion of programming by public television stations.

PUBLIC STATION PROGRAM PHILOSOPHY

Public television, its mission and its public service objectives occupy a unique position in American broadcasting. Contrary to broadcast development in nearly every other country in the world, public service broadcasting in the United States developed long after the commercial system was in place. This fact has had an immense effect on the general public's attitude toward American public television programming and on public broadcasters' self-definition.

The public debates whether or not public television programs are even necessary and whether they should occupy the time and attention of the nation's communications policymakers in the Congress, the Executive Branch and the Federal Communications Commission. Some argue that the advent of the new technologies of cable, direct satellite broadcasting, multipoint distribution systems, videotapes and discs and so on in the marketplace obviate the need for public television. Others counter that the marketplace fails to provide the special audience programming that public television offers and that any belief that emerging technologies will be different from existing media is unfounded. They point to CBS's and RCA's failures when they offered arts and cultural programming on cable and to the very limited success of Bravo and Arts & Entertainment, who supply cultural programming on pay and basic cable. Marketplace critics also state that only public television programming has special audience services for children, the elderly and ethnic minorities.

The debate over programming content has persisted within the industry since public television began. For stations, the debate centers on the meaning of **"noncommercial educational broadcasting,"** which is what the Communications Act of 1934 and the Federal Communications Commission call public television's program service. Noncommercial service came into existence in 1952 when educational interests lobbied the FCC into creating a special class of reserved channels within the television allocations—exclusively dedicated to "educational television."

One extreme argument defines *educational* in the narrow sense of *instructional*. From that viewpoint, public television (PTV) should teach—direct its programs to school and college classrooms and to out-of-classroom students; the last thing PTV should do is to compete for commercial television's mass audience. At the other extreme are those people who define *educational* in the broadest possible sense. They want to reach out to viewers of all kinds and generate mass support for the public television service. This group perceives "instructional" television as a duty that sometimes must be performed, but their devotion goes to the wide range of programming the public has come to think of as public television.

The Carnegie Commission on Educational Television introduced the term *public television* in 1967. The commission convinced many in government and broadcasting that the struggling new service had to generate wider support than it had in its fledgling years. One of the impediments to such support, the Commission felt, was the word *educational*, which gave the service an unpopular image. They suggested *public television* as a more neutral term. Thus, a distinction has grown up between **instructional television (ITV)** and **public television (PTV)**—a distinction not altogether desirable or valid.

Lacking a truly national definition for public television's program service, a public television station's programmer must deal with the unresolved, internal questions of what it means to be a "noncommercial educational broadcasting" service. The PTV programmer must come to grips with a particular station's particular program philosophy. Philosophies vary widely from one station to the next, but one common theme persists: being **noncommercial.** This term implies that public television must directly serve "the people"; it must be, at the very least, different from— if not better than—commercial television. One of the implications of such a fundamental difference is that public television programming need not pursue the largest possible audience at whatever cost to programming. Public broadcasting has a special mission to serve audiences that would be otherwise neglected because they are too small to interest commercial broadcasting. This difference in outlook has great programming significance. It means that the public station programmer is relieved of one of the most relentless constraints limiting a commercial programmer's freedom of choice.

At the same time, public television cannot cater only to the smallest groups with the most esoteric tastes in the community. Broadcasting is still a mass medium, whether commercial or noncommercial, and can justify occupying a broadcast channel and the considerable expense of broadcast facilities only if it reaches relatively large numbers of people. As explained in Chapter

17, public broadcasting achieves this goal cumulatively by reaching many small groups. As long as they add up to a respectably large cumulative total in the course of a week, the PTV programmer has a "large" audience. Moreover, it is typically the general entertainment viewer who is able and willing to subscribe to public television.

TYPES OF STATION LICENSEES

One of the difficulties in describing PTV programming strategies is that the stations are so diverse. The 168 **licensees** (as of 1988), operating 325 **stations,** represent many management viewpoints.[1] Much of this diversity is explained by the varying auspices under which they operate. Licensees fall into four categories: community, university, public school and state agency, and each constrains programming in different ways.

Community Licensees

In larger cities—particularly those with many educational and cultural institutions but without a dominant institution or school system—the usual licensee is the *nonprofit community corporation* created for the purpose of constructing and operating a public television station. Because the governing board of such a station exists solely to administer the station (as compared with university trustees who have many other concerns), many feel community stations are the most responsive type of licensee. As of the late 1980s, 79 such stations operated in the United States.

Compared with other licensees, community stations derive a higher proportion of their operating support from *fund-raising activities*—about 50 percent, compared with 32 percent for licensees overall. As a result, much of their programming reflects the urgent need to generate funds from the viewers they serve. Programmers at these stations, therefore, are more likely to be sensitive to a proposed program's general appeal. They will lean toward high-quality production values to attract and hold a general audience. These stations cannot grow or improve without a rapidly ascending curve of community support.

Reductions in federal funding for public television during the Reagan administration's first term forced a greater reliance on public donations. Most stations came to rely more heavily on revenue from nonfederal sources in general and on public donations in particular. Searching for alternative ways to finance public television, Congress authorized a one-year *advertising experiment*. Ten public television stations, including all types of licensees, were allowed to sell and broadcast advertising from April 1982 through June 1983. Studies showed minimal objection from the public, and some participating stations reported substantial profits (direct cost of sales commissions averaged only 30 percent of gross sales). But advertising revenues are based directly on the size of a station's audience, and because public television ratings are comparatively small, gross sales (and profits) provided stations only a fraction of their annual budgets. The public television industry could find no cause for enthusiasm in the outcome, and no authorizing legislation resulted. Instead, hoping to stimulate corporate support another way, the FCC loosened their **underwriting**

guidelines to permit, among other things, the display of products and animated corporate logos in program underwriter credits.

Within the community category, *eight* stations stand somewhat apart because of their metropolitan origins, their large size and their national impact on the entire noncommercial service as producers of network-distributed programs. These flagship stations of the public broadcasting service are located in New York, Boston, Pittsburgh, Washington, Chicago, Los Angeles, San Francisco and Philadelphia. The first *four*, as mentioned in Chapter 17, are particularly notable as production centers for the nation, originating such major programs as *MacNeil/Lehrer*, *Nova* and the *National Geographic Specials*. Although other public stations and commercial entities often participate in their productions and financing, these large, community-licensed producing stations generate most of the PBS schedule.

University Stations

In many cases, colleges and universities activated public television stations as a natural outgrowth of their traditional role of providing extension services within their states. As they see it, "The boundaries of the campus are the boundaries of the state,"[2] and both radio and television can do some of the tasks extension agents formerly did in person. Fifty-three licensees make up the *university* group.

Here, too, programmers schedule a fairly broad range of programs, often emphasizing adult continuing education and culture. Some, typically using student staff, produce a nightly local newscast, and many produce a weekly public affairs or cultural program. None, in recent history, has produced a major PBS series for the prime-time core schedule. University-licensed stations such as WHA (Madison, Wisconsin) and KUHT (Houston, Texas) contribute occasional specials and single programs to the PBS schedule. WUNC-TV at the University of North Carolina in Chapel Hill produced *The Woodwright Shop* series, and other university licensed stations have supported short-run series aired in the daytime PBS schedule.

As operating costs mount and academic appropriations shrink, university stations also ask their communities to supplement their budgets from their licensee institutions. Expanded fund-raising efforts are generally accompanied by broadening program appeal.

Public School Stations

Local school systems initially became licensees to provide new learning experiences for students in elementary school classrooms. From the outset, some augmented instructional broadcasts with other programming consistent with the school system's view of its educational mission. By the late 1980s only 13 of these *school licensees* remained. Most of them have organized a broadly based community support group whose activities generate wider interest and voluntary contributions from the community at large. As a result, the average local licensee now draws from 15 to 20 percent of its income from subscriber contributions. Naturally, programmers at these stations are heavily involved with in-school programming (instructional television on ITV), but because they desire community support, they are also concerned with programming for children out of school and for adults of all ages. Other than ITV series, most rarely produce original entertainment programs for PBS, and they obtain most of their schedules from national, state and regional suppliers of instructional programming. Of course, they usually carry *Sesame Street* too.

State Television Agencies

More than a hundred of the nation's public television stations are part of *state networks* operated by legislatively created public broadcasting agencies. Networks of this type exist in 23 states. Most of them were authorized initially to provide new classroom experiences for the state's schoolchildren. Most have succeeded admirably in this task and have augmented their **ITV** service with a variety of public affairs and cultural programs furnished to citizens throughout their states.

State networks, such as those in South Carolina, Maryland, Kentucky, Nebraska and Iowa, are very active in the production and national distribution of programs. Their efforts range from traditional school programs for primary and secondary grades to graduate-degree courses offered in regions where colleges and universities are few. These production efforts are the counterpart to the national production centers of the community-based licensees. Although state networks rarely produce prime-time PBS series, they frequently join *consortia* generating specific programs for series such as *Great Performances* and *American Playhouse*. Others, such as the Maryland Center for Public Broadcasting and the South Carolina ETV Commission, have produced many long-lived PBS series such as *Wall Street Week* and *Firing Line*.

Although in recent years these state network stations have gotten more foundation, underwriter and even viewer support, state legislatures still appropriate more than three-fifths of their budgets. This fact, plus the perception of their "community of service" as an entire state rather than a single city, gives programmers at these stations a different perspective.

It should be evident from these brief descriptions that each category of public television station poses special problems and special opportunities for programming strategies. Each station type is ruled by a different type of board of directors—community leader boards, university trustees, local school boards, state-appointed central boards. Each board affects program personnel differently. University boards, preoccupied with higher education programs, tend to leave station professionals free to carry out their job within broad guidelines. School boards likewise are preoccupied with their major mission and in some cases pay too little attention to their responsibilities as licensees. State boards must protect their stations from undue political influences. Community representatives try to balance local power groups. All licensees struggle to function with what they regard as inadequate budgets, but there are wide funding discrepancies between the extremes of a large metropolitan community station and a small local public school station.

Significantly, all types of stations have broadened their financial bases in recent years to keep up with rising costs and to improve program quality and quantity. Licensees having the greatest success in securing new funding have, in general, made the strongest impact on national public television programming, partly because the firms or agencies that underwrite programs want to get maximum favorable impact from their investments. In turn, successful public television producer-entrepreneurs are motivated to create attractive new public television programs with broad audience appeal in the hope of securing still more underwriting. These kinds of programs increase viewership and draw more support in the form of memberships and subscriptions. Although this trend has its salutary aspects, it has also diverted noncommercial television from some of its original goals. For example, controversial public affairs programs and programs of interest only to specialized smaller audiences now tend to be eliminated.

THE PROGRAMMER'S AUDIENCE INFORMATION SOURCES

Before attempting to build a public television station's program schedule, a programmer must know the people who live in the area the station serves—not as objects for commercial exploitation but as constituencies entitled to special program services. An in-depth study originally undertaken in 1977 under the auspices of the television station managers themselves, and supported by subsequent studies, shows much about how programming decisions are actually made. It revealed the kinds of information on audience needs programmers have available and the programming sources that fill those needs.

Robertson Associates, Inc., studied how local stations developed their program service and the role that PBS and other nonlocal program sources played in the total local offering. On-site visits were made to 20 PBS member stations, carefully selected to make the sample group proportional to the total PBS membership in several respects: UHF versus VHF facilities, geographic location, licensee type and size of market. The results of those interviews were measured against questionnaire responses from program managers at 20 other stations, equally representative of total PBS membership. Thus, the study's findings (many of which are reported in this chapter) were based on a sample that included more than 25 percent of all public television station *programmers* in the country. The study revealed that public television programmers secure information on the public's needs and interests in at least seven ways. The information sources are ranked by importance, and the general pattern has remained constant through the 1980s.

1. *Rating Services.*   About three-quarters of U.S. public television stations use commercial ratings services, most of which now include profiles of commercial and public channel viewing within a given market. Public television programmers use this information to plan their schedules. For example, the Pacific Mountain Network, a regional public television organization, formed PMN-TRAC (Television Ratings Audience Consortium), a *program scheduling advisory service* for some 40 participating stations, operated by David and Judith LeRoy.

2. Station-Commissioned Local Studies.   Since many public television stations are licensed to educational institutions with research capabilities, they can enlist faculty members and students to measure program impact and to ascertain community needs. Several stations in metropolitan areas retain professional polling organizations to conduct periodic studies for them. About two-thirds of stations use specially commissioned research today.

3. Formal and Informal Ascertainment.   Between 1977 and 1984, the FCC required noncommercial as well as commercial television stations to determine—through interviews of key community leaders and random sampling of the general public—the needs, interests and problems of the station's local community (**formal ascertainment**). Since 1984, only **informal ascertainment** has been required (the method determined by the station). Stations must still file a quarterly list of local issues and the programming undertaken in response to those needs, interests and problems.

4. Mail and Phone Calls from Viewers.   Public television stations generally keep fairly detailed records of viewer mail and phone calls. Many stations keep very specific records and furnish reports to program decision makers on numbers of letters and calls, topics mentioned and attitudes expressed—both positive and negative.

5. Viewers' Evaluations through Questionnaires and Screening.   Nearly half of U.S. public television stations use questionnaires (often published in their program guides) to solicit viewer responses to programs already aired and suggestions as to types of programs desired in the future. Some stations hold screening sessions for program advisory groups to tap a more representative sampling of opinion than can be acquired from the staff alone.

6. Exchange of Information with Other Programmers.   Program executives of public television stations can exchange information on programming strategies when they meet at frequent executives conferences and during the annual PBS Station Program Cooperative (SPC).

7. PBS-supplied Information.   PBS acquires audience information from both stations and national ratings services and shares it with stations. As of the late 1980s, PBS supplied *National Audience Reports* (based on one-week Nielsen surveys) on a monthly basis, and *Station Audience Reports* following each Nielsen **sweep** (four per year). This information is crucial to program decision-making at large-market stations wanting to attract big subscribing audiences.

PROGRAM SOURCES FOR STATIONS

After discovering the *needs* of their service areas, program managers face a second task: evaluating the full range of program *sources* at their disposal. Public broadcasting sets out to be different from commercial broadcasting, and the development of unique program sources has been one of its most difficult problems. PTV stations have to have a national program service but do not want a network organization that would dominate station programming (as

Figure 18-1 Public Television Station Programming Sources

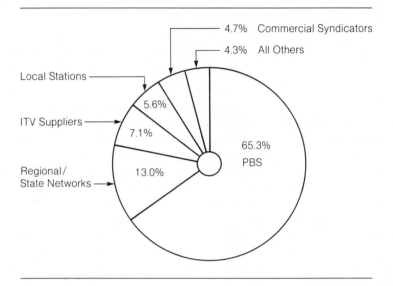

4.7% Commercial Syndicators

4.3% All Others

Local Stations

5.6%

ITV Suppliers

7.1%

65.3%

PBS

Regional/
State Networks

13.0%

Source: Corporation for Public Broadcasting, Policy Development and Planning.
Used with permission.

happens with the three commercial broadcast networks). PTV needs commercially syndicated material but cannot always compete with commercial broadcasters for it. It needs the revenue from syndicating its instructional programming but lacks the backlog typical of syndicated entertainment programs. And finally, PTV needs to produce local programs since commercial programming neglects them, and PTV has a special obligation to serve local needs and interests.

As shown in Figure 18-1, the Public Broadcasting Service distributes the largest proportion of all programming hours aired by public stations (65.3 percent). Stations in major markets produce many of the series PBS offers, but *local programming* (produced locally for local audiences) fills just under 6 percent of airtime. Locally-produced *instructional* programming is less than 1 percent of local programming but instructional hours *not* produced locally amount to 7.1 percent of airtime. Regional and state networks, commercial syndicators and miscellaneous others supply the remainder. Five sources, then, supply most PTV programming.

The National Program Service

Clearly, the satellite-delivered PBS programming is the most significant program source for most public television stations. As explained in the preceding chapter, PBS is not a network organization in the customary commercial sense. It does not have "affiliates"; it undertakes no program production itself; it does not own or operate any stations. It is a membership organization to which nearly every public television licensee belongs and for whom it administers and distributes the national program service according to policies and patterns the stations themselves set.

Most of the PBS schedule is determined each season through an unusual mix of member station preference and PBS Program Advisory Committee action. The mechanism is far from simple but assures the needs and interests of the local licensee will not be overlooked as the national schedule takes shape. (See the discussion of the **SPC** in Chapter 17.) PBS develops a programming book containing production proposals for the stations to consider about a year and a half in advance of when the programs are to air. After individual station programmers respond to it, the book proposals are refined and reduced in number. Every October, local station programmers gather to meet with program producers to discuss program offerings and suggest how to make the programs offered even more attractive to the local audiences. PBS calls this its annual **Program Fair.**

PBS's Program Department takes the information gathered at the Program Fair, works with the producers to incorporate the station recommendations and then meets with a group of station programmers the entire system has elected. Their purpose is to create a national program schedule to recommend to the stations for purchase. Since the money for program purchases flows from the stations to the national organization, everyone concerned wants to buy the best programs possible at the lowest cost to meet the greatest number of licensee needs. The amazing thing is that it seems to work. The ultimate program decisions rest with the *local stations*. Their programming staff must decide whether or not to purchase the offered program package. They may refuse by withholding their money, or they may buy only a few of the offered programs, giving them the opportunity to program their station as they believe makes the most sense for the audience they serve.

Subnational Networks

Programmers are not limited to PBS for network programs. As mentioned in Chapter 17, four regional telecommunications associations exist: the Eastern Educational Television Network (**EEN**) with members from Maine to Virginia; the Southern Educational Telecommunications Association (**SECA**) including stations from Maryland to Texas; the Central Educational Network (**CEN**) in the upper Midwest from Ohio to the Dakotas; and the Pacific Mountain Network (**PMN**) serving stations from the Rockies to the West Cost. These associations serve not only as forums for discussions of stations' policies and operating practices but also as agents for program production and acquisition. Set up to make *group buys* of instructional series, the regionals' role in providing nonlocal programming for general audiences as well as for ITV use was firmly established by the early 1980s. This trend was accelerated by the availability of the *public television satellite distribution system*, enabling these organizations to deliver a program to any public television station in the country.

The state networks in 23 states, as mentioned earlier, provide both instructional and general audience programming, including legislative coverage and special events of statewide interest. In some states (such as Kentucky,

Georgia and Nebraska), a central office makes programming decisions for the entire state. In other states (such as New York, Ohio and Florida), station program managers within the state jointly plan the schedule on the state interconnect. Although state networks are another program source for local stations, materials they produce do not usually serve stations beyond the state's boundaries.

Noncommercial Syndication

Because of its role in formal education, public television has had to develop its own unique body of *syndicated* material to meet instructional television needs (**ITV**). The only precedent for such program stockpiling is the audiovisual film distribution center, an educational adjunct that came into being long before television. Public television gradually created a new appetite for instructional material, introduced technological resources for its production and stimulated the founding of new centers for program distribution that perform the same function as commercial syndication firms except on a noncommercial or cooperative basis.

The **Agency for Instructional Technology (AIT)** in Bloomington, Indiana, for example, produces series for primary grades, high school use and postsecondary students. Among the best known are *Ripples, Inside Out, Trade Offs, Thinkabout* and *Give & Take*. AIT took the lead in developing innovative instructional programming for classrooms that operate in conjunction with microcomputers, creating the first interactive lessons on videodiscs.

The **Great Plains National Instructional Television Library (GPN)** in Lincoln, Nebraska, offers dozens of series for elementary and junior high use along with a great many materials for college and adult learning. Titles in the 126-page catalog for 1988 range from *The Big A* (an art series) and *Reading Rainbow* for first graders to *Dollar Scholar* and *Ways of the Law* for high schoolers and adults.

The **International ITV Co-op,** Inc., Falls Church, Virginia (known to most programmers for *Cover to Cover, Write On!* and other widely used instructional series) has won international awards for its earth-space science series, *L-4.* And **Western Instructional Television,** Los Angeles, offers more than 500 series in science, language arts, social studies, English, art and history. **TV Ontario** also supplies U.S. schools with dozens of instructional series, especially in science and technology. The abundance of ITV materials means that most instructional programming is no longer produced locally, except where certain subject matter is unique to a local area or community.

Local school authorities usually select instructional materials for inschool use, although the public television station's staff often serves as liaison between sources of this material and users. The state may appropriate funds for instructional programs, giving them to public stations within the state, or school districts may contract with a local public station to supply particular ITV programs at certain times. Stations that serve schools usually employ an "instructional television coordinator" or "learning resources coordinator" to work full-time with present and potential users, assist teachers in proper use of the materials, identify classroom needs and select or develop materials to meet the specific goals of local educators.

More quality programming for *adult learners* is now available to public stations than in the earlier decades of public broadcasting. Beginning in the late 1970s, consortia efforts in higher education turned out television courses (**telecourses**) to be integrated into the curriculums of most postsecondary institutions, yet produced in a way that made them attractive to the casual viewer as well. Budgets for such series now range from $100,000 to $1 million for a single course. These efforts center particularly in community colleges, led by Miami-Dade (Florida), Dallas (Texas) and Coastline Community College (Huntington Beach, California).

Meanwhile faculty members at other leading postsecondary institutions began developing curriculum materials to accompany several outstanding public television program series distributed nationally through PBS for general viewing. The first of these was *The Ascent of Man* with the late Dr. Jacob Bronowski, a renowned scholar as well as a skillful and effective communicator on camera. More than 200 colleges and universities offered college credit for that course. Quickly others followed (*The Adams Chronicles, Cosmos, Life on Earth, The Shakespeare Plays* and so on) as programmers discovered such series furnished the casual viewer with attractive public television entertainment and simultaneously served more serious viewers desiring to register for college course credits.

This experience led many public television programmers to realize that too much had been made of the supposed demarcation between ITV and PTV. Too often during earlier years, many program producers would not even consider producing so-called instructional television. The first Carnegie Commission in 1965 strengthened this presumed gap by not concerning itself with television's educational assistance to schools and colleges and by adopting the term *public* television to mean programming for general viewing.

In 1980 PBS began its *adult learning service*. After three years of development, 230 stations offered this service, eventually growing to over 6,000 colleges and universities and enrollments of 75,000 per semester. This service offers public television programmers one of the most challenging additions to the program schedule. Because such programs require close cooperation with institutions offering the credit, they require a reliable repeat schedule that permits students to make up missed broadcasts, while the quality of the programming must also interest the general viewer who may not sign up for credit.

The **Annenberg/CPB Project** has had enormous impact on delivering college credit courses to *nontraditional adult learners*. The Annenberg School of Communications (Walter Annenberg owns *TV Guide*) gave $15 million annually for ten years to CPB to fund college-level instruction via television and other new technologies. The Project has resulted in such high-visibility public television series as *Constitution: That Delicate Balance, French in Action, Planet Earth, The African* and *Economics USA* (more than 40 courses as of 1988), with subject matter ranging from the humanities to science, mathematics and business. Colleges and universities wanting to offer credit for these telecourses normally arrange for local public television stations to air the series, and all registration, fees, testing and supplementary materials are handled by the school. Some of the courses use computers, and all are keyed to special texts and study guides. These adult-oriented programs have budgets far above the norm for previous instructional programs, resulting in innovative, high-quality television programming for the general audience as well as the for-credit student.

Recent experience has demonstrated that ITV and PTV programs can appeal to viewers other than those for which they were especially intended. The Annenberg/CPB series is only one example. Another is *Sesame Street*, initially intended for youngsters in disadvantaged households, prior to their school years. Yet one of the significant occurrences in kindergarten and lower elementary classrooms throughout America in the 1970s and 1980s was the *in-school* use of *Sesame Street*.

Commercial Syndication

More extensively tapped sources, however, are such *commercial syndicators* as Time-Life, David Susskind's Talent Associates, Wolper Productions, Granada TV in Great Britain and several major motion picture companies including Universal Pictures. Public television stations sometimes negotiate individually for program packages with such syndicators; at other times they join with public stations through regional associations to make group buys. Commercially syndicated programs obtained in this way by PTV include historical and contemporary documentaries, British-produced drama series and packages of highly popular or artistic motion pictures originally released to theaters.

The proportion of commercially syndicated programming in specific public television station schedules may range from none at all to as much as 25 percent. The variation has two derivatives. First, those commercially-syndicated programs public television stations find appropriate are relatively expensive. Unless outside underwriting is secured to cover license fees, many stations simply cannot afford them. The second factor is philosophical. Although much commercially syndicated material has strong audience appeal, its educational or cultural value is arguable. Today, however, the *Avengers, Lawrence Welk, Lassie* and even *Leave It to Beaver* appear on large public stations because these shows meet some community needs, are relatively cheap and have the mass appeal so necessary in metropolitan areas.

Local Production

The percentage of airtime filled with *locally produced* programming has gradually *decreased* over the years, as both network and syndication programming have increased in quantity and quality. The percentage of total on-air hours produced locally by public television stations declined from 16 percent in 1972 to just under 6 percent in 1987. Moreover, production quality expectations have risen. More time and dollars and better facilities must be used to produce effective local programs than before. A medium-sized station intending to produce 200 to 320 hours of local programs per year (or up to 1 hour a day, six days a week) should have at a minimum the following equipment.

- One studio of 3,000 square feet
- Three broadcast-standard color cameras

- Six broadcast-standard videotape machines
- Three programmable videotape editing units
- Two film islands
- One graphic font character generator
- One 35-mm still camera
- Three electronic newsgathering (ENG) units

The total cost for this equipment can range from $1.5 million to $4 million. With such equipment and a reasonably proficient engineering and production staff, a station should be able to turn out *an hour a day* of creditable local programming.

Increasingly, programmers now spend their limited local budgets on regular, nightly broadcasts devoted to activities, events and issues of local interest and significance. These newscasts are somewhat different from those of the network-affiliate. Commercial broadcast television stations concentrate on spot news and devote only a minute or less to each story; public television stations see their role as giving more comprehensive treatment to local affairs. (As of the late 1980s, a few local cable systems were adopting a similar style of local news coverage.) Further, the use of ENG units has made live and recorded news coverage outside the station studio (**remotes**) easier to handle.

Many stations and consortia of stations produce unique public affairs programs covering their state governments, exemplified by the weekly *Inside Albany* from WMHT in Schnectady and the long-running nightly (January to March) *Indiana Lawmakers* from WPVI in Indianapolis. Public television's commitment to in-depth local public affairs is without counterpart in commercial broadcasting.

THE SEQUENCE OF SCHEDULE BUILDING

No PTV programmer ever builds an entire schedule from scratch. A public television program schedule is a series of compromises meant to serve the total audience in the best manner possible but doomed to serve no single viewer's needs entirely. The program schedule is built on what the programmer thinks the audience will watch at a particular time.

A public television programmer must consider and balance these elements: *licensee type* (each carries its unique program priorities), *audience demographics, competition* from commercial and other public television signals, *daypart targeting* (such as afternoons for children's programming, daytime for instructional services), *program availability* and *equipment capacity.* No single element overrides the others, but each affects the final schedule.

Public television programmers seek programs that meet local audience needs and schedule those programs at times most likely to attract the target audience. Since all audience segments cannot be served at once, the mystery and magic of the job is getting the right programs in the right time slots. High ratings are not the objective; serving the appropriate audience with a

Figure 18-2 Types of Programming Broadcast by Public Television Stations

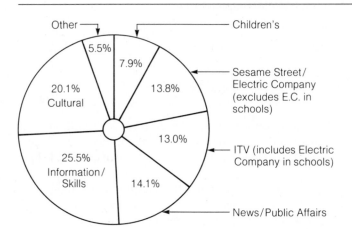

*1984 data, most recent available.
†Excluding the ITV portion of the *Electric Company*.

Source: Corporation for Public Broadcasting, Policy Development and Planning. Used with permission.

show they will watch that adds to the quality of their life is. (See Figure 18-2 for a breakdown of PTV program types.)

Instructional Programs

Over 80 percent of public television stations carry some *in-school instructional* programs. Broadcasting is still the least expensive way to reach millions of students in elementary schools scattered across the nation. In 1987 over 18 million students watched instructional programs each week on public television stations.

State agency licensees and school board stations carry the heaviest instructional schedules, but most public television stations have contracts with state school boards or local districts to provide instructional services. For the programmer this means that instructional programming is often the first part of the program schedule to be filled since it can only be broadcast during specific hours of the day and times of the year. Moreover, instructional telecasts are *income-producing;* the school district *pays* the station for airing specific programs.

PBS Programs

Another major element most stations schedule early on is *network* programming from PBS because (1) about two-thirds of PTV stations depend on PBS programs to *generate their largest audiences* and (2) a number of PBS series have become staples in the local audience program diet, and viewers expect them to remain *in the same time period* from season to season. For these reasons as well as *to capitalize on national promotion,* local programmers usually carry major PBS features in the prime-time spot PBS programmers propose (the **core**) so that a given telecast is seen more or less simultaneously on all PBS stations.

Member stations, however, control PBS and are free, without fear of reprisal, to rearrange PBS programs in any way they wish. As explained in Chapter 17, when the satellite is feeding two programs simultaneously, the station has *three* scheduling choices: to air Program A without delay, recording Program B; to air Program B without delay, recording Program A; or to record both for later use. Programmers cannot always take advantage of these options, however. Videotape recording machines are expensive to operate and maintain and may be tied up with other functions when needed to record off the network.

More than 155 earth terminals feed public television stations in the United States and associated territories, and as a result, individual stations now control access to national programs. Today, every public television station has its own earth station, shares one or has access through a network to satellite signals.

Commercially Syndicated Programs

Programs acquired from *commercial syndicators* are usually the next priority in building a schedule. These features possess the same high quality and broad appeal as PBS's best offerings and add variety to a station's schedule (as long as they remain consistent with its philosophy). In many cases they are motion pictures of artistic or historical value as well as strong audience appeal. In other cases, such as *Lawrence Welk,* they are shows no longer airing on commercial television.

Local Programs

Locally produced programs do not necessarily come last in the sequence of schedule building. In fact, some stations block in time for certain local programs (for example, the nightly magazine programs devoted to local activities and interests) before considering anything else in their proposed schedule. The appropriate maxim is, however: Secure the best of whatever is needed from elsewhere, then use local production resources to make programs that cannot be obtained elsewhere precisely because they are local.[3]

Just *where* in a public television station schedule should the programmer insert local programs? Practices of PTV stations across the country vary on this point. For example, some schedule their local nightly news-and-feature magazine adjacent to *The MacNeil/Lehrer Newshour,* an in-depth news interview program PBS supplies. Because viewing habits differ from one time zone to another, some stations cannot do this without running opposite local commercial news programs. Some stations air their local news-and-feature programs twice, once in early evening and again late at night. Here, as in other instances, the public television programmer must make a judgment based on local viewing habits and preferences, programs on other local channels and programs available from the incoming PBS satellite channels.

COUNTERPROGRAMMING BY STATIONS

PTV station programmers do *not* engage in fierce head-to-head warfare with their commercial colleagues. For example, most station programmers avoid putting their strongest dramatic program opposite another station's strongest drama, preferring to play theirs at an hour when other stations are not appealing to the drama devotee. Instead, against a commercially broadcast drama they may play their strongest public affairs features or their strongest programming of some other type. In areas with more than one public television channel as well as the usual array of commercial channels, the public television programmers usually confer and develop schedules designed to give viewers the greatest possible choice of viewing times for programs. Most PBS member stations play most PBS programs at least *twice*, and some also repeat selected local features a second time since there is always a potential audience for repeats.

AUDIENCE FLOW WITHIN THE LOCAL SCHEDULE

Public television programmers wrestle with the question of how to keep an audience tuned to their station just like commercial programmers do. For the PTV programmer, however, the question is more difficult since the programs most often appeal only to a particular or special audience. It is possible, with due regard for related interests and tastes, to schedule a sequence of programs that holds viewers from one time period to another (creating **audience flow**). One musical program followed by another, for example, may keep viewers interested in music tuned to a PTV station. The same principle applies to public affairs programs, science and natural history broadcasts, drama and performing arts productions, business and economic reports.

Some station programmers consider it unwise to devote an entire evening to one type of programming (**block programming**) because it excludes viewers not interested in that particular program type. Others contend that within the course of a week, it is possible to attract all audience segments. Every programmer faces the dilemma of deciding between greater *diversity* in program offerings versus the desirability of increasing the *time* viewers with a particular interest spend watching public television programs.

FUTURE DEVELOPMENTS

Many people in the noncommercial field believe the public television station of today will become the public telecommunications center of tomorrow—a place where telecommunications professionals handle the production, acquisition, reception, duplication and delivery of all types of noncommercial educational-cultural-information materials and stand ready to advise and counsel people in the community. In this scenario, existing public television stations will transmit programs of broad interest and value to relatively large audiences scattered throughout their coverage areas; but they will also feed these and other programs to local cable channels and transfer programs of more specialized interest to videocassettes or videodiscs for use in schools, colleges, libraries, hospitals and industry or for use on home video equipment. Because of its high quality, *high-definition television* (**HDTV**) may give public broadcasters the special edge they need—if its adoption proves practical.

SUMMARY

The disparate philosophies guiding public television programmers have in common the elements of noncommercialism and special audience service. The four types of licensees—community, university, public school and state agency—follow different mandates in programming to serve their constituencies, although all tend to appeal more and more to the general, entertainment-oriented audience that supports public television with subscriptions. The public television station programmer draws information from seven sources to evaluate the success of the station's programming strategies. Ratings are only one indicator since so few public stations have large enough one-time audiences to receive ratings. Public stations count their cumulative audience rather than per program as commercial stations do. PBS is the main source of PTV programming; regional and state networks, local production, commercial and noncommercial syndicators and other sources supply only about 30 percent of station programs. Although audience flow, counterprogramming and blocking strategies affect program placement on public stations, actual PTV practices differ somewhat from those of commercial television. In selection and scheduling, station programmers must consider license priorities, audience demographics, commercial competition, dayparting, program availability and equipment capacity.

Notes

1. More stations (325) than licensees (168) exist because in 20 states a legislatively created agency for public broadcasting is the licensee for as many as 11 separate stations serving its state. Also, in several communities, one noncommercial educational licensee operates two television channels. In these cases (Boston, Pittsburgh, San Francisco and Milwaukee, among others), one channel usually offers a relatively broad program service while the second channel is used for more specialized programming, often instructional material. Montana is the only state without a public television station.

2. This particular expression was coined by President Charles Van Hise of the University of Wisconsin in the early 1900s, but all land-grant colleges espouse similar traditions.

3. Percentage of total on-air hours public television stations produced locally, as reported by the Corporation for Public Broadcasting, was 16.1 percent in 1972, 11.4 percent in 1974, 10.1 percent in 1976, 7.4 percent in 1978 and 6.8 percent in 1980.

Selected Sources

Alternative Financing Options for Public Broadcasting, Vols. I & II. The Temporary Commission on Alternative Financing for Public Telecommunications, Report to the Congress of the United States, 1982.

Frank, Ronald E., and Greenberg, Marshall G. *Audiences for Public Television*. Beverly Hills, Calif.: Sage Publications, 1982.

Koughan, Martin. "The Fall and Rise of Public Television." *Channels* (May/June 1983):23–31.

LeRoy, David and Judith. "TV Intelligence: Introduction to TV Ratings Concepts," monthly series on audience measurements beginning in 1987 in *Current*.

Lewis, Raymond J. *Meeting Learners' Needs Through Telecommunications: A Directory and Guide to Programs*. Washington, D.C.: Center for Learning and Telecommunications, American Association for Higher Education, 1983.

The Project Team in Instructional Television. Washington, D.C.: Corporation for Public Broadcasting, 1983.

Schenkkan, Robert F.; Thurston, Carol M.; and Sheldon, Alan. *Case Studies in Institutional Licensee Management*. National Association of Educational Broadcasters, 1980.

Witherspoon, John, and Kovitz, Roselle. *The History of Public Broadcasting*. Washington, D.C.: Current, 1987.

CHAPTER 19 PUBLIC RADIO PROGRAMMING

Wallace A. Smith

A Guide to Chapter 19

Wallace A. Smith, vice-president and general manager of WNYC-Radio in New York, has been involved in public radio broadcasting, communications teaching and university administration and counseling for nearly two decades—first at Occidental College, then at the University of Southern California, then in New York. A graduate of Waynesburg College and Pittsburgh Theological Seminary, both in Pennsylvania, he holds a master's degree and Ph.D. in telecommunications from the University of Southern California. He has been active in public radio locally, statewide and nationally. As general manager, he shepherded KUSC-FM through its transition from a low-powered student-run operation to its position as one of the leading public radio stations in the nation. He served as a member of the board of directors of National Public Radio and two terms as president of the board of directors of the California Confederation of the Arts. He is a founding member of the American Public Radio Associates and a member of its board of directors. He has served as chairman of the radio advisory committee of the California Public Broadcasting Commission, has been on the executive committee of the Association of California Public Radio Stations, and is past president of Alpha Epsilon Rho, the national radio/television honor society. In 1987 he moved to New York to head one of the country's top noncommercial stations. Dr. Smith uses the station he managed, KUSC, as a dramatic case study of public radio's potential.

PHILOSOPHY AND FORMAT

Of the four types of *noncommercial* radio stations—public, religious, college and community—255 highly visible stations receive funding (*Community Service Grants* and *National Program Production and Acquisition Grants*) from the Corporation for Public Broadcasting, making them **public** broadcasters. Qualifying for CPB grants necessitates a large budget (over $150,000 annually), at least five full-time, paid staff members, a powerful transmitter, complete production facilities (a studio and control room), an 18-hour daily program schedule and commitment to public service. The remaining 1,000 or so noncommercial stations operate on smaller budgets and with smaller facilities and staffs than **CPB-qualified** stations. Most low-power stations are either **religious** broadcasters serving a sectarian group or **college/university** stations reaching a tiny geographic area such as a college campus, even a dormitory. The fourth group, free-form **community** stations pioneered by Lorenzo Milam, emphasizes public access. Only about four dozen or so community stations remain active broadcasters today, though some survive on cable FM (see Chapter 12).

This chapter focuses on the programming strategies of **public radio,** relating a station's philosophy to its audience and fundraising capability, its degree of localism and its integrity. The author describes the six main public radio formats, concentrating on their program selection and scheduling strategies, and the effects of satellite relay of programming on public radio networking. Using the adoption of a classical music format by KUSC-FM as a case study, the chapter illustrates how public radio programmers do their jobs, showing the roles of promotion, fund raising, financial accountability and ongoing evaluation in achieving success.

Audiences and Fund Raising

The purpose of noncommercial, educational (**public**) broadcast licenses is intentionally different from the purpose of commercial broadcast licenses, but *both* licensees are challenged to use their channel assignments in the most productive manner to reach the *largest possible audience given their program services*. Even though a public broadcast station may serve a disparate audience with highly specialized programs, its overall objective is to reach as many listeners as possible. Commercial broadcasters want to attract large audiences to generate operating revenue and profits for their stockholders. Public broadcasters have the same objective but reinvest their profits (*nonprofit revenue*) in the program service.

One ongoing, even acrimonious, controversy within public radio concerns *target audiences:* Most public stations today target **adults,** not children. A recent widespread practice, copied from commercial broadcasting, of creating smooth, seamless formats appealing to a targeted demographic group, killed off several award-winning series for children and minorities, among them *Kids Alive* from WNYC in New York. Only 26 out of more than 300 broadcasters could fit a children's show within their schedules because so many now try to increase **time-spent-listening** (see Chapter 2) rather than total cumulative audience as public television does. The reality is that narrow programming for a targeted adult group generally does better in attracting listener support than more varied public radio programming.

The challenge to the public radio programmer, then, is to design an alternative program service that differs significantly from program formats other commercial and noncommercial stations in the market offer. The selected format must attract sufficiently large audiences to generate **direct listener support** of the station and encourage philanthropists, government agencies, foundations, business, industry and corporations to invest. Motivating support for a public radio station requires evidence that substantial numbers of people in a community use, want and need the program service.

Localism and Integrity

A unique sound captures the imagination of the potential listening audience. Programming elevates a public station into a position competitive with other radio services. It is not enough to say, "We are public, therefore we are better," or to rely on the lack of commercial announcements to build an audience. *Localism* is a key factor in developing radio formats. Radio is a flexible medium using lightweight equipment that enables it to respond quickly to spontaneous events. The more *live* local events and happenings included in a broadcast schedule, the higher the probability for success.

Public broadcasting's most valuable assets are the *integrity* and *quality* of its programs. Whatever format is selected, success is predicated on the delivery of a program service that will inform, entertain and enhance the life of each listener and improve the quality of life in the community. Those goals are idealistic, but they create the margin of difference that will attract listeners to public broadcasting regardless of the station format. Commercial broadcasters are less able to pursue such lofty ideals. They must turn a profit, so even their most deliberate attempts to achieve excellence are often compromised.

FORMAT OPTIONS

Public radio uses six basic formats: classical music and fine arts, jazz, news and public affairs, community service and public access, eclectic and instructional; another option mixes two in a dual format. Americans are accustomed to selecting radio stations according to format. Nothing annoys radio listeners more than tuning to a news station *for news* only to hear classical music. Educating the public to accept more than one sound from radio is a slow process. Most public as well as commercial broadcasters therefore deliver the expected format. In the 1980s, however, some evidence had emerged that radio audiences were beginning to listen to radio for individual programs and that public radio stations were challenging the rigid rule that people listen to radio stations, not programs. The extraordinary success of programs such as *All Things Considered*, *Prairie Home Companion* and its replacement, *Good Evening*, and radio adaptations of *Star Wars* and *The Empire Strikes Back*, inserted in any of the basic formats discussed below, suggests a change in the audience's expectation of uniformity in radio programming. It is still too early to decide if these programs indicate a new trend or are the exceptions that prove the rule.

Classical Music and Fine Arts

All-music formats depend on prerecorded music for the majority of their broadcast schedules. Public radio stations choosing the **classical music and fine arts** format have a competitive edge over their commercial counterparts because they can broadcast *long, uninterrupted performances* of classical works. They can surround these performances with informational modules to enhance the audience's listening experience but avoid the abrasive intrusion of advertisements. Public radio stations' ability to put aside time restraints contributes substantially to the quality of presentation of classical music.

The classical music format has become a staple in public broadcasting. Because it is considered a *safe* format, many social activists criticize managers that select it. Their criticism is usually a result of misplaced values. The priority for arts and music in our society is low; music and arts are tolerated, but most people have a limited understanding of their value in stimulating many higher aspirations. And a format that feeds those aspirations is as important as any service public radio provides. The size of audiences and financial support for the classical music and fine arts format are sufficient evidence of the need for them.

The classical music and fine arts format can take several forms. WNED-FM (Buffalo, New York) broadcasts all classical music with only the briefest interruptions for information about the performers.[1] KUSC-FM (Los Angeles), licensed to the University of Southern California, schedules 85 percent classical music. The other 15 percent includes news, fine arts modules on subjects besides music and programs about classical music. NPR's Performance Today, a daily arts and performance magazine show, aids this effort. Then, in the late 1980s, WFMT-FM in Chicago began syndicating the Beethoven Satellite Network, an overnight classical music service for noncommercial and commercial stations. Public broadcasters from Minnesota to Florida pick it up, because it allows them to expand to 24-hour service at low cost while retaining high quality.

Live classical music *concerts* have also returned to radio. Unlike the stereotypical classical music jukebox using scholarly announcers to introduce one record after another, public radio now produces major programs featuring live concert music from concert halls throughout the world. KUSC, for example, records more than 90 live concerts each year, including the seasons of the Los Angeles Philharmonic and other major orchestras and chamber ensembles in southern California. Minnesota Public Radio, WGBH in Boston, KQED in San Francisco and WNYC in New York also record many live concert events and major American music festivals. Moreover, live broadcasts from Bayreuth, Salzburg and other European cities now arrive via satellite for listeners throughout the United States.

Jazz

A new public radio format emerged during the late 1970s as certain stations began featuring **jazz music** programming. Like the classical station, these stations combine recordings with live events. Although they often record concerts in clubs and from concert stages, they also produce jazz events themselves—which are then recorded or transmitted live to local and national audiences.

KLON-FM, Long Beach, California, and WGBO in New Jersey are the two public radio stations currently producing the largest number of jazz concert events. The Long Beach Blues Festival, featuring some of the nation's best-known blues performers, has become a national event as a result of KLON's efforts to record and promote the annual day-long concert.

National Public Radio was once again a pioneer in regenerating interest in live radio broadcasts of jazz performances. *Jazz Alive* presented jazz concerts from all over the United States. The program went under during NPR's financial crisis in 1982, but producing stations such as KLON and WGBO continue to make original jazz programming available to other public radio stations.

Public stations selecting the jazz format have a particular problem they must address: They usually do not find much audience support for this program service. The audience for jazz music tends to be less affluent than the classical listening audience, and listeners usually do not join stations as members or participants in fund-drives. As a result, many public stations emphasize jazz programming but include other program elements to attract financial support. The all-jazz format is popular with some university-licensed public radio stations, such as WRTI-FM at Temple University in Philadelphia, which do not seek financial support from their audiences.

News and Public Affairs

The **news and public affairs** format, although seemingly a natural for public radio, is less used than one might expect. National Public Radio supplies most news programs for public radio. Most stations integrate local news into NPR's 90-minute daily news magazine, *Morning Edition,* using pre-established cutaways from the national news service. Most stations also use *All Things Considered* on weekday afternoons and weekends. A few stations, however, completely dismantle the national service and build a local news service that includes segments from the national programs.

Only two public radio stations use an *all-news* format. WEBR-AM in Buffalo, New York, was the first to do so, but it fills out its broadcast day with jazz. Minnesota Public Radio has one station, KSJN-AM, carrying largely news. WEBR-AM and KSJN-AM follow the traditional, commercial, all-news format described in Chapter 15, using cycles of national and local headlines, local news coverage, commentary, public policy discussions, business news coverage, agriculture, sports, weather and so on. The major difference between noncommercial and commercial all-news stations is that public stations have no commercial restraints. Thus, topics local advertisers might consider touchy are not given "kid glove" treatment, and individual item length can be as long as necessary to adequately cover the topic.

Several statewide, public radio news gathering organizations emerged in the 1980s. California Public Radio (CPR) produces statewide coverage of major news events, and public radio stations use this service much in the way they use NPR programs. KSJN-AM in Saint Paul, Minnesota, is the anchor station for the owned-and-operated stations of Minnesota Public Radio that has also developed a statewide hourly news service for commercial stations. This business venture is an imaginative way for a public radio organization to use its resources to earn revenue through a commercial business whose profits then subsidize its noncommercial programming.

The **Pacifica stations**—WBAI-FM (New York), WEFW-FM (Washington, D.C.), KPFT-FM (Houston, Texas), KPFA-FM (Berkeley, California) and KPFK-FM (Los Angeles)—pioneered the news and public affairs format for noncommercial public radio.[2] The Pacifica Foundation, licensee of the stations in this group, has a specific social and political purpose that influences their approach to news and public affairs. The listener has little difficulty recognizing the bias, and Pacifica is open about its philosophy. These stations were especially successful during the late 1960s and early 1970s when the nation was highly politicized over Vietnam and Watergate. They demonstrated the vital role of broadcasting that is free from commercial restraints in their reporting of the war and surrounding issues.

WEBR, KSJN and the Pacifica stations differ in both format and point of view. WEBR and KSJN concentrate on hard news reporting and investigation, similar to all-news commercial stations. They use their noncommercial status to provide more complete news coverage than is possible in commercial all-news operations. The Pacifica stations present a variety of news and public affairs programs in a somewhat eclectic format. One may hear an in-depth news report on Third World nations, followed by a program on automobile maintenance with a consumer emphasis, followed by a dialogue on Marxism, followed by a gay symphony concert, followed by a lecture on socialism. Listeners cannot predict what they will hear but can usually expect the ideas expressed and programs broadcast to reflect a nonestablishment, nontraditional point of view, whether the content is hard news reporting, commentary, news analysis, documentaries or public affairs programs. Although the majority of program ideas are oriented to the political left, the managers of the Pacifica stations recognize their responsibility to present unrepresented right-oriented political philosophies. They tend to leave the broad middle, the traditional point of view, to other noncommercial and commercial broadcasters.

News and public affairs programming has become increasingly viable in public radio because an information society demands high-quality news programs. The extraordinary popularity of NPR's news programs, *All Things Considered, Morning Edition* and *Weekend Edition,* has created audiences for news programs on public radio. These programs have won many awards for broadcast journalism, and they provide a prestigious base for local station newscasts and supply sufficient national and international coverage to support expanded news programming in all public radio formats.

NPR's news programs also attract private and corporate financial support. News programming was difficult to underwrite locally or nationally until NPR pioneered a fund-raising strategy, the News & Public Information Fund, that enabled corporations, foundations and individuals to invest jointly. This fund in turn supports individual news programs.

Community Service and Public Access

Often considered the only legitimate format for public radio, **community service and public access** programming is essentially directed at the specific needs of unserved or underserved minorities. The programs provide information needed for social and economic survival and the opportunity for the public to use radio to vent emotions or solicit political support. KBBF-FM (Santa Rosa, California) is one of the few minority-owned public radio stations in America.[3] Its programming is directed at Spanish-speaking and bilingual audiences in the Santa Rosa Valley, and it has become a major production center for the network of radio stations serving the Spanish-speaking farm workers in California and other special interest constituencies within the Latino community.

KYUK-FM (Bethel, Alaska), licensed as a community station to Bethel Broadcasting Co., serves its community with programs that include the broadcast of personal messages to individuals isolated by weather and geography. Moving from ice to deserts, KEDB-FM (Ramah, New Mexico) is licensed to the Ramah Navaho School Board and provides instructional services and specific education in the culture and history of the Navaho Indians.

One of the best examples of a more diversified community service format station is KPBS-FM (San Diego). It leads the nation in the development of bilingual programs for local and national distribution. For example, KPBS produces National Public Radio's *En Folke Nacionale.* Because San Diego, California, and Tijuana, Mexico, are border cities poised to become a truly international city, their social, political and economic lives are inextricably woven together. Recognizing this reality, the manager of KPBS-FM boldly discarded the station's evening classical music service, replacing it with a bilingual news and information service targeting the needs of the vast Hispanic community that hears KPBS on both sides of the border. The station also multiplexes SCA **subcarrier services** for the print-handicapped.[4] Its daily program services include city council hearings and comprehensive local news coverage. The program format is carefully designed to meet the needs of subsets of the San Diego community. No matter how obvious the justification for selecting this format appears to be for public broadcast stations, few managers successfully merge the components of community service and broadcasting. KPBS-FM is a rare example of success with the public service format.

The community service and public access format is highly individualized. As such, it is often so specialized that it fails to serve the community's broader needs. It frequently becomes the instrument of a vocal minority and fails to reach the people who need it. When people scream at people about a need that the people who are being screamed at already know exists, it accomplishes little beyond catharsis for the speaker. Those who could actually do something about the need being expressed listen to a different radio format, and those in need are likely to be so bored by discussion of issues they are already familiar with that they also listen to something else.

Eclectic

The most common public radio format is the **eclectic** format, which operates on the premise that public radio should have a little something for everyone. Although eclectic stations will occasionally emphasize one theme, listeners expect anything from a symphony concert to a school board meeting, to jazz, to cooking lessons, to folk music, to news, to soul music, to lectures on almost any topic. Increasingly, public radio stations are turning to narrower formats (or a two-part format) finding eclectic hard to program and weaker at generating listener support than more narrowly focused formats. Many listeners, however, enjoy turning on a radio station knowing it might broadcast a concert, a lecture by Herbert Marcuse, a community forum or a discussion of motorcycle riding. Essential requirements for this format are good quality and a logical program sequence. Listeners will depend on a program service that delivers a variety of programs as long as they can reconcile its scheduling logic and theirs.

The key to an eclectic format is achieving *continuity*—making the diverse parts a whole. The eclectic is the most difficult to design of all radio formats because it requires a logical program sequence that enables the listener to follow from one program to another with a sense of appropriateness. This logic comes from carefully planned program blocks that lead from one set of ideas or listening experiences to another. Listeners must be able to anticipate what they will hear when tuning to the station. The program manager must satisfy that expectation by programming so that listeners identify that station whenever they tune that frequency on the dial.

The critical difference between a successful eclectic format and an unsuccessful one is whether the listener gets a meaningful sequence of diverse programs or a program hodgepodge broadcast at the whim of a programmer attempting to keep the listener off balance. In communities where the commercial stations rely primarily on popular or beautiful music, the eclectic public radio service provides an interesting option for listeners who will be attracted by the station's diversity.

KCRW-FM (Santa Monica, California) is one of the best examples of an eclectic station.[5] It programs jazz, classical music, folk music, esoterica, coverage of local school board and city council meetings, Santa Monica College sports, political opinion, arts, news and music/talk mixes, such as its *Morning Becomes Eclectic* and *Evening Becomes Eclectic*. Although this format may seem to be the hodgepodge for which public broadcasting is notorious, people who listen regularly to KCRW know what to expect when they tune to the station.

Instructional

The **instructional** format was at one time the dominant format for noncommercial educational licensees. Some public radio stations licensed to school boards still broadcast classroom instruction, but in-school programming has generally moved to public television to gain the visual element. KBPS-AM in Portland is the prime example of the radio instructional format. It broadcasts other public radio program material but designates a part of its broadcast day for instructional broadcasts.

The Dual Format

Dual format stations appeared in public radio in the 1970s and have become increasingly common in the 1980s. This format is similar to the eclectic but concentrates on two specific program forms—such as news and jazz or classical and news. The dual format station focuses on building two distinct but comparable audiences for the station. WEBR-AM, Buffalo, for example, is allnews during the day and jazz at night; no attempt is made to mix the two formats. WUWM-FM in Milwaukee is also news and jazz. During the early morning and late afternoon drivetimes, WUWM broadcasts news; late morning, afternoons and evenings are for jazz. But WUWM's manager includes one or two jazz recordings in the news wheel to provide continuity and tries to maintain similar announcing styles for news and jazz. Continuity of style and an occasional reminder of both formats during the news and music segments provide the essential glue for both versions of the dual program format.

NATIONAL NETWORKS

Although one network, **National Public Radio (NPR),** has had long visibility as the national noncommercial service, other radio networks emerged in the 1980s to compete for public radio affiliates, the most successful of which was **American Public Radio (APR).** This section describes the economics and programming of these two networks.

National Public Radio

About one-fifth of noncommercial radio stations are members of National Public Radio (NPR). This system of about 347 nonprofit radio stations broadcasts to communities in 48 states, Puerto Rico and the District of Columbia. Each station, itself a production center, contributes programming to the entire system. Each station mixes locally produced programs with those transmitted from the national production center.

NPR, a private nonprofit corporation, distributes informational and cultural programming by satellite to member stations daily. Funds for the operation of National Public Radio and for the production, acquisition and distribution of radio programs come from corporate underwriting, private foundations, government agencies and member stations.

From 1970 to 1987, CPB contributed directly to NPR's budget, supplying funds for operation and production. Following a 1987 reorganization of public radio, CPB paid all programming funds directly to CPB-qualified stations (NPPAG grants). In response, NPR **unbundled** its programming in 1988. Instead of each member-station paying for the entire schedule, irrespective of need, stations now choose to purchase one (or all) of three NPR chunks: the *morning news service*, the *afternoon news service* or the *performance programming*. Partial-users pay only for the programming unit desired, but at much higher than previous rates. As recently as 1984, most public radio stations paid almost nothing for NPR programs, but as of the late 1980s, costs ran from $25,000 to over $300,000, depending on the amount of federal financial support and amount of programming used. Rates increased for two reasons: Two-dozen large public stations dropped NPR programming in the late 1980s/early 1990s, leaving fewer stations to pick up programming costs, and CPB ended direct financing of NPR programs, meaning that stations now pay full production and transmission costs (plus a portion of the network's overhead).

NPR programs news, public affairs, art, music and drama to fit into whatever formats member stations choose. The news and information programs already discussed—*Morning Edition, All Things Considered* and *Weekend Edition*—are NPR's most distinguished trademark and the core of its program service. It also has provided leadership in music and arts programming for the public radio system, such as *Performance Today, The World of F. Scott Fitzgerald, Jazz Alive, NPR Playhouse* (featuring new radio dramas), live broadcasts of musical events from Europe and from around the United States. NPR has also provided stations with in-depth reporting on education, bilingual Spanish news features and live coverage of Senate and House committee hearings. Satellite distribution of the NPR program service has meant better-quality transmission of existing programs and the distribution of up to a dozen stereo programs simultaneously. The high quality of national programs frequently entices stations to use NPR programs.

In addition to Programming, two other NPR divisions, Representation and Distribution, also provide valuable services to member stations. The Representation Division, like a trade organization, represents NPR and public radio before the FCC, the Corporation for Public Broadcasting, Congress and any government agency involved with matters of importance to public radio.

Member stations pay dues to support the Representation Division since it acts as an advocate for member stations in disputes with NPR and so must be funded separately. The Distribution division operates and maintains the satellite relay system. It also works with some autonomy within NPR because it has broad responsibility for the overall management of the information system. Stations also pay separately for program distribution (transmission).

NPR's Financial Crisis. In the early 1980s, the Reagan administration advocated a phaseout of federal funding for public broadcasting. In response, NPR began a campaign to end its reliance on federal dollars. One part of that effort was the creation of NPR Ventures in 1983, a company joining commercial partners in new business activities to develop profits to replace federal dollars. Because the new ventures business is highly risky, many of NPR's first ventures failed to materialize.

A naive optimism on the part of NPR management was the major cause of a serious financial crisis in 1983. The attempt to realize huge profits from venture activities distracted NPR's officers from the daily operation and administration of the company, allowing a major failure of the budget control and financial accounting system to nearly destroy NPR.

Nonprofit organizations traditionally downplay the importance of financial *accountability,* moving revenue from budget category to budget category without careful controls on dollar flow. NPR's imaginative attempts to stretch income to serve too many budget purposes created a revenue shortfall that resulted in an insurmountable deficit. Another related characteristic of nonprofit companies affecting NPR's deficit was overly *optimistic income projections.* That NPR had no plan to reduce operational costs in the event of a financial crisis was also typical of nonprofit company problems.

NPR was saved from bankruptcy by a $9 million loan from the Corporation for Public Broadcasting. NPR member stations agreed to pay $1.6 million annually for three years (1984–86) to NPR to assist in repaying the loan. Some member stations also agreed to forego their entire annual Community Service Grant to collateralize the loan. The Corporation for Public Broadcasting forced NPR to sell its satellite equipment to a special public trust to secure the future of the public radio interconnection system in the event of a loan default or other financial crisis.

NPR's president and several NPR officers were forced to resign as a result of the financial crisis, and more than 140 NPR employees lost their jobs. *All Things Considered* and *Morning Edition* were given top budgetary priority, but most of NPR's cultural and arts programs were lost. Recovery in the mid and late 1980s allowed NPR to expand back to 24 hours of classical music, seven days a week, add a daily ten-hour jazz service and reinstate its news and public affairs and add news performance programs. But by the late 1980s, two dozen large stations had stopped carrying any NPR programs.

The Public Radio Satellite System. In the 1970s public radio switched from land-line interconnection to satellite interconnection. The Corporation for Public Broadcasting, NPR and public stations created a system of earth satellite stations (**PRSS**) that freed public radio from dependence on low-quality, monaural telephone lines. Public radio leased 24 channels of full fidelity stereo transmission on Westar I to transmit and receive radio programs and data information. Sixteen uplinks and 280 downlinks were built.

The main originating terminal was constructed in Washington, D.C., and NPR was to manage the new distribution system. The system's primary purpose is to provide high-quality NPR programming to public radio stations, but the system is interactive, permitting origination of whole or partial elements of programs from all 16 uplinks. Through the Extended Program Service (EPS), producing stations and independent producers can distribute their programs by satellite to interested stations. Interconnection with European and Canadian satellite systems also enables U.S. public radio to use live programs originating outside the country.

The introduction of the satellite distribution system greatly increased the number of high-quality programs available to individual public radio stations. It also provides public radio with its best opportunity for generating commercial revenue to support NPR. By *selling* unused satellite time (*excess capacity*) to commercial users, public radio generates badly needed revenue without decreasing program availability.

American Public Radio

In 1982 a group of five stations formed a second national radio network. American Public Radio Associates, composed of Minnesota Public Radio, KUSC-FM in Los Angeles, KQED-FM in San Francisco, WNYC AM/FM in New York and WGUC in Cincinnati, joined together to market and distribute programs they produced and to acquire other programming to distribute to affiliates.

American Public Radio (APR) differs from NPR in two ways. First, APR is not a membership organization but a network of affiliated stations paying fees to become the primary or secondary outlet for APR programs in their community. Unlike NPR (but like commercial networks), APR offers its programs to only one station in each market (**exclusivity**) and fees are based on market size. However, when a primary affiliate refuses a program, it is offered to the secondary affiliate, much in the way small-market affiliations operate in commercial television. Second, APR's charter does not permit it to become a national production center. Like PBS, all its programs are *acquired* from stations or other sources. A program fund, supported by major foundations and corporations and administered by the APR board of directors, provides revenue for producers with ideas that fit the APR program schedule.

The most successful program APR distributed in its first year, 1982, was *A Prairie Home Companion*, produced by Minnesota Public Radio. When the host Garrison Keillor left *Prairie Home* in 1985, Minnesota Public Radio created *Good Evening*, as a replacement. The majority of its schedule consists of original performances by orchestras, soloists and ensembles. It also carries the BBC's World News Service. Like commercial network affiliates, APR affiliates select programs individually for use in their schedules. APR does not supply a continuous long-form schedule. Over 318 public radio stations are APR affiliates, most also continuing their membership in NPR.

Other national distribution organizations, such as WFMT's Beethoven

Satellite Network and U.S. Audio (formed by eastern Public Radio), Audio Independents and Longhorn Network, began in the 1980s. Like APR, the new
networks and syndicators market and distribute programs nationally.

A variety of station programming consortia also have emerged in
public radio, paralleling those in public television, commercial broadcasting
and cable. The Public Radio Cooperative (PRC), a joint venture of individual
public radio stations largely in the northeastern United States, supplies programs to stations that pay a broadcast fee. Member stations produced many of
the programs; the rest come from commercial syndicators. The appetite for
more programming than NPR can supply is strong.

A CASE STUDY

The largest class of public radio stations in America is that licensed to
colleges and universities. The emergence of public broadcasting generated a
substantial dilemma for many of those institutional licensees. Traditionally,
campus radio stations were training grounds for journalism and broadcasting
students and assorted radio freaks—students interested in careers in broadcasting or looking for an extracurricular activity. When the Corporation for
Public Broadcasting, under a mandate from Congress in 1969, began to develop
a national public radio system, it found many of the most desirable noncommercial licenses were held by colleges and universities. CPB provided special
grants to selected holders of educational and noncommercial licenses to explore their institutions' and communities' support of a public radio service.
Forming a **public** station generally meant relinquishing many educational opportunities for students.

The University of Southern California has held the license for KUSC-
FM since 1946. Captain Alan Hancock—an oil wildcatter, marine biologist and
amateur musician—decided it would be nice to share the concerts his string
ensemble played with the citizens of California, or at least those few with FM
receivers in 1946. Over the years the station served as an outlet for Captain
Hancock and variously as laboratory for the Broadcast Communications Department of the university and toy for any given generation of students. The
station was on the air from 4 to 24 hours per day, and the budget seldom exceeded $4,500 per year. It was typical of most college campus radio stations: It
fluctuated between ingenuity and disaster.

In 1972 USC hired the first full-time employee to manage its radio
station. The general manager's mandate was (1) to provide management continuity, (2) to work with the students operating the station and (3) to explore
the station's potentials for the university and the community. The students
had great ambitions for the station and encouraged the manager to expand
KUSC's service to the broader public and to build the station into a strong public radio station.

The first requirement was to convince the university to adequately
fund the operating budget and invest in capital improvements. Second, it was
necessary to plan the transition of the staff from students to professionals.
Third, a format had to be chosen that would have the greatest potential for suc-

cess in a market saturated by more than 80 radio stations, 6 of them public. After four years of advocacy, the university invested $150,000 in capital improvements and dramatically increased the operating budget from $26,000 to nearly $100,000. CPB granted KUSC $775,000, and in December 1976 new facilities became operational.

Objectives

The strategies employed to achieve success in radio are grounded in the very nature of the medium. People listen to *radio stations*, not *radio programs*. They compare stations with stations, not programs with programs. Therefore, the successful radio broadcaster builds a sound image that distinguishes one station from all the others. KUSC's management set an ambitious goal: It wanted KUSC to become the *premiere* fine arts and classical music broadcast station in America—the standard against which all public or commercial classical music stations would be measured.

The format includes a significant number of nonmusic features and programs with an overall emphasis on quality in performance, language and writing. A careful integration of high-quality news, cultural affairs and modular features on the arts, drama, poetry and literature enables KUSC to develop a consistent sound image with a variety of aural experiences. Although 85 percent of its programming is music, the format also uses local, national and international news about the arts. Working on the premise that arts are not an escape from everyday life but rather a vital part of it, KUSC also airs significant news and public affairs programs from NPR.

Competition

The Los Angeles market has 83 commercial and noncommercial radio stations, sharing an audience of nearly 12 million, the second largest in the United States. Establishing a new service and building an audience in such a market were major challenges.

KUSC's primary competition is a commercial classical music service with a long and well-established tradition as "the" classical AM and FM music source in Los Angeles. Changes in ownership over the years left the stations in the hands of individuals who did not take seriously the broadcast audience for traditional classical music. First shorter works, then movements of major works, then themes from movements of major works took over programming. An increasing number of commercials offended dedicated classical music and casual listeners.

In the mid-1970s, KUSC decided to counter with a program service emphasizing *quality* in all programming aspects—signal, performance, information about the music and nonmusic broadcast programs. The result was that many classical listeners alienated by the commercial AM and FM services began to listen. KUSC's audiences grew from 30,000 to 230,000 in less than two years, but the commercial FM station also maintained its audience or grew slightly in listenership. This phenomenon suggests that KUSC shares a large part of its audience; that KUSC provides an alternative classical format for listeners to select if they are dissatisfied with a given program on the competition; and that listeners turned away from the classical format to another format such as beautiful music before KUSC emerged.

In addition to entering a crowded radio market, KUSC had a *dial location* problem. The main FM competition was adjacent to KUSC on one side of the broadcast band and KPFK—the Pacifica station that programmed a lot of classical music until KUSC emerged—on the other. Creating a sound image that would make it impossible for listeners to confuse KUSC with either of the other stations was enormous.

While KUSC's *primary competition* is from commercial stations, the growing number of noncommercial stations in the Los Angeles market has become an additional challenge. By 1983 the noncommercial stations numbered seven, three offering serious competition to KUSC. KPFK, the Pacifica station, is the oldest challenger. KCRW, licensed to Santa Monica College, is the newest and most formidable competitor for the public radio market. A change in its transmitter facilities provided KCRW with a coverage area identical to KUSC's, and careful positioning in the market has attracted some of the audience that used to rely solely on KUSC for its NPR programming. The dilemma facing KUSC was whether to concede certain programs to KCRW and build competitive alternative program offerings or to continue to share the audience for many programs with KCRW. This is called the **duplicator dilemma,** alleviated in part by the unbundling of NPR programs and the use of APR and other noncommercial radio program services.

This situation illustrates the conflicting strategies among both public radio and public television programmers. One view holds that a community should have several options for hearing public radio programs (or seeing public television programs). By presenting the same program at different times, a larger number of people are able to hear each program (and the *cumulative* audience builds). On the other hand, by presenting the same program on several stations, the audience has fewer total program choices than if each station had a unique schedule (eliminating some *diversity,* although increasing diversity is an acknowledged goal of public broadcasting). In addition, stations airing the same programs *divide the audience* rather than lure new listeners from commercial radio or other activities. And most crucial for community-supported stations, sharing programming *blurs station image* and *divides financial support.*

As of 1984, KUSC had taken a middle ground, offering both duplicate and some alternative programs. This strategy let it maintain its competitive position by keeping all major NPR programs in the schedule, while counting on KCRW's NPR schedule to free it to present some alternative programs. The new programs give KUSC something unique to promote and a chance to build new audience loyalties.

KLON, Long Beach, is the third station making significant progress in the Los Angeles market. It has a weak signal in much of the area KPFK, KCRW and KUSC serve, but is nonetheless significantly increasing its audience within the area. KLON's format combines jazz and local news. It includes NPR's national news programs as more of a courtesy than as competition since all NPR programming is available to KLON's audience on other stations. As KLON produced more original programming, it became a major threat to the Los Angeles–based stations.

By the late 1980s, duplication of NPR programming had become a substantial problem, and alternative program sources such as APR could fill KUSC's needs. In 1987 KUSC became the first major CPB-qualified station to drop its membership in NPR, including membership for its satellite outlets, KCPB-FM in Thousand Oaks and KSCA-FM in Santa Barbara. This necessitated an even greater increase in local production of concerts and specials and a greater commitment to news.

Staff

The transition from a completely *volunteer* staff (mostly students) to paid *professionals* was tedious and long. Fortunately, students suggested that a fully professional staff was needed to provide a high-quality, competitive public broadcast service. Tying salaries for professional staff to university faculty and staff pay scales also complicated staff development. (Public radio in general has disproportionately lower salaries than public television.)

The first staff under the new management combined volunteers, students and full-time paid employees. But as community expectations for a high-quality broadcast service increased, upgrading the professional experience and specialized skills of the staff was necessary. As KUSC drew more sophisticated listeners, the mail regarding employee errors and mistakes increased in volume and intensity. Staff unable to meet audience expectations for informed opinion, commentary and programming were let go. The need for excellence in performance and content forced the station to search for personnel in all areas of operation who were knowledgeable about concert music. All of the persons presently working at KUSC know, understand and love classical music. Even administrative, clerical and engineering personnel are expected to have a working knowledge of classical music and fine arts. Many successful commercial and noncommercial radio stations employ as few as four or five employees. KUSC's 38 people are the margin of difference in its service, and the station makes a substantial financial and personal investment in its employees.

Promotion and Development

The critical role of *promotion, advertising* and *public relations* in establishing a public radio service cannot be overemphasized. All the program strategies in the world are useless if people do not know that the program service exists. A major public relations firm was engaged to develop KUSC's promotional and public relations programs. The senior officers of the firm were fans of the station, believed in its potential and agreed to handle KUSC at a rate far below charges made to commercial clients.

Their first assignment was to design and implement a graphic image to complement the sound image. Next they embarked on a campaign to get every inch of print copy and electronic media coverage possible. The judicious use of meager sums of money to purchase the best possible advertising space was helpful in introducing new listeners to the station. The radio editor of a major trade paper once commented that in his career with that trade paper, he had never seen any radio station get as much ink as KUSC.

KUSC eventually internalized its public relations department and staffed it with one officer from the public relations firm. An aggressive public relations campaign is still a major component of the station's management strategy.

Fund Raising

Another major component of the KUSC strategy is *fund raising*. A fatal flaw in most public broadcasting entities is the failure to provide for a diversified financial base. Developing a competent fund-raising department requires time and professional leadership. Success comes to any public broadcasting station only through the commitment and support of the *local* community. The amount of support that a station generates is relative to the size, wealth, support of nonprofit organizations and the pure pride of its community. But no community can expect federal and state revenues if it does not demonstrate its willingness to invest its own resources in its public broadcast service. Either the licensee fully subsidizes the station or commits itself to fund raising.

However, some institutions prohibit their public broadcasting stations from fund raising. Such a decision deprives the institution and its station of money essential to station growth and community service. Academic institutions are typically the most restrictive of the public broadcasting licensees. They usually fear that fund raising for the public broadcasting station will compete with the institution's other fund raising activities. This attitude is shortsighted and fails to acknowledge that public broadcasting and education are distinct and separate businesses. Donors are able to make distinctions between gifts to a university and gifts to a broadcast station licensed to the university.

The University of Southern California allowed and encouraged KUSC to raise funds. As a result, KUSC has generated substantial operating funds. Careful coordination between KUSC and the university's development office avoids embarrassing conflicts with potential donors.

Accountability

Finally, a major failure of many public broadcasting entities is *financial accountability*. NPR's near disaster, described earlier in this chapter, underscores the need for sound fiscal management. Public broadcasters often get so caught up in the design and development of their program service that they neglect to establish sound business practices, especially financial record-keeping. Lionel van Deerlin, former chairman of the House Communications Subcommittee, told a gathering of public radio managers in 1978 that the state of financial record-keeping in public broadcasting was appalling, and it has improved little in the last decade. Other government agencies, corporations and foundations also show concern about the lack of sound business procedures in the administration and accounting practices of nonprofit organizations, including public broadcasting.

The call for *accountability* in public programs by consumer activist organizations, the reduction of tax revenues and changes in tax laws greatly reduce the amount of revenue available for nonprofit entities. As a result, government agencies, foundations, corporations and individual donors are increasingly interested in the best use of their investments. Financial accountability serves as one measure of the effective management of limited resources. It also provides additional security against wastefulness, duplication of services and misappropriation of funds.

KUSC maintains its own business office working in tandem with the business offices of the university to keep accurate records of business transactions and administer finances. KUSC's decision to hire a full-time business manager has been repaid a thousandfold.

Evaluation

KUSC has established *goals* for its service. The station believes it should reach at least 0.5 percent of the available audience of 12 million people in southern California and a weekly cumulative audience of 750,000. The initial goal was to reach that number in five years, and it was achieved. Every scrap of available data is used to evaluate reaction to the program service. Mail response, telephone response, program guide questionnaires, direct-mail solicitation, personal contact and Arbitron ratings are basic *evaluative tools*.

A radical change in listenership between one rating period and the next revealed the importance of these data in program evaluation. During one year the station had a very high weekly cume followed by a rating period with significantly lower numbers. The staff noted several factors contributing to the ratings decrease, and most of them were tied to programming. First, the commercial station broadcast a program unavailable to KUSC that greatly reduced the Saturday morning audience. Second, KUSC aired a series of programs on experimental composer Arnold Schoenberg during the same ratings period. Because of the low audience appeal of experimental music, that program registered the lowest ratings ever for a series on KUSC. Third, the afternoon classics program had a drop in ratings because the announcer had included more than the normal quantity of new and unfamiliar music.

The strategy for combating such ratings vagaries is, first of all, to identify the few programs the competition has that are not available to KUSC. If it is not possible to secure rights to those programs, KUSC must broadcast stronger programs opposite them. Second, during a ratings period the station will not broadcast a series of programs that is likely to draw a limited audience. This tactic does not imply that only "safe" programs will be broadcast, only that the timing of the broadcast of limited appeal programs will be more carefully selected. One can afford such programs when other programs are stronger and the overall ratings are higher. Third, the daily programming will be corrected to maintain the proper balance of familiar music.

As a whole, public radio station managers are devoting more effort to *audience research*. Many stations subscribe to the Radio Research Consortium, a company created to provide detailed analyses of Arbitron data for individual public radio subscribers. Audience data enables programmers to make informed decisions about audience flow and listening trends when creating program schedules and so build audience size.

Some persons argue that public broadcasting stations should not seek high ratings. Nonsense. Ratings provide a relative measure of success, and success is a desirable objective. The more individuals public radio serves, the better. Although public broadcasters may rely less on the number of people they reach than on the delivery of alternative program services to special audiences, it is imperative that they serve the largest number of individuals within those areas of special interest. To aim for less is to misuse a public trust and underutilize a scarce commodity—the broadcast spectrum.

TRENDS

Public radio grew considerably in the 1970s and has grown more in the 1980s. Both public and commercial radio audiences will continue to expand as long as radio provides local, personal, informational, educational and entertaining services. Public radio audiences, especially, will increase as public stations mature and become more professional.

The introduction of the Public Radio Satellite System opened up opportunities for independent producers, production companies, syndicators and public radio centers. This inexpensive distribution means created competing networks of program suppliers, increased the program market and diversified program offerings. The emergence of American Public Radio and the fall of National Public Radio from dominant supplier of public radio programs mean more variety within public radio. Although NPR will continue as a major programming producer, new networks supply alternative programming, thus increasing the competition for funds from listeners and corporations for program support. The new competition has three positive side effects: (1) more and diversified programs are available to local communities through their public radio stations, (2) increased competition stimulates donor interest in public radio, and (3) public radio no longer relies on a single programming source, minimizing the effects of any future NPR financial problems.

The chief threats to public radio continue to be lack of funding and the government bureaucracies that manage the system. Public radio is relatively inexpensive. Because it costs less, it is often difficult to convince the persons and agencies that finance public broadcasting to allocate sufficient funds to accomplish the quality of service listeners demand. Bureaucrats also tend to consider *radio* and *television* as one—lumping them together as "the media"— ignoring their subtle but substantial differences. This view is as disastrous as expecting a basketball team to use a football because both basketball and football are sports that use a ball. If public radio is left with its existing structure intact, it has a great future.

SUMMARY

Public radio seeks to combine localism and programming integrity to attract big cumulative audiences that will actively support its fund raising activities. Public radio stations use six formats to meet this challenge. The classical format, illustrated here by the case study of KUSC, shows how a clear set of objectives, a high-quality staff and ongoing evaluation help a public station meet its commercial competition in the ratings. Although only two public stations use the all-news format, news itself is playing a greater role in all public radio, partly due to the strong news base NPR provides. Jazz is one of the most recently developed public radio formats among public licensees, but its listeners are not usually financial donors. Community service and public access programming typify public radio in many people's minds, and the format generally serves minority audiences with informational rather than entertainment programming. Eclectic programming is the most common and most difficult format to succeed with, whereas the instructional was once the easiest, usually having a built-in market. But radio now plays a diminished role in schools; television has preempted its function. The dual format combines programming for two separate audiences by shifting from a daytime format to a nighttime format. Promotion, development, fund raising and strict accountability are the major tools that assist the public radio broadcaster to high levels of achievement in programming. NPR's high-quality news and arts programming occupied center stage in public radio programming for a decade, but partly as a result of NPR's financial crisis and partly as a result of cheap satellite distribution technology, joint ventures, consortia and new networks such as APR, its role has changed. Because CPB now funds public radio program production and acquisition directly (NPPAG grants) and NPR unbundled its programs, programmers today can choose only the programs that best suit their needs, creating more diversity and differentiation, as well as more competition in public radio.

Notes

1. WNED-FM is one of three stations licensed to Western New York Educational Foundation. WNED-FM and WEBR-AM were commercial stations the foundation purchased to operate as noncommercial broadcast stations. The price of approximately $1.8 million is believed to be one of the highest outright purchase prices ever paid for a noncommercial station.

2. The Pacifica stations were founded in 1949 in Berkeley, California. All of the stations qualify for financial support from the Corporation for Public Broadcasting, but only one—KPFT-FM in Houston—is a member of the national public radio system. Primary support for Pacifica stations comes from listener donations, and the stations generally refuse support from business and industry.

3. KBBF-FM is licensed to the Bilingual Broadcasting Foundation. The station was established by funding from the National Campaign for Decency of the Roman Catholic Church and was set free to develop its own support in the community. While the station struggles to survive, it has become a major training center for Spanish-speaking personnel for local public radio stations and National Public Radio.

4. The FCC authorizes FM stations to transmit two or more signals in the same channel (multiplex), and expanded this opportunity in 1983 to include commercial ventures for public stations.

5. KCRW-FM is licensed to Santa Monica Community College. The majority of the staff are professionals or community volunteers; however, some students work at the station for college credits.

Selected Sources

Freiberger, Paul. "Western Public Radio: The Independent Producer Gets a Chance," *Public Telecommunications Review* 7 (September–October 1979):12–14.

Giovannoni, David. "Radio Intelligence: The Economics of Programming," a multipart series on programming in *Current*, 1987 and 1988.

Josephon, Larry, editor. *Telling the Story: The NPR Guide to Radio Journalism*. Washington, D.C.: National Public Radio Publications, 1983.

Listening to the Future: Cable Audio in the 80s. Washington, D.C.: National Public Radio, 1982.

Lukoff, Manny. "The University and Public Radio: Who's in Charge?" *Public Telecommunications Review* 7 (September–October 1979):22–26.

Milan, Lorenzo. *The Radio Papers: From KRAB to KCHU*. San Diego: Mho & Mho Works, 1986.

Public Radio and State Governments, Vol. 1 & 2. Washington, D.C.: National Public Radio, 1981.

Williams, Wenmouth, Jr., and Krugman, Dean M. "Innovativeness and the Public Radio Audience," *Journal of Broadcasting* 25 (Winter 1981):61–69.

ABBREVIATIONS AND ACRONYMS

Boldface terms are explained further in the Glossary. See the Index for text page references.

AAA	Association of Advertising Agencies	CBC	Canadian Broadcasting Company
AC	Adult contemporary (radio music format)	CBN	Christian Broadcasting Network
ACE	Awards for excellence in cable programming	CD	Compact disc
		CEN	Central Educational Network
ACT	Action for Children's Television	CHN	Cable Health Network (now Lifetime)
ADI	**Area of dominant influence**		
AFTRA	American Federation of Television and Radio Artists	**CHR**	Contemporary hit radio (radio music format)
AGB	Marketing company collecting peoplemeter ratings	CM	Commercial matter
		CNN	Cable News Network
AID	Arbitron Information on Demand	CP	Construction permit
		CPB	**Corporation for Public Broadcasting**
AIT	Agency for Instructional Technology	CPM	Cost per thousand (used in advertising)
AOR	Album-oriented rock (radio music format)	**CRT**	Copyright Royalty Tribunal
AP	Associated Press (news service)	C-SPAN	Cable-Satellite Public Affairs Network
APR	**American Public Radio** network	CTAM	Cable Television Administration and Marketing Society
AQH	Average quarter hour		
ARB	Arbitron Research Bureau	**DBS**	**Direct broadcast satellite** (also direct satellite services)
ASI	Market research company (does program testing)	DJ	**Disc jockey**
ASCAP	**American Society of Composers, Authors and Publishers**	DMA	**Designated market area**
		EEN	Eastern Educational Television Network
ATC	American Television & Communications Corp.	EEO	Equal Employment Opportunity
		ENG	Electronic newsgathering
BEA	Broadcast Education Association	ERP	**Effective radiated power**
BM	**Beautiful music** (radio music format)	**ESF**	Expanded sample frame
		ESPN	Entertainment and Sports Programming Network
BMI	**Broadcast Music, Inc.**		
CAB	Cable-Television Advertising Bureau	FBC	Fox Broadcasting Company
		FCC	Federal Communications Commission
CATV	Community antenna television		
C-BAND	Low-power communications satellites	FNN	Financial News Network
		FTC	Federal Trade Commission

G	Movie code: general audiences	PG	Movie code: parental guidance suggested
GPN	Great Plains National Instructional Television Library	PMN	Pacific Mountain Network
HBO	Home Box Office	PPV	Pay-per-view cable services
HHs	**Households having sets**	PRSS	Public Radio Satellite System
HUTs	**Households using television**	PSA	Public service announcement
ID	Station identification	PTAR	**Prime-time access rule**
INN	Independent Network News, now *USA Today.*	PTL	Praise The Lord (religious program service)
INTV	Independent Television Station Association	PTV	**Public television**
		PUT	Persons using television
IRTS	International Radio Television Society	R	Movie code: restricted
		RAB	Radio Advertising Bureau
ITFS	Instructional Television Fixed Service	RPC	Radio Programming Conference
		RTNDA	Radio Television News Directors Association
ITNA	Independent Television News Association	SCA	Subsidiary Communications Authorization (permission to use subcarriers by the FCC)
ITV	**Instructional television**		
KU-BAND	High-power communications satellites	SECA	Southern Educational Communication Association
LIFO	Last in, first out	SESAC	Society of European Songwriters, Artists and Composers
LO	Local origination cable programming		
LPTV	Low-power television	SIN	Spanish International Network
LULAC	League of United Latin American Citizens	SIP	Station Independence Program (service of PBS)
MBS	Mutual Broadcasting System	SMATV	Satellite master antenna television
MDS	Multipoint Distribution Service		
MFTV	Made-for-TV (movies for broadcast use)	SMPTE	Society of Motion Picture and Television Engineers
MMDS	Multichannel Multipoint Distribution Service	SPC	**Station Program Cooperative** (PTV's programming bidding system)
MNA	Multi-Network Area Report		
MOR	Middle-of-the-road (radio music format)	SRA	Station Representatives Association
MSO	Multiple System Operator	SSS	Southern Satellite Systems
MTV	Music Television cable network	STV	Subscription television service
NAACP	National Association for the Advancement of Colored People	TBN	Trinity Broadcasting Network (religious network)
NAB	National Association of Broadcasters	TCI	Tele-Communications, Inc.
		TNN	The Nashville Network (cable service)
NAEB	National Association of Educational Broadcasters (now BEA)	**TSL**	Time spent listening (to radio)
		TvB	Television Bureau of Advertising
NARB	National Association of Radio Broadcasters	TVPC	Television Programmers' Conference
NATPE	National Association of Television Program Executives	**TVRO**	TV receive only (backyard dish owners)
NCTA	National Cable Television Association	**TvQ**	Television quotient (program and performer ratings)
NET	National Educational Television	UPI	United Press International (news service)
NFLCP	National Federation of Local Cable Programmers	USA	USA Network (cable service)
NOW	National Organization of Women	VBI	Vertical blanking interval (unseen portion of television scan)
NPR	**National Public Radio**		
NSI	Nielsen Station Index	**VCR**	Home videocassette recorder
NTI	Nielsen Television Index	VHS	Video Home System, the leading consumer videocassette format
O&O	**Owned-and-operated station**		
OPT	**Operation Prime Time**		
PBS	**Public Broadcasting Service**	VJ	Video jockey
PDG	Program Development Group	WCA	Wireless Cable Association (MMDS operators)

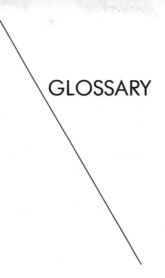

GLOSSARY

Italicized words in the definitions also appear as defined terms. See the Index for text page references.

Above-the-Line Costs Production costs related to concept, script, producer, director, stars.

AC Adult contemporary, a soft rock music format targeting the 25 to 54 age category.

Access Public availability of broadcast time. In cable, one or more channels reserved for public use, possibly requiring fees to cover facility costs. See also *Prime-Time Access Rule, Access Time, Free-Form Community Stations* and *Community Access Channels.*

Access Syndication Not-for-profit distribution of public access programs.

Access Time Hour between 7 and 8 P.M. (EST) which the broadcast networks cannot program and when the affiliates cannot air off-network programs. See also *Prime-Time Access Rule.*

ACE Awards sponsored by the National Cable Television Association for original cable programs.

Action News Television news reporting style emphasizing films, rapid pace and visuals; frequently includes informal dialogue among anchors.

Actuality An on-the-spot news report or voice of a newsmaker (frequently taped over the telephone) used to create a sense of reality or to enliven news stories.

Adaptation A film or video treatment of a novel, short story or play.

Addressability Remote control equipment that permits the cable operator to activate,

disconnect or unscramble signals to each household from the cable *headend;* provides maximum security; usually associated with the potential for *pay-per-view* channels.

Ad Hoc Networks Temporary national or regional hook-ups among stations for the purpose of program distribution; especially common in radio sports.

ADI See *Area of Dominant Influence.*

Adjacencies A commercial or promotional spot next to a specific program or type of program, especially spots next to prime-time programs.

Affiliate A commercial radio or television *station* receiving more than ten hours per week of *network* programming, but not owned by the network. Occasionally applied to individual cable operators contracting with *pay* or *basic* networks, or to public stations airing noncommercial programming from the *Public Broadcasting Service, National Public Radio* or *American Public Radio.*

Affiliate Agreements Contracts between a network and its individual affiliates specifying the rights and responsibilities of both parties.

Aided Recall In survey research, supplying respondents with a list of items to stimulate their memory.

Air-Lease Rights Permission to broadcast a program.

Alphanumeric News Service Television news created on a character generator and distributed as lines of text to be displayed on television receiver screens.

American Public Radio A not-for-profit radio network serving public radio stations.

American Society of Composers, Authors and Publishers (ASCAP) An organization licensing musical performance rights. See also *Broadcast Music, Inc. (BMI)*.

Amortization The allocation of syndicated program series costs over the period of use to spread out total tax or inventory and to determine how much each program costs the purchaser per airing; a station may use straight-line or declining value methods.

Ancilliary Markets Secondary sales targets for a program that has completed its first run on its initial delivery medium. Also called "back-end" markets.

Ancillary Services Revenue-production services other than the main broadcast or cable programming.

AOR Album-oriented rock, a rock music format appealing to a strongly male audience, ages 18 to 34, consisting of less well-known songs by avant-garde rock artists and groups as well as their most popular works.

Area of Dominant Influence (ADI) One of about 210+ geographical market designations defining each television market exclusive of all others; indicates the area in which a single station can effectively deliver an advertiser's message to the majority of homes. ADI is Arbitron's term; Nielsen's comparable term is Designated Market Area (DMA).

Ascertainment An examination of local community needs the FCC requires to retain broadcast television licenses.

ASI Market Research Los Angeles company specializing in program and commercial testing using invited theater audiences.

Aspect Ratio The ratio of the television screen's width to its height, about 4:3 for traditional broadcast television sets, about 5:3 for *high-definition television*.

Audience Flow The movement of audiences from one program or time period to another, either on the same station or from one station to another; includes turning sets on and off. Applied to positive flow encouraged by similarity between contiguous programs.

Audimeter Nielsen's in-home television rating meter, used until 1987. See also *Peoplemeter*.

Auditorium Research In radio, mass testing of song *hooks* to measure their popularity.

Automation Use of equipment, usually computerized, that reproduces material in a predesignated sequence; includes both music and commercials and produces a *log* of airings acceptable to advertising agencies. Also used for traffic and billing and in some television production processes.

Avail Short for a sales *availability*.

Availability Spot advertising position ("avail") offered for sale by a *station* or a *network*; also, syndicated television show or movie ready for station licensing. See also *Inventory* and *Program Availabilities*.

Average Quarter Hour (AQH) Rating showing the average percentage of an audience that tuned a radio or television *station*.

Backfeed Line A line from the production site or studios to the cable *headend* for the purpose of delivering the program.

Barter Licensing of syndicated programs in exchange for commercial time ("*inventory*") to eliminate the exchange of cash.

Barter Incentive Extra inducement to encourage negotiation of a barter deal.

Barter Spot Time in a syndicated program sold by the distributor.

Barter Syndication The method of program distribution in which the *syndicator* retains and sells a portion of a syndicated program's advertising time. In *cash-plus-barter* deals, the syndicator also receives fees from the station licensing the program.

Basic Cable Those cable program channels supplied for the minimum subscriber rate, including most local broadcast stations and assorted advertiser-supported cable networks. See also *Basic Networks*.

Basic-Cable Households Number or percentage of total television homes subscribing to cable service.

Basic Networks Those cable services for which subscribers do not pay extra on their monthly bills (although the cable system may pay to carry them); usually supported by advertising and small per-subscriber fees paid by the cable operator. Contrast with *Pay-Cable Networks*.

Beat The geographic area or topic-related area in which a reporter gathers news (for example, White House, state government, northern suburbs).

Beautiful Music A format emphasizing low-key, mellow, popular music, generally with extensive orchestration and many classic popular songs (not rock or jazz).

Bicycling Transfer of *syndicated* or *group* program tapes or films by means of wheeled delivery services or mail (in contrast to wired, microwave or satellite transmission).

Big Seven The major Hollywood studios: Columbia, Disney, MGM-UA, Paramount, 20th Century–Fox, Universal and Warner Bros.

Blackout A ban on airing an event, program or *station's* signal. Also FCC rules for blocking imported signals on cable that duplicate local stations' programs.

Block Booking Licensing several programs or movies as a package deal.

Blockbusters Special programs or big-name films that attract a lot of attention and interrupt normal scheduling; used especially during sweeps to draw unusually large audiences; usually exceed 60 minutes in length.

Blocking Placing several similar programs together to create a unit with *audience flow*.

Block Programming Several hours of similar programming placed together in the same *daypart* to create *audience flow*. See also *Stacking*.

Boilerplate Syndicated program packages using low-cost *formats*.

Break Averages Ratings for the breaks between programs, usually calculated by averaging the ratings for the programs before and after the break.

Breaks Brief half-hourly interruptions of programming to permit station identification and other messages.

Bridging Beginning a program a half-hour earlier than competing programs to draw their audiences and hold them past the starting time of the competing programs.

Broadband Having a wide bandwidth capable of carrying several simultaneous television signals; used of coaxial cable and fiber optic delivery.

Broadcast Music, Inc. (BMI) A music-licensing organization created by the broadcast music industry to collect and pay fees for musical performance rights; competes with *American Society of Composers, Authors and Publishers (ASCAP)*.

Broadcast Window Length of time in which a program, generally a feature film that was *made-for-pay* cable, is made available to broadcast stations in syndication. See also *Pay Window* and *Window*.

Broken Network Series Cancelled network series that has been revived for syndication, mixing *off-network* and *first-run* episodes of the series; usually a *sitcom*.

Bumping Canceling a showing, as in *preempting*.

Bundling Grouping several cable services on a pay tier for a single lump monthly fee.

Burnout Song that is no longer popular with target radio listeners.

Buying Renting by station of programs from *syndicators*. See also *License Fee, Prebuying* and *Presold*.

Buy Rate Sales per show, or the rate at which subscribers purchase *pay-per-view* programs, calculated by dividing the total number of available PPV homes by purchases. For example, if 50 of 100 PPV households ordered one movie, the buy rate would be 50 percent; if 50 of 100 PPV households ordered two movies, the buy rate would be 100 percent.

Cable Audio FM radio signals delivered to homes along with cable television, usually for a separate monthly fee; same as *Cable Radio* or *Cable FM*.

Cablecasting Distributing programming by coaxial cable as opposed to broadcast or microwave distribution; also, all programming a cable system delivers, both pay and basic, except over-the-air signals.

Cable FM FM radio signals delivered to cable subscribers, usually for a small installation or monthly fee; same as *Cable Audio* or *Cable Radio*.

Cable Franchises Agreements between local franchising authorities (city or county government) and cable operators to install cable wires and supply programs to a specific geographic area; usually involves payment of a franchise fee to the local government.

Cable Network National service distributing a channel of programming to cable systems.

Cable-Only Programming or services available only to cable subscribers; also, basic and pay networks that supply programming to cable systems but not to noncable households.

Cable Penetration The percentage of households subscribing to basic cable service.

Cable Radio Radio signals converted to FM and delivered to homes along with cable television, usually for a separate monthly fee; same as *Cable Audio* or *Cable FM*.

Cable Service Same as *Cable Network* or *Cable System* or both; also including local offerings such as an *access* or *local-origination* channel and alarm or security signals.

Cable Subscriber A household hooked to a cable system and paying the monthly fee for *basic cable* service.

Cable System One of about 8,500 franchised, nonbroadcast distributors of both broadcast and cablecast programming to groups of 50 or more subscribers not living in dwellings under common ownership. See contrasting *SMATV*.

Cable System Operator The person or company managing and owning cable facilities under a *franchise*. See *MSO*.

Cable Television All programming, both *basic* and *pay*, transmitted to subscribers by a cable system.

Cabletext Text such as alphanumeric news on an otherwise unoccupied cable channel.

Call-Ins People telephoning the station.

Call Letters FCC-assigned three or four letters beginning with *W* or *K*, uniquely identifying all U.S. broadcast stations. (Stations in other countries are assigned calls beginning with a different letter, as in *X* for Mexico and *C* for Canada.)

Call-Out Research Telephone surveying of audiences initiated by a station or research consultant; used extensively in radio research especially to determine song preferences in rock music. Contrast with *call-in* research referring to questioning listeners who telephone the station.

Call Screener Person screening incoming calls on telephone call-in shows and performing other minor production functions as assistant to a program host.

Camcorder A portable video camera and videotape recorder in one unit.

Canned Prepackaged or prerecorded; commonly applied to *syndicated* mini-lectures, automated music, commercials and other program elements that arrive at a station preproduced.

Capsules Brief news headlines within prime-time programs.

Carriage Charges Fees paid to a cable network or, hypothetically, a television station for the right to carriage.

Cash Call Radio giveaways requiring listeners merely to answer the phone or call in.

Cash Flow Revenues minus expenses and taxes, or cash in minus cash out; depreciation, *amortization* and other noncash charges have not been figured in, unlike most accounting methods.

Cash-Plus-Barter A syndication deal in which the station pays the distributor a fee for program *rights* and gives the syndicator one or two minutes per half-hour for national advertising sale, the remaining advertising time being retained by the station.

Casting Tape A videotape showing prospective actors in various roles; used especially for proposed soap operas and *live* action children's programs.

CATV The original name for the cable industry, standing for "community antenna television" and referring to retransmitting of broadcast television signals to homes without adequate quantity or quality of reception.

C-Band The frequencies used by most communications satellites, specifically from 4 to 6 gigaHertz (billions of cycles per second). See also *Ku-Band*.

Channel Balance Carrying several cable services having varied appeals.

Channel Piggybacking See *Piggybacking*.

Charts Music rankings as listed in trade publications.

Checkerboarding Scheduling five *stripped* programs alternately, one each day in the same time period; that is, rotating two, three or five different shows five days of the week in the same time period; a prime-time access strategy on some *affiliates*.

Cherrypicking In cable, selecting individual programs from several cable networks to assemble into a single channel (as opposed to carrying a full schedule from one cable network).

CHR Contemporary hit radio, a format that plays the top songs but uses a larger playlist than top 40.

Chromakey The special-effect mechanism for inserting one picture on top of another by electronically eliminating background of a specific frequency (usually blue).

Churn Turnover; in cable, the addition and subtraction of subscribers or the substitution of one pay-cable service for another; in broadcast network television, shifting of the prime-time schedule; in public broadcasting, changes in membership.

Churn Rate A cable industry formula that takes account of subscriber connects, disconnects, upgrades and downgrades.

Clearance Acceptance of a *network* program by *affiliates* for airing; the total number of clearances governs a network program's potential audience size.

Clear Channel AM radio station the FCC allows to dominate its frequency with up to 50kw of power; usually protected for up to 750 miles at night.

Clipping Illegally cutting off the beginning or end of programs or commercials, often for the purpose of substituting additional commercials.

Clocks Hourly program schedules, visually realized as parts of an hour. See also *Wheel.*

Clone A close copy of a prime-time show, usually on another network. Compare *Spinoff.*

Closed Captioning Textual information for the hearing impaired—transmitted in the vertical blanking interval—that appears superimposed over television pictures; requires special decoders for reception.

Clutter Excessive amounts of nonprogram material during commercial breaks; includes credits, IDs, *promos,* audio tags and commercial spots.

Coding In radio, classifying songs by type or age of music and/or frequency to be played.

Commentary Background and event interpretation by a radio or television on-air analyst.

Commercial Load The number of commercial minutes aired per hour.

Common Carriage Simultaneous airing of prime-time PBS programs.

Common Carriers Organizations that lease transmission facilities to all applicants; in cable, firms that provide *superstation* signal distribution by microwave and satellite.

Common Channel Lineup Identical service arrays on cable channel dials/tuners/converters on most cable systems within a market.

Community Access Channels Local cable television channels programmed by community members, required by some franchise agreements.

Community Service Grants Financial grants from the *Corporation for Public Broadcasting* to public television and radio stations for operating costs and the purchase of programs.

Compact Disc A 5-inch digital recording read optically by a laser; may be used for computer data, visuals or sound.

Compensation A broadcast network payment to an affiliate for carrying network commercials (usually within programs, but sometimes radio affiliates carry only the commercials embedded in a local program).

Compensation Incentive Usually a cash payment by a network or syndicator to encourage program *clearance.*

Composite Week An arbitrarily designated seven days of program logs from different weeks, reviewed by the FCC in checking on licensee program performance versus promise (until 1982 for radio).

Compulsory Licensing Mandatory fees paid by cable operators for the right to retransmit copyrighted material (such as broadcast station and *superstation* signals); amounts set by government rather than private negotiations. See also *Copyright.*

Contemporary FCC radio *format* term covering popular music, generally referring to rock; generally called adult contemporary (AC) or urban contemporary (black-oriented).

Continuity Acceptance Station, network or system policies regarding the technical quality and content claims in broadcast advertising messages, especially important within children's programs.

Continuous Season Network television scheduling pattern spreading new program starts across the September to May year (rather than concentrating them in September/October and January/February).

Conus A national news service for television stations using satellite delivery of timely news stories from all over the country.

Converter An electronic device that shifts channels transmitted by a cable system to other channels on a subscriber's television set.

Cooperation Rate In ratings, the percentage of contacted individuals or households agreeing to participate, such as by filling out a diary or agreeing to have a meter installed in the home.

Coproductions Agreements to produce programs in which costs are shared between two or more corporations or stations.

Copyright Registration of television or radio programs or movies (or other media) with federal Copyright Office, restricting permission for use.

Copyright Fee In cable, mandatory fee paid by cable operators for reuse of broadcast programs.

Copyright Royalty Fee paid for permission to use copyrighted material.

Copyright Royalty Tribunal (CRT) A small federal agency that collects and distributes royalties from the compulsory cable license.

Core Schedule In the early 1980s, two hours of programs fed to PBS member stations for simultaneous airing four nights a week; begun in 1979, ended in 1986; term now loosely refers to prime-time programs on public television.

Corporate Underwriters National or local companies that pay all or part of the cost of producing, purchasing or distributing a noncommercial television or radio program; they may fund programs on *PBS, NPR* or local public broadcast stations. See also *Underwriter.*

Corporation for Public Broadcasting (CPB) Government-funded financial and administrative unit of national public broadcasting since 1968.

Correlator An inside or telephone reporter on radio who aids the editor; frequently responsible for *actualities* for news broadcasts.

Cost per Episode The price of licensing each individual program in a syndicated series.

Cost per Thousand How much it costs an advertiser to reach a thousand viewers or listeners or subscribers.

Counterprogramming Scheduling programs with contrasting appeal to target unserved demographic groups.

CPB-Qualified Stations Public radio stations receiving *Community Service Grants* from the *Corporation for Public Broadcasting;* has prerequisites of large budget, paid staff, strong signal and so on.

Cream Skimming Marketing only to high-return portions of an audience, generally upper-income households.

Critical Information Pile A quantity of important news breaking simultaneously that causes massive alterations in planned news coverage.

Crossmedia Ownership Owning two or more of broadcast stations, cable systems, newspapers or other media in the same market; prohibited by FCC unless exception granted (temporary or grandfathered).

Crossover Temporarily using characters from one program series in episodes of another series. Compare *Spinoff* and *Clone.*

Crossover Points Times when one network's programs end and another's begin, usually on the hour and half-hour, permitting viewers to change channels easily (although a long program such as a movie may *bridge* some hour and half-hour points).

Crossownership Rules FCC rules prohibiting control of broadcast, newspaper or cable interests in the same market.

CRT See *Copyright Royalty Tribunal.*

Cume Cumulative rating; the total number of different households that tune to a *station* at different times, generally over a one-week period; used especially in commercial and public radio, public television and commercial sales.

Cycle Span of news flow between repeat points in all-news radio.

Daypart Period of two or more hours, considered as strategic unit in program schedules (for example, morning *drivetime* in radio—6 to 10 A.M.—and *prime time* in television—8 to 11 P.M.).

Dayparting Altering programming to fit with the audience's changing activities during different times of the day (such as shifting from music to news during *drivetime*).

Daytimer An AM radio station licensed to broadcast only from dawn to dusk.

DBS Programming from *direct broadcast satellites* going from satellite to home receiving dishes, bypassing a ground-based distributor such as a broadcast station or cable system. See also *TVRO*.

Dedicated Channel Cable channel restricted to a single type of program or aimed at a single audience (for example, sports, news or children's channels).

Deficit Financing Licensing television programs to the broadcast networks at an initial loss, counting on later profits from *syndication* rights to cover production costs; practiced by the major Hollywood studios.

Delayed Carriage Taping a live program for later airing.

Demographics Descriptive information on an audience, usually the vital statistics of age and sex, possibly including education and income.

Demo Tape Demonstration tape of a program, used for preview without the expense of producing a *pilot*.

Designated Market Area (DMA) Nielsen's term for local viewing area. See also Arbitron's *Area of Dominant Influence (ADI)*.

Diary Instrument for recording hours of listening or viewing of a station or cable service, used by Arbitron, Nielsen and other research firms; filled out by audience members.

Differentiation Perceived separation between networks, stations or services by the audience and advertisers, generally based on programming differences and promotional images.

Digital Delay Unit Electronic device to delay programs for a few seconds between studio and transmitter to permit dumping of profanity, personal attacks and other unairable material; used on all call-in programs.

Direct Broadcast Satellites Special satellites intended for redistribution of high-powered television signals to individual subscribers' receiving dishes, requiring only small dishes. See *DBS* and *TVROs*.

Disc Jockey (DJ) A radio announcer who introduces records.

Disconnects Cable subscribers who have cancelled service.

Dish Receiving or sending antenna with bowl shape, intended for transmitting satellite signals; also called *earth station*.

Disjunctures Places in the television schedule where successive audiences do not overlap.

Distant Independents Television signals from *independent* stations in other markets, especially *superstations*.

Distant Signals Broadcast station signals imported from another market and retransmitted to cabled homes; usually *independents*. See also *Superstations*.

Distribution Window A period of time in which a movie or television program is available to another medium. See also *Window, Pay Window* and *Broadcast Window*.

Docudrama Fictionalized drama of real events and people.

Documentary Program that records actual events and real people.

Dolby A circuit incorporated in audio equipment to improve the ratio of *signal-to-noise*.

Dominant Satellites Communication satellites used by the most popular cable networks (Satcom III-R, Galaxy I).

Downgrading Reducing the number or value of pay services by a subscriber.

Downlink Satellite-to-ground transmission path, the reverse of *uplink*; refers also to the receiving antenna (*Dish*).

Download Transmission and decoding of signals at receiving end; used of satellite program (and computer) signals.

Downscale Audience or subscribers with lower than average socioeconomic demographics, especially low income. See also *Upscale*.

Downtrending A pattern of declining ratings/shares over time.

Drama Prime-time series program format, usually one hour long, contrasting with situation comedy; includes action-adventure, crime, doctor, adult soap and other dramatic forms.

Drivetime In radio, 6 to 10 A.M. (morning drive) and 4 to 7 P.M. (afternoon drive).

Duopoly Rule FCC rule limiting ownership of stations with overlapping coverage areas.

Early Fringe In television, the period preceding the early news, usually 4 to 6 P.M. See *Fringe*.

Earth Station Ground receiver/transmitter of satellite signals; when receiving, the purpose usually is to redirect satellite signals to a broadcast station or to cable *headend* equipment; also used to receive signals directly without a broadcast or cable intermediary; see *TVRO*. Most are receive-only stations; also called antennas or *dishes*.

Eclectic Mixed; applied to varied programming in radio incorporating several types of programs; a recognized *format* in public radio.

Editorials In broadcasting, statements of management's point of view on issues.

Effective Radiated Power (ERP) Watts of power measured at receiving antennas on average; used to measure the strength of antennas.

Electronic Text Alphanumeric video representations of words and sometimes diagrams, excluding moving video images; includes *teletext*, *videotex* and *cabletext* news services such as those supplied by Associated Press and United Press International wire services.

Emmys Awards to top broadcast television programs and performers.

ENG Electronic news gathering; refers to portable television equipment used to shoot and tape news stories on location.

Entering Stations In public broadcasting, those stations participating in an SPC bid or a production venture.

Episode One show out of a series.

Equal Employment Opportunity (EEO) Federal law prohibiting discrimination on the basis of race or sex in employment.

Equal Time An FCC rule incorporated in the Communications Act of 1934 requiring equivalent airtime for candidates for public office.

Equity Holdings A financial interest from part ownership of a business; same as "equity interest" or *Equity Shares*.

Equity Shares Ownership shares offered as compensation or incentive to cable operators for making *shelf space* for a cable network, especially newly introduced networks such as *shopping services*.

ERP See *Effective Radiated Power*.

Ethnic Programming by or for minority groups (for example, Spanish-speaking, American Indians, blacks).

Exclusivity The sole right to air a program within a given period of time in a given market.

Expanded Basic Tier A level of cable service beyond the most basic *tier*, offered for an additional charge and comprising a package (or bundle) of several cable networks—usually advertiser-supported services.

Expanded Sample Frame (ESF) The base unit for a sampling technique that includes new and unlisted telephone numbers.

Extraneous Wraps Reusable closings for radio news, prerecorded by an announcer or reporter for later on-air use.

Facilities Physical buildings, equipment and other technical characteristics of a broadcast license, such as permissible antenna height, power and frequency.

Fairness Doctrine A former FCC policy requiring that *stations* provide airtime for opposing views on controversial issues of public importance; ended in 1987.

Family Viewing Time A short-lived NAB code reserving the first two hours of television prime time—7 to 9 P.M. (EST)—for programs suitable for both children and adults; later determined to be illegal (if done at the FCC's behest) by a federal court.

Feature Radio program material other than hard news, sports, weather, stock market reports or music; also called *short-form*. In television and cable, generally short for theatrical feature films.

Feature Film Theatrical motion picture, usually made for theater distribution; feature films occupy about one-fifth of the total syndication market.

Feature Syndicator Distributor of short, stand-alone programs or series, as contrasted with long-form (continuous) programming; used in radio, television and cable.

Financial Interest Rules FCC regulation prohibiting broadcast networks from owning an interest in the domestic syndication rights of most television and radio programs they carry.

First Refusal Rights The legal right to consider a program proposal until reaching a decision on producing or not producing it; can stymie a program idea for years.

First-Run The first airing of a television program (not counting theatrical exhibit of feature films).

First-Run Syndication Distribution of programs produced for initial release on stations, as opposed to the broadcast networks. Compare *Off-Network Syndication*.

Flat Fee Method of payment involving a fixed lump price; contrast with sliding scale (usually based on number of viewers).

Flip Card Filing system for record rotation at radio stations. `

Flipping Changing channels frequently during programs.

Flow See *Audience Flow*.

Focus Group People participating in a joint interview on a predetermined topic; a method of research.

Formal Ascertainment A no-longer required method of collecting information on the public's needs, interests and problems by interviewing community leaders and randomly surveying the general public. Compare *Informal Ascertainment*.

Format Overall programming design of a station, cable service or specific program, especially used of radio and cable program packages.

Formula The elements that define a format.

Foundation Services In cable, the earliest established and most widely carried *cable networks*.

Franchise License granted by local government to provide cable service, based on local government's right to regulate public rights of way; cable requires installing wires in a community or portion of a community. The franchise agreement delineates geographic area to wire.

Free-Form Community Stations Public *access* radio format, begun in the 1960s most notably by Lorenzo Milam.

Frequency In advertising, the number of times the audience was exposed to a message. Also, the portions of the electromagnetic spectrum used for broadcasting and satellite *uplinks* and *downlinks*; see *C-Band* and *Ku-Band*.

Fringe The television time periods adjacent to *prime time*—from 4 to 7 P.M. and 11 P.M. to midnight or later (EST). *Early fringe* means the time preceding the early local newscast; late fringe usually starts after the end of late local news at 11:30 P.M.

Front-and-Backend Deal A program licensing agreement in which the station pays a portion of the fees at the time of the contract and the remainder at the time the program actually becomes available; see *Futures*.

Frontload In *pay television*, to schedule all main attractions at the beginning of the month.

Futures Projected episodes in a series that have not yet been produced; typically, network series programming intended for syndication that may be purchased while the series is still on the network for a negotiated price that takes account of the purchaser's risk.

General Premium Channels Cable movie networks targeted at a broad audience, seeking appeal to all or nearly all demographic groups.

Gold A hit song or record generally with lasting appeal; in sales, a song selling a million copies, an album selling 500,000 copies.

Gold Book List of gold (classic) records for use in radio programming.

Graphics Titles and other artwork used in a program, promo or commercial spot.

Gross Rating Points In advertising and promotion, system of calculating the size of the delivered or anticipated audience by summing the rating points for all airings of a spot.

Group Parent corporation, owners of several broadcast stations or cable systems.

Group-Owned Station Radio or television station licensed to a corporation owning two or more stations; cable system owned in common with many other cable systems. See also *MSO*.

Group Owner An individual or company having the license for more than two broadcast facilities. Compare *MSO*.

Guides Program listings, published in printed or electronic form.

Hammocking Positioning a weak program between two successful programs; they support a new or less successful program by lending their audience to it.

Hard News Daily factual reporting of national, international or local events. Compare *Soft News.*

Headend Technical headquarters for receiving and transmitting equipment for a cable system, where signals are placed on outgoing channels.

High-Definition Television (HDTV) Various technical systems for distributing video with higher quality and a wider aspect ratio than standard television broadcasting; generally uses a greater bandwidth in the spectrum and has more scanning lines. See also *Aspect Ratio.*

Homes Passed The total number of buildings cable wires pass, irrespective of whether the occupants are or are not cable subscribers.

Hook A plot or character element at the start of a program that grabs audience attention; also, in radio research, a brief song segment characterizing a whole song.

Horizontal Documentaries Multipart treatment of a news subject spread over several successive days or weeks. Compare *Vertical Documentaries.*

Host Personality who moderates a program or conducts interviews on radio, television or cable.

Hot Clock See *Wheel* or *Clocks.*

Households Having Sets (HHs) Ratings industry term for the total number of homes with receiving sets (AM or FM radio, UHF or VHF television or cable hookups); that is, total potential audience.

Households Using Television (HUTs) Ratings industry term for the total number of sets turned on during an *average quarter hour;* that is, actual viewing audience to be divided among all stations and cable services in a market.

House Show Program produced in the station's studios rather than purchased as a syndicated property; usually called *in-house.*

Hyping Extended promotion of a program or airing of special programs to increase audience size during a *ratings* period.

Ideal Demographics The theory that a particular age and sex group should be the target of prime-time network television programs.

Impulse Systems Technology permitting a cable viewer to punch up and purchase a *pay-per-view* program or merchandise using a hand-held remote control.

Incentive Enticement to make a deal or sign a contract, as in additional local *avails* offered to stations or cable systems by a syndicator or network, or payments for clearing a program; also, discounts and prizes offered to lure potential cable subscribers.

Indecency A subcategory of the legal definition of obscenity, enforced by the FCC; refers generally to prohibited sexual and excretory language and depictions of behavior.

Independent A commercial television broadcast *station* not *affiliated* with one of the national *networks* (by one FCC definition, carries fewer than ten hours of network programming per week).

Independent Producers Producers of television series, movies or specials that are legally separate from the Hollywood movie studios.

Infomercial A long commercial, usually incorporating a demonstration and sales pitch lasting from 3 to 15 minutes, typically presented on cable television or teletext.

Informal Ascertainment Determining a community's needs, interests and problems in order to file a report with the FCC showing how a station responded with programming; method of collecting information determined by the station. Compare *Formal Ascertainment.*

In-House Programs produced in the station's own facilities, as opposed to network or syndicated shows; also shows such as soap operas, newscasts amd public affairs that the broadcast networks produce themselves.

Instructional Television (ITV) Programs transmitted to schools for classroom use by public television or radio stations.

Instructional Television Fixed Service (ITFS) A television distribution system delivering programs by line-of-sight microwave to specific noncommercial and commercial users within a fixed geographic area; usually, the means for delivering instructional programming to schools by public television stations.

In-Tab Diaries that are actually returned in usable form and counted in the sample.

Interactive Cable Two-way cable that permits each household to receive one stream of programming and also to communicate back to the cable headend computer.

Interconnection Grants Funds from the *Corporation for Public Broadcasting* for public television stations to cover satellite transmission costs.

Interconnects Transmission links among nearby cable systems permitting shared sales and carriage of advertising spots.

Interstitial Programming Short programs intended to fill the time after an odd-length program is completed. Also called *shorts*.

Inventory The amount of time a station has for sale (or the commercials, records or programs that fill that time).

Iris Awards for television advertising commercials.

Jock See *Disc Jockey* and *Video Jockey*.

Joint Venture Cooperative effort to produce, distribute or market programs.

Key-Pad Hand-held remote control device for selecting television channels; also used for purchasing *pay-per-view* programs and merchandise on shopping channels.

Kiddult Television programs appealing to both children and adults.

Kidvid Television programs for children.

Ku-Band Frequencies used for transmitting some high-powered satellite signals; refers to the band between 11 and 14 gigaHertz (billions of cycles per second); requires smaller receiving dishes than C-band. Compare *C-Band*.

Large-Market Stations Broadcast stations in markets 1 to 25, as defined by the ratings companies. Compare *Mid-Market Stations*, *Small-Market Stations* and *Major Market*.

Latchkey Children Children whose parents work who are given their own keys so that they may return home by themselves after school.

Lead-In Program preceding others, usually intended to increase *audience flow* to the later programs. Called *Lead-off* at start of prime time.

Lead-Off See *Lead-In*.

Leapfrogging Importing distant (noncontiguous) signals without importing all intervening station signals; used of cable systems picking up independent station signals.

Leased Access Channels available for commercial lease, occasionally required by cable franchise agreement, sometimes voluntarily offered by large-capacity cable systems.

Least Objectionable Program (LOP) A theory holding that viewers select not the most appealing program among those available at one time but the one that offends fewest viewers watching together; presumes that channel switching requires an active effort occurring only when the channel currently being viewed presents something new and objectionable.

Legs Slang meaning that a program will provide dependably high ratings, as with *blockbuster* off-network television series.

Leveraged Buyout Acquisition of a company, usually by its management, in which the buyers borrow against the company's assets, usually requiring subsequent sale of some assets to cover purchase costs.

Licensees Entities legally holding broadcast licenses.

License Fee Charge for the use of a syndicated program, feature film or network service.

Lifespan In television, the number of years a series stays on network television.

Lifestyle The way different people live; in research, measures of people's attitudes, interests and opinions.

LIFO "Last in, first out"; idea that the most recently added cable network will be the first removed from the system, having had the least time to develop a following; also applies to subscribers, meaning subscribers added most recently are often the first to cancel.

Lift Added audience gained by combining popular and less popular cable services in marketing.

Limited-Run Series A television series having only a few episodes for airing.

Liners Brief ad lib comments by *disc jockeys* between records on music radio.

Live Not prerecorded; or in the record industry, recorded as performed, not edited.

Live Assist Programming combining disc jockey chatter and automated music programming on tape.

Live Feed A program or insert coming from a network or other interconnected source without prerecording and aired simultaneously.

Local Programs or commercials generated 50 percent or more within a station's broadcast coverage area.

Localism FCC policy of encouraging local ownership of broadcasting and community-oriented programming.

Local Origination Cable programs the cable system produces or licenses from syndicators to show locally, including *access* programs, as contrasted with *basic cable networks* or *pay-cable networks*.

Log The official record of a broadcast day, kept by hand or automatic means such as tape, noting opening and closing times of all programs, commercials and other non-program material and facts mandated by the FCC.

Long-Form Longer than the usual length of 30 minutes for most television series and 60 minutes for *dramas* or *specials* (for example, a 90-minute fall season introduction to a new prime-time *series*) or playing the entire two or three hours of a feature film in one evening; also, in radio, nationally distributed programming using a single musical format, as in automated beautiful music or rock, as opposed to syndicated feature programming or *short-form* news.

Long-Form Nights Evenings on which a two-hour movie or special is scheduled by a network.

Loss Leader A program (or *format*) broadcast because management thinks it is ethically, promotionally, culturally or aesthetically worthwhile rather than directly rewarding financially; in cable, carrying cultural channels; used in image building.

Lotteries Contests involving the three elements of prize, consideration (payment of some kind) and chance, prohibited on broadcast stations by the FCC.

Low-Power Station A class of broadcast television stations with limited transmitter strength (usually covering less than ten miles), generally assigned in areas where a full-power signal would interfere with another station using the same channel.

Made-for-Pay Programs, usually feature films, produced for pay-cable distribution; may later be syndicated to broadcast stations.

Made-for-TV (MFTV) Movie feature produced especially for the broadcast television networks, usually fitting a 90-minute or two-hour format with breaks for commercials.

Magazine Format A television or radio program composed of varied segments within a common framework, structurally resembling a printed magazine.

Major Market One of the 100 largest metropolitan areas in number of television households.

Mandatory Licensing Nonvoluntary fees cable operators must pay for the right to re-use copyrighted broadcast programming; fees returned by CRT to rights holders; usually called *Compulsory Licensing*. See also *Copyright*.

Matching In cable, assigning the same cable channel number as a station's over-the-air channel number. See also *Repositioning*.

MDS Multipoint distribution service; a system of distribution of pay television using microwave to rooftop antennas; generally distributes pay-cable networks (without using cables outside buildings). See also *MMDS*.

Merger Legal joining of two separate corporations or companies into one legal entity.

Metered Cities Fifteen or so largest markets in which the stations pay Nielsen or Arbitron to provide *overnight* ratings from metered households.

Metro Most densely populated center of a metropolitan area, defined by Arbitron and Nielsen for rating a geographic subset of a market.

Midband Channels on a coaxial cable falling between broadcast channels 6 and 7, requiring a converter, cable-ready television set or VCR to tune.

Mid-Market Stations Broadcast stations in markets 26 to 100, as determined by the ratings companies. See also *Large-Market Stations* and *Small-Market Stations*.

Minicam A small, portable television camera. See also *ENG* and *Camcorder*.

Mini-Doc A short documentary.

Minipay A basic cable network that charges cable systems a small amount per subscriber per month for its programming.

Miniseries Prime-time network television series shorter than the traditional 11 episodes.

MMDS Multichannel Multipoint Distribution Service, also called wireless cable; distributes up to 33 channels in a market. See also *MDS*.

Monopoly Excessive concentration of ownership or means of distribution.

Movie Libraries Those *feature films* under contract to a station with *plays* still available.

Movie Licenses Contracts for the right to play a movie a fixed number of times; contract lengths average five years nowadays.

Movie Repetition Repeating movies on a cable network.

Movie Rotation Scheduling movies at different times of the day and days of the week on a cable network.

MSO Multiple system operator; owner of more than one cable system; see also *Group Owner*.

Multiaffiliates Stations with affiliation contracts with two or more networks, generally specifying a primary and a secondary affiliation; only in very small markets.

Multibasic Cable environment of many competing basic cable services.

Multichannel Multipoint Distribution Service See *MMDS*.

Multipay Cable environment of many competing premium services.

Multiple Franchising Licensing more than one cable company to wire the same geographic area and compete for subscribers; occurs very infrequently. See *Overbuild*.

Multiple Networks In radio, several co-owned services such as ABC's six radio networks or Westwood's five networks.

Music Sweep Uninterrupted period of music on music radio.

Must-Carry Rule An FCC requirement that cable systems had to carry certain qualified local broadcast television stations, ruled unconstitutional in 1987.

Narrowcasting Targeting programming, usually of a restricted type, to a nonmass audience, usually a defined demographic or ethnic group; used when either the programming or the audience is of a narrow type.

National Program Production and Acquisition Grants (NPPAGs) Funds paid to *public radio* stations by the *Corporation for Public Broadcasting* for making and licensing programs.

National Public Radio (NPR) The non-commercial radio *network* service financed primarily by the *Corporation for Public Broadcasting (CPB)*; serves *affiliated* public radio stations.

National Representative See *Station Rep(resentative)*.

Negative Cost Actual production cost of a movie, exclusive of marketing and advertising expenses.

Network An interconnected chain of broadcast stations or cable systems that receive programming simultaneously; also refers to the administrative and technical unit that distributes (and may originate) preplanned schedules of programs (for example, ABC, CBS, NBC, Mutual, PBS, NPR, HBO, ESPN, Showtime).

Network Compensation Payments by broadcast networks to affiliated stations for airing network programs and commercials.

Network One Stop Marketing service controlled by TCI supplying a package of 16 satellite-delivered networks for backyard dishes (*TVROs*).

Network Parity Equality in network audience sizes, usually calculated by comparing numbers of affiliated stations in large, middle and small markets. See also *Parity*.

Network Syndication Rule FCC rule prohibiting the broadcast networks from syndicating their programs themselves in the domestic U.S. market.

New-Build Recently constructed residential area in which cable wires pass all houses.

News Block Extended news programming; in radio, the time immediately before and after the hour when stations program news; in television, the period between 5:30 and 7:30 P.M. (varies with market).

Nonclearance Written refusal to carry a particular network program by an affiliate.

Noncommercial Broadcasting The system of not-for-profit television and radio stations, and the networks that serve them, that operate under educational licenses; includes public broadcasting, public access stations and many religious and state or city-operated stations.

Nonduplication FCC policy prohibiting airing of the same program material on two co-owned radio stations (such as an AM and FM) in the same market (exceptions granted in some very small markets or grandfathered cases).

Nonentertainment Programming News and service information such as weather and traffic reports.

Nonprime Time In network television, the hours outside of prime time, especially morning, day and late night; nonprime-time programming usually excludes news and sports since they are handled by separate network departments.

Nontraditional Scheduling Putting news or other blocks of programs in times other than the ones normally used by network-affiliated stations.

Off Line Use of program elements as they are fed from a network or other source.

Off-Network Program Former broadcast television network show now syndicated.

Off-Network Syndication Selling programming (usually series) that has appeared at least once on the national networks directly to stations or cable services.

One-to-a-Market Rule FCC policy limiting ownership to a single broadcast station in a market.

Operation Prime Time (OPT) An association of stations and producers contributing funds on a prorated basis for the production of high-quality, *first-run* drama intended for prime-time airing.

Oscars Awards for feature films and performers.

Overbuild A second cable system built where another firm already has one. See also *Multiple Franchising*.

Overmarketing Persuading people to subscribe to more cable services than they can readily afford.

Overnight Radio airtime in the small hours, usually from 1 to 4 A.M.; television programming from 1 or 2 A.M. to 4 or 6 A.M.

Overnights National television *ratings* from metered homes in major cities, available the following day to network programmers.

Owned-and-Operated Station (O&O) Broadcasting station owned and operated by one of the major broadcast networks.

Parity Audience equivalence; in network television, having equal numbers of affiliates with equal reach so that each network has a fair chance to compete for ratings/shares based on programming popularity. Also applied in comparing VHF and UHF stations and broadcast stations with and without cable carriage. See also *Network Parity*.

Passive Viewing Watching television without actively consulting all the competing program options.

Pay Cable Cable television programming services for which the subscriber pays an optional extra fee over and above the normal monthly cable fee. See also *Pay Television, Premium Networks* and *Pay-per-View*.

Pay-Cable Households Number or percentage of total television households subscribing to a *premium* cable service.

Pay-Cable Networks National satellite-distributed cable programming for which subscribers pay an extra monthly fee, over and above the monthly fee for basic cable service. See also *Premium Networks*.

Pay Channel *Pay cable* and *pay-per-view* channels supplying mostly movies, sports and specials to cable subscribers for an optional extra monthly or per-program fee.

Payola Illegal payment for promoting a recording or song on the air.

Pay-per-View Cable or subscription television programming that subscribers pay individually for, purchased per program viewed rather than monthly.

Pay Run Length of a movie's license (*rights*) on a cable network.

Pay Television An umbrella term for any programming for which viewers pay a fee; includes *pay cable, subscription television, pay-per-view, MMDS, DBS* and *TVRO* packages.

Pay Window A period of time in which a program, usually a feature film, is made available to pay cable, generally from 6 to 12 months. See also *Broadcast Window* and *Window*.

PBS See *Public Broadcasting Service*.

PEG Public, educational and governmental *access* channels on cable television.

Penetration *Reach;* in a given population, the percentage of households using a product or receiving a service.

Peoplemeter Electronic meter attached to television sets measuring both tuning and audience demographics; viewers push buttons to identify themselves; variants used by Nielsen, Arbitron's ScanAmerica, AGB and R.D. Percy & Co.

Pick Off Preempt.

Piggybacking Scheduling two part-time cable networks on the same channel, usually one in daytime and one in nighttime; also, two cable networks carried on same satellite *transponder.* Also, in advertising, promoting two cable services as if carrying one (or subscribing to one) were conditional on carrying (or subscribing to) the other.

Pilot A sample first program of a proposed television series, often longer than regular episodes; introduces characters, set, situations and style of the program, generally accompanied by heavy promotion when aired.

Pilot Testing Comparing audience reactions to new television programs under controlled conditions prior to the program's appearance in a network schedule.

Plateauing Leveling off in successive ratings; can characterize a single program or an entire *station's* or *network's* programming.

Play A showing or *run* of a program. Also, one to two showings of each episode of a program until all rights are exhausted as specified in a licensing agreement.

Playlist Strategically planned list of records to be played on music radio.

Playoffs Last games in a sports series; also, last showings of episodes of a licensed program series to get full value for the program expenditure.

Plugola Inclusion of material in a program for the purpose of covertly promoting or advertising a product without disclosing that payment of kind was made; penalties for violating *payola* or plugola regulations may be up to a $10,000 fine and/or a year in prison for each offense.

Population All homes with television sets or radios. See also *Universe.*

Positioning Making the audience believe one *station* or cable service is really different

from its competitors; especially important for *independent* television stations, rock music radio stations and cable shopping services.

Prebuying Financing a movie or television series before production starts in order to obtain exclusive future telecast rights.

Preemption Cancelation of a program by an *affiliate* after agreement to carry the program, or cancelation of an episode by a *network* to air a news or entertainment *special;* also applied to cancelation of a commercial sold at a special preemptible price to accommodate another commercial sold at full rate.

Premiere Week Start of the new fall prime-time season.

Premium Networks In television and radio, pay services costing subscribers an extra monthly fee over and above basic cable; in cable, called *pay cable;* also includes *STV, SMATV, MMDS* and *DBS* services; in radio, called premium *cable FM.*

Prerun Showing before network television air date (usually on pay television).

Presence Quality of audio that seems close to the speaker (rather than far away).

Presold Series episodes or film idea sold before being produced (generally related to high reputation of the producer). See also *Buying* and *Prebuying.*

Prime Time Television *daypart;* in practice, 8 to 11 P.M. (EST) six days a week and 7 to 11 P.M. Sundays. Technically, any three consecutive hours between 7 P.M. and midnight.

Prime-Time Access Rule FCC rule forbidding network affiliates from carrying more than three hours of network programs and *off-network* reruns (with some exceptions) in the four hours starting at 7 P.M. EST.

Production Fee License the broadcast networks pay for new programs.

Product-Purchase Data Information from electronically-scanned lines on most retail merchandise; correlated with television viewing patterns by ratings such as ScanAmerica.

Program Availabilities Syndicated programs not yet under contract in a market, therefore available to stations for license.

Program Department Division of *PBS* that develops and handles new programs, scheduling and long-range program planning.

Program Fair Annual fall meeting for public television program directors to screen pilot programs and read program proposals for public television programs.

Program Operations Department of *PBS* that handles daily scheduling of satellite *transponders.*

Program Practices Department Network department that clears all programs, *promos* and commercials before airing, responsible for administration of network guidelines on such subjects as sex, race and profanity. Also called "standards and practices" or "continuity acceptance department." Function also performed at every station.

Promo A broadcast advertising spot announcing a new program or episode or encouraging viewing of a *station's* or *network's* entire schedule.

Promotion Informational advertising of programs, *stations* or *networks.*

Prosocial Behavior and ideas that appear to provide constructive role models and uphold the highest traditional social values.

Psychographics Descriptive information of the lifestyles of audience members, includes attitudes on religion, family, social issues, interests, hobbies and political opinions.

Public Broadcasting Service (PBS) The noncommercial, federally supported interconnection service that distributes programming nationally to member public television stations; serves as a representative of the *public television* industry.

Public Radio The noncommercial radio stations in the United States qualifying for grants from the *Corporation for Public Broadcasting;* mostly FM licensees.

Public Station Television or radio station receiving a grant from the *Corporation for Public Broadcasting;* prior to 1967 called educational station; licensed by the FCC as a noncommercial educational broadcast station.

Public Television (PTV) Overall term replacing educational television to describe federally funded noncommercial television.

Qualitative Research Systematically gathered information on broadcast and cable audiences and program viewing other than ratings collected by the industry; also used in sociological research to contrast with other quantitative research methods.

Qube Warner Communications' two-way, interactive cable system installed in Columbus, Ohio, Pittsburgh and other cities.

Radio Superstation FM broadcast station retransmitted by satellite or microwave to distant cable systems for local subscribers.

Rankings In radio, lists of songs and albums by popularity, commonly published in trade magazines; in television, share rankings are lists of television shows with highest to lowest percentages of homes watching (out of homes using television).

Rate Structure Arrangements for revenue paybacks or licensing rights between cable operators and cable program suppliers.

Rating Audience measurement unit representing the percent of the potential total audience tuned to a specific program or station for program or time period.

Reach Cumulative audience or total circulation of a station or service.

Recaps Recapitulation of news events or news stories.

Recurrents Songs that have been number one on *playlists* in the recent past; used in scheduling songs on popular music stations.

Redundant Carriage In cable, distributing two stations with overlapping program content, as in two affiliates of the same broadcast network; sometimes applied to carriage of more than one public television station on a cable system.

Remote Live production from locations other than a studio (such as football games, live news events).

Remote Controls Hand-held devices for television set or VCR channel changing.

Rep See *Station Rep(resentative).*

Repositioning Moving stations and networks to different positions on a cable channel array; generally refers to moving broadcast stations away from channel numbers corresponding to their over-the-air channel numbers. Compare *Matching.*

Rerelease Second round of theater showings of a recently made movie.

Rerun Repeat showing of a program first aired earlier in the season or some previous season. Commonly applied to series episodes.

Resale Rights Permission from wholesaler to offer copyrighted material for retail sale (republication or retelecasting).

Reselling Offering a program to the public for purchase as in the videocassette rental and sales business. See also *Resale Rights*.

Reserve Price The minimum acceptable bid for a syndicated television program.

Residual Rights Royalty payments for reuse of shows or, in the case of radio, voiced announcements, news features and other content.

Rest Length of time a feature film or other program is withheld from cable or broadcast syndication (or local station airing) to avoid losing appeal from overexposure.

Resting Shelving a movie or series for a period of time to make it seem fresh when revived.

Retransmission Consent Control by originating station of right to retransmit that station's signals for use by cable systems; also a proposal to require agreement from copyright holder before programs can be picked up by resale carriers (*common carriers*); issue particularly affects *superstations*, cable operators and writers/producers.

Reuse Fees *Royalties* for replay of recorded material.

Revenue Split Division of pay revenues from subscribers between cable operator and cable network (usually 60/40 or 50/50).

Reverse Telephone Directory A phone book arranged by addresses instead of names; can be purchased from urban telephone companies.

Rewrite Proposed redrafting of the Communications Act of 1934, introduced in early 1970s but dropped in 1979.

Rights Legal authority or permission to do something, especially with copyrighted material.

Rip and Read Simplest form of newscasting; announcer rips copy from wire service and reads it on the air.

Road-Blocking The simultaneous airing of a program or commercial on all three networks to gain maximum exposure for the content (for example, presidential addresses, political campaign spots and commercial spots).

Rocker Colloquial term for a radio station with a rock music *format*.

Rolling Averages In radio research, using different daily audience samples and averaging them together; used in telephone ratings research by Birch.

Rotation Scheduling Repeating programs (usually movies) four to six times during a month on different days and often in different dayparts to encourage viewing, creating a cumulatively large audience; used by pay cable and public television services.

Royalty *Compensation* paid to copyright holder for the right to use copyrighted material. See also *Copyright* and *Compulsory Licensing*.

Run The *play* of all episodes of a series one time.

Run-Through Staging of a proposed show for preview by program executives; often replaces script for game shows.

Sample Size Number of people surveyed (in radio or television, asked to fill out a diary or have a meter installed). See *In-Tab*.

Sampling Frame Population from which ratings sample is drawn.

Sandwich For affiliate news, splitting the local news into two sections placed before and after the network newscast; in promotion, standardized opening and closing segments of a *promo*.

Satellite Master Antenna Television See *SMATV*.

Satellite Piggybacking See *Piggybacking*.

Satellite Placement Location among various communication satellites used by cable program services.

Schedule The arrangement of programs in a sequence.

Scrambling Altering a television transmission so that a proper picture requires a special decoder; purpose is to prevent unauthorized reception.

Screener An assistant who preinterviews incoming callers or guests on participatory programs; also called *call screener*.

Screening In research, locating individuals fitting specific age or gender criteria.

Second Season Traditionally the 11 to 13 weeks of episodes (of new or continuing programs) beginning in January.

Self-Transmitting Reporter One with a "lunchbox" or miniature transmitter; does not need telephone lines to reach the broadcast studios.

Sellout Rate The percentage of advertising inventory sold.

Semipilot Sample videotape version of a proposed game show with audience and production devices (such as music) but no finished set.

Series Program that has multiple *episodes* sharing a common cast, plot line and situation.

Service Information Hourly reports (in some dayparts) on weather, traffic, school closings and so on, matters of practical value to local listeners.

Share A measurement unit for comparing audiences; represents the percentage of total listening or viewing audience (with sets on) tuned to a given station; total shares in a designated area in a given time period equal 100 percent.

Shelf Space Vacancies on the channel array of a cable system.

Shock Jocks Talk-show *hosts* and *disc jockeys* who attract attention with controversial material; generally targeting adult males with off-color patter and jokes, usually in major markets.

Shopping Services Cable networks supplying merchandise for purchase as long-form programming.

Short-Form Program material in less than 30-minute lengths on television; typically one to five minutes long for radio.

Shorts Very brief programs, usually five minutes or less in length; see also *Interstitial Programming*.

Signal-to-Noise Ratio Relationship between the amount of transmission noise in a signal and the intended sounds or data.

Sitcom See *Situation Comedy*.

Situation Comedy A program (usually a half-hour in length) in which stereotyped characters react to new plots or altered situations.

Skew Graphs Bar graphs showing the percentage of each of six demographic groups a station reaches; used to compare all stations in a market.

Slivercasting Very narrowly targeted programming, used of cable networks that distribute only to small total audience, especially programming in foreign language or appealing to a hobby group.

Slow Builders Programs acquiring a loyal audience only after many months on the air.

Small-Market Stations Broadcast stations in markets 101 to 210+, as defined by the ratings companies. See also *Large-Market Stations, Mid-Market Stations* and *Major Market*.

Small Sweeps July ratings period. See *Sweeps*.

SMATV Satellite master antenna television; satellite-fed television serving multiunit dwellings through a single satellite earth station; service distributed within a restricted geographic (private property) area not requiring a franchise to cross city streets or public rights-of-way; otherwise similar to cable service; charges a monthly fee and usually delivers a mix of satellite-distributed pay and basic networks.

Soap Opera A serial drama generally scheduled on broadcast networks during weekday afternoons. Advertisers (such as laundry detergent manufacturers) targeting homemakers dominate advertising time.

Soft News Opposite of *hard*, fast-breaking news; consists of *features* and reports that do not depend on timely airing (for example, medical reports, entertainment industry stories, hobby material).

Sound Bed Musical background; an instrumental beginning and ending for commercials, station identifications or other on-air talk; applied especially to radio.

Special One-time entertainment or news program with special interest; usually applied to *network* programs that interrupt regular schedules.

Specialized Premium Networks *Pay cable* services targeting a less broadly defined audience than a *general premium service*, usually carrying a more restricted schedule of programs (all adult, all culture and arts, all sports).

Spectacular Older term for network television one-time-only programs interrupting regular scheduling. See *Special*.

Spinoff A series using a secondary character from another series as the lead in a new prime-time series, usually on the same network. Compare *Clone*.

Stacking Sequential airing of several hours of the same kind of programs; similar to *block programming*.

Standard Error Statistical term accounting for unavoidable measurement differences between any sample and the population from which it was drawn.

Standards and Practices Department See *Program Practices Department*.

Station Facility operated by licensee to broadcast radio or television signals on an assigned frequency; may be *affiliated* by contract with a *network* (for example, ABC, NPR) or may be *independent* (unaffiliated); may be commercial or noncommercial.

Station Program Cooperative (SPC) The vehicle for public television station participation in choosing the national program schedule carried by *PBS*.

Station Rep(resentative) Firm acting as sales agent for client station's advertising time in the national market.

Staying Power A series idea's ability to remain popular year after year.

Step Deal Agreement to supply funds to develop a program idea in stages from expanded concept statement to scripts to *pilot* to four or more episodes.

Stockpiling Preemptive buying of *syndicated* programs for future use that also keeps them off the market and unavailable to competitors. See also *Warehousing*.

Stop Set Interruption of music on radio to air commercials or other nonmusic material.

Stringer A free-lance reporter paid per story rather than by hour or month.

Stripping Across-the-board scheduling; putting successive episodes of a program into the same time period every day, five days per week (for example, placing *Star Trek* every evening at 7 P.M.).

Strip Run/Strip Slot See *Stripping*.

Stunting Frequent adding of *specials* and shifting of programs in schedule; also using *long-form* for a program's introduction or character *crossovers*; goal is to attract audience attention and consequent viewership; frequently used in the week preceding the kickoff of a new fall season combined with heavy *promotion*; also used in *sweeps*.

STV See *Subscription Television*.

Subscription Television (STV) Over-the-air *pay television* (scrambled).

Subsidiary Communications Authorization (SCA) FCC permission to use subcarriers for an FM channel to piggyback other material, such as readings for the visually handicapped or computer data transmissions; requires a special decoder.

Substitution Cable subscribers replacing one cable pay service with another.

Superband Channels on a coaxial cable between the broadcast frequencies of channels 13 and 14 (above VHF and below UHF); requires a converter or VCR tuner.

Superstation An *independent* television *station* that has its signal retransmitted by satellite to distant cable companies for redistribution to subscribers (for example, WTBS-TV, formerly WTCG, from Atlanta, Georgia).

Sweeps The periods each year when Arbitron and Nielsen gather audience data for the entire country; the ratings base from a sweep determines the network and station rates for advertising time until the next sweep. For television, the four times are November (fall season ratings most important, becomes ratings base for the rest of the year); February (rates fall season again plus replacements); May (end-of-year ratings); and July, when a small sweep takes place (summer replacements). Radio sweeps occur at different times and vary from 48 weeks to two to six occasions annually depending on market size.

Switch-In Adding a new cable service to an established lineup (usually involves canceling one existing service).

Switch-Out Dropping one cable service from an established lineup, generally to replace it with another service.

Syndex *Syndicated Exclusivity Rule* governing the syndication of television programs.

Syndicated Exclusivity Rule Called "*syndex*," a former FCC rule (reinstated for 1989) that requires cable systems bringing in *distant signals* to block out syndicated programming (usually on *superstations*) for which a local broadcaster owns exclusive rights.

Syndication The marketing of programs on a station-by-station basis (rather than through a *network*) to *affiliates*, *independents*, or *cable systems* for a specified number of plays; *syndicators* are companies that hold the rights to distribute programs nationally or internationally. See also *Off-Network Syndication*.

Syndication Barter Practice in which advertiser rather than *station* buys rights to *syndicated* program and barters remaining spots to stations in exchange for free airing of its own spots in the program. Same as *Barter Syndication*.

Syndication Window Length of time a program, usually a feature film, is made available to broadcast stations, generally ranging from three to six years, may be as short as two months for pay television. See also *Pay Window*.

Syndicator A company marketing television or radio programs to stations and cable systems within the United States and other countries.

Talk Radio *format* characterized by conversation between program hosts and callers, interviews and monologues by personalities.

Targeting Aiming programs (generally by selecting appropriate appeals) at a demographically or psychographically defined audience.

Tease A very brief news item or program spot intended to lure potential audience into watching or listening to the succeeding program or news story; referred to as the "teaser" when used as a program introduction.

Telecourses Instructional courses viewed on public television or a cable network, offered for credit in conjunction with local colleges and universities.

Teletext One-way electronic publishing service, using the vertical blanking interval of the broadcast signal. See also *Videotex* and *Cabletext*.

Tent-Poling Placing a highly rated program between two series with lower ratings (often new programs); intended to prop up the ratings of the preceding and following programs.

Theme Weeks Daily movies grouped by genre or star on independent television stations.

Tiering Combining cable channels to sell at a package price; may be only basic services or a combination of pay and basic networks.

Time-Buyers Advertising agency executives who purchases station time on behalf of their client advertisers.

Titles Text portion of a program with the name of the program or stars or credits or source.

Tonnage Raw audience size (as opposed to demographic subgroups); used in advertising.

Top 40 Radio music *format* consisting of continuous replay of the 40 highest-rated popular songs; generally superseded by CHR and AC except in the largest markets.

Tracking Monitoring a syndicated or local program's ratings over time, often in several different markets if syndicated.

Trafficking Rules Former FCC prohibitions against resale of a station license for a period of three years; no longer in effect.

Transponder One of several units on a communications satellite that both receives *uplink* signals and retransmits them as *downlink* signals (amplified on another frequency). Some users lease the right from satellite operators to use entire transponder (40 MHz bandwidth); others lease only a part of a transponder's capacity. Most satellites have 24 transponders nowadays.

Treatment Outline of a new program (applied especially to *soap operas*); describes characters and setting of program (before a script is prepared).

Trending Graphing ratings/shares over a period of time or on a series of stations to anticipate future ratings/shares, especially of syndicated series; same as *tracking*.

TSL Time spent listening; a measurement of continuous tuning to one radio station.

Tuning Inertia A theory that viewers tend to view the next program on a channel without switching until moved by unacceptable programs to actively switch.

Turnover Changes in the numbers of subscribers, listeners or viewers; in cable, the ratio of disconnecting to newly connecting subscribers. See also *Churn*.

TvQs Program and personality popularity ratings, typically measuring familiarity and liking, characterized by viewer surveys asking respondents to tell if a program or personality is "one of their favorites."

TVRO Television Receive-Only, referring to (owners of) backyard satellite dishes and the home satellite market. See also *DBS, Downlink* and *Network One Stop*.

UHF Ultra high frequency television signals having less advantageous positions on the broadcast band than *VHF*, requiring separate receiving antennas in the home. Most public and many commercial independent television stations are UHF.

Unbundling Breaking apart previously grouped programs, services or channels for separate licensing or member purchase; used in cable and public radio.

Underwriter Foundation or private corporation giving grant to cover costs of producing or airing a program or series on public television or radio.

Unduplicated Said of programming that is not available on any other local or imported station signal in a market.

Universe In cable, the total *population* of cable subscribers within all franchises.

Uplink Ground-to-satellite path; also the sending antenna itself (the reverse of *downlink*).

Upscale Audiences or subscribers with higher than average socioeconomic demographics, especially income. See also *Downscale*.

Uptrending A pattern of increasing ratings/shares over time.

VCR Videocassette recorder; used for playback and recording of television programs.

Vertical Documentaries In-depth factual treatment of a subject in many segments broadcast on the same day. See also *Horizontal Documentaries*.

Vertical Ownership Owning both the program supply and means of distribution; in cable, owning a cable program network as well as cable systems.

VHF Very high frequency; the segment of the electromagnetic spectrum in which television channels 2 to 13 fall, the most desirable broadcast television stations.

Videocassette Packaged videotape unit for recording or playback.

Videodisc Prerecorded video information on disc for playback only; usually read by laser.

Video Jockeys (VJs) The announcer/host on rock music programs, corresponding to a radio *disc jockey*.

Videos Taped musical performance shorts used for promotion and programming (on MTV and others).

Videotex Two-way interactive electronic signals requiring telephone line or cable to connect a central computer with the home user's computer screen. Compare *Teletext* and *Cabletext*.

Voicers Stories prerecorded by someone other than the announcer or *disc jockey*.

VTR Videotape recorder, also used for playback by television stations and networks.

Warehousing Purchasing and storing series and movies primarily to keep them from competitors. See also *Stockpiling*.

Weighting Statistically matching a sample to the population by increasing the numerical weight given to responses from one or more subgroups.

Wheel Visualization of the contents of an hour as a pie divided into wedges representing different content elements; used in radio to visualize a program *format*, showing designated sequences and lengths of all program elements such as musical numbers, news, sports, weather, *features*, *promos*, PSAs, commercials, IDs and time checks.

Window Period of time within which a network or distributor has the *rights* to show a feature film or other program (generally after the first theatrical distribution if the program was not made-for-pay); windows vary from a few months to many years. See also *Pay Window, Syndication Window* and *Broadcast Window*.

Wireless Cable See *MMDS*.

Zapping Erasing commercials on home-taped videocassettes; sometimes used synonymously with *flipping*—changing channels by remote control to avoid commercials.

Zipping Fast-forwarding through commercials on home-taped videocassettes.

BIBLIOGRAPHY OF BOOKS, REPORTS AND ARTICLES ON PROGRAMMING

This is a selective, annotated listing of recent books, articles, guides, reports, magazines and dissertations on broadcast and cable programs and programming. An item is included if it contributes unique or otherwise useful insights into the factors affecting television, radio or cable programming strategy for the 1990s. The bibliography lists major trade publications, books published since 1980 and scholarly research about programming theory and practice, but brief articles and industry reports only appear if they have unusual value to the study of programming. Additional citations of short or timely trade articles appear at each chapter's end under "Notes" and "Selected Sources." For publications prior to 1980, consult the bibliographies and chapter sources to the first and second editions of this book. Other useful sources are the annual bibliographies of the National Association of Broadcasters, scholarly journals, *Topicator* and computer indexes to the trade and popular press such as Infotrac.

Adams, William J.; Eastman, Susan Tyler; Horney, Larry J.; and Popovich, Mark N. "The Cancelation and Manipulation of Network Television Prime-Time Programs." *Journal of Communication* 33 (Winter 1983):10–27. Multipart analysis of new and established program cancelations by the three commercial networks in the last decade showing some effects of program schedule manipulation.

Agostino, Don. "Cable Television's Impact on the Audience of Public Television." *Journal of Broadcasting* 24 (Summer 1980):347–365. Scholarly analysis of Arbitron ratings data showing improved cumulative audiences for public broadcasting as a result of cable carriage.

Alternative Financing Options for Public Broadcasting, Vol. I & II. The Temporary Commission on Alternative Financing for Public Telecommunications, Report to the Congress of the United States, 1982. Major report on the options in new technologies, advertising and fund raising for public television and radio for the 1980s.

Arbitron Ratings/Radio. *Arbitron Radio Market Report Reference Guide: A Guide to Understanding and Using Radio Audience Estimates.* Laurel, Md.: Arbitron Ratings Company, 1987. A readable reference to Arbitron's radio ratings and how a station can use them; includes quiz and glossary.

Arbitron Ratings. *How to Read Your Arbitron Television Market Report.* Laurel, Md.: Arbitron Ratings Company, 1987. A revised and readable reference to Arbitron's television ratings books, including sample pages, glossary and other services provided by Arbitron.

Arnall, Gail. *Instructional Television Fixed Services: An Analysis of ITFS Operations*. Washington, D.C.: Corporation for Public Broadcasting, 1984. Analysis of ITFS finances, audiences and schedules intended for public broadcasters.

Attracting Minority Audiences to Public Television. Washington, D.C.: Corporation for Public Broadcasting, 1981. Report prepared by Booz-Allen & Hamilton based on data collected in conjunction with public television studies by Ronald E. Frank and Marshall G. Greenberg; segments minority audience on common interests and needs.

Aumente, Jerome. *New Electronic Pathways: Videotex, Teletext, and Online Databases*. Newbury Park, Calif.: Sage, 1987. Analysis of latest trends in text-oriented technologies, based on first-hand interviews, site visits and unpublished materials.

Austin, Bruce A. "People's Time in a Medium-Sized Market: A Content Analysis." *Journalism Quarterly* 57 (Spring 1980):67–70. Analysis of commercial network-affiliate programming during the 4:00 to 8:00 P.M. time period.

Austin, Bruce A., ed. *Current Research in Film: Audiences, Economics and Law, Vol. 1 & 2*. Norwood, N.J.: Ablex, 1985, 1986. Scholarly research studies on feature films and made-for-television films.

Baldwin, Thomas F., and McVoy, D. Stevens. *Cable Communications*. Second edition. Englewood Cliffs, N.J.: Prentice-Hall, 1988. Definitive text on the technology, regulation and operations of cable systems and cable program suppliers, including the Cable Act of 1984; detailed, readable and scholarly.

Barnouw, Erik. *Tube of Plenty: The Evolution of American Television*. Revised edition. New York: Oxford University Press, 1982. Condensed version of his monumental *History of Broadcasting in the United States* in three volumes, this is a one-volume, authoritative and readable history of television and the influences on it.

Barrett, Marvin, ed. *Broadcast Journalism 1979–1981: The Eighth Alfred I. Dupont–Columbia University Survey of Broadcast Journalism*. New York: Everest House, 1982. Biennial survey of trends in news programming at the network and local level.

Bedell, Sally. *Up the Tube: Prime-Time Television and the Silverman Years*. New York: Viking Press, 1981. An informal, anecdotal excursion through recent network entertainment programming.

Bellamy, Robert V., Jr. "Impact of the Television Marketplace on the Structure of Major League Baseball." *Journal of Broadcasting & Electronic Media* 32 (Winter 1988):73–87. An historical and analytic examination of the relationship between Major League Baseball and the broadcast television and cable industries.

Besen, Stanley M., and Johnson, Leland L. *An Economic Analysis of Mandatory Leased Channel Access for Cable Television*. Santa Monica, Calif.: Rand Corporation, 1982. Analyzes cable regulation and the access issue from an economic standpoint; prepared for the Markle Foundation.

Beville, Hugh M., Jr. *Audience Ratings: Radio, Television and Cable*. Hillsdale, N.J.: Lawrence Erlbaum Associates, 1985. Comprehensive text on the generation, interpretation and application of industry ratings; includes history, ratings methodologies, qualitative ratings, cable ratings and current uses and problems with ratings.

Beyond the Ratings. Laurel, Md.: Arbitron Ratings Company, 1977 to date. Monthly trade newsletter on developments in and applications of Arbitron local radio and television ratings for broadcasters.

Billboard: The International Newsweekly of Music and Home Entertainment. New York, 1888 to date. Weekly trade magazine of the record industry.

Billboard. *Billboard Salutes Westwood One*. Los Angeles: MCA Records, 1986. Special report on the growth and achievements of Westwood One radio, including Mutual services.

Blau, Robert T. "To Franchise or Not to Franchise: Is That Really the Question?"

Journal of Broadcasting & Electronic Media 31 (Winter 1987):95–101. Comment on Thomas Hazlett's article, criticizing his lack of concern for political economics.

Blum, Richard A., and Lindheim, Richard D. *Primetime: Network Television Programming.* Boston: Focal Press, 1987. Comprehensive examination of network programming theory and strategy, the development process, personnel structures and organizations affecting prime-time television on ABC, CBS and NBC.

Boemer, Marilyn Lawrence. "Correlating Lead-In Show Ratings with Local Television News Ratings." *Journal of Broadcasting & Electronic Media* 31 (Winter 1987): 89–94. Scholarly study showing moderate to high positive correlations between lead-in show ratings and local news ratings for three major-market network-affiliates over a two-year period.

Bortz, Paul I. *Great Expectations: A Television Manager's Guide to the Future.* Washington, D.C.: National Association of Broadcasters, 1986. Projections on the television station and network business, including impacts of cable and new technologies, leading into the 1990s.

Bortz, Paul, and Mendelsohn, Harold. *Radio Today—and Tomorrow.* Washington, D.C.: National Association of Broadcasters, 1982. In-depth analysis of the radio audience and usage patterns, assessing the trends affecting radio in the 1980s.

Broadcaster: The Magazine for Communicators. 1942 to date. Canadian trade magazine on the radio, television and cable industries, with especial emphasis on news.

Broadcasting. 1931 to date; cable added in 1972. Major weekly trade magazine of the broadcasting industry; see "Special Reports" on cable, children's television, independents, journalism, media corporations, radio, reps, satellites, sports, syndication and television programming listed in this bibliography.

Broadcasting and the Law. Knoxville, Tenn.: Perry Publications, 1972 to date. Twice-monthly newsletter and supplements explaining findings of the Federal Communications Commission, courts and Congress affecting broadcast operations.

Broadcasting/Cablecasting Yearbook. Washington, D.C.: Broadcasting Publications, 1935 to date, annual. Basic trade directory of radio and television stations and support industries; added cable in 1980.

Brooks, Tim, and Marsh, Earle. *The Complete Directory to Prime Time Network TV Shows: 1946–Present.* Third edition. New York: Ballantine, 1985. Annotated directory of most network television programs with details on casts and content of the program; updated from 1981 edition.

Brotman, Stuart N. *Broadcasters Can Negotiate Anything.* Washington, D.C.: National Association of Broadcasters, 1988. Practical manual on negotiating ploys, covering advertising sales, radio ratings and syndicated television program contracts; includes exercises and worksheets.

Broughton, Irv. *The Art of Interviewing for Television, Radio and Film.* Blue Ridge Summit, Penn.: TAB Books, 1981. Anecdotal guide to eliciting entertaining live interviews.

Broughton, Irv. *Producers on Producing: The Making of Film and Television.* Jefferson, N.C.: McFarland, 1986. Entertaining interviews with TV writers, producers and program executives on their daily problems, personal philosophies and decision-making practices.

Brown, Les. *Les Brown's Encyclopedia of Television.* New York: Zoetrope, 1982. Expanded version of the *New York Times Encyclopedia of Television;* descriptive and analytic comment on facts of network television programming, economics and personalities in the 1970s.

Browne, Bortz and Coddington. "The Impact of Competitive Distribution Technologies on Cable Television." *Cable and Its Competitors: An Analysis of Services, Economics and Subscribership.* Washington, D.C.: National Cable Television Association, March 1982. Report commissioned by NCTA assessing the demand for single channel STV in competition for cable; also examines the findings of the Arthur D. Little DBS Study.

Bryant, Jennings, and Anderson, Daniel R., eds. *Children's Understanding of Television: Research on Attention and Comprehension.*

New York: Academic Press, 1983. Compendium of funded research reports covering the process aspects (rather than the effects) of children's television viewing and learning.

Burke Marketing Research, Inc. *The Effects of Station Environment on Television Advertising Communications: Independent Stations vs. Affiliated Stations, 1981*. Washington, D.C.: Association of Independent Television Stations, 1981. Analysis of telephone survey comparing audience response to and perception of ads on independent television stations and network-affiliated stations.

Burns, George A. *The Burns Media Report on AM Radio*. Studio City, Calif.: Burns Media Consultants, 1982. Assessment of the future of AM radio, stressing format marketability.

Cable Marketing. New York, 1981 to date. Monthly trade magazine covering the marketing and promotion of cable systems and cable network programming for cable executives.

Cable Services Directory. Washington, D.C.: National Cable Television Association. 1978 to date, annual (title varies). Annual directory of information on individual cable systems including amounts and types of local origination.

Cable Strategies: The Operations and Marketing Journal of the Cable Television Industry. Englewood, Colo., 1986 to date. Monthly trade magazine published by Communications Technology Publications Corp., featuring brief articles on hot aspects of cable television management and marketing.

Cable Television Business (formerly, *TVC*). Colorado, 1963 to date. Semimonthly cable-industry trade magazine published by Cardiff Publishing Company, focusing on issues and events affecting cable system managers.

"Cable Television Symposium." *Comm/Ent: A Journal of Communications and Entertainment Law* 3 (Summer 1981):557–767. Special issue devoted to legal concerns in cable television touching on programming.

CableVision. Denver, Colo., 1975 to date. Biweekly cable-industry trade magazine published by International Thompson

Communications, devoted to programming, economics and marketing of cable and related new technologies; in-depth articles and monthly series and cable industry statistics.

Cantor, Muriel G. *Prime-Time Television: Content and Control*. Beverly Hills: Sage, 1980. Research-based text on prime-time entertainment using a verbal model of constraint patterns; covers program forms, legal and organization contexts and audiences from a sociological perspective.

Cantor, Muriel G., and Pingree, Suzanne. *The Soap Opera*. Beverly Hills: Sage, 1983. Scholarly overview of research on the soap opera format, content and audience, placing them in a social and historical context.

Carey, John; Gherardi, Thomas; Kappes, Harold; and Moss, Mitchell. *Modularization and Packaging of Public Television Programs*. Washington, D.C.: Corporation for Public Broadcasting, 1983. Description of the distribution chain for noncommercial entertainment and instructional programs.

Carey, John, and Moss, Mitchell. *Telecommunications Technologies and Public Broadcasting*. Washington, D.C.: Corporation for Public Broadcasting, 1984. Advice on the use of alternative technologies such as cable, electronic text, videocassettes, videodiscs, teleconferencing and home computers for the delivery of public broadcasting services.

Cassata, Mary, and Skill, Thomas. *Live on Daytime Television: Tuning-In American Serial Drama*. Norwood, N.J.: Ablex, 1983. Scholarly content analyses of daytime network soap opera genre, including lifestyles, social issues and interactions.

Chambers, Everett. *Producing TV Movies*. New York: Prentice-Hall, 1986. Anecdotal look at the made-for-TV movie development process, including how a project is conceived, sold, written, produced and broadcast.

Channels: The Business of Communication (formerly, *Channels of Communication*), New York, 1980 to date. Monthly magazine focusing on television programming for the broadcast industry and informed consumers, edited by Les Brown, former *New York Times* television critic.

Channels Field Guide. Annual since 1983. End-of-year prospective on the coming year in broadcasting, cable and new media technologies; charts, tables and graphs.

Childers, Terry L., and Krugman, Dean M. "The Competitive Environment of Pay Per View." *Journal of Broadcasting & Electronic Media* 31 (Summer 1987):335–342. Results of a field test comparing users' perspectives of pay-per-view, pay cable and videocassette rentals.

Clift, Charles III, and Greer, Archie, eds. *Broadcasting Programming: The Current Perspective*. Seventh edition. Washington, D.C.: University Press of America, 1981. Facsimile reprints from trade and scholarly programming literature on ratings, network primetime programming schedules, network program types, local television programming, public broadcasting, radio programming, program regulation, and the role of citizen groups in broadcasting.

Christensen, Gary L., chairman. *Cable Television: Retrospective and Prospective*. Washington, D.C.: Practicing Law Institute, 1985. Handbook on cable law, organized to serve cable professionals as well as attorneys; contains readable introductory analyses by single authors on aspects of cable technology, finance, copyright, regulation, labor, public access, First Amendment and antitrust; includes Cable Communications Act of 1984.

Cole, Barry G., ed. *Television Today: A Close-Up View: Readings from "TV Guide."* New York: Oxford University Press, 1981. Compendium of reprints of *TV Guide* articles from the 1970s.

Comm/Ent: A Journal of Communications and Entertainment Law. San Francisco: Hastings College of the Law, 1978 to date. Law journal, published quarterly, containing articles summarizing the law on specific issues including broadcasting and new technologies.

Community Television Review. Washington, D.C.: National Federation of Local Cable Programmers, 1979 to date. Bimonthly newsletter of the NFLCP for local cable programmers, covering public, educational and governmental access television on cable and local cable origination.

Compaine, Benjamin M., ed. *Anatomy of the Communications Industry: Who Owns the Media?* Second edition. White Plains, N.Y.: Knowledge Industry Publications, 1982. Original edition subtitled "Concentration of Ownership in the Mass Communication Industry"; contains eight original articles providing tabular and text information on ownership of the major media, including radio, television and cable.

Corporation for Public Broadcasting. *A Report to the People: 20 Years of Your National Commitment to Public Broadcasting, 1967–1987, and 1986 Annual Report*. Washington, D.C.: Corporation for Public Broadcasting, 1987. Brief history of public broadcasting and report on current programming and economics in public television and public radio.

Cosell, Howard, with Bonventre, Peter. *I Never Played the Game*. New York: William Morrow, 1985. Insider's controversial look at the business of network television sports by the celebrity sportscaster.

Current. Washington, D.C., 1981 to date. Weekly Washington newspaper focusing on public broadcasting.

Daily Variety, Trade Newspaper of the Film and Television Industries. Hollywood/New York: Variety, 1905 to date. Daily version of *Variety* magazine oriented toward film and television production and programming.

David, Nina. *TV Season*. Phoenix, Ariz.: Oryx, 1976 to 1979, annual. Annotated guide to the previous season's commercial and public network and major syndicated television programs.

De Luca, Mariann. *Survey of Radio Stations*. New York: Torbet Radio, 1983. Series of 1983 surveys of radio managers on their programming practices.

DeMaeseneer, Paul. *Here's the News: A Radio News Manual*. Kuala Lumpur, Malaysia: Asia-Pacific Institute for Broadcasting Development, 1982. Practical handbook on the basics of radio news announcing and reporting.

DeSonne, Marsha L. *Radio, New Technology and You.* Washington, D.C.: National Association of Broadcasters, April 1982. Overview of new radio technologies as revenue-producing options for radio broadcasters.

DiGiacomo, Frank. "Independent Television: Today's Questions, Tomorrow's Answers." *View* (5 January 1987):91–120. Trade-oriented analysis of the state of independent television, including predictions on television programming options.

Dominick, Joseph R., and Fletcher, James E. *Broadcasting Research Methods.* Boston: Allyn & Bacon, 1985. Comprehensive text on survey research methods and their application to industry ratings.

Dranov, Paula. *Inside the Music Publishing Industry.* White Plains, N.Y.: Knowledge Industries Publications, 1980. Overview of the structure of the music publishing industry, covering copyright, royalties, contracts, domestic and foreign markets; with charts, tables and a directory of music publishers.

Duncan, James H., Jr., ed. *American Radio.* Indianapolis, Ind.|: Duncan Media Enterprises, semiannual. Reference source on Arbitron and Birch audience, programming and sales ratings and statistics on both national and local market levels; spring and fall editions annually.

Duncan, James H., Jr. *American Radio, Tenth Anniversary Issue, 1976–1986: A Prose and Statistical History.* Indianapolis, Ind.: Duncan's American Radio, 1986. Commentary and historical statistics on a decade of radio formats.

Durham, Dona A., and Meyer, Timothy. "TV and Prosocial Behavior: A Critical Review of Key Issues and Literature." Paper presented at the International Communication Association, May 1983. Analysis, based on dissertation research, of the issues, concepts and literature of prosocial behavior, especially in children's television programming.

Eastman, Susan Tyler. "Policy Issues Raised by the FCC's 1983 and 1984 Subcarrier Decisions." *Journal of Broadcasting* 28 (Summer 1984):289–303. Description of uses of radio and television subcarriers and analysis of policy questions.

Eastman, Susan Tyler, and Klein, Robert A. *Strategies in Broadcast and Cable Promotion.* Chicago, Ill.: Waveland, 1988 (originally published by Wadsworth, 1982). Text on strategic planning for marketing networks, stations and cable systems to audiences and advertisers; includes strategies and tactics for promoting images, personalities, formats, programs and audience and sales contests written by industry experts.

Eisner, Joel, and Krinsky, David. *Television Comedy Series: An Episode Guide to 153 TV Sitcoms in Syndication.* Jefferson, N.C.: McFarland, 1984. Handy synopses of each episode of widely syndicated, long-running situation comedies intended for television station programmers.

Electronic Media. Chicago, 1982 to date. Weekly trade periodical published by Crain Communications, covering topical news in broadcasting, cable and new media technologies.

Eliot, Marc. *Televisions: One Season in American Television.* New York: St. Martin's Press, 1983. Anecdotal overview of the people, programs and events of the 1981–82 season as seen by a producer and critic.

An Evaluation of 'Over Easy': A Television Series for and About Older People. Washington, D.C.: Corporation for Public Broadcasting, 1980. Evaluation of this targeted and purposive program series prepared by the Office of Communication Research using innovative program evaluation methodologies.

Fang, Irving E. *Television News, Radio News.* Third edition. Minneapolis: Rada Press, 1980. Overview of news reporting, presentation and delivery.

FCC Sensitivity Training Guide for TV Program Directors. Washington, D.C.: National Association of Broadcasters, 1979. Handbook on FCC rules and practices pertaining to programming, especially Fairness Doctrine and equal time regulations.

Fisher, Michael G. "A Survey of Selected Television Station Program Managers:

Their Backgrounds and Perceptions of Role." Master's thesis, Temple University, 1978. Survey of 160 members of the National Association of Television Program Executives on personal experiences, background and position in management hierarchies.

Fletcher, James E. *Broadcast Research Definitions*. Washington, D.C.: National Association of Broadcasters, 1988. Most recent guide to the terminology used in broadcast ratings and research.

Fletcher, James E., ed. *Handbook of Radio and TV Broadcasting: Research Procedures in Audience, Program and Revenues*. New York: Van Nostrand Reinhold, 1981. Compendium of rating and survey research procedures for television and radio researchers; includes reprints of articles and ratings.

Fletcher, James E. *Music and Program Research*. Washington, D.C.: National Association of Broadcasters, 1987. Updated review of methods and practices in radio programming research.

Fletcher, James E. *Squeezing Profits out of Ratings: A Manual for Radio Managers, Sales Managers and Programmers*. Washington, D.C.: National Association of Broadcasters, 1985. A self-guided course in understanding and using radio audience ratings; includes exercises, lectures, examples, readings and a computer program.

Fletcher, James E., and Wimmer, Roger D. *Call-Out Research in Managing Radio Stations*. Washington, D.C.: National Association of Broadcasters, n.d. Manual for telephone surveys of listener song preferences to aid in construction of music playlists.

Fletcher, James E., and Wimmer, Roger D. *Focus Group Interviews in Radio Research*. Washington, D.C.: National Association of Broadcasters, August 1981. Practical guide to conducting focus group interviews on radio listener preferences and lifestyles using a facilitator.

Forbes, Dorothy, and Layng, Sanderson. *The New Communicators: A Guide to Community Programming*. Washington, D.C.: Communications Press, 1980. Originally published by the Canadian Cable Television Association, written to aid local cable programmers in focusing community television efforts.

Foster, Eugene S. *Understanding Broadcasting*. Second edition. Reading, Mass.: Addison-Wesley, 1982. Introductory text on the technology, economics, regulation and programming of television and radio.

Fowler, Mark S., and Bresser, Daniel L. "A Marketplace Approach to Broadcast Regulation." *Texas Law Review* 60:207 (1982):250–255. Statement of the legal and policy implications of the competitive market approach to broadcast regulation by the former chairman of the Federal Communications Commission.

Frank, Ronald E., and Greenberg, Marshall G. *Audiences for Public Television*. Beverly Hills: Sage, 1982. Analysis of national survey data on the viewing habits and leisure patterns of the public television audiences, translated into strategies for programming public stations.

Frank, Ronald E., and Greenberg, Marshall G. *The Public's Use of Television: Who Watches and Why*. Beverly Hills: Sage, 1980. Interest segmentation analysis of the public television audience.

Fuller, John W. *Who Watches Public Television?* Alexandria, Va.: Public Broadcasting Service, 1986. Report on the audiences for national public television, written by PBS's director of research.

Gantz, Walter, and Eastman, Susan Tyler. "Viewer Uses of Promotional Media to Find Out About Television Programs." *Journal of Broadcasting* 27 (Summer 1983):269–277. Report of survey of viewers' uses of promotional media such as guides, listings and promos and the value placed on them.

Gianakos, Larry James. *Television Drama Series Programming: A Comprehensive Chronicle, 1982–1984*. Metuchen, N.J.: Scarecrow Press, 1988. Cross-referenced encyclopedia of dramatic series and special programs on the three commercials television networks, including date, day and cast; supplements earlier volumes covering programs since 1947.

Gitlin, Todd. *Inside Prime Time*. Revised edition. New York: Pantheon, 1985. Mass market book based on 200 interviews with network executives, producers, writers, agents and actors, delving into the process of prime-time program selection and cancelation; updated.

Goodhardt, G.J.; Ehrenberg, A.S.C.; and Collins, M.A. *The Television Audience*. Lexington, Mass.: Lexington Press (Saxon House), 1975. Classic scholarly analysis of research on program scheduling assessing audience flow, lead-in effects, loyalty and viewing patterns, published originally in Great Britain.

Gordon, Meryl. "Colossus of Cable." *Channels* (6 October 1986):26–33. Speculative analysis of the role of Tele-Communications Inc. in the cable industry; report on TCI president, John Malone.

Greenberg, Bradley S. *Life on Television: Content Analyses of U.S. TV Drama*. Norwood, N.J.: Ablex, 1980. Studies of the content of dramatic series on prime-time network television.

Greenberg, Bradley S.; Neuendorf, Kimberly; Buerkey-Rothfuss, Nancy; and Henderson, Laura. "The Soaps: What's On and Who Cares?" *Journal of Broadcasting* 26 (Spring 1982):519–535. Analysis of soap opera content and survey of soap viewers to determine viewing motives, involvement and possible effects.

Gross, Lynn Schafer. *The New Television Technologies*. Second edition. Dubuque, Iowa: Wm. C. Brown, 1986. Overview textbook describing the technical workings and recent history and issues of traditional broadcasting, satellites, computers, cable, videodiscs, videotext, direct broadcasting and other new media technologies; revised and expanded.

Grossman, Gary H. *Saturday Morning TV*. New York: Dell, 1982. Popular essay on the cartoon fare delivered by the three commercial networks to children on weekends.

Grote, David. *The End of Comedy: The Sit-Com and the Comedic Tradition*. Hamden, Conn.: Shoe String Press, 1983. Scholarly tracing of the historical evolution of the comedic form from its origins to the present forms of comedy in network television programs.

A Guide to Understanding and Using Radio Audience Estimates. New York: Arbitron Ratings Company, 1987. Instructional manual for users of Arbitron radio ratings reports.

Hadden, Jeffrey K., and Swann, Charles E. *Prime Time Preachers: The Rising Power of Televangelism*. Reading, Mass.: Addison-Wesley, 1981. Brief overview of the major religious television personalities and their audiences.

Halberstam, David. *The Powers That Be*. New York: Alfred A. Knopf, 1979. Analytic history of four of the largest media institutions in America including CBS; emphasizes the role of Paley and his influence on CBS's programming.

Hazlett, Thomas W. "The Policy of Exclusive Franchising in Cable Television." *Journal of Broadcasting & Electronic Media* 31 (Winter 1987):1–20. Scholarly analysis of the grounds for cable franchises as natural monopolies. See also, in the same issue (pp. 95–101) Blau, Robert T. "To Franchise or Not to Franchise: Is That Really the Question?" and (pp. 98–101) Wirth, Michael O. "Comment on 'The Policy of Exclusive Franchising in Cable Television.'"

Head, Sydney W., and Sterling, Christopher H. *Broadcasting in America: A Survey of Electronic Media*. Fifth edition. Boston: Houghton Mifflin, 1987. Basic reference text on American broadcasting, covering technology, economics, regulation, history, social effects and programming; newest edition contains three chapters on program strategies, network and non-network programs by Susan Tyler Eastman.

Heeter, Carrie, and Greenberg, Bradley S. *Cableviewing*. Norwood, N.J.: Ablex, 1988. Unusual examination of the process of choosing channels to view in cable television homes; introduces concepts of viewing style and reports results of several scholarly studies of cable viewers.

Heighton, Elizabeth J., and Cunningham, Don R. *Advertising in the Broadcasting Media*. Second edition. Belmont, Calif.: Wadsworth, 1984. Expanded text on the history, campaign strategies, and principles of electronic media from the perspective of the advertiser and agency; includes case studies.

Henriksen, Frank. "A New Model of Duplication of Television Viewing: A Behavioral Approach." *Journal of Broadcasting & Electronic Media* 29 (Spring 1985): 135–145. Scholarly application of the author's model applied to adjacent programs on Denmark's single national television network.

Hiber, Jhan. *Hibernetics: A Guide to Radio Ratings and Research.* Los Angeles. R & R Books, 1984. A radio consultant's practical handbook to the programming and sales use of Arbitron and Birth ratings for radio stations.

Hiber, Jhan. *Winning Radio Research: Turning Research Into Ratings and Revenues.* Washington, D.C.: National Association of Broadcasters, 1987. Tips and techniques for conducting and interpreting radio audience research.

Hollowell, Mary Louise, ed. *The Cable/Broadband Communications Book, Vol. 3, 1982–1983.* Washington, D.C.: Communications Press, 1983. Most recent in a series tracing policy changes and problems in cable and related technologies.

The Home Video & Cable Yearbook, 1982–83. White Plains, N.Y.: Knowledge Industries Publications, 1982. Compendium of statistics on cable systems, networks and program services, operators and other aspects with brief summaries.

Howard, Herbert H. *Group and Cross-Media Ownership of Television Stations, 1987.* Washington, D.C.: National Association of Broadcasters, annually. Continuing series of reports on television station ownership commissioned by the National Association of Broadcasters; useful statistical profiles as of the first of each year.

Howard, Herbert H. *Ownership Trends in Cable Television, 1987.* Washington, D.C.: National Association of Broadcasters, annually. Continuing comparative series on the 50 largest cable multiple-system-operations; tables and charts.

Howard, Herbert H., and Kievman, Michael S. *Radio and TV Programming.* New York: Macmillan, 1983 (originally published by Grid). Station-oriented text on broadcast programming, covering history, appeals, audience, station management and criticism for commercial and noncommercial stations.

How to Read Your Arbitron Television Market Report. New York: Arbitron Ratings Company, 1987. Instruction manual for using Arbitron's local television station ratings, updated annually.

Intinoli, Michael. *Taking Soaps Seriously: The World of Guiding Light.* New York: Praeger, 1984. Ethnographic investigation of the production of the oldest network soap opera, CBS's *The Guiding Light,* owned and produced by Procter & Gamble.

INTV Journal: The Magazine of Independent Television. New York: View Communications, 1985 to date. Bimonthly (seven times a year) trade magazine for members of the Association of Independent Television Stations and others interested in the nonnetwork television business.

Jesuale, Nancy, ed., with Smith, Ralph Lee. *The Community Medium: Vol. I.* Arlington, Va.: Cable Television Information Center, 1982. First of two parts (second: *A Guide for Local Policy*), this book discusses cable technology and services within an historical perspective, including state-of-the-art options, intended for local government regulators.

Jeter, James Phillip. *A Comparative Analysis of the Programming Practices of Black-Owned Black-Oriented Radio Stations and White-Owned Black-Oriented Radio Stations.* Madison, Wis.: University of Wisconsin, 1981. Ph.D. dissertation on the influences of the owner's race on radio programming for the black audience.

Johnson, Rolland C.; Groth, Gary; and Lynch, Edith. "Trends in Broadcasting, Broadcast-Related Media, and Film." In *A Study on Creative Personnel in the Media Fields of Radio, Television and Film,* by Robert J. Anderson, Gary Groth, Rolland C. Johnson, Edith Lynch, Sonia P. Maltezou, and Robert J. Wuthnow. Washington, D.C.: National Endowment for the Arts, 7 July 1980. Chapter summarizing trends in industry structure and economics, including programming, emphasizing the impact of new technologies.

Johnston, Jerome, and Ettema, James S. *Positive Images: Breaking Stereotypes with Children's Television*. Beverly Hills: Sage, 1982. Review of the creation and audience viewing of the PBS series *Freestyle*.

Josephson, Larry, ed. *Telling the Story: NPR Guide to Radio Journalism*. Washington, D.C.: National Public Radio Publications, 1983. Practical handbook on radio reporting and announcing for public broadcasters.

Josephson, Larry. "Why Radio?" *Public Telecommunications Review* 7 (March/April 1979):6–18. Addresses Carnegie Commission's request for justification of public funding of public radio; this issue of *PTR* focuses entirely on radio and includes several articles on the future of public radio in the 1980s.

Kaplan, Barry. "Cable TV: The New Freedom Arrives." *Cable Strategies* (15 November 1987):30–33. Financial analyst's assessment of ancillary revenue sources and regulatory issues, reprinted from *The Cable Television Industry*, an investment publication of Goldman, Sachs & Co.

Katzman, Natan, and Wirt, Kenneth. *Public Television Programming Content by Category: Fiscal Year 1982*. Washington, D.C.: Corporation for Public Broadcasting, 1984. Latest in biennial series on national and local programming trends in public television, including ITV; tables and charts.

Katzman, Solomon; Katzman, Natan; and Mendel, Robin. *Public Radio Programming Content by Category: Fiscal Year 1982*. Washington, D.C.: Corporation for Public Broadcasting, 1985. Latest statistical report analyzing the programming of CPB-qualified public radio stations; tables and charts.

Keith, Michael. *Radio Programming: Consultancy and Formatics*. Boston: Focal Press, 1987. Industry-oriented analysis of current strategies and tactics for commercial radio stations, written by a radio programming consultant.

Kierstead, Phillip O. *All-News Radio*. Blue Ridge Summit, Penn.: TAB Books, 1980. Handbook for programming the all-news format on commercial stations.

King, Larry. *Larry King*. New York: Simon & Schuster, 1982. Popular, anecdotal autobiography by the nationally known late-night talk personality.

King, Larry, with Occhiogrosso, Peter. *Tell It to the King*. New York: Putnam, 1988. Anecdotes from 30 years of talk broadcasting and writing for *USA Today*.

Kirkley, Donald H., Jr., *Station Policy and Procedures: A Guide for Radio*. Washington, D.C.: National Association of Broadcasters, 1985. A manual on personnel policies for employees of broadcast stations.

Klein, Paul. "When Men Who Run TV Aren't That Stupid . . . They Know Us Better Than You Think." *New York*, January 25, 1971, pp. 20–29. Statement of Klein's programming strategy at NBC including the concept of the least objectional program.

Koughan, Martin. "The Fall and Rise of Public Television." *Channels*, May/June 1983. An informal overview of the political strengths and weaknesses of public television from a popular perspective.

Krasnow, Erwin G.; Longley, Lawrence D.; and Terry, Herbert A. *The Politics of Broadcast Regulation*. Third edition. New York: St. Martin's Press, 1982. Introduction to the five determining institutions in regulatory policy; includes five case studies, one of which deals with format changes, another with comparability for UHF television stations.

Leroy, David, and Leroy, Judith. *Impact of Cable Television on Public Television*. Washington, D.C.: Corporation for Public Broadcasting, 1983. Description of cable's impact on public television station audiences and memberships.

Levin, Murray B. *Talk Radio and the American Dream*. Lexington, Mass.: Lexington Books, 1987. Analysis of conversation by talk show participants in the Boston area, illustrating the types of callers and range of political perspectives.

Levinson, Richard, and Link, William. *Stay Tuned: An Inside Look at the Making of Prime-Time Television*. New York: St. Martin's Press, 1981. Insiders' view of the history of selected prime-time series by two commercial television producers.

Lewis, Raymond J. *Meeting Learners' Needs Through Telecommunications: A Directory and Guide to Programs.* Washington, D.C.: Center for Learning and Telecommunications, American Association for Higher Education, 1983. Guide to programs and projects completed and underway for the commercial and noncommercial instructional markets.

Liebert, Robert M., et al. *The Early Window: Effects of Television on Children and Youth.* Second edition. New York: Pergamon Press, 1987. Analysis of the research literature on children and television, including the 1972 Surgeon General's Report.

Lindlof, Thomas R. *Natural Audiences: Qualitative Research of Media Uses and Effects.* Norwood, N.J.: Ablex, 1987. Scholarly volume covering theory and techniques from symbolic interactionism, ethnomethodology, cognitive and ecological psychology and semiotic critical studies as adapted by mass media studies; authoritative academic contributors; indexed.

Listening to the Future: Cable Audio in the 80s. Washington, D.C.: National Public Radio, 1982. Report of research conducted principally by NPR's staff on the potential of cable audio, especially for public radio broadcasters.

Lloyd, Mark L. "A Descriptive Analysis of the Syndicated Religious Television Programs of Jerry Falwell, Rex Humbard and Oral Roberts." Ph.D. dissertation, the University of Michigan, 1980. Examination of the production of three nationally syndicated evangelical or fundamentalist television programs and their on-air personalities.

Lotteries & Contests: A Broadcaster's Handbook. Washington, D.C.: National Association of Broadcasters, 1985. Updated review of the common legal problems in on-air contesting, including recent FCC rulings.

Lull, James. *Popular Music and Communication.* Newbury Park, Calif.: Sage, 1987. A dozen essays commenting on commercial radio, videos, education and political communications as reflected in popular music.

Mahler, Richard. "Special Report: The State of Syndication." *Electronic Media.* 22 February 1988, pp. 1, 56–74. A detailed look at the television program syndication marketplace from a trade perspective, concluding that the gap between successful and scrambling companies is growing and that syndication has become another industry supported by blockbusters.

Mahony, Sheila; Demartino, Nick; and Stengel, Robert. *Keeping PACE with the New Television: Public Television and Changing Technology.* New York: Carnegie Corporation, 1980. Review of the developments in new technologies as they affect public television, prepared by three members of the Carnegie Commission's staff, proposing a nonprofit cable network for performing arts, culture and entertainment.

McCabe, Peter. *Bad News at Black Rock: The Sell-Out of CBS News.* New York: Arbor House, 1987. A former CBS senior producer details the rise and fall of the *CBS Morning News.*

McCavitt, William, and Pringle, Peter. *Electronic Media Management.* Boston: Focal Press, 1986. Text covering managerial issues and functions, including programming, at broadcast stations and for cable systems.

McNeil, Alex. *Total Television: A Comprehensive Guide to Programming from 1948 to the Present.* Second edition. New York: Viking Penguin, 1984. Brief factual backgrounding on all network television programs aired from 1948 to 1983.

Metzger, Gale D. "Cable Television Audiences: Learning from the Past and the Present." *Journal of Advertising Research* 23 (August/September 1983): 41–47. Review of the history of the impact of television on radio and the 1982 CONTAM report, concluding that cable will have little impact on radio and total television viewing and no impact on prime time viewing.

Miles, Daniel J.; Miles, Betty T.; and Miles, Martin J. *The Miles Chart Display of Popular Music.* New York: Arno Press, 1985. Week-by-week graphs of the chart history of nearly 10,000 records and 2,300 artists; one of the bibles of music radio programming.

Morgenstern, Steve, ed. *Inside the TV Business*. New York: Sterling, 1979. Eight chapters by outstanding experts on aspects of network television programming.

Multichannel News: The Newspaper for the New Electronic Media. New York, 1979 to date. Weekly trade newspaper of regulatory, programming, financial and technical events affecting the electronic media.

NAB/BFM. *1987 Radio Employee Compensation and Fringe Benefits Report*. Washington, D.C.: National Association of Broadcasters and Broadcast Financial Management Association, 1987. Tables of salary and compensation figures compiled from information reported by about half of commercial radio stations.

NAB/BFM. *1987 Television Employee Compensation and Fringe Benefits Report*. Washington, D.C.: National Association of Broadcasters and Broadcast Financial Management Association, 1988. Tables of salary and compensation figures compiled from information reported by 502 stations in May 1987.

NAB Legal Guide to FCC Broadcast Rules, Regulations and Policies. Washington, D.C.: National Association of Broadcasting, 1988. Regularly updated. Loose-leaf one-volume compilation of selected FCC broadcasting regulations (many on programming) with analysis and commentary designed for station managers.

National Federation of Local Cable Programmers. *Cable Programming Resource Directory 1987*. Washington, D.C.: Broadcasting Publications, 1987. A guide to local cable program centers and organization supplying full-length noncommercial programs and public service announcements.

Newcomb, Horace. *Television: The Critical View*. Fourth edition. New York: Oxford University Press, 1987. Provocative compilation of critical articles on issues in television.

Newcomb, Horace, and Alley, Robert S. *The Producer's Medium: Conversations with Creators of American T.V.* New York: Oxford University Press, 1983 (paper, 1985). Interviews with eight producers of commercial television programs critically analyzing their work and perspectives.

The New Television Technologies: The View from the Viewer-II, An American Consensus Report. New York: Benton & Bowles, May 1983. Second of two mail surveys on new television technologies focusing on cable and home video recording.

O'Donnell, Thomas, and Gissen, Jay. "A Vaster Wasteland?" *Forbes* (24 May 1982):109–116. Popular assessment of the direction of cable programming emphasizing economic limitations.

Oringel, Robert S. *The Access Management's Handbook: A Guide for Managing Community Television*. Boston: Focal Press, 1987. A guidebook for operating a cable television access channel, covering construction, training, management and audience measurement; includes highlights of community access station practices across the country.

Orton, Barry, ed. *Cable Television and the Cities: Local Regulation and Municipal Uses*. Madison: University of Wisconsin–Extension, 1982. Booklet on the process of municipal franchising.

Paiva, Bob. *The Program Director's Handbook*. Blue Ridge Summit, Penn.: TAB Books, 1983. Practical tips to guide production, scheduling, promotion, personnel, sales and research for radio programmers.

Paley, William S. *As It Happened: A Memoir*. New York: Doubleday, 1979. Personal reminiscences of an important figure in broadcast history; includes remarks on programming strategy with numerous anecdotal examples.

Palmer, Edward L., and Dorr, Aimee, eds. *Children and the Faces of Television*. New York: Academic Press, 1980. Collection of contributed articles on children's television emphasizing research and policy making.

Paper Tiger Television. *Deep Dish Directory: A Resource Guide for Grass Roots Television Producers, Programmers, Activists and Cultural Workers*. New York: Paper Tiger TV, 1986. A guide to public access television, describing the first public access satellite network and a listing of producers and access coordinators across the country who make or program the kind of programming featured in the Deep Dish series.

Parsons, Patrick. *Cable Television and the First Amendment*. Lexington, Mass.: Lexington Books, 1987. Detailed, scholarly review of court decisions and interpretations of freedom of speech and the press as applied to cable television.

The Project Team in Instructional Television. Washington, D.C.: Corporation for Public Broadcasting, 1983. Booklet describing options in personnel structures for production teams creating instructional series for schools, including functions and responsibilities.

Rader, Benjamin G. *In Its Own Image*. New York: Free Press, 1984. Scholarly history of television's role in the growth of sports in America.

Radio In Search of Excellence: Lessons from America's Best-Run Radio Stations. Washington, D.C.: National Association of Broadcasters, 1985. McKinsey & Company's analysis of the management practices of the top-rated radio stations in the U.S., identifying the characteristics of superior performance; includes chapters on radio programming, music research and community involvement by academic and industry consultants.

Radio & Records: The Industry's Newspaper. Los Angeles, weekly to date. Trade magazine of the record industry ranking songs and albums; also, *R&R Ratings Report*, a twice annual comparison of ratings for popular formats by region and station, including a comparison of Arbitron and Birch ratings.

Radio Only: The Monthly Management Tool. Cherry Hill, N.J., 1981 to date. Monthly trade magazine covering issues of concern to radio station managers and programmers.

Rapping, Elayne. *The Looking Glass World of Nonfiction TV*. Boston: South End Press, 1987. Popular comment on current soap operas, talk shows, documentaries and miniseries.

Regulatory Trends in the 1980's: More Owners—More Stations. New York: Station Representatives Association, 1980. Trade association report covering the history of the Federal Communications Commission's ownership rules and policies, current practices and proposals in hand.

Reis, Al, and Trout, Jack. *Positioning: The Battle for Your Mind*. New York: McGraw-Hill, 1981. Advertising experts' strategies for market recognition and image.

Religious Broadcasting. 1968 to date. Monthly magazine emphasizing evangelical broadcasting on radio and television with informal style.

Report on Prime-Time Network Television, and Report on Daytime Network Television. New York: Batten, Barton, Durstine & Osborn, Inc., annual. Booklet reporting on the upcoming network season, stressing details of interest to advertisers on upcoming trends.

Reymer & Gersin Associates. *Radio WARS I: How to Survive into the '80s*. Washington, D.C.: National Association of Broadcasters, 1983. Results of a national survey of 1300 radio listeners, including nine separate format reports.

Reymer & Gersin Associates. *Radio WARS II: How to Push Listeners' Hot Buttons*. Washington, D.C.: National Association of Broadcasters, 1985. Description of different psychological types that listen to radio.

Rice, Jean, ed. *Cable TV Renewals & Refranchising*. Washington, D.C.: Communications Press, 1983. Guide to municipal options and procedures, access programming and legal considerations from the perspectives of the cable operator and the local government.

Robards, Brooks. "Situation Comedy and the Structure of Television: A Structural Analysis." Ph.D. dissertation, University of Massachusetts, 1982. Application of four tenets of structural analysis (transformation, intelligibility, self-regulation, formalization) to television situation comedies.

Robertson Associates, Inc. *Local Station Utilization of PBS Programming: A Study for the TV Manager's Council of NAEB*. Washington, D.C.: National Association of Educational Broadcasters, 1977. 1977 study of public television station programming.

Rose, Brian G. *Television and the Performing Arts: A Handbook and Reference Guide to American Cultural Programming*. Westport, Conn.: Greenwood Press, 1986. Overview of the role of high culture programs on network television and cable, including brief program descriptions.

Rothenbuhler, Eric W. "Programming Decision Making in Popular Music Radio." *Communication Research* 12 (April 1985): 209–232. A case study of a rock music radio station examining the process of decision making about song selection, concluding that national, industry-wide criteria were more important than local criteria.

Routt, Edd; McGrath, James B.; and Weiss, Frederic A. *The Radio Format Conundrum.* New York: Hastings House, 1978. A wealth of detail on radio formats and factors affecting format decisions written from the point of view of the station manager.

Satellite Times: The News Source for the Home TVRO and Cable Industries. Shelby, North Carolina: Triple D Publishing, 1986 to date. Biweekly trade periodical concentrating on home satellite and cable-only industries.

Shaffer, William Drew, and Wheelwright, Richard. *Creating Original Programming for Cable TV.* Washington, D.C.: National Federation of Local Cable Programmers, 1983. Guide for producing local origination on cable for community groups and individuals; includes a case study of the Iowa City system.

Shane, Ed. *Programming Dynamics.* Washington, D.C.: National Association of Broadcasters, 1984. Practical guide to monitoring a radio station's programming and interpreting Arbitron ratings.

Shapiro, Mitchell E. "The Changing Nature of AM Radio in the 1980s: Talk, Ethnic & Religious Formats." Unpublished paper. Coral Gables, Fl.: University of Miami, 1987. Paper presented to the 1987 Speech Communication Association citing evidence of the profitability of talk, ethnic and religious formats to AM radio and the likelihood of AM's popular formats moving to FM.

Shooshan, Harry M. III, and Jackson, Charles L. *Radio Subcarrier Services, Com/Tech Report,* Vol. 2, No. 1. Washington, D.C.: National Association of Broadcasters, May 1983. Legal restrictions and technical potential of subcarrier services for commercial broadcasters.

Sigel, Efrem. *The Future of Videotext.* White Plains, N.Y.: Knowledge Industries Publications, 1983. Survey of the history and status of electronic information services, covering the legal and technical problems a new industry faces; includes summary tables.

Sklar, Rick. *Rocking America.* New York: St. Martin's Press, 1984. Popular insider's look at the development of top-forty radio in America, describing the impact of rock music on radio and record companies; anecdotal behind-the-scenes stories of performers, promotions and disc jockeys.

Sklar, Robert. *Prime-Time America: Life On and Behind the Television Screen.* New York: Oxford University Press, 1980. Entertaining criticism of network television as a popular art form.

"Special Report: Cable." *Broadcasting* (10 May 1982): 40–91; (15 November 1982): 48–68; (22 November 1982): 59–67; (20 June 1983): 47–69; (24 March 1986): 52–87; (7 July 1986): 75–80. Reports on cable networks, cable systems technology and operations, national and regional conventions and competitive prospects.

"Special Report: Children's Television." *Broadcasting* (9 July 1984): 38–54; (6 August 1984): 41–50; (4 August 1986): 53–63. Overviews of federal and industry actions and issues regarding children's television programs.

"Special Report: Independents." *Broadcasting* (1 February 1982): 36–48; (11 October 1982): 43–54; (17 January 1983): 55–70; (24 January 1983): 66–73; (27 June 1983): 49–70; (23 January 1984): 62–82; (22 October 1984): 54–82; (7 January 1985): 72–90; (14 January 1985): 130–158; (30 September 1985): 55–74; (6 January 1986): 78–88; (13 January 1986): 148–174; (5 January 1987): 90–112. Analyses of the growth of independent television stations, including superstations, UHFs and programming.

"Special Report: Journalism." *Broadcasting* (16 November 1981): 39–48; (26 July 1982): 39–91; (27 September 1982): 43–71; (25 July 1983): 78–84; (19 September 1983): 50–76; (27 August 1984): 47–108; (3 December 1984): 47–90; (17 December

1984):47–62; (7 April 1986):45–123; (28 April 1986):46–65; (31 August 1987):41–52. Overviews of broadcast news, concentrating on the impact of new field equipment on news gathering, reporting and distribution.

"Special Report: Journalism." *Electronic Media* (31 August 1987):J1–J19. Overview of trends in electronic journalism from various trade perspectives.

"Special Report: Radio." *Broadcasting* (25 August 1980):39–103; (17 August 1981): 39–78; (14 December 1981):39–43; (8 February 1982):45–56, 80–88; (8 March 1982):118–128; (6 September 1982):30–40; (20 September 1982):40–51; (27 September 1982):81–82; (4 October 1982):39–47; (11 October 1982):43–54; (15 August 1983):47–52; (29 August 1983):48–104; (5 September 1983):48–66; (19 September 1983):50–56; (23 July 1984):49–89; (17 September 1984):39–80; (24 September 1984):42–75; (4 February 1985):51–59; (22 July 1985):43–79; (11 November 1985):35–52; (28 July 1986):46–79; (27 July 1987):45–64. Analyses of all aspects of commercial radio broadcasting including formats and programming.

"Special Report: Radio." *Electronic Media* (7 September 1987):R1–R8. Trade report on disc jockeys, jingles and formats in commercial radio.

"Special Report: Satellites." *Broadcasting* (9 April 1984):43–68; (14 July 1986):42–57; (20 July 1987):33–61. Special reports on the use of space transmissions.

"Special Report: Sports." *Broadcasting* (1 March 1982):47–52; (9 August 1982):38–49; (27 February 1984):45–52; (4 March 1985):43–62; (25 March 1985):42–50; (3 August 1987):39–58; (19 October 1987):43–55; (30 November 1987):47–50; (15 February 1988):59–66; (7 March 1988):53–64. Analyses of professional and college sports on television.

"Special Report: Sports." *Channels* (1 April 1986):45–58. Three articles on the economics of sports and the impact of television on games.

"Special Report: Sports." *Electronic Media* (21 September 1987):S1–S8. Series of brief reports on various televised sports.

"Special Report: TV Programming." *Broadcasting* (13 February 1984):96–107; (20 February 1984):42–67; (21 May 1984):68–76; (28 May 1984):78–85; (22 October 1984): 68–76; (21 January 1985):42–75; (6 June 1986):49–119; (7 September 1987):35–41; (12 October 1987):40–72. Reports on syndication, network owned and operated stations, barter, first-run programming and peoplemeters.

Station Representatives Association. *The Station Representative: His Role in Broadcast Advertising.* New York: Station Representatives Association, September 1980. Trade association booklet describing the functions and responsibilities of the rep.

The Television Audience. Northbrook, Ill.: A.C. Nielsen Company, 1959 to date, annual. Trends in television programming and audience viewing patterns.

Tiedge, James T., and Ksobiech, Kenneth H. "Counterprogramming Primetime Network Television." *Journal of Broadcasting & Electronic Media* 31 (Winter 1987):41–55. Analysis of the mean shares of prime-time series aired from 1963 to 1985 showing the effects of counterprogramming among the three commercial broadcast networks.

Topper, Judith. "Putting Channels in Their Place." *Cable Marketing,* January 1987, pp. 22–29ff. An informal look at the goals behind the new channel lineups.

Tramer, Harriet, and Jeffries, Leo W. "Talk Radio—Forum and Companion." *Journal of Broadcasting* 27 (Summer 1983):297–300. Report of a survey of callers to three talk shows on radio investigating their motivation for calling.

United States Congress. House Committee on Energy and Commerce. Subcommittee on Telecommunications, Consumer Protection, and Finance. *Children's Television Programming: Hearings before the Subcommittee on Telecommunications, Consumer Protection, and Finance, October 25, 1985.* Washington, D.C.: U.S.G.P.O., 1986. Reprint of House hearings raising issues in children's programming and advertising to children.

Van Petten, Vance Scott, ed. *Television Syndication: A Practical Guide to Business and Legal Issues.* Los Angeles: Los Angeles

County Bar Association, 1987. Handbook covering contracts for syndicated television programs and movie packages.

Variety. New York and Hollywood, 1925 to date. Weekly trade newspaper covering the stage and the film, television and recording industries published in New York; also *Daily Variety* published in Hollywood covering the film and television industries.

Verna, Tony. *Live TV: An Inside Look at Directing and Producing.* Boston: Focal Press, 1987. Anecdotal look at the live production of the nightly news, telethons, sports and local TV talk shows.

Verta, Paul. "Television Entertainment Gatekeeping: A Study of Local Television Program Directors' Decision-Making." Ph.D. dissertation, University of Iowa, 1979. Analysis of types of decision-makers based on strategies used in purchase and retention of a hypothetical syndicated program series by 28 midwestern station programmers.

View: The Magazine of Television Programming. New York, 1979 to date. Monthly trade magazine.

Wakslag, Jacob J.; Agostino, Donald E.; Terry, Herbert A.; Driscoll, Paul; and Ramsey, Bruce. "Television News Viewing and Network Affiliation Changes." *Journal of Broadcasting* 27 (Winter 1983):53–68. Analysis of audience flow and repeat viewing based on ratings before and after network affiliation changes.

Webster, James G. "Audience Behavior in the New Media Environment." *Journal of Communication* 36 (Summer 1986):77–91. A scholarly comparison of channel content and availability in cable and traditional television broadcasting, concluding that the new media foster audience polarization.

Webster, James G. *Audience Research.* Washington, D.C.: National Association of Broadcasters, 1983. Primer on basic research methods for broadcasters.

Webster, James G. "Program Audience Duplication: A Study of Television Inheritance Effects." *Journal of Broadcasting & Electronic Media* 29 (Spring 1985):121–133. Scholarly study of determiners of audience duplication.

Webster, James G., and Saxon, Judy. *Audience Research: A Workbook.* Washington, D.C.: National Association of Broadcasters, 1983. Practice in understanding the concepts of ratings and research for broadcasters.

Webster, Maurice. *1987 Radio Survey.* New York: Radio Information Center, 1987. Booklet reporting results of a survey of radio station programmers.

Williams, Wenmouth, Jr., and Krugman, Dean M. "Innovativeness and the Public Radio Audience." *Journal of Broadcasting* 25 (Winter 1981):61–69. Results of a mail survey that did not demonstrate a relationship between innovativeness and listening to public radio.

Wimmer, Roger D., and Dominick, Joseph R. *Mass Media Research: An Introduction.* Second edition. Belmont, Calif.: Wadsworth, 1987. Revised text on research methods in mass media, emphasizing broadcasting; includes survey methods and peoplemeter ratings.

Wirth, Michael O. "Comment on 'The Policy of Exclusive Franchising in Cable Television.'" *Journal of Broadcasting & Electronic Media* 31 (Winter 1987):98–101. Comment on article by Thomas Hazlett.

Witherspoon, John, and Kovitz, Roselle. *The History of Public Broadcasting.* Washington, D.C.: Current, 1987. A brief history of the development of public television and public radio focusing on funding and programming.

Zorn, Eric. "Radio's Super Superstation." *Channels* (September/October 1984):30–31. A quick look at the most widely distributed FM station, Chicago's WFMT, a commercial classical music station delivered by satellite to cable systems in nearly 300 cities across the country.

Zuckerman, Laurence, and Brown, Les. "Autumn of the Networks' Reign." *Channels* (September/October 1983):45–48. Insiders' analysis of the effects of cable and independent television station audience shares on the power of the three commercial television networks.

INDEX TO PROGRAM TITLES

This is a guide to specific television, radio and cable **programs** and **movies** mentioned in the text. (Cable **networks** and radio and television **networks** appear in the General Index.)

GENERAL INDEX

Definitions and major text references appear in **boldface.**

Independent television stations, 123, **133,** 207, 223, 227, **229–248,** 258; children's programs, 218; costs, 230, **236–238,** 240–242, 244; carriage charges, 246, 279; local programs, **239–244;** positioning, 231–233; ratings, 241–242; repositioning, **275;** strategies, 30, **229–248;** superstations, 257–258, 265, 275, **287–290;** talk, 243
Independent Television Station Association (INTV), 32, 95
Infinity Broadcasting, 117
Information radio, 444, **423–442, 444–460**
INN (Independent Network News), 194. *See also USA Today* in Index to Program Titles.
Inspirational Network, 208, **310**
Instructional formats, adults, **494–496;** radio, 511; television, **486,** 488, 489, 494, 498
In-tab diaries. *See* Diaries.
Interactive cable, 261. *See also* Addressability.
Interconnects, 255, **265–266,** 278, 299, 351. *See also* Advertising, cable.
Interconnection grants, 462
International ITV Co-op, 494
International Radio and Television Society (IRTS), 32, 38
Interstitial programming, 32, 251, 339, **353–354**
Interviewing, radio, **452–456**
INTV, 32, 95
Inventory, ads, **237–238;** programs, **102.** *See also* Commercials.
IRTS (International Radio and Television Society), 32, 38
ITV (Instructional television), **486,** 488, 489, 494, 498

Jankowski, Gene, 16
Jazz music format, **507,** 511
The Jazz Network, 364
Jennings, Peter, 193
Joint ventures, 126. *See also* Group owners; MSOs.
Jones Galactic Radio, 364
Jones Intercable, 305, 364

KABC, 65–66, 117, 214, 444, 445, 447, 451, 457
KABL, 417
Katz Agency, 88, 98–99, 101
KBBF-FM, 509
KPBS-AM, 511
KCBS, 65–66, 117, 424
KCPB-FM, 518
KCRW-FM, 511, 517
KEDB-FM, 509
KEGL-FM, 417
KFWB, 424
KGO, 444, 447
KHJ, 65–66
Kiddult programming, 215, **226,** 234, **235,** 239
Kidvid (children's programming), 232

King Features, 26
KKDA, 419
KKGO, 364
KLIF, 419
Klein, Paul, 136, 137–138
KLON-FM, 507, 517, 518
KNBC, 65–66, 117, 214
KNX, 424
KOST, 417
KPBS-FM, 509, 510
KPFA-FM, 508
KPFK-FM, 508, 517
KPFT-FM, 508
KPHO, 243
KPIX, 220
KQED-FM, 507, 514
KRLD, 419
KSCA-FM, 518
KSJN-AM, 508
KTLA, 65–66, 240, 290
KTRH, 451
KTTV, 65–55, 240
KTVT, 290
Ku-band satellites, **267–268,** 279
KUHT-TV, 488
KUSC-FM, 504, 506, 507, 514, **515–521**
KWGN, 243
KVIL-FM, 419
KYUK, 509
KYW, 424, 438
KZEW, 417

Late fringe daypart, **223**
Late night programming, **194–197, 223–224**
Lead-in strategy, **150**
Lead-off strategy, **150**
Lear, Norman, 39
The Learning Channel (TLC), 303, **304–305**
Leased channels, 359, **365–366**
Least objectionable program (LOP), **137–138**
Libel, **37–38,** 207
Liberty Broadcasting Network (LBN), 311
Licenses, **206, 216–217;** affiliate, 205–207, 215–216; cable, 256, **262–265, 283,** 284; compulsory, **265;** copyright, **35–36;** futures, **235–238;** independent, 233, **234;** movies, 234, **238;** program, 103, **109–113,** 141, 144–146; public station, 487–490; sports, 240. *See also* Music, royalties.
Lifestyle/psychographics, 8, 10–11. *See also* Ratings.
Lifestyle (cable radio network), 364
Lifetime, 16, 24, 76, 126, 127, 208, 263, 271, 272, 276, 284, 307, **308**
Lift, **269,** 272, 278, 284, **308,** 322
Lineups. *See* Channel lineups.
Live assist, 378
LO, cable, 251, 256, 274, 348–369; syndication, **349**
Localism, **35,** 123, 315, 505–506
Local programs, television, **27–28, 124,** 211, 219, **220–221, 239–244**